Robert Tomes

Battles of America by sea and land:

Consisting of the colonial and revolutionary battles, the War of 1812, and the Mexican

campaigns; with biographies of naval and military commanders, and illustrative anecdotes -

Vol. 1

Robert Tomes

Battles of America by sea and land:
*Consisting of the colonial and revolutionary battles, the War of 1812, and the Mexican campaigns; with
biographies of naval and military commanders, and illustrative anecdotes - Vol. 1*

ISBN/EAN: 9783337814656

Printed in Europe, USA, Canada, Australia, Japan

Cover: Foto ©ninafisch / pixelio.de

More available books at **www.hansebooks.com**

BATTLES OF AMERICA

BY

SEA AND LAND:

CONSISTING OF

THE COLONIAL AND REVOLUTIONARY BATTLES,

THE WAR OF 1812, AND THE MEXICAN CAMPAIGNS;

WITH

BIOGRAPHIES OF NAVAL AND MILITARY COMMANDERS,

AND

ILLUSTRATIVE ANECDOTES.

BY ROBERT TOMES, M.D.,

JOINT EDITOR OF COMMODORE PERRY'S "EXPEDITION TO JAPAN," ETC., ETC.

ILLUSTRATED BY A SERIES OF STEEL ENGRAVINGS OF NAVAL AND MILITARY
INCIDENTS AND BATTLE SCENES, CHIEFLY FROM ORIGINAL DESIGNS BY
F. O. C. DARLEY, ALONZO CHAPPEL, AND OTHER EMINENT ARTISTS.

VOL. I.

NEW YORK:

VIRTUE, YORSTON AND COMPANY,

12 DEY STREET.

LIST OF PLATES,

VOL. I.

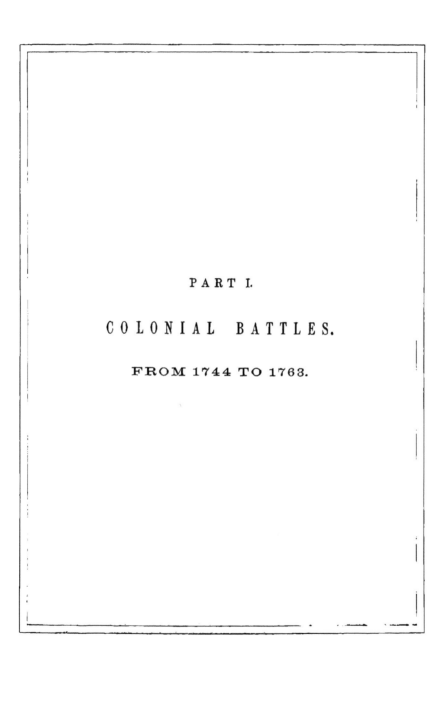

PART I.

COLONIAL BATTLES.

FROM 1744 TO 1763.

BATTLES OF AMERICA.

PART I.—COLONIAL BATTLES.

CHAPTER I.

The Rivalry between England and France in the Old World revived in the New.—France's Lust of Dominion in America.—Jealousy of English Colonists.—Frequent Conflicts, with no Results but Spilling of Blood.—Louis the Fourteenth's Contemptuous Disregard of his American Subjects.—His Fatal Concessions to Great Britain by the Treaty of Utrecht.—The Consequent Danger of Canada.—The French guard against it by the Founding of Louisburg.—Its Extensive Fortifications.—The Jealousy of the English Colonists excited.—Their Trade endangered.—The French deemed a Horde of Dangerous Interlopers.—Anxiety to get rid of them.—The French commence Hostilities.—Canseau attacked by the French and captured.—Annapolis repels the Invaders.—New England aroused.—Governor Shirley, of Massachusetts, boldly resolves upon a Secret Expedition against Louisburg.—The Secret disclosed by a Pious Member of the General Court.—Shirley asks the Aid of the Home Government for the Defence of Nova Scotia.—Solicits the Assistance of the English West-India Fleet.—Shirley opposed by the Legislature.—He finally triumphs over the Opposition.—Massachusetts foremost in voting Men and Money.—Land-Forces and the Fleet of New England.—Embarrassment of the Governor in the Choice of a Commander of the Expedition.—Colonel William Pepperell finally chosen.—Governor Wentworth passed over, on the Score of Ill-Health.—Wentworth, disappointed, declares he has thrown away his Crutches, and offers his Services, but too late.—Pepperell hesitates to accept.—The famous Whitefield advises him religiously.—The Expedition against Louisburg a Religious Crusade.—The Pious Enthusiasm of the People.—Pepperell's Origin, Life, and Character.—A Great Merchant.—Immense Popularity.—Military Experience.—Recruits crowd to his Standard.—Shirley, anxious to take Louisburg by a *Coup de Main*, cuts off all Communication with the Place.—The Expedition prepares to sail.—A Heavy Blow, and Great Discouragement.—Admiral Warren, of the West-India Station, at the Last Moment, refuses to co-operate.—Prayers and Sermons.—Expedition sails for Canseau.

THE rivalry between England and France in the Old World was revived in the New under circumstances calculated no less to excite jealousy, and stir up contention, than those which had for ages brought these two nations in another hemisphere into almost constant conflict. As in Europe, so in America, the English and French were near neighbors; and with this proximity of two different and aspiring people, came naturally a clashing of interests, and repeated struggles for supremacy. France, in possession of Canada and Louisiana, was, with its usual lust of dominion, eager to enlarge the boundaries of its American territory: with this view, she claimed the whole region which extended back of the original British colonies from the mouth of the St. Lawrence to that of the Mississippi, and strove on every occasion to make good her claims by military possession. The English settlers, with their rapidly-developing commercial and trading interests, looked at these encroachments with a jealous eye, and sought every opportunity to check the advances of their French rivals. Frequent collisions ensued in consequence, and the colonial annals are full of recorded conflicts between the two competitors for American dominion. The temporary military triumph of the one or the other was the only result of these repeated contests, and the combatants were left, for the most part, in the possession of their original territorial claims.

1713. In 1713, however, Louis XIV., with a contemptuous disregard of the interests of his American subjects, ceded to Great Britain, by the treaty of Utrecht, the province of Nova Scotia—called by the French *Acadie*—Newfoundland with its wealth of fisheries, and the territory bordering Hudson's bay.

This concession was a fatal blow to French dominion in America. Newfoundland and Nova Scotia should have been retained at all hazards by France, as they were, from their position off the mouth of the St. Lawrence, the natural guards to Canada. It is true that the island of Cape Breton, to the west, was reserved for the protection of the Canadian possessions; but its proximity to the coast of New England, and to Nova Scotia from which it was only separated by a narrow strait, exposed it to attack from those quarters.

The French were alive to the danger incurred by the concessions of the treaty of Utrecht, and strove to secure the safety of their Canadian territory by strongly fortifying Cape Breton, as their only means of guarding the approach to the St. Lawrence, and thus protecting the extensive territory of which that river is the outlet. They accordingly founded a walled town on a tongue of land, at the southeastern part of Cape Breton, and called it Louisburg, in honor of their monarch. The most skilful engineers of France were commissioned to fortify it on the most extensive plan, and according to the best approved systems of defence.

The site of the town and fortifications embraced a circumference of no less than two and a half miles; while a solid rampart of masonry, with a height of more than thirty feet and a ditch of the width of eighty feet, was constructed to protect every part that was approachable. Toward the sea, there was no occasion for more than the defence of a dike and pickets, since the water here was so shallow and so underspread with dangerous reefs, that there was no danger from the approach of armed vessels. The entrance to the harbor was only four hundred yards wide, and this was defended by the construction of a battery of thirty twenty-eight pounders upon a small island which was conveniently situated in the very centre of the strait. Another battery was built on the land bordering the upper part of the harbor, and directly facing the town. This was termed the Royal battery, and was provided with twenty-eight forty-two and two eighteen-pound cannon. On the elevated ground of the main-land opposite to the fortified island, stood the lighthouse, and at some distance to the north were built the necessary magazines and storehouses.

The town itself was handsomely constructed of wood and stone, and was entered through a gate at the west over a drawbridge, which was defended by a circular battery containing thirteen twenty-four pounders. The cost of the whole construction, of town and fortifications, amounted to no less than six millions of dollars; and such had been the deliberate care with which the works were conducted, that they required twenty-five years for their completion.

The English colonists of the New England coast naturally beheld the rising of this strongly-fortified citadel with anxious alarm. They began to fear for the safety of their trade and commerce: they saw, in Louisburg, a cover for French cruisers and privateers, which, on the least pretence of hostility, might sail out and pounce upon their merchantmen and fishing-vessels. The English, with a natural instinct for trade, had largely developed the Atlantic fisheries and commerce, while the French, more intent upon military possession, seemed eager only for the glory of dominion. The latter, therefore, were regarded by the former as a horde of dangerous interlopers, whom it was necessary to get rid of at all hazards, as fatal obstacles to British colonial prosperity.

Odious, however, as the threatening aspect of the fortified Louisburg was to the New-Englanders, and eager as they were to rid themselves of so dangerous a neighbor, it was not before the French had provoked the attack, that the English prepared to commence hostilities.

Nova Scotia, in possession of Great Britain, was poorly defended by two small English garrisons: one on the island of Canseau, at the mouth of the strait of that name, which separates Nova Scotia from Cape Breton; and the other at Port Royal, or Annapolis, situated to the north. The French commander at Louisburg, anticipating a declaration of war between France and England, sent out a detachment of nine hundred men against the garrison **1744.** of Canseau. The English, consisting only of a single company of soldiers, and suspecting nothing, were taken by surprise and conveyed to Louisburg as captives. A similar attempt was made upon Annapolis; but William Shirley, governor of Massachusetts, anticipating the danger, had sent a small force from Boston to the aid of the garrison, which succeeded with much difficulty in repelling the French attack.

The colonists of Massachusetts were greatly provoked by these invasions, and prepared to take revenge. Their thoughts naturally turned to Louisburg, the possession of which by the French was believed to be so dangerous to the British colonial interests. The prisoners who had been captured at Canseau and taken to Louisburg, had been set free. On their arrival in Boston, their imprisonment became naturally a general topic of conversation, and served to stimulate the desire for an attack upon the place of their captivity. They, moreover, were enabled to give the exactest information in regard to Louisburg and its fortifications. With this definite knowledge, Governor Shirley conceived the bold idea of getting up a secret invasion of the French citadel, with the view of taking it by surprise and capturing it at once by a *coup de main*. Shirley was so bent upon his scheme,

and so convinced of the necessity of secrecy, that he extorted from each member of the general court a solemn oath
not to divulge his plan. The secret was,
however, only kept for a few days; it
having been disclosed through the piety
of one whose voice was heard, not only
in the legislature, but the church. In
his capacity as member of the latter, being called upon to pray, he piously invoked the blessing of Heaven upon Shirley's scheme, and thus disclosed the governor's important secret. The subject
now became the common talk, and general opinion was freely expressed against
the proposition, as reckless and impossible.

Shirley strove even to mystify the
British ministry; and, while he invoked
their aid, he carefully concealed from
them the exact purpose of his demand.
He wrote to the home government, asking for the assistance of a naval force, on
the plea that Nova Scotia was threatened
by the French; and addressed also a letter to Warren, who had the naval command on the West-India station, and was
then at Antigua, soliciting his aid.

The indefatigable Shirley was not to
be balked of his favorite purpose by the
opposition of the legislature, which had
reported, through a committee, unfavor-
ably to the attack on Louisburg. He
accordingly used his influence with the
traders of New England, to prevail upon
them to get up a petition to the legislature to reconsider its former vote. This
was done, and had its effect; for a new
committee was appointed, which reported in favor of the expedition. Upon the

report being warmly and longly discussed,
the governor's plan was finally carried
by the majority of one. The vote was
given; there was no longer any opposition to carrying out its object; and all the
colonists warmly seconded the efforts of
Shirley for the execution of the proposed
attack upon Louisburg.

New England, and particularly Massachusetts, felt naturally the greatest interest in the enterprise, and the share borne
in it by that portion of the colonies was
accordingly the greatest. Massachusetts
was foremost, and voted to contribute
more than three thousand men. Next
came Connecticut, with five hundred;
and then Rhode Island and New Hampshire, with three hundred each. Aid was
solicited from the other colonies, but
there was little active sympathy shown
with the cause, and New England was
left to bear the chief burden. Pennsylvania, however, sent some provisions, and
New York contributed a small supply of
artillery. In addition to the land-forces,
there were fourteen small armed vessels,
with an aggregate of two hundred and
four guns, made up of the various cruisers kept always in service by the seaboard colonies. With the transports, the
whole fleet amounted to no less than a
hundred sail. A provincial, of the name
of Edward Tyng, was appointed commodore of this colonial squadron.

It was a matter of greater difficulty to
find a commander for the land-forces, and
a general leader of the expedition. The
governor of Massachusetts seemed embarrassed in making a choice, as might
naturally have been expected among a

people whose occupations were of commerce and trade. It was not difficult to find among the fishermen, lumberers, sailors, and mechanics, of New England, hardy and bold men enough for any undertaking requiring courage and endurance; but who among them had that knowledge of military art necessary to discipline their rude force into the order required for regular warfare? It is true, there were not wanting those who had gathered their countrymen together from the bench, the field, and the fishery, and led them against the savages, in defence of their lives and property. These were, however, mere Indian skirmishes in which there was no occasion for military art.

Governor Shirley was supposed to have hesitated for some time between two distinguished New-Englanders: Wentworth, governor of New Hampshire, and Colonel William Pepperell, president of the council of Massachusetts. He finally chose the latter, but evidently not without some compunctions of injustice toward the former, to whom he wrote, after the appointment of Pepperell, to this effect: "It would have been an infinite satisfaction to me, and done great honor to the expedition, if your limbs would have permitted you to take the chief command." Shirley alluded to Wentworth's gout, as his reason for passing him by. The governor of New Hampshire, however, did not care thus to be invalided, and wrote in reply that he had thrown away his crutches, and was ready, in spite of the gout, to march at the head of the expedition. But it was too late, as Pepperell had already received his appointment.

No better selection could probably have been made, in the want of any regular military tactician. Pepperell, however, was very doubtful of his own capacity for the undertaking, and hesitated to accept the position. Governor Shirley strenuously urged him to comply, on the ground that his influence with those upon whom the expedition depended for its success could not be dispensed with. He, however, still pondered the matter, and determined to consult his friends before coming to a final conclusion.

At this time, the celebrated George Whitefield, the eloquent Methodist preacher, had reached New England, in the course of his evangelizing labors in America, and was stopping at the house of Pepperell, in Maine. The host took this occasion of consulting his famous guest in regard to his appointment, and is supposed to have been influenced by Whitefield's advice, in his resolution to accept. The divine said, he did not think the scheme very promising; that the eyes of all would be upon him; that if it should not succeed, the widows and orphans of the slain would reproach him; and if it should succeed, many would regard him with envy, and endeavor to eclipse his glory; that he ought, therefore, to go with a single eye, and he would find his strength proportioned to his necessity.

This was good religious advice, and gave a holy sanction to the enterprise, which seems to have had its influence in determining Pepperell to undertake it, and in inspiring many of the New-England people with a pious ardor in favor of the cause. Many of Whitefield's own

2

converts offered themselves with enthusiasm as recruits, and all began to consider the expedition as a sanctified one.

There is no doubt that the Puritan feeling of New England was aroused in religious hostility to the French, in consequence of their Romish Catholic faith. Whitefield himself seems to have given such a direction to the sentiment of New England by the motto which he furnished for the flag of the expedition. *Nil desperandum, Christo duce*—" With Christ for our leader, nothing is to be despaired of" —were the words supplied ; and none could have been better chosen, to give the tone of a religious crusade to the undertaking. That such, in effect, was the result, may be gathered from the fact that clergymen, with axes on shoulder, prepared to demolish popish images, readily enlisted for service ; and from such letters as this from one Deacon Gray, addressed to Pepperell : "O that I could be with you and dear Parson Moody in that church, to destroy the images there set up, and hear the true gospel of our Lord and Saviour there preached! My wife, who is ill and confined to her bed, yet is so spirited in the affair, on hearing of your taking the command, that she is very willing all her sons should wait on you, though it is outwardly greatly to our damage. One of them has already enlisted, and I know not but there will be more. She sends her duty to you, and says, so long as she has life she shall importunately pray for you."

There was no man in the whole colony more popular than Pepperell. He was a thorough New-Englander, by birth, education, religion, habits, and occupation. His father, at an early age, had emigrated from Wales and settled at Kittery, on the banks of the Piscataqua, the river which separates Maine from New Hampshire. Commencing as a fisherman, he finally reached the more imposing position of a merchant, and became colonially famous for wealth and integrity.

His son William was born in 1696 at Kittery. His early education was the best that could be supplied by the village school, and consisted only of the elementary reading, spelling, and arithmetic. Having soon exhausted these academic resources, he was taken into his father's trading establishment, and there finished his education, which was, of course, more of a practical than scholastic character. The Pepperells were great merchants for those times, and dealt largely in timber, fish, and West-Indian molasses, rum, and negroes.

The elder Pepperell, from a fisherman's apprentice, had passed rapidly through the various transitions of fisherman, proprietor of fishing-boats, shopkeeper, and factor, until he finally became ship-owner and merchant. He had his coasters to send to the West Indies with lumber, in exchange for sugar and other tropical productions ; his ships to take these and other colonial produce to Europe, and bring back manufactured goods ; and, in fact, he carried on as important commercial transactions as the colonial trade allowed. His son William soon became a partner in the paternal house, and added rapidly to its importance and wealth. On his father's death, he succeeded him as the principal member of the firm, and in a few years was known throughout New England as the wealthiest and most influential of its merchants.

Taking an active part in the public concerns of the colony, he soon secured a large share of colonial honor. He successively became justice of the peace, a captain, major, lieutenant-colonel, colonel, and commander-in-chief, of the militia of Maine, and finally member of the council of Massachusetts. It was his military prominence, combined with his great personal influence and popularity, which had induced Governor Shirley to give him the command of the expedition about to set out for the attempt upon Louisburg.

Pepperell's command as colonel of the militia seems to have inspired him with considerable military ardor. He devoted himself with great spirit to his duties, and, by frequent drills, musters, and parades, imparted to his miscellaneous regiment of fishermen, lumberers, and mechanics, all the discipline of which they were capable. As the neighborhood was particularly exposed to the incursions of surrounding savages, there was the motive of constant and imminent danger to prompt to alertness of military preparation. The ardor of their commander was thus readily shared by his fellow-colonists; and it may well be conceived that the troops of Maine were as effective as the best of the irregulars. None could have surpassed them in courage and endurance, and few equalled their skill in the use of the firelock. In the frequent skirmishes with the Indians, they had become practised in savage warfare; while not only their occupations as fishermen and lumberers, but their amusements on the sea and in the forest, served to inure them to danger and fatigue, as well as to accustom them to the exercise of their strength and skill. All they required was the practice of acting together in large bodies; and this they were about learning, for the first time, in the hazardous attempt upon Louisburg.

The recruits came in rapidly, as soon as it was known that Colonel Pepperell had accepted the command of the proposed expedition. His personal influence was so great, that all his immediate neighbors capable of bearing arms seemed eager to join his standard. The whole town of Berwick turned out almost to a man. There was no difficulty in obtaining the necessary quota of soldiers for the ranks, but there was some trouble in reconciling the officers to assuming certain subordinate positions. Some of these, even in Berwick, were accordingly backward in offering their services. Pepperell, referring to this remissness, wrote: "I have not the least doubt that the commissioned officers in Berwick are as brave and as good men as any in this province, and would willingly venture their lives with their colonel. Please to tell them all I sincerely value and love them, and that should there be occasion for forces to be sent after us, I don't doubt in the least but they will be ready to come. I beg all their prayers."

Governor Shirley was still bent upon his scheme of taking Louisburg by surprise; and accordingly, although he had failed to keep the purpose of his expedition a secret from his own people, he resolved to use every precaution to mystify the French. All communication with Louisburg was cut off, by prohibiting the sailing of colonial vessels to that place; and it was strictly forbidden for copies to be taken of the orders read to the companies, or for any soldier to disclose their purport. Shirley's plan of taking Louisburg by surprise, and carrying it by a *coup de main*, was based upon his knowledge, not only of the strength of that citadel, but of the weakness of the colonial forces. He naturally supposed that an undisciplined militia had not the necessary skill, or even the patience, for executing the operations of a systematic siege. He knew, moreover, that the colonists, to a man, would do all that enterprise and courage could do in the want of art, and accordingly trusted for success to these well-known characteristics of the New-England troops. It was, therefore, no Quixotic scheme of Shirley to design a rapid movement, a sudden surprise, and a quick execution, by which the skilled soldier in command of the French fortress would be thrown off his guard, and be prevented from bringing to bear the resources of military art against his undisciplined opponents. The governor of Massachusetts, accordingly, as Bancroft says, "wisest of all, gave instructions for the fleet of a hundred vessels to arrive together at a precise hour; heedless of the surf, to land in the dark on the rocky shore; to march forthwith, through thicket and bog, to the city and beyond it;

and to take the fortress and Royal battery by surprise before daybreak."

The troops all being raised within the brief period of two months, and to the number of over three thousand, prepared to sail in the fleet now at anchor in the roads of Nantucket. Some of the fleetest of the provincial cruisers were sent in advance, to hover about Louisburg, and intercept all French vessels bound thither. The rest were detained to transport the provincial forces. A day was now set apart for prayer, and to invoke the blessing of Heaven upon the expedition. Large crowds gathered together on the shore, on the Sunday preceding the day of embarkation; solemn prayers were offered up to the God of battles, imploring his aid in the coming struggle; and sermons were delivered in every church, setting forth the holiness of the cause, and urging the duty of each soldier to do his "manfullest in the service of the Great Captain of our salvation."

On the day before the departure, a heavy blow and great discouragement came, in an answer from Warren, the commodore of the West-India squadron, to Governor Shirley, refusing to give the aid solicited. The colonial forces had expected to be reinforced by this squadron before sailing; but the cause of the non-arrival of Warren with his ships having been kept a secret by the prudent governor, and only disclosed to Pepperell (now lieutenant-general) and his second in command, General Wolcot, the troops embarked in ignorance, and expected merely a temporary delay of the naval assistance still confidently hoped for.

The small settlement of Canseau, in the strait of that name dividing Nova Scotia and Cape Breton, having been determined upon as the rendezvous, the various vessels set sail. The troops of Massachusetts, which formed the larger proportion of the forces, sailed first, on the 24th of March, and were succeeded at brief intervals by those of New Hampshire and Connecticut.

1745.

CHAPTER II.

Arrival at Canseau.—Detained by Ice.—A proposal to float into Louisburg upon Icebergs.—Encouraged by a Capture.—The Judicious Pepperell keeps his Troops busy.—The Encouraging Arrival of a British Squadron.—Admiral Warren.—His Life and Character.—His Nephew, Sir William Johnson.—Pepperell superseded in the Naval Department.—His Judicious Behavior.—Shirley's Letter.—His Desire to give Warren the Pre-eminence.—Pepperell tenacious of his Rights.—Anxious to secure the Glories of the Coming Conquest for the New-Englanders.—The Ice clears away.—Departure for Louisburg.—The French unexpectant of the Attack.—Sailing into the Bay.—Landing.—The Alarm of the Fortress.—The Enemy put to Flight.—The Capture of Morepang.—Encampment before the Town.—Admiral Warren doing Good Service on the Coast.—Colonel Vaughan sent to reconnoitre.—The Garrison of the Grand Battery frightened by a Smoke.—Their Flight.—The Hoisting of a Red Coat.—A Sortie from the Fort.—The French driven back.—The Grand Battery reinstated and held by the New-Englanders.—The French strive by a Brisk Cannonade to make it too hot to hold.—Their Want of Success.—The Siege regularly begun.—Erection of Batteries.—The Difficulties spiritedly overcome.—The Island Battery a Great Annoyance.—The Attempt upon it postponed by the Advice of Pepperell.—The Town summoned to surrender.—The Defiant Answer of the French.—Councils-of-War.—A Determination to carry Louisburg by Storm.—Postponement.—The Siege expected to be long.—The New-Englanders, however, still hopeful.—The Sufferings of the Besiegers.—Pepperell forced to send to Shirley for Reinforcements.—A Heavy Fire opened against the Walls.—A Breach made.—Compliments passed between the Hostile Parties.—Splitting of Cannon.—Captures by the Fleet.—Impatience of the Admiral.—Pepperell cautious and temporizing.—Another Attempt upon the Island Battery proposed, and again postponed.—A Small Triumph for the Enemy.—A Great Triumph for the British Fleet.—The Capture of the Vigilant.—A General Attack by Sea and Land proposed.—An Unsuccessful Attempt upon the Island Battery.

1745. THE vessels with the Massachusetts troops on board reached Canseau on the first of April, and were in a few days joined by the rest. Here they were unfortunately detained, in consequence of the ice, which, breaking up in that season, had drifted in such masses in and about the harbor of Louisburg, that it was impracticable to attempt its entrance. There was great disappointment felt at this untimely detention, by the ardent and sanguine; and it was even gravely suggested by some, more impulsive and impatient than the rest, to float the troops into Louisburg on the ice! The men, however, kept up their spirits successfully, in spite of the untoward delay. An opportune chance at an enemy's vessel served to occupy their minds and reinvigorate their hopes. A French colonial vessel, laden with tropical produce, rum, and molasses, appeared off the coast, making its way to the port of Louisburg. The New-England cruisers at once pounced upon it, and, making an an easy capture, brought the prize into Canseau, much to the satisfaction of the impatient invaders.

Care was taken by the judicious Pepperell to keep his men busy. Some were put to preparing the ammunition; some were set to building fortifications, structures, and hospitals, for the more effective protection of the small garrison of Canseau; and others were sent out in detachments to practise themselves in skirmishes with the neighboring savages and French. Important information in regard to Louisburg was gathered from those taken captive in these engagements.

Three weeks had thus passed with the troops still at Canseau, in consequence of the ice, when the appearance of three large vessels off the harbor was announced. These, to the great satisfaction of the colonists, proved to be British men-of-war, under command of Warren. Soon after this officer had written to Governor Shirley, refusing to co-operate on his own responsibility with the colonial expedition, he received orders from the British government directing him to render with his squadron all the aid in his power to the New-England enterprise.

Warren, who was a prompt officer, immediately set sail in the Superbe, accompanied by the Launceston and the Mermaid. He was making for the port of Boston, quite unaware of the proposed attack on Louisburg, when he fell in with a New-England vessel, from which he learned that the troops had sailed for Canseau. He accordingly directed his course at once for that place, where the arrival of his three effective men-of-war was now hailed with joyful acclamation.

Warren was a brave, impulsive Irishman, and a most skilful sailor and judicious commander. His long service on the American coast had made him familiar with its navigation, and no naval officer accordingly could be better fitted to guard provincial seaboard interests. He was, moreover, bound by a family tie to the colonies, having married the daughter of James Delancy, lieutenant-governor of New York. He had become also a large landed proprietor, owning an extensive territory watered by the Mohawk.

His nephew was the well-known Sir William Johnson, who, having been invited by his uncle to take charge of his American estates, became so enamored of the wild life on the borders, that he passed the remainder of his years among the Indians, over whom he exercised an influence perhaps never equalled by any European. These various circumstances served to identify Warren with colonial interests, and caused him to support them with ardor.

Warren and his ships were a great accession to the colonial troops, and their arrival gave increased confidence to all. Pepperell might, perhaps, have been pardoned a little feeling of jealousy, on the arrival of the English admiral, who was to supersede him in part of his command. Pepperell had been appointed lieutenant-general and commander-in-chief of both the land and sea forces. He was now requested, by a letter from Shirley, to make over the command of the colonial fleet to Warren. "You will perceive," says Shirley to Pepperell, "upon your perusal of his majesty's orders to me, that in any attempt against the enemy's settlements, he has plainly given Commodore Warren the command of the shipping or naval force with which I am ordered to assist him; hence in general upon any expedition, which you are sensible must supersede any commission from me, as to any sea-command; and doubtless Commodore Warren will expect and insist upon the armed vessels with which, since my receiving his majesty's orders, I am assisting him in obedience to the royal commands, the command of those ships; and I doubt not, sir, from the extraordinary conduct and vigilance with which you have hitherto acted for his majesty's service, that you will instantly give orders to Tyng and the other cruisers to follow the commodore's directions and orders to them, the omitting of which may create a most unhappy disagreement and variance between you and Mr. Warren, which may prove fatal to the service. Had I not received these precise orders from his majesty, which so evidently give Mr. Warren a general command at sea, in all expeditions from hence, I should have insisted upon my command given you over the sea-forces (which, as it is, is only suspended during Captain Warren's presence, and would revive upon his going off), against every person whatsoever; and you must be sensible that this is not a preference given to him by me, but only acting in obedience to his majesty's orders."

It is quite evident that Shirley was particularly anxious to shift the responsibility of this change from himself, and at the same time not the less desirous of securing as large a share of the command as possible for Warren. It has even been asserted that the governor was desirous of giving the English commodore the entire control of the expedition. There is no occasion, if this be true, to attribute Shirley's conduct to jealousy of his friend Pepperell. It was quite natural that, in his anxiety for the success of the expedition, of which he was the originator, the governor should have more faith in the leadership of one who, like Warren, was of established fame, than in Pepperell, who, with all his well-known qualities as a good and true man, had had no opportunity of giving proof of his capacity as a military commander.

Pepperell, though tenacious of his own rights, was the first to welcome Warren's arrival, and did not hesitate to yield his naval command to the English commodore, although he brooked no interference with his leadership of the land-forces. In Pepperell's first letter to Warren, in which he hurried to congratulate him upon his arrival, he took at once to define what he supposed to be the especial function of the naval branch of the service: "I am confident," he says, "that nothing which the strictest vigilance and prudence can foresee or bravery execute will be wanting on your part, and doubt not you will succeed in *preventing the introduction of provisions and succors into Louisburg*, and that we shall soon have the pleasure of a meeting there."

Pepperell was a positive, self-confident man, and relied, with all his inexperience and that of his troops, upon his and their efforts mainly for the attempt upon Louisburg. He, however, was a prudent man withal, and was not disposed, upon a mere question of etiquette, to quarrel with Warren, to whom and whose ships he looked for such important aid in the approaching enterprise. It was now agreed between the two commanders that the naval squadron should proceed to blockade the harbor of Louisburg, and thus cut off all communication by sea; while the troops should be transported at the earliest moment, and, disembarking at the most convenient point, should attack by land the French citadel.

The ice did not clear away sufficiently until toward the close of the month of April, to allow of the sailing of the troops. It was thus as late as the 29th of April when the transports weighed anchor and sailed for Louisburg. In accordance with Governor Shirley's design, it was intended to reach that place in the dead of night, and therefore the departure from Canseau had taken place early in the morning. Though starting with a fair breeze, the wind in the course of the evening so far lulled, that the vessels did not arrive at their destination until an early hour next day. It was hoped that they would have reached the bay of Chapeaurouge, or Gabarus as it was called by the English, upon the shores of which it was determined to land, without being discovered by the inhabitants of Louisburg. Every precaution had been taken to prevent a knowledge, on the part of the French, of the proposed attack, and with complete success. The English men-of-war had been observed cruising in the neighborhood, but their purpose was not suspected; while their diligent capture of coasting and other vessels bound to and from Louisburg, put a stop to all communication from without, by which the French might have been made aware of their impending danger, and have protected themselves accordingly.

It was not until the New-England fleet of a hundred sail, soon after daybreak on the morning of the last day of April, came sailing into their bay under full canvas, that the French were conscious of their danger. Great was the alarm and great the confusion at Louisburg when the approach of so formidable an enemy was observed. There can be little doubt that if the colonial troops (so unexpected was the invasion) had arrived as was intended, marched to the town, and made an assault under cover of the night, Louisburg would have fallen at once, and Shirley's bold design been fully justified by a triumphant success.

The provincial troops were no less eager for the attack than the French were dejected at its prospect. The vessels had hardly come to anchor in the bay, when the boats were lowered and **May 1.** pulled off, loaded down with soldiers, eager to reach the shore and commence the affray. As they neared the land within a short distance of the walls of the town, the fort was aroused to a great state of excitement. The bells began to sound a general alarm, and the signal-guns were fired in quick succession. Finally, a detachment of French troops appeared issuing from the gates of Louisburg, and marching rapidly to the point where the provincials seemed about to land. These latter, however, having made a feint of pulling their boats to a certain spot, suddenly changed their course, and disembarked farther inland, before the enemy could arrive and dispute their landing.

They had some difficulty in getting safely in with their boats, in consequence of the great surf, but finally succeeded; and had no sooner sprung to the shore, than they became the pursuing force, and rushed eagerly to meet the French, whom they defeated at the first collision, killing seven or eight, and wounding and capturing as many more, among whom was the French commander Morepang. The rest of the enemy took to their heels and fled back in panic to the town. The provincials came out of the encounter without any loss, and with only one or two wounded; and, being in fine spirits, their commander was eager to give them a " time for a general push." The troops now succeeded in landing, without fear of molestation; and in the course of a few days, the whole force had disembarked, and encamped before the town. In the meantime, Pepperell kept up almost daily communication by letter with Warren, who, with his squadron off the mouth of the bay, was doing good service in blockading the harbor, and protecting by the cover of his guns the provincial camp on shore.

As soon as a sufficient number of the soldiers had landed, Pepperell sent, on the very first day of their arrival, Colonel Vaughan (the same man who had proposed the bold expedient of floating the troops upon the ice into Louisburg), at the head of a company, to reconnoitre Louisburg and its environs. This officer approached as near as possible to the garrison, and, having let them hear the sound of three hearty cheers, he marched his men to the acclivity of an eminence called Green hill, which overlooked the Royal battery, at some distance from the town, to the northeast of the harbor. Here Vaughan, having arrived at nightfall, found several dwellings and structures, to which he set fire, making a most portentous-looking blaze and smoke. During the night Vaughan sent back most of his men, and encamped with thirteen only on the spot; and at break of day next morning, ascending the summit of Green hill, to make a survey of the Grand battery, which was situated within distinct view below, he was surprised to find that there was every appearance of its being deserted. There was no flag flying, no smoke rising from the barrack-chimneys, and in fact no indication of its containing a single soldier. He now descended and entered the battery with his thirteen men, and sent back immediately to the provincial camp, asking for a reinforcement to aid in holding the position, and a British flag to fly from the fort. In the meantime, one of the thirteen, stripping off his red coat, and taking it in his teeth, climbed the staff, and nailed it to the top.

It seems that the smoke and blaze from the conflagration on the acclivity of Green hill, during the night before, had been observed from the Grand battery, and had so frightened the soldiers of the garrison, who supposed that the whole force of the enemy was approaching, that they deserted their post and fled into the town.

The French soon discovered their mistake, and sent out boats, with a hundred men or so, to regain possession of the

3

battery before Vaughan and his handful of men could be reinforced by the provincial camp. The brave Vaughan, however, leading out his thirteen to the shore, succeeded in keeping the Frenchmen at bay, and prevented their landing, until aid from Pepperell arrived, when the enemy were forced to betake themselves hurriedly to the town.

The provincials, finding that the cannon had been spiked by the French previous to deserting the battery, set some twenty smiths, under the supervision of one Pomeroy, a gunsmith by trade, and now a major of a Massachusetts regiment, to work at drilling the guns. They thus found themselves in possession of twenty-eight serviceable forty-two pounders, besides a good supply of shells, balls, and other ammunition. The powder, however, had been thrown into a well. With the Grand battery thus reinstated, the provincials were enabled to turn upon the enemy their own guns with great effect. The French were much vexed at the result, and strove, by keeping up a brisk fire, to render the position too hot for the provincials to hold; but the latter succeeded in maintaining possession, and in returning more than they received. The Grand battery remained, impregnable, in the hands of the colonists, to the end of the siege.

The *coup de main* suggested by Shirley having been now abandoned, there was every prospect of a long siege; and Pepperell accordingly made preparations for a systematic attack. He began erecting batteries at various points, from which he might direct his fire upon the town.

One was constructed on Green hill, fifteen hundred yards from the northwestern wall; another in the same direction, some six hundred yards nearer; and a third within seven hundred yards of the town. These batteries were composed of brush-wood, fagots, and turf, which naturally suggested themselves to the militia, who made no pretension to skill in military art, and who in fact ridiculed its technicalities. It was a labor of great difficulty to land the cannon and place them in position. In consequence of the boggy nature of the soil, the wheels of the gun-carriages sank deeply into the morasses; and it was found necessary to transport them upon sledges, which were constructed by a New-Hampshire colonel, of the name of Messerve. The men, having harnessed themselves to these by means of straps drawn over their shoulders, dragged them, as they sank knee-deep into the mud, to the batteries. For a full fortnight, by day and by night, they were thus occupied in this fatiguing work of getting the cannons into place.

The provincials were much annoyed by a strong battery of the enemy, built on an island situated at the opening of the harbor, and facing the town. This island battery was keeping up constantly a brisk fire upon Pepperell's works, and he was of course anxious to silence its guns at his earliest chance. Commodore Warren had soon discovered the importance of carrying it, and proposed to aid Pepperell in the undertaking. Councils-of-war, on land and on shipboard, were held from day to day, to devise some plan for this purpose. The commodore was

for attempting it at once; but Pepperell, more cautious and prudent, insisted upon waiting until his battering cannon and mortars were ready to play on the town. The attempt, therefore, was postponed; while the provincials, in the meantime, busied themselves in completing and furnishing their batteries, and bringing them nearer and nearer to the walls of the citadel.

May 7. The two commanders now determined to send a flag of truce to the town, with a summons to surrender. To the demand of the English the French returned the defiant answer that their reply would be at the cannon's mouth. After a momentary cessation of hostilities, during this brief parley, the firing was renewed with greater vigor than ever; and the provincials, with the addition of a fourth fascine battery, within two hundred and fifty yards of the west gate of the town, were now enabled to send such a shower of balls and shells against the walls as to do the enemy great mischief.

Warren now urged again his favorite project of an attack upon the island battery. The war-council, however, did not approve of it, considering it too hazardous, although Pepperell favored the commodore's proposition. The objections of the army were overruled, and, for several nights in succession, boats were got ready for an attack; but it was found impracticable, in consequence of the weather. The two commanders were in constant communication, and for the most part in harmony in regard to the operations of the siege. Councils-of-war were daily held on sea and land, and the results of their deliberations communicated through Pepperell and Warren.

It was finally agreed that the **May 9.** town of Louisburg be attacked by storm, in the night, with all the vigor possible. Before the night set in, however, it was found advisable to postpone the assault, "inasmuch as there appears a great dissatisfaction in many of the officers and soldiers at the designed attack of the town by storm this night; and as it may be attended with very ill consequences if it should not be executed with the greatest vigor whenever attempted, the said attack of the town be deferred for the present, or until the cannon are all mounted and in full play, and the enemy more reduced by the siege."

"Louisburg is an exceedingly strong place," wrote Major Pomeroy, the gunsmith, to his wife, "and seems impregnable. It looks as if our campaign would last long; but I am willing to stay till God's time comes to deliver the city into our hands." The good dame answered in the same spirit of patriotic and pious confidence: "Suffer no anxious thought to rest in your mind about me. The whole town is much engaged with concern for the expedition, how Providence will order the affair, for which religious meetings every week are maintained. I leave you in the hand of God."

The spirit of the Pomeroys was that of the whole provincial force; and the men went on, day by day and night by night, toiling without a murmur and with a pious resignation, waiting for the "coming of God's good time." Their labors were heavy and their sufferings great, but their energies never flagged and their spirits were equal to every trial. Without regular tents, they were obliged to house themselves under temporary erections of turf and brushwood, and to sleep upon the ground. The weather, fortunately, was unusually dry; but, notwithstanding, the men suffered from disease in consequence of their severe hardships and exposure. Pepperell found so many of his men disabled, that he was forced to send to the governor of Massachusetts for another reinforcement of a thousand men, for the bringing of whom he had despatched fourteen transports, which he took occasion to load with a number of the prisoners that had been taken.

The provincials continued their labors, adding battery to battery, and keeping up a brisk fire night and day from the works already erected. "Yesterday," writes Pepperell, "we gave **May 16.** the west gate about one hundred shot from our fascine battery," and concludes hopefully: "I hope that, under God, we shall soon be masters of this island, and that I shall have the pleasure of writing you from within the walls of Louisburg." He had now raised his fourth fascine battery, termed Titcomb's, in honor of one of the bravest and most daring of the New-England captains. Having mounted this with some of the heavy French guns taken from the Grand battery, the provincials were enabled to open a destructive fire upon the town. As they were only distant two hundred and fifty yards, they could point their guns with such effect, that they succeeded in de-

stroying the western gate, with its drawbridge, and making a small breach in the walls. The soldiers on both sides, on this occasion, were brought into each other's view, and so closely, that they passed mocking compliments, with invitations to take a glass of wine, and exchanged volleys with their muskets, by which some Frenchmen were toppled off dead from the walls.

The enemy did not appear to be doing as much damage to the besiegers as the besiegers seemed to be doing to themselves, for the latter reported several as wounded by the "splitting" of their own cannon. Pepperell was apparently very well satisfied with the progress of his operations, and wrote: "We have had considerable success hitherto, having cleared three forty-twos at the Grand battery, and have done some execution, lodging several shot in the citadel; the mortars and cohorns throw into the town in most instances." Warren, however, was not so well satisfied with the state of affairs, and complained of the apparent delay. Still, the two commanders remained on the most friendly terms with each other, and we find Pepperell thanking the commodore for the "claret and lemons, and repeated kind offers."

Warren took care to keep his squadron busy; and, with an occasional capture of an enemy's privateer and some dozen merchantmen, and a bombardment of two neighboring French settlements, his activity told to a good purpose. Pepperell went on in his usual patient way with the batteries, to which, having found thirty cannon in the east harbor at low-water mark, he added another near the light-house. Here he hoisted an English flag, and sent a regiment to guard the position. The French crossed over in boats from the town opposite, and attempted to dislodge them, but were repulsed with loss.

Warren was getting more and more impatient, and continued to urge Pepperell daily by letter to more active operations, and particularly to an attack on the island battery. The latter answered these suggestions courteously, but never failed to justify his own conduct. "It is my great concern," he says, May 17th, "that our progress against our enemies on shore is so slow; but when the difficulties of attacking the island battery are duly considered, there being but critical moments in which it can possibly be done with hopes of success; also the difficulty of scaling walls, without a breach, by undisciplined troops; of landing our cannon in so bad a harbor; of getting them conveyed on such bad grounds in the face of our enemy's fire, while we can not annoy them at all; and a general illness through the army: these and such like things considered, I hope your patience will not tire. The probability of the speedy arrival of a French sea-force I duly consider, but I hope the best, and nothing in my power shall be wanting toward the greatest despatch and most vigorous attack."

Warren had proposed another plan for the attack on the island battery, which Pepperell laid before his council-of-war. The provincials did not seem to approve of it, as the commodore wished to bring in his squadron and trust chiefly to the naval forces for the enterprise. The troops were desirous, if honor was to be won, that they should secure for themselves a fair share of it. Pepperell, accordingly, went on with his systematic siege, and seemed satisfied with its progress. "We have continued," he says, "our fire on the enemy from the west-gate battery, which has shattered the wall considerably; but we were so unfortunate last night as to split one of the forty-two pounders."

May 20.

The enemy about this time enjoyed a small triumph, in the arrival of a Bordeaux merchantman, laden with provisions, which succeeded, under the cover of a dark and stormy night, in escaping the vigilance of Warren and his cruisers, and reaching the harbor of Louisburg in safety. At the same time there arrived a less welcome visiter in the shape of a fire-ship, which Pepperell, taking advantage of the darkness of the night, had sent in, and which did considerable damage to the enemy's shipping.

Commodore Warren, however, won the greatest triumph of all, having taken a French man-of-war of sixty-four guns, manned by six hundred men, and laden with military stores. The capture of the Vigilante, as she was named, produced a burst of joy in the army, and animated the soldiers with fresh courage to persevere. Pepperell himself seemed now to tire of the slowness of his own operations, and proposed a general consultation, in order to determine upon a speedy and vigorous attack with the whole united forces, both sea and land. Warren received this suggestion with a hearty welcome, and, with the advice of his council, proposed a plan for an attack upon the town.

It was proposed that all his majesty's ships, and all the colonial cruisers except two, with the schooners and transports, should sail into the harbor and attack the town and batteries with the utmost vigor, "with his majesty's ships in such order of battle as shall be agreed on, and that all the unarmed vessels anchor in the northeast harbor, out of gunshot." It was, moreover, proposed that sixteen hundred of Pepperell's men should go on board the vessels of the squadron, to aid in the attack, while the marines should be landed under the command of M°Donald, their colonel, who was to lead the attack on shore, and be sustained by the provincial troops.

This proposition was by no means welcome to Pepperell and his army, as its whole scope was to place the provincials in a very subordinate position, and deprive them of all chance of glory in the proposed undertaking.

Pepperell and his council had other reasons to urge. The Indians, they contended, might come in upon their backs, while the troops were on board the ships, and attack what forces remained in the camp and hospitals. Moreover, they declared that the army was so reduced by sickness, that the soldiers were unfitted for such service as proposed; and that if the plan should miscarry, as it probably would from this inefficiency, the result would be disastrous to the colonies. Pepperell's council then proposed that a general attack be made upon the town by the land and naval forces forthwith; that five hundred men be impressed from the cruisers and transports, to embark in the Vigilante (the vessel captured from the French), and that the other men-of-war follow her into the harbor; that five hundred provincials put off in boats from the Grand battery at a given signal, to land and scale the walls in front of the town, under cover of the guns of the squadron and the land-batteries; that the marines and sailors of the fleet should put off and join them; that five hundred of the troops should scale the walls at the southeast part of the town, and that the same number should make a breach at the western gate, leaving half a thousand disposable men to aid any party that might need their services.

This plan of Pepperell's council was not sent at once to Warren, in consequence of a dense fog. The commodore became impatient, and wrote, asking why he had not received an answer to the proposition sent two days before; and, after reiterating some **May 26.** of its details, peevishly remarked, "For God's sake, let us do something, and not waste our time in indolence!"

The provincials began to sympathize with Warren's anxiety to do something, and the council-of-war proposed that the general should go on board the commodore's ship, and try to decide upon some mutual plan for immediate action. Warren, although he had been reinforced by several additional men-of-war, which had joined him from the various American and West-Indian stations, was fearful that the arrival of the French fleet, daily expected, would give him so much to do in looking after it, that he would no longer have it in his power to aid in the attack upon Louisburg. He therefore pressed this enterprise with all his energies. As a preliminary to the general assault, Warren thought it necessary to silence the island battery, which guarded the approach to the town, and was seriously in the way of his ships making an attack. He accordingly prevailed upon Pepperell to make an attempt on the island, though the army generally was averse to it, as too hazardous, and as likely to result in disappointment.

A volunteer party of provincials was now enlisted for the purpose, and started with scaling-ladders to make the assault. Although it was in the darkness of the night, and every precaution was taken to elude the vigilance of the enemy, the garrison of the island battery caught the alarm, and began to fire upon the boats before they reached the shore. On the provincials now attempting to land, they got so wetted in the heavy surf that many of the firelocks could not be discharged, and some of the party were driven back at once in confusion to their boats; others succeeded in making a stand on the shore for awhile, but were, after an hour's hard struggle, compelled to yield to the French. Sixty were killed, and no less than a hundred and sixteen taken prisoners. "Providence seemed remarkably to frown upon the affair," as one of the pious provincials wrote, in giving an account of this melancholy disaster to his friends in New England.

CHAPTER III.

Exultant Shouts of the Enemy.—Pepperell discouraged.—A more Vigorous Push.—A General Attack proposed.—Opposed by the Admiral.—A French Deserter reports the Enemy in Good Spirits.—A Plan to dash them.—A Successful Ruse. —An Attack upon the Island Battery again proposed.—Opposed by Pepperell.—The Bombardment of the Town brisker than ever.—The General Assault decided upon.—The " Three Smokes and Dutch Flag."—Great Preparations. —Louisburg suffering more than ever.—The Attempt begun.—Stirring Addresses from the General and the Commodore.—The Enemy sends out a Flag of Truce.—Proposes to capitulate.—Terms of Surrender agreed upon.—Pepperell and Warren disputing about the Keys.—The General triumphs.—Louisburg entered.—Its Strength and its Weakness. —Glorification.—Dinner.—Parson Moody agreeably disappoints his Friends with a Short Grace.—Pepperell and Warren Joint Governors.—The French Flag hoisted as a Decoy.—Fat Prizes.—Glorification and Thanksgiving in New England.—Ditto in Old England.—The King delighted.—The Admiral promoted, and Pepperell made a Baronet, the first and last in New England.—The Effect of the Victory.

THAT night's repulse of the attack on the island battery was a sad blow to the provincials, who, as the morning dawned upon them in their camp, heard the exulting shouts of the enemy over the first success they could claim since the beginning of the siege. Although Pepperell had made fair progress in investing the citadel with his batteries, by which he had succeeded in doing much damage to the town, and had beaten back the French on every sortie from their walls, he was, after the defeat of the previous night, evidently somewhat disheartened.

May 28. "It is now," says Pepperell himself, "the twenty-ninth day since the army invested Louisburg and drove in the inhabitants. Five fascine batteries have been erected, with hard service to the men, who have drawn the cannon and mounted them; the enemy has been distressed, some breaches have been made in their walls," and it is not doubted but that "we shall soon reduce the circular battery. Five unsuccessful attempts have been made upon the island battery, in the last of which one hundred and eighty-nine men and many boats were lost. Scouts have been sent out, and have succeeded in destroying the enemy's settlements and in preventing surprise. Fatigue, however, has brought on disease, and left not more than two thousand one hundred men fit for duty, six hundred of whom are gone in pursuit of two large bodies of French and Indians eastward and westward of the provincial camp."

This was the not very encouraging state of things, when Pepperell resolved upon a more vigorous push. He was anxious now for a consultation with Warren, but was prevented for several days by the fog from going on board the commodore's ship. He finally, however, succeeded in reaching him, and proposed a joint attack on the town. Warren, however, was not now disposed to concur in this proposition, although it had originally been made by him. He thought it better not to send his ships into the harbor until further execution had been done against the enemy's batteries.

Pepperell, in the meantime, continued to do his best in pushing on the siege. He, however, was in great straits for want of ammunition and effective men. In his despatch to Governor Shirley, he says: "Powder and balls are nearly used up, on account of which many of our guns are silent. We have one thousand five hundred sick, and a reinforcement therefore of three thousand men is absolutely necessary." The French, on the other hand, seemed to be in excellent condition, and by no means discouraged as to their ability to hold out against the besiegers.

A French soldier deserts, and, **June 4.** reaching the provincial camp, reports that there are within the garrison three thousand six hundred that bear arms, seven or eight hundred of whom are soldiers; that they have provisions to last till October, and considerable ammunition; that the enemy judged variously the provincial forces from one thousand to four thousand five hundred men; that they have burst one of their mortars and several cannon; that they are prepared to receive an attack every night in all parts of the town; and that if their expected ships are taken they will have to surrender, but they do not expect the British ships will venture into the harbor.

Commodore Warren, learning from this deserter, who was sent to him by Pepperell, how well the French kept up their spirits, resolved upon a plan to try and dash them somewhat. The inhabitants of Louisburg had not yet heard of the capture of the Vigilante, although she had been in the hands of the English for nearly three weeks. Warren thought if this intelligence could be conveyed to the French commander, it would naturally have the effect of lowering his hopes of a continued successful resistance. The commodore, accordingly, pretending that he had heard of the cruel treatment of some of the provincials held by the enemy's garrison as prisoners, suggested to the former commander of the Vigilante, who was now a captive of the English, to write to Duchambon, the governor of Louisburg, and interpose in their behalf. The Frenchman readily complied, and prepared this letter :—

"ON BOARD THE VIGILANTE, WHERE I AM A PRISONER, BEFORE LOUISBURG, *June 8*, 1745.

"Herewith I send you, sir, the copy of a letter written me by Mr. Warren, commander of a squadron, who informs me that the French have treated some English prisoners with cruelty and inhumanity. I can scarcely believe it, since it is the intention of the king our master that they should be well treated on every occasion. You are to know that on the 20th of May I was taken by the squadron, as I was about to enter your harbor; and it is fitting you should be informed that the gentlemen, the captains and officers, treat us not as prisoners, but as their good friends, and take a very particular care that my officers and equipage should want nothing. To me it seems just you should treat them in the same manner, and see that those be punished who act otherwise, and offer any insult to those whom you may make prisoners.

"Yours, &c.

"DE LA MAISON FORTE."

4

To carry out his *ruse* more effectually, Warren selected one of his officers, who understood the French language, Captain Macdonald, and intrusted the letter to him to deliver. This officer was accordingly sent to Louisburg under a flag of truce, and was duly received by the governor, who was greatly startled by the letter, which gave him the first intelligence of the capture of the Vigilante. Captain Macdonald, who communicated with the French officers only through an interpreter, was supposed to be ignorant of their language; and accordingly they freely expressed their thoughts and opinions in their native tongue, without the least fear of being understood. The English officer was thus enabled to bring back to Warren a faithful account of the fright occasioned by this untoward news of the capture of that large man-of-war, the Vigilante, the safe arrival of which they had been expecting, with supplies of men, provisions, and ammunition.

The French were further disheartened by learning of a large accession to the British squadron, and disappointed at the delay of their own expected fleet. Pepperell, too, had been reinforced, by a timely arrival of recruits and ammunition, not only from the neighboring British settlements of Canseau and Annapolis, but from Massachusetts; and was thus enabled to keep up, by a more effectual fire from his batteries, the lively apprehensions of the French, first aroused by a knowledge of the fate of the Vigilante.

By a council-of-war held in the squadron, it was determined that **June 8.** it was not practicable or advisable to attack the town of Louisburg, without the island battery should be first taken. It was therefore proposed that, if proper pilots could be found, the ships should be anchored within half a cable's length of the island, and General Pepperell having supplied the commodore with five hundred provincials, that these, together with the sailors and marines of the squadron, should land under cover of the ships, and attack the island fortress.

Pepperell, on being consulted, did not altogether approve of this plan, being especially opposed to the attack on the island by embarking the troops in the whale-boats, which a few musket-balls might sink. He therefore urged again his former proposition of a general attack upon the town. As for the island battery, the squadron, he suggested, might bombard it from the outside, and be safe to retreat. Pepperell sent accordingly three pilots from his own transports, to take charge of the ships and bring them to a safe anchorage as near as possible to the point of attack.

While this plan of Pepperell is being considered, the provincials set to work, with renewed energy, in their bombardment of Louisburg, and threw into the citadel a continued shower of red-hot balls. The French, too, were not backward, and returned the fire with great spirit. They succeeded in planting six cannon, during the night, to protect the west gate, which was the chief object of attack; but the provincials had the good fortune to silence them early the next morning.

Warren finally consented to bring in his ships, in accordance with Pepperell's plan; and it was agreed that, as soon as the wind was fair for the squadron to sail into the harbor, the attack upon Louisburg should be made. The commodore was to hoist a Dutch flag under his pennant at the maintop-gallant masthead, as the signal of his having weighed anchor; and Pepperell was to answer, when he should be ready, with " three smokes."— " When I hoist a Dutch flag," says Warren in his communication, " you should march toward the town, drums beating and colors flying; when I hoist the red flag on the flagstaff, you may then be assured I shall be in and begin the attack in about half an hour."

Pepperell was as eager as the commodore, and was making ready with all possible despatch. He ordered all the transports out to join the squadron, the boats to be fitted with oars and ladders, and sent to Warren a supply of cohorns and shells, and what oakum and moss could be collected. He got ready three more forty-twos to play upon the circular battery, and prevent it from annoying the ships. He was keeping up a constant fire from his lighthouse battery upon the island fortress, and had succeeded in almost silencing it. His other batteries, too, were kept busy; and Louisburg was evidently suffering more than ever it had done during the whole six weeks of the siege.

Everything was now in readiness for the general "push." The **June 14.** provincial vessels had sailed out of the bay to join the squadron; the brushwood had been gathered and placed on the summit of Green hill, preparatory to the raising the signal of "three smokes ;" and all was now eager expectation of the coming event.

June 15. Warren hoisted his Dutch flag; Pepperell answered with his "three smokes" from Green hill; Warren replied with his red flag; and soon the fleet sailed in before the wind, and anchored in a line near the town. The commodore pulled off at once for the shore, and, meeting the general, they were received by the troops on parade. Both Pepperell and Warren, having addressed them in a few stirring words, prepared to assume their several positions, and fulfil the duties of the day. Before they had parted, however, it being late in the afternoon, a flag of truce was seen advancing from the west gate of the garrison. The bombardment ceased at once, and the captain of the foremost of the provincial batteries approaching half way, met the French officer who bore the flag, and received from him a proposal for the suspension of hostilities, in order to give the garrison an opportunity for the consideration of terms of capitulation. Pepperell and Warren sent back their answer as follows, having written it in the camp as late as half-past eight at night :—

"*June 15th.*

" GOVERNOR DUCHAMBON :

" We have yours of this date, proposing a suspension of hostilities for such a time as shall be necessary for you to determine upon the conditions of delivering up the garrison of Louisburg, which arrived at a happy juncture to prevent the effusion of Christian blood, as we were together, and had just determined upon a general attack. We shall comply with your desire until eight o'clock to-morrow morning ; and if in the meantime you surrender yourselves prisoners-of-war, you may depend upon humane and generous treatment.

" We are your humble servants,

" PETER WARREN,

" WILLIAM PEPPERELL."

Next morning, Duchambon sent back his terms for the surrender of Louisburg, but they were rejected by Warren and Pepperell, who insisted upon conditions less favorable to the enemy. These were accordingly accepted by the French, who, however, demanded that their troops might be allowed to march out of the garrison with their muskets and bayonets, and colors flying. This privilege was freely granted by Pepperell and Warren, who thought it not worth while to "stickle at trifles." Terms of capitulation having been agreed upon, hostages delivered, and all preliminaries arranged, the two commanders prepared to take possession. There now sprang up a feeling of rivalry between Pepperell and Warren, as to who should enter Louisburg first and receive the keys of the fortress. Both seemed anxious for awhile to frustrate the other; and each wrote to Duchambon, demanding that the town should be given up to him. Pepperell, to whom probably precedence belonged, wrote to the French governor that he would send Colonel Bradstreet with a detachment at four o'clock in the afternoon, to **June 17.** take possession of the town and forts, to whom he desired that the keys be delivered.

Warren, having stolen a march upon his rival, had previously written to Duchambon, demanding that the **June 16.** keys of the town be delivered to such officers and troops as he should appoint. The French governor seemed inclined rather to yield to the commodore, who probably passed with him as the superior officer. Duchambon accordingly showed Pepperell's letter to Warren, who was so angered by its purport, that he wrote reproachfully to the provincial general, telling him he was sorry to find by his "letter a kind of jealousy which I thought you would never conceive of me, after my letter to you of last night. And give me leave to tell you I don't want at this time to acquire reputation, as I flatter myself mine has been pretty well established long before."

After this little spirt of rivalry between the two commanders, the affair was finally adjusted by Warren conceding to Pepperell—what fairly belonged to him as commander-in-chief of the expedition— the right of receiving the keys. The **1745.** French fortress was now delivered up; and, as the troops entered, they were so struck with the strength of the fortifications, that they considered their own success as a marvel of God's goodness. " God," wrote an eye-witness, " has gone out of the way of his common providence, in a remarkable and almost miraculous manner, to incline the hearts of the French to give up and deliver this strong city into our hands."

Strong as it was, however, Pepperell had succeeded with his batteries in shattering its strength very effectually. In his despatch to Shirley he said : " I believe such ruins were never seen before, which, however, is not to be wondered at, as we gave the town about nine thousand cannon-balls and six hundred bombs before they surrendered, which sorely distressed them, especially the day before they sent out a flag of truce, when our incessant fire on the town prevented their showing their heads or stirring from their covert ways; and from lighthouse battery we played upon the island battery with our cannon and large mortar, so that some of them ran into the sea for shelter."

On entering Louisburg, it was found to contain two thousand inhabitants, in addition to about four thousand troops, of whom about six hundred and fifty only were regulars. All these, by the terms of the surrender, were to be sent to France, and pledged not to bear arms against Great Britain or its colonies for the period of twelve months. A large quantity of provisions, sufficient to have lasted the garrison for half a year, and immense supplies of ammunition and military stores, were taken possession of by the captors.

The occasion of the capture was celebrated by a public dinner, given by Pepperell to his officers, of which a clerical anecdote is recorded as the most memorable incident. The general had been accompanied by a number of the New-England clergy, among whom was his wife's brother, one Parson Moody. This divine being the eldest, was entitled to the honor of saying " grace before meat." As he, however, was apt to be very long-winded on such occasions, the company were in a state of nervous anxiety, lest he should inflict upon them his usual prolixity. Moody, however, only gave vent to the following brief invocation, much to the relief of the anxious and hungry guests: "Good Lord! we have so many things to thank thee for, that time will be infinitely too short to do it; we must therefore leave it for the work of eternity. Bless our food and fellowship upon this joyful occasion, for the sake of Christ our Lord. Amen."*

Pepperell and Warren became the joint governors of Louisburg on taking possession of the city in the name of his majesty George II.; but they continued to fly the French flag from the fortress, with the view of deceiving the French vessels expected to arrive. By this deception, they succeeded in ensnaring a large number of prizes, amounting in all to no less than a million of dollars. There were two East-Indiamen supposed to be worth one hundred and seventy-five thousand pounds sterling, and a South-sea ship of the enormous value of eight hundred thousand pounds. This prize-money, however, much to the dissatisfaction of the provincials, fell exclusively to the naval forces.

When they heard in New-England of the success of the expedition, there was great joy throughout the colony. Boston was illuminated as it had never been before. "There was not a house in town,

* "The Life of Sir William Pepperell, Bart., by Usher Parsons. Boston: Little, Brown, & Company, 1855." A work of careful research, to which the author of the "Battles of America" has been indebted for much valuable information.

in no by-lane or alley, but joy might be seen through its windows." The bells rang, the cannons roared, and the people shouted the whole day, while bonfires burnt and houses blazed with light all the night. A day was set apart throughout the province to return thanks "to God for his appearance on our behalf."

Nor did the news of the victory excite less joy in Old England. "We are making bonfires for Cape Breton," wrote Horace Walpole. George II., who was on a visit to his Hanoverian possessions when he received the intelligence of the capture of Louisburg, was aroused to an unusual pitch of enthusiastic delight. He made Warren an admiral at once, and governor of Louisburg; and issued his letters-patent, dating them from Hanover, by which he conferred a baronetcy upon Pepperell. Sir William was the first and only native New-England colonist ever raised to that dignity.

In London the news created great excitement; the tower and park guns were fired, and the city illuminated. On the return of George II. to his British dominions, he was met by congratulations and addresses of the towns and public bodies, upon the happy event. The ministry of the duke of Newcastle had involved Great Britain in a war with France, which had hitherto only resulted in disgrace to the former and glory to the latter. The English had now the conquest of Louisburg, "the *Dunkirk* of America," as a set-off to the French triumph at Fontenoy.

The Americans became exalted at once in the estimate of their British fellow-subjects, as they alone had succeeded in vindicating the fame of their country by a great victory over its enemies. The reduction of Cape Breton, said a contemporary writer, "by the people of New England, was an acquisition so unexpected and fortunate, that America became on that remarkable event a more general topic of conversation. Of such consequence to the French was the possession of that important key to their American settlements, that its restitution was in reality the purchase of the last general peace of Europe."

The effect upon the future destinies of America was no less than upon the actu-al position of affairs in Europe. At the siege of Louisburg, the American colonists learned their first lesson in regular warfare, and acquired that self-confidence which did not hesitate, in behalf of their own great cause of independence, to try the chances of battle with European troops. At Louisburg, too, were schooled those famous officers, Wooster, Whiting, Gridley, and others, who became as heroic Revolutionary leaders in the battle for "life, liberty, and happiness," as they had been faithful soldiers in the service of their king, whom they only loved the less because they loved their country more.

CHAPTER IV.

The New-Englanders eager for Conquest.—Proposal to invade the Canadas.—The French burning with Revenge.—An Avenging Fleet.—Its Fate.—A Second French Fleet.—Met and conquered by the British.—Peace.—The Concession of Louisburg to the French.—New-Englanders dissatisfied.—France again lusting for Dominion.—Desires to unite the St. Lawrence and the Mississippi.—Who shall be supreme, France or England?—Might not Right.—Marquis Du Quesne, Governor of Canada.—His Activity.—Forts built.—Ohio Company alarmed.—Appeal to Governor Dinwiddie, of Virginia.—A Commissioner sent to expostulate with the French.—Failure of the Mission.—George Washington appointed.—A Bootless Errand.—The Ohio Company constructs a Fort.—Dinwiddie sends a Force to protect it.—Washington declines the Honor of the Chief Command, but accepts the Second Rank.—His March to the Ohio.—The French Invasion.—Washington and his Difficulties.—Spirited Conduct.—The American Fort on the Ohio attacked and the Virginians routed.—The Garrison arrive in Washington's Camp at Will's Creek.—Their Story and Adventures.—Monsieur Contrecœur.—A Wily Old Indian.—Washington perplexed.—A Council-of-War.—March to Redstone Creek.—Road-Making.—Little Meadows.—Excessive Labors.—The Indians propose the River Route.—The River found impracticable.—Road-Making resumed.—Rumors of the French.—Arrival of the Enemy.—Washington goes in Pursuit.—Finds the French, attacks and beats them.—The Death of Jumonville.—A Spy or an Embassador?—Washington slandered by the French.

1745. The New-Englanders were so elated by their success at Louisburg, that their minds were stirred with a desire for further conquests. They were now prepared to carry the war into Canada; and a plan for a campaign was actually devised, by Shirley, the governor of Massachusetts, and the two heroes of Louisburg, Pepperell and Warren, within the walls of that citadel. The British minister, the duke of Newcastle, seemed to favor greatly the American design; and, having conferred colonelcies upon Shirley and Pepperell, ordered them to recruit their regiments to the number of a thousand each, preparatory to the invasion of the French possessions in Canada.

The French, on the other hand, having heard with great vexation of the loss of their famous citadel, determined to take revenge. They accordingly fitted out a large fleet, at an immense expense, in the port of Brest, and, placing it under **1746.** the command of the duke d'Anville, despatched it to America, with the view of reconquering Cape Breton, and striking a severe blow upon the coasts of the British provinces in America. Great preparations were made in New England to defend it against this formidable enemy. Forts were erected along the coast, the militia of the various provinces gathered to protect the exposed points, and sentinels were placed on the hilltops to watch for the first signs of the coming of the French ships. Sir William Pepperell, the hero of Louisburg, had now returned to Maine, and assumed his old command of its militia. He was full of martial spirit on the occasion, and had his companies mustered by their captains, their accoutrements put in order, and every possible arrangement made for the approaching emergency.

D'Anville and his fleet did not arrive, however. They had put to sea in great force, with no less than eleven ships-of-the-line, thirty small vessels-of-war, and various transports containing three thousand regular troops. Nova Scotia, then as now in possession of the English, was to be the first point of attack. Calculating upon the sympathy and active aid of the French residents of this the former Acadie, they anticipated an easy conquest. Once in possession of this peninsula, they proposed to retake Louisburg, and thence invade the New-England coasts. The design was extensive, and the preparations had been on a scale of grandeur in accordance. But man proposes and God disposes.

The fleet had hardly sailed out of Brest in gallant trim, and fairly got to sea, when a storm arose, which wrecked many of the vessels, and separated the rest. The duke d'Anville succeeded in reaching the American coast in his own ship, and was soon joined by a few of the smaller vessels. His sudden death, however, put a stop to all his plans; and the command fell, by succession, to the vice-admiral. This commander resolved upon returning to France, in consequence of the diminished number of his vessels and their shattered condition; but his council-of-war overruled him. So excited was the vice-admiral by the opposition of his officers, that he ran himself through the body with his sword.

The aged De la Jonquierè now succeeded, who, in spite of his nearly seventy years, had not only advocated the bolder policy in opposition to the vice-admiral, but now, in command, was prepared to carry it out with the greatest energy. All, however, was in vain: another storm arose, off Cape Sable, and the few vessels that escaped returned in a damaged state, to give testimony of the fatality which had attended the great French expedition.

The government of France, however, was not discouraged, and soon had in readiness another fleet to invade the British colonies. England, early conscious of this renewed attempt, had **1746.**

also equipped a large naval force, by which it was proposed to intercept the French. Anson was made admiral of the English fleet, and Warren, the naval hero of Louisburg, rear-admiral.

On hearing that the French were about to sail, the English put to sea, and awaited the enemy off Cape Finisterre, on the coast of France. The two met on the 3d of May, 1746, and immediately began battle. The French were worsted after a severe struggle, leaving all their ships-of-the-line in the hands of the British, with a large quantity of bullion, and Admiral de la Jonquierè, the newly-appointed governor of Canada, to reward and grace the English triumph.

There was now, with the exception of an occasional brush between the English and French on the frontiers, an almost entire suspension of hostilities. The British finally disbanded the provincial army; and the colonists were thus prepared, in anticipation, for the event which now occurred, that of the declaration of peace by the treaty of Aix-la-Chapelle. **1748.** By this treaty, the island of Cape Breton, with the hard-won fortress of Louisburg, was given up to the French, much to their satisfaction, and to the vexation of the New-Englanders, who considered the possession of this town as essential to their own security. It was true, the right of Great Britain to Nova Scotia was acknowledged; but the French inhabitants of that peninsula—under the advice, as was suspected, of the government of France—resisted the English claim. The treaty, therefore, was very distasteful to New England, and natural-ly, for its best interests had been sacrificed by the mother-country, in her anxiety to bring to a close a war which had cost so much, and profited her so little.

The French, in spite of the peace, began soon, not only covertly, as in Nova Scotia, but openly, to encroach upon English colonial rights. France had long entertained the grand idea of connecting its northern possessions in Canada with those she held on the gulf of Mexico. Her possession of Louisiana, with its then widely-extended boundaries, gave her the command of the Mississippi; while her Canadian territory, stretching from the mouth of the St. Lawrence to the great lakes, brought her upper dominion so close to the Ohio, that nothing was wanting but the mastery of that river to give her the united power, north and south, which she coveted.

The English colonies could not look calmly upon this scheme, which was, if consummated, destined, as has been ingeniously said, to catch them in a net, that, being tightened at either end, would inevitably bring them entirely within the power of the French. There were claims and counter-claims urged by France and Great Britain to the territory watered by the Ohio, but those of the one and the other were equally baseless. The question was not one of disputed rights, but of contending powers. The whole matter resolved itself into this: "Who shall be supreme in the West, France or England?" It was of little importance that the latter claimed unlimited territory from the Atlantic to the Pacific, and that the former insisted, by the right of discovery and the command of the Mississippi, on the possession of all its tributaries, and the rich land west of the Alleghany mountains watered by them. It was clear, with such unbounded claims on each side, that neither could secure its supposed right but by an appeal to might.

The French first threw down the gauntlet. The marquis du Quesne was appointed governor of the French dominions in America—and was instructed to make good the widest claims of his country, by military possession. He accordingly hurried to carry the orders of his government into effect. He organized the militia of Quebec and Montreal, and placed all the forces under his command on the most effective footing. He now sent various detachments to the banks of the Ohio, for the purpose of establishing forts and securing the command of that river, that he might thus unite it with the Mississippi by military posts, and complete the cordon from Canada to Louisiana. Such was the activity of Du Quesne's movements, that, before the end of the year, he had established a line of forts from Montreal to the Rivierè aux Bœufs, now known as a small stream, in Pennsylvania, by the name of French creek.

1752.

1753.

The "Ohio Company" was the first to complain of what they called an invasion of their rights. This company was an English association chartered some time in the year 1749, and was composed of a large number of native and colonial Englishmen. Its purpose was to colonize, and trade, principally for furs, with the Indians; and accordingly five hundred thousand acres of land west of the Alleghanies had been granted to the company. It was this extensive territory which had been encroached upon by the French, and the Ohio Company therefore called upon Dinwiddie, the governor of Virginia, to take some action toward dispossessing the intruders. Dinwiddie, who was a proprietor of the company, saw at once the necessity of interference, and sent a commissioner to expostulate with the French on their invasion of the rights of Virginia. Captain William Trent, who had been selected to perform this duty, returned without having fulfilled it, but came back with more alarming accounts than ever of the French invasion.

George Washington, who was only twenty-two years of age, was then selected by the governor of Virginia. His profession as a surveyor had led him into the uncultivated parts of the country, and made him familiar with the wild life of the savage and the borderer. He had had also some experience as a military disciplinarian, having served, before he was of age, as one of the adjutant-generals of the province, whose duty it was to organize and drill the militia. He was now appointed adjutant-general and commissioner to bear the summons of the governor of Virginia to the French commander on Lake Erie, requiring him to retire from what was claimed to be English territory. The errand of Washington proved bootless, and the French continued to seize and disperse the English traders, and prepared to descend the Ohio and take military possession, by

5

establishing forts at each available point on the river.

The Ohio Company had commenced the construction of a fortified post on the Ohio river, at the junction of the Alleghany and Monongahela. This was supposed to be a point that would attract the invaders at once. It was therefore determined by the governor of Virginia to send a force there, to aid in the construction of the fort, and defend it against every attack. Captain Trent was accordingly despatched at the head of a hundred militiamen on this service.

The youthful Washington was also called upon again by Dinwiddie, and offered the chief command of the 1754. three hundred men whom it was proposed to enlist. Washington, however, modestly declined the honor, and gave way to a Colonel Joshua Fry, under whom he served as lieutenant-colonel. Washington, preceding his colonel, set out for the fork of the Ohio on the 2d of April, at the head of two companies, numbering one hundred and fifty men. Fry was to follow with the rest and the artillery.

The French at this time were in possession on Lake Erie, within the limits of the present town of Erie, of a log-fort, which had been built for several years, and which was well protected with pickets, bastions, and ditch, and a strong garrison of soldiers. They had also taken possession of a spot where now stands the village of Waterford, and constructed a fort on the Rivière aux Bœufs, so called from the numerous herds of buffalo which fed upon the fertile meadows watered by that stream, now known as the French creek, in Pennsylvania. Farther on, again, toward the Ohio, they had also lately established another fortified post, which was called Venango. This was situated on the Alleghany, at the mouth of the "Rivière aux Bœufs," or French creek. A strong garrison was maintained during the whole winter at the fort on the Rivière aux Bœufs, and large additional forces were ordered to rendezvous there the subsequent 1754. spring. Accordingly, at this time, some five hundred to a thousand well-organized French-Canadian soldiers had mustered, and prepared, under the command of Monsieur de Contrecœur, to advance down the Ohio and take military possession of its banks.

It was to meet this anticipated invasion that Washington was now marching with his one hundred and fifty men. He found his progress obstructed by every possible difficulty. On reaching Winchester, he was forced, in order to obtain the necessary horses and baggage-wagons, to put into effect the militia-law of Virginia, which authorized him to take by compulsion what could not be gotten from the free will of the reluctant farmers. With all this arbitrary exercise of power, he had to wait more than a week for only ten horses, which was literally but a tithe of the number demanded. At this disadvantage, Washington was forced to continue his march, over a country that was mountainous and unsupplied with roads. The men were obliged, in consequence of the sorry condition of the horses impressed from the farmers, to put their shoulders constantly to the wheels of the wagons, and assist them over the steep passes and through the boggy soil. They were not disheartened, however, and proceeded bravely on their toilsome march, until they reached Will's creek, now the Cumberland river, where they found Captain Trent. From him they learned that he had left his men under the command of one Lieutenant Frazier, all well, and hard at work in finishing the fort on the Ohio. Washington was anxious to push on; but as Trent had failed to provide the pack-horses expected, he was forced to send and make another levy upon the reluctant patriots of Winchester. As this town was at a distance of forty miles, the youthful colonel was obliged, much to his dissatisfaction, to repress his impatience to move. In the meantime, all uncertainty about the fate of the men at the Ohio fork was settled by their appearance, on the 25th of April, at Will's creek, loaded down with their working-tools, and commanded by one Ensign Ward.

The cause of this unexpected arrival was soon explained. While the men— only fifty in number, thirty-three of whom alone were effective—were busily engaged on the works of the fort, Monsieur Contrecœur suddenly made his appearance, at the head of a thousand men, and well provided with artillery and other means of attack. He had just come from the fortified post of Venango, on the Alleghany, having floated his force down that river, in sixty batteaux and three hundred canoes. He now summoned Ensign Ward, who in the absence of Trent and Frazier had been left in command, to surrender, and gave him one hour in which to give his answer. Ward was perplexed, as in the absence of his superiors he hardly cared to take the responsibility of making any capitulation, however urgent might appear its necessity. In this dilemma, he consulted the Indian half-king Tanacharisson, who was an ally of the English, and happened at that time to be in the fort. This wily old savage suggested to Ward to plead want of authority, and to ask the French commander to be polite enough to postpone the affair for the present. The ensign followed the advice of his Indian counsellor; but Monsieur Contrecœur was not to be dissuaded from his purpose, and insisted more urgently than ever upon immediate surrender. There was no alternative for Ward; for what could he do, with only thirty-three men able to bear arms, and a half-built fort, against a thousand soldiers, and a whole park of artillery? The fort was accordingly given up, the men being allowed to depart with their tools. These were the visiters who had arrived at Will's creek, and such the story they had to tell of their adventures.

Washington, with his handful of men, was sadly perplexed as to his movements. The French greatly outnumbered him in force, and had succeeded by liberal presents in winning over to their side the larger tribes of the Indian savages of the wilderness. The French were, moreover, in daily expectation of receiving reinforcements from Canada and their southern possessions; and no less than six hundred warriors of the Chippewa and Ottawa nations were said to be making their way to join the camp of Contrecœur. All that Washington could calculate upon, in addition to his own small troop, were the hundred and fifty men with the artillery under Fry. These, however, might yet be detained for a long time. As for Trent and his men, no reliance could be put in them. The captain himself was timid and improvident, and his followers a set of independent vagabonds, who, having been enlisted as volunteers, exercised their volition in doing nothing, and interfering with the general good discipline of the troops.

Washington now called a council-of-war, in which it was resolved to march to Redstone creek, where the Ohio Company had a post. It was proposed to proceed thither, and, having encamped, to fortify their position as best they could, until reinforcements should arrive, or some expedient should suggest itself in the course of events to extricate themselves, or to justify action. Two Indians had come into Washington's camp in company with Ensign Ward and his men. These savages had been sent by Tanacharisson, the chief of the western tribes of Indians, who were friendly to the Virginians. The two Indian warriors bore a speech, pledging fidelity to the English, and a belt of wampum as a symbol of friendship for the governor. The wampum was forwarded, under the care of its Indian bearer, to Dinwiddie; and Washington sent back the other Indian with a return speech, in which he invoked the aid of the half-king in council, and called upon him to come down, in company with an-

other sachem, and meet him at a certain point on the road.

Washington's march began, but was exceedingly toilsome and slow, as he was obliged to make the road on which he moved, not only for his own present purposes, but for the future passage of Fry's artillery. He had sent some sixty men in advance, several days before he set out with the remainder of his whole force, numbering, all told, only one hundred and sixty. The advance party was soon overtaken, as they had made but slow progress in their labors. The rest of Washington's men, on coming up, fell to work also; but, with all their combined efforts, it was found that they could not get on at the best with more than four miles a day. It took them ten days to reach Little Meadows, only twenty miles from Will's creek, whence they had set out. They, however, continued their laborious undertaking, and labored day after day, slaving (as Washington himself describes it) through woods, rocks, and mountains.

They finally reached the river Youghioney, where they were obliged to build a bridge. While engaged in this work, which was an affair of several days, some friendly Indians entered the camp of Washington. On hearing of his plan of constructing a road over the mountains to Redstone creek, they remonstrated with him upon the impracticability of such a work. He then, by their advice, set out, in company with a guard and an Indian guide, to try the practicability of the river-route. This was found, however, so full of rocks and shoals, and so interrupted by rapids and falls, that it was useless to attempt to navigate it with boats sufficiently large for military purposes. Washington accordingly resolved to continue his arduous land-route.

From day to day, as the Virginians remained encamped on the banks of the Youghioney, and were going on with their work upon the bridge, Indian scouts and white traders came in with every variety of rumor in regard to the enemy. Some told how the French commander was building a strong fort at the fork of the Ohio; some reported that he had received large reinforcements from Canada, and was preparing to come down the river; others, however, declared that the French were only eight hundred strong, and that one half of them had been sent out from the fort on a secret expedition, the object of which was suspected to be an attack upon the English.

This latter suspicion was confirmed by a direct message from Tanacharisson, the Indian chief, who said: "It is reported that the French army is coming to meet Major Washington. Be on your guard against them, my brethren, for they intend to strike the first English they shall see. They have been on their march two days. I know not their number. The half-king and the rest of the chiefs will be with you in five days to hold a council."

This was information that could not be disregarded, and Washington made preparations to act in accordance. As he was examining the neighborhood for a proper position in which to entrench his force, and to await the coming up of the French, he heard that they had already arrived within eighteen miles, and were fording the very river upon the banks of which the Virginians were at that moment encamped. Washington now decided at once upon his position, which was at a spot called the Great Meadows, and with which he was so pleased, that in his journal he terms it "a charming field for an encounter." The space being cleared of its scattered trees, long grass, and thick brushwood, the Virginians were here encamped, and protected by entrenchments. Although scouts were sent out, who diligently coursed the surrounding country, there was no sign of an enemy. Washington's men were, however, in a state of excited expectation, and were prepared for an attack at any moment. There were frequent alarms; and on one occasion, in the middle of the night, the sentinels fired upon some men in the dark. Next morning, it was discovered that six soldiers had deserted.

All doubt now of the approach of an enemy was removed by the arrival of an Indian messenger, who reported that his chief and some of his tribe had reached the neighborhood, and were now only six miles distant. The half-king sent word that he had fallen in with the track of Frenchmen, and did not doubt that they were lurking near by, awaiting a good chance to attack Washington and his party. Washington now determined to go at once, although it was night, to meet his friend the half-king, and accordingly started with forty men, and the Indian messenger as guide, to the chief's lodge.

It was morning before Washington reached the end of his journey, which, as it was through a rough and unbroken country, and during an unusually dark night, with a heavy, pouring rain, was necessarily tedious and fatiguing. The half-king received Washington with a warm welcome, and was ready to comply at once with his plans. At his request, Indian scouts were sent out, who soon came back, with the report that they had tracked the French to their encampment.

With these Indian scouts as his guides, Washington now started with his forty men, and accompanied by the Indian chief Tanacharisson and a small number of his warriors. As they approached the position of the enemy, Washington drew up his men in single file to the right, with himself at their head, and sent the Indians to the left. As the object was to take the French by surprise, the force moved on in perfect silence, so that their approach was not suspected until they met face to face, within gunshot. The French, though taken off their guard, promptly sprang to their arms, and began returning the fire of the Virginians.

Washington, at the head of his men, had been the first to show himself from behind the rocks and trees which concealed the path that led into the hollow where the enemy was encamped. He accordingly was exposed to the first and hottest fire of the French; one of his men was killed by his side, and three wounded, at the first volley. There was not much difference in the numbers of the two opposing parties; but the French, taken at a disadvantage, were forced to give up the struggle, and took to their heels. They were immediately pursued and overtaken, and about a score of prisoners thus secured, whom Washington had some difficulty in keeping out of the merciless hands of his savage allies, who were eager to exercise their tomahawks upon them for the sake of " a little blood-ying the edge of the hatchet," as the Indian chief himself, in his broken English, expressed it.

A young Frenchman, of the name of Jumonville, the leader of the French party, was killed at the first fire. As he was much beloved, and was from his influential connections of considerable social importance, his early death was the subject of much expressed grief and remark. M. de Villiers, who held a command under De Contrecœur, was the brother-in-law of Jumonville, and, from his desire to screen the memory of his young connection, determined to give a complexion to the affair in which he was engaged that is not at all borne out by the facts.

De Villiers and the French generally declared that Jumonville was only sent out as an embassador, to warn the English from territory claimed by France; and that the attack upon him by Washington was unjustifiable, and the fatal result only deserved to be termed an assassination, as in fact it was termed in all the French reports.

It might be enough for us to know that the great and good Washington was an actor in the affair, to denounce the French statement as a base slander; but we have, in his own words, the true version of the character of Jumonville's party, which settles the matter beyond any chance of doubt. In his despatch to Governor Dinwiddie, Washington says: "I doubt not but they [the prisoners] will endeavor to amuse you with many smooth stories, as they did me; but they were confuted in them all, and, by circumstances too plain to be denied, almost made ashamed of their assertions.

"I have heard since they went away, they should say, they called on us not to fire; *but that I know to be false*, for I was the first man that approached them and the first whom they saw, and immediately they ran to their arms, and fired briskly till they were defeated. I fancy they will have the assurance of asking the privileges due to an embassy, when in strict justice they ought to be hanged, as *spies of the worst sort.*"

They were spies undoubtedly, but they may have been embassadors as well. It seems, in fact, to have been the object of their orders, to give Jumonville and his force this double character. The written instructions, found on the body of the young French leader, directed him to use every secret means he could to obtain information of the proceedings of the English, and send it back to his chief in command as soon as obtained. It is true he was also ordered to summon the English to retire from what was claimed to be French territory, but only after he had exhausted his resources as a spy was he expected to begin upon his more dignified duty of an embassador. Jumonville was caught in the act of his preliminary and less honorable functions, and was dealt with by Washington accordingly.

CHAPTER V.

Washington wins his Spurs.—"A Brave Braggart."—The Death of Jumonville declared by the French an Assassination.—Plans for Revenge.—Fort Du Quesne.—Expedition against Washington.—He fortifies himself at Great Meadows.—Nothing daunted, but prudent withal.—Tanacharisson's Blood up.—Promises to come to the Rescue.—Fort Necessity.—Sufferings and Trials.—Famine approaching.—Arrival of Indians.—Relief.—Promotions.—Van Braam a Captain.—Captain Mackay and his Independent South-Carolinian Volunteers.—The French approach.—Return of Washington.—Stops at Great Meadows.—Fortifications.—The Idle Carolinians.—Washington puts his own Hands to the Work.—Fort Necessity described.—Desertion of the Half-Chief and his Indians.—Tanacharisson's Excuse.—The Approach of the Enemy.—Attack begun.—A Parley proposed.—Washington consents to treat.—Van Braam appointed Negotiator.—His Knowledge of French and English.—Capitulation.—Washington made to call Himself an Assassin.—Van Braam a Blunderer or a Rogue.—How Washington was deceived.—He marches out with Colors flying.—The French Slanders.—Washington's Arrival at Williamsburg.—Vote of Thanks.—Tanacarisson's Opinion of Washington.—Fort Necessity destroyed by the French.—Honors paid to the Memory of Jumonville.—De Villiers's Return to Monsieur de Contrecœur.—A Reverse in the State of Affairs at Fort Du Quesne.—A Reinforcement from Canada.—Champagne and Costly Velvets.—The Court at Versailles exultant over French Successes in the Wilderness.—Jumonville called a Hero, Washington an American Farmer and Assassin.—A Fanfaron.—Louis XV. resolves upon pushing his American Conquests.—England feebly remonstrates.—The Duke of Cumberland indignant.—An accomplished Secretary of State.—The Young Gates.—General Braddock.

THE Virginian colonel had now first "won his spurs," and no ancient knight better deserved to wear them. Young as Washington was, being only twenty-two years of age, he had borne the brunt of the battle with the steadiness of a veteran, although he had exposed himself perhaps with the too reckless spirit of a youthful adventurer. In writing to a brother, he gives vent to the heat of his young blood in the following burst of enthusiasm : " I fortunately escaped without any wound ; for the right wing, where I stood, was exposed to and received all the enemy's fire ; and it was the part where the man was killed and the rest wounded. *I heard the bullets whistle, and, believe me, there is something charming in the sound."* Horace Walpole termed this the rhodomontade of " a brave braggart ;" and George II. is said to have remarked, when he heard of it, " He would not say so if he had been used to hear many [bullets]." Washington, at a later period of life, when time had subdued the reckless daring of youth into the prudent courage of age, replied, when asked if he had ever made the remarks about the whistling of bullets, " If I said so, it was when I was young."

A French Canadian, having escaped the fate of most of his companions, succeeded in reaching the headquarters of Contrecœur, and gave in his account of the death of Jumonville, and the fatal result of his expedition. De Villiers, the brother-in-law of Jumonville, was greatly excited by these tidings of wo, and, swearing revenge, declared at once in favor of the most violent and vindictive measures. He was, however, overborne by the more judicious of his fellow-officers ; and it was finally agreed in the council that six hun-

dred men should be despatched immediately, under Monsieur de Villiers as chief in command, to meet the Virginians.

Contrecœur had, ever since he had ejected Ward and his thirty men from the fork of the Ohio, been busy in strengthening that important point. The works had been placed under the supervision of Mercier, an artillery-officer of merit, and he had succeeded in completing a very substantial fort, which Contrecœur had called, in honor of the governor of Canada, Fort Du Quesne. Mercier's work being over, he was in readiness to join De Villiers, to whom he was appointed second in command ; and the French force sallied forth, without more ado, in search of Washington.

Washington, in the meantime, had returned to his camp at the Great Meadows, and, having sent off his prisoners and despatches to the governor of Virginia, prepared to strengthen his position with the expectation of an early attack by the French. He had heard of the completion of the new fort of Du Quesne, and of the large number of troops gathering there. He knew that Contrecœur would not be long in striking a blow, in return for the death of Jumonville and the defeat of his party. He was therefore in daily expectation of an attack — and an attack in which he would be at the disadvantage of an inferior force. He, however, was nothing daunted. " I shall expect every hour to be attacked," he writes, " and by unequal numbers, which I must withstand, if there are five to one." Young and daring as he was, Washington was not wanting, even at

---

* This letter is endorsed by Washington Irving, in his "Life of Washington," as genuine, although the expression italicized has been hitherto suspected to have been a mere bit of idle scandal propagated by the gossip Walpole.

that early age of self-confidence, in the prudence and foresight which marked his subsequent life. "Your honor," he declares in his despatch to the governor of Virginia, "may depend I will not be surprised, let them come at what hour they will." His deeds confirmed his words, and he set about diligently making every preparation for the coming attack. He finished his entrenchments at Great Meadows, and began to erect a palisade. He sent a messenger with all despatch to Colonel Fry, who was ill at Will's creek, with a request that he would send at once as many of his men as he could spare. The half-king Tanacharisson did not require much urging, as his savage blood, having become heated in the late fight with the French, was now boiling fiercely for another struggle. The chief accordingly, having sent the scalps taken from the French dead, and the significant hatchet, to his Indian allies, the Mingoes and Shawnees, strove to engage them to take up arms for his brothers the English. He himself went away to join his own people, promising soon to return with forty or more of his own warriors.

Having completed his fortification at the Great Meadows, Washington gave it the name of Fort Necessity, as well he might, from the compulsory trials to which he had been subjected in the course of its construction. Here he was forced to make a stand to await the approach of an enemy that far outnumbered his own small force. Here he heard of the death of Fry at Will's creek; and here his men, worn out with daily

6

toil, were deprived of their daily bread. The small camp almost suffered from famine in consequence of the neglect of the trader Croghan, who had contracted to supply the troops with flour. For nearly a week they were deprived of this essential staff of life. The scarcity, moreover, which was so great as to bring Washington's men to the verge of starvation, was further increased by the arrival at the camp of the half-king, his forty warriors, and all their families. Supplies, however, fortunately soon reached the almost famished garrison.

Washington succeeded to the chief command by the death of Fry, upon the arrival of whose detachment from Will's creek the force at Fort Necessity was increased to three hundred. A further addition was expected from South Carolina, which had enrolled an independent company of one hundred men, under the command of a Captain Mackay, whose arrival was daily looked for.

Some changes in rank occurred among the other officers in consequence of Washington's advancement. Captain Adam Stephen was promoted to a majority, and Jacob Van Braam, Washington's old companion and interpreter, was made a captain.

Fort Necessity having been put in a tolerable condition, Washington (leaving the hundred men of South Carolina and their captain, Mackay, who had lately arrived, as a garrison to defend it) took up again his old route for Redstone creek. Washington had so much trouble with Mackay's troop, as they considered themselves in the light of volunteers, and thus relieved from the obligation of ordinary military duty, that he determined to proceed without them in the toilsome labors of completing the military road. The Virginians had not been many days gone, when intelligence was received of the approach of the force which we have seen was sent out from Fort Du Quesne. Washington sent immediately for Captain Mackay, and on his arrival a council-of-war was held, at which it was resolved that it was necessary to take up some more secure position than that where they were then encamped, although they had protected themselves by hurriedly throwing up entrenchments.

The whole force now began to retire; and, after a toilsome retreat, for want of a sufficiency of pack-horses and wagons, **July 1.** finally reached Fort Necessity. The Virginians complained loudly during the whole route of the Carolinians, who left all the work of clearing the road, carrying the baggage, and dragging the artillery, to them, while those independent military gentlemen considered it inconsistent with their dignity to do anything else but march in battle array. When Washington reached the fort, he found that his own men, either worn down with fatigue, or influenced by the bad example of the Carolinians, would not move a step farther, and was fain to rest at the Great Meadows, and there await the coming of the French.

There was no time to spare, and Washington set his men at work at once upon the fort, which he strove to strengthen by a breastwork of timber. The Carolinians still looked idly on, while the Virginians, with Washington himself putting his own hands to the work, laboriously cut down the trees, and rolled up their great trunks to protect the small entrenchment.

Fort Necessity was a rude stockade, about a hundred feet square, and surrounded by trenches. It stood in the middle of the Great Meadows, on a level spot hemmed in by hills mostly covered with wood. A small stream ran near the place, and continued its course along the base of the high ground and through the valley which opened into the Great Meadows.

Washington, while thus manfully preparing to defend himself with his handful of men against the larger force which was coming to attack him, was further weakened by the desertion of the half-chief and his Indians. Tanacharisson pretended to be disaffected in consequence of not having been sufficiently listened to by Washington in the formation of his plans. It was, however, suspected that the Indians wished only to secure the safety of their families; and, as they were aware of the overpowering numbers of the French, they feared the fatal result of an encounter at such odds. As some few of the Indians who had no wives still remained, it was supposed that the motive just given was the real cause of the desertion of those who went away.

The first sign of the approach of the enemy was the arrival, early in the morning, of a wounded sentinel, who **July 3.** came staggering in from the outposts. Washington immediately drew up

his men on the plain to meet the anticipated attack, which was now made certain by the arrival of the scouts with information that a large body of French
and Indians was within a few miles, and
rapidly approaching. Toward noon the
enemy had taken possession of a neighboring hill, and commenced a fire from
under cover of the trees. Their shots at
first fell short, and were not returned by
the provincials. The fire, however, of the
French soon began to tell more effectually, and Washington was forced to order
his men within the fortifications; and
here they kept up a straggling fire with
the enemy, seldom securing a good aim
at them, as they were hid among the
trees. This kind of skirmishing lasted the
whole day, the English having already
lost thirty while the French had only
three killed, when, night coming on, De
Villiers proposed a parley.

After some hesitation on the part of
Washington, who suspected a *ruse*, he
consented to send an officer to treat with
the French commander. Van Braam, who
had some pretensions to the knowledge
of the language, was selected. He made
several journeys backward and forward,
between the fort and the enemy's camp,
before he brought terms of capitulation
to which Washington was willing to as-
sent.

These were sent by the French commander, written out in due form; and,
upon being delivered to Washington by
Van Braam, that officer was called upon
to translate them. This he undertook
to do, and how far he was equal to the
undertaking will be found by the result.

Washington and his officers, neither of
whom understood a word of French, believed that they had got a fair idea of
the terms of capitulation proposed, although Van Braam was evidently not
quite at his ease either in French or English. There was no objection made to
any of the stipulations as translated, with
the exception of that which proposed
that Washington should give up all his
artillery and ammunition to the enemy.
This he would not concede, and De Villiers accordingly altered it.

The besieged were in a condition not
very favorable certainly for insisting upon the most liberal terms. Their cattle
had fallen into the hands of the enemy,
and Washington had only two bags of
flour and a little bacon left to feed his
whole three hundred men upon; while
all were so worn out with the hard and
hurried labor upon the works during the
three days and nights previous, that it
required all the undaunted spirit of their
young commander to cheer on their flagging energies. The weather, too, was
unfavorable. The rain poured in such
torrents, that it overflowed the trenches,
and, wetting the firelocks of the men,
prevented them often from returning the
fire of their assailants.

Washington, however, was, even under such circumstances of discouragement, not disposed to make any but the
most honorable terms of capitulation with
the enemy. He accordingly insisted that
he should be allowed to depart with all
the honors of war, with drums beating
and colors flying. That Washington,
therefore, could have been aware, when

he signed the capitulation, that it contained the expression, " the *assassination* of
Jumonville," is preposterous.   The death
of that young Frenchman, however, was
thus described, and Washington had signed the paper upon which the base word
was written ! Of course, no one now believes that Washington ever knowingly
was made to condemn his own honorable
action, which resulted in the death of Jumonville, as the deed of an assassin. The
French at the time, however, made a great
deal of this admission, which appears to
have been particularly sweet to De Villiers's desire to revenge his young relative.   In his report of the affair at Fort
Necessity, he says : " We made the English consent to sign that they had assas-
sinated my brother in his camp."

It has been suspected that the cunning
French commander had bribed Van Braam
to misconstrue purposely the word *assassinal*, in order that the French might indulge a stolen pleasure of revenge. It
is, however, more probable that the stupid Van Braam, who knew very little
English and much less French, made an
unintentional blunder in the translation.
Still, the French word *assassinal* corre-
sponds so nearly with our own "assassination," that we could hardly conceive
how Washington himself, even with his
ignorance of the French language, should
have been misled, were it not from this
fact. The paper with the written stipulations was brought in at night, and read
in the trenches, by means of a candle
held close to the face of the blundering
Van Braam, who was undertaking to read
and explain its purport in broken English. The rain was pouring in torrents at
the same moment, and Washington and
his officers were gathered in a confused
group about the reader, while there was
the greatest difficulty to see with sufficient distinctness to make out the writing, or even to keep the candle burning.
Washington probably, in the confusion
and uncertain light, never saw the original word, and intrusted implicitly to his
interpreter.

Early next day, Washington,
having destroyed his artillery,   **July 4.**
and hid away his military stores, as had
been agreed upon, led out his men, with
all the honors of war. Van Braam, who
could be well spared, and a Captain Stobo,
who was a man of different and more genuine metal, were left with the French
commander as hostages for the fulfilment
of the terms of the capitulation.   De Villiers, in his report, utters a contemptuous
lie, declaring that " the English, *struck
with panic*, took to flight, and left their
flag and one of their colors." They did
leave their regimental flag, because it was
too burdensome to carry, but their colors
they bore away flying, as they were entitled to by the concession made by this
same De Villiers who forged the lie.

The French had been better occupied
in keeping their own word than in de-
vising false accusations against others.
They had pledged themselves that Washington and his men should be allowed to
march out without molestation ; and yet
they had hardly got out of the fort, when
the Indians from De Villiers's camp began plundering the baggage, and it was
found necessary, in consequence, to de-

stroy the greater part of it, in order to get rid of these ravenous savages. In a few days, after a toilsome journey, Washington succeeded in leading his jaded and disheartened force to Will's creek, where, with abundant provisions, and in a snug encampment, they were left to recruit their strength and health, until they might be in proper condition to march homeward. Washington himself pushed on directly for Williamsburg, to give in his report of the unfortunate but honorable results of the expedition. His own province justly estimated Washington's services, and he received a vote of thanks from the Virginia house of burgesses for his courage and the prudence of his conduct.

The old chief Tanacharisson, however, who had deserted his "white brother" in his emergency, took, as it seems, a very different view of Washington's management. "The colonel," he said, "was a good-natured man, but had no experience; he took upon him to command the Indians as his slaves, and would have them every day upon the scout, and to attack the enemy by themselves, but would by no means take advice from the Indians. He lay in one place from one full moon to the other, without making any fortifications, except that little thing in the Meadow; whereas, had he taken advice, and built such fortifications as he (Tanacharisson) advised him, he might easily have beat off the French. But the French, in the engagement, acted like cowards, and the English like fools."

De Villiers, having taken possession of Fort Necessity on its surrender, set about destroying its rude and incomplete works, and then started on his return to Fort Du Quesne. As there was little to be done in demolishing the simple defences of the English provincials, the French were enabled to get through their labors in a single morning, and marched out on the very same day that Washington departed. Their force was now divided into two parties, and both went to work destroying all the English trading-posts and stockades met with in the course of their different routes. De Villiers led his detachment to the scene of Jumonville's defeat and death, and, with pious affection, seeking out from among the mangled corpses of the slain (who, in accordance with Indian warfare, lay scattered about with their skulls bared by the tomahawk) his brother's body, buried it with the honors of a soldier's grave. This pious duty performed, De Villiers hastened on to Fort Du Quesne, where he arrived on the 7th day of July.

Monsieur de Contrecœur and his garrison on the Monongahela were not found by De Villiers in such a flourishing condition as when he had left them on his expedition down the Ohio. Supplies, which had been sent out for the provision of the fort, had been delayed on the route. Those who had charge of them had wandered from their way, and, not succeeding in finding horses and wagons to carry their burden, were obliged to bear it themselves. With the fatigue, the delay, and the scarcity of provisions, the men sickened; and no less than four hundred of the party died from the effects of hunger, exhaustion, and the scurvy.

Those who escaped finally broke open the packages with which they were charged, and helped themselves freely to their contents. They thus got an abundant supply of the generous wines of Champeaux and Bordeaux, and in their wild orgies dressed themselves, in the midst of the wilderness, in the costly velvet uniforms sent to grace the dignity of Monsieur de Contrecœur and his fellow-officers. When they arrived at the fort, they had hardly anything to offer but themselves, tricked off in the gaudy suits of their superiors. Fresh instalments, however, from Canada, soon put Fort Du Quesne on a more satisfactory footing, and its commander was enabled to carry out his plans, for the possession of the Ohio, in a manner to gratify the unbounded appetite of his sovereign for dominion.

The court at Versailles were in raptures with French success in America; and, while they slandered the young Washington, they elevated the unfortunate Jumonville to the rank of a hero. His death was mourned in story, as that of the brave and the good; while Washington, *ce planteur Americain*—that American farmer who in a few years afterward was to be hailed as the regenerator of the human race by the people of France — was held up to scorn, by the minions of a lewd king and his shameless mistress, as an assassin!

In England, there was hardly any more disposition to do Washington justice; and we are not surprised to find Walpole recording, in one of his gossiping letters, that "the French have tied up the hands of an excellent *fanfaron*, a Major Washington, whom they took and engaged not to serve for a year." Throughout England, however, the ill success of the Virginian expedition, whatever may have been thought of its young and heroic leader, was received with undisguised vexation. The government remonstrated, through their embassador at the court of Versailles, the dissolute Albemarle, against the aggressions of the French in America. These remonstrances, however, produced no effect. Louis XV. continued to send reinforcements to Canada, and made no secret of his determination to follow up his successes at Fort Necessity with further attempts upon the territory west of the Alleghanies. Great Britain, with unusual equanimity of temper, contented itself with opposing these overt acts of hostility by sending a little advice to its colonies. These were urged to unite for their common protection, and defend themselves against the whole power of France. The languid hands of Pelham, and the weak grasp of the incapable duke of Newcastle, then held the reins of power, and the active aid necessary could hardly be expected from the indolent prime minister and his feeble brother.

The duke of Cumberland was indignant at the inaction of his government, and swore that, rather than lose one foot of ground in America, he would oppose the enemies of his country in that part of the world himself. To this prince, in fact, the colonies were finally indebted for the aid, such as it was, that they received. Little, certainly, could be expected, when left to himself, from the duke of Newcastle, " a statesman without capacity, or the smallest tincture of human learning ; a secretary who could not write ; a financier who did not understand the multiplication-table ; and the treasurer of a vast empire who never could balance accounts with his own butler." Such a man could be of little assistance anywhere, and least of all in a country of which he knew so little, that, when it was suggested that Annapolis should be defended, replied : " Annapolis, Annapolis ! Oh, yes, Annapolis must be defended ; to be sure, Annapolis should be defended : where is Annapolis ?"

After considerable delay, when nothing was done, the necessity of doing something was agreed upon, but how to do it was the puzzling question. The duke of Newcastle, in his ignorance, was reduced to all sorts of makeshifts for his want of knowledge and capacity. Having heard of a young officer of the name of Gates, who had just returned from America — where he had, while on duty in Nova Scotia, learned something of American affairs — his grace of Newcastle sent for him.

On being closeted with the minister, Gates was asked for a plan for an American campaign ; but he pleaded his youth and inexperience, and modestly declined. Others were resorted to in the emergency. Pitt, on being asked his views, slyly answered : " Your grace knows I have no capacity for these things ; and therefore I do not desire to be informed about them." Sharpe, who had been a lieutenant-governor of Maryland ; Hanbury, the chief of the Ohio Company ; Lords Townshend and Walpole, had all been consulted in turn — when, finally, it was found advisable to leave the whole regulation of the American difficulty to the duke of Cumberland. This martial prince was for sending out immediately a military force to drive the French from the banks of the Ohio. Two regiments of the line were accordingly detached at once for service in Virginia, and the command bestowed upon General Braddock.

CHAPTER VI.

General Braddock.—His Life and Character.—Braddock's Family.—His Sister, Fanny Braddock.—Her Love, and Tragic Death.—A Brother's Tribute to a Sister's Memory.—An Iroquois.—Braddock's Military Career.—His Life in London.—Mrs. Upton and her Last Shilling.—Braddock's Duel with the Earl of Bath.—A Poor Dog !—His Farewell of a Frail but Constant Friend.—Braddock exiled by Poverty.—Recalled by the Duke of Cumberland, and given the Command of the American Expedition.—His Age and Military Character.

1754. " DESPERATE in his fortune, brutal in his behavior, obstinate in his sentiments, he was still intrepid and capable," are the few, biting words in which Walpole sums up the character of the general appointed to command the regiments now about to be sent out to America. Six feet high, of Atlantean shoulders, of good appetite, and a lover of his bottle, he was equal to any effort of personal vigor. He was a match for the best swordsman in the army, and could drink his whole mess under the table! He swore copiously, as troopers were wont to do in those days. Turbulent and pugnacious, he was never so much at his ease as in the hurly-burly of war. Intrepid and loyal, he was always ready to fight for his king or his great master, his royal highness the burly duke of Cumberland, whom he was proud to copy as the model soldier.

Of Braddock's early history little is known, although there is sufficient proof that he was not altogether the low adventurer it has been the habit of historians to represent him. His father himself was a soldier, and possessed of sufficient patronage or desert to have reached the rank of major-general, with a colonelcy in the guards. He was known as a retired veteran officer, living in his old age at the fashionable town of Bath, where he died on the 15th of June, 1725. He was evidently a man of competent fortune, for on his death he left no less than six thousand pounds as a provision for his two daughters, and probably a much larger sum to his only son, Edward Braddock.

One of the daughters died early, and her sister, Fanny Braddock, became possessed of her share of the father's legacy. Goldsmith, in his life of Beau Nash, has told the romantic story of Fanny, under the name of "Miss Sylvia S——," with his usual sweetness of narrative and gentle kindness of sympathy. She was descended, he says, from one of the best families in the kingdom, and was left a large fortune upon her sister's decease. Whatever the finest poet could conceive of wit, or the most celebrated painter imagine of beauty, were excelled in the perfections of this young lady. She was naturally gay, generous to a fault, good-natured to the highest degree, affable in conversation; and some of her letters and other writings, as well in verse as in prose, would have shone among those of the most celebrated wits of this or any other age, had they been published.

But these qualifications were marked by another, which lessened the value of them all. She was imprudent. "By which," says the kind biographer, "I only mean she had no knowledge of the use of money." She was arrived at the age of nineteen, when the crowd of her lovers and the continued repetition of new flattery had taught her to think that she could never be forsaken, and never poor. "Young ladies are apt to expect," wisely moralizes Goldsmith, in a strain that reminds us of a passage in the "Vicar of Wakefield," "a certainty of success from a number of lovers; and yet I have seldom seen a girl courted by a hundred lovers that found a husband in any. Before the choice is fixed, she has either lost her reputation or her good sense; and the loss of either is sufficient to consign her to perpetual virginity."

Among the number of this young lady's lovers was a handsome, good-natured, easy kind of fellow, of whose name we can learn nothing beyond its initial "S." He was "constitutionally virtuous," but practically it appears quite the contrary, for he followed the "dictates of every

newest passion." He loved Fanny Braddock, and Fanny Braddock loved him.
The vices of the man (Goldsmith gently
terms them "imprudences") soon ruined
him, and he was thrown into prison for
debt. Fanny Braddock, with the disinterestedness of a pure and loving woman,
was resolutely bent on freeing him, and
sacrificed her whole fortune in relieving
her lover from his obligations to his cred-
itors, and thus restored him to liberty.
S——, instead of improving in friendship
or affection, only studied to avoid a cred-
itor he could never repay ; for, "though
small favors produce good will, great ones
destroy friendship," says Goldsmith, who
could utter maxims worthy of Solomon,
while he lived as riotously as the Prodigal Son.

Poor Fanny, however, was ruined, in
reputation as well as in fortune, by this
profuse generosity to her ungrateful lover. Beau Nash, then meeting with her
among some of his friends in London,
prevailed upon her to go with him to
Bath, where the Beau, being paramount
in power, might introduce her to the
best company, and leave it to her merit
to do the rest. People of distinction
courted her acquaintance, and strove to
divert her with the social enjoyments and
fashionable frivolities of the place ; but it
was apparent that a settled melancholy
had taken possession of her mind, and she
moved among, but was not of, the gay
throng. With loss of love, loss of fortune, loss of friends, and loss of health,
she was finally induced, as a mere refuge
from her own wretchedness, to yield to
the invitation of a Dame Lindsey, who

desired to secure so much beauty, as an
additional temptation to those who resorted to her gambling-rooms. Although
she yielded to Dame Lindsey's invitation,
Fanny Braddock is believed never to
have been tainted with any other vice
than that of presiding at the hazard-table
for the advantage of others.

She could not long, however, endure
this disgrace, and preferred the humble
condition of a housekeeper in a gentleman's family, to which her poverty now
reduced her. Here she remained, always
sad, but faithful to her duty. The gentleman with whom she lived now went
up to London with his wife, leaving the
children and the house to her care. On
the day when he was expected to return,
Fanny, after the discharge of her daily
household duty, went into the dining-
room and wrote these lines upon one of
the window-panes :—

> "O Death ! thou pleasing end of human wo !
> Thou cure for life, thou greatest good below !
> Still mayst thou fly the coward and the slave,
> And thy soft slumbers only bless the brave."

Some visiters coming in, she entertained
them cheerfully, and, on their going out,
she went to the library, where she had
ordered supper. Here "she spent the
remaining hours preceding bed-time in
dandling two of Mr. Wood's (the gentleman in whose family she lived) children
on her knees. In retiring thence to her
chamber, she went into the nursery, to
take her leave of another child, as it lay
sleeping in the cradle. Struck with the
innocence of the little babe's looks, and
the consciousness of her meditated guilt,
she could not avoid bursting into tears,

7

and hugging it in her arms. She then bade her old servant a 'Good-night,' for the first time she had ever done so, and went to bed as usual.

"It is probable she soon quitted her bed. She then dressed herself in clean linen and white garments of every kind, like a bridesmaid. Her gown she pinned over her breast just as a nurse pins the swaddling-clothes of an infant." She then took a pink-silk girdle, and, lengthening it with another made of gold thread, she made a noose at one end, and tied three knots at a small distance from each other.

She now sat down to read that passage in Ariosto's "Orlando Furioso," where Olympia is abandoned by her bosom friend, and ruined. Having laid aside her book, she arose, took the girdle she had prepared, and, tying it about her neck, stepped upon a stool, and, throwing the end of the girdle over a closet-door, attempted to hang herself. The girdle, however, broke with her weight; and she fell with such a noise, that a workman, who was passing the night in the house, was awoke. He, nevertheless, thinking nothing more of it, turned over and fell asleep again. She now made another attempt, with a stronger girdle, made of silver thread, and succeeded. Her old maid next morning waited as usual the ringing of the bell, and protracted her patience, hour after hour, till two o'clock in the afternoon, when the workmen, at length entering the room through the window, found their unfortunate mistress still hanging, and quite cold.

Such is the history of Fanny Braddock, for the most part as related by Goldsmith. "Hundreds in high life," says he, "lamented her fate." Her brother, when he heard of it, remarked, "Poor Fanny! I always thought she would play till she would be forced to tuck herself up." Horace Walpole might well say, "Braddock is a very Iroquois in disposition."

Braddock was early led to a military life, by its being his father's profession. He probably entered the army, as is the custom with "young bloods" in England, before he had got out of his teens, and too soon to have acquired much education. His first commission dates from the 11th of October, 1710, when he became ensign in the Coldstream guards. His promotion, although not very rapid, was sufficiently so to show that he had either the command of money or the benefit of patronage. He probably had both, as his father was an officer of high rank, and withal tolerably rich. The fact of the son beginning in a crack regiment, like that of the Coldstream, proves that his career must have opened with the advantage of either family, favor, or fortune. In six years from the date of his first commission he becomes a lieutenant; in twenty years more he is a captain; and, in the brief period of seven years, we find him with the high rank of lieutenant-colonel in the line, and second major in his own regiment, the second of the Foot-guards.

Braddock had considerable opportunities of seeing service. He had served in Flanders and Spain, and distinguished himself at the battle of Fontenoy, where the French won so brilliant a victory, and the Guards, of whom Braddock was an officer, fought so furiously in the action, and drew off with such cool courage and steady discipline in the retreat, as to win for the English soldier almost enough credit to compensate for his being beaten. Braddock was promoted, immediately after the battle of Fontenoy, to the first majority of his regiment, and in a few months later to a lieutenant-colonelcy. He served under the duke of Cumberland in Scotland, when that "sanguinary" prince was engaged in his cruel raid against the Young Pretender and his Jacobite defenders. Braddock had evidently won the esteem of Cumberland, who sought every opportunity to serve him. After service in Scotland, and a further campaign in the Low Countries, peace was declared, and Braddock returned with his regiment to London.

While in the capital, Braddock, like most officers, lived a gay life. He was known about town as a gallant blade, reckless of every virtue save that of courage, and as prodigal of his money as he was careless of character. He gambled, as did all the men of the world of his day; and his losses at hazard often placed him in such strait, that he was tempted to resort to means to replenish his purse, if we can believe some of the stories told of him, which proved him to be far from the gallant gentleman that he doubtless wished to be considered.

It is said that a certain Mrs. Upton, well known to (ill) fame in London, was a paramour of Braddock, and we are told this anecdote of his relations with her: "One day, Mrs. Upton frankly answered a demand for money by pulling out her purse, with but twelve or fourteen shillings in it. With the keen eye of an experienced forager, Braddock saw cause to suspect that this was not all its contents. 'Let me see that!' he cried, and snatched it from her hand. In the farther end he found five guineas. Coolly emptying all the money into his pocket, he tossed the empty purse into his mistress's lap. 'Did you mean to cheat me?' cried he; and he turned his back upon the house, to see her no more." This piece of dirty meanness was freely talked about in every coffee and club house in London; and, finally, Fielding held Braddock up to public contempt, by bringing him on the stage, as Captain Bilkum, in the "Covent-Garden Tragedy."[*] The author of the book just quoted has ferreted out this interesting literary item, and gives the following passage from Fielding's play, in which Braddock's dirty transaction with Mrs. Upton is supposed to be alluded to:—

"Oh! 'tis not in the power of punch to save
My grief-strung soul, since Hecatissa's false —
Since she could hide a poor half-guinea from me!
Oh! had I searched her pockets ere I rose,
I had not left a single shilling in them!"

Braddock's inveterate habits of gambling kept him constantly in debt, and often involved him in quarrels with some of his fellow-debauchees. It was in consequence of some dispute at the hazard table, or some refusal to settle a claim

[*] The History of the Expedition against Fort Du Quesne, &c., by Winthrop Sargent, M. A.: Philadelphia, 1855. A valuable work, to which we have been indebted for many of the facts in this narrative.

incurred there, which brought him a challenge to fight from a Colonel Gumley, the brother-in-law of the earl of Bath. When they reached the ground and were going to engage, Gumley, who had good humor and wit, said: "Braddock, you are a poor dog! Here, take my purse; if you kill me, you will be forced to run away, and then you will not have a shilling to support you." Braddock refused the purse, insisted on the duel, was disarmed, and would not even ask for his life.

Braddock, as a man of wit and pleasure, and, moreover, with the reputation of a brave officer and a good swordsman, could have had no difficulty in making his way in the best society of London. He, however, suffered in the estimation of those whose virtues were no better, but whose manners were; and he consequently was shunned by the refined for the brutality of his conduct and the rudeness of his behavior. Yet he has found an apologist, in a fair but frail lady,* with whom Braddock was an intimate. She says, in giving an account of her last interview with him, on the night before his setting out for America: "Before we parted, the general told me he should never see me more, for he was going with a handful of men to conquer whole nations; and, to do this, they must cut their way through unknown woods. He produced a map of the country, saying, at the same time, 'Dear Pop, we are sent like sacrifices to the altar.' The event

* George Anne Bellamy, the actress, from whose Apology for her Life this passage is quoted in the Appendix of Sargent's "History," &c.

of the expedition too fatally verified the general's expectations. This great man," she adds, "having been often reproached with brutality, I am induced to recite the following little anecdote, which evidently shows the contrary. As we were walking in the Park one day, we heard a poor fellow was to be chastised, when I requested the general to beg off the offender. Upon his application to the general officer, whose name was Dury, he asked Braddock how long since he had divested himself of brutality and the insolence of his manners. To which the other replied: 'You never knew me insolent to my inferiors. It is only to such rude men as yourself that I behave with the spirit which I think they deserve.'"

It was doing the handsome thing for Miss Bellamy, the pretty actress (for she was the fair apologist), to come to the rescue of the fame of Braddock; but we must not forget that she was a prejudiced party, as the general had been one of her most favored and devoted lovers, had bestowed upon her putative husband the profitable agency of his regiment, and left him by his will his whole property, amounting to something like thirty-five thousand dollars.

Braddock, as Gumley had said, was "a poor dog," and had got so deeply in debt, that he was obliged to leave England. His influential friends, however, secured him an honorable exile, by obtaining for him the rank of colonel in a regiment then at Gibraltar. While there, his old patron, the duke of Cumberland, was mindful of him; and, upon the expedition for America being determined

1754. upon, Braddock was recalled, elevated to the rank of major-general, made commander-in-chief of all the British forces on the western continent, and given the command of the troops now ordered there for the especial service we shall recount.

That Braddock was a good soldier in the European sense, there could be no doubt. He was now advanced in years (having reached threescore), and a veteran in service, having served no less than three-and-forty years as an officer in the Guards, during which time he had been engaged in most of the great battles of his country. He was a martinet in discipline, and, however loose in private life, no one could find fault with him for want of strictness in the field or on parade. His regiment was always among the most effective in the army, and had under his command gained undying laurels for its steady behavior and brave bearing in the unfortunate field of

Fontenoy as well as in the cruel triumphs of Culloden.

At St. James's park, too, in days of peace and holyday, Braddock's men were marked and admired as among the most orderly and soldierly looking of all the household troops in London. He was just the man to please the duke of Cumberland, who, brought up in the school of the great Frederick, was a devoted believer in the powdered, bewigged soldier and the formal tactics then prevailing in all the camps of European warfare. Braddock had undoubtedly courage, and had besides a most thorough schooling, under the eye of Cumberland himself, in those very formalities and methods which were thought to be the necessary framework of all military art. The selection, perhaps, could not have been better, for a regular European campaign; but how it suited the eccentricities of American warfare, will be shown in the course of our narrative by the result.

CHAPTER VII.

BRADDOCK had frequent conferences with the ministry, and especially with the duke of Cumberland, who was the master-spirit of the American enterprise. These resulted in the formation of a plan for the campaign, the objects of which, in accordance with the policy of the government and the advice of the military authorities, were—

To eject the French from the lands which they held unjustly in the province of Nova Scotia.

To dislodge them from a fortress which they had erected at Crown Point, on Lake Champlain, within what was claimed as British territory.

To dispossess them of the fort which they had constructed at Niagara, between Lake Ontario and Lake Erie.

To drive them from the frontiers of Pennsylvania and Virginia, and recover the valley of the Ohio.

It was more particularly, however, the last object which was reserved for Braddock; and his instructions were so far specific in this respect, that he was ordered to march as soon as possible after his arrival in America and attack the French fort of Du Quesne, situated on the fork of the Ohio.

Lieutenant-Colonel Sir John St. Clair was sent out in advance to Virginia, as deputy quartermaster-general, to obtain every possible information, and to make the preliminary arrangements for the furtherance of the objects of the proposed expedition.

Braddock himself, soon after his arrival in London, hurried to Cork, where the troops were to embark. He, however, got impatient at the delay in recruiting the soldiers and fitting out the expedition, and went to Portsmouth, whence he **1755.** soon after sailed. The general was on board the Norwich, in company

* Life of Washington, by Irving.

with one of his aids, Captain Robert Orme, and his military secretary, Mr. William Shirley, the son of the governor of Massachusetts. Two other vessels, the Centurion and the Siren, with a small military guard and a company or so of the soldiers, sailed with the Norwich. The transports, with the rest of the troops, the artillery, and supplies, were to follow as soon as ready.

There was considerable delay in getting the troops off, notwithstanding they were so few in number; it having been determined to send out only two regiments—the forty-fourth, with Sir Peter Halket as colonel, and the forty-eighth, Colonel Thomas Dunbar. These were to make up their numbers each to no more than five hundred before leaving, with the intention of adding three hundred by recruits in America. One thousand, therefore, was the whole force of regulars sent out by the government, and these were to form a nucleus about which it was hoped to gather, in the provinces, an army of some four thousand. The soldiers were finally recruited; the stores, artillery, and ammunition, prepared and put on board; the whole force embarked; and the fleet of transports, amounting to more than a dozen, sailed under the **1755** convoy of two men-of-war, on the 14th of February, three weeks subsequent to the departure of the commanding general.

The hopes of England were not very sanguine about the success of this expedition to America, if we can trust what that gossip Walpole wrote: "The French have taken such liberties with some of our forts that are of great consequence to cover Virginia, Carolina, and Georgia, that we are actually despatching two regiments thither. As the climate and other American circumstances are against these poor men, I pity them, and think them too many if the French mean nothing further, too few if they do. Indeed, I am one of those who feel less resentment when we are attacked so far off: I think it an obligation to be eaten the last."

After a voyage of nearly two months, Braddock arrived in Hampton roads, in Virginia, and proceeded at once to Williamsburg, to join Governor Dinwiddie, and consult with him in regard to the details for carrying out the proposed expedition. Sir John St. Clair, the deputy quartermaster-general, and Commodore Keppel, commander of the British fleet, soon after repaired to Williamsburg also. On consultation with these officers, it was determined by Braddock that the troops should disembark at Alexandria. Orders were now sent for the transports, as they should arrive, to sail up to that place. They came in at slow intervals, the last vessel being as late as the 14th of March, and, as was directed, after anchoring in Hampton roads, proceeded up the Potomac to Alexandria, where the troops disembarked in fine condition, in spite of the long voyage.

The colonies hailed this aid from the mother-country with great joy, and gave an enthusiastic welcome, after their propitious voyage, to those ships—

"Freighted with wealth, for noble ends designed ;
So willed great George, and so the Fates inclined,"

as a native poet, in anticipatory poetical enthusiasm of the great event, had written.

Braddock, soon after the arrival of his troops, had invited the governors of the different British colonies to meet him at Alexandria; and accordingly, on the 14th of April, a great council was held. Here were Robert Dinwiddie, governor of Virginia; General William Shirley, governor of Massachusetts; and here also were the three lieutenant-governors, James Delancey, of New York; Sharpe, of Maryland; and Morris, of Pennsylvania. Braddock the general and Keppel the commodore completed the number of this august council. The various governors were first reminded, by the reading of the orders of the home government, of the duty of their several provinces to raise a colonial revenue, and make provision for the expenses of the expedition. They all, however, without an exception, had a most unsatisfactory account to give of their endeavors to fulfil the obligations that had been imposed upon them. Their several assemblies had been diligently urged, but had refused to vote the tax necessary to establish the fund; and the governors now convened declared unanimously that "such a fund can never be established in the colonies without the aid of Parliament. Having found it impracticable to obtain in their respective governments the proportion expected by his majesty towards defraying the expenses of his service in North America, they are unanimously of opinion that it should be proposed to his majesty's ministers to find out some method of com-

1755.

pelling them to do it, and of assessing the several governments in proportion to their respective abilities."

Braddock's arbitrary spirit was chafed by this colonial recreancy, and he stormed loudly, with anger, that "no such fund had been yet established." He sent the resolves of the council to the home government, accompanying them with a letter from himself, in which he fiercely complained of the neglect of their duty by the colonies, and urged the necessity of compelling them, by taxation, to do it effectually for the future. Here was the little fire by which the great flame of revolution was kindled, and which finally, after a period of unsettled, nebulous light, concentrated in the glorious stars of American Independence.

The opinion of the governors in council in regard to some other matters, showed a wiser discretion. They proposed that New York should be the point from which the movements of the campaign should be directed. Braddock would not or could not listen to such suggestions. It was supposed that he had received positive orders to march upon Fort Du Quesne, and that he was thus obliged to carry on the expedition across the Alleghanies, with all the disadvantages of a wild country. It would have been wiser, doubtless, to have attacked the French settlements in Canada, as they could be reached by sea, and the land-forces might have been sustained by a naval squadron. Fort Du Quesne, however, was the point proposed, and against this Braddock determined to lead his forces. The two battalions raised and commanded by Governor Shirley

and Sir William Pepperell, the hero of Louisburg, were directed upon Niagara; General Johnson was ordered to muster his Indians for an attack upon Crown Point, at Lake Champlain; and the British colonel Monckton, with the provincial colonel Winslow, were sent to do service against the French in the bay of Fundy.

Sir John St. Clair had succeeded in obtaining the Virginian recruits before the arrival of the British troops, and they now, on Braddock's men landing, prepared to join them. They were, however, taken hold of at once, for drill, by an ensign of the forty-fourth, who had been ordered by the general "to make them as like soldiers as possible."

There was one greater than all the rest who at this time offered himself as a volunteer, in a cause in which his beloved Virginia was so deeply concerned. This was Washington. "The din and stir of warlike preparation," says Irving, "disturbed the quiet of Mount Vernon. Washington looked down from his rural retreat upon the ships-of-war and transports, as they passed up the Potomac, with the array of arms gleaming along their decks. The booming of cannon echoed among his groves. Alexandria was but a few miles distant. Occasionally he mounted his horse and rode to that place; it was like a garrisoned town, teeming with troops, and resounding with the drum and fife. A brilliant campaign was about to open, under the auspices of an experienced general, and with all the means and appurtenances of European warfare. How different from the starveling expeditions he had hitherto been doomed to conduct! What an opportunity to efface the memory of his recent disaster! All his thoughts of rural life were put to flight. The military part of his character was again in the ascendant; his great desire was to join the expedition as a volunteer."

When General Braddock heard of this desire on the part of young Washington, and learned who he was—his high social position in Virginia, his great personal worth, and the experience he had already had in border warfare—he invited him to become one of his aids. This is the letter bearing the invitation:—

"WILLIAMSBURG, 2d March, 1755.

"SIR: The general, having been informed that you expressed some desire to make the campaign, but that you declined it upon some disagreeableness that you thought might arise from the regulations of command, has ordered me to acquaint you that he will be very glad of your company in his family, by which all inconveniences of that kind will be obviated.

"I shall think myself very happy to form an acquaintance with a person so universally esteemed, and shall use every opportunity of assuring you how much I am, sir, your most obedient servant,

"ROBERT ORME, Aid-de-Camp."

Orme was a young lieutenant of the Guards, of a good English family, which had supplied many a brave soldier for the service of their king. He had now nominally the rank of captain, and, being a great favorite of Braddock, had been appointed by him one of his aids-de-camp. He was a spirited, well-educated, and high-bred young fellow, and commended himself greatly to the friendship of Washington, with whom during the campaign he became very intimate.

The offer of Braddock was gladly accepted by Washington; and, in spite of his mother's entreaties, and all the household interests of Mount Vernon which had gathered about him during his retirement, he determined, as soon as he could settle his affairs at home, to join the expedition. He was greatly gratified at the appointment he had received. He was fond of a military life, and had only been prevented from taking a position, as an officer in the Virginian troops, in consequence of the contempt of those bearing colonial commissions implied by a parliamentary act, which gave all the British officers the precedence of them in rank and pay. Washington's pride, as a Virginian gentleman, revolted at this, and naturally; for he might thus, at any moment, be placed in an inferior position to some ignorant, low-bred person, suddenly elevated above him by a commission which had been either bought for money or truckled for by fawning servility. The young Washington had consequently smothered all his burning ardor for military glory, rather than sacrifice his own self-respect.

The offer of Braddock now came to give him, what he so much desired, an opportunity for honorable service. The position as aid-de-camp, which he had accepted, gave him rank among the highest of his years, and was one of those

8

gentlemanly offices—for there was no pay—that particularly commended itself to a disinterested Virginian cavalier. There was the further advantage that, as aid-de-camp, Washington would have the best opportunity of improving himself, and that this was a great object with him he confesses in writing to Orme: "I wish earnestly to obtain some knowledge in the military profession; and believing a more favorable opportunity can not offer than to serve under a gentleman of General Braddock's abilities and experience, it does, you may reasonably suppose, not a little influence my choice."

Washington did not join the army for several weeks after receiving his commission. When he presented himself he was warmly welcomed by the general, and received into the intimate friendship of Braddock's two aids-de-camp and secretary, Orme, Morris, and Shirley, who were of about the same age as the young Virginian.

While the congress of governors was being held at Alexandria, Sir John St. Clair, the deputy quartermaster-general, was sent again along the proposed route of the army, to look up the contractors, and find out how far they had kept their engagements. He soon discovered that their promises, of which so favorable an account had been reported to Braddock, were far from being fulfilled. The road that was to have been made by Pennsylvania, had not yet been begun; and there was no sign of the provisions required of that province.

Sir John became highly indignant at this remissness, and stormed like a lion rampant. He declared to the Pennsylvania commissioners that, instead of marching to the Ohio, he would in nine days march the army into Cumberland county to cut the roads, press horses and wagons; that he would not suffer a soldier to handle an axe, but by fire and sword oblige the inhabitants to do it; and to take away to the Ohio every man that refused, as he had some of the Virginians. He would kill all kind of cattle, and carry away the horses, and burn the houses. If the French defeated the troops by the delays of the province, he would with his sword drawn pass through it, and treat the inhabitants as a parcel of traitors to his master. He would write to England immediately by a man-of-war, shake the proprietorship of Mr. Penn, and represent Pennsylvania as a disaffected province. He would not stop to impress the assembly; his hands were not tied, Sir John said, and they should find it out. He did not value a d——, the wrathy baronet declared, what the governor or assembly did or resolved, as they were dilatory, and had retarded the march of the army, and that the commissioners might tell them so; and, moreover, go to the general if they pleased, who, if they did, would give them ten bad words for one he gave! He (Sir John) would do their duty himself, and not trust to them; but he declared with an oath that they should have to pay dearly for it, and "by G–d" he was in earnest! Even Braddock, as little mealy-mouthed as he was, could not approve St. Clair's violence, and, on its being reported, rebuked him severely. It seemed not to have been without its effect, however, upon the Pennsylvanians, who set about the road, though dilatorily, and did not make much progress in sending forward the promised supplies.

Other provinces were equally backward with Pennsylvania. Only twenty wagons, two hundred horses, and some utterly worthless provisions, came in, out of the twenty-five hundred horses, two hundred and fifty wagons, and eleven hundred head of cattle, which had been promised by Maryland. Braddock was thus detained at Alexandria, with the artillery and military stores, for want of means to convey them. He finally resolved to proceed to Fredericktown, in Maryland, to endeavor to hasten the levy of horses and wagons. He left behind him, at Alexandria, four companies of the forty-fourth regiment, under the command of Lieutenant-Colonel Gage, who was ordered to forward the artillery, ammunition, and stores, as means should arrive for their conveyance. The main body of the troops were at Fredericktown, where the general now joined them. The Virginian regiments had, however, been ordered to Winchester, with the exception of the rangers, sent to build stockade forts on Greenbrier river, under Captain Lewis, subsequently, in our revolutionary struggle, a brigadier-general, and an especial favorite with Washington for his soldierly qualities. Six companies of the forty-fourth regulars soon after moved on also, under the command of Sir Peter Halket, to Winchester, where they were ordered to remain, with the Virginians, until the road was in proper condition, and then to march to Fort Cumberland.

Commodore Keppel had also detached a number of seamen from his ships, who by their knowledge of the use of ropes and tackle, and practice in rowing and hauling, might assist in ferrying the army over the rivers, making the bridges, and moving the heavy artillery up and down the acclivities of the steep roads. This naval detachment awaited at Alexandria the movements of the companies left there, to come on with the guns and military stores.

When Braddock reached Fredericktown, he found the troops in great want of provisions, there being no cattle laid in as yet. He applied to Governor Sharpe, of Maryland, in the emergency; but so little influence had this official in his own province, that he could not get either wagons or provisions. The general sent round the country, however, and succeeded in purchasing a few head of cattle. While Braddock was thus harassed, and his movements almost entirely stopped, Benjamin Franklin fortunately arrived at Fredericktown. The nominal purpose of his visit, as he was then at the head of the colonial postoffice department, was to make suitable provision with Braddock for the conveyance of despatches to and from the provincial governments. Franklin's real object, however, was undoubtedly to acquaint himself with the details of the expedition, and to reinstate if possible, his own province of Pennsylvania in the good opinion of the army.

On Franklin's arrival in Fredericktown, Braddock expressed a particular desire to see him, and, from the first interview, was greatly impressed with the superior sagacity of his visiter, and solicited his advice. Franklin now became a daily guest at Braddock's table, and has left in his autobiography an interesting record of his occasional talk with the general: "One day, in conversation with him," says Franklin, "he was giving me some account of his intended progress. 'After taking Fort Du Quesne,' said he, 'I am to proceed to Frontenac, if the season will allow time; and I suppose it will, for Du Quesne can hardly detain me above three or four days: and then I can see nothing that can obstruct my march to Niagara.'

"Having before revolved in my mind," Franklin observes, "the long line his army must make in their march by a very narrow road, to be cut for them through the woods and bushes, and also what I had heard of a former defeat of fifteen hundred French, who had invaded the Illinois country, I had conceived some doubts and some fears for the event of this campaign; but I ventured only to say: 'To be sure, sir, if you arrive well before Du Quesne with these fine troops, so well provided with artillery, the fort, though completely fortified, and assisted with a very strong garrison, can probably make but a short resistance. The only danger I apprehend of obstruction to your march, is from the ambuscades of the Indians, who, by constant practice, are dexterous in laying and executing them; and the slender line, nearly four miles long, which your army must make, may expose it to be attacked by surprise on its flanks, and to be cut like thread into several pieces, which from their distance can not come up in time to support one another.'

"He smiled at my ignorance, and replied: 'These savages may indeed be a formidable enemy to raw American militia, but upon the king's regular and disciplined troops, sir, it is impossible they should make an impression.' I was conscious," adds Franklin, "of an impropriety in my disputing with a military man in matters of his profession, and said no more."

This was just the advice wanted, and the general, with his wrong-headed obstinacy and old-fashioned camp prejudice, was just the man to disregard it. In another matter, however, where his military self-conceit did not interfere, the general listened to Franklin, and, as we shall see, to advantage. "It is a pity the troops had not landed in Pennsylvania, where every farmer has his wagon," remarked Franklin. "Then, sir," answered Braddock, "you, who are a man of interest there, can probably procure them for me, and I beg you will."

Franklin undertook to obtain at once what was wanted, and was as good as his promise. A paper being drawn up by the general, giving Franklin due authority to hire for the use of the army, fifteen hundred saddle or pack horses, and one hundred and fifty wagons, to be drawn by four horses each, that man, so prompt and full of resource, had them all in readiness to send in less than a fortnight. The means he adopted were characteristic of Franklin's shrewd knowledge of mankind, and his business tact. He had a handbill printed, and sent everywhere about the country. In this document Franklin shrewdly appealed to the fears of the people, by reminding them that "it was proposed to send an armed force immediately into the various counties, to seize as many of the best carriages and horses as should be wanted, and compel as many persons into the service as should be necessary to drive and take care of them."—"I apprehended," says Franklin, "that the progress of a body of soldiers through these counties on such an occasion, especially considering the temper they are in and their resentment against us, would be attended with many and great inconveniences to the inhabitants; and therefore more willingly undertook the trouble of trying first what might be done by fair and equitable means." He concluded with the most telling point when he said, "If this method of obtaining the wagons and horses is not likely to succeed, I am obliged to send word to the general in fourteen days; and I suppose *Sir John St. Clair*, the hussar, with a body of soldiers, will immediately enter the province, of which I shall be sorry to hear, because, *I am, very sincerely and truly, your friend and wellwisher,*   B. FRANKLIN."

The inflammatory Sir John had already made himself, by his explosive wrath on former occasions, sufficiently formidable to those who had been exposed to it; but this threatening aspect of him as "the hussar," was calculated to make him still more terrific, particularly to the German farmers of Pennsylvania, who re-tained a very lively dread of the summary proceedings of the hussars of their fatherland. This home-thrust had such an astonishing effect, that the Germans, from being the most remiss before, suddenly became the most forward, and contributed more than their share of the required supplies.

Braddock was so gratified with the success of Franklin's exertions, that, in his despatches to the British government, he said emphatically it was almost the first instance of integrity, address, and ability, that he had met with in all the provinces.

Franklin volunteered to do another act of gracious service to the army, and did it with the same promptitude. While at Fredericktown, he was supping with Colonel Dunbar, the second in command, when that officer remarked that his subalterns were hard put to it, with their small pay and the dearness of everything on the route of an army on the march, to provide themselves with what was necessary to their comfort. Franklin, on his return to Philadelphia, bore this in mind, and succeeded in squeezing out of the assembly sufficient money to buy a small stock of luxuries for each of the subalterns, of whom there were a score, under Dunbar and Sir Peter Halket. Packages were accordingly made up, containing tea, good butter, some dozens of old Madeira, a couple of gallons of Jamaica, six dried tongues, and various smaller comforts for the inner man, and despatched. These timely supplies were very welcome, and the officers who received them gratefully returned their hearty thanks to those who "had been so good as to think of them in so genteel a manner."

The general, having sent forward the forty-eighth regiment under Colonel Dunbar, soon after followed, accompanied by his aids-de-camp and secretary. Braddock had purchased a coach from Governor Sharpe, of Maryland, in which he now travelled, with considerable state, having, as he dashed along,

April 31.

a bodyguard of light-horse, with his staff at their head, galloping on either side. In this style the general reached Winchester, and, not finding the Indians he expected there, started for Fort Cumberland. Coming up with the forty-fourth regiment, under Dunbar, the general entered, with the troops following him, and their drums beating "The Grenadiers' March;" and, on his arrival, was saluted with a volley of seventeen guns.

CHAPTER VIII.

The Hard March to Fort Cumberland.—The General swears terribly.—Delay.—What is thought of it in England.—Arrival of the Artillery.—Their Hard Experience by the Route.—A Rattlesnake Colonel.—Braddock's Force smaller than expected.—British Contempt of Provincial Troops.—The Grand Display of Braddock's Camp.—Order.—Exercises.—Amusements.—Death.—Good Cooks and Good Eating at Headquarters.—Good Morals.—Arrival of Indians.—White Thunder and his Daughter Bright Lightning.—Entertainment of the Savages.—"Drams round."—The Indians disaffected.—The Indian Women the Cause of the Trouble.—Departure of the Indians.—An Occasional Delaware shows Himself.—Delawares suspected of Villany.—Captain Jack and his Indian-Killers.—The Captain's History.—Braddock's Contempt.—The Consequences.—Captain Jack goes off in a Huff, and all his Indian-Killers with him.—Arrival of Horses and Wagons sent by Franklin.—First Appearance of Daniel Morgan on the Field of History.—Daniel and the British Officer.—No Flour and Beef.—A Detachment of Cavalry and Wagons ordered out for Supplies.—Braddock in a Rage.—The March begun.—The Hard Road.—Five Miles in Two Days.—Lightening the March.—Women and Baggage sent back to the Fort.—Shades of Death.—Arrival at Little Meadows.

THE army had had a tedious march to Will's creek, or Fort Cumberland, as it was now called, in honor of the British prince. The general himself, having had a good opportunity of seeing the absurdity of the route, and, as Washington writes, "of damning it very heartily," was determined now to abandon his fine coach and his stately progress, and submit himself to the hard requirements of the wild country in which he had begun his campaign.

Twenty-seven days had been already consumed in the march, and there was every prospect of a long detention now at Fort Cumberland. The British ministers, when they heard of the delays, were greatly vexed. "The duke of Cumberland," says Walpole, "who is now the soul of the regency, is much dissatisfied at the slowness of General Braddock, who does not march as if he was at all impatient to be scalped. It is said for him that he has had bad guides, that the roads are exceedingly difficult, and that it was necessary to drag as much artillery as he does. . . . . This is not the first time," adds the malevolent gossip, "that the duke has found that brutality did not necessarily constitute a general."

Braddock, however, was not to blame for these delays, which fretted his impetuous temper as much as they could possibly have annoyed his patron the duke of Cumberland. The general had met with disappointment at every point and turn. Here at the fort, where he had been promised the greatest plenty of all kinds of provisions, none that were fresh could be obtained. The men had already marched through an uninhabited wilderness, without anything but salted meat, and there was every reason to fear that their health would suffer in consequence. The general did all in his power to remedy these deficiencies by offering large rewards and lending money out of his own pocket to several people, in order to enable them to provide the camp. By these means some supplies were procured, but not in sufficient abundance to satisfy their wants.

May 20. The artillery, after being detained at Alexandria a whole fortnight, awaiting wagons and horses, now came in, under the command of Lieutenant-Colonel Gage. The party, which was accompanied by the naval detachment of seamen, had suffered greatly on the route. They had been often without provisions for themselves and fodder for their horses. The men, worn out with hauling the guns over "prodigious mountains," and exposed to the fitful changes of the spring weather, now suffering from the sultry heat and again from the damp cold and heavy dews, became ill, and some so disabled, that they were obliged to be left on the route. They found little encouragement from the various semi-barbarous frontiersmen at whose log-houses and forts they stopped on their march. There was "one Cressop, a rattle-snake colonel and a d——d rascal," whom they had a particular reason for remembering for his roguery and ill service.

The forces were now all collected at Fort Cumberland. There were the two regiments sent out from England, composed of a few hundred more than their original strength of a thousand, but not up to their full complement of fifteen hundred, as the expected recruits from Maryland and Virginia had not been obtained. There was the troop of Virginia light-horse; the two independent companies from New York, under Captain Horatio Gates; two companies of "hatchet-men," or pioneers; a company of guides; the detachment of sailors, and a few Indians, making in all about two thousand men.

The British officers, with their set notions about military order and appearance, were not very well pleased with the looks of the provincials. They had been submitted to a systematic drill. Ensign Allen, their drill-master, "had taken great pains with them, and they performed their evolutions and firings as well as could be expected; but their languid, spiritless, and unsoldier-like appearance, considered with the lowness and ignorance of most of their officers, gave little hopes of their future good behavior." Their "future good behavior," however, was such as to put to the blush the boasted superiority of the regulars, and to prove how little they deserved this contempt, which was common to British general and British subaltern.

Braddock shared in this depreciation of the provincial soldier, and wrote: "The American troops have little courage or good will. I expect from them almost no military service, though I have employed the best officers to drill them." He became so rude in his denunciations of the provincials, that Washington's patriotism was wounded, and he warmly took up the defence of his countrymen. He, however, gave up the general, as of impracticable obstinacy and prejudice, and as one who was "incapable of arguing without warmth, or giving up any point he had asserted, be it ever so incompatible with reason or common sense."

Doubtless the provincial troops did appear, during these comparatively holyday times at Fort Cumberland, to great disadvantage with the British regulars. During the compulsory detention here, Braddock had a fine opportunity of displaying some of his London-park tactics, and even Washington was struck with admiration at the effective show and strict discipline of the British grenadiers. The general himself kept up considerable state. He held a daily *levee* at his tent every morning from ten to eleven o'clock, and expected his various officers to present themselves in full uniform. The camp was arranged on the most approved principles of military.art, and the strictest system and most regular order everywhere established. The troops were daily exercised and submitted to the severest discipline. None of the usual ceremonies were omitted, but all as strictly celebrated as if the troops had been stationed under the Tower-guns at London, instead of being encamped in a wilderness.

A Captain Bromley dies, and his funeral takes place, with every detail of military order and respect, notwithstanding the discomforts of the camp on "an excessively hot day." A captain's guard marched before the corpse, with the captain of it in the rear, the firelocks reversed, and the drums beating "The Dead March." On coming near the grave, the guard formed two lines, facing each other, resting on their arms with the muzzles downward, and leaning on the butts of their muskets. The body, with the sword and sash of the dead captain on the coffin, was now carried between the two lines of soldiers, and followed by the officers, walking two and two. The chaplain, a Mr. Philip Hughes, having read the service, the guard fired three volleys over the grave, and marched back to the camp.

There was, however, with all this strictness of discipline, an effort made to keep up the spirits of the camp by occasional amusements. The young officers got up races and hunting-parties; and the general, who had his cooks from Europe, and prided himself upon his kitchen, gave frequent invitations to dinner. There was, however, a strict attention paid to the morals of the troops. No sutler was allowed to sell more than one gill of spirits a day to each man, and this was to be diluted with three gills of water; and every soldier found drunk was sent immediately to the guardhouse, and when sober, next morning, received two hundred lashes. Theft was punished with death. Gambling was prohibited to the non-commissioned officer and common soldier, under a penalty of three hundred lashes; and all lookers-on were deemed principals, and punished the same.

Of all the Indians who had been promised, only thirty as yet had arrived at the fort. These were some chiefs and warriors belonging to the Six Nations. There was Monicotoha, the wise man, whose duty it was to do all the speaking; White Thunder, who had "a daughter called Bright Lightning;" he it was who had charge of the wampum-belts; and there were also Silver-Heels and Great Tree, all potent men in their various tribes. As soon as they arrived, the general received them at his tent, surrounded by all his officers in full uniform, and with his guard drawn up and presenting arms. The interpreter was instructed to tell the assembled chiefs that their brothers the English, who were their old friends, were come to assure them that every misunderstanding that had been in former times should now be buried under that great mountain, which was throwing its shadow over the camp. A belt of wampum was then passed, with still further assurances of friendship, and the whole concluded with "the ceremony of drams round."

Again, on the next day, the general had another reception of his Indian friends, when he expressed his great sorrow at the death of the half-king, old Tanacharisson, Washington's capricious friend, and his desire that they should take up the hatchet for the great king of England, their father, against the French.

Presents of rings, beads, knives, and paint, being distributed, the Indians went off, greatly rejoicing, and, to "show they were pleased, made a most horrible noise, dancing all night."

"For a time all went well," says Washington Irving, whose description of the issue we borrow; for when he once gets upon his favorite subject of the Indians, his narrative becomes so charmingly picturesque and humorous, that we listen to it with such delight as not to care to investigate its accuracy. "The Indians had their separate camp," writes Irving, "where they passed half the night, singing, dancing, and howling. The British were amused by their strange ceremonies, their savage antics, and savage decorations. The Indians, on the other hand, loitered by day about the English camp, fiercely painted and arrayed, gazing with silent admiration at the parade of the troops, their marchings and evolutions; and delighted with the horse-races, with which the young officers recreated themselves.

"Unluckily, the warriors had brought their families with them to Will's creek, and the women were even fonder than the men of loitering about the British camp. They were not destitute of attractions, for the young squaws resemble the gipsies, having seductive forms, small hands and feet, and soft voices. Among those who visited the camp was one who no doubt passed for an Indian princess. She was the daughter of the sachem, White Thunder, and bore the dazzling name of Bright Lightning. The charms of these wild-wood beauties were soon acknowledged. 'The squaws,' writes Secretary Peters, 'bring in money plenty; the officers are scandalously fond of them.'

"The jealousy of the warriors was aroused; some of them became furious. To prevent discord, the squaws were forbidden to come into the British camp. This did not prevent their being sought elsewhere. It was ultimately found necessary, for the sake of quiet, to send Bright Lightning, with all the other women and children, back to Aughquick. White Thunder and several of the warriors accompanied them for their protection."

The Indians, for some reason or other, never returned with their warriors in such numbers as they had promised. Some have blamed the general, saying that he underrated their services. It is probable, with his contempt for everything but "regular" warfare, he did; but, at the same time, he seems to have treated his savage visiters always with great consideration. Franklin says, "He slighted or neglected them, and they gradually left him, although they might have been of great use to his army as guides or scouts, if he had treated them kindly." It was not, however, so much the fault of the general, as the treacherous character of the people he had to deal with. Some of the Indians evidently were acting faithlessly from the beginning, and only coquetting with the British, to obtain gifts, or awaiting the result of the struggle with the French, in order to give in their adherence to the stronger.

Delaware warriors were, almost daily, coming into the camp, with offers of service, and pretended information of the enemy. The British officers were from the beginning suspicious; and the outspoken sailor, who has left a journal of the expedition, says, "These people [the Delawares] are villains, and always side with the strongest." This he says just after some of them had come into the camp and told the general that they would return home, collect their warriors, and meet him on their march. Another Delaware turns up again, with some dubious information about Fort Du Quesne, when our sailor declares, "I believe this fellow is a villain, as he is a Delaware, who never were our friends." Whatever may have been the cause, Braddock had never at any time over half a hundred Indians with him, and of these only eight were left at the close of the expedition.

The general, however, was more to blame for another loss, that of Captain Jack and his band of "Indian-killers." This man was an early settler on the frontiers of Pennsylvania, where with his family he lived the life of an occasional hunter and farmer. During the season for game, he was abroad in the forest-wilderness, with his gun upon his shoulder, and in his leathern suit, engaged in the chase for deer, the bear, and the fox. He thus supplied his family with wild meat, and gathered skins for barter at the various trading-posts with the fur-dealers, who supplied him in exchange with guns, ammunition, Jamaica spirits, and articles of food and clothing required by himself and family. When not occupied in the chase, he busied himself in cultivating the patch of cleared ground which surrounded his rude log-house, and planting it with potatoes and Indian corn. Though roughened by the wild life he led on the frontier, he had taken to himself a wife, who had borne him several little ones, and his independent and somewhat reckless disposition was thus still in subjection to the ties of civilization.

One day, the hunter returns, loaded with game, in eager expectation of a warm welcome from wife and children, when, as he reaches the familiar spot of his home, he finds his log-house burned to the ground, and his family lying dead and mangled amid the ashes! This cruel work he knew at once to have been that of the ruthless savage. The rude elements of the man's character now swelled up with a violence that overmastered all the gentler emotions, which were once, but alas! no longer called forth, at the soft entreaty of wife and child. He swore revenge against the whole race of Indians; and, gathering about him other frontiersmen, broken loose like himself from the bonds of kindred and civilized life, he commenced a career of such fierce onslaught upon his savage enemies, that "The Black Hunter of the Forest"—for thus he was called, from the swarthiness of his visage—was a terror from the northern lakes to the Chesapeake.

Such was the Captain Jack, who with his men had now offered himself to Braddock, and been rejected, because forsooth the British guardsman would not bate a jot of his Hyde-park rules of discipline, even in the wilderness! Jack had made it a condition of his services that he and his men should not be subjected to the routine of military discipline. Braddock, with an absurd obstinacy, refused compliance. The captain and his "Indian-killers" moodily departed. The general made a great mistake. These bold woodsmen, familiar as they were with the wild life of the borders, and the habits of the Indians—whom they even resembled in appearance, their faces being blackened by exposure to sun and weather, and their garb being of the rude Indian material and make—would have been the best force to act as guides through the forest, and as a protection against the chances of a savage ambuscade.

The horses and wagons which, as will be recollected, Franklin had undertaken to supply, and had so promptly got ready, now reached the camp, **May 20.** after considerable detention on the rough roads. There came with the wagons a remarkable man, of whom we shall hear more in the progress of our history of the battles of America. This was Daniel Morgan, of Pennsylvania. Living a somewhat reckless and dissipated life, but being sufficiently well to do in the world as to own a wagon and horses, he had joined the expedition. He was a person of humble position, but of high spirit; and had hardly started in this new enterprise, when an officer, taking advantage of the former, had an opportunity of finding out the latter. Daniel, being behind time one day with his horses, was severely reprimanded by the military gentleman in command, to whom he answered in terms not usually addressed in the British army to a superior. The officer drew his sword. Daniel brandished his whip.

The officer made a thrust. Daniel knocked the weapon out of his hand, and lashed him with his whip. The teamster was accordingly arrested and punished. Five hundred lashes was the sentence; but, as Daniel fainted after the first four hundred and fifty, the last half-hundred were remitted. Daniel has reported that the officer subsequently acknowledged that the fault was his own, and handsomely apologized.

Although the wagons and horses had arrived, they did not bring with them the supplies of food and stores expected. That "rattlesnake colonel" Cressop had allowed the teams to pass his fort at Conegogee without sending the flour contracted for; and the fellow's father turned out to be as great a rogue as the son, for, although he had sent the beef, it was necessary to bury it as soon as it reached the camp. The father had been paid to salt this beef, whereas the old rascal had put it up without pickle, and in dry casks which could never have contained any.

Without flour and beef, the general was obliged to send thirty wagons, with a detachment under Washington, to Winchester, over sixty miles of mountainous and rocky country, for a supply. Three hundred pack-horses were also ordered off for flour; and a troop of light-horse to bring up the rascal Cressop from Conegogee, full ninety miles distant.

Braddock became every day more and more inflamed against the provinces, and with reason, for they all failed in their engagements toward him. Governor Morris's secretary, Mr. Richard Peters, came in for a large share of the general's anger, having just arrived in camp when the raging storm was at its height. Peters asked for a guard to protect the laborers on the road which was being made, in accordance with Braddock's requisition, to connect Fort Cumberland with the high-roads of Pennsylvania, in order to secure a communication for reinforcements and provisions from that province. He would not supply guards for wood-cutters, not he, declared the general, with an oath; let Pennsylvania do it. Subsequently, however, Braddock did do it himself, as without his aid the road would never have made any progress; for the laborers were so constantly harassed by their fears, and occasionally by the Indians themselves, that they hardly ventured to go to their work in the wilderness.

Everything that was done had to be done by the general himself. It was only after he had thus taken the work into his own hands, that he got the necessary supplies, and was prepared to march. Six weeks of valuable time had been already lost, in awaiting the slow and reluctant action of the provincial governments. He was again detained a month afterward in doing what ought to have been done long before by the colonial authorities.

Toward the close of May, a council-of war having been called, the plan of march was agreed upon. The first preliminary step was accordingly made immediately after, by sending a detachment of six hundred men, under the **May 29.** command of Major Chapman, to act as pioneers and open the way. They started at daybreak, and when night came they had only got about two miles from the camp, and no wonder; for there was a mountain in the way, the ascent and descent of which were almost a perpendicular rock. Three wagons were entirely destroyed in the operation of getting past this obstruction, and "many more were extremely shattered,"although three hundred men, with a company of miners, had been engaged several days previously in making that hill passable. A passage, however, was soon after discovered through a valley by Lieutenant Spendlowe of the naval brigade, by which the "great mountain" could be avoided, and this was adopted by the general for the march.

June 7. Sir Peter Halket was the next to follow Major Chapman, with his brigade, artillery, and baggage-wagons. Three days subsequently, Colonel Dunbar marched with his division; and **June 10.** a few hours afterward, General Braddock, accompanied by his aids-de-camp, set out with the remainder of the forces.

The general was not long in discovering that he had engaged in an undertaking full of difficulty and danger. The march was over a rough country—now through a deep forest, which required to be cleared at every step; and again over mountains, which demanded all the skill of the sailors, and the constant labor of the soldiers, to scale with their heavy artillery and baggage. Lieutenant-Colonel Burton had ridden back to the general, and reported that he had been two days in marching about five miles, on a better

road than they were to expect afterward. This induced Braddock, on consultation with his officers, to diminish the heavy load with which the army was encumbered. Two six-pounders, four cohorns, and a considerable quantity of stores and ammunition, were sent back to the fort, and twenty wagons thus cleared; the load of each man was reduced, and the horses' allowance of two hundred weight it was found necessary to diminish one half, as most of the animals were sorry nags, incapable of full duty. Even the officers determined to rid themselves of much of their personal baggage, and, giving up the marquees and their luxurious appointments, resolved to content themselves with the common soldier's tent and its bare necessities. They were thus enabled to make over their superfluous horses for the common service. The general himself gave up twenty, which proves him to have had rather an exorbitant stud. The weakest men in the ranks, together with all the women, with the exception of two to each company, were also sent back to the fort.

Lightened and relieved even as they were now, the march continued to be exceedingly difficult and slow, and the whole force did not reach Little Meadows, twenty-four miles only from Fort Cumberland, until the 18th of June. During this march, although "all possible care was taken," the line was sometimes extended to a length of four or five miles. So soon came to pass what Benjamin Franklin foretold of the army making "a slender line nearly four miles long, which may expose it to be attacked by surprise on its flanks, and to be cut like thread into several pieces, which from their distance can not come up in time to support one another."

Thus they toiled along, sickened with hard work, exposure, and bad fare; and thus they passed sadly and slowly through that forest of pines, aptly termed "The Shades of Death," and ominous of a terrible future, until they finally came to a halt and pitched their tents at Little Meadows.

CHAPTER IX.

Braddock disposed to change his Tactics.—Consults Young Washington, his Aid-de-Camp.—The Army divided.—Sir John St. Clair in advance.—A Foretaste of the Future.—An Indian Ambuscade.—Braddock advances with the Choicest of the Troops.—Dunbar left behind, to proceed leisurely with the Rest.—Braddock still indulging in his Old-fashioned Notions.—Great Crossings in a Week.—Indians skulking about.—Sickness among the Troops.—Washington ill.—Obliged to halt.—Tracks of Indians and French.—Braddock becomes cautious.—Encampment at Thickety Run.—News and Scalps from Fort Du Quesne.—Gist's Report.—Smoke in the Valley.—Washington rejoins Braddock.—Monakatuca Camp.—The Unfortunate Death of the Young Monakatuca.—The Reverence paid by Braddock to the Dead.—The Monongahela Route.—Crossing the Monongahela.—The Brilliant Display of the Troops.—The Virginians in the Rear.—The Conflict.—The Brave Struggle.—The Courage of Braddock.—Four Horses shot under Him.—The General falls.—The Retreat.—Its Horrors.—Washington unhurt, though exposed to the Hottest Fire.—Havoc of Officers.

At Little Meadows, the various brigades came in in slow succession, at intervals of two or three days of each other; and the men, fatigued and dispirited by the tedious, laborious, and melancholy march, were glad to tent themselves within the camp, which had been fortified by Sir John St. Clair and his advance-party. Braddock now became conscious of the necessity of waiving some of his old-fashioned, European notions of military progress. His line he found was dangerously weakened by the great extent of baggage; his men were worn out by the fatigue of remaining so many hours under arms; and the horses grew fainter every day, and many died.

The proud British general now descended from his high state of dignified self-sufficiency, and deigned to consult his young provincial aid-de-camp. Washington's advice was solicited, and given straightforwardly, but with a discreet modesty. The garrison at Du Quesne, he reminded the general, was weak at this time; and there was little prospect, while the rivers were low, of any addition to its strength from the coming in of more men and supplies. Now was the time, urged the young Virginian, to make a rapid march and strike an irresistible blow. He would advise, therefore, that the general should push on at once with a light division, and leave the heavy troops and baggage to follow after. Braddock approved of this view, and determined to lay it before his council-of-war, where Washington himself, of course, from his position, had no voice. The plan of the young Virginian aid-de-camp was adopted, and preparations made at once to carry it into effect.

June 18. Sir John Sinclair, the deputy quartermaster-general, whose duty it was to act as pioneer, now set out with four hundred men, under Gage, to cut and make the road to the "Little Crossings," situated on a small stream emptying into Casselman's river. They took with them the pack-horses, laden with tools and provisions, and two six-pounders for defence. The Indians also accompanied them, to act as scouts. Sir John St. Clair's detachment had not proceeded far, when the peculiar hazards of the march were strikingly exhibited. The Indian chief Monokatuca, or Scaro-vyadi, as he was sometimes called, had strayed, in company with his son, in advance of the party, when he fell into an ambuscade of French and savages. The former were for killing him at once; the Indians, however, refused, and declared that they would join the English if they did so. They then agreed to tie him to a tree, and leave him there. The son escaped, and, bringing word to his Indian brethren of the whereabouts of his father, the old chief was released at once.

June 19. Braddock himself set out the next day after the departure of St. Clair, taking with him the two veteran grenadier companies and five hundred rank and file of the best of the remaining troops, under the various commands of Sir Peter Halket, Lieutenant-Colonel Burton, and Major Sparks, which, with the eighteen Virginia light-horse and the small party of seamen, made up a division of eight hundred, all told. Dunbar and others left behind were sorely vexed at the preference given by the general to the troops with which he marched as it was well understood that his purpose had been to select those he believed to be the best.

Disencumbered as the general comparatively was, his march was still slow. He had rid himself of much of his artillery and baggage, taking with him only four howitzers, each drawn by nine horses; four twelve-pounders, with seven horses each; and thirty wagons, with four horses each. Braddock was still too set in his old military notions, to adapt himself to the requirements of the country; for, as Washington says, "instead of pushing on with vigor, without regarding a little rough road, they were halting to level every molehill and to erect bridges over every brook, by which means we were four days in getting twelve miles." With this deliberate kind of procedure, there was little chance of reaching Fort Du Quesne by the 28th of June, the time proposed, in order to anticipate the arrival of the half-thousand regulars who were reported to be on their march to the aid of the French garrison. They did not, in fact, reach the "Great Crossings" on the Youghiogeny river until the 24th of June, although it was but seventeen miles, which had taken a week to march.

Braddock found himself always on the heels of the advance-party under Sir John St. Clair, with whom he was constantly coming up. The general was thus obliged to halt until the sides of a mountain were cut through, or the swamps were made passable. He was not without disturbance, too, from daily rumors of the approach of the enemy, and occasional harassment by hostile Indians. At one time the guides came running in, extremely frightened, and reporting that a great body of the enemy were marching to attack the advanced guard. This alarm over, intelligence was brought that some men, who had roamed beyond the outposts, had been shot and scalped; while Indians were constantly observed skulking about, to waylay a straggler, or to watch the progress of the march. Horse-thieves abounded, too; and it was with the greatest difficulty that the fatigued nags, after a hard day's work, could get a nibble of pasture, before they were driven off by some of the freebooters of the forest.

Sickness also prevailed among the officers and soldiers, in consequence of the fatigue and bad provisions. One of the commanders of the naval brigade was prostrated by fever, and sent back to Little Meadows. Washington fell ill, and, being unable to sit any longer on his horse, was obliged to allow himself to be conveyed in a covered wagon. He was finally forced by his disease to give in, and was induced at the earnest solicitation of Braddock—to whom he had become greatly endeared from his virtues, and was now almost indispensable from the excellence of his judgment and the value of his opinions—to stay behind. Washington's ardor to go on was only appeased by the solemn promise of Braddock that he should have a chance of joining him before he engaged with the enemy.

As Braddock moved on slowly from the "Great Crossings," he had more and more proof that he was in the Indian country, and greater reason to be on his guard against the ambuscades of the wily savages. During one day's march, an Indian camp was discovered, that had been just abandoned, and which, from the number of huts, proved that some hundred and seventy of these savages had lately occupied them. They had stripped the barks from the trees, and inscribed upon them with paint all kinds of threats and bravadoes, in the Indian and French languages.

They now passed the Great Meadows, and encamped about two miles on the other side. Some Indians **June 25.** making their appearance in the neighboring woods, the general sent the light-horse, a few Indian scouts, and some volunteers, to surround them; but they returned without success. On taking up their march again, next day, they had made but a quarter of a mile from their late encampment, when they reached the summit of so steep a hill, that it was necessary to call in the aid of the sailors, and let down the wagons with tackle.

On this day, in consequence of the badness of the road, the **June 26.** army could only make four miles. At the halting-place, which was situated where the Indian path to the Monongahela terminates, was found an Indian camp which had been so recently abandoned, that the fires were still burning. Triumphant bravadoes were seen written upon the trees, with the number of scalps that had been taken two days before. There had evidently been some French with them, for they had inscribed also their names, and many insolent expressions, in their own language. The position of the Indian camp was strongly fixed upon a high rock, with a narrow and steep ascent to the top. In the middle flowed a spring. It was by the Indian pass, which led to this camp, that the French and Indian force had come which attacked Washington at Fort Necessity. Traces were discovered of the route taken by those who had so recently abandoned the place, and some ninety volunteers, provided with guides, issued out at night, toward the Monongahela, in pursuit; but although they found by the way some provisions and a batteau, which they destroyed, they saw no men.

Great precautions were now taken, at every halting-place on the march, lest the Indians and the French should come upon them unawares. The pickets were doubled; the men kept constantly under arms, with fixed bayonets; and no fire, on any account, allowed to be lighted in front of them. In cleaning the guns, the soldiers were strictly ordered to draw the charges, and not fire them off, lest the enemy should be within hearing, and thus be made aware of the approach of the troops. The cartridges were carefully examined, and, when injured by the wet, exchanged for fresh ones. Although it was the 30th of June when the line had crossed the Youghioney—the men wading through a depth of three feet, and across a breadth of water of two hundred yards—it was not before the 4th of July, so slow was the progress, the march frequently not exceeding two miles a day,

10

that they came up to "Thickety Run," where they encamped. The country now became less mountainous and rocky; and the white-oak woods less dense, and not offering so good a cover for a skulking enemy.

A couple of Indians, who had been sent out toward Fort Du Quesne, now returned, bringing the scalp of a **July 6.** French officer, whom they had fallen in with while he was out shooting, and the intelligence that there were few men or tracks about, and no additional works at the fort. Gist, the general's provincial guide, brought back a very similar report, with the additional and most important information, however, that he had observed some smoke in a valley between the English encampment and Fort Du Quesne. Gist had had a narrow escape; for while attempting at night to get closer to the fort, he had been observed by a couple of Indians, who pursued and came very near catching him.

While encamped at Thickety Run, the captain with his detachment of one hundred men, who had been sent to Dunbar's camp at Little Meadows for provisions, came in with a very welcome supply. The delay incurred in waiting for this seemed absolutely necessary, but, as the sequel will prove, was disastrous to Braddock. With the party, however, came Washington, who had so far recovered as to join the troop on its way to the general's camp. He was warmly welcomed on his arrival by Braddock and his fellow-aids-de-camp, Morris and Orme, who had kept him during his absence well informed, by frequent letters, of every detail of the march. He came in the very nick of time, for the army was only distant fifteen miles from Fort Du Quesne, and might expect hot work at the earliest moment. The next day after Washington's arrival had been, in fact, appointed as the day of attack.

The place where Braddock had now halted was styled "Monakatuca Camp," from an unhappy accident that occurred in its neighborhood. A few stragglers in the rear of the march had been attacked by hostile Indians, and ruthlessly scalped. A company of grenadiers having been ordered out to look after these savages, met with a party of Indians belonging to the English line, and, mistaking them for the enemy, fired upon them—notwithstanding the countersign agreed upon, raising a bough and grounding arms, was made—and killed the son of the chief Monakatuca. When his body was brought to the camp by the wailing Indians, the general did everything in his power to console the father and the rest. The usual presents were bestowed, a military funeral with all its solemnities was ordered, the officers attended, and a volley was fired over the forest-grave where the young chief was laid. This marked respect to their dead seemed to have greatly won for Braddock the attachment of the few Indian followers left to him.

July 8. On taking up his march, Braddock strove, in order to avoid the dangerous pass called "The Narrows," to cross the narrow stream known as Turtle creek. He had not, however, proceeded far, when he reached a precipice that it was impossible to descend. Sir John St. Clair was therefore ordered to take a captain and a hundred men, some light-horse, and Indian guides, and reconnoitre thoroughly the country round about. The main body having in the meantime encamped for the night, the reconnoitring party returned with the report that another route, by fording the Monongahela, had been discovered, by which both the precipice and the narrows might be avoided.

It was determined, therefore, to pursue the Monongahela route, by which the army would be obliged to cross that river twice in order to reach Fort Du Quesne. The road through the Narrows was the more direct one; but, as it was but a narrow pass of two miles in length, with a river on the left and a very high mountain on the right, and in such a rough condition that it would require much time and labor to make it passable for carriages, it seemed right to abandon it.

The next morning, therefore, **July 9.** Braddock, who had been encamped the previous night within two miles of the Monongahela, made his arrangements for passing his forces across the two fords, one of which would take them to the opposite bank, and the other bring them back to the side whence they started, but in the immediate neighborhood of the fort. Accordingly, at daybreak, Lieutenant-Colonel Gage was ordered to march with two companies of grenadiers, one hundred and sixty rank and file of the forty-fourth and forty-eight, Captain Gates's independent company of New-Yorkers, some four hundred men in all, two six-pounders, and proper guides. His instructions were, to pass the two fords of the Monongahela, and on crossing the second to post himself so as to secure the passage of the river. Washington is said to have ventured to propose that the rangers, of Virginia, accustomed to the wild country and Indian warfare, should lead the advance; but that Braddock peremptorily and angrily refused to listen to any such proposition, and, to show his superior confidence in the regulars and his contempt for the provincials, ordered the Virginians to the rear. Gage advanced and crossed the fords, as had been ordered, meeting with no opposition but a show of hostility from some thirty Indians, who, however, took to their heels at once and disappeared.

The general now moved his main body, and it marched across the two fords in admirable order. The troops were in full uniform, their colors were flying gayly, the drums were beating, and the fifes playing "The Grenadiers' March." The provincials were struck with admiration at the gallant martial display, and the whole line thrilled with confident hope of a speedy and glorious termination to their long march. Both passes having been got over in such gallant array, without any disorder or interference, they began to think that the enemy would not even venture to make an attack, "as they might have done with so many advantages a little time before."

"Washington," says Irving, "with his keen and youthful relish for military affairs, was delighted with the perfect order and equipment of the troops, so different from the rough bush-fighters to which he had been accustomed. Roused to new life, he forgot his recent ailments, and broke forth in expressions of enjoyment and admiration, as he rode in company with his fellow aids-de-camp, Orme and Morris. Often in after-life he used to speak of the effect upon him of the first sight of a well-disciplined European army, marching in high confidence and bright array, on the eve of a battle."

From early morning, the advance party under Gage having moved before daybreak, until the afternoon, it being nearly two o'clock when the rear-guard passed the second ford, Braddock had been engaged in getting his forces again in the line of march toward the fort. As soon as all were over, there was a general halt, and then the army fell into marching order. First went an engineer, three guides, and six light-horsemen, to lead the way, followed closely by the grenadiers, and flanking-parties distributed along the edge of the wood which bounded the march. Next came the working-force, under Sir John St. Clair. Then marched the main body with Braddock himself, while the unappreciated Virginians sullenly brought up the rear.

The banks of the river along which the army was now formed rose gradually from the water in natural terraces, gently sloping from one to the other, until suddenly bounded by the steep, rocky wall of the mountain-range. The ground upon which they halted, immediately on the border of the Monongahela, where it was crossed by the second ford, was for a fourth of a mile almost level, with an open, park-like growth of hickory-trees spread over it, and clear of vines and brushwood. When the van took up its march, however, the road of only twelve feet in width soon led through a forest, which crowded the rising ground back to the hills. On either side was a ravine, and each so shrouded with tangled vines and spreading trees as to be unnoticed from the road.

At two o'clock, Lieutenant-Colonel Gage had been ordered to begin his march with the advance and working parties, and continue it until three. He had now proceeded about a quarter of a mile in advance, when the general ordered the rest of his forces to move. The word had hardly, however, been given, when the sound of an excessively quick and heavy firing, coming from the farthest front, reached the ears of all those in the rear. The general, at once supposing that the advanced parties were very warmly attacked, ordered the vanguard, eight hundred strong, to march to their relief; and the rest of the line, composed of some four hundred only, to halt and guard the artillery and baggage.

Braddock was correct in his surmise. The advance party had been attacked, and warmly too. As the engineer, followed by a party of "hatchet-men," had gone ahead to make his survey and mark out the route, he caught a glance of a large number of Indians, led on apparently by a chief dressed in a gay hunting-suit, and who, from the silver gorget glistening from his neck, was supposed to be an officer of rank. With a wave of their leader's hat, the savages scattered to the right and left, forming a semi-circular line, and then disappeared in an instant. Now came forth, from the dark ravines about, a terrible volley, by which three fourths of those in advance were struck down at once. The grenadiers, coming up, were aghast at this frightful blow from an unseen enemy. Gage, however, awaiting a moment the arrival of St. Clair and his working-party who were immediately behind him, rallied and led his men on to meet the foe. They had hardly advanced a step, when, with terrible yells, came another volley out of the thick covert of wood in front, as well as on the right and the left, staggering the whole force, and striking down the British grenadiers, one after the other, with the rapidity and mystery of the thunderbolts of heaven.

True to discipline, the soldiers fixed their bayonets, advanced, levelled their muskets, and fired, but fired in vain, for they hardly saw an enemy, and merely shot at random into the thick forest and deep ravines, where their foes were supposed to be lurking. The artillery was brought up, and grape-shot was showered about, and not without effect, for all the Indians who had ventured from their hiding-place were killed; and their leader, more daring than the rest, fell dead at the very first fire. The Indians were now momentarily discouraged by the loss of their commander, the chief with the silver gorget, who proved to be De Beaujeu, a gallant French officer. They accordingly retreated through the thicket, in scattered flight, but were rallied successfully by the loud and spirited appeals of another young Frenchman, of the name of Dumas, who had succeeded to the command of Beaujeu.

The Indians now recommenced their "bush" firing, and with such certainty of death to their opponents and security to themselves, that the hitherto firm ranks of the grenadiers began to yield; and at last, finding that their officers were falling rapidly, one after the other, and that their own fire was without effect, they fled from the spot. As they fell back, they were met by the vanguard, under Lieutenant-Colonel Burton, who had been sent by the general to the relief of the advance-party. This produced inextricable confusion. Burton was striving to form his men on the ground for an advance, while the panic-stricken force under Gage was trying to save itself by a retreat to the rear. The two forces now became so mixed together, that it was impossible to separate them; and, with all the spirited efforts of the officers to keep up discipline, there was nothing but disorder: and soon, as the French and Indians were still continuing their deadly fire from their hiding-places, Burton's troops became as discouraged as those of Gage, and shared in the common panic.

The general, in the rear, became every moment more and more anxious, as the firing continued, and it was evident that the struggle was getting more serious. He first sent an aid-de-camp, to bring back intelligence of the nature of the attack. Getting impatient, however, he did not await the return of his messenger, but, leaving the command of the baggage to Sir Peter Halket, galloped forward himself.

When the general reached the scene of struggle, he strove to rally his panic-stricken army. He rode after the flying men, and fiercely called upon them to stand their ground and fight. "We would fight," they said, "if we could see the enemy, but it was useless to fire at trees and bushes, and we can not stand to be shot down by an invisible foe." He succeeded in rallying some of them, and strove to form the men in small, detached parties, which might thus gain the neighboring hills and dislodge the enemy. The officers, however, having been mostly killed or wounded—for the Indians had aimed their deadly shots first at them—there was not a sufficient number left to carry out this manœuvre. The general, notwithstanding, still rode madly about, raving at the cowardice of the men. He had had already four horses shot under him, and, although wounded, had mounted the fifth. The surviving officers strove equally with their undaunted commander-in-chief to form the ranks and bring them to the charge. All, however, seemed vain. The officers continued to come gallantly on, but the men quailed before the demoniac howl of the savages, and the fatality of their hidden aim. The soldiers, distracted by the confusion, either fired wildly into the air, or shot in any direction where they beheld smoke, thus often killing their own comrades on the flank or in advance.

That this unequal warfare could not last long was early foreseen by the provincials; and Washington, familiar with Indian fighting, begged the general to let the men shelter themselves under the cover of the trees, and thus wage an equal battle with the enemy. Braddock was so maddened by the ill conduct of his men, or so wedded to system, that he would not listen to such a proposal, and insisted upon his soldiers keeping the ranks. Moreover, whenever he found a poor fellow covering himself behind a tree, he would ride up to him, and, striking him with the flat of his sword, and fiercely calling him a coward, drive him back to the open ground. A company of Virginians, however, familiar with the Indian warfare, succeeded in gaining the cover of a large trunk of a felled tree, and thence fired upon the enemy with excellent effect. The British soldiers, unable in their fright and confusion to distinguish friend from foe, no sooner saw the flashes and smoke of the provincials' firelocks, which were doing such good service, than they turned their guns upon them, and thus killed fifty out of the whole Virginian company of eighty, and forced the small remnant to fly for their lives!

Everything had been done that courage could do by the officers, hardly one of whom was now able to keep the field. Sir Peter Halket had been struck down soon after arriving upon the ground; and his son, a young subaltern, was shot by his side, and fell dead across his father's body. Not a single one of the general's aids, with the exception of Wash-ington, escaped; all being either wounded or killed. Shirley, Braddock's secretary, was shot dead by a musket-ball, which struck him in the head. Orme and Morris, the two aids-de-camp, were severely wounded, and so early in the engagement, that the duty of carrying the orders of the general devolved solely upon Washington, whose escape seemed marvellous. He was everywhere, and exposed to the hottest fire throughout the action. He had two horses shot under him, and four bullets passed through his coat; and yet he did not receive a single wound.

Amid the terrible massacre which was going on about him, Braddock himself remained in the centre of the field, bravely struggling for a long time against fate. At last, when almost all his officers had fallen — when nearly two thirds of the army had been slain, and the rest so panic-stricken as to be hardly capable of keeping their ranks, in formal obedience to his command — the general saw that all was lost, and gave the order to retreat. The retreat became at once a precipitate flight. "They ran as sheep pursued by dogs, and it was impossible to rally them."

Braddock had hardly given the order, when he was struck with a musket-ball, which passed through his right arm into his lungs. He fell immediately from his horse to the ground.

CHAPTER X.

Braddock prostrate on the Field.—The Affectionate Devotion of the Surviving Officers.—The Panic of the Soldiers.—Men bribed to bear away the Fallen General.—Braddock's Desponding Courage.—Demands his Pistols, and threatens Suicide.—The Coolness of Washington in Covering the Retreat across the Monongahela.—Braddock still mindful of Duty.—Attempts to rally the Fugitives.—His Failure.—Washington sent in Advance to summon Dunbar to the Rescue.—Braddock continues the Retreat, lying on a Litter.—Kindness of the Dying General.—Arrival at Dunbar's Camp.—Its Disorder.—Last Words, Death, and Burial, of Braddock.—A Retrospect.—The French at Fort Du Quesne.—The Works at the Fort.—The Despair of Contrecœur.—The Daring Proposition of a Subaltern.—De Beaujeu and his Indian Allies.—De Beaujeu's Effective Appeal.—The Cruelty of the Conquerors.—A Scene of Ferocious Barbarity.—Dunbar's Fright and Pell-mell Flight.—What he did do, and what he might have done.—Preparations in Philadelphia for the Celebration of the Expected Victory of Braddock.—Franklin's Wet Blanket.—News of the Defeat, and its Effect upon the Philadelphians.—Shirley and Fort Niagara.

1755. In the general, helter-skelter flight which succeeded the order to retreat, the wounded Braddock lay upon the ground, abandoned by all but those few of his officers who were still alive and yet able, in spite of their wounds, to bestow upon him their affectionate and faithful services. His aid-de-camp Orme, though disabled, succeeded in reaching the side of his fallen general, and called upon the flying soldiers to come to his aid and bear him from the field. He ordered; he urged; he begged; he finally strove to bribe, with a purse of gold, the panic-stricken fugitives, but in vain: they continued their flight—throwing away their arms and ammunition, and even their clothes, to escape the faster from the deadly aim and the ruthless tomahawk of their savage enemy.

Orme was almost in despair for the safety of his general, when Captain Stewart, the commander of the Virginia lighthorse, came up, and, sharing with the young aid-de-camp his kind and devoted sympathy for their wounded chief, offered his services. They at last succeeded, by the assistance of some servants attached to the army, who were bribed by a guinea and a bottle of rum to each, in placing the helpless Braddock in a tumbril, and thus bore him off the field. The general, however, at first refused to be carried away, declaring that he wished to be left on the spot where he had fallen. He even became impatient of the death which was fast coming, and begged the pistols of a bystander, that he might thus, like an ancient Roman, put an end, by suicide, to the torturing reflections of a despairing courage.

The retreat continued; the British soldiers flying in confused fright, and the Indians following after, howling in fierce pursuit, and only ceasing their deadly fire when they stopped to scalp some prostrate fugitive. The retreat was thus harassed to the bank of the Monongahela river, which, however, was crossed with mitigated suffering, thanks to the coolness of Washington, who succeeded in rallying a small force of men, sufficient to keep at bay the pursuing savages, while the remnant of the troops were hurriedly crossing the ford.

When about a quarter of a mile on the other side of the Monongahela, although most of the soldiers still continued their flight, Braddock succeeded in bringing to a halt about a hundred men. The general, though his life was ebbing fast, and though his pride had been so mortally wounded by the disgrace of the day, did not lose his sense of duty. He still, though prostrate under the hands of the surgeon, gave his orders, and strove to hold the position where he was until he might be reinforced by Dunbar, with the hope of yet revenging himself for the defeat he had suffered from the enemy.

Washington was sent accordingly to Dunbar, with orders for that officer to hasten on immediately with his troops. Braddock in the meantime moved his few men to an advantageous spot about two hundred yards from the road. Small parties and sentinels were then posted about, and it was intended to keep possession of that ground until the arrival of Dunbar. All the men, however, before they had been there an hour, ran off, leaving the general and his wounded officers, with none but a small remnant of the vanguard. It was of course useless, after this desertion, for Braddock to remain; and, trying at first to mount a horse, but finding himself unable from his increasing weakness, he was obliged to be carried on a litter. Borne thus, and accompanied by Orme and Morris, his wounded aids-de-camp, on litters like himself, the general began his sad jour-

ney. He had left the field at five o'clock in the afternoon, and the shades of evening began now to fall. He travelled slowly on, with the darkness of night gathering, to throw an added gloom upon his saddened heart.

On crossing the second ford of the Monongahela, Braddock was joined by Lieutenant-Colonel Gage, who had succeeded in rallying some eighty men, who now offered themselves as a timely escort to the dying general and his wounded officers. Thus reinforced, they marched all that night and the next day until ten o'clock in the evening, when they reached Gist's Plantation. Here they found a timely supply of wagons, provisions, and hospital-stores, which had been brought on from Dunbar's camp by Washington, who, having fulfilled his commission, was now on his return to meet the general. After a slight halt for refreshment at Gist's Plantation, they all proceeded to Dunbar's camp, some thirteen miles distant. The first thing done by Braddock, on arriving there, was to send a sergeant's party back with provisions, to be left on the road from the Monongahela, for any stragglers who might have lost their way on the route. It is pleasing to record this proof of a kindly impulse on the part of a man who, like Braddock, was so often accused of brutality.

At Dunbar's camp all was disobedience and confusion. Many of those, principally the Pennsylvania wagoners, who had fled from the fatal field without ceasing a moment their flight, had come in here, with the sad tidings of the defeat, which they hurried to communicate in despairing cries, exclaiming, "All is lost! Braddock is killed! Wounded officers have been borne off from the field in bloody sheets! The troops are all cut to pieces!" Dunbar's camp itself became infected with the panic, and many of his men had run away, while those who were left seemed to have forgotten all discipline. The presence of the general secured a little more order in the camp, and he had still hoped so far to reassure his troops as to be able to march them again toward Fort Du Quesne. Finding, however, Dunbar and his men in a condition of hopeless disaffection and disorder from fright, the dying Braddock resolved to give up all hope of redeeming the disgrace of the fatal defeat, and sadly but firmly from his camp-bed, where he lay prostrate, ordered the troops to retire to the seaboard. The military stores were now destroyed, much of the artillery was buried, the wagons burned, the powder-casks stove in, and the powder emptied into a spring of water. Nothing was preserved but what was actually wanted for the march.

Braddock lingered on, though growing weaker and weaker. His heart seemed to give way before his life-blood ceased to run; and he was heard to utter, in accents of despair, "Who would have thought it!" He, however, occasionally rallied in spirits, and exclaimed, with a gleam of hope, "We shall better know how to deal with them another time."

July 13. The march having been begun, the troops succeeded in reaching Great Meadows in tolerable order, the general and his wounded officers having been conveyed to that place on litters borne by horses. A halt had hardly been ordered, and the prostrate Braddock borne to his tent, when the brave but unfortunate general died. He, however, retained his self-possession to the last, and availed himself of the few remaining moments of his life to thank those who were about him, and who had been devotedly kind and faithful to him during the struggle on the battle-field, as well as in the agony of death. Washington he particularly signalled out, asking his forgiveness for his irritable temper toward him, and, to prove his gratitude for the young Virginian's fidelity and friendship, left him his favorite horse and his negro-servant Bishop.

The last sad duty to the remains of the general was paid, in consequence of the chaplain being wounded, by Washington, who read the funeral-service over the grave. The burial was conducted with the greatest reverence, although the usual drum-beat and the volley of guns were omitted, for fear that the watchfulness of some lurking savages in the neighborhood might be aroused, and that they might thus seek out the spot and desecrate the last resting-place of the unfortunate Braddock. "Whatever may have been his faults and errors," says Irving, "he in a manner expiated them by the hardest lot that can befall a brave soldier, ambitious of renown—an unhonored grave in a strange land; a memory clouded by misfortune; and a name for ever coupled with defeat."

Let us now turn back, in regard to

time, and observe the condition and conduct of the enemy when anticipating the approach of the English on that expedition against Fort Du Quesne which resulted in the disastrous defeat we have just recorded.

The French fort, which was situated on the triangular piece of land at the junction of the Monongahela with the Alleghany, had been tolerably well constructed, and was, with a strong garrison, able to endure a long and vigorous siege. It was well protected on one side, and naturally, by the river Monongahela, on the eastern bank of which it stood; and its more exposed points, facing the land, were fortified with bastions built up of great logs to the height of a dozen feet, and filled in with firmly-packed earth and sod. These bastions were joined by a strong stockade of piles driven deep into the ground, and fenced with thick, transverse poles, between which interstices were left for loopholes for cannon and muskets. A ditch, with a stockade to support it, surrounded the whole on the land-side. The inner part of the fort, containing the magazines and the officers' and men's quarters, was made of heavy logs; and its walls were so deeply laid down in the ground, that the earth almost reached the top. The roof, which was the only part exposed, was thickly covered with clay. The whole fortification was deemed so strong as to be only pregnable to hot shot or bombs thrown upon it from the neighboring hills; and here Sir John St. Clair, after his preliminary survey, had proposed to Braddock to mount his artillery, and thence direct his attack — a plan which, it is supposed, had obtained the concurrence of the general.

During the spring of 1755, at the time when Braddock's forces were originally intended to have reached Fort Du Quesne, Contrecœur, who was in command, had only two hundred men, including French and Indians, to garrison the place. Reinforcements were urgently solicited from Canada; and, although there were rumors which had reached the English camp that a large force was on its march to strengthen the garrison, none had arrived when Braddock approached.

As the English drew near, and no word came of aid from Canada, Contrecœur so far despaired of defending himself, that he had almost made up his mind to surrender without striking a blow. He had, in fact, prepared the solitary gun, to march out with, on his being granted — which was evidently intended to be the extent of his demand — the honors of war on capitulation. Contrecœur had been kept well informed of all the particulars of Braddock's march by means of the Indians in the French interest, who were constantly skulking about the British line; and it was not until the 8th of July, when an Indian scout brought in word that the army was about to ford the Monongahela, that there was entertained the least hope of successful opposition. It was at this time that De Beaujeu, a young and spirited French officer, proposed to prepare an ambuscade, by which he might surprise the English forces, and attempt to stop their progress as they recrossed the second ford of the Monongahela.

The old French commander shrugged his shoulders doubtingly as he listened to his youthful subaltern's hazardous proposal. He was, however, so far won over by the urgent enthusiasm of the young officer, that he consented, provided he could get volunteers for his rash enterprise. De Beaujeu took his commander at his word, and submitted the plan to the garrison. The whole, to a man, immediately declared themselves ready to join him.

The Indians, however, were more backward, and said to young Beaujeu, tauntingly, after he had laid before them his plans: " We are only eight hundred men, and you ask us to attack four thousand English !" They then told him plainly that what he had said showed he had no sense. They promised, however, to sleep over the proposition for a night, and give in their final answer next morning. Accordingly, on the succeeding day, at an early hour, De Beaujeu started out with a handful of French, and, arousing the Indians, asked them whether they were ready to go. They answered him with a very decided negative. Beaujeu, who was prompt in an emergency, and ready-witted, then exclaimed : " I shall go out myself against the enemy ; I'm sure of victory ! Will you allow your father to go out alone ?" They then, with one accord, answered the implied rebuke with a burst of enthusiastic devotion to their leader, and expressed their willingness to follow him. We know the result, so fatal to Braddock and the English, and so successful to the French, though it brought death to the gallant De Beaujeu. Out of

the fourteen hundred and sixty English, four hundred and fifty-six were killed, and four hundred and twenty-one wounded ; giving a total of eight hundred and seventy-seven, of whom sixty-three were officers. The French only had three officers killed and four wounded, and lost besides some score of Indians and soldiers. Everything in the way of baggage had been lost by the English, even to their personal clothing. Artillery, cattle, provisions, military treasure amounting to more than a hundred thousand dollars, and all the private letters and despatches contained in Braddock's chest, fell into the hands of the French.

The conquerors shamed the chivalry of their country, and their own fame, by permitting the Indians to glut their savage instincts, in the torture of the English prisoners. Contrecœur and his French garrison are described as having looked from the bastions of the fort, if not unmoved, still without interference, upon a terrific scene, which an observer has described as if " Hell had given a holiday, and turned loose its inhabitants upon the upper world !" Here is the spectacle, with all its details of horror elaborately wrought up by the fervid pen of an annalist :*—

" An hour before sunset, the French and Indians, returning to the fort, halted within a mile's distance, and announced their success by a joyful uproar, discharging all their pieces, and giving the scalp halloo. Instantly the great guns responded, and the hills around re-echoed to their

* The History of an Expedition against Fort Du Quesne, &c., by Winthrop Sargent, M. A. Philadelphia, 1855.

roar. Pushing hastily on, the majority of the savages soon appeared, blood-stained and laden with scalps, and uncouthly arrayed in the spoils of the army. Tall grenadiers' caps surmounted their painted faces, and the regimental colors trailed disgracefully at their heels. With less disordered pace the French succeeded, escorting a long train of pack-horses borne down with plunder. Last of all, and while the parting light of day lingered on the beautiful bosom of the Ohio, appeared a small party who had dallied behind to make the needful preparations for the crowning scene of horror. Before them, stripped perfectly naked, their faces blackened and their hands bound behind their backs, with reluctant steps were driven twelve British regulars, on whom God's sun had shone for the last time.

"Delirious with excitement, their barbarous conquerors could hardly wait for the tardy night, to consummate their unhallowed joy. A stake was at once sunk on the opposite bank of the Alleghany, whither the crew repaired; the prisoners lost in dumb sorrow at the surprising fate which they now began to comprehend. Here, one by one, they were given to the most cruel and lingering of deaths. Bound to the post under the eyes of their remaining comrades and of the French garrison, who crowded the ramparts to behold the scene, they were slowly roasted alive! Coals from an adjacent fire were first applied to various parts of the victim's person. Sharp splinters of light, dry pine-wood were thrust into his flesh, and ignited, to consume and crackle beneath the skin, causing the most exquis-

ite tortures. His trunk was seared with red-hot gun-barrels; blazing brands were thrust into his mouth and nostrils; boiling whiskey was poured in flames down his throat; and deep gashes made in his body, to receive burning coals. His eyeballs were gradually consumed by the thrusts of pointed sticks or the application of a heated ramrod; and the warrior was prized the most highly who could farthest prolong sensibility in his prey, and extract a renewed cry of anguish from the wretch who had almost ceased to suffer—'his weary soul hanging upon his trembling lips—willing to take its leave, but not suffered to depart!' The last expedient was generally to scalp the poor creature, and on his bare, palpitating brain, flash gunpowder or throw a handful of live embers!.... The horrors of this night endured till dawn."

After Braddock's death, Colonel Dunbar, who had succeeded to the chief command, seemed to have lost all self-possession, and, without regard to duty or to the consequences of its neglect, began and continued one of the most disgraceful retreats on record. If he had made a stand upon the frontier, and reassured his troops, it would not have been difficult, with reinforcements from the provinces, to have again marched upon Fort Du Quesne; and probably, with the benefit of the experience of Braddock's disastrous faults, the English would have struck a successful blow, as the enemy, though cheered by their unexpected victory, were awaiting in timid anxiety another attack, against which they were ill prepared. Dunbar himself, however, was panic-stricken, and had no control over his men. He was despised by his own soldiers for his cowardice; and, as they neither feared nor respected, they would not obey him. The consequences showed themselves in the retreat, in which the soldiers, loosened from all control, wandered at their will over the country, and devastated it with a wantonness which left its inhabitants nothing to dread from an enemy.

The provinces were not prepared to hear of Braddock's defeat. They were, in fact, so confident of victory, that in Philadelphia they had begun to prepare for its celebration. The preliminary subscription had even begun to circulate, when the shrewd Franklin threw the wet blanket of his prudence upon the scheme, and effectually put out the kindling enthusiasm of his fellow-citizens. "I looked grave," Franklin writes, in his own account of the premature affair, "and said it would, I thought, be time enough to prepare the rejoicing when we knew we should have occasion to rejoice. They seemed surprised that I did not immediately comply with their proposal. 'Why, the devil!' said one of them, 'you surely don't suppose that the fort will not be taken?'—'I don't know that it will not be taken; but I know that the events of war are subject to great uncertainty.'"

Governor Morris, who, while on the frontier, supervising the construction of the Pennsylvania road, had learned the melancholy news, hastened to Philadelphia to carry it, but on his arrival was insulted for venturing to give out that General Braddock was defeated! The people began, however, to suspect the truth when the frightened fugitives came in, one after another, and told with trembling lips the story of the disaster. And yet they were not finally persuaded of the fact until Braddock's own messengers passed from post to post, from tavern to tavern, from "The Whip" to the "Indian Queen," with that open letter, which authoritatively published the catastrophe.

Dunbar himself finally came in with his fifteen hundred men, and took up his winter-quarters in Philadelphia in midsummer, where we hear of him and his gallant officers getting up a military ball, to do honor to the beauty of the Pennsylvania dames.

Smollett has truly said of the French success and of the English retreat: "On the whole, this was perhaps the most extraordinary victory that ever was obtained, and the farthest flight that ever was made."

The effect of Braddock's unfortunate campaign was something far greater than the loss of a battle, with its waste of life and treasure. It so weakened the tie between the colonies and mother-country, that it finally gave way in the American Revolution. The provinces now no longer trusted to the courage and skill of British regulars, and had learned to confide in the strength of their own forces, which had shown themselves so much superior as allies, that they had no reason to dread the possible position of enemies. The British contempt for the provincial militiaman had been proved to be so little merited, that the American, no longer humbled, became assured of his own power; while his pride, inflamed by the humiliating treatment it had received, burned to vindicate itself against those who had wantonly offended it.

Shirley, of Massachusetts, one of the most energetic and able of the provincial governors, had the command of the expedition ordered for the reduction of Fort Niagara. His force consisted principally of the two provincial regiments of New England known as those of Shirley and Pepperell, both of whom had been made British colonels, in reward for their services in the conquest of Louisburg. This energetic commander had reached Albany, and was preparing to move on to Oswego, when the news of Braddock's misfortune reached him, and struck a panic to the hearts of his men. Many of his troops deserted him, and all the native boatmen and fur-hunters whom he had engaged to man his batteaux for the conveyance of his force and its supplies westward, fled away, and could not be pre-

vailed upon to return. Shirley, however, with the remnant left him, boldly pushed on, and, being reinforced by a detachment of Royal artillery spared him from the troops disheartened by the defeat of Braddock and the inglorious retreat of Dunbar, reached Oswego, with **Aug. 18.** some hope of a successful attempt on Niagara. At Oswego, on the southeast side of Lake Ontario, there was a fortified trading-post in the English interest. Here it was hoped to obtain a large accession of Indians; but these wary savages, having heard of the French success on the Monongahela, were not disposed to join those whom they believed to belong to the weaker party. Deprived of this Indian aid, and finding the season advanced and provisions scanty, Shirley was forced to return from Oswego, without proceeding to Niagara. He, however, strengthened the Oswego fort, and left a garrison of seven hundred men, under Mercer, for its more effectual protection against the French.

CHAPTER XI.

Colonel William Johnson at Crown Point.—Johnson's Career, Character, Magnificence, and Influence upon his Savage Dependants.—His Baronial Hall and its Guests.—Partial Success at Lake George.—Surprise.—Repulse of the French. —Great Rewards and Small Deeds.—Johnson made a Baronet.—An Indian in London.—One Shilling Each Person.— A Spirited Subaltern.—The Easy Triumph in Acadia.—A Garden turned into a Desert.—The Energy of the French. —The Gallant Bradstreet.—His Desperate but Successful Expedition to Oswego.—The Pertinacious Resistance of the French.—The British Government making a more Vigorous Demonstration.—The Earl of Loudoun's Appointment. —Grand Preparations.—Major-General Abercrombie arrives in Advance.—Does nothing.—The Earl of Loudoun arrives, and does likewise.—British Contempt of Colonial Troops.—The French make Great Preparations.—The Marquis de Montcalm.—His Life and Character.—His Heroism at Exilles.—Montcalm's Energy.—A Winter Attack on Fort Ontario.—Victory.—Canadian Exultation.—"Bring Lilies with Full Hands."—The English in Despair.—Inactivity of Lord Loudoun.—The Massacre at Kittanang.

COLONEL WILLIAM JOHNSON commanded the third expedition. This set out to attack the French fort at Crown Point, on Lake Champlain. Johnson was selected, not from any proof he had given of military skill, but in consequence of the wonderful influence he was known to possess over the Indians. Having been early induced to leave his native Ireland by his uncle, Admiral Warren, who had large possessions in the western part of the province of New York, and who wished him to take charge of them, the young Irishman came over to America. His home was now fixed on the banks of the Mohawk, then almost a wilderness, with no inhabitants but the roaming Indians. Johnson became fond of this wild life, and sought to share with his savage neighbors in their untrammelled habits.

His personal appearance—as he was tall, well-proportioned, and possessed of a handsome face, with an expression of calm dignity such as belongs to those born to command—commended him at once to Indian admiration, which is freely extended to those who can claim pretensions to manly strength and beauty. He was, moreover, so cool, that he never seemed to lose his self-possession; and, although ordinarily a man of few words, yet, when the occasion prompted, he was fervid and even eloquent in speech. He was fond, too, of the exciting dangers of the chase. He excelled as a marksman, with his rifle; while, incapable of fatigue, he could follow the game with as long and untiring an endurance as that of the most practised native hunter. The Indians found, in these characteristics of the young Irishman, so much that was congenial to their own nature, that they readily welcomed Johnson among them as one of themselves. His powers of command soon effected the rest; and, from appreciation of him as a companion, came naturally admiration of his superior nature, and a ready subjection to his will.

With a lingering attachment, in spite of his love of a forest-life, for the luxuries and comforts of civilization, he built on the banks of the Mohawk two spacious mansions, known as his castle and his hall. In the former he shut himself up in the winter, and the latter was his summer residence. Here he received all British officers or adventurous travellers whom duty or love of travel had brought there, and entertained them with the free hospitality of an old English baronial hall. Here, too, the Indians came in tribes; and five hundred of them have been known to be welcomed by him to the profuse conviviality of the hall by day, and to have thrown themselves at night on the ground, with their liberal host in their midst, and thus have slept over the effects of the carouse. Johnson had won such an influence over the Indians, that he never feared, though the only white man present, thus to trust himself unguarded to his savage neighbors. With the Five Nations he ruled almost supreme; and now that he was called upon to do service for his country, Hendrik, a Mohawk chief, followed him at his bidding, with three hundred warriors of his tribe.

Besides his Indian allies, Johnson had mustered at Albany a large provincial force, consisting of several thousand men, chiefly from Connecticut and Massachusetts. Most of these were sent forward, to establish a post between Lake George and the Hudson river. This was done, and the place was called Fort Edward. Johnson himself followed after with his Indians and the rest of the troops, and, joining the advance-party at the fort which they had completed, marched on, with all his force, excepting a small garrison of three hundred left to guard Fort Edward. Passing through the wilderness, where there was neither house nor fort, Johnson halts his men on the southern borders of a lake, to which he gives the name of his sovereign, and which has ever since been known as Lake George.

Bancroft, with his usual artistic skill, paints a picture of the scene thus: "The lake protects him on the north; his flanks are covered by a thick wood and a swamp. The tents of the husbandmen and mechanics, who form his summer army, are spread on a rising ground; but no fortifications are raised, nor is even a trench thrown up. On week-days, the men, accustomed to freedom, saunter to and fro in idleness; or some, weary of inaction, are ready to mutiny and go home. On Sunday, all come forth and collect in the groves for the worship of God; three hundred men, also, regularly enlisted under the English flag, and paid from the English treasury, seat themselves on the hillock, and, while the light of a summer's afternoon is shedding its sweetest influence on the tops of the forest-clad mountains and on the still waters of the deep, transparent lake, they listen gravely to the interpretation of a long sermon. Meanwhile, wagon after wagon brought artillery, and stores and boats for the troops that were listlessly whiling away the season."

This idle state of existence was, however, interrupted by the return of some scouts with the intelligence that Dieskau was approaching with a large force; but what were their exact numbers, the scouts (who were Indians, and unable to count) could not tell. Johnson now resolved upon sending out a force to check the French advance. Accordingly, one thousand provincials and two hundred Indians were despatched for this service, under the command of Colonel Ephraim Williams. Among his private soldiers was Israel Putnam, of Connecticut, of whom, in the course of our history, we shall have much that is memorable to relate. They had hardly gone three miles from the camp on Lake George, and fairly entered the ravine through which the narrow road passed, when they were attacked by the French and Indians, who had awaited them in ambush among the forests and wooded swamps extending on either side of the long line of march. With this disadvantage, the English provincials, though they resisted bravely, were utterly routed, and pursued to within a short distance of the camp, where the French were brought to a check by a vigorous onset of a party of three hundred men sent by Johnson to drive off the pursuers.

The camp had not been intrenched. So, while the enemy was brought to a pause, Johnson began to prepare a temporary defence, by cutting down trees and rolling them together, in order to form a breastwork, behind which several cannon were dragged and placed in position. The wagons and baggage were also arranged so as to serve as a cover for the provincial marksmen.

Johnson had hardly time to make these hasty preparations, before Dieskau and his French and Indians made a rush for the camp. The English artillery now began to play with such good effect, that the savages were scattered at once, and hid themselves in the pine-wood covert on the neighboring rising ground, from which they kept up a desultory and almost harmless fire. The Frenchmen, however, under their gallant commander, still advanced in the very mouth of the cannon, until finally almost every man was struck down, and among the foremost fell the baron Dieskau himself, mortally wounded. Two of his soldiers hurried to his relief, and one being shot down, the other was ordered away; and the dying commander, crawling to the fallen trunk of a tree, seated himself upon it, and calmly awaited, amid a shower of bullets, the issue of the struggle. The result was a complete victory, the French having lost no less than eight hundred men, while the Americans suffered only to the extent of two hundred and twenty killed and nineteen wounded. Johnson himself was wounded early in the struggle, and was obliged to retire to his tent. Lyman, his second in command, completed the success of the day by pursuing the enemy for a short time at the close with great slaughter.

The Canadians and Indians, as they retreated, were met by a party of a hundred and twenty New-Hampshire men, under a youth of the name of M'Ginnes, and, being attacked, were put to the rout, although the young American leader was killed.

This small success of Johnson was such an exceptional case of triumph during that year for the English arms in America, that the British government was disposed to make the most of it. A baronetcy was accordingly bestowed upon Colonel Johnson, and a grant of five thousand pounds, as a reward for his services.

The public interest in England in Johnson's success was kept alive by the exaggerated importance given to it by the authorities; and in this contemporary advertisement in the *Public Advertiser* of the year 1755, we read the appeal of a showman, which illustrates the general curiosity of London on the occasion:—

"THE ONLY INDIAN IN ENGLAND SINCE THE REIGN OF QUEEN ANNE!

"JUST ARRIVED FROM AMERICA, and to be seen at the NEW YORK AND CAPE BRETON COFFEE-HOUSE, in *Sweeting's Alley*, from 12 to 3, and from 4 till 6, to the latter end of next week, and then will embark for America in the '*General Webb*,' Captain Boardman, a famous MOHAWK INDIAN WARRIOR! the same person who took M. DIESKAU, THE FRENCH GENERAL, prisoner at the BATTLE OF LAKE GEORGE, where GENERAL JOHNSON beat the French, and was one of the said General's Guards. He is dressed in the same manner with his native Indians when they go to war; his face and body painted, with his SCALPING-KNIFE, TOMAXE, and all other implements of war that are used by the Indians in battle; a sight worthy the curiosity of every TRUE BRITON.

"PRICE, *one shilling each person*."

The conduct of Colonel Johnson was hardly such as to merit all the distinction and public notice it received. However brilliant his success at Lake George, his proceedings afterward showed less energy and spirit than might have been expected from the supposed courage and activity of this remarkable man. Instead of pushing on, while his troops were in the full tide of victory, and making a bold stroke for the position at Crown Point, which was the object of the expedition, Johnson remained at Lake George. Here it is true he kept his men busy, for he built a fort, which he named Fort Henry, and garrisoned it with a small detachment of provincial troops; he then moved the main body of his forces back to Albany, and sent the men to their several homes.

A spirited subaltern, of the name of Rogers, who was left at Lake George, did something, however, by his activity and boldness, toward retrieving what was lost by the remissness of Johnson. Rogers made frequent sallies against the French in the neighborhood of Crown Point, by which he succeeded in cutting off many of their detached parties, and keeping a watchful eye upon their proceedings. Thus, he learned that the French had collected together some two thousand Canadians and Indians, and a good force of artillery, at Ticonderoga, situated at the northern end of Lake George, and that they were busy in fortifying that post.

To this partial success of Johnson, the British could only add that of the cruel expulsion of the Acadians from Nova Scotia. It is not for us, however, to do more than make a passing mention of what certainly can not properly be included in "The Battles of America." It is true that New England sent its two thousand men, and some heavy artillery served by British regulars, to compel by force, if need be, the submission of the French inhabitants of the English province of Nova Scotia. The troops were landed without interruption; they paraded gayly upon the shores, and, after a night's quiet repose, marched deliberately against the Acadians, who hardly ventured to oppose them. The fort of Beausejour surrendered in four days. That of St. John was abandoned and burnt; and the other small fortresses capitulated without resistance. The inhabitants were declared traitors, their possessions forfeited, and all the men, women, and children, exiled for ever from their homes and their altars, their gardens and their pastures! This was persecution, not war. Hate tortured her victims. Courage did not strike a blow. The tears of the weak and innocent were poured out. Not a drop of blood was shed by the strong in the might of resistance. We pass, therefore, gladly from woman's tears and children's cries, wrung by cruelty, to listen to the shouts of men and heroes battling for right or might. Our duty, thank Heaven, is to record the deeds of the manly brave, not the work of the inhuman persecutor!

The French were prepared to recommence hostilities with the opening of another year, and their first move-
1756. ment was a success. There was a small English fort on the Oswego route. This was now the point of attack. Three hundred and fifty Canadians, under M. Chaussegros de Lèvy, arrived before the fort. Lieutenant Ball, in command, with two dozen men, was summoned to surrender. He refused, determined to resist to the last. The French began their attack, and overpowered their handful of opponents, who, with the exception of two, were mercilessly scalped by the French savages.

Another expedition from Canada now set out to attack the provincial fort at Oswego; but, before reaching it, the French halted at a short distance, and erected a small fortification of their own, so hid in the forest as to be unseen by their opponents; and thus succeeded in greatly harassing them, by cutting off supplies and preventing reinforcements. Lieutenant-Colonel Bradstreet, who had won the confidence of Sir William Pepperell in the famous siege of Louisburg, by his prowess, now went to the rescue of Oswego. His men were chiefly raw Irish recruits, but Bradstreet knew how to control their irregular impulses, and succeeded in getting a great deal of effective work out of them. He succeeded in reaching Oswego, and supplying the garrison with provisions. A French force of seven hundred men tried to intercept him, but, having lost their way in the forest, did not discover, until it was too late, that Bradstreet was in advance of them. They now determined to lay in wait for him on his return.

Bradstreet, having relieved Oswego, now commenced to retrace his steps. His route lay by the river Onondaga, on the banks of which the French had concealed themselves, awaiting his approach. He, either conscious of this danger, or from his experience of American warfare, became exceedingly wary, and hit upon an excellent expedient for avoiding the dangers of an ambuscade. Bradstreet accordingly took the precaution of dividing his men into three parties, each one of which was placed in a separate fleet of canoes, which were ordered to ascend the Onondaga at small distances apart. In this way, if one party was attacked suddenly, the others might come up prepared to sustain it. Bradstreet himself took the lead, in the very first canoe; the others followed after, bold and eager enough for a fight; and it was with the greatest difficulty that their prudent leader could keep the Irish blood of his men sufficiently cool for the discreet conduct that was necessary.

Bradstreet's experience in border warfare led him to expect, at any moment, to see the flash of the Canadian musket, or hear the war-whoop of the savage, from the dark clumps of cedars, and the crags of the rugged banks which bordered the river.* It was on the 3d of July when they embarked. The stream was low, and difficult of navigation; and the trees and underwood, luxuriant with their midsummer foliage, afforded complete concealment to the enemy. For a length of nine miles the canoes were forced up the Onondaga with great toil, but with no interference. They had thus reached a point where there was a small island surrounded by rapids, and the banks of the river were thickly shaded by a dense forest-growth, when suddenly a volley of musketry and an Indian war-whoop burst through the silence of the wilderness. The effect upon those in the advance-canoes was terribly fatal; but Bradstreet and six of his men pushed at once for the island, where a score of the enemy,

* The Conquest of Canada, by the Author of "Hochelaga," &c. New York: Harper and Brothers.

having plunged into the river and made their way through a ford, had arrived before him. So spirited, however, was the onset of the colonel and his half-dozen men, that he succeeded in driving back the enemy to the mainland.

The French, however, now came up again to the attack with increased numbers. Bradstreet, too, in the meantime had been reinforced by fourteen other men, who had just landed from those canoes which had brought up the rear of the advance-party. The French were forced again to retire; and, renewing for a third time the attack, with more men still, a fierce struggle ensued, which lasted nearly an hour. Bradstreet was again victorious, and with his twenty men succeeded in putting to a complete rout all who were left of the seventy Frenchmen who had attempted to dislodge him from the island.

The rest of Bradstreet's forces had landed on the shore lower down, and were marching to the relief of their comrades on the island. The main body of the French, observing this movement, crossed the stream, to prevent the junction. But Bradstreet, having now succeeded in beating off the enemy's attack on the island, was free to join the rest of his troops which he succeeded in doing, and led them with a vigorous onslaught against the main body of the French, who were forced back into the river. Many fell dead before the brisk fire of Bradstreet's men, but many more were drowned in their attempts to cross the river.

The enemy, in spite of these repeated defeats, still pertinaciously prolonged the struggle. A number, while Bradstreet was below, on the mainland, began to cross the ford below, near the small island; but they had hardly reached the opposite bank, and made ready for an attack, when the English came rushing down, and with one impulsive effort drove them back into the stream. The French lost more than a hundred men, who were either shot or drowned, while seventy were taken prisoners. The loss of Bradstreet, too, was no less than sixty killed or wounded.

The English troops were too much fatigued to continue the pursuit immediately; and when, next morning, they were reinforced by a company of grenadiers on their way to Oswego, and some two hundred men besides who had come to their aid from that fort, Bradstreet found that the Onondaga was so flooded with the pouring rain during the night, that it would be quite impracticable to follow the enemy. The company of grenadiers, therefore, accompanied the detachment from the fort back to Oswego, and Bradstreet with the rest of his forces went on his way to Albany.

The British government, having now at last declared an open war against the **1756.** French, was disposed to carry on hostilities in America with greater vigor. The earl of Loudoun, a great stickler for the prerogatives of the crown, and a proportionate opponent of all colonial disenthralment, was sent out to America, with unusual powers. He was made general-in-chief of all the forces on the American continent, and colonel of a regiment of four battalions, to be composed principally of the Swiss and German Protestants in America, and to be commanded by officers of their own native countries. To give additional dignity to his lordship's appointment, he was also made governor of Virginia.

Previous, however, to the setting out of the earl of Loudoun, Major-General Abercrombie had been ordered to precede him, and hold the command until his lordship's arrival. Abercrombie was now at Albany, with four regiments of British regulars, two of which **June.** had accompanied him from England, the New-England battalions, eight independent companies, and a large body of provincial militia, making all together the formidable army, for those days, of ten thousand men. At Albany, too, was assembled the council of governors from the various provinces, to confer with the British general in regard to the plans of a campaign against the French in America. Abercrombie resisted the urgent appeals of the council to carry out a scheme of general attack, on the plea that his force was not sufficiently large for so extensive an undertaking. He, therefore, declined to act on his own responsibility, and determined to await the arrival of his superior in command, the earl of Loudoun. He, however, was prevailed upon to send General Winslow, with the provincial forces, to the English fort William Henry, on Lake George, where he was to await reinforcements, and then march against the French post at Crown Point, on Lake Champlain.

On the arrival of the brave Bradstreet at Albany, he hurried to the quarters of

General Abercrombie, and, giving in the report of his own successes, laid before him the dangerous position of Oswego, and earnestly urged the necessity of despatching immediate relief. The British officer, Colonel Webb, was accordingly ordered to hold himself in readiness to march with his regiment on this service; but, for some reason or other, a long and fatal delay ensued. The provincial council and Abercrombie were supposed to be at loggerheads. The former declared for Crown Point: the latter favored the march to Oswego. So, to settle the difference, nothing was done.

July 29. Lord Loudoun now arrived at Albany, and assumed command at once; but, full of his own dignity, and reserved in his communications with others, he would listen to no suggestions from those who knew so much of a country about which he knew so little. He had the proverbial contempt of his countrymen for the colonies, and had no faith either in the wisdom of the colonial governor or the courage of the colonial soldier. The force at Albany was large — amounting, as we have seen, to ten thousand men; but more than half of these were provincials — "mostly vagabonds picked up by the New-Englanders at random," wrote Abercrombie, who exclaimed, "With such troops, what can we do?" Loudoun no doubt echoed, with fellow-contempt, these opinions so disparaging to the colonists. They could not learn the simple lesson of experience, which, if they had, would have taught them that all the victories had been won in these colonial battles by the "vagabonds," while the de-feats were to be set down to the boasted "regulars." Abercrombie did nothing: Lord Loudoun did no more.

The French, however, were not inactive. The court at Versailles had sent out a considerable force of regulars to America, under the command of the marquis de Montcalm. A better leader could not have been chosen. Montcalm had a wise head and a dauntless spirit. Born of a noble family, he had inherited the traditional chivalry of his race. On his escutcheon he bore the motto of "Extinguisher of the Dragon," as a perpetual record, handed down from generation to generation, of the prowess of an ancestral Templar of St. John, who had delivered the isle of Rhodes from the ravages of some mysterious monster. He was descended from a long line of heroes, and was destined to illustrate, in his own career the heroic temperament of his family.

His education was carefully conducted by a distinguished man of science, who bore the name of Dumas. Under his tuition, the young Montcalm was so endued with a love of study, that, although he entered the army at the early age of fourteen, he preserved his taste for science and literature amid all the tumultuous life of the camp, and became remarkable for his mental acquirements.

Montcalm's military career was rapidly made brilliant by his gallant behavior. He was wounded three times at the battle of Plaisance, and twice in the heroic struggle at Exilles. This latter was the battle where was enacted a scene that has only been paralleled since by the charge of the English "Light-Brigade" at Balaklava, when—

> "Into the valley of Death
> Rode the six hundred!"

The count of Belleisle had been promised the baton of a marshal if he should succeed in the campaign in Piedmont. Meeting the enemy at Exilles, the count began an imprudent attack, which resulted in the defeat of the French. He felt so greatly the ill success of an attempt which had been disapproved of by all experience, that in his desperation he put himself at the head of his officers, and led them in a column against the intrenchments within which the enemy had withdrawn! Few only escaped. Belleisle himself, wounded in both hands, madly strove to tear down with his teeth the palisades of the wall, when he received a mortal shot. Montcalm was one of this heroic brigade, which, true to discipline, obeyed even the insane command of their leader.

But a few years past forty, Montcalm, although full of the enterprising spirit of youth, was, from his long service in the army, a veteran in experience. He was short in person, but of a wiry structure. Active, and of great powers of endurance, he possessed all the gay vivacity of his countrymen, and was lively in times of social enjoyment as he was all activity in business. He was quick to observe, and bold and prompt in action. He soon proved that he was the right man in the right place.

There was no dilly-dallying about Montcalm. He had not been at Quebec a week before he was ready to set out with his French troops for Oswego, which had been so disgracefully neglected by the dilatory Abercrombie and the self-sufficient Lord Loudoun. De Vaudreuil was sent in advance with a considerable force of Canadian militia, raised at Montreal. Montcalm was not long behind him, with his regulars, and ready to commence operations. The French commander's first object was to attack Fort Ontario, which was situated on the river Onondaga, at its mouth, where it empties into Lake Ontario, and opposite to the more important Fort Oswego. Here accordingly he opened his trenches at once, and, with his usual promptness, **Aug. 12.** beginning at the dawn of day, succeeded in overcoming the resistance of the besieged before nightfall. Taking possession of Fort Ontario, from which the garrison had fled to Oswego, without spiking all the cannon in their hurry, Montcalm turned the remaining guns with great effect upon the fort opposite. It was not long before the walls of Oswego gave way; and the English seeing, with their leader Mercer struck down, and a breach made in their fortress, no hope of a longer resistance, capitulated.

The victory for the French was a great one. They became possessed of an important post, took captive twelve hundred prisoners, and obtained several armed vessels, two hundred batteaux, and a vast quantity of treasure, military stores, and provisions. They made the most of their triumph, sending the British flags to be hung in the churches of Quebec and Montreal; erecting crosses at Oswego, with the inscription, "This is the banner of victory;" and raising triumphant columns, upon which their joy was illustrated by the exultant words, carved in stone— " Bring lilies with full hands !"

Montcalm razed the fort at Oswego to the ground, and began a desolating march eastward, burning the dwellings and the crops of the frontier settlers of New York, and killing and scalping all the unfortunate inhabitants he met. Colonel Webb, in the meantime, with his seventeen hundred men, who had been kept back until it was too late to render any service to the neglected fort at Oswego, was slowly making his way, until he heard of the French success, when he precipitately took to flight. Walpole might well say, when this disastrous news reached England : " The negligence and dilatoriness of our government at home, and the little-minded quarrels between the regular and irregular forces, have reduced our affairs in that part of the world [America] to a most deplorable state. Oswego, of ten times more importance even than Minorca, is so annihilated, that we can not learn the particulars."

Something was naturally expected from the expedition of General Winslow, an able officer, who had acquired great renown in the siege of Louisburg ; but, although the French fort at Crown Point, on Lake Champlain, was its original destination, it got no farther than the English forts Edward and William Henry. These Winslow strengthened by leaving a portion of his force ; but was prevented from striking a blow against the enemy by the inactivity and pusillanimous conduct of his superiors. Lord Loudoun having so far done nothing, now seemed resolved to do nothing for the future ; and, after an inglorious inactivity at Albany, he sent the provincials to their several homes.

The English colonists obtained some consolation for their repeated ill fortune, by a small success against the Indian town of Kittanang, lying in a valley among the Alleghanies. This was the nest of a horde of Indian savages, who had stolen upon the English settlers scattered about the western frontier, and massacred a thousand of them. About three hundred men now hurriedly collected together, and, choosing one Armstrong for their leader, determined to revenge the merciless murder of their countrymen. They pushed on, forgetting the fatigues and perils of the hard and dangerous road of some hundred and fifty miles in length, in their eagerness for revenge. On arriving at the Indian settlement at night, they heard the savage murderers exulting, in songs and dances, over their late massacre. Armstrong awaited until dawn the next morning, when, suddenly presenting himself, he offered the Indians quarter, on their immediately surrendering. The savages dared not accept it; and then the provincials began an attack, which resulted in a slaughter and a cruelty that could have only been equalled by the Indians themselves. Some of the savages were shot, some beaten down with the butt-ends of muskets, some shut up in their huts and burned to death, some blown up with gunpowder, and others seized and scalped as the Indians themselves would have seized and scalped the English if they had been victims instead of avengers.

This was one of the pitiful successes which were to weigh against the preponderating victories of the French during the whole campaign of 1756.

CHAPTER XII.

1757. WITH the successes of the previous year, the French, under the ever vigilant and active Montcalm, were emboldened to begin 1757 with great vigor. It was January. Canada was bound with the fetters of winter. The waves of those great inland seas, the northern lakes, were stilled. The rivers ceased to flow. The waters everywhere had turned to ice. The snow covered the mountain-tops, and filled in the valleys. Fields, roads, and by-paths, had departed with the life of the year, and were now overspread with the universal shroud of winter. The smoke of a few hamlets, under the cover of the hillsides, scattered distantly over the wide, wintry expanse, betokened the existence of occasional home warmth and comfort; but for the most part the scene was one of universal wintry desolation.

It was not in the nature of Montcalm's active spirit to grow torpid, even under the influence of a North-American winter. In the very depth of this season of frost and snow, he determined to send a force against the English fort William Henry, at the southern end of Lake George. Fifteen hundred men, four hundred of whom were Indians, were accordingly selected for this service, and placed under the command of Rigaud de Vaudreuil.

The route was a long one. One hundred and fifty miles were to be travelled before reaching the fort. Sledges were made ready, and dogs harnessed to them with thongs, as in the arctic regions, to drag the provisions and stores through the snow and over the ice. Each man was clad like an Esquimaux, in furs, and given a leathern mask to protect his face from the fatal touch of the biting wind and the frost, and a bearskin within which

13

to enfold himself when encamped at night upon the snow. Thus equipped, they set out, passing rapidly over the frozen surface of Lake Champlain and of Lake George with their sledges and their snow-shoes. As they approach the English fort, they await the coming of night, and are more cautious in their movements. Pioneers are sent in advance, with axes in hand, to try the strength of the ice, and to guide the force in safety to the walls of the enemy. With cautious steps they reach the spot in the dead of night, and are lifting the scaling-ladders against the fortifications, when the sentry observes them, and gives the alarm. The garrison are in a moment on their defence, and, with a brisk volley from their cannon and musketry, drive back the assailants.

Next morning the French renew the attack, but without effect; and again make an attempt later in the day, but are once more driven back. They now summon the officer in command, a Major Eyres, to surrender. He resolutely refuses. The French continue the assault, and, after making in all five unsuccessful efforts, they give up in despair. The stronghold can not be taken. The enemy, however, revenged themselves for their repulse, by destroying such outworks of the fort as were within their reach. Vaudreuil now sent reinforcements to the French forts at Ticonderoga, Crown Point, and Niagara, and then returned to Montreal.

The garrison at Fort William Henry does not allow the winter to pass in idleness. Its rangers accordingly sally out, under the gallant subaltern Stark, and succeed in falling in with sledges on their route, with men and provisions, for the French forts. Stark, with some seventy men, takes a party thus by surprise, attacks them, and comes off victorious. He is, however, intercepted by a considerable force on his return to the fort, with his prisoners and booty, and a third of his adventurous rangers are laid low; but Stark and the survivors so gallantly defend themselves, that the enemy are obliged to retreat, and the English come off with all the glory.

Lord Loudoun, having done nothing where he could do something, now undertook to do something where he could do nothing. Taking a large provincial force from the colonies, where they were needed, he embarked them on board an English fleet consisting of numerous men-of-war and transports, and sailed with them to Halifax, in Nova Scotia. With nineteen ships-of-the-line and a large number of smaller vessels in that harbor, and no less than thirteen battalions of troops landed after a prosperous voyage, Loudoun was in a condition to have undertaken anything, no matter how formidable. The time was, nevertheless, wasted in parade and mock-fights. Louisburg, which, after the famous conquest by Sir William Pepperell, had been ceded to France, was supposed to be the object of attack of this magnificent armament. News arriving, however, to the effect that the French, with some three thousand troops, a considerable body of Indians and militiamen, and a fleet of eighteen ships-of-the-line, were prepared to defend themselves, it was determined by the prudent Loudoun to postpone the attempt upon Louisburg.

When Loudoun sailed away from the place where he was most wanted, Montcalm took occasion to avail himself of his absence, by making an attack upon Fort William Henry, on Lake George. Gathering some eight thousand men at the French fort at Ticonderoga, he marched with his usual rapidity against Fort William Henry, and met with a brave resistance from the English commander, Munro, who, to a haughty demand to surrender, answered thus spiritedly: "I will defend my trust to the last extremity!" It was, however, in vain. The English, disappointed in their hope of relief from the timid Webb, who was running away, instead of coming to their assistance, were obliged to capitulate.

Lord Loudoun, while at Halifax in a state of inaction, heard this disastrous news of the capture of Fort William Henry, and immediately returned, with a large proportion of his troops, to New York; but, with what purpose, it would be difficult to conjecture. He left the English admiral at Halifax; but that officer did nothing but sail to Louisburg and back again. When this intelligence reached England, Walpole wrote, on the 3d day of September, 1757: "We had a torrent of bad news yesterday from America. Lord Loudoun has found an army of twenty thousand French, gives over the design on Louisburg, and retires to Halifax. Admiral Holborne writes that they have nineteen ships to his seventeen, and that he can not attack them. It is time for England to slip her own cables, and float away into some unknown sea."

Lord Loudoun arrived at New York, and thence made his way to Fort Edward, the only northern post left to the English. Here he gave some directions for defence, and prudently retired to Albany. Nothing, however, was done; and the British people and the British government became aware at last that, without some change in men and measures, British dominion in the West would be lost to them for ever.

"My lord, I am sure that I can save this country, and that no one else can!" were the proud, self-reliant words of the great commoner, William Pitt. His country took him at his word; and, with the power to execute what his comprehensive genius had conceived, he made good his grand promise. The incapable duke of Newcastle, deserted by Fox, was forced to let drop from his feeble hands the reins of government. Fox himself now strove to form a ministry; but, with all his great talents, he felt himself incapable of the charge of administration without the aid of Pitt, and solicited his alliance. The "great commoner," however, rejected all overtures from his superior, in wealth and rank, but by far his inferior in moral influence. Pitt, conscious of the faith of the British nation in him, and him alone, was determined to share with no other the glory of delivering that nation from her agony of shame and disgrace.

"Whoever is in or whoever is out," writes Lord Chesterfield, in despair of his country, "I am sure we are undone, both at home and abroad: at home, by our increasing debt and expenses; abroad, by our ill luck and incapacity...... The French are masters to do what they please in America. We are no longer a nation. I never yet saw so dreadful a prospect." The British people, however, still had a hope: that hope was William Pitt. The lords were in despair, and yet resisted, in their mad pride of birth, the aid of a commoner. But such was the resolute will of the nation to be governed by Pitt, that king and peers were obliged to yield, and suffer him to take hold of the helm and guide the ship of state.

With Pitt's administration began a new era for British arms in America. His first act was to get rid of the incapables, and to put the right men in the right place. The weak and capricious Loudoun, as well as the over-cautious and inactive Admiral Holborne, were recalled, and men of sterner stuff sent to America to replace them. Amherst, the resolutely brave, the spiritedly active, and the coolly judicious, was, in spite of the formalities of military precedence, promoted to the rank of major-general, and given the command of the land-forces destined for America. Boscawen, a dashing naval officer, of known skill and courage, was made admiral of the fleet then off Halifax, in Nova Scotia.

Louisburg was marked out in the plan of the campaign as the first object of attack. Amherst sailed with a large armament on the 19th of February for **1758.** Halifax, but was delayed in his voyage by storms and unfavorable winds, and did not arrive off that port until the 28th of May, when he met the impatient Boscawen coming out, with all his ships, on his way to Louisburg.

The two forces, land and naval, thus combined, presented a formidable array. There floated the grand fleet, with twenty-two ships-of-the-line, fifteen frigates, and one hundred and twenty smaller vessels. There gathered the eleven thousand six hundred troops, mostly British regulars, with their battalions of infantry, their formidable artillery, and their skilful engineers. Amherst's land-force was divided into three brigades, under the several commands of the brigadier-generals Whitmore, Lawrence, and Wolfe. This effective armament now sailed **June 2.** for Cape Breton, and in a few days reached Gabarus bay, within cannon-shot of Louisburg.

There was one in this expedition whose subsequent career of heroism entitles him to more than a mere enumeration among a list of other gallant officers. This was Wolfe.

JAMES WOLFE was the son of a soldier. His father had won an honorable name as an officer under Marlborough. The elder Wolfe had sought—after his marriage with a Miss Thompson, the sister of the member of Parliament for York—a temporary retreat in the neighborhood of that city, in the quiet village of Westerham. Here his son was born, on the 2d of January, 1727, at the modest vicarage-house, which the father had rented for his temporary residence. At Westerham the young Wolfe was sent to a good private school, where he remained until he was fourteen years of age. As a boy, he was spirited and clever, but not remarkable for his devotion to work.

His father being now ordered to join Lord Cathcart's expedition to Flanders, he took with him his son, although but fourteen years of age. On the journey, the lad, who was always feeble in health, fell ill, and was landed at Portsmouth. In a short time, however, he recovered his strength, and rejoined his father at the camp, where he entered at once with youthful ardor upon all the duties of a military life. A commission was secured for him, and the boy of fourteen became an officer in a battalion of marines as early as 1741. In another year he was made ensign, and then fought his first battle at Dettingen. In 1743, he becomes a lieutenant, and is engaged in active service in Flanders. He next receives the command of a company, and we hear of the youthful officer fighting under the duke of Cumberland at Fontenoy, and redeeming, by his gallant behavior, in common with the other British officers, the misfortunes of that day.

The young Wolfe's merit was so obvious, that nothing could resist his advancement, and he was rapidly promoted. Every step he took in rank was more than justified by his progress in the path of glory. A major under Cumberland at the battle of Feldt, his conduct was so admirable, that his general-officer loudly thanked him, in the presence of the whole army, on the battle-field.

Pitt, who was ever alive to merit, had his eye upon young Wolfe, who plucked fresh laurels on every occasion. It was not only that the youthful officer was dashingly gallant in battle, but he was remarkable for his judgment, and the careful study of his art. He was, moreover, not purely a professional routinist, but possessed of a general culture, which had liberalized and refined his whole life and character.

When General Sir John Mordaunt and Admiral Barker were sent against Rochefort, with a large force, Pitt chose Wolfe, for his merit alone, as the quartermaster-general. The expedition **1757.** arrived in the Basque roads. The leaders were quarrelling, and nothing was being done. Wolfe, impatient of this sluggishness, takes a boat and lands alone upon the shore. He now quietly walks into the enemy's country for a mile or more, observing with a soldier's eye its weaknesses and its strength. He returns on board the admiral's ship, and reports the result of his observations to the leaders of the expedition. He urges them to land and begin an attack on Rochefort at once, as there was no obstacle sufficient to resist it. His advice is scorned. He now, in his earnestness, declares that if three ships-of-war and five hundred men are given him, he will carry the place himself. His proposition is rejected.

The expedition, making no attempt upon Rochefort, returned ingloriously home. Wolfe's conduct becoming known to Pitt, confirmed that statesman in his high estimate of him. The public welcomed him as the only hero of the occasion, and the minister elevated him to the rank of colonel.

On the 23d of January, Wolfe was appointed a brigadier-general, **1758.**

under Amherst, and now has arrived off Louisburg, in command of one of the three divisions of the large force about to attack that citadel.

It was hoped to take Louisburg by surprise. Arriving before the break of day, Amherst gave orders that not a light should be shown, and no noise be made, in order that the transports might work their way silently into the harbor, and the troops be landed so suddenly as to come upon the garrison unexpectedly. As the morning broke, however, a thick fog shrouded the land so completely, that it was impossible to attempt to disembark the troops. As the day advanced, the fog dispersed; but a strong wind then began to blow, bringing in with it from the Atlantic a great swell, which broke in such a high surf upon the shores of the bay, that it was quite impossible for a small boat to ride through it in safety to the land. The general, however, in the company of Wolfe and another officer, ventured to approach the shore during the night, for the purpose of reconnoitring, and saw that the French had been very busy in adding to the defences, by outworks and posts, which greatly increased the risks of landing.

For a week the Atlantic continued to pour in its great waves, so as to cause such a swell in the harbor, and dash such a surge upon the beach, that no attempt was made during that whole time to land. On the eighth day, however, the sea went down, but still leaving a dangerous surf. A naval officer having made a preliminary survey, and reported a favorable place for disembarking, the troops were ordered out before daybreak into the boats, to prepare for the attempt. There were three divisions. The right and centre were under the commands of Whitmore and Lawrence. Wolfe led the left at the head of his grenadiers, five hundred infantry, and a company of provincial rangers. He was the first to approach the shore. The French gathered in large force to oppose the landing, but withheld their fire until their enemy came close in; and, as the boats rose in the white crests of the surf, as it curled up from the shore, they began a near and murderous fire: the English suffered greatly, but, retaining their coolness, and not returning a shot, vigorously drove their boats through the surf, into the very mouths of the French muskets. Wolfe now succeeded in landing his troops, and began an onslaught which soon drove the enemy in disorder from their outworks, to the very walls of the city. The pursuit was continued with great slaughter, until checked by the cannon of the citadel, when Wolfe retired to a position near where he had landed, bringing back with him seventy prisoners. The other divisions had succeeded also in landing, but not until they had lost a hundred boats, and a large number of men, from the violence of the sea.

Another severe storm coming on, the artillery was not brought on shore for two or three days. This postponed the siege, which, however, was soon commenced in good earnest. The guns in position and the intrenchments dug, the bombardment began. Day and night the English poured from their batteries on land, and their ships in the bay, such a tempest of balls, bombshells, and red-hot shot, that finally, the citadel having been on fire, the barracks burnt to the ground, and the walls so crumbled and brought so close within the approaching land-batteries, that the enemy were unable to stand to their guns; and the French commander was forced, after a spirited resistance, which was prolonged for several weeks, to make an unconditional surrender.

The shipping of the harbor, and a fine French fleet at anchor in the bay, were almost annihilated. Two of the vessels-of-war, toward the close of the siege, still remained secure; when a volunteer party, in a number of small boats, moved into the harbor, in spite of a hot fire kept up by the enemy, and, boarding the surviving ships, gallantly took them. With this volunteer party was Cook, then a petty officer on a British ship-of-war, afterward the famous Captain Cook, who sailed round the world.

The victory was a great one. England rejoiced at it, and did honor to the gallantry of her soldiers. The French flags were hung, with solemn ceremonies, on the walls of St. Paul's cathedral; and thanks and honors were decreed by Parliament to the brave officers and soldiers who had so valiantly won a victory in their country's cause. Wolfe, having performed a painful duty in expelling a remnant of Acadians, still in Nova Scotia, from their homes, was attacked with a severe illness, and was obliged to return to England. On his arrival there, his first act was to address a letter to Mr. Pitt, in which he modestly but spiritedly offered his services for the ensuing campaign in America.

The British government, under the administration of Pitt, had expressed its resolution to redeem, at every hazard, the disasters which had sullied English fame in the North and West. England voted men, arms, ammunition, provisions, and all that was necessary for a campaign; and for the first time, at the suggestion of the able Pitt, bestowed upon provincial officers the rank and pay of regulars. The American colonies sympathized with these liberal measures of the home government, and raised a large force of provincial militia: seven thousand men came from Massachusetts, five thousand from Connecticut, nine hundred from New Hampshire, and large numbers from Rhode Island, New York, and New Jersey, and gathered together at Albany, under the command of Abercrombie, who, since the departure of Lord Loudoun, had become commander-in-chief. In addition to the large provincial force, amounting to over nine thousand, there were nearly seven thousand British regulars, well officered by some of the most brilliant of England's military chiefs, among whom was the young Lord Howe, "the idol and soul of the army."

This great force now set out. "On the fifth day of July," says Bancroft, 1758. "the whole armament of more than fifteen thousand men, the largest body of European origin that had ever been assembled in America, struck their tents at daybreak, and in nine hundred small boats and one hundred and thirty-five whale-boats, with artillery mounted on rafts, embarked on Lake George. The fleet, bright with banners, and cheered by martial music, moved in stately procession down the beautiful lake, beaming with hope and pride, though with no witness but the wilderness. They passed over the broader expanse of waters to the first narrows; they came where the mountains step down to the water's edge, and, mantled with forests, enhance the picturesque loveliness of the scene; and, in the richest hues of evening light, they halted at Sabbath-day point. Long afterward, Stark (who was now a captain) remembered that on that night, Howe, reclining in his tent on a bearskin, and bent on winning a hero's name, questioned him closely as to the position of Ticonderoga, and the fittest mode of attack."

At Sabbath-day point they halted but a few hours; and, while it was yet night, the troops took to their boats again, and sailed along the lake until they reached the Narrows, where they arrived at break of day. Here the brave Colonel Bradstreet was put ashore at once with two thousand men to reconnoitre, who, finding no enemy, were followed immediately by the rest of the forces.

The French fort of Ticonderoga, against which the English were now marching, was placed on the narrow strip of land between Lake George and Lake Champlain. Montcalm was vigilant, and, aware of the approach of the British, had sent out a small force to the borders of Lake George, to oppose their landing. This force, however, observing the large numbers advancing, began to retire; but, in attempting to return, they got lost in the forests, which crowded thickly the surrounding country. A small party of the English, under Lord Howe, being in advance, reconnoitring, fell in with the French; and a desperate struggle began at once, in the midst of the tangled woods and in the yielding swamp. The English fought gallantly, and the enemy stoutly resisted. The heroic Howe was foremost in the fight, but, struck early by a musket-ball, fell instantly dead. The loss of their good and chivalrous young leader gave the intensity of revenge to the courage of his men, and they battled more desperately than ever with the enemy; but such was the obstinate fierceness with which the French held their ground, that they did not yield until they were nearly all exterminated, with but a single hundred out of their whole force of half a thousand left!

The death of Howe was so discouraging to the troops and to their general, that both seemed to lose heart. Abercrombie himself acted almost like a madman. With no purpose that was intelligible, he marched his forces back again to the spot whence they had come the day before, with the greatest trial to their spirit and endurance. He, however, soon recovered sufficient courage to act, but only to act with reckless imprudence. He marched upon Ticonderoga, and, encountering the French, to the number of four thousand or more, in an intrenched camp at Cerrillon, in front of the fort, gave them battle. With an unreflecting audacity, Abercrombie led his troops against the impregnable centre of the enemy's position, though the flanks were exposed, and would have readily yielded to an assault. The British fought gallantly, but they dashed themselves in vain against the enemy's defences, like an angry sea upon a granite coast. They were driven back with fearful slaughter. They came up again and again to the attack; but so useless seemed their efforts, and so great their loss, that the survivors at last fled in confusion from the place. Montcalm had earned a great victory: Abercrombie had suffered a disgraceful defeat. The loss of the English amounted to nineteen hundred and fifty, among whom was a large number of officers. The French, protected as they had been by their strong breastwork, had lost less than four hundred. Pitt, when he received intelligence of this British defeat, was almost inconsolable. "I think this check, my dear Pitt," wrote Bute, "affects you too strongly."

Abercrombie returned now to the safe quarters of Fort Edward, and busied himself in strengthening its defences. With an unaccountable stupidity, however, he sent away the artillery and ammunition to New York, and thus deprived himself of the means of acting on the offensive, which his large number of troops would so fully have justified. The gallant Bradstreet fretted at this inactivity of his general, and begged that he might be permitted to lead a force against the French post of Frontenac, on Lake Ontario. Abercrombie yielded to the solicitations of his spirited subaltern, and sent him out with several thousand men and a detachment of artillery.

Bradstreet moved rapidly on. Clear-

ing with immense labor the logs from Wood creek, with which Webb, with stupid officiousness, had obstructed its navigation, he embarked his artillery and stores, and marched his men by land to Lake Oneida. Thence he sailed up the Onondaga to Lake Ontario, and landed within a mile of Fort Frontenac. He now approached, and, gaining possession of an old intrenchment near the French position, threw up some additional works, and began a vigorous attack.

The French commander soon surrendered, and Bradstreet succeeded in the object of his expedition without the loss of a single soldier. While Abercrombie was securely intrenched within Fort Edward, keeping his large body of troops in almost complete inactivity, a British expedition was being carried on with great spirit to the West.

General Forbes had been intrusted with the command of a large force, with which to march against Fort Du Quesne, and strove to redeem the disgrace of Braddock's defeat. In addition to five thousand provincials—among whom was a corps of Virginians, under Washington—Forbes had with him a regiment of Highlanders, and a number of officers, like himself, who were brave but hot-headed Celts. These were the reclaimed Jacobites, of whom Pitt said, and by his own wise policy was enabled to say, "They cheerfully bled in defence of those liberties which they had attempted to overthrow but a few years before."

Starting from Philadelphia, the army had a long and difficult march over the Alleghanies; but Forbes had learned, by

14

the sad experience of Braddock, to provide against the trials and dangers of a passage through the wilderness. He met with no reverse until within about ninety miles of the fort, when one of his too impulsive Scotch officers, while in advance to reconnoitre the enemy's position, sounded his bagpipes and challenged the French to battle. The challenge was accepted; and the impatient Highlander, with his eight hundred kilted followers, was worsted. He had to pay for his rashness by his own captivity and that of three hundred of his men.

The Highlanders—who were raw recruits, fresh from their mountain-fastnesses—were constantly, by their ignorance and disregard of military discipline, getting into all sorts of serious difficulties. On one occasion, a man was seen coming out of the woods, with his long hair all awry, and his body wrapped in some dark-colored drapery. The sentinel challenged him, but receiving no answer, or not understanding it, shot him dead. It turned out that the poor fellow, who was supposed to be a skulking Indian in a blanket, was no more than a raw, unkempt, and innocent Hielander, in his mountain-plaid, astray in the woods. He had probably answered the sentinel's challenge in his native Gaelic, his only tongue; and the Saxon soldier had mistaken it for Choctaw, or some other Indian dialect!

Again, on another occasion, several of these Highland soldiers, by their undisciplined habits of wandering, fell into an ambush of Indians. These savages began their cruel tortures, when one Allan Macpherson, finding his turn had come, was resolved upon escaping, if not death, at any rate the lengthened agonies of savage torture. He accordingly hit upon this ingenious expedient: He gave out that he knew the secret of a great medicine, which, if applied to the skin, would make it invulnerable. He was believed by his barbarous listeners, who allowed him to gather the necessary herbs, with which Allan made a decoction, and applied it to his neck. "Strike, now," he told them, "with all your might, and you'll see the power of the great medicine!" The savage raised his tomahawk, and, bringing it down with all the force of his arm, sent poor Allan Macpherson's head rolling off several yards! The Indians saw the trick, by which the shrewd Highlander had saved himself the torments of a lingering death. They were so tickled with Macpherson's ingenuity, that they became sufficiently good-natured to spare his surviving comrades, not from death, but from a long and painful journey to it. Torture was not inflicted upon the rest of the victims.

In spite of the mishap in which the recklessness of his officers had involved him, Forbes persevered in his advance, and had the satisfaction of finding, on reaching Fort Du Quesne, that the French had fled. The British took possession of the deserted fort, with Washington and his "really fine corps" of Virginians among the first to plant the **Nov. 25.** English flag, and called the place Pittsburg, in honor of the great statesman who was now redeeming everywhere the glory of his country. Thus ended the campaign of 1758.

CHAPTER XIII.

Pitt determines to wrest America from the Dominion of France.—Expedition to Canada, under Amherst.—Its Failure.—Johnson's Success at Niagara.—Wolfe appointed to command the Expedition against Quebec.—His Interview with Pitt.—Wolfe's Enthusiasm.—His Better Qualities.—Poet and Soldier.—Honor and Piety.—The Expedition sails.—The Force.—The Officers.—The Voyage.—Arrival on the American Coast.—Off Quebec.—Wolfe's Impetuosity of Temper.—Promptitude of Action.—Landing of a Small Detachment on the Island of Orleans.—Audacity stronger than Numbers.—The Whole Force debarked.—Wolfe's Contemplation of the Scene of the Coming Struggle.—His Reflections.—A Storm, and an Overshadowed Heart.—Clear Weather, and Bright Hope.—A Nocturnal Incident.—A Fire-ship in the Night.—Wolfe's Proclamation.—A Gentle Nature curdled by Blood.

1759. THE attention of England was now concentrated upon its American colonies. Pitt, encouraged by the triumphs which his active administration had succeeded in winning, and cheered by the sympathies of the whole British nation, resolutely bent all his energies toward wresting completely the dominion of America from the grasp of France. The English Parliament seconded, almost with one mind, this spirited design of their leader, and, to carry it out, generously voted the large sum of two hundred thousand pounds. The great object was, to conquer Canada; and, with this purpose, he determined to send three expeditions against those strongholds of French power in America — Niagara, Montreal, and Quebec.

Amherst, who had been so successful at Louisburg, was appointed commander-in-chief of the British forces in America, and ordered to advance toward Canada, by the northern lakes. He accordingly marched, with an immense force, and, although with much toil, delay, and occasional opposition, succeeded in possessing himself of the two French forts of Ticonderoga and Crown Point, and, after a most unaccountable procrastination, sailed at length to the north of Lake Champlain. The enemy had feared to meet the preponderating numbers of the English on their march; and, as the latter came near Montreal, the inhabitants of that city, although making every effort to prepare for resistance, were in a state of great alarm. The English, however, turned back again when within reach and almost certain of victory.

The expedition against Niagara had, with the aid of Johnson and his Indian force, been successful, and that important position had surrendered also to the English.

It was to Wolfe that Pitt intrusted the expedition against Quebec. In January, 1759, the young officer was gazetted a major-general, and given the command-in-chief of the troops destined for Canada. Wolfe was now thirty-two years of age. He is not described as being particularly well-favored in looks. His frame was meager, and indicative of a feeble constitution. His features were sharp and angular, his forehead receding, his complexion coarse and freckled, and his hair reddish. His mouth, however, bore a refined and gentle expression, while his large blue eyes beamed with intelligence and a sweet sensibility. His manner was not particularly engaging to strangers, but all who knew him well loved him well. He was frank and sincere. Warm in his affections, and of a loving nature, he clung to his parents, and particularly to his mother, with the devotion of a pure and fond heart. He was naturally domestic in his tastes, notwithstanding his military life, and in writing to his mother he says of himself: "I have a turn of mind that favors matrimony prodigiously; I love children, and think them necessary to people in their later days."

He became enamored of a beautiful woman at an early age, but his love was not at first returned. Persisting, however, in his suit, he was finally accepted by Miss Lowther, a celebrated beauty (subsequently the duchess of Bolton), whom he was to marry on his return from the Canadian expedition. He gave his betrothed, on his last farewell, a necklace of pearls. She wore it ever after, but, in a few months, always wrapped in *black* velvet.

Wolfe was excitable in manner, and somewhat impetuous in temper. His nature was an enthusiastic one, and he pursued with ardor whatever touched his heart. His warmth occasionally caused those, who did not know him well, to doubt his discretion. A day or two after he had received his command, he dined with Pitt. After dinner, the subject of his expedition to Quebec naturally coming up, Wolfe became so excited, that he sprang from his seat, strode about the room, flourishing his sword, and spoke of what he would do in such a boastful manner, that Pitt was said to have been frightened for a moment at having intrusted to apparently such a frivolous character so weighty a matter as the fate of nations.

Wolfe's mercurial temper was, however, balanced by a strong and well-cultivated intellect. He was fond of study, and, by diligent application, though most of his life had been spent in the camp, had become no mean scholar. He wrote both prose and verse with facility. That famous camp-song is his which still echoes in every tent where the British soldier is serving his country:—

> "How stands the glass around?
> For shame! ye take no care, my boys,
> How stands the glass around?
> Let mirth and wine abound,
> The trumpets sound,
> The colors they are flying, boys:
> To fight, kill, or wound,
> May we still be found
> Content with our hard fate, my boys,
> On the cold ground!
>
> "Why, soldiers, why,
> Should we be melancholy, boys?
> Why, soldiers, why?
> Whose business 'tis to die!
> What, sighing? fie!
> Don't fear, drink on; be jolly, boys!
> 'Tis he, you, or I!
> Cold, hot, wet, or dry,
> We're always bound to follow, boys,
> And scorn to fly!
>
> "'Tis but in vain—
> I mean not to upbraid you, boys—
> 'Tis but in vain
> For soldiers to complain:
> Should next campaign

> Send us to Him who made us, boys,
>   We're free from pain!
>   But, if we remain,
> A bottle and a kind landlady
>   Cure all again!"

Wolfe's affectionate and domestic nature, in sympathy with the devotional sentiment of his pious mother, whom he so strongly loved, was religiously disposed. He had even the reputation of being fanatical. A courtier remonstrated with the king on the appointment of Wolfe, saying, "He is mad" (meaning by "mad," over-religious). "If he be mad," replied the sovereign, "I wish he would bite some of my other generals!" Wolfe tells his mother, in a letter from Scotland: "I have observed your instructions so rigidly, that, rather than want the word, I got the reputation of being a very good Presbyterian, by frequenting the kirk of Scotland till our chapel opens."

1759. On the 14th of February, the British land-forces, under Wolfe, sailed for America. The transports which bore them were convoyed by a large English squadron, commanded by Saunders, "that admiral who was a pattern of most sturdy bravery united with the most unaffected modesty. No man said less or deserved more. Simplicity in his manners, generosity, and good nature, adorned his genuine love of his country." On the 21st of April, the whole armament arrived off Cape Breton, but could not enter the harbor of Louisburg, as was originally intended, in consequence of the large quantity of floating ice. They set sail for Halifax, in Nova Scotia, and anchored in that port. Here were now gathered a magnificent fleet of twenty-two ships-of-the-line, five frigates, nineteen smaller vessels, and a crowd of transports, under the flag of Admiral Saunders. General Wolfe mustered eight thousand troops under his command. A detachment of artillery and engineers, ten battalions of infantry, and six companies of rangers, made up the whole force, which, however, was afterward increased by the addition of several companies from the garrison at Cape Breton, and which formed what was called the corps of Louisburg grenadiers.

"On board one of the ships," says Bancroft, "was Jervis, afterward Earl St. Vincent; another which followed bore as master James Cook, the navigator who was destined to explore and reveal the unknown paths and thousand isles of the Pacific. The brigades had for their commanders the brave, open-hearted, and liberal Robert Monckton, afterward governor of New York and conqueror of Martinico; George Townshend, elder brother of Charles Townshend, soon to succeed his father in the peerage, and become known as a legislator for America, a man of quick perception but unsafe judgment; and the rash and inconsiderate Murray. For his adjutant-general Wolfe selected Isaac Barré, an old associate at Louisburg; an Irishman of humble birth, eloquent, ambitious, and fearless. The grenadiers of the army were formed into a corps, commanded by Colonel Guy Carleton. A detachment of light infantry were to receive orders from Lieutenant-Colonel, afterward Sir William Howe."

The ice having cleared, Admiral Saunders bore away for Louisburg. He detached from his fleet, however, a small squadron, under Admiral Darrell, to intercept the French vessels which were said to be making their way to the St. Lawrence, in order to carry relief to Quebec. On the arrival of the ships and troops in the harbor of Louisburg, the two commanders (Saunders and Wolfe) counselled together in regard to the plans of the proposed attack on Quebec; and orders were soon after issued to all the vessels, in case of separation, to make Gaspé bay, in the gulf of St. Lawrence, the first, and the island of Bic, one hundred and fifty miles up the river St. Lawrence, the second rendezvous.

All the forces, land and sea, were in a state of high confidence, and impatient for action. They were just ready to start, when bad news arrived. Darrell had lost his chance at the French squadron, which had given him the slip and sailed up the St. Lawrence. This, however disappointing, did not bate a jot of the confident enthusiasm which filled the heart of every British soldier and sailor. On the 6th of June, as the splendid fleet cleared the dismal, snow-covered shores of Cape Breton, the troops drew up on the decks, and the crews manned the yards of each vessel, from the proudest ship-of-the-line to the humblest tender, and gave one shout of joyful hope of soon meeting the enemy. There was victory in the full sound of this burst of confident enthusiasm. The men relied upon their own strength and courage, and trusted in the skill of their leaders. Each tar knew Saunders to be every inch a sailor. No soldier doubted the courage and ability of young Wolfe. Affection, too, warmed the faith of every follower into devotion to his leaders. Saunders, and more especially Wolfe, were beloved by their men.

With fine weather and favorable winds the fleet moved on gallantly past Newfoundland, in its mantle of snow; along the Bird islands, with a "ten-knot breeze;" and, on the 11th of June, came up with the Gaspé headland. One frigate, however, had pushed on ahead, the Richmond, which bore the impatient Wolfe, and which with his eagerness to be foremost he had selected as the fastest in the fleet. On the 13th of June, the dangers of the island of Anticosti, lying threateningly at the mouth of the gulf of St. Lawrence, were safely passed; and, on the 18th, the fleet came to anchor not far from the island of Bic. At this point, although the ships had "kept well together," the Richmond, with Wolfe aboard, had already arrived, having been to this moment far in advance of all the rest.

The fleet moved on again the next day. There was a calm off the mouth of the Saguenay, where there was some danger of wreck to the small vessels from the current-drifts, but from which they were fortunately relieved by the evening wind blowing off the land; there was a capture of a French vessel, with a distinguished lady belonging to the family of the marquis de Vaudreuil, governor of Canada, and some nuns, all of whom were most courteously treated, and sent to Quebec; and nothing more of incident until the whole fleet came to anchor in the evening of the 23d of June, off the village of St. Joseph. Here there was a slight brush with the enemy. Some survey-boats were shot at by the inhabitants, and the English took summary revenge with a company of grenadiers, who, with fire and slaughter, laid waste the Canadian hamlet.

On the 26th of June, the whole fleet of men-of-war and transports anchored off the island of Orleans, from which could be distinctly seen the lofty cliffs of jagged slate on which QUEBEC stood, with its citadel grimly defiant. Wolfe's love of action—for, although judicious, he was impetuously prompt—would not allow him to waste a moment. He ordered his troops at once to make ready to land; and on the very first night he sent a small reconnoitring force of forty rangers, under the command of a lieutenant, to make their way silently to the island, and gain what intelligence they could. The rangers landed cautiously and without observation, but, in groping their way quietly over the ground, came suddenly upon a large number of the inhabitants, busily engaged in burying in the earth their valuables, to secure them against the invaders. The British officer looked somewhat aghast at the overpowering crowd, but, finding that his only safety was in audacity, boldly confronted them, and began at once an onslaught. The Canadians struggled manfully for awhile, but, fearful of a larger body of the enemy in reserve, soon gave way and fled.

The English were too glad at their happy escape, to risk anything by pursuit, and, quietly making their way to a neighboring farmhouse, rested there until the next morning. During the night all the inhabitants made their escape, leaving the island in possession of the lieutenant and his twoscore of rangers. They were, however, soon joined by the whole of Wolfe's troops, who landed early in the day. The boats had made for a cove, and the men landed on a spot near a church, on the walls of which the priest had reverently inscribed an appeal "to the worthy officers of the British army," invoking them to spare the holy edifice and its sacred altars. The church was spared.

While the men encamped on the beautiful island, and, when off duty, lingered with delight over its fertile fields and rich gardens, all in the freshness and bloom of early summer, their anxious commander was thoughtful only of duty. His first impulse was to make his way, in company with the chief-engineer and an escort, to the farthest west of the island, that he might look upon the scene of the great work in which his whole mind was now absorbed.

"A magnificent but disheartening scene lay before him," says Warburton. "On the summit of the highest eminence, over the strait in the great river from whence the basin before him opened, the French flag waved. The crest of the rocky height was crowned with formidable works, redoubted and flanked. On every favorable spot, above, below, or on the rugged ascent, were batteries bristling with guns. This stronghold formed the right flank of a position eight miles in extent; the falls and the deep and rapid stream of the Montmorenci was the left. The shoals and rocks of the St. Lawrence protected the broad front; and the rich valley of the St. Charles, with the prosperous and beautiful villages of Charlesburg and Beauport, gave shelter and hospitality in the rear. A crested bank of some height over the great river marked the main line of the defences from east to west; parapets, flanked at every favorable spot, aided their natural strength. Crowded on the embattled bank, swarming in the irregular village-streets, and formed in masses on the hills beyond, were twelve thousand French and Canadian troops, led by the gallant Montcalm."

Wolfe looked on with momentary feelings of despair; and, as he gazed, pondering upon the undertaking which loomed in such immensity before his imagination, there came up a heavy cloud, which had gathered over the city, and now burst in a violent storm over his head. The hurricane blew with great fury; and, as the lightning flashed, the terrible effects of the raging wind were visible. The fleet of vessels were in a state of great commotion, being thrown about almost at the mercy of the agitated waters. The iron chains which moored the transports were rent in twain as if they had been of straw; the small boats were reft from their moorings, and dashed in useless wrecks upon the shore; and the great ships-of-the-line could hardly hold to their heavy anchors.

Wolfe, almost overwhelmed with what appeared to be an omen of fatal disaster to his great enterprise, turned away from the melancholy scene in deep thought, full of sad presage for the future. His mind, however, soon turned in retrospect to the land he had left, and to that country which had intrusted him with the guardianship of its glory.

Other feelings now stirred his heroic soul; despair and irresolution gave way to hope and firmness. He had promised that " no dangers or difficulties should discourage him," and he now determined that none should. As the calm self-reliance which belongs to genius settled upon his mind, and all the disordered fancies which had momentarily vexed his thoughts were scattered, Nature, as if in sympathy with the noble Wolfe, became also lulled to quiet. The storm passed suddenly away; and, as night darkened, all was in repose, with but a star here and there gently twinkling a faint light.

The British soldiers now encamped, and all soon were sleeping on their arms, except the watchful sentinels who passed to and fro along the shore. As the night advanced, the darkness deepened, and the quiet became more still. Nothing was heard but the ripple of the water, and nothing seen but the waving glimmer of scarcely a star, here and there, in the slight surf where the waves beat at the feet of the sentinels. Some dark objects appear suddenly, however, like black clouds, floating on the surface of the river. Those on the watch are bewildered as they look upon the strange phenomenon, and exchange whispering words of surprise and doubt. In a moment, before the sentinels have decided to arouse the drowsy camp, there burst from those dark objects, which had now floated, with the tide, into the neighborhood of the anchored fleet, a terrible volley of hissing bombs, rattling muskets, and booming cannon. Louder and more frequent was heard the noisy cannonade; nearer and nearer approached the dreaded objects. Now, in an instant, when almost within reach of the English fleet, the mystery was revealed by one burst of lurid light. The sentries did not pause to look, where all was now as bright as noonday, but turned and fled in fright toward the camp, arousing every soldier in confused alarm. The whole army was panic-stricken, and each affrighted man wandered about, lost in bewilderment, and regardless of discipline and order.

Some officers, more cool than their comrades, hurried to the farthest extremity of the island looking toward Quebec. Here, in the blaze of light, which threw its bright glare over the whole scene, they could see that the cause of the commotion was the appearance of a number of fire-ships, which the enemy had sent down to destroy the English fleet. The contrivance had failed, for the "diabolical machines" had blazed prematurely, and thus failed of their intended effect. Admiral Saunders had coolly, but with bated breath, watched the threatening approach; and when he saw that the fire-ships, from the premature discharge of their explosives, had been deprived of their chief means of injury, he coolly ordered out boats to grapple with them, and tow them far out of reach of harm to his fleet.

Order in the course of the night was restored to the camp on the island of Or-

leans. Next day, before commencing a systematic attack, Wolfe sent forth to the inhabitants of Canada this proclamation:

"WE HAVE A POWERFUL ARMAMENT. WE ARE SENT BY THE ENGLISH KING TO CONQUER THIS PROVINCE, BUT NOT TO MAKE WAR UPON WOMEN AND CHILDREN, THE MINISTERS OF RELIGION, OR INDUSTRIOUS PEASANTS. WE LAMENT THE SUFFERINGS WHICH OUR INVASION MAY INFLICT UPON YOU; BUT, IF YOU REMAIN NEUTER, WE PROFFER YOU SAFETY IN PERSON AND PROPERTY, AND FREEDOM IN RELIGION. WE ARE MASTERS OF THE RIVER: NO SUCCOR CAN REACH YOU FROM FRANCE. GENERAL AMHERST, WITH A LARGE ARMY, ASSAILS YOUR SOUTHERN FRONTIER. YOUR CAUSE IS HOPELESS, YOUR VALOR USELESS. YOUR NATION HAVE BEEN GUILTY OF GREAT CRUELTIES TO OUR UNPROTECTED SETTLERS; BUT WE SEEK NOT REVENGE: WE OFFER YOU THE SWEETS OF PEACE AMID THE HORRORS OF WAR. ENGLAND, IN HER STRENGTH, WILL BEFRIEND YOU: FRANCE, IN HER WEAKNESS, LEAVES YOU TO YOUR FATE."

This was a clever production, undoubtedly from Wolfe's own pen. Nothing could have been more judiciously worded; but its author hardly expected any other effect from it than it produced. It was more for the purpose, as is usual with military conquerors, to give a coloring of right and a tone of confidence to his new enterprise, than to persuade those to whom it was addressed to forsake their own country in its adversity, and to embrace with affection that country's bitterest enemy. The proclamation was met, on the side of the French, by an earnest appeal to the Canadians from their priests, to fight for their faith, against the heretic

English; and counter-manifestoes from the fierce Montcalm, containing some terrible threats against traitors.

The Canadians, of course, remained faithful to their country, and proved their devotion by liberal contributions of men and means to the cause. More than this: they became so ferocious in their enmity, that they joined with the Indians in inflicting savage cruelties upon all the English who fell into their hands. Wolfe appealed to the humanity of Montcalm, to stop these atrocities; but the French general could not, or would not. The almost feminine sensibility of the brave and humane Wolfe was so far worked into a fermentation of cruel anger by the result of his appeal to the humanity of Montcalm, that he issued this order:—

"THE GENERAL STRICTLY FORBIDS THE INHUMAN PRACTICE OF SCALPING, *except* WHERE THE ENEMY ARE INDIANS OR CANADIANS DRESSED LIKE INDIANS."

Such is war, that even the gentlest spirit is curdled into cruel rage by its touch of blood!

CHAPTER XIV.

The British Fleet draws nigh Quebec.—Point Levi taken.—De Vaudreuil and Montcalm quarrel.—The French strive to drive away the British Fleet.—Quebec not yet taken.—Wolfe's First Manœuvres.—The British Rangers in the Forest.—Pursued by the Savages.—The Murder of the Innocents.—Failure of Wolfe on the Montmorenci.—De Chassier's Night-Attack.—Its Catastrophe.—Admiral Holmes moves his Ships farther up the St. Lawrence.—Consternation of the French.—Wolfe takes a Survey, and does not admire the Prospect of the Heights of Quebec.—Wolfe's Second Attempt and Failure.—A Touching Incident.—Ochterlony and Peyton, the Two Friends.—Escape from the Savages.—Death of Ochterlony, and Safety of Peyton.—Wolfe unsuccessful, but not despondent.—News from Johnson and Amherst, and its Effect.—Wolfe's Illness.—The General commands, and forms Plans, on his Sick-Bed.—A French Priest arouses his Flock to Action.—Mutual Barbarity.

1759. ADMIRAL SAUNDERS, made aware by the effects of the storm, from which his ships had so greatly suffered, of their insecurity, was now anxious to move them from the channel between the island of Orleans and the south shore, where they were moored, to the safer anchorage of the "Basin," facing the city. Point Levi, however, which commanded the place to which he proposed to take the fleet, was held by the enemy, with a considerable force of artillery, by which they could keep up an annoying fire. Monckton was accordingly ordered by Wolfe to pass over from the island of Orleans with his brigade, and drive away the French from the point. After some difficulty, and two or three repulses, Monckton finally succeeded in his object, and the village of Levi fell into his possession. The Canadian troops and Indians were forced to fly, and, crossing the St. Lawrence, took refuge within the walls of Quebec.

The loss of Point Levi was severely felt by Montcalm, who had, with his usual judgment, early discovered the importance of the position, and had strongly

urged upon the marquis de Vaudreuil the necessity of so strengthening it as to resist any attempt of the English. The governor had, however, obstinately objected; and when the result that Montcalm had feared occurred, and the town of Levi was taken by his enemy, he was so vexed, that he never forgave De Vaudreuil. From that time, the two were no longer friends. This quarrel fatally interfered with the success of the French arms.

The English, once in possession of Point Levi, began to fortify it with batteries, placed upon various elevations which commanded Quebec; and were able, although the distance across the river was three quarters of a mile, to throw a damaging fire upon the city. The French for awhile made a useless effort to dislodge Monckton's force, by means of floating batteries moored in the river; but they were soon silenced by the guns of one of Saunders's frigates, sent to drive away the annoyance.

Wolfe daily increased his fortifications on Point Levi, and continued to fire with great effect upon the city. With red-hot balls and bombshells he succeeded in setting fire to over forty houses in one night, destroying the greater part of the lower town, and so angering the inhabitants, that they volunteered to cross the St. Lawrence in a body and drive away the invaders. This was, however, but a temporary fit of enthusiasm; and the citizens, becoming more discreet, thought better of their rash determination, and retired from their ruined habitations to the security of the citadel, which, perched on the heights, the English guns could not reach.

The British had now been a fortnight before Quebec; and, although they had made good their possession of the St. Lawrence, and had succeeded in keeping up a brisk fire from the Point-Levi batteries, no impression had been made upon the citadel itself, and the object of the expedition seemed almost as remote from accomplishment as ever. **July 9.**

Wolfe now determined upon a plan of operations by which he hoped to get at the enemy more effectually. Montcalm had extended his camp from the citadel, along the northern bank of the St. Lawrence, as far as the river and falls of Montmorenci. Wolfe proposed to land his forces on the side of this river and these falls opposite to the farthest eastern extremity of the French encampment. In order to divert the enemy, while Wolfe was engaged in crossing the St. Lawrence to the Montmorenci, the smaller vessels of the fleet were worked in close to the northern shore, and began to play their guns upon the French, and with such success, that they were forced to draw back their troops from the border of the river to the higher ground behind.

Monckton, too, was ordered to make a diversion, on Point Levi, toward Quebec. He accordingly sent out a small company of his rangers, under Lieutenant Rogers, to prepare the way for a larger movement on the southern shore of the river. The rangers pushed on with such zeal, that they got lost in the thick woods, and, night coming on, were forced to pass it in the forest, sleeping on their arms. Next morning, while making their way to Monckton's camp, they observed, in some rising smoke, signs of habitation, and accordingly, having cautiously advanced, came upon a log-house, where they found a Canadian settler and his three children, the eldest of whom was less than fifteen years. They were taken captive, and were being led back to the camp, when suddenly the whoop of the Indian sounded upon their ears, and they discovered that a large body of these savages were close upon their track.

There was no hope now but in concealment and flight. The rangers, skilled in forest-warfare, plunged at once into the woods, and strove to dodge the Indian pursuit among the trees and undergrowth. They moved on with the greatest possible haste, dragging their prisoners with them, and endeavored to keep so silent as not to be heard by the savages, who were beating the woods like so many bloodhounds. Silence, however, was impossible. The Canadian father and his eldest son were readily kept quiet; but the two younger children, who were almost infants, kept up such a continual cry of fear and anguish, that it was found impossible to stop them. Threats were tried in vain, and persuasions were found equally useless. They were urged by Lieutenant Rogers to leave him, and find their way home; but they would not be entreated, and continued their lamentations, so that the woods rang with their cries. The savages, guided by the noise, were fast approaching. Rogers was al-

most in despair. His only hope was now in a terrible sacrifice. The children must be silenced; and silenced they were, by death! A sword was plunged into the heart of each of the innocents, and their bodies cast aside, to be eaten by the wolves. Rogers now succeeded in reaching Monckton's camp in safety with all his rangers and the bereaved remnant of his prisoners. .

Wolfe succeeded without difficulty in conveying a large force from the island of Orleans to the opposite bank of the river, and there encamped them. The river and the falls of Montmorenci were now between him and the enemy: he was on the east side of the stream, whose course is north and south, and they on the west. The falls, with a descent of three hundred feet, and the rapids of the river, near where Wolfe was encamped, formed an impassable barrier between the two camps. The ground which the English, after a slight struggle with the Indians and bush-rangers, now held, was in a commanding position, and so lofty, that from its cliffs the eye readily looked down within the intrenchments of the enemy on the opposite side. A crossing-place was now searched for, and a ford found some three miles distant from the mouth of the Montmorenci. But the French side was so well protected by the natural barriers of precipice and thronging woods, and the strong intrenchments which the alert Montcalm had thrown up, that it seemed almost impracticable to attempt it. Several efforts were, notwithstanding, made — which, however, were repulsed each time by a murderous fire from the Indians hidden in the forest covert. Wolfe now abandoned for ever all hope of crossing at that point.

Montcalm became confident and more daring when he found Wolfe's plan had failed; and, believing that the English had made a fatal error in dividing their force, tried to profit by it. He accordingly sent a body of troops from Quebec to the south bank of the St. Lawrence, to the west of Point Levi, where Monckton was encamped, and gave orders for a night-attack. Wolfe, hearing of this movement, made his way across at once, and took command in person of the troops in Monckton's camp. Not conscious of the dangers which were pressing to overwhelm them in the darkness, the British soldiers threw themselves down, after a day's hard duty at the works, and now lay in profound repose.

Two thousand French, Canadians, and savages, as soon as the shades of evening had begun to fall, took up their silent march. De Chassier, a brave man, lord of the domain of Point Levi, and familiar with every landmark and forest-path, led the force. This was separated, as it approached the British camp, into two divisions. One was sent in advance, and the other followed at some distance in the rear. As the first proceeded through the wood in the increasing darkness, the men became suddenly alarmed, and fled back in confusion. The other division coming up, and hearing the approaching footsteps of their retreating comrades, took them for the enemy, and commenced a deadly fire, which was returned; and the awful mistake was not discovered until seventy had been killed, and both parties had been put to flight in opposite directions! The only result of this unfortunate expedition was this sad suicidal slaughter.

While the British troops were busily engaged on Point Levi and the bank of the Montmorenci, in throwing up their intrenchments, Wolfe continued active in studying the defences of the enemy, and the natural position of the surrounding country. A portion of the fleet, under Admiral Holmes, having been moved during the night, much to the surprise and alarm of the inhabitants of Quebec, up the St. Lawrence, and even beyond that city, where they were anchored, Wolfe seized the opportunity of taking a survey of the northern bank of the river, to the west of the town. He accordingly took a barge and pushed off from the shore to the nearest ship in the stream. The barge was observed, and immediately the enemy's guns began to play upon her; but she happily succeeded, with only the loss of her mast, in carrying her precious freight to the safe guardianship of a seventy-four. Wolfe did not like the look of things above Quebec. The northern banks of the St. Lawrence rose in rugged precipices from the shore, there as elsewhere, about the site of the formidable citadel. Moreover, the French had defended the approach by intrenchments and a strong battery at Sillery, which crowned the high ground of the northern shore of the river. Wolfe, therefore, for the present, turned his attention elsewhere.

Near where the Montmorenci empties

into the St. Lawrence, the stream, after its turbulent course over the falls and rapids, becomes smooth, and at low tide so shallow, that it can in some places be crossed on foot. Montcalm, conscious of the natural facilities here for the approach of the enemy, had fortified the place with a redoubt below the bank; while the bank itself rose so precipitately, and was so strongly intrenched, that even if an opposing force should succeed in gaining the shore, they would have a tough work before them in an attempt to scale the precipitous heights in the very mouths of a threatening battery. Wolfe, however, growing impatient—as he had already been five weeks before Quebec, and had done nothing to satisfy the impulsive energies of his restless spirit—was now resolved upon the desperate undertaking of throwing his troops across to this very point, so strongly resisting, and presenting so little hope, even to the most daring and resolute. The general, notwithstanding, undertook it, and failed. The brigades succeeded in getting across from the opposite side of the Montmorenci, and Monckton's force landed in fine order from Point Levi. But the grenadiers were in too great a hurry, and, pushing with too much eagerness for the intrenchments, were repulsed, and came flying back in disorder; although Monckton's men, with admirable coolness, formed and held the ground where they had landed, and thus prevented a precipitate and confused retreat. The attack had been delayed by the grounding of some of the boats. Night was now approaching, and the tide rising fast; so Wolfe withdrew his men, and give up the attempt as futile.

In this unfortunate repulse, there occurred an incident which so beautifully illustrates the manly affection of comrade for comrade, and affords so bright a revelation of the gentle goodness of brave hearts, while even steeled to the cruel duties of war, that we interweave with heightened pleasure this pure page of brotherly feeling with the leaves of the "Battles of America," stained as they are by fratricidal blood:—

Captain Ochterlony and Ensign Peyton belonged to the regiment of Royal Americans. They were nearly of an age, which did not exceed thirty. The first was a North Briton, the other a native of Ireland. Both were agreeable in person and unblemished in character, and connected together by the ties of mutual friendship and esteem. On the day that preceded the attempt which we have just related, Captain Ochterlony had been obliged to fight a duel with one of the German officers of the mercenary troops employed under Wolfe, in which, though he wounded and disarmed his antagonist, yet he himself received a dangerous hurt under the right arm, in consequence of which his friends insisted on his remaining in camp during the action of the following day. But his spirit was too great to comply with this remonstrance. He declared it should never be said that " a scratch," received in a private rencounter, had prevented him from doing his duty when his country required his service; and he took the field, though he was hardly able to carry his arms. In lead-

ing up his men to the enemy's intrenchments, he was shot through the lungs
with a musket-ball; but he still continued advancing, until, by the loss of blood,
he became too weak to proceed farther.

About the same time, Mr. Peyton was
lamed by a shot, which shattered the
small bone of his left leg. The soldiers,
in their retreat, earnestly begged, with
tears in their eyes, that Captain Ochterlony would allow them to carry him and
the ensign off the field. Mr. Peyton, with
a generous disdain, rejected their good
offices, declaring that he would not leave
his captain in such a situation; and in a
little time they remained the sole survivors on that part of the field.

Captain Ochterlony sat down by his
friend; and, as they expected nothing
but immediate death, they took leave of
each other. Yet they did not altogether
lose hope of protection as prisoners; for
the captain, seeing a French soldier with
two Indians approach, started up and ac-
costed them in the French tongue, which
he perfectly understood, and expressed
his expectation that he and his companion would be treated as officers and gentlemen. The Frenchman, however, came
up to Mr. Peyton, as he lay upon the
ground, and snatched his laced hat from
him, and robbed Ochterlony of his watch
and money. This outrage was a signal
to the Indians, who seemed to be entirely under the control of the French mis-
creant, to begin. Accordingly, one of
these savages struck at the captain behind with the butt-end of his musket, but,
missing his head, at which he aimed, the
blow fell upon his shoulder. At the same
moment the other Indian, with his muzzle
to the breast of the unfortunate Ochterlony, poured its contents into his chest.
"O Peyton," cried out the captain, "the
villain has shot me!" The savage, not
yet satiated in his cruelty, then sprang
upon him and stabbed him in the belly
with his tomahawk. The captain was
without a single weapon of defence. The
Frenchman and his associate savages now
strove to strangle him with his own sash;
and he seemed completely at their mercy, struggling upon his knees with all his
might.

Peyton, observing the position of his
friend, lifted himself from the ground,
and, levelling his double-barrelled musket, brought one of the savages down,
who fell dead upon the spot. The surviving Indian now made for Peyton, who,
seeing the savage coming, fired with a
sure aim his second barrel at him, but
apparently without effect. The Indian
then returned the fire, which wounded
Peyton in the shoulder; and, to complete
his bloody work, rushed upon him and
thrust his bayonet through his body.
The young English officer was, however,
not yet despatched; and, as a second attempt was being made with the bayonet,
he seized the musket of the Indian, and,
dragging him close to him, succeeded in
drawing the dagger at his side, and
plunged it into his antagonist. Now ensued a fierce struggle for life or death;
but Peyton managed to get the better of
the Indian, and with another thrust with
the poniard the savage rolled over, and,
with one last agony, breathed no more.
At this moment the young British officer

was seized with an uncontrollable curiosity to find out whether his shot, which had seemed to be a sure one, had taken effect. On stripping the blanket off the dead body of the savage, he discovered that his ball had passed quite through the chest!

Peyton now managed to raise himself on one leg, and to hobble toward the place where he saw his friend Ochterlony standing up, with the Frenchman at his side, not far from the French battery. "Captain, I am glad to see," cried out his friend, "that you have at last got under protection; but beware of that villain with you, who is more barbarous than the savages themselves! God bless you, my dear fellow! I see some Indians coming this way, and expect to be murdered immediately."

The Indians were, indeed, coming—some thirty of them—who, having left off pillaging and scalping the dead who had fallen in the late unfortunate attempt, were now making for Peyton. He, disabled as he was, made a run for life, but had not proceeded far, when he found himself unable to continue his flight. He now came to a stop, and had just loaded his musket, when two of the Indians, ahead of their fellow-savages, came almost within range of his fire; but, as he aimed at them, they suddenly paused, awaiting the coming up of the others. The French, in the meantime, began to play with their cannon and musketry upon the poor, solitary, and maimed Peyton! This was his almost hopeless position, when he caught a sight in the distance of a Highland officer, to whom he waved his hand, in signal of distress. It was fortunately noticed, and three men were immediately sent to his aid.

The three British soldiers, in spite of a terrible fire, succeeded in reaching Peyton, and one of them bore him off on his shoulders. The Highland officer was his kinsman, and, having heard that Peyton had dropped on the field, had come out with a party; and, driving off the opposing French and savages, had thus succeeded in bringing him rescue, and carrying him off in triumph. Ochterlony was conveyed as a prisoner to Quebec, where he soon after died of his wounds —the surgeons declaring that he might have recovered of the two shots in his breast, if it had not been for the fatal plunge of the savage's tomahawk in the belly.[*]

The failure at the Montmorenci so wrought upon the sensitive nature of Wolfe, and his feeble constitution had been so broken by fatigue and exposure, that he now fell ill, and was prostrate in his camp with fever and dysentery. His proud soul recognised death alone as the alternative of conquest; and, while there was life, he resolutely strove for victory. He now, stretched as he was on the bed of sickness, bated not a jot of his energy and resolute courage. He issued his orders with his usual promptness, and exercised his command with the same strictness of discipline. The impetuous rush of the grenadiers had lost the day, and he now sternly rebuked them:—

"The check which the grenadiers met

* Smollett tells this story, and we have repeated it very nearly in his own words.

with will, it is hoped," said Wolfe, " be a lesson to them for the time to come. Such impetuous, irregular, and unsoldier-like proceedings, destroy all order, and put it out of the general's power to execute his plans. The grenadiers could not suppose that they alone could beat the French army; therefore it was necessary the corps under Brigadiers Townshend and Monckton should have time to join them, that the attack might be general. The very first fire of the enemy was sufficient to have repulsed men who had lost all sense of order and military discipline. Amherst's and the Highland regiment, by the soldierlike and cool manner in which they formed, would undoubtedly have beaten back the whole Canadian army if they had ventured to attack them. The loss, however, is very inconsiderable, and may be easily repaired when a favorable opportunity offers, if the men will show a proper attention to their officers."

Wolfe, however, was not the man to linger despondingly upon the errors of the past. His impulsive spirit was ever looking forward with hope to the future, and his sense of duty prompted him to act as long as there was any chance of doing something for the cause to which he had pledged his service and his honor. There was no hesitation in his conduct; and he promptly sent Murray, immediately after the repulse on the Montmorenci, with twelve hundred men, to aid Admiral Holmes in effecting a landing above Quebec. Little, however, was accomplished by this movement, as Montcalm had so strongly fortified every point,

16

and so diligently guarded against surprise, that it was found impossible to do more than destroy the small village of Dechambault in the course of the passage up the river. Some prisoners of distinction were here taken, and letters found upon them, which gave the first information of the success of Amherst at Crown Point, and that of Johnson at Niagara. This news was brought back by Murray exultingly, with the hope of cheering his general; Wolfe, however, derived but little comfort from the intelligence, as he saw at once that there was no hope now of aid from either Johnson or Amherst, so dilatory had been their progress.

Wolfe now became so ill, that he could no longer bear the daily presence of his officers; but his mind continually dwelt upon the great undertaking, the fate of which rested on him alone. He devised plans of attack, and from his bed dictated their several details, with this general letter to his brigadiers :—

" That the public service may not suffer from the general's indisposition, he begs the brigadiers will meet and consult together for the public utility and advantage, and consider of the best method to attack the enemy.

" If the French army be attacked and defeated, the general concludes that the town would immediately surrender, because he does not find that they have any provision in that place.

" The general is of opinion that the army should be attacked in preference to the place, because of the difficulties of penetrating from the lower to the upper town; in which attempt neither the guns of the shipping nor of our own batteries could be of much use."

Wolfe's plans, which accompanied this letter, were all—in accordance with his view of attacking the army and not the citadel—based upon operations against the French encampment extending along the northern shore from the city of Quebec to the river Montmorenci. The brigadiers met and deliberated, and finally determined on another and bolder project, said to have been suggested* by Colonel George Townshend, that heroic officer who had abandoned rank, position, parliamentary influence, and the endearments of domestic life, to share in the hardships and dangers of the American campaign. Wolfe did not hesitate to adopt the daring suggestion of his inferior in command, and now bent all his energies to crown it with triumph.

The whole army welcomed the prospect of some decisive action. They had been harassed by the irregular warfare with the Indians and Canadians, who were constantly provoking them into skirmishes, which merely fevered cruelty with a thirst for blood, and brought them no nearer to the settlement of the great struggle. The Christian soldier was lapsing into the barbarity of the heathen savage. In fact, the conversion would seem already to have been made. For example: A French priest armed some eighty

of his flock, and fortified himself in a large stone-house, about ten miles eastward of the British camp at Montmorenci. Thence he sent a message, challenging to combat, an English detachment posted in his neighborhood. At the same time, with eccentric French courtesy, he sent a polite invitation to the English commander to do him the honor of dining with him, offering him a safe-conduct for the occasion. The invitation was courteously refused. Soon after, a company of light-troops, with a fieldpiece, was sent against the belligerent French priest and his flock. The English placed themselves in a wood near by, and by a stratagem succeeded in enticing the French out of their fortified house; and, surrounding some thirty of them, killed and scalped the whole, including the gallant priest! That the victims were disguised as Indians, was pleaded as an excuse for the savage cruelty with which they were treated!*

With such unholy and unsatisfactory warfare to noble spirits, it was not surprising that the whole army was eager for a change. The soldiers, too, suffered from hardships and want of provisions. Horseflesh had already been served out as occasional rations. Moreover, two months had been passed in vain, and all felt the impatience which awaits unsatisfied expectation.

* Warburton.

* Warburton.

CHAPTER XV.

Wolfe's Letter to Pitt.—The Great Commoner's Dismay.—Walpole's Babble.—Townshend suggests a Plan for the Campaign.—Wolfe adopts it.—Reconnoitres the Heights.—Finds a Place of Landing.—Wolfe's Cove.—The Army kept in Ignorance.—The Wisdom of the Caution.—A Deserter from the French.—The Enemy losing Heart.—Montcalm writes despairingly to Count Molé.—His Remarkable Prophecy.—The British proceed to the Attack.—Wolfe's Night-Sail.—His Song.—The Plan of the Attack.—Wolfe and Gray's Elegy.—Wolfe on the Shore.—The British on the Heights of Abraham.—Montcalm doubtful.—Assured at last.—The Battle.—Gallantry on Both Sides.—Wolfe falls.—The British victorious.—Wolfe dies "happy."—De Bougainville blusters loudly, and flies.—Montcalm's Heroic Death.—News of the Victory reaches England.—Joy and Sorrow.—Honor to the Brave.—End of the Canadian Campaign.

1759. WOLFE, after several weeks of illness, had sufficiently recovered his strength to present himself again to his troops. He showed, as always, the same undaunted air of confidence to his soldiers, cheering them by his inspiriting words, and encouraging them by his self-reliant example. His tone, however, to the British government was more distrustful. "I am so far recovered," he wrote, "as to do business; but my constitution is entirely ruined, without the consolation of having done any considerable service to the state, or without any prospect of it." Pitt was dismayed at these despairing words, and began to tremble for the glory of his country, and to fear lest he had intrusted it to the guardianship of feeble hands. The unfavorable news began to circulate in London, and its great people to quake with fear. Walpole caught up the echo from the aristocratic circle which gathered about the personages of state, and repeated it in a gossiping letter: "In short, you must not," he says, "be surprised that we have failed at Quebec, as we certainly shall.... How this little army will get away from a much larger, and in this season, and in that country, I don't guess —yes, I do." Walpole's "guess," which was sure, in accordance with his small, tittle-tattle spirit, to take a mean direction, was very far from doing justice to the great character of Wolfe. Walpole "guessed" that the British would run away!

The plan which Wolfe had adopted, at the suggestion of Townshend, was to convey a large force above the town, and thus draw Montcalm from his citadel to an open fight. This was the general design: the details were now to be settled.

Wolfe allowed no weakness or tardy convalescence to interfere with the activity of his movements. He started himself at once on board one of the frigates in Admiral Holmes's squadron, and, sailing up the stream, landed in a cove on the northern bank of the St. Lawrence, three miles above Quebec, while **Sept. 9.** the men-of-war diverted with a busy fire the various French batteries, and covered the landing of the general and his brigadiers who accompanied him. The place where they had driven in the boat was slightly hollowed out in the course of that great volcanic movement which, ages ago, had reft in two the land, and made way for the rush of the waters, which now calmly flow, in the beautiful river St. Lawrence, between its rugged banks of slate. The place has ever since been called "Wolfe's Cove." From the scant spot of alluvial shore where Wolfe landed, there led up the precipice, which frowned high above, a narrow and winding way to the summit. Once at the top, the ground becomes almost like a table-land, and stretches with but gentle elevations to the walls of Quebec, which stands upon a part of this high level, and defiantly from its guarded height, raised upon steep sides of stone, would seem to scorn all invaders.

Wolfe resolved upon taking his troops up the path at the foot of which he had landed, and which led to the "Plains of Abraham," as the level land at the top of the headlong cliff was called. This was such a daring resolve — so hazardous, so remote from probability and apparent possibility — that even Montcalm, with all his vigilant foresight, could not anticipate it. Secrecy was absolutely necessary, and it was therefore determined to land the troops in the dead of night. Wolfe took great care to keep his own counsel; and, although he at once made active and thorough preparations for carrying out his design, he let no word escape, by which the precise object of his operations might be known to the soldiers, and his plans thus exposed to the chance of reaching the enemy through a deserter. In his orders to the **Sept. 11.** troops, he spoke of their embarkation and disembarkation, specifying the hours of the night; and directed the men to be quite silent, and not on any account, when about to land, to fire from the boats. He said nothing, however, about the specific object of his design, but confined himself to the general order to "the army to hold themselves in readiness to land and attack the enemy."

Wolfe's caution was wise; for, on the very morning which preceded the night of his proposed attempt, one of **Sept. 12.** his soldiers deserted to the enemy. Knowing nothing, however, this fellow had nothing to communicate to the French. One of Montcalm's regulars, who in his turn deserted to the English camp, had more to say. From him it was learned that the French general believed the attack would only be made on the Montmorenci side, and accordingly still kept his main force below the town; that a large detachment of troops had been sent off (thus weakening the garrison of Quebec) to meet Amherst, whose success at Crown Point, and that of Johnson at Niagara, had greatly alarmed the Canadians; that M. de Bougainville, with fifteen hundred men, was watching the movements of the British fleet above the town; and, finally, that the French were in great want of provisions, and much disheartened.

The French had too much occasion to lose heart. The British fleet rode in their waters, in triumphant mastery of the St. Lawrence, cutting off all hope of aid by sea. Amherst and Johnson threatened the Canadian frontier by land. And, worse than all, the able Montcalm was thwarted by the obstinate resistance to his plans by the less capable De Vaudreuil. "You have sold your country!" cried out the general, in excited rage against the governor; "but while I live," added the resolute Montcalm, "I will not deliver it up!" He wrote, almost in the bitterness of despair, to M. de Molé, president of the Parliament of France: "The enemy are in a condition to offer battle when they please, and I can not refuse them, although I shall be beaten. My Canadians, without discipline, and deaf to the call of the drum, will fly at the first charge; and what will be left for me, but to be overwhelmed without a resource? Such is my position—a position so terrible for a general, that it gives me some awful moments of reflection! But, come what will, be assured I shall not survive the loss of the colony. There are times when all that is left for a general is to die with honor." He then "consoles" himself, as he declares, with a remarkable prophecy of the fatality which should attend British dominion by the conquest of Canada: "I shall console myself," writes Montcalm, with the serious earnestness of a prophet of wo, "for my defeat, by the certain conviction that that defeat will one day be worth more to my country than a single victory, and that the conqueror, in widening his dominion, will but open for himself a tomb." Montcalm was conscious that his chief danger lay above Quebec, and wrote: "Unless Wolfe lands above the town, and forces me to a battle, I am safe." Yet, on the very night that the danger he feared threatened him, he knew nothing of its approach!

The British troops were embarked. Wolfe himself was on board. The night had set in. The evening was clear. The wind was fair, with the promise of a fresh breeze to carry the ships rapidly up the St. Lawrence. The plan of sending the larger vessels, with the mock show of landing a force on the northern bank of the river, near the Montmorenci, had been successful, and the enemy were still unsuspicious of Wolfe's real design. The British general now issued his last orders, in which, having reminded his army that the fate of Canada might be determined by a vigorous blow struck at this moment, he tells them mysteriously, still keeping his secret, that they are to land where the French would least expect it. "The first body that gets on shore is to march directly to the enemy. The battalions must form on the upper ground with expedition, and be ready to charge whatever presents itself..... The officers and men will remember what is expected from them, and what a determined body of soldiers, inured to war, is capable of doing, against five weak French battalions, mingled with a disorderly peasantry."

Wolfe, absorbed as he was in the preparations for his great enterprise, and anxiously disturbed with thoughts of its hazards, and the importance of the stake, still preserved his cheerful, confident tone in the presence of all. At his evening mess he was even joyous in the company of his fellow-officers, and sang his own song—

> "Why, soldiers, why,
> Should we be melancholy, boys?

Why, soldiers, why?
Whose business 'tis to die !" *

The ships, with a part of the troops, now sailed, and, with a favorable breeze, soon passed up the St. Lawrence to the rendezvous, eight miles above Quebec, where they joined the fleet stationed there under Holmes. That portion of the army at Point Levi moved simultaneously along the southern bank of the river, and, halting opposite to the ships, embarked. The troops, to the number of sixteen hundred, were then removed into flat-bottomed boats, in the utmost silence. Everything promised success. The enemy were evidently quite unconscious of the English movement, although an event occurred which had nearly exposed the whole affair, and might have spoiled the enterprise. A couple of French deserters had sought refuge on board one of the ships-of-war, and, giving information of an expected convoy of provisions, destined to Quebec, from De Bougainville's force up the river, the captain of the ship was on the lookout, and determined to stop the supplies. The movement among the English, while the troops were getting into the small boats, was observed by the French deserters, and it was supposed that they were the convoy preparing to make for Quebec. The British captain, whose vessel was at some distance, and who was unconscious of Wolfe's plan, had pointed his guns and was about to fire, when fortunately his

preparations, in consequence of the noise and bustle, were observed by Wolfe, who succeeded in setting the zealous naval officer aright, and thus preventing him from killing his countrymen and alarming the French.

About an hour before daybreak, the fleet of flat-bottomed boats began to move down with the ebbing tide. Wolfe, in company with some of his officers, led the van. The rowers, with muffled oars, just touched the rippling stream, and they glided silently and calmly on. The stars shone out bright in the clear sky. The stillness and darkness of the night, the gentle movement, the regular dip of the oar, the pulsation of the tide against the ribbed gunwale of the boat, the stifled throbbings of the expectant hearts, naturally subdued all to quiet and serious thought. Wolfe was the first to break the silence, by uttering, in a tone of gentle melancholy, this verse of Gray's Elegy :—

" ' The boast of heraldry, the pomp of power,
   And all that beauty, all that wealth e'er gave,
   Await alike the inevitable hour—
   The path of glory leads but to the grave !'

"Now, gentlemen," said Wolfe to his officers, "I would rather be the author of that poem than take Quebec." *

The boats now approached the land, and, cautiously floating under the overhanging cliffs, they at last reached the cove which Wolfe had selected for the place of disembarkation. The general

---

* We have already quoted the whole of this song, as given in that most excellent and accurate work of the brothers Duyckinck, "The Cyclopædia of American Literature." The song is supposed to have been composed on the night when it was first sung by Wolfe, that of the attack.

* This incident is told by a gentleman who was a midshipman, doing duty on board Wolfe's boat on that night, and became afterward Professor John Robinson, of the University of Edinburgh.

himself, in the foremost boat, was the first to leap ashore. Some of the boats, carrying a company of Highlanders, had been borne by the tide to some distance below. Donald Macdonald, their captain, however, without hesitation, leaped on shore, and, nothing daunted by the steep ascent above him, sprang at an overhanging tree; and, bidding his men to follow, climbed up the jagged precipice to the top, with his soldiers close behind him. On the summit was a French sentinel, who, hearing approaching steps, cried out, "*Qui vive?*"—"*La France!*" was the quick reply of Macdonald, who fortunately understood the French language. "*A quel régiment?*" pertinaciously inquired the Frenchman. "*De la Reine!*" answered the captain, who knew that was De Bougainville's. And the French soldier, muttering, "*Passe*," continued to pace his round. The Highlanders, however, as they scrambled up among the bushes, and the loosened slate of the precipice, made a rustling noise, which alarmed the enemy's guard, who, after rushing toward the edge of the cliff, and firing a volley, took to their heels.

Wolfe, with his brigadiers Monckton and Murray, and the first division of the army, were not less successful below. They all clambered along the precipitous path, so narrow that but two could go abreast, and reached the top without opposition. The French pickets stationed on the summit were overpowered at once, and the rest of the forces continued to come up in rapid succession, without resistance. As the day broke, the whole army had reached the "Plains of Abraham," and, being formed on solid ground, were ready for the enemy at any moment.

When a messenger arrived at Montcalm's quarters with the intelligence of the English army being drawn up on the plains of Abraham, he would hardly believe it, and contemptuously declared, "It can be but a small party, come to burn a few houses and retire." After more explicit information, however, he became assured of the fact, and cried out, angrily: "Then they have, at last, got to the weak side of this miserable garrison. I must give battle, and crush them before noon!" Montcalm acted accordingly, and unwisely. His gallantry misled him. His true policy would have been the discreet one of retiring within the citadel, and awaiting there, safe within its walls, until he had exhausted the patience and resources of his enemy. He recklessly determined, however, to give battle; and, hastily collecting his forces from Quebec and from below, along the northern shores of the St. Lawrence, to the Montmorenci, he drew them up, and marched to face the foe.

At eight o'clock in the morning, the French column was observed from the English camp to be advancing up the rising ground from the river St. Charles to the plains of Abraham. Wolfe had succeeded in dragging up the cliff but a single piece of artillery; but this solitary gun was made to play with such effect upon Montcalm's forces, that they were obliged to alter their line of march.

At ten o'clock, Montcalm had reached the battle-field, and began to form his

army. As he came up, however, De Bougainville, who had been summoned by
the French general to his aid, sent up, in
advance of his own march, a body of light
cavalry, which made a show of attack upon Wolfe's left, but were easily checked
by Townshend, at that post. Montcalm
formed his centre of seven hundred and
twenty regulars, of the regiments of
Bearne and Guienne, with twelve hundred militia, and led it in person. To
his right he placed the regiments of La
Sasse and Languedoc, some sixteen hundred strong, all veteran soldiers; with
these was a militia force of less than five
hundred, and a single small fieldpiece.
On the left were thirteen hundred infantry of the Royal Rousillon regiment, together with twenty-three hundred Canadian militia and a marine battalion. The
whole French force thus amounted to
half a hundred less than eight thousand,
without counting the Indians, who were
distributed about, to hide themselves in
the neighboring bush, and thus execute
what annoyance they could by their usual mode of warfare. Less than a half of
Montcalm's force, however, were regulars,
and the rest were raw Canadians, in whom
he had no confidence. Wolfe himself
enumerated his enemy thus contemptuously—"Five weak French battalions,
mingled with a disorderly peasantry!"
But this was his statement to his own
men, for the sake of encouragement. He
knew that he had one of the most skilful
generals of the age, with some of the
most experienced soldiers, pitted against
him.

The English from an early hour had
awaited, in battle array, the coming up
of the enemy. Wolfe himself led the
front line, on the right with Monckton,
and Murray the left. The second line
was under the command of Townshend,
who, with his light-infantry and the Royal
Americans, took position at the extreme
left. A reserve was thrown back in a third
line, under Burton and Howe. Wolfe's
whole force was less than five thousand,
but each man was a trained soldier.

Montcalm had sent in great haste for
De Bougainville and De Vaudreuil to
come up with their troops, and in the
meantime checked his impatience for the
onset by a diversion with his three small
pieces of artillery, which, in his hurry,
were all he had brought with him. For
an hour he continued firing his cannon
upon the British, who rejoined with their
single gun; and thus, during that time,
an ineffective fire was kept up.

Montcalm now lost all patience, and
began the attack in earnest. His first
attempt was, by a flank movement, to
crowd the English down the precipice.
With this purpose in view, the French
veterans on the right swept round the
English left, under Murray, with impetuous force, and poured in a murderous fire
upon the light-infantry in the rear, under
Howe. This young officer gave them a
warm reception, and stayed their progress until Townshend came up to his relief with his infantry and the Royal Americans, and drove the French back to their
lines in greatly-diminished numbers.

The attempt upon the light-infantry in
front of the British centre was more successful, and came near deciding the day

disastrously for Wolfe. Observing these troops yielding before the French marksmen, and fearing lest, as they fell back in their flight, they might force the main body into confusion, Wolfe hurried along the line, and, encouraging his men, bade them to hold back their fire, and not to move a step until ordered. He was none too soon; for the soldiers in the rear, having become conscious of the confused movement in front, were in a state of anxious excitement. Wolfe's presence, however, and his few inspiriting words, calmed them at once, and they again firmly stood their ground.

Now Montcalm, encouraged by the success of his skirmishers, bore down with his whole centre toward the English right wing. The French, as they halted, poured in a terrible fire. The British fell fast before it; and Wolfe himself, who was in the foremost van, was among the first to suffer. A shot wounded him in the wrist; but hastily wrapping a handkerchief around it, he continued to pass from rank to rank, exhorting each man not to fire. The troops, true to discipline, obeyed; and these "unknown demigods" coolly bore the murderous attack of the enemy without a waver, moving only to step over the dead bodies of their heroic comrades, into their empty ranks.

Wolfe waited until the enemy had reached within a distance of forty yards, and then ordered the whole line to fire. The effect was terrific. The French columns seemed to stagger as one body under the shock. Whole ranks fell in heaps together—leaving to the view, as the smoke cleared away, the scattered sol-

diers standing aghast here and there, and marking, like monumental stones, the places of the dead. Officers and men had suffered alike. St. Ours and De Zenczergnes were dead, and Montcalm himself severely wounded. The French veterans, a ghastly remnant, still stood their ground, but the Canadian militia had fled in fright. The victory was won, but the gallant Montcalm would not give up the fight. Though deserted by all the Canadians, and though his own faithful Frenchmen had been fearfully diminished in numbers, the general brought together the scattered remnant of his regulars, and cheered them on for another attack. They halted, and prepared to fire.

Wolfe at this moment ordered his line to advance, and the whole army moved forward and calmly returned the volley which just came from the enemy. The British soldiers, however, provoked by the resistance of the shattered French ranks, could no longer restrain themselves, and began, in spite of discipline, to run with an impetuous rush at the enemy, sweeping all before them. Wolfe was leading on the twenty-eighth and the Louisburg grenadiers, as with fixed bayonets they charged the steady French veterans (who, though falling fast, kept up an obstinate fire), when he was wounded a second time, in the body, but carefully concealed it. Again, as he bravely bore on in front, a ball from the enemy's redoubt struck him in the breast. Staggering with the shock, he quietly said to an officer by his side, "Support me, that my brave fellows may not see me fall." He, however, after an effort to rally his strength, sank im-

17

mediately into the arms of his friend, and with the aid of some soldiers was borne to a short distance in the rear.

Monckton was sent for, to take command; but he had been wounded, and could no longer do duty. Townshend was then summoned, and, coming up to the spot where his general lay in agony, cast a momentary glance of despair, and then hurried away, as chief, to complete the victory of the day. The French still gallantly resisted, for Montcalm was yet on the alert, and impetuously urging his troops to form and to fight. He was everywhere, riding about among them, and shouting out brave words of encouragement. His troops did continue to struggle manfully, but it was useless; the English, thronging up, drove all before them. Montcalm himself was now struck down, and his soldiers fled in dismay.

The dying Wolfe struggled against the agonies of death, with his mind still intent upon duty. As his strength weakened, he made a strong effort to bring back his departing vitality. With his hand he strove to brush away the web which Death was busily weaving before his eyes, and at the same moment succeeded in raising himself to a sitting posture. At this instant, an officer cried out, "See! see! how they run!"—"Who runs?" exclaimed Wolfe. "The enemy, sir; they give way everywhere," was the answer. "Go, then, one of you, to Burton, and tell him to march Webb's regiment to the bridge, and cut off the retreat," said the dying general, who to the last was mindful only of his duty. "Now, God be praised, I shall die happy!" he faintly uttered; and, turning over his body, shuddered with the last agony: his eyes closed; and the brave Wolfe lived only, but for ever, in memory.

The rout of the French was complete; the English pursuit fierce and pertinacious. The Highlanders, with their claymores, made a great havoc among the fugitives, some of whom begged piteously to be spared, as they had not been among those at Fort William Henry.* Many of the enemy made for the citadel, and were not safe until they had succeeded in getting within its walls. The British troops, in the ardor of the pursuit, were in a state of confusion; but Townshend, expecting the coming up of De Bougainville with his fresh force, took care to recall his disordered battalions, and draw them up in readiness for the still-unconquered portion of the enemy.

De Bougainville had hurried up with his fifteen hundred men; but, so rapid had been the defeat of Montcalm's troops, that he found none to co-operate with. So complete, moreover, had been the English victory, that De Bougainville's forces, although composed of the choicest of the French grenadiers and light-infantry, were so discouraged by the total rout of their countrymen, that they hardly dared to show an opposing front to the troops Townshend sent against them. Their advance was checked at once by a couple of regiments and two fieldpieces; and the French scarcely caught a glimpse of them, before they were off in a precipi-

* The conduct of the victorious French at Fort William Henry had been cruel, and the English burned to retaliate upon the enemy for their ferocity on that occasion.

tate retreat along the northern bank of the river, above Quebec. De Vaudreuil was still more in a hurry; and, as soon as he heard of Wolfe's success, he made off with his fifteen hundred Canadians, leaving behind him his artillery, ammunition, and all his stores. De Vaudreuil was conscience-stricken, and feared greatly lest he should fall into the hands of the English, who, as Walpole says, "were determined to scalp him, he having been the chief and blackest author of the cruelties exercised on our countrymen. Some of his letters were taken, in which he explicitly and basely said that 'peace was the best time for making war on the English!'"

The whole loss of the British on the plains of Abraham was only fifty-five killed and six hundred and seven wounded; while that of the French could not have been less than fifteen hundred in all.

The brave Montcalm, when he was wounded, was borne to the citadel; and when the surgeon began to examine his wound, he was asked by the general if it was mortal. Being told that it was, Montcalm calmly rejoined, "I am glad of it," and asked, "how long can I survive?" —"Perhaps a day, perhaps less," was the surgeon's answer. "So much the better; I shall not live to see the surrender of Quebec!" exclaimed the gallant Montcalm. He now prepared for death, and, when asked for his commands in regard to the citadel, he refused to give them, saying: "My time is very short, so pray leave me. I wish you all comfort, and to be happily extricated from your present perplexities." The priest was then summoned, who performed extreme unction, and remained by his side until he breathed his last. With his dying words he paid this tribute to his foe: "Since it was my misfortune to be discomfited and mortally wounded, it is a great consolation to be vanquished by so great and generous an enemy. If I could survive this wound, I would engage to beat three times the number of such forces as I commanded, with a third of their number of British troops."

De Vaudreuil, on reaching Cape Rouge, where he had retreated and joined his forces to those of De Bougainville, grandiloquently expressed the opinion to the assembled officers, that "they should take their revenge on the morrow, and endeavor to wipe off the disgraces of the day." The council, however, more discreetly resolved upon continuing the retreat, and De Vaudreuil himself was not backward in giving in his adhesion to the prudent resolve. They retired to Point aux Trembles, where they were soon joined by De Levi and his troops from Montreal, whence he had commenced his march as soon as he heard of Montcalm's defeat. After this junction there was a momentary feeling of hope, and the generals wrote to Ramsay, in command of the garrison at Quebec: "We exhort you by all means to hold out to the last extremity. On the 18th [September] the whole army shall be in motion. A disposition is made to throw in a large supply of provisions, and to relieve the town." It was too late: Quebec was surrendered on the very morning (September 18, 1759) that De

Vaudreuil's messenger reached the gates of the citadel.

The joyful news of Wolfe's great victory was received in England with a universal acclamation of delight. " You may now give yourself," writes Walpole to the British embassador at the Hague (Sir H. Mann), " what airs you please ; you are master of East and West Indies..... It was a very singular affair, the generals on both sides slain, and on both sides the second in command wounded—in short, very near what battles should be, in which only the principals ought to suffer. If their army has not ammunition and spirit enough to fall again upon ours before Amherst comes up, all North America is ours!.... What a scene! an army in the night dragging itself up a precipice by stumps of trees, to assault a town and attack an army strongly intrenched and double in numbers. Adieu! I think I shall not write to you again this twelvemonth; for, like Alexander, we have ño more worlds left to conquer."

Pitt, the great minister, in the affluence of his glowing rhetoric, spoke to the British senate of " the horror of the night; the precipice scaled by Wolfe; the empire he with a handful of men added to England; and the glorious catastrophe of contentedly terminating life where his fame began.... Ancient story may be ransacked, and ostentatious philosophy thrown into the account, before an episode can be found to rank with Wolfe's!" These eloquent words of Pitt prefaced his motion that a monument should be erected in Westminster Abbey to the memory of the hero. The British people,

pious, grateful, and exultant, joined in public thanksgiving to God for the victory; bestowed, through their representatives in Parliament, a liberal largess upon Wolfe's family; and raised with one voice, throughout England's wide dominions, a burst of triumph on a day set apart for holyday rejoicing. In Westminster Abbey, sculptured art and classic learning record the gratitude and sorrow of Great Britain. A tall column of stone rises above the heights of Quebec, to testify to the taste and feeling of a noble Englishman. A small stone, planted on the plains of Abraham, tells the traveller that " HERE WOLFE DIED VICTORIOUS." But the memory of Wolfe requires neither sculptured art, nor lofty column, nor tablet of stone: it is fixed for ever in the hearts of all who love the good and the brave.

" Who the deuce was thinking of Quebec?" asks Walpole. " America was like a book one had read and done with, or, at least, if we looked at the book, one just recollected that there was a supplement promised, to contain a chapter on Montreal, the starving and surrender of it; but here we are on a sudden reading our book backward. An account came two days ago" (Walpole is writing on the 20th June), " that the French, on their march to besiege Quebec, had been attacked by General Murray, who got into a mistake and a morass, attacked two bodies that were joined when he hoped to come up with one of them before he was enclosed, embogged, and defeated." The gossiping Walpole thus tells the whole story in a pleasant way. All we have to add is,

1760. that Murray, who had been left in command, did foolishly march out with his small force against De Levi's troops, ten thousand strong, and was beaten back within the walls of Quebec, which would probably have fallen, had not a British fleet arrived, sailed up the St. Lawrence, and driven away the French besiegers encamped upon its banks.

General Amherst (now Sir Jeffrey Amherst), calm, cautious, and slow, had moved too deliberately to satisfy the impulsive spirit of Wolfe. He had, however—in time to complete the conquest of Canada—succeeded in concentrating his large force of over ten thousand men, including the provincials under Gage and the Indians led by Sir William Johnson, on the shores of Lake Ontario, from the waters of which two British ships had driven the French cruisers, and forced them to seek refuge in the intricate and labyrinthine channels of the "Thousand Isles."

On the 7th of August, the grenadiers and light-troops, including a battalion of Highlanders, were sent forward, to post themselves at the end of the lake, where the St. Lawrence receives its waters. On the 10th, Amherst in person followed, with the remainder of the regulars and the Indians; but the lagging Gage did not come up with his provincials until the 12th, when the whole army was gathered at La Galette, on the banks of the St. Lawrence.

Embarked once more, the whole force dropped down the river to Isle Royale, capturing on their way a French cruiser, which was spiritedly attacked by some soldiers in the whale-boats, and gallantly carried. Fort Levi, on the island, was still in possession of the enemy, and, though invested by Amherst's immense force, with all the reg- **Aug. 23** ularities of a siege, and a severe cannonade opened, was so spiritedly defended by its little garrison, that one of the British vessels was obliged to strike her colors. Amherst, checked by this unexpected vigor on the part of the French, put off the assault until the next day. In the meantime, the French commandant, finding that it was impossible to hold out long against the overwhelming force of his assailants, surrendered at discretion.

When the fort was given up, Johnson's Indians, who had been thirsting to wreak their vengeance upon the Frenchmen, would have begun their cruel work, had not Amherst, with a noble humanity, interposed. He immediately gave orders to Sir William to deter the savages, if possible, from their purpose, promising them all the stores found in the fort; but warning them, at the same time, that if they persisted, he would restrain them by force. The Indians, in sullen submission, returned to their camp, but fiercely resented the interference; and Sir William Johnson informed the general that they would probably quit the army. Amherst answered: "Although I wish to retain their friendship, I will not purchase it at the expense of countenancing barbarity; and tell them that, if they commit any acts of cruelty on their return home from the army, I will assuredly chastise them."[*] The Indians left him, but the humane

* Warburton.

Amherst won a triumph worth more than hundreds of bloody victories.

Levelling the captured works on Isle Royale, the troops descended the stream, and entered the turbulent and dangerous passage of the Cedars. As the heavily-laden boats got among the broken rocks and boiling eddies, they were so crowded and tossed together, that some were swamped, and others dashed to pieces. Sixty-four, laden with artillery and stores, were in this manner lost, and eighty men drowned.

Sept. 6. On landing upon the island of Montreal, the French retired within the walls of the city, and Amherst invested the place. Murray in the meantime had sailed from Quebec, with all the disposable force which could be spared, and joined Amherst on the 7th of September, with twenty-four hundred and fifty of the conquerors of Quebec. Colonel Haviland, who had come from Crown Point, arrived the next day with another body of troops, and now upon the island of Montreal were gathered sixteen thousand British. The marquis de Vaudreuil, who had fled to Montreal after Wolfe's conquest of Quebec, now gave up all in despair, and signed a **Sept. 8.** capitulation, by which all Canada was lost to France for ever.

After long negotiations, protracted by the expansive demands of the imperious Pitt, the war between Great Britain and France ceased with the treaty of peace at Paris, in 1763. The **Feb. 10.** French ministry yielded with reluctance; and the proud Choiseul, who resigned his place, asked, despairingly: "But what can we do? The English are furiously imperious; they are drunk with success; and, unfortunately, we are not in a condition to abase their pride."

END OF PART I.

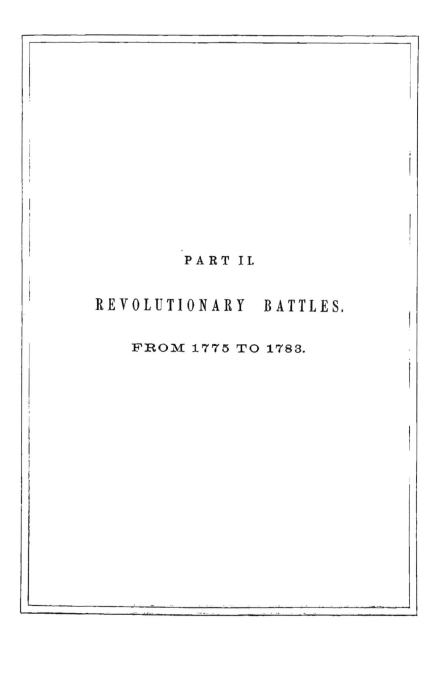

PART II.

REVOLUTIONARY BATTLES.

FROM 1775 TO 1783.

PART II.

BATTLES OF THE REVOLUTION.

CHAPTER I.

1774. "THEY say you have no right to tax them without their consent. They say truly. Representation and taxation must go together: they are inseparable."* This was the American cause: *Representation and taxation must go together* —a cause which the colonists, almost with one voice, had now determined to seal with their blood. British Tyranny resolved to force submission. American Liberty determined to oppose resistance. The struggle began. Battles were fought, and continued to be fought, until independence was won. These it is our purpose to record, to which we shall proceed now without further preface.

General Thomas Gage, having been appointed captain-general and governor of Massachusetts, was now at Boston, in command of the British troops; while English men-of-war floated threateningly in the harbor. He had been selected by the government of Great Britain to en-

force, by threats if possible, by violence if necessary, the obedience of New England to the tyrannical edicts of the mother-country. The people of Massachusetts had been the first—although the other colonies showed the same spirit of independence—to resist, by overt act, the tyrannical exercise of British authority. They, in common with the rest of the people of the provinces, had contented themselves with opposing, by petition and protest, the stamp-act; and, on its repeal, only exhibited their spirit of independence by a burst of joy. The exultation of these lovers of liberty was, however, soon vexed into the excitement of passionate resistance by other tyrannical acts of Great Britain. The colonists now, almost with one voice, determined upon retaliation. They would punish the mother-country by not consuming her products, and thus weaken her strength by diminishing her revenue. Great Britain, in spite of her suffering trade and

* Earl Chatham's speech in the house of lords.

18

commerce, and the urgent appeals of her men of business to change her odious colonial policy, madly persisted, and strove to compel where she had failed to persuade.

An effort was made to force upon the colonies the consumption of tea. A cargo arrived at Boston. A "tea-party" was formed, composed of fifty men—"very dark-complexioned persons, dressed like Mohawks, of very grotesque appearance." With an Indian whoop, these Bostonians —and "solid men" they were—rushed to the wharf, boarded the ships, and in the course of two hours threw into the river three hundred and forty-two chests of tea. This was no impulsive act of riot, but the deliberate proceeding of men of determined character, appointed to carry out the calm resolutions of their fellow-townsmen.

The tea-proceeding, when heard of in England, was received with applause by the friends of liberty, and with indignation by the government and its favorites. Tyranny now suggested an act of oppression as a punishment for those who had dared to disobey its caprices. It was readily acceded to, with the object of reducing the people of Boston to "starvation"—a word then first coined, in the British Parliament, by a tory member, whose inveteracy of hate could find no expression in the English language sufficiently strong to bear the impress of his cruel purpose. The punishment of Boston came in the form of the "Boston port-bill," the object of which was to deprive the refractory town of its privileges and rights as a place of commerce. Gage

and his British soldiers were now on the spot to carry that bill into execution.

Gage had proved himself a gallant soldier in the unfortunate campaign of Braddock; but he was nothing else than a soldier, with all the decided sentiments in favor of absolute authority engendered by a long military life. He was, moreover, a thorough aristocrat in feeling, and a tory by political association. He did not understand what "the mob" (as he called the people), as long as they had enough work, and could eat and drink abundantly, had to do with political principles. Their whole public duty, he believed, was obedience. To govern, or even to say who was to govern, was not their vocation. Gage, however, should have learned something of the character of the American colonists. He had been a good deal among them, and had married a native lady of New York. But, nevertheless, he did not understand them, and seemed as unconscious as the khan of Tartary of the devotion of Americans to liberty, and of their resolute firmness to defend it against any oppressor. His associations in the colonies were too much with the loyalists, who were always fawning about royal governors, and whispering into their ears what would flatteringly exaggerate the self-importance of the dignitary, and contemptuously depreciate "the rabble." In New York he had found among his kindred, and the pretentious aristocracy of its tory society, a more obsequious courtiership than ever licked royal hands at the court of St. James. He was now in Puritan New England; and while among his own suite, and surrounded by a few exceptional Massachusetts tories, he did not seem to be conscious of the difference in his position. He took no account of the great body of the Puritan people, who had learned from their ancestors, under the orders of Cromwell, and the teachings of Milton, those principles of liberty which they carried with them to America, and taught their children not only to venerate, but to guard, at all hazards of life or fortune, against the oppressor.

It was claimed for Gage that he was a man naturally frank, and of a gay, social disposition. This he may have been, among those he considered his "equals," but to his "inferiors" he was haughty and arrogant. He was, in fact, in everything except capacity, a perfect instrument to compel "a full and absolute submission" to the tyrannical acts of his masters. With his British troops to back him, he did not hesitate at fulfilling the most cruel purpose of despotism.

Gage, in common with most British officers and many British statesmen, held the colonial opposition in great contempt. The American leaders were, in his opinion, without capacity, their followers without courage. While he thus increased the hostility against him, he diminished his power of resistance. Gage never justly appreciated the sentiments or rightly measured the strength of his enemies.* While the Americans declared—"No danger shall affright, no difficulties shall intimidate us; and if, in support of our

* "General Gage, in his private letters, encouraged the ministers to be firm, and that if they would be so, they would prevail."—WALPOLE.

rights, we are called to encounter even death, we are yet undaunted, sensible that he can never die too soon who lays down his life in support of the laws and liberties of his country"—Gage called the authors of these heroic resolves "a despicable rabble," and undertook to keep them quiet with five regiments, saying, "The Americans will be lions only as long as the English are lambs!" So, too, a Colonel Grant, who until then was only known in America by his folly—which had nearly ruined the expedition under Forbes against Fort Du Quesne—now, with the attempted wisdom of a counselor, declared that the Americans were cowards. "With five regiments," said this braggadocio to the assembled Parliament of England, "I could march through all America." Truth, however, was bursting from the eloquent lips of Lord Chatham almost at the same moment and within the same walls: "My lords," said the great orator, "there are three millions of whigs. Three millions of whigs, my lords, with arms in their hands, are a very formidable body." But English Tyranny closed its ears and eyes to truth, and rushed recklessly on to destruction. The king said loudly, and with a scornful laugh, that "he had as lief fight the Bostonians as the French."—"Corruption," wrote Walpole in England, "smiled, and was not afraid of swords at such a distance."

On the first day of the operation of the "Boston port-bill," the people contented themselves with signifying their affliction at this invasion of their 1774. rights by tolling their church-bells, by fasting and prayer, and by hanging their houses and public buildings with crape. It was not until those further acts of the British Parliament—which virtually destroyed the charter of Massachusetts—deprived the people of the right of public meetings, thus cutting away the scaffolding of English freedom, and interfered with the trial by jury, that an armed resistance was determined upon. A meeting was held at Faneuil hall, composed of delegates from various parts of Massachusetts. It was by them resolved that "a provincial Congress is necessary to counteract the systems of despotism, and that, as a necessary means to secure the rights of the people, the military art ought to be attentively practised." A provincial Congress was accordingly held; the militia mustered, and, arming themselves, prepared for resistance.

August.

Gage, not satisfied with dissolving meetings at Boston with his soldiers, seized the artillery and ammunition which belonged to the city, and thus greatly excited the indignation of the townspeople. The seizure of the powder was magnified, by the excited imaginations of the Massachusetts men, into a cannonade of Boston; and the neighboring colonists began to ring their alarm-bells, light up the beacon-fires, and hurry in armed crowds to the scene of the supposed danger. Gage himself became anxious, and wrote to the government at home that "the flames of sedition had spread universally throughout the country, beyond conception;" that "civil government was near its end;" and that "the time for conciliation, modera-

tion, reasoning, was over." Nothing now, he believed, could be done but by force, and this he resolved upon using. "The torrent should be stemmed, not yielded to."[*] The Massachusetts people were, in their turn, making preparations for the struggle, by disciplining their militia, and collecting together their arms and ammunition.

Gage, strengthened by additional troops, had fortified Boston neck, and turned the city into a camp, where his four thousand men stacked their guns in Faneuil hall, and converted the churches into mess-rooms. He now decided upon a movement, by which he hoped to overwhelm the Massachusetts men, and put an end to their means of mischief. His plan was, to take the colonists by surprise, and destroy their magazine of arms and ammunition at Concord, some eighteen miles from Boston. Gage employed every possible means to keep his purpose secret. He sent out his officers in disguise to make sketches, and to bring back reports of the position of Concord, its strength, and the various approaches to the place. He also determined, in order to further conceal his design, to make the attack under the cover of the night.

1775.

The patriots were vigilant, and became conscious of Gage's movements. They accordingly strengthened their guard at Concord, and removed some of their stores secretly to other places. Gage continued

[*] Gage was, however, seemingly not without some sense of discretion, for Walpole records: "It was said, on General Gage receiving orders to seize and send over hither the chief patriots, he had for answer that, should he attempt to do any such thing, that would be the last letter they would ever receive from him, for he should be knocked on the head."

his preparations, but each act of his was watched closely by the alert patriots; and, seeing the boats one night launched and moored under the sterns of the British men-of-war, took care to send intelligence of the fact to Concord. A few days after, some English officers were sent out on the roads leading from Boston, to prevent any messengers going out to carry information of the proposed expedition.

April 15.

The night finally arrived. When eleven o'clock struck, some nine hundred of the choicest of the British troops, under the command of Lieutenant-Colonel Smith, embarked in small boats at the foot of Boston common, and, landing near Lechmere point, began their silent march to Concord.

April 18.

The patriots, however, were on the alert. Warren, the Boston physician — whose whole soul was in the cause, and who was one of the most active members of the committee of safety — had already sent messengers to his friends at Concord; and when the British embarked, he ordered the lantern, which was agreed upon as the signal, to be hoisted from the steeple of the North church in Boston. Gage, much to his surprise, discovered that his secret was known. Having communicated his design in the evening to Lord Percy, that officer retired, and was on his way to his quarters, when, crossing the common, he fell in with a group of citizens in earnest conversation, in the course of which one was heard to say, "The British troops have marched, but will miss their aim!" — "What aim?" asked his lordship. "Why, the cannon

at Concord," was the answer. Percy returned at once to Gage, and told what he had heard, when orders were immediately issued that no person should be allowed to leave the town. It was, however, too late: the vigilant Warren had already despatched a couple of messengers, and given orders for the hoisting of the warning lantern.

The whole country was aroused. The town of Lexington, through which the road to Concord passed, was especially on the alert; and its minute-men, to the number of about a hundred and thirty, turned out in the middle of the night, and were assembled together on the common until two o'clock in the morning, with their guns "loaded with powder and ball." At this time a messenger returned, with the word that no troops had yet shown themselves on the road. Accordingly, as the morning was chilly, the men were dismissed to a neighboring tavern, with orders to make their appearance on the first sound of the drum. The two messengers, who had been sent on to give Concord the alarm, were met by a party of British officers, when a scuffle ensued, and one of the patriots was taken prisoner; while the other succeeded in escaping by leaping a stone-wall, and, running off, made his way to the place where Hancock and Samuel Adams had temporarily concealed themselves.

These two, Hancock and Adams, both men of distinction in Boston, had early made themselves conspicuous as earnest friends of the popular cause; and, as their safety was regarded as of the utmost importance, they were induced to hide themselves from observation, lest they should be taken prisoners by the British. Dorothea Quincy, Hancock's betrothed, insisted upon accompanying them, and she was now with the two patriots; and the three were sitting down to an "elegant dinner" at the house of a friend, when suddenly a man broke in upon them with a shriek, and the alarm was given that the regulars were upon them. Hancock and Adams were then led along a cartway to another and more humble house, where they were glad to make up for their lost spread of good things, by a dish of "salt pork and potatoes."

In the meantime, the British troops, under Lieutenant-Colonel Smith, were fast approaching. The route they had taken led them through a morass, into which the men plunged waist-deep until they reached the high-road to Charlestown. Their midnight march was cautious and stealthy; not a drum was allowed to beat, nor a fife to sound. Some members of the provincial Congress, stopping at a roadside inn, where they had been holding a "rebel" conclave, aware of the approach of the troops, were up, and silently watching the soldiers as they came on. The front ranks passed by steadily, but with measured tread. The centre, however, no sooner reached a point opposite to the tavern, than there was a halt; and, directly, an officer and a file of men were seen advancing to the house. But the "rebels" were too quick for them; and, while the soldiers were ransacking the tavern, those of whom they were in search were in a field hard by, securely hid from their pursuers.

The British commander soon discovered that all the precautions which had been taken to keep the expedition a secret had failed. Although it was night, the whole country was aroused. Every church was ringing its bells, beacon-fires were blazing, and signal-guns firing. The British officers who had been on the road, on a tour of observation, now joined the troops, and reported that at least five hundred of the "rebels" were in arms, in readiness for the attack. Smith sent Major Pitcairn forward with six companies of light-infantry, to secure the bridges at Concord; and an orderly back to Gage, at Boston, for a reinforcement. Pitcairn pressed on hurriedly, only stopping on the road to capture any straggler he could pick up. One man, however, was too much on the alert to be caught; for, getting a glimpse of the British coming up the road, he turned his horse, and, laying on his whip, galloped into Lexington, with the news that the "red-coats" were at hand.

Captain Parker ordered his drums to beat, and alarm-guns to be fired immediately; and soon the minute-men began to turn out and to muster on the ground about the meetinghouse. These men formed a part of that resolute band— "the constitutional army"—which had been authorized to make a forcible and regular resistance to any hostility by the British soldiery; and there they were ready to do their country's bidding. Before they had fairly mustered and formed, the British were in sight, at a short distance from the ground.

Pitcairn, seeing the assemblage, and

hearing the drums of the patriots, halted his troops and ordered them to load. He then brought them on in double quick time. Some sixty or seventy only of the minute-men had mustered and found time to present an orderly rank in front, when the regulars rushed forward, shouting, with their commander at their head, waving his sword, and crying out: "Ye villains! ye rebels! disperse! Lay down your arms! Why don't you lay down your arms?" Two or three shots were now fired, but without effect. Then ensued a general volley, by which some of the minute-men were killed and wounded. Their fellow-patriots now no longer withheld their fire, which they had hitherto done in obedience to the command of Parker, their captain. Their shots, however, were straggling, and did little damage, only wounding two of the privates and the horse of the British major. The regulars fired with much greater effect, killing eight, wounding ten, and putting the rest to flight. One daring fellow, who had always said "he never would run from the British," though wounded, stood his ground, and, while loading his piece, was thrust through and through by a bayonet, and died on the spot where he had so firmly planted himself. Another was pursued to the road facing the common, and was struck down by a shot within view of his own house. The blood was gushing from his breast, but he started up, and stretching out his hands toward his wife, who was at the window, staggered a moment, and fell again. Striving once more to stand, he could only succeed in raising himself upon his hands and knees, and thus crawled toward the door of his dwelling. His wife was there to meet him, but only to see him dying at her feet.

The British now formed on the common, and, exulting in their "victory," fired a *feu-de-joie*, gave three loud huzzas, and marched on toward Concord. There were two thoughtful observers of this Lexington affair, in a house near by, who could have told the British that this was no time for exultation. They knew, with the foresight of wisdom, that no defeat ever suffered by English troops, was so disastrous as this "victory." Samuel Adams and John Hancock saw, in the blood which flowed at Lexington, that which was to cement the colonies into an indissoluble union, and thus secure a foundation upon which to establish the great hope of their patriotic hearts—the independence of America. "Oh, what a glorious morning is this!" exclaimed Adams, as he walked abroad; for, although his countrymen were falling, and he and his companion were driven from home and fortune by the cruelty of tyrants, he saw that that morning would be "glorious" for all time, as the first gleam of the perpetual light of American liberty.

The provincials, though put to flight, did not lose heart. Some retreated along the road, but the most gathered again on a height to the north of the Lexington common, formed readily under their leader, and eagerly awaited his orders to go when and where their country required their services. The British, once again on the road to Concord, were joined by the rest of the troops, under their colonel.

Concord, as it appeared in those days, was a town covering considerable space, between two hills which completely commanded it. It had its church, jail, and courthouse; and its dwellings, though not very numerous, were scattered over a large expanse of ground. Through the town winds sluggishly the Concord river, which was crossed by two bridges, the north and the south, as they were called. The British had determined to possess themselves of these bridges, so that they might cut off all approach to the town, while they should be engaged in destroying the magazines and military stores there collected and guarded by the provincials.

The town, however, was on the alert. The people had been timely warned, and, when they heard of the skirmish at Lexington, were roused to fierce indignation. The militia were for marching immediately to meet the British on the road, and they accordingly started; but, on discovering that the numbers of the enemy amounted to treble their own force, they fell back and took up their position on a high ground which rises to the north, not far from the centre of the town. There they stood, around the liberty-pole lately raised, and awaited the approach of those who came as determined enemies to that freedom of which it was the emblem.

Concord was but six miles distant from Lexington; and it was still early when the British troops came marching in, with **April 19.** drums beating, flags flying, and with the light of the morning sun reflected glitteringly upon their polished guns and gilded accoutrements.

Many of the militia were for giving fight at once; but their commander, Colonel Barrett, checked their reckless enthusiasm, and prudently withdrew his men when the enemy were seen advancing, within a quarter of a mile. Barrett conducted his force along the road which led to the north bridge, and, having crossed the Concord river, drew them up on the high ground about a mile from the centre of the town.

On the British now coming up, one division posted itself on the hill just left by the provincials, and the rest of the troops continued their march along the main road until they reached the centre of the town. The enemy now began their work. Two hundred men were detached to hold the north bridge, and prevent the advance of the militia; another party took possession of the south bridge. The rest of the troops were occupied in carrying out the especial object of their visit. Some were sent to the house of Barrett, the militia-colonel, on the outskirts of the town, to destroy the military stores concealed there. The remainder went about their work of destruction in the town itself. Threescore or less of barrels of flour were staved in, three cannon were spiked and otherwise maltreated, some sixteen carriage-wheels were burnt to cinders, three or four barrelsful of wooden spoons reduced to ashes, the liberty-pole felled, the courthouse set on fire, but put out by a woman with a pail of water, and half a thousand iron balls rolled into the river. "These," says Gordon, "were all the stores they could discover and destroy; on the account of

which a civil war has commenced between the colonies and the parent-state. The inhabitants of Britain may see reason, for many ages, to curse the memory of the man or men who has or have been at the foundation of this fatal catastrophe, should they ever be known." While the British troops were thus occupied for a couple of hours, the provincials were not less busy.

The neighboring towns and country, fully alive to the doings of the English soldiery, began to send in their "minutemen," as the militia were called, until the force of patriots on the hill numbered nearly five hundred. These, in addition to the Lexington people, were composed of men from Carlisle, Chelmsford, Westford, Littleton, and Acton. They were farmers, tradesmen, mechanics, from sixteen years of age to sixty, who came in with their guns with which they had often followed the Indian, the bear, and the wolf; and many of them were dressed in the homespun suits which had been woven at their own winter firesides. Even the clergy presented themselves, and, although debarred by their calling from active hostilities, did what they could in giving advice to the men, and quieting the alarms of the women and children.

The militia-officers joined in council, when it was proposed to dislodge the enemy from the north bridge. One ardent captain declared that he "hadn't a man that was afraid to go." The British soldiers could be easily seen, and their doings were watched with painful anxiety. As the fires began to blaze, and it was observed that the meetinghouse had already caught, the people began to fear for their town and their homes. The militia were eager to rush to their rescue; and accordingly, without more ado, Colonel Barrett ordered his men to the north bridge, and to strive to pass it, but not to fire a shot unless they were first attacked. In double file, and with trailed arms, the detachment moved on.

The British on the bridge, observing the advance of the provincials, retired to the east side of the river, and began to remove the planks. The American major in command of the militia, as he approached, cried out to the enemy to stop doing what he claimed they had no right to do, and hurried on his men to prevent it. When the provincials had reached within a few feet of the bridge, the British troops began to fire, but with no effect, as but few guns were let off, and with no fixed aim. A second and fuller volley succeeded, and with a different result, killing two of the provincials and wounding a third. Their captain now cried out, "Fire, fellow-soldiers! for God's sake, fire!" when his men, true to the word, did fire, and brought down a number of the enemy. The British then fled, and the provincials after them, when a thoughtless lad, coming up with a wounded grenadier, struck him on the head and dashed out his brains.

The provincials did not continue their pursuit far; but, dividing, one party went back with their dead and wounded, while the rest proceeded on the road and took up their position on a height which overlooked it. Smith, the British colonel, now gathered together his force, and pre-

19

pared to return to Boston, but lingered at Concord nearly two hours before he commenced his march. This delay nearly proved the total destruction of his whole force.

All the country round was now in a state of great excitement, and every man was eager to rush to the rescue of the patriot cause. Each village was alive with preparation. All the inhabitants turned out, and there was hardly a man under seventy and above sixteen years of age who did not shoulder his musket and present himself for parade on the church green. Thence, after a blessing from their pastor, they were marched off to the scene of action. Although the most were fresh from their farms and shops, and knew little of military discipline but what they had learned in an occasional militia muster, there were among them some gray-headed veterans who had fought at Louisburg and Quebec. They were all, however, more or less familiar with the use of firearms, and had become practised shots in pursuit of the game which abounded in the yet uncleared forest-wilds. With a sober determination to make the cause of their country a holy one, each man dwelt with pertinacious conscientiousness upon the fact that "the regulars had fired the first." The blow having been given, they all prepared to return it. None now talked of forbearance or peace. Every voice was urgent for war.

It was mid-day before the British colonel began his march, and he was soon convinced of and greatly startled by the hubbub he had created throughout the country. So full were the roads and hillsides of the armed provincials, that it appeared to the British as if "men had dropped from the clouds." Smith threw out a flank-guard on the side of the main road, to protect his march; but in the woods, on each hill, and behind every wall, there were gathered the vigilant provincials, who with a sure aim were bringing down a British soldier at every step. The enemy suffered terribly as they advanced for miles between two fires, which were incessant from both sides of the road. The British quickened their march almost to a run, but this only served to hasten their death, as they offered themselves more rapidly to the successive shots of the American marksmen. Smith, the British colonel, was severely wounded; and another officer, on a fine blood-horse, while brandishing his sword and urging on his men, was killed by a shot from behind a rail-fence. As his rider fell dead, the horse ran in his fright toward the fence, leaped it, and joined the provincials. Just as the troops were hastening into Lexington, one of the British soldiers lagged behind, and, falling in with a militia-man, levelled his musket and cried out, "You're a dead man!"—"So are you!" was the answer. Both fired at the same instant, and both were killed.

The British troops, thus constantly galled by this incessant and most fatal fire along the road, began to lose all self-command, and, as they approached Lexington, became so confused and disordered by their suffering and despair, that they would have fled precipitately, had not their officers placed themselves in front, and threatened the men with instant death if they moved without orders. At this moment a welcome relief presented itself, in a reinforcement from Boston.

CHAPTER II.

Lord Percy to the Rescue.—Dancing to "Chevy Chase."—His Lordship's Arrival at Lexington.—General Heath arrives and takes Command of the Provincials.—Doctor Warren on the Alert.—The British retreat to Boston.—The Slaughter on the Route.—The British arrive at Charlestown.—The Panic in the Town.—Arrival at Boston.—The Killed and Wounded.—The General Excitement.—Meeting of the Provincial Council.—Their Remonstrance.—General Artemas Ward appointed Commander-in-Chief.—The Whole Country aroused.—Israel Putnam.—Benedict Arnold.—American Troops called out.—Cambridge made Headquarters.—A Second Continental Congress.—Washington's Reflections on the Lexington Affair.—Canada.—Ticonderoga and Crown Point.—Action of Connecticut.—Ethan Allen and the Green-Mountain Boys.—Expedition to Ticonderoga.—Arnold volunteers.—Fall of Ticonderoga.—Skeensborough.—The Meeting of the Continental Congress.—Washington chosen Commander-in-Chief.—The Army organized.

1775. GENERAL GAGE, having received Colonel Smith's request for a reinforcement, sent to his relief nine hundred men and two pieces of artillery, under the command of Lord Percy, "a penurious,* undignified young man," as Walpole called him. At nine o'clock in the morning, **April 19.** this detachment marched out of Boston, the bands "playing, by

---

* "When Lord Percy was in Ireland with his regiment, the fifth infantry, he consented, after much consideration, to give a dinner to the officers in garrison at Limerick. The gallant but cautious earl ordered the repast at a tavern, specifying that it should be for fifty persons, at eighteen pence per head. The officers heard of the arrangement, and they ordered the landlord to provide a banquet at a guinea per head, promising to pay the difference in the event of their entertainer declining to do so. When the banquet was served, there was but one astonished and uncomfortable individual at the board, and that was the earl himself, who beheld a feast fit for the gods, and heard himself gratefully complimented upon the excellence of both viands and wines. The astonished earl experienced an easily-understood difficulty in returning thanks when his health was drunk with an enthusiasm that bewildered him ; and, on retiring, early sought out the landlord, in order to have the solution of an enigma that sorely puzzled him. Boniface told the unadorned and unwelcome truth ; and the inexperienced young earl acknowledged his mistake, and discharged the bill with a sigh on himself and a check on his banker." — DORAN, "Table-Traits, and Something on Them."

way of contempt, 'Yankee Doodle,' a song composed in derision of the New-Englanders, scornfully called Yankees." A "smart" boy, observing it as the troops passed through Roxbury, made himself extremely merry with the circumstance, jumping and laughing so as to attract the notice of his lordship, who, it is said, asked him at what he was laughing so heartily ; and was answered, "To think how you will dance, by-and-by, to Chevy Chase !" It is added that the repartee stuck by his lordship the whole day.*

Percy suffered but little annoyance on his march to the relief of Smith and his men. At Charlestown he found the bridge taken up, but, as the planks were discovered near by, they were readily replaced ; and he marched on without difficulty un-

---

* Gordon's History of the American Revolution. The allusion to Chevy Chase will be understood by the reader, if he calls to mind that a Lord Percy is the hero of that old ballad. The Lord Percy spoken of in the text is the one afterward duke of Northumberland, of whom Halleck writes :

——" who, when a younger son,
Fought for King George at Lexington,
    A major of dragoons."

til he reached Lexington, where he found the retreating force "so much exhausted with fatigue, that they were obliged to lie down for rest on the ground, their tongues hanging out of their mouths, like those of dogs after a chase." Percy, bringing his fieldpieces to bear from a commanding position upon the provincials (who were hanging upon his troops, prepared to gall them with their shots whenever they took up their march), there was a brief cessation of hostility.

The friends of the patriot cause had, in the meantime, been busy in Boston. General Heath, who had been authorized by the provincial Congress to take command of the minute-men whenever called out, now hurried to the scene of action; having in his route given orders suitable to the emergency, and directed the Charlestown people to form a barricade of the planks of their bridge, and there post themselves to oppose the British as they returned to Boston. When he arrived at Lexington, Heath took command of the provincials, and strove to form them in military order. Warren, too, the patriotic physician of Boston, was active in cheering and advising his countrymen, as he rode forward to meet the British. "Keep up a brave heart," he said to one. "They have begun it— that either party could do; and we'll end it—that only one can do." To another, who exclaimed, "Well, they are gone out," he answered, "Yes, and we'll be up with them before night!"—"His soul," as it was justly said, "beat to arms as soon as he learned the intention of the British troops."

Percy did not halt long, as he found the provincials gathering so fast, and so bent upon resisting him to their utmost. He had now over eighteen hundred well-disciplined men under arms; but he had evidently determined upon no act of hostility, beyond what might be necessary to protect his retreat to Boston. So, after proper refreshment of his men, and placing the harassed force of Colonel Smith as far as possible under the cover of his fresher troops, he began his retreat. The British, however, no sooner began to move, than the Americans renewed their harassing attacks. The soldiers, in spite of the efforts at restraint of Lord Percy, were excited to such a pitch of uncontrollable rage, that they began to retaliate by acts of devastation and cruelty. They rushed into the houses and murdered the sick, the helpless, and even mothers with their babes at the breast! They drove the inhabitants away at the point of the bayonet, and burned their dwellings. But the provincials, nothing daunted, kept up their harassing fire, and did not hesitate to come out in throngs upon the road and skirmish with the regulars. Fierce slaughter raged on both sides. The British fell fast, and Lord Percy himself nearly lost his life from a musket-ball which shot off a button from his coat. The provincials, too, suffered greatly, but continued to hang on the rear of the British troops, and harass them with their sharp-shooting. Harris and Warren were constantly cheering on the men, and bravely taking the lead in every struggle. Warren barely escaped with his life, a musket-shot having struck his hair, and driven out the pin by which it was gathered behind his ears.

When the British troops were about entering Charlestown, and had reached the base of Prospect hill, the attack of the provincials became terribly severe; but Percy, after playing his fieldpieces with effect, hurried on his men to a run, until they reached Charlestown neck, and were protected by the guns of the men-of-war. Charlestown had been the whole day in a state of great excitement. The schools had been dismissed; the men had marched to the relief of their fellow-patriots; the shops had been closed; and the old and feeble, the women and children, huddled together in anxious groups in the houses, or gathered in knots about the streets, discussed with alarm the terrible events of the day. Now that the enemy were returning, a general panic ensued, and the people scattered in all directions, crying out, "The British are coming, with fire and slaughter!" Lord Percy had his troops under sufficient control during his march through Charlestown to keep them from doing much mischief, and the inhabitants were accordingly more frightened than hurt. None were harmed, and all the troops insisted upon was "something to drink." The main body of the British occupied Bunker's hill, and the rest entered Boston, perfectly worn down with fatigue. The officers immediately thronged the tavern in the square, and called upon "mine host" for supper and wine; while the men were ordered to their quarters, to sleep off the effects of their hard day's work. General Gage strengthened the guards throughout the city, and, posting a party at the neck, ordered them to allow no one to leave Boston that night.

The whole loss of the Americans was computed at forty-nine killed, thirty-nine wounded, and five missing, with a destruction of property amounting to about three thousand pounds. The British had seventy-three killed, one hundred and seventy-four wounded, and twenty-seven missing. Among these were no less than eighteen officers. In the record of battles, the affairs of Concord and Lexington rank merely as skirmishes. In the history of America, they are the great events which began the War of the Revolution. Gage and his chief officers, now aware of the evil consequences of the rash attack which had been made upon the provincials, affected great indignation at the conduct of Pitcairn, in his charge upon the militia at Lexington. Startled as they were, they might well be solicitous about incurring the responsibility of an act which had inflamed the indignation of the whole country, and which, in the foresight of the wise, was the commencement of a revolution which was destined to tear from the crown of Great Britain the American jewel, without which, Lord Chatham declared, it would not be worth the wearing.

The inhabitants were now everywhere in arms; and they collected in such numbers about Boston, that they seemed effectually to invest the city, and created great anxiety on the part of General Gage and his British troops. The provincial Congress met almost immediately after these occurren- **April 22.**

ces at Lexington and Concord, and drew up a " narrative of the massacre," which, with an address, they sent to the British throne. Yet disposed to be loyal, if the king could only be just, they declared that " these marks of ministerial vengeance" had not yet detached them from their royal sovereign, whom they were still ready to defend in " person, family, crown, and dignity." They were, however, resolutely determined, as they said, not to submit tamely to tyranny; but, with God on their side, to die or be free. The Congress, moreover, prepared for the worst, by everywhere organizing the militia, and by the appointment of General Artemas Ward as commander-in-chief.

The feeling in Massachusetts was soon communicated to all the colonies. Every colonist felt that the cause of the Boston people was his own; and crowds flocked in, to unite with those who had already struck a blow on the memorable day of Lexington and Concord. They came from every part of New England. Old Israel Putnam, now threescore years of age, who had seen service in the French war, had retired to his Connecticut farm, and, like another Cincinnatus, was ploughing his field, when one of his sons ran up to him with the last news from Boston. The veteran dropped the handle of the plough, unharnessed his horses, and, saddling one of them, galloped away to join the Massachusetts patriots. Stark, too, of New Hampshire, an old campaigner, came in, offering his services. The people now looked up to these veterans for counsel, and readily submitted to the guidance of the one, who from a private had reached

the militia rank of general; and of the other, who was known as colonel in the same service.

Another and more remarkable man still, whose life supplies the darkest page in American annals, was then among the first to devote himself to the patriotic cause. This was *Benedict Arnold*, of New Haven, a Yankee skipper and small trader. He had been chosen the captain of a volunteer company; and no sooner did the Lexington news reach him, than he called his men together, and asked them whether they would march off with him, the next morning, for the neighborhood of Boston, distant about one hundred and fifty miles. They agreed to a man, and mustered at the time appointed, in front of the tavern where the Connecticut committee of safety were in session. Arnold applied to these gentlemen for a supply of powder and ball. They demurred, on the ground that he was not duly authorized. He then proposed to his soldiers to help themselves, by force, if necessary, to which they agreed. Arnold next sent word to the committee, of his resolution. Colonel Wooster now came out, and tried to persuade him to wait until he had received proper orders. The impetuous Arnold answered, " None but Almighty God shall prevent my marching !" He got his ammunition, and marched to Boston.

The provincial Congress, still in session, resolved that thirty thousand men be immediately raised, and that all New England be urged to add their quota of men to the Massachusetts troops. Cambridge, near Boston, was made the headquarters;

and the college there (the venerable Harvard) was emptied of its students, that room might be made for the provincial militia.

The appeal of Massachusetts to the other New-England provinces was responded to with spirit. Connecticut voted six thousand men, two thousand of whom were for its own defence, and the rest to send in aid to the neighboring colony, under the command of the veteran Putnam (already on the ground), and Spencer and Wooster. New Hampshire did not, as yet, organize an army, but expressed an ardent sympathy with the cause, and recommended supplies to be sent to the gallant Stark and his volunteers. Rhode Island was already represented by Nathaniel Greene, a blacksmith by trade and a Quaker in religion—now, however, "read out of meeting," for his warlike propensities. This little province, notwithstanding, voted an army of observation, numbering fifteen hundred men, and invested the bellicose young "friend" with the chief command. Pennsylvania held public meetings, appointed a "committee of safety," with Benjamin Franklin as its chairman, enrolled volunteer companies, and expressed the most patriotic resolutions. The people of New York, struggling against the adverse influence of a tory assembly, met together in spite of strong opposition, and united in an "association for the defence of colonial rights," and recommended the early meeting of a provincial Congress, "to deliberate on and direct such measures as may be expedient for our common safety." At the South, too, each province—Delaware, Virginia, the Carolinas,* and all—was firm for the patriotic cause, and prepared to act in its defence.

To give unanimity to the action of the colonists, a second continental Congress was to be held, at Philadelphia. Washington was at Mount Vernon, preparing to set out as a delegate to this assembly, which was to meet in May, when he received news of the affair at Lexington.

"Washington's feelings," says Irving, "were of a mingled nature. They may be gathered from a letter to his friend and neighbor, George William Fairfax, then in England, in which he lays the blame of this 'deplorable affair' on the ministry and their military agents; and concludes with the following words, in which the yearnings of the patriot give affecting solemnity to the implied resolve of the soldier: 'Unhappy it is to reflect that a brother's sword has been sheathed in a brother's breast; and that the once-happy and peaceful plains of America are to be either drenched with blood or inhabited by slaves. Sad alternative! *But can a virtuous man hesitate in his choice?*'" The impression produced in England may be learned from this record of Walpole in his journal, after the victories of Concord and Lexington were announced: "Stocks immediately fell. The provincials had behaved with the greatest conduct, coolness, and resolution. One circumstance spoke a thorough determination of resistance. The provincials had sent over affidavits of all that had passed, and a colonel of the militia had sworn in

* In North Carolina they even precipitated matters, by a "Declaration of Independence."

an affidavit that he had given his men order to fire on the king's troops if the latter attacked them. It was firmness, indeed, to swear to having been the first to begin what the Parliament had named rebellion; thus was the civil war begun, and a victory gained, the first fruits of which were on the side of the Americans, whom Lord Sandwich had had the folly and rashness to proclaim cowards." Let us, however, pass from what was said to what was done by the patriots; for the purpose of our history is to tell how they fought, and not what they thought.

When the struggle between the colonies and the mother-country became imminent, the attention of some thoughtful men in New England was directed to the probable position of Canada in the coming contest. Few doubted but that it would remain loyal under any circumstances; and, with such a disposition, it was quite evident that Canadian territory would offer to the British a firm holding-ground, upon which they might establish a basis of military operations, and through which they could do continued mischief to all the colonies, and particularly to New England and New York. The main route from the Canadas to the provinces south was over Lake Champlain; and upon this lake were the two forts of Ticonderoga and Crown Point, held each by a British garrison. These, accordingly, commanded the way. To acquire them, therefore, was thought of great importance to the patriot cause by the wise in counsel. The bold in action were not wanting to offer to do what was deemed advisable to be done. The necessity of securing Ticonderoga and Crown Point had been urged by many throughout New England, but Connecticut was foremost in proposing a plan of action, and sending out an expedition.

Several members of the assembly of Connecticut got up the enterprise, but kept it a secret, as it might not have been safe to intrust a knowledge to those who, however patriotically disposed, had not yet declared themselves boldly for war. Money was obtained, and a few volunteers enlisted in Connecticut and Massachusetts. The projectors of the undertaking, however, looked for the main staple of their force to the "Green-mountain boys" of the "New-Hampshire grants." This territory was then a wild region: it is now the state of Vermont. In those early days it was settled by a few hardy men, who joined to the strong attachment of the farmer to his land, the wild and fierce characteristics of the forest-borderer. The territory in their possession was derived from New Hampshire. New York, however, claimed the title, which was confirmed, on appeal, by royal authority. The latter province then attempted to eject the settlers of the "New-Hampshire grants," but found itself resisted by a band of resolute fellows who called themselves "The Green-mountain boys." The legislature of New York now outlawed these bold resistants, and offered a reward for their apprehension.

Ethan Allen, born in Connecticut, but living from childhood among the Green mountains, was the chosen leader of these "New-Hampshire grant" outlaws. He advised arming and defiance: his followers adopted his counsel, and pledged themselves to resist New York to the death. Allen was bold almost to fierceness, a natural contemner of authority, yet one who, with all his reputed disregard of traditional religious opinion, was of the strictest integrity. "An anecdote is related of him," says Lossing, "which illustrates the purity of his principles. He owed a citizen of Boston sixty pounds, for which he gave his promissory note. It was sent to Vermont for collection. It was inconvenient for Allen to pay, and the note was put in suit. Allen employed a lawyer to attend the court, and have the judgment postponed until he could raise the money. The lawyer determined to deny the genuineness of the signature, as the readiest method of postponing the matter, for in that case a witness at Boston would have to be sent for. When the case was called, it happened that Allen was in a remote part of the courthouse, and to his utter astonishment heard his lawyer gravely deny the signature of the note. With long and fierce strides he rushed through the crowd, and, confronting the amazed 'limb of the law,' rebuked him in a voice of thunder: 'Mr. ———, I did not hire you to come here and lie! That is a true note—I signed it—I'll swear to it—and I'll pay it! I want no shuffling; I want time. What I employed you for was to get this business put over to the next court; not to come here and lie and juggle about it!' The result was, the amicable postponement of the claim, arranged between the two lawyers."

The style of the man as a speaker—
20

for he had some pretensions to a rude eloquence—is described as that of "a singular compound of local barbarisms, scriptural phrases, and oriental wildness; and, though unclassic and sometimes ungrammatical, highly animated and forcible." And Washington said there was "an original something in him which commanded admiration."

The small force collected together in Connecticut and Massachusetts now rapidly pushed on to join the "Green-mountain boys," who readily flocked to the call of their old leader, Ethan Allen. Castleton was the rendezvous, and here soon the whole force was gathered, amounting to two hundred and seventy, all of whom, with the exception of forty, were "Green-mountain boys." Now a council-of-war was held. On the road, the small Connecticut detachment had met with one who was apparently a countryman, from whom they had gathered such an account of the formidable position of things in Ticonderoga, that their hearts almost failed them. This incident was laid before the council, and was thus reported by the witnesses: While they were on their way, they fell in with one who appeared to be an undesigning, honest traveller. They addressed him. "From whence came you?"—"From *Ty*" (so Ticonderoga was called, for shortness); "left it yesterday," at such an hour.—"Has the garrison received any reinforcements?"—"Yes; I saw them: there were a number of artillerymen and other soldiers."—"What are they doing? Are they making fascines?" —"*Fascines?* I don't know what you call *fascines*. They are tying up sticks and brush in bundles, and putting them where the walls are down."

This account so alarmed many of the party, that there was some thought of returning; and it was only determined by a majority of one, that they should push on. And well they did; for the "countryman" was a shrewd fellow, affecting not to know anything, and yet knowing enough to deceive, by giving such information as he thought would save the British forts, and which information was very far from the truth. Ethan Allen was no sooner appointed to command the whole expedition, by the council of officers at Castleton, than there came one, in great haste, to dispute the honor with him. This was Benedict Arnold.

Arnold, fresh from Connecticut, where the expedition against Ticonderoga and Crown Point was the subject of talk among the patriots, no sooner arrived at Boston—and not finding much there at that moment for the occupation of his busy activity—than he laid before the Massachusetts committee of safety a proposition for an attack upon the British forts. He was readily listened to when he spoke of the dismantled condition of Ticonderoga, its great stock of cannon and military stores, and of how easily it might be taken, defended as it was by only two-score men. The committee approved of his proposition, and appointed him colonel, with the authority to raise four hundred men. Arnold, however, knowing that Allen was before him, did not wait for recruits, but pushed on and arrived at Castleton with a single servant. Here he showed his Massachusetts commission,

and claimed the supreme command; but, finding that the men, who were mostly " Green-mountain boys," insisted upon being led by their old commander, Allen, he was fain to content himself with the position of second.

One Captain Noah Phelps now came in with certain intelligence in regard to Ticonderoga. This bold fellow had disguised himself as a rustic laborer, and had gone into the fort, requesting to be shaved by the barber of the garrison. Suspecting nothing, he was readily admitted; and, as he was searching for the man of the razor, he went all about the fort, prying into every nook and corner, and asking, with the affected greenness of a countryman, all sorts of questions. After spending the better part of the day thus, and getting rid of his beard at the hands of the barber, he left, and returned to his fellow-patriots, with the fullest information of what he had seen and heard. It was determined to make the attack at once, and the adventurous Noah Phelps undertook to guide the party to the fort.

On the 9th of May, Allen began his march, and reached Lake Champlain, at a point opposite to Ticonderoga, in the middle of the night. There were but few boats to be had, but Allen was too impatient to wait until more could be obtained; so he and Arnold, with eighty-three men, crossed at once. When on the other side, it was suggested that they should await the arrival of the rest of the force; but Allen would not listen to it for a moment, and declared that he was for striking a blow on the instant. " It is a desperate attempt, I know," said he, "and I ask no man to go against his will. I will take the lead, and be the first to advance. You that are willing to follow, poise your firelocks!" Every firelock was "poised."

The fort stood upon a height above them, and they now rapidly climbed the hill, with Phelps and a farmer's lad they had picked up, guiding the way. On reaching the top, a sentry on the outer wall snapped his fusee at Allen, and then retreated within. A dispute now took place between Arnold and Allen. The former "became assuming, and swore he would go in first; the other swore he should not." At last it was agreed that they should go in together; so Allen and Arnold entered the port leading to the fort side by side. It was in the early gray of the morning, as they silently marched in, followed by their handful of men. A soldier on guard struck at one of the officers, but was soon brought to his knees by a blow from Allen's sword upon the head, and forced to beg for quarter.

May 10.

As the provincials, with a loud shout, rushed into the parade within the walls, the garrison came flying out, and were easily made prisoners. Allen now made his way (with the aid of the farmer's lad, who knew every turn in and out of the fortress) to the quarters of Captain Delaplace, the commander, who was still in bed. Allen gave a thundering rap at the door with the hilt of his sword, which at once aroused Delaplace, who came out half-dressed, "with the frightened face of his pretty wife peering over his shoulder," and demanded, with an air and tone of affected firmness, what the disturbance meant. Allen insisted upon his instant surrender. "By what authority?" asked Delaplace. "In the name of the Great Jehovah and the continental Congress!" was the memorable answer, rounded off with the usual oath of the leader of the wild "mountain-boys." It is true, at that moment there was no continental Congress; and it might be very questionable whether a profane character like Allen could justly claim divine authority: but there was the provincial force in possession, to which their leader had only to point, which settled the matter, and put an end at once to all questions. Delaplace had nothing else left him but to surrender; and accordingly Ticonderoga was immediately given up, with all its effects, including the captain with his forty men, and a large stock of artillery and military stores.

Arnold, with his usual uneasy longing for power, insisted impetuously upon the command of Ticonderoga being given to him; but was forced to yield to Allen, who had the advantage of being seconded by the predominating majority of his "Green-mountain boys," with whom he was so great a favorite. Arnold, however, protested, and sent a letter of complaint to the Massachusetts committee. The rest of the force now coming up from the lake, they were detached to take possession of Crown Point, in which they succeeded without firing a gun. It surrendered on the 12th of May, being almost without defence, as the garrison numbered only a dozen men, under the command of a sergeant. Its hundred cannon and various stores were, however, a timely addition to the meager supplies of the provincials.

Arnold's restlessness now found vent in an enterprise that was concocted in council at Ticonderoga. A small detachment, composed of some thirty men, had been sent to Skenesborough, to secure the son of Major Skene, who was an ardent royalist, and a man of large wealth and influence, by which he was enabled greatly to serve the cause to which he was devoted. They had succeeded in taking young Skene by surprise, while out shooting. Otherwise, they might have had tough work in effecting their object; for Skene was quite a lord in his way, with his numerous tenants and negroes, who were ready to do his bidding at all hazards, and to defend him and his family to the death. The provincials seized the son—known, as well as his father, as a Major Skene—his strong stone-house and fortress, a number of his dependants and slaves, and his boats, among which there was a good-sized schooner. They likewise made another capture, of which they had but little expectation. It was that of the elder Skene's wife, who had not accompanied her husband, as might naturally have been expected, to England, where he had gone. On ransacking the great stone-house, they found the mistress of the mansion in the cellar. She had been there, it seems, many years. The good lady, however, was dead, and had been so for a long time; but her husband, having a strong attachment to an annuity which was to be continued to her " while she remained above-ground,"

had taken care to secure the object of his affection, by keeping his wife's body out of the grave. The provincials reverentially removed the remains, and buried them behind the great stone-house.

It was now determined that Arnold should lead the men who had been so successful at Skenesborough, and, embarking them on the boats which they had captured, sail with them down Lake Champlain, and take St. Johns, a Canadian post on the river Sorel. Arnold himself, who had been a sailor in early days, took command of the schooner, and with a fair wind succeeded in outsailing the batteaux, which were left so far behind, that he had landed and captured the place with his small advance-party before the rest could come up. Arnold, now learning that the troops from Canada were coming, destroyed what he could not carry away, and, taking with him an armed vessel and some military stores, set sail up the lake again. He had not got far, when he was met by Ethan Allen and his men, in the slow-moving batteaux. Arnold exultingly saluted his rival commander with a broadside of cannon, which Allen returned with a volley of musketry from his militia. An interview on board Arnold's royal " man-of-war" of seventy tons followed, when Allen was informed of the particulars of the late success. The latter then determined to continue his course for St. Johns, and make an attempt to hold it. He was, however, forestalled by a superior British force, and had to turn back to Ticonderoga.*

* This account is derived from Irving, who gives rather a different version from other writers.

1775. The second continental Congress assembled in Philadelphia on the 10th of May. Almost the first subject which came before them was, the state of things in Massachusetts. In the attitude of the British government toward that province, they saw a subversion of its charter, and advised the organization of a government which might restore, as far as possible, the former laws of Massachusetts. The Congress, however, so far assumed a conciliatory tone, as to resolve upon another petition to the British throne. The New-Englanders, with whom the spirit of independence was rife, opposed all further efforts at conciliation; and John Adams was among the foremost to denounce them as "imbecile." The petition to the king was, however, carried. Still, the Congress continued to act as if the colonies were already independent, and proceeded to deliberate upon measures of offence and defence as if they constituted a separate nation.

That the people of New England were in arms to resist the British government, was a fact that could not be concealed; and that their interest was the common interest of the whole country, every one felt, and determined to sustain it. The question now came up, as to who should be commander-in-chief to lead the forces which were fast gathering to the rescue of their country. There was no little jealousy, even at this early period, between the North and the South. The Massachusetts men were greatly in favor of Hancock, of Boston, and he himself undoubtedly aspired to the high position. Colonel Washington was the choice of the South. That great man, however, modestly thought not of himself, but of his country only. John Adams now, with the consent of most of the New-Englanders, made a concession to the southern provinces, by proposing Mr. George Washington, "a gentleman whose skill and experience as an officer, whose independent fortune, great talents, and excellent universal character, would command the approbation of all America, and unite the cordial exertions of all the colonies better than any other person in the Union." As soon as Adams had uttered these words, "Mr. Washington, who happened to sit near the door.... with his usual modesty, darted into the library-room."

There were many New-Englanders opposed to this nomination, and one who was particularly chagrined. It was Hancock, who was sitting at that time as president of the Congress, in the absence of Peyton Randolph, who had returned to Virginia, to preside at the assembly of his own province. Adams says: "While I was speaking on the state of the colonies, the army at Cambridge, and the enemy, Hancock heard me with pleasure; but when," he adds, "I came to describe Washington for the commander, I never remarked a more sudden and striking change of countenance. Mortification and resentment were expressed as forcibly as his face could exhibit them."

The election was delayed for a few days, in consequence of the opposition; when, finally, GEORGE WASHINGTON was unanimously chosen commander-in-chief of the provincial forces. On his election being announced **June 15.**

Washington arose and modestly said, after thanking the Congress for the honor conferred upon him: "Lest some unlucky event should happen unfavorable to my reputation, I beg it may be remembered, by every gentleman in the room, that I this day declare, with the utmost sincerity, I do not think myself equal to the command I am honored with. As to pay, I beg leave to assure the Congress that, as no pecuniary consideration could have tempted me to accept this arduous employment, at the expense of my domestic ease and happiness, I do not wish to make any profit of it. I will keep an exact account of my expenses. These I doubt not they will discharge, and that is all I desire."

In the congressional resolution to appoint a commander-in-chief, a provision was made for his support to the amount of five hundred dollars a month. The army which had been gathering, principally from the various parts of New England, was now formally adopted by the continental Congress; and a commander-in-chief having been appointed, they proceeded to organize the whole military staff. Artemas Ward was chosen second in command, Charles Lee the third, Philip Schuyler the fourth, and Israel Putnam the fifth, all with the rank of major-general. Seth Pomeroy, Richard Montgomery, David Wooster, William Heath, Joseph Spencer, John Thomas, John Sullivan, and Nathaniel Greene, were the eight appointed as brigadier-generals. Horatio Gates had the same rank, with the especial function of adjutant-general. There was a good deal of opposition to the appointment of Lee and Gates, but Washington's earnest advocacy secured their elections. They were both Englishmen, and were looked upon with suspicion as military adventurers, more concerned about their own private interests than the public good of a country to which they were comparatively strangers.

CHAPTER III.

The Provincial Camp before Boston.—Men and Officers.—The Country round.—Charlestown and Boston: their Aspect.—The British reinforced.—Burgoyne, Clinton, and Howe.—Gage's Proclamation.—Indignation of the People.—Breed's and Bunker's Hills.—Taken Possession of by the Provincials.—The Fortifications.—Colonel Prescott.—His Martial Air.—Character.—The Labors and Anxieties of the Night on Bunker's Hill.—The Morning.—The Surprise of the British.—The Bombardment of the Works by the British Ships.—Colonel Prescott encourages his Men.—The British Troops prepare to attack.—Activity of Putnam.—Lord Howe.—His Character.—The Preparations for the Struggle.—The Excitement of the People.—The Stir in the Provincial Camp.—Putnam on the Move.

1775. SIXTEEN thousand New-England patriots were now in arms before Boston. Of these, about three fourths were from Massachusetts; and the rest from Connecticut, New Hampshire, and Rhode Island. One common sentiment of patriotism united them all in a firm resolve to defend their country against the oppressor. This was their strength, which was sure to give them the ultimate victory over their enemies. They had their weaknesses, however;—and these greatly diminished their efficiency as an army gathered to resist the disciplined troops of Great Britain. With the exception of a few veterans, who had fought in the British ranks at Louisburg and Quebec, most of the men were fresh from the shop and the field. All varieties of trades and occupations had their representatives in the American ranks. There was even a divine, the Reverend John Martin,* of Rhode Island, who, having delivered a stirring sermon on the text —" Be not ye afraid of them : remember the Lord which is great and terrible, and fight for your brethren, your sons, and your daughters, your wives, and your houses" (Neh. iv. 14), shouldered his musket, and took his position as a private in the line. Most of the Americans, at best, had had but a few days' militia-training, and knew nothing of war but its " first steps." They could form ranks, face to the right and left, and march, keeping an irregular step to the village drum and fife, to the undisguised ridicule of the critical looker-on.

There was hardly a man, however, in those early days, who could not steadily poise his gun and bring down his game with the sure aim of a " good shot." In appearance, they had none of the look of a soldier. In dress they pretended to no uniformity, and civilized broadcloth coats, homespun jackets, and coarse shirt-sleeves, indiscriminately diversified the patriot ranks. Some shouldered fowling-pieces rusty from neglect, or polished

* He fought bravely at Bunker's hill.

smooth with long use ; some carried blunderbusses ; others implements of peaceful husbandry, sharpened into weapons of war ; and but few were provided with the " regulation" musket and its efficient bayonet.

There was a general scarcity of military stores. The artillery was scanty, the ammunition small in quantity, and there was a great want of tents, clothing, and even roofs, to protect the troops from exposure to the weather. There was, moreover, worse than all, an absence of unity in command. " The Massachusetts men had their own commander, Connecticut and the other provinces theirs ;" and each insisted upon being governed exclusively by his own leader. They were all, however, ready to fight for the one cause ; and we shall see how this unanimity of feeling, in the time of trial, smoothed many of the irregularities which came from a want of discipline.

Among the officers there were men of military experience, and well able, with proper *materiel*, and under favorable circumstances, to organize an army, and to command it. Artemas Ward, the general of the Massachusetts men, had fought gallantly under Abercrombie. "Old Put," of Connecticut, had learned a good deal of war while serving as a private in the French campaign. Pomeroy had distinguished himself at Louisburg, and so had Gridley, where he had shown great skill as a military engineer. Prescott and Stark, too, were veterans, who had fought bravely while serving in the British ranks against the French. The men looked up with veneration to these leaders, and condently obeyed their orders. Such was the patriot force now loosely scattered over some ten miles of country surrounding Boston, and holding that city in a state of siege.

The town itself and the suburbs were emptied of their inhabitants. Charlestown was almost entirely deserted, but one or two hundred out of two or three thousand of the population being left. A few only of the citizens returned occasionally, to plant their gardens, mow their grass, and look after the property which they could not take away with them. The removals of the citizens from Boston into the country were so frequent, that General Gage became alarmed; and, although he had pledged himself to give passes to those who desired to leave, he threw all kinds of obstructions in their way to prevent their departure. The passes were made out in such a manner as to prevent those who bore them from carrying anything with them. "All merchandise was forbid; after awhile, all provisions were forbid; and now all merchandise, provisions, and medicine. Guards were appointed to examine all trunks, boxes, beds, and everything else, to be carried out." The passports, too, were often so worded as to separate men from their wives and children, whom the governor was particularly desirous of retaining as pledges for the "good conduct" of the patriots. Passes finally were refused altogether. The whole city was given up almost entirely to the British soldiery. Occasional skirmishes occurred between Gage's outposts and the American patriots, but nothing was effectually done un-

til the arrival of reinforcements from Great Britain.

A large number of British troops now arrived, which, added to Gage's previous force, gave him an army of ten thousand well-disciplined soldiers, mostly by long service inured to war. Three British generals of renown also arrived—Howe, Clinton, and Burgoyne. As the Cerberus man-of-war, on board of which these officers came, was entering the harbor, she spoke a coaster; and the skipper, being asked what news there was, replied, "Boston is surrounded by ten thousand country-people."—"How many regulars are there in the town?" asked General Burgoyne; and, being told there were about five thousand, he cried out, with astonishment: "What! ten thousand peasants keep five thousand king's troops shut up? Well, let *us* get in, and we'll soon find elbow-room!" This expression, "*elbow-room*,"* stuck by Burgoyne during all the time he remained in America. The British generals might well be surprised at the state of things in Boston; for, when they left England, they had no thought of being obliged to draw the sword, and supposed that their mere appearance would settle all the difficulties. They had accordingly prepared themselves with fowling-pieces and fishing-rods, with the view

June.

* "General Burgoyne is designated by *Elbow-room* in the satires of the times. It is said that he loved a joke, and used to relate that, after his Canada reverses, while a prisoner-of-war, he was received with great courtesy by the Boston people, as he stepped from the Charlestown ferry-boat; but he was really annoyed when an old lady, perched on a shed above the crowd, cried out at the top of a shrill voice: 'Make way, make way—the general's coming! Give him *elbow-room!*'"—FROTHINGHAM.

of "good sport" in America, during their leisure hours, when off duty.

Gage, thus reinforced, prepared for active hostilities. As a beginning, he issued a proclamation which excited the indignation of each patriot, and fixed him more firmly in his resolve to fight for his country. The British fretted greatly at the idea of being shut up within Boston, and now resolved to extend their "elbow-room." It was accordingly proposed, in council, to take possession of Dorchester and the other heights which surrounded the city.

The provincial leaders heard of these designs of the enemy, and prepared to counteract them. Several plans of operation were considered, and, among others, that of occupying Bunker's hill. This hill formed, with that of Breed's, the heights which, overlooking the northern end of Boston, were at the back of Charlestown, and gradually descended to the neck of the peninsula upon which that town is situated. The object was, to hem the British in effectually on that side, and prevent all sallies. Many, however, opposed the plan, as too hazardous, deeming the militia not sufficiently expert as yet to be capable of a sustained military operation. But others contended that the country was growing discontented with the inactivity of the army, and that the soldiers themselves were eager for work. The veteran Putnam and the martial Prescott strongly advocated the possession of Bunker's hill, by which means they might draw out the British and have a fair fight with them. These officers professed great faith in the provincials,

21

and Putnam said: "The Americans are not afraid of their heads, though very much afraid of their legs; if you cover these, they will fight for ever." General Ward and Warren (who had been appointed a brigadier-general, but had not yet received his commission) opposed the plan. The advice of Putnam and Prescott, however, carried the day.

The American forces were much scattered about the neighborhood of Boston. General Thomas was at Roxbury, with four thousand Massachusetts men; General Greene was at Jamaica Plains, with the Rhode-Islanders; where also was General Spencer, with the larger portion of his Connecticut regiment. The main body of the American militia, consisting of some nine thousand men and four artillery-companies, was in and about Cambridge, where General Ward had his headquarters. This part of the forces was distributed over a considerable surface of ground, and, extending through most of the villages over Charlestown neck, with its outposts it reached even the base of Bunker's hill.

With the main body, besides General Ward of Massachusetts, were Putnam of Connecticut, Stark and Reed of New Hampshire, and Gridley the engineer. The officers and men were quartered in the college-buildings, churches, taverns, farmyards, and in tents under the few breastworks which had been hastily erected here and there. It may be well here to give a more specific description of the scene of the struggle which we are about to record. We borrow it from Frothingham, who says:—

"The peninsula of Charlestown is situated opposite to the north end of Boston, and is separated from it by Charles river. It is about a mile in length from north to south; and its greatest breadth, next to Boston, is about half a mile, whence it gradually becomes narrower until it makes an isthmus, called 'The Neck,' connecting it with the mainland. The Mystic river, about half a mile wide, is on the east side; and on the west side is Charles river, which here forms a large bay—a part of which, by a dam stretching in the direction of Cobble hill, is a millpond. In 1775, the Neck, an artificial causeway, was so low as to be frequently overflowed by the tides. The communication with Boston was by a ferry where Charles-river bridge now is, and with Malden by another called 'Penny Ferry,' where at present Malden bridge is....Bunker hill begins at the isthmus, and rises gradually for about three hundred yards, forming a round, smooth hill, sloping on two sides toward the water, and connected by a ridge of ground on the south with the heights now known as Breed's hill. The easterly and westerly sides of this height were steep; on the east side, at its base, were brick-kilns, clay-pits, and much sloughy land; and on the west side, at the base, was the most settled part of the town.....The easterly portions of these hills were used chiefly for hay-ground and pasturing; the westerly portions contained fine orchards and gardens."

1775. Friday night (16th of June) was the time appointed for taking possession of and fortifying Bunker's hill. Accordingly, orders were issued for the assembling of the troops drafted for the purpose; and, at six o'clock in the evening, they mustered ready for duty. They were some twelve hundred men in all, mostly of the Massachusetts regiments, although Connecticut supplied a fatigue-party of two hundred. Colonel William Prescott, of Pepperell, was appointed to command the Massachusetts detachment; Captain Thomas Knowlton, a favorite of Putnam, and an officer in his regiment, led the Connecticut men. The two field-pieces and forty-nine artillerymen were in charge of Captain Samuel Gridley, a son of Colonel Richard Gridley, who was the chief-engineer of the enterprise, and was to plan the fortifications about to be constructed.

The men came, as had been ordered, provided with all the intrenching-tools that could be found in the camp, and with packs, blankets, and provisions for twenty-four hours (it was supposed, for that had been the order). They were not informed of the precise object of the enterprise in which they were about to engage. Their leader, Prescott, had received a written order from General Ward, directing him to proceed that evening to Bunker's hill, build fortifications there, and to defend them until relieved. This order was, however, not to be communicated to his force until they had reached Charlestown neck.

Colonel Prescott presented himself in full uniform, "being equipped with a three-cornered hat, a top-wig, and a single-breasted blue coat, with facings, and lapped up at the skirts;" and, as he paraded his men, his tall figure, thus magnificently arrayed, and his military bearing—for he was a veteran, having served as a lieutenant at the siege of Louisburg—were the admiration of his raw and miscellaneously-clothed troops. He had, moreover, not only the look and spirit of a good soldier, but was known to be a most determined patriot. A few months before this time, while he commanded a regiment of min-ute-men, his brother-in-law, Colonel Wil-lard, was at his house, and endeavored to dissuade him from the active part he was taking against the king's government. Upon his being reminded that if he should be found in arms against his sovereign, his life and estate would be forfeited, Pres-cott replied: "I have made up my mind on that subject. I think it probable I may be found in arms, but I will never be taken alive. The tories shall never have the satisfaction of seeing me hanged." Such was the resolution of the man who was intrusted with the important com-mand at Bunker's hill.

The men having been reviewed on the common by General Ward, President Langdon offered up an earnest prayer, and dismissed the force with a blessing. It was nine o'clock when they began their march, which had been purposely delayed until that late hour, in order that it might be under the cover of the dark-ness of the night, and that the enemy might thus remain unsuspicious of the movement. Each man was ordered to keep the utmost silence; and, with two men carrying dark lanterns in front, they thus continued their still and groping march to Charlestown neck, where they came to a halt. Here the veteran Put-

nam rode up, and Major Brooks joined them. A guard now having been de-tached to the town of Charlestown, the main body cautiously continued their march along Charlestown neck, to the base of Bunker's hill, where there was another halt, when Prescott communi-cated his orders to his chief officers.

A question now arose as to the hill to be fortified. Bunker's hill was the place specified in the written orders; but, as Breed's hill was nearer Boston, it was thought by most of the officers to be the most suitable for the purpose intend-ed. There seemed considerable difficul-ty in coming to a decision; but, as the night was passing, Gridley declared there was no longer any time to spare, and it was finally determined to proceed to Breed's hill, and there erect the main fortifications—although, at the earnest persuasion of General Putnam, it was al-so agreed to raise some works on Bun-ker's hill as well. The men were now marched farther along to the heights of Breed's hill, and, when near the top, they halted, stacked their guns, threw off their packs, and prepared for the duty of the night. Gridley marked out the lines rap-idly, and at twelve o'clock had his men fairly at work.

In the meantime, Prescott was greatly anxious lest the labors of the provincials should be detected by the British. He sent a party below to patrol the shore, and keep a close watch upon the men-of war lying in Charles river, within gun-shot, and upon the battery at Copp's hill, at the north end of Boston, just across the river. Prescott might well be anxious, with the enemy so threateningly near, and who, if once aroused, before the American works were completed, would be sure to defeat the whole enterprise. The patriots had so far succeeded, by their exceeding caution, in escaping every danger. They had passed the neck in safety, under the very guns of a man-of-war stationed to guard that approach. There was now more occasion than ever for watchfulness, as their present position was commanded by no less than three armed vessels and several floating batteries, whose guns pointed directly at the height where the Americans, as they busily worked, were totally unprotected. As their thousand spades were diligently plied, the progress was rapid; and the men continued their labor without interruption, listening with eager ears to the bell-watches of the British men-of-war, and the "All's well!" of the sentries on the opposite shores. Prescott himself, as the night was passing, became more and more anxious. He continued to urge on his men constantly to increased effort; and went down himself to the shore, to watch the enemy, and try if he could catch the least sound of movement among the ships or the troops. He could hear nothing, in the quiet summer night, but the hour-watches striking, and the sentries' cry, and returned up the hill with words of renewed encouragement and hope. The men went to work with greater spirit than ever; and Colonel Prescott saw, with great satisfaction, as the dawn of morning approached, the intrenchment rising fast: for he was particularly anxious to have a screen for his raw troops,

since he believed it would be difficult to keep them, however firm in their patriotism, steady enough to stand for the first time in an open field against artillery and well-disciplined soldiers.

When morning broke, so diligent had been the Americans, that they had already fortified their position with a redoubt almost complete, and an intrenchment of six feet in height. All this, moreover, had been done in such silence and secrecy, that nothing was observed or suspected by the British, until the sailors, as day dawned, saw from the decks of the men-of-war the American fortress, which had risen upon the hill during the night as if by magic. The captain of the Lively immediately put a spring on his cable, and, hauling in, opened a fire on the works. This was done without orders; and, upon the admiral being made aware of it, it ceased momentarily, and then each of his ships opened its broadside and played unceasingly upon the hill. The British battery on Copp's hill also joined in with a brisk cannonade.

The firing aroused all Boston and the neighboring suburbs; **June 17.** and the inhabitants poured out, taking their positions on the housetops, the roofs of the churches, and the hills, looking anxiously at what was going on. The patriots continued their work, in spite of the fatigue of the night's labor and the heat of the summer sun, as it came out, darting its burning rays upon them. For awhile, the firing from the British ships and the battery on Copp's hill did no damage, as the provincials were protected by the intrenchments. A private, however, having ventured out, was struck down by a ball and instantly killed. This created quite a panic among the raw troops, and some of the men made off in fright.

Colonel Prescott, in order to reassure his inexperienced soldiers, now mounted the parapet, and, walking deliberately upon it, encouraged them at their work, and talked laughingly of the chances of war. At this moment, General Gage was watching with his glass the patriot movement on the hill, and, seeing a tall person on the top of the works, asked Councillor Willard, at his side, "Who is that person, giving orders?"—"It's my brother-in-law Prescott," was the answer. "Will he fight?" inquired the general. "Yes, sir," replied Willard; "he's an old soldier, and will fight while there is a drop of blood left in his veins!"—"The works must be carried," was all that Gage said in rejoinder.

Colonel Prescott, succeeding in allaying the panic, and getting his men again at work, the fortifications continued to make fair progress; although the day, as it advanced, became fearfully hot, and the troops suffered greatly, not only from the heat, but from excessive fatigue and want of refreshments, which they had strangely neglected to provide themselves with. The men at last began to grow discontented, and some murmured loudly. The officers took up their cause, and urged the colonel to send to General Ward, at Cambridge, for other men to take the place of those who had worked all night. Prescott refused, saying: "The enemy will not dare to attack us; and if they do, they will be defeated. The men who have raised the works are the best able to defend them; already they have learned to despise the fire of the enemy. They have the merit of the labor, and shall have the honor of the victory."

The patriots were certainly becoming fast inured to warfare, under the severe discipline of Prescott, who gave them a foretaste of the summary mode of doing business in the time of war, by the manner in which he disposed of their comrade, the first killed by a cannon-ball. His death was reported to the colonel by one of the subaltern officers, who asked what was to be done with the body. "Bury it," replied Prescott. "The chaplain," says Irving, describing this scene, "gathered some of his military flock about him, and was proceeding to perform suitable obsequies over the 'first martyr,' but Prescott ordered that the men should disperse to their work, and the deceased be buried immediately." The object of the colonel was, no doubt, to remove as soon as possible from the thoughts of his agitated men this by no means unusual event of battle, upon which they were disposed to dwell with a persistency of grief quite unsuitable and inconvenient to the occasion.

The British troops now began to move, and evidently with the view of attacking the American works on Breed's hill. General Gage had held a council of his officers in the morning, when there was a dispute respecting the plan of operations. Some, of whom Clinton was one, had expressed themselves strongly in favor of landing in the rear, and, by thus cutting off the retreat of the patriots from the hill, proposed to hem them in within the peninsula between two British fires: others, and among them Gage, who decided the question, were for crossing directly from Boston, and attacking them in front. This was the bolder expedient, but far the more dangerous, and which would probably never have been entertained, had it not been for the general's absurd contempt of the prowess of the provincials.

The Americans heard the commotion in the British camp with some degree of anxiety. As the sound of the wheels of the artillery-wagons rattling in the streets of Boston, and of the beating to quarters of the troops with drum and fife, came across the waters, it startled the raw militia with such an alarming expectation of approaching battle, that they began to show considerable solicitude for relief. Their officers now urged again upon Prescott to send to General Ward for fresh men as substitutes for those on the ground, who were completely worn out by the night's fatigue and the want of refreshment. Prescott would not listen to anything which should deprive the men then under his command of the glory which he earnestly believed would be the result of the day, but was induced to send a messenger, soliciting reinforcements and a supply of provisions.

Ward had been already urged to send aid to Prescott early in the morning, by General Putnam, whose experienced eye saw that the struggle was to be on the hill, and that the day would be a hard one. The general had consented, some-

what unwillingly, and had ordered Stark and Reed, with the New-Hampshire men, to reinforce Prescott. These were on their march when the messenger arrived from the hill. Ward now refused to send any more, as he was convinced that the British attack was to be in his own direction, and not against the American fortifications on Breed's hill.

As the day advanced, the British succeeded, by means of the flood-tide, in floating in toward the Charlestown peninsula several batteries, by which, in addition to the ships, they were enabled greatly to increase their fire. The provincials, however, took no further notice of the cannonade, than by an occasional return-shot from a single gun in their redoubt. They went on with their work until eleven o'clock, when they stopped from their labors, and, having laid aside their intrenching-tools, anxiously awaited the arrival of the expected refreshments and reinforcements from Cambridge.

General Putnam now rode up to the redoubt, and, hurrying to Colonel Prescott, told him that the intrenching-tools must be sent off, or they would be lost. The colonel replied that, if he sent any of the men away with the tools, not one of them would return. To this the general answered, "They shall every man return!" A large party was then sent off with the tools, and not one of them returned! Some of the tools, however, and men to use them, got no farther than Bunker's hill, where Putnam put them to good service in raising a breastwork.

At about noon, the British became active in their preparations for attack. The men-of-war were hauled closer in toward the Charlestown shore, and their guns began to play briskly along the low lands opposite to the north end of Boston, where the British troops were embarking in their boats and barges. Under the cover of this fire from the ships, and a continued cannonade from the battery on Copp's hill, the troops left the **June 17.** Boston side, and began to cross the river. The barges, twenty-eight in number, crowded with soldiers, moved regularly across in parallel lines. It was a bright summer's day, and the mid-day sun was pouring down a flood of light, which glowed brilliantly in the stream, and upon the flashing accoutrements of the English officers and soldiers in their uniforms of scarlet, and with their polished arms and gilded ornaments. The troops were three thousand of the choicest of Gage's army, and were led by Major-General Howe.

WILLIAM HOWE was a younger brother of the gallant earl who fell at Ticonderoga in 1758. So greatly had that youthful nobleman endeared himself, by his amiable qualities, to the Americans, while fighting with them in the common cause against the French, that they now saw with exceeding pain his brother presenting himself as their enemy. "America is amazed to find the name of Howe in the catalogue of her enemies; she loved his brother," were the warm words of an address of the continental Congress to the people of Ireland. William Howe himself, however, was not the man to sympathize strongly with any sentimental affection. He was a careless, good-

natured man, "the most indolent of mortals, and never took further pains to examine the merits or demerits of the cause in which he was engaged than merely to recollect that Great Britain was said to be the mother-country; George III. king of Great Britain; that the king and Parliament formed the supreme power; that a supreme power is absolute and uncontrollable; that all resistance must consequently be rebellion; but, above all, that he was a soldier, and bound to obey in all cases whatever."[*] Being a younger son, he was "provided for" by a commission in the army, and, confidently trusting to the influence of his aristocratic family for advancement, gave himself little anxiety about the present or the future. He was brave, like all his race, and with his handsome figure, six feet in height, and his frank, chivalrous air, made a gallant-looking officer. He had no pretensions, however, to the genius which can conceive great enterprises, and bring them to triumphant results. He had neither the active sympathy with the good, of the young lord who fell at Ticonderoga, nor the administrative ability and energy of Admiral Howe (at this time the earl); but, like his two brothers, he possessed courage, and, as that was all that was required in the present emergency, he had the spirit equal to the occasion. Lee dashes off his character thus: "He is naturally good-humored, complaisant, but illiterate and indolent to the last degree, unless as an executive soldier, in which capacity he is all fire and activity, brave and cool as Julius Cæsar. His un-

[*] General Charles Lee.

derstanding is rather good than otherwise; but was totally confounded and stupefied by the immensity of the task imposed upon him. He shut his eyes, fought his battles, drank his bottle, had his little .... advised with his counsellors, received his orders, shut his eyes, fought again."

Howe succeeded in landing his men in admirable order on the Charlestown shore, and drew them up in three **June 17.** lines. Covered as they were by the British men-of-war and batteries, no attempt was made by the patriots to dispute their landing; and they quietly took up their position at the bottom of Breed's hill at the north, without even a musketshot being fired. Howe now reconnoitred the American fortifications, and, finding them more formidable than he had supposed, thought it would be necessary to have reinforcements before he could effectually perform the duty of the day, which was, " to drive the rebels from their works." He accordingly sent to Gage for more troops and ammunition, as, by a stupid blunder, the cartridges he had brought with him were too big for his fieldpieces! In the meantime, refreshments were plentifully distributed to the men, who were allowed to stack their arms, and gather in groups upon the grass, while they ate and drank to their fill.

The landing, however, of the British troops at Charlestown, though unresisted, created a great commotion in Cambridge, where General Ward had his headquarters, and where were gathered, not only the main body of the provincial troops, but large numbers of old men, women, and children, whose sons, husbands, and sires, had shouldered their muskets, and were awaiting a struggle which, brought it victory or defeat, would certainly bring death and sorrow to many a loving heart. The bells of the churches and college at Cambridge were ringing; drums beat in the American camp; and horses clattered through the streets, bearing messengers with orders for the commanders to assemble their regiments and prepare to march. Adjutants were seen riding fast from point to point. One comes by at full gallop. " What is the matter ?" shouts a youth, coming quietly out of his lodgings after dinner. " Have you not heard ?' — " No." —" Why, the regulars are landing at Charlestown, and we are all to meet and march immediately to Bunker's hill, to oppose the enemy." The adjutant puts spurs to his horse, and is away, shouting, " Turn out! turn out !" The youth waits not, but runs, gets his arms and ammunition, and hastens to his company in the church where it has its barrack, and finds his comrades almost ready for the march. They are soon equipped with their frocks and trousers of "blue turned up with red," drawn over their other clothes; for they are loth, with a rising martial pride, to expose themselves in other than a military trim. Thus prepared, off they start.

General Putnam, who seemed to be everywhere that day (riding hurriedly now to Bunker's hill and urging on his favorite work there, now to Breed's, and then to Cambridge), at this moment came galloping his horse to headquarters, and, ordering out those of the Connecticut men that were left, led them forward to the aid of Prescott on the heights. General Ward, retaining two or three regiments to protect Cambridge, sent on the remainder of the Massachusetts troops to Charlestown.

The patriots on the hill, still without reinforcements, and with but a scanty supply of refreshments, looked down from their intrenchments upon the brilliant array of the enemy below them with respectful awe, and almost with envy, as, half famished themselves, they beheld the "red-coats" making jolly over their abundant food and " bucketfuls of grog." The patriots became irritable and suspicious, and even charged their leaders with wantonly exposing them to destruction. The men were almost exhausted by fatigue and hunger; they were conscious of their inexperience as soldiers; they saw a formidable British force, with its immense resources of art, threatening them. It

was natural that a raw militia, under such circumstances, should be disheartened, and, wanting self-confidence, should temporarily lose trust in their leaders. As the reinforcements did not come, as the supply of provisions failed them, they not unnaturally became disaffected. They were, however, now cheered by the timely arrival of Generals Warren and Pomeroy, who as they came in were welcomed with loud hurrahs. These were true patriots, whom none, the most suspicious, ever doubted. Their assurances of approaching aid, and their own resolute declaration to share as volunteers in the dangers of the day, soon dispelled all suspicion, and encouraged the men to renewed hope and confidence. The ever-active Putnam, too, came riding in, cheering all by his hearty words and his undaunted bearing, and then galloping away again, to hurry on the approaching reinforcements.

CHAPTER IV.

The Works on Bunker's Hill described.—The Approach of the British Troops.—Arrival of Warren.—Howe's Address to his Soldiers.—The Struggle.—The British repulsed.—"Old Put" at the Guns.—Cheers of Victory.—The British again driven back.—Charlestown set on Fire.—General Clinton volunteers.—Another Attack and Repulse.—The Sublimity of the Scene.—A Final Rally of the British.—The Last Struggle, and Retreat of the Provincials.—Howe does not pursue.—The Dead and Wounded.—The Moral Victory of the Provincials at Bunker's Hill.—Death of Warren, and the Public Grief.—His History.—The English Loss.

1775.   THE patriots, with renewed spirit, indulged less in despairing reflections about the formidable aspect of the enemy which threatened them, and set to work in making further preparations for defence.   Although it was as late as

22

three o'clock in the afternoon,   June 17. and the British might be expected at any moment, the fortifications on Bunker's hill were by no means complete. The redoubt which had been built was small, being only eight rods square; and although tolerably strong in front, with its projecting angles, it was weaker on the other sides. On the east was a large field, which was commanded by the guns of the redoubt on that side. Continuous with this eastern side of the redoubt, a breastwork extended a hundred yards north, to what was called "The Slough." Beyond this slough there was a space of some three hundred feet entirely unprotected; while, still farther on, there was a rail-fence. The redoubt and the breastwork were cannon-proof. The rail-fence merely offered a partial cover to a marksman, and could not be styled a defence, though it might slightly obstruct the approach of the enemy. Thus, to the north of the breastwork from the ridge of the hill down to the water's edge of the Mystic river, there was nothing but a rail-fence; and in this direction there offered an opportunity for the British to approach in security.

Howe began now to move his troops; and, as his right wing seemed to be taking a direction along the shore, which was thought to indicate the design of making a flank movement through the unprotected approach at the north, Prescott ordered Captain Knowlton, with his Connecticut men, to go down the hill and prepare to oppose the British advance in that direction. Knowlton marched and took up his position to the rear of the redoubt, on the low ground which separated like a shallow valley the two hills of Bunker and Breed. Here he found a rail-fence, which topped a foot-wall of stone, and, with ready Yankee ingenuity, turned it into a very tolerable breast-work. Having gathered together a number of rails, he erected another fence, behind the original one, and filled in the space between them with new-mown hay which he found ready to his hand in the neighboring fields.

While the Connecticut men were thus engaged in their novel style of constructing a fortification, Stark came to their aid with his New-Hampshire men. He had been long in crossing from Medford, whence he had set out early by the orders of General Ward. As he was coming deliberately along Charlestown neck, and the British man-of-war which commanded that point was blazing at him and his troops, an officer suggested to Stark that it might be well to quicken their march. But the veteran shook his head, and replied, "One fresh man in action is worth ten fatigued ones." His troops continued their slow and regular step as before. When Stark reached the ground, he addressed a few pithy words to his men, and, after sending some of them to aid General Putnam at the works upon Bunker's hill, set the rest to labor with Knowlton's party at the rail-and-hay battery.

When the struggle was about to commence, Warren stationed himself in the redoubt. As he came in, he was offered by Prescott the chief command, but declined, saying, "I am come to fight as a volunteer, and feel honored in being allowed to serve under so able a commander." Pomeroy went down to do duty at the rail-fence, and here Warren had also gone and remained momentarily, when the command there was likewise offered him. "No," he replied; "I only wish to know where I can be of most service as a private soldier."—"The redoubt," said General Putnam, who also remarked that he would be there under cover. "Don't think I seek a place of safety! where will the attack be the hottest?" sharply rejoined Warren. Putnam again replied: "The redoubt, for that is the enemy's object; and, if that can be maintained, the day is ours." This decided Warren, and he returned to the redoubt; but nothing would induce him to take the command, as, although he had been chosen general, he had not yet received his commission.

This was now the disposition of the American force at the moment of acting. Colonel Prescott was at the redoubt and breastwork, with the Massachusetts part of the detachment which had arrived on the ground the evening before, and had raised the fortifications. The Connecticut troops, under Knowlton, together with the New-Hampshire men, commanded by Stark, were at the rail-fence battery; and here also, for a time, was General Putnam. Captains Gridley and Callender had their artillery-company and fieldpieces posted at the exposed space between the breastwork and the rail-fence. As a reinforcement of Massachusetts troops came up at the last moment, some of them entered the redoubt, while others planted themselves on the outside, to the right.

The British forces having remained at Moulton's point, where they landed, until they had received the reinforcements and ammunition which had been sent for to Boston, now prepared, at three o'clock in the afternoon, to make the assault on the American works upon Breed's hill. His troops being drawn up, General Howe rode in front and addressed them:—

"Gentlemen, I am very happy in having the honor of commanding so fine a body of men. I do not in the least doubt but that you will behave like Englishmen, and as becometh good soldiers.

"If the enemy will not come from their intrenchments, we must drive them out, at all events; otherwise the town of Boston will be set on fire by them!

"I shall not desire one of you to go a step farther than where I go myself at your head!

"Remember, gentlemen, we have no recourse to any resources, if we lose Boston, but to go on board our ships, which will be very disagreeable to us all!"

These spirited words were received by the soldiers with a hearty cheer, and then the army began to move. The left wing, under General Pigot, was to advance up the hill in face of the redoubt, and attempt to take it by assault. Howe himself was to lead the right wing against the American lines at the rail-fence, and thus endeavor, by a flank movement, to surround the rear and cut off the retreat from the works.

This disposition having been made, the march began. Howe orders his artillery on the flank to fire; and simultaneously the English ships, the floating batteries, and Copp's hill, join in with a furious cannonade, in order to cover the British advance. The people in Boston, crowding the tops of the houses and churches, are listening to the thundering cannon with stifled hearts; and watching, at every break in the thick smoke, with eager glance, to catch a sight of the slightest movement. On Copp's hill stand the two British generals Clinton and Burgoyne, coolly contemplating with professional interest the military manœuvres, and not for a moment doubting the success of the British regulars.

Howe's artillery soon ceased its fire; not, however, before it had silenced the guns of Gridley and Callender on the hill. The latter even withdrew to Bunker's hill, declaring that his cartridges were useless from being too large. Here he was confronted by the ubiquitous Putnam, who would listen to no excuses, and ordered him back to his post on Breed's. The panic-stricken Callender, however, did not return, and his men abandoned him in contempt. His fieldpieces were then, by the order of Putnam, dragged by some of his own men to the rail-fence, and there posted for its defence. Howe's artillery had ceased its fire, on account of another stupid blunder, twelve-pound balls having been for the most part supplied in lieu of six-pound, which the guns required. They were then ordered to be charged with grape. The artillery-wagons, however, got mired at the base of the hill, and became fixed in a position where the guns were of little service.

General Pigot was now advancing up the hill, at a deliberate and regular pace. His men began at once to fire, although they were at a great distance, and continued to discharge their muskets as fast as they could load them, and at every step forward. The Americans had been ordered not to return a shot until the British were within thirty or forty paces. "Powder is scarce, and must not be wasted!"—"Fire low: aim at the waistbands!"—"Wait until you see the white of their eyes!"—"Aim at the handsome coats!"—"Pick off the commanders!" Such were the expedient but rather unmilitary orders hurriedly given by raw officers to raw men. Some of the provincials, however, lost patience, and began to return the British fire. Colonel Prescott angrily rebuked them for their disobedience; and some of his officers sprang on the top of the parapet of the redoubt, and kicked up the muskets which the men were levelling, and about to let off.

Pigot had now brought his grenadiers quite close to the works, when Prescott ordered his whole line to fire. The effect of the volley was murderous, for, as each American was a marksman, hardly a gun missed its aim. The British, however, quickly filled in the empty places of their dead, and, firmly holding their ground, returned the fire, but with little damage to the Americans, who were protected by their redoubt and breastwork. The second volley, which is even more effective than the first, is so terrible, that the enemy are staggered, confused, and driven back in flight. The officers run down after their men, and, brandishing their swords, passionately urge them back. They succeed in rallying them again to face the redoubt, but are once more repulsed; and Pigot, agonized by the carnage, and hopeless of success, orders a retreat. The Americans shouted out a loud and triumphant hurrah as the enemy retired.

While Pigot was thus repulsed in front, Howe was marching his right wing in confidence against the left of the Americans. These latter were ready for the enemy; and as soon as the British showed themselves, General Putnam ordered the artillery abandoned by the inefficient Callender to fire, which was done with excellent effect, "Old Put" himself pointing the pieces. As the enemy advanced, but when still at some distance, several of the provincials, contrary to orders, began to fire. Putnam, however, soon put a stop to this, declaring he would strike down the next man who dared to disobey. The premature musket-balls succeeded in drawing the fire of the British lines, which then began a regular succession of volleys; but their shots were too high, and passed over the heads of the Americans.

The eager provincial marksmen were now permitted to return the enemy's fire, which they did with the usual efficacy of such good shots. Each man rested his musket upon the fence, and, deliberately taking aim, did not fail to bring down his victim. The officers were here, as at the redoubt, picked off the first. "There! see that officer!"—"Let us have a shot at him!" they cried, in their eager rivalry to shoot. The execution was as terrible as it was sure; and the British ranks were so affrighted by the carnage, that they began to retreat in disorder, after the very first volley. The Americans were in high spirits, to which they gave vent in cheers of victory.

When these repulses, so disheartening to the British, were observed by Gage, he determined to fulfil a purpose which he had resolved upon before the struggle. This purpose was, to burn Charlestown. Orders were now given to the battery at Copp's hill to shower shells upon the town; and soon, as the houses and buildings were of wood, the whole place was in a blaze. Simultaneously, Howe and Pigot had rallied their troops, and were commencing a second assault. General Clinton, who had been so coolly looking on from the heights of Copp's hill in the beginning, no sooner observed the repulse of his boasted regulars, than, without awaiting orders, he jumped into a boat, crossed the river, and hurried to the aid of his comrades.

The Americans, too, in confident enthusiasm, were spiritedly preparing for the renewed struggle. Colonel Prescott was encouraging his troops with well-deserved praise, and urging them to obedience in regard to the reserve of their fire. The busy Putnam had galloped off for reinforcements, and was back with a few stragglers only. He inspirited his men, however, who had done their duty so well before, with promises of the same success on the same good conduct in the coming action.

The struggle again began. The British troops seemed resolved on victory, but did not alter their plans of attack. As before, Pigot was moving up the hill in front of the redoubt, and Howe was renewing his flank movement. The well-disciplined regulars marched slowly and steadily to their work.

To the beholder, the whole scene of action was terrific. General Burgoyne, who was a looker-on from the battery at

Copp's hill, said: "Sure I am, nothing ever has been or can be more dreadfully terrible than what was to be seen or heard at this time. The most incessant discharge that ever was heard by mortal ears!... Terrible indeed was that scene," he repeats, "even at our distance. The western horizon was one huge body of smoke, and in the evening a continued blaze; and the perpetual sound of cannon and volleys of musketry worked up our imaginations to a high degree of fright." The scene was no doubt terrific, but the patriots beheld it without dismay, though not without indignation. The provincial troops were not even inconvenienced, for, as the summer breeze quickened toward evening, the dark clouds of smoke were driven aside, and the enemy so revealed to view, that each American musket could mark its victim in the clear light of the summer afternoon.

The British came on as before, firing at every step as they advanced. The Americans, more obedient than on the former occasion, reserved their fire until the enemy were close to them, and then sent forth a murderous volley. The British troops bore it well, notwithstanding its fatal effect upon their ranks, and held their ground. The second volley staggered them, however, and sent them flying back. Their officers did their best to rally them—ordering, threatening, and even trying to goad them back to their duty with the points of their swords. It was, however, all in vain: the men fled to the bottom of the hill. Howe was conspicuous among the officers in their efforts to encourage the troops by their words

and own daring example. He was constantly in the van during the attack upon the fence; and, as one after another of his aids was shot down, and his men were falling back, he was left almost alone, exposed as a prominent mark to the whole American line of sharp-shooters. But neither his example, his commands, nor his threats, could induce his troops to advance in the face of the terrible fire of their foes. They continued their retreat, and in great disorder; some even rushed to the shore, and sprang into the boats.

At this moment, the thousands of patriots who beheld the scene, from every neighboring point of view, were cheered with almost certain hope of final victory; while the British looked on from Boston with anxious alarm. Burgoyne, who was a witness of the whole action from Copp's hill, acknowledged that the moment was critical, for he saw that Howe's forces were staggered. He declared loudly that it would require the utmost exertion of all the officers, from the generals down to the subalterns, to repair the disorder which the hot and unexpected fire of the Americans had produced. A long pause now ensued, while Howe and his generals were striving to reform their disordered troops.

Prescott, in the meanwhile, pointing to the heaps of the dead and dying, which lay scattered on the hill to within a few yards of the works, reminded his men of the good service they had done, and encouraged them to meet with the same spirit the next attack. "If they are driven back once more," said he, "they will never rally again." The men answered him with a cheer, and cried out, "We are ready for the red-coats again!" The colonel, however, felt more anxiety than he cared to express. He knew that the ammunition was failing; and so long had he been expecting in vain the arrival of reinforcements, that he almost gave up all hope of any aid reaching him in time. The British still hesitated about renewing the attack; and the pause appeared so long, that the Americans began to hope that the work of the day was over, and that the victory was theirs.

While Prescott was anxiously awaiting reinforcements, Putnam was doing his best to bring them. He rode to the rear of Bunker's hill, and, meeting with a regiment of Massachusetts men, detailed some for work on the fortifications, and sent the rest to do duty at the fence. He found Gridley falling back, with the view of covering, as he said, the retreat of the patriots, and tried to bring him to the ground again, but did not succeed. Putnam was indefatigable, but failed to get the aid which he hoped, and returned to his post.

Howe now determined upon another assault. Some of his officers loudly opposed it, saying it would be downright butchery to lead the men against the terrible American fire. The general, however, insisted, declaring that British honor was at stake. They must "fight, conquer, or die," as it would never do for "English soldiers to give way before a rabble rout of rustic rebels; and, besides," he continued, "there is no chance now to retreat, as all the boats are on the other side of the river." General Clinton arriving at this moment, and bringing with him a timely reinforcement of four hundred marines, the men were encouraged, and resigned themselves, though with a disheartened air, to the seemingly desperate orders of their commander. Howe had learned wisdom from the "rustics," and prudently assumed their mode of warfare. His troops were ordered to reserve their fire until close to the works, which it was now determined to make the main object of attack. The artillery was, moreover, to be applied more effectually, and to be brought up in such a position as to rake the breastwork and fence. Clinton and Pigot were to lead the left division, against the redoubt; while Howe had reserved for himself and his grenadiers and light-infantry the attack on the breastwork.

The British officers were determined to carry the American works at all hazards of toil and death. They were encouraged by the discovery that the "rebels" were almost without ammunition, and the fact—from the raking fire which the English ships and batteries succeeded in keeping up across Charlestown neck—that the Americans had but little chance of receiving reinforcements. The troops were ordered, if their fire should prove ineffectual, to carry the works at the point of the bayonet. To lighten them for this active service, the men were told to throw off their knapsacks; and some of the soldiers, on that hot day, stripped themselves to their shirt-sleeves.

Prescott now beheld the steady approach of the British with unusual anxiety. His ammunition was reduced to a few artillery-cartridges. These he ordered to be opened, and the powder they contained to be distributed to his troops, begging them "not to waste a grain of it, and to be sure to make every shot tell." A few only of the Americans had bayonets to their muskets, and these were stationed at the most exposed points of the redoubt. Such were the desperate straits to which the rest were reduced for want of means of defence, that they collected together heaps of stones, to use as missiles against the enemy; and the men, laying hold by the barrels, brandished their muskets, and declared that they would beat back the British with the butt-ends.

Howe first made a show of attack on the rail-fence, but he soon concentrated his force against the works. His artillery was so brought to bear, that it swept the breastwork from end to end, and drove its defenders into the redoubt. Prescott saw the success of this manœuvre, and feared the fatal result. He was, however, firm in his determination to resist to the last, and continued resolutely to give his orders, with his usual calmness. His men, whose powder was reduced to little more than a single charge each, were again and again ordered to reserve their fire until the latest moment. When the enemy had reached within twenty yards of the redoubt, the word "Fire!" was given, and the Americans sent forth another of their volleys, with the usual terrific effect: the British ranks were broken by the numerous dead, and the whole body staggered

momentarily; but the columns quickly formed again, and, without returning the fire, advanced steadily forward. As usual, the English officers suffered the most by the American fire, several of them having been killed, and General Howe himself wounded in the foot. He continued, however, to lead on his troops, without giving a momentary regard to his own suffering.

The Americans, with hardly any ammunition left, could no longer fire their fatal volleys; and their shots were so scant, that the British troops succeeded in marching up to the redoubt, and began to scale its walls. A spirited young Irish officer was the first to mount the parapet, which he had just reached, shouting, "The day is ours!" when he was shot down, and with him fell those who had immediately followed. Major Pitcairn, who commanded the British in the skirmish at Lexington, was among the earliest on the wall, and, as he mounted, cried out, "Now for the glory of the marines!" when he was toppled over by a mortal shot, from a negro volunteer.

The British soldiers now began to swarm over, while the Americans ineffectually attempted to resist them by hurling stones at them. This only encouraged the enemy, for they were conscious that the ammunition of the redoubt was exhausted. The struggle now was hand to hand. The British had the advantage of their bayonets and reserved fire, but the Americans made a manful resistance with the stocks of their muskets. It was, however, in vain. General Pigot had succeeded, by the aid of a tree, in mounting the wall; and, springing down into the redoubt, was followed by swarms of his men, whose bristling bayonets filled the space within; and their thronging steps, stirring up the ground, raised such a cloud of dust, that the outlet of the fortress could scarcely be seen. Colonel Prescott, seeing that all hope of further successful resistance was gone, ordered his men to retreat. Driven as they were into a corner, it was difficult for them to get out. Some scrambled over the top of the walls, and others had to cut their way through the opposing enemy. Prescott himself was the last to retire, and only succeeded in escaping by striking down, with his sword, bayonet after bayonet, thrust at his life. He retained his martial bearing throughout. "He did not run, but stepped along, with his sword up." Notwithstanding his cool and deliberate movements, he got off unharmed, although both his "banyan and waistcoat were perforated in several places."*

As the British took possession of the American works, they set up a loud huzza of triumph. They then reformed, and began to fire upon the retreating provincials, doing more havoc than they had yet done. Warren was at this moment killed by a shot through the head; and, as he was among the last to leave the works, there were none to carry him from the field. Colonel Gardner was killed; Gridley and Bridge were wounded; and a number of other officers, with many privates, suffered.

The Americans at the rail-fence, in the meanwhile, had gallantly held their posi-

tion, having resisted all attempts to turn their flank. When, however, they saw that the redoubt was in possession of the enemy, and that their comrades were in full retreat, they also retired, but with wonderful regularity for such raw troops. Their steady courage and excellent order saved Prescott's force from being exterminated; for, by defending the rear, they prevented the British troops from surrounding the American main body, and thus cutting off its retreat. General Putnam steadily withdrew his men, from their position at the base, up the ascent of Bunker's hill, where he strove to bring the rest of the retreating forces to a stand. He rode to the rear of the troops, while the British bullets were flying thick and fast about his head, and entreated them to turn again and front the enemy. "We can make a stand here!" he cried; "we can stop them yet. In God's name, form and give them one shot more!" The slaughter continued dreadful; and still "Old Put," nothing daunted, stopped an artillery-piece, and, pointing it against the pursuers, stood by it until the British bayonets were almost at his breast. Pomeroy, too, another veteran, planting himself with his broken musket in his hand at the side of the resolute Putnam, endeavored by his words and example to rally his retreating comrades. The torrent, however, could not be stayed: the patriots continued their flight over the top and down the side of Bunker's hill, across Charlestown neck (terribly galled as they fled by a fire from the English men-of-war and batteries), and into the country, until they reached Cambridge.

* Frothingham.

23

The British did not continue the pursuit, although General Clinton earnestly begged Howe to follow up his success by pushing on his troops to Cambridge. He seemed, however, satisfied at present with his hardly-earned victory. His men were exhausted by the day's work, and discouraged by the loss of their comrades, among whom the carnage had been so terrible. It was getting late, moreover, it being past five o'clock when the British in pursuit reached Bunker's hill. Here they paused, and, receiving additional forces from Boston, spent the night in raising a breastwork to protect the position.

When Colonel Prescott reached Ward's headquarters at Cambridge, he found the general in great alarm, lest the enemy should advance upon him and catch him when so ill prepared for resistance. Prescott, however, set his mind somewhat at ease, telling him he did not think that the British would be in a very exulting mood after that day's success. The colonel, after receiving Ward's thanks for his gallant conduct, declared that it was true he had been vanquished, but that the enemy had no reason to triumph; for, if the handful of men under his command, though exhausted by fatigue and hunger, had been supplied with sufficient ammunition and with bayonets, he could have held his position. He offered, moreover, to retake the hill that very night, if fifteen hundred men, properly equipped and supplied, should be given him. But the more cautious Ward was not disposed to accede to this daring proposition.

The loss of the British in killed and wounded, in this momentous conflict, was at least one thousand and fifty-four, while that of the Americans was no more than four hundred and fifty.

Though forced to retreat, the Americans gained a great moral victory, while the British sustained equally a defeat. The raw militia had proved that they could not only stand the fire of regular troops, but that they could resist them effectually, with a fair hope of victorious success. Critical judgments severely condemned the conception of the enterprise as rash, but all united in praising the courage and steadiness with which it was executed. An orator in the British house of commons could not withhold his admiration of the American gallantry on the occasion: "To a mind," he said, "which loves to contemplate the glorious spirit of freedom, no spectacle can be more affecting than the action at Bunker's hill. To see an irregular peasantry, commanded by a physician, inferior in number, opposed by every circumstance of cannon and bombs that could terrify timid minds, calmly wait the attack of the gallant Howe, leading on the best troops in the world, with an excellent train of artillery, and twice repulsing those very troops, who had often chased the chosen battalions of France, and at last retiring for want of ammunition, but in so respectable a manner that they were not even pursued—who can reflect on such scenes, and not adore the constitution of government which could breed such men?"*

The struggle on Bunker's hill might

* Governor Johnstone, in a speech in the house of commons, October 30, 1775.

well be condemned on strategic principles, for nothing was gained in a purely military point of view. It had, however, a great influence in promoting the patriotic cause; it gave increased hope to the defenders of that cause, and lessened the confidence of its opponents. The most inveterate tories in Great Britain acknowledged, when they heard of this dearly-bought victory, that "affairs wore a serious aspect in America;" and none now pretended that "with a couple of regiments" the whole of the colonies could be subjected. The friends of America were no less elated than its enemies were depressed. When Washington heard of the struggle at Bunker's hill, his first question was, whether the militia had stood the fire of the British regulars. On being told that they had, he answered, "The liberties of the country are safe."

Though joy was the more common feeling throughout the country at the result of the contest, there was a universal grief at the loss sustained in the death of Warren. Howe passed the highest eulogium on him when he said, as he saw the body of the illustrious patriot lying upon the battle-field, that "his death was worth to the British five hundred of the provincials." WARREN was still a young man when he gave up his life to the cause of his country. He was born in 1740, at the farmhouse of his father in Roxbury. Though of comparatively humble origin, he enjoyed the best opportunities of culture that his country afforded. He graduated at Harvard college, and studied medicine under the most eminent physician at Boston, where he himself prac-

tised his profession, and rapidly reached its highest rank. Though devoted to his art, his impulsive nature soon exhibited a warm sympathy with the patriot cause, and he took an active part in the liberal colonial politics of his day. He boldly joined the bands of the "Sons of Liberty," and became conspicuous as a leader among this brotherhood pledged to the cause of freedom. He was a man cool and judicious in counsel, and yet fervid and even eloquent in utterance. He had so much the reputation of an orator, that he was chosen to deliver, in 1771, the oration commemorative of the Boston massacre. In 1775, he volunteered to perform the same duty, for no other reason than because the British officers had threatened to take the life of any man who should venture upon its performance. Warren's offer was accepted, and the day arrived. The meetinghouse was the place appointed, and the British officers seemed determined upon executing their threat, for they filled the pews, the aisles, and even the pulpit, with armed soldiers. The young orator was obliged to make his way, by means of a ladder, through a window, to a back part of the pulpit. The audience, though threatening in look, kept a profound silence, while Warren began his oration. Such was the power of his earnest eloquence, that even his military auditors, who had come steeled to vengeance, were softened to tears of sympathy and compassion for those martyrs of freedom whose sacrifice the youthful orator so feelingly described.

Warren was so highly esteemed in New England, that he was chosen to succeed

John Hancock as president of the provincial Congress; and when hostilities with Great Britain were imminent, he received the commission of major-general. A contemporary of Warren has said: "He was valued in private life for his engaging manners, and as a physician for his professional abilities. The death of an amiable consort had made his life of the greatest importance to his children; he was willing, however, to risk it in the service of the public. His intrepidity and zeal for the cause he had espoused, together with the electing voice of the provincial Congress, induced him to enter upon the military line. Within four days after his appointment to a major-generalship, he fell a noble sacrifice to the natural rights of mankind. He was of a middling size, and of a lowish stature. The ladies pronounced him handsome."

There were memorable officers, too, who fell on the British side. Lieutenant-Colonel Abercrombie was killed while leading on his grenadiers up the hill. As his soldiers were bearing him from the field, he begged them to spare his old friend Putnam. "If you take General Putnam alive, don't hang him, for he's a brave man," were among his dying words, which showed how his brave heart was beating true to a noble gallantry in its latest pulsations. Major Pitcairn was also greatly beloved, and his death sincerely mourned. "I have lost my father!" cried his son, who was of the same regiment. "We all have lost a father!" was the utterance of each soldier in it. Spendlove and Addison, too, were gallant men; the former a veteran of forty years' service, and the latter a worthy collateral descendant of the gentle author of "The Spectator." Only a single aid-de-camp of Howe, so fatal to the British officers had been the struggle, lived to reach England —Lieutenant Page— whose escape from the bloody conflict on Bunker's hill made him memorable.*

CHAPTER V.

A Sad New-England Sabbath.—The Anxieties of the British at Boston.—The Stir in the American Camp.—Arrival of Washington.—His Life.—Personal Appearance.—The Effect of his Presence in the Camp.—A Council of War.—Organization of the Army.—Reform and Discipline.—Wants.—Want of Government.—Want of Respect.—Want of Uniformity.—Want of Clothing.—Want of Powder.—Want of Money.—No Lack of Spirit.

1775. It was an unusual Sunday for New England, the day after the bloody struggle on Breed's hill. The British cannonade disturbed the peace of the sabbath with its threatening roar. "It has not ceased yet, and it is now three o'clock, sabbath afternoon," writes Mrs. Adams. "It is expected they **June 18.** will come out over the Neck to-night, and a dreadful battle must ensue. Almighty God! cover the heads of our

* Frothingham.

countrymen, and be a shield to our dear friends." A rumor was abroad that the British were about to march to Cambridge, and take dreadful revenge for the slaughter they had suffered on the previous day. From the whole country round crowds were hurrying to the American camp. Some were volunteers, coming with their muskets on their shoulders, to proffer their aid in the approaching danger; and many were fathers, too old to bear arms, mothers, wives, and daughters, who, with hearts stifled with compressed doubts and fears, anxiously sped on their way, and breathlessly caught the joyful word of hope or the agonizing sentence of despair. They came to hear of the life or the death of those they loved. It was a day of mourning to many, and not a joyful sabbath to a single soul. The country was in the agony of its trial, and the throes of its suffering sorely wrung the hearts of the bravest.

The British, however, were in no humor or condition to execute the vengeance which was feared. Their victory, with its terrific slaughter, had staggered them more than an ordinary defeat. As the dead, during that whole day, were borne through the streets of Boston, officers and soldiers looked upon the remains of their comrades with gloomy thoughts, to which they gave utterance in murmurs against their leaders, on account of the sacrifice they had wrought.

Those inhabitants still left in the city whose sympathy was with the patriotic cause, could not conceal their indignation at an army which seemed determined, at any cost of blood, to crush out American liberty. It was feared by the British generals that the "rebels" of Boston would arise in their rage, attack and burn the town. All "unsuspected" citizens were called upon to relieve the military guards by establishing night-patrols. Governor Gage issued a proclamation, requiring the inhabitants to surrender up their firearms, and declaring that "all persons in whose possession any firearms may hereafter be found shall be deemed enemies to his majesty's government." Gage was alarmed, and only thought now of defence, and not of active hostilities. He had good occasion for anxiety, when he saw from day to day the increased animation of the patriotic spirit, and the activity with which the Americans prepared to sustain the cause of their country.

The American camp was soon astir with the daily arrivals of fresh troops from all parts of New England. The patriots, although anxiously expectant of an attack from the British, were now in high spirits, and they even longed to "speak with them again." The militia had learned a great deal at Bunker's hill, and they became not only more cautious and vigilant, but tolerably skilful in availing themselves of the means and appliances of military art. They at once set about throwing up various kinds of defence, and busied themselves in intrenching the heights which they commanded in the neighborhood of Boston. General Putnam, as usual, was indefatigable. After the retreat from Bunker's hill, he had posted his Connecticut men on Prospect hill, and at once began throwing up fortifications. Such was the untiring energy of this aged veteran, that here he was found, as described by his son, two days after the battle, hard at work with his own hands, without having " put off his clothes or washed himself" since. At Roxbury, Winter hill was newly fortified, and Cambridge strengthened by additional works.

June 19.

Little was done, by either the Americans or British, for a fortnight, in the way of hostility. There was an occasional skirmish. At one time, a couple of Indians, belonging to a Massachusetts tribe which had joined the Americans, had surprised, in ambush, an outpost of British soldiers, and shot down with their arrows four of them. This brought in revenge a cannonade from Boston. Bombs were frequently thrown by the enemy, which, however, beyond setting a house or a barn on fire, did little damage. The patriot army was now awaiting the arrival of their new general, GEORGE WASHINGTON, whose reputation, as a gallant officer in the colonial battles, gave great hopes to every man in the American ranks.

Most biographers have fondly traced back the origin of Washington to a William de Hertburn, who lived in the middle of the thirteenth century. This gentleman came into the possession of a manorial estate, in the county of Durham, in England, called Washington, which name he thence assumed, and his descendants after him. A long line of reputable doctors, divines, lawyers, and squires, followed. Among them there was even a knight, a gallant Sir Henry Washington, who fought loyally for King Charles I., bravely sustained the siege of Worcester

against the parliamentary forces, and distinguished himself at the taking of Bristol. Diligent investigators have discovered that, in 1538, there was a Lawrence Washington, who had been a lawyer of Gray's Inn, and mayor of Northampton, to whom the manor of Sulgrave, in Northamptonshire, was granted. Two great-grandchildren of this gentleman went as settlers to the colony of Virginia, about the year 1657. Their eldest brother remained at home; and proof is given of his importance, by the statement of the fact that he married a half-sister of the duke of Buckingham. John and Lawrence were the names of the two emigrants to Virginia, who, being younger brothers, were forced to shift for themselves.

The American hero was immediately descended from Augustine Washington, the second son of Lawrence, the elder of the first two settlers in the colony. Augustine was married twice. By his first wife, Jane Butler, he had four children: Butler, who died in infancy; Lawrence; Augustine; and Jane, who did not survive her childhood. By his second wife, Mary Ball, whom he married on the 6th of March, 1730, he had six children: George, Betty, Samuel, John Augustine, Charles, and Mildred.

GEORGE WASHINGTON was born on the 22d of February, 1732, on an estate which his father held and cultivated as a planter, on the banks of the Potomac, in Westmoreland county. The father died at the age of forty-nine, leaving landed property of sufficient extent to bequeath to each of his sons a plantation, and to make suitable provision for his widow and daughter. Mrs. Washington, upon whom the care of five children devolved, the eldest of whom at the time of the death of her husband was only eleven years, showed herself equal to her charge, and was rewarded for her tender and wise management by a long life, which was graced by the virtues of all her offspring, and rendered triumphant by the glory of her eldest son.

The young George was sent to one of the best schools in Virginia, where, however, there was little in those days to be acquired beyond the elementary reading, writing, and arithmetic. He was a docile child, and soon learned all that the humble learning of his teacher could impart. He was of a kindly, affectionate disposition, and, though somewhat hot-tempered, was a great favorite with his schoolfellows. Strong in constitution, and active and supple in movement, he took the lead in the playground, and few could equal him in wrestling, running, and jumping. He is said even in his boyhood to have shown a martial taste, and to have frequently got up mimic battles, in which he always bore a prominent part, as the leader of one of the fighting-parties.

He was remarkable, at a very early age, for his love of system and order. His copy-books were always written and kept with great neatness; and he seems to have shown, while yet a child, a taste for business. A manuscript book exists, written when he was but thirteen years of age, in which page after page contains copies of bills of exchange, leases, receipts, and land-warrants, all penned with the greatest care, and with hardly a scratch or a blot. He was no less systematic, it would appear, in his study of the proprieties of conduct; for in the same manuscript book there is a part devoted to "Rules of Behavior in Company and Conversation." This consists of written maxims of manners and morals.

Arithmetic was his favorite study, and as he advanced in age he pursued diligently the elements of the higher mathematics, and became proficient in geometry, trigonometry, and surveying. These latter studies were his chief occupation during his last two years at school, which he quitted just before he reached his sixteenth birthday.

His brother Lawrence, who had served with credit as a British officer in the West Indies, and had won the respect and friendship of General Wentworth and Admiral Vernon (from whom he called his plantation "Mount Vernon"), was enabled, through the influence of these distinguished friends, to obtain for George a midshipman's warrant. The lad was all eagerness at this prospect of being a young officer; but his mother would not consent, and Washington was reserved for another and more glorious destiny.

The boy, disappointed of his naval buttons, went to live with his brother Lawrence at Mount Vernon, and there passed the winter in the study of mathematics, with the purpose of preparing himself for the profession of a surveyor. Lawrence had married the daughter of William Fairfax, of a noble English family, and high colonial distinction. Fairfax resided at Belvoir, near Mount Vernon, and at this period he had as a guest at his house no less a personage than Lord Fairfax. His lordship, an accomplished Oxford man, and a writer for "The Spectator," was fond of study, and, becoming naturally a recluse in his habits, had lately arrived with the intention of living upon one of his Virginian estates. Lawrence Washington presented his brother to the Fairfaxes, and an intimacy at once ensued, which in the course of a few months was turned to the profit of the young surveyor.

Lord Fairfax held a large tract of territory lying among the valleys of the Alleghany mountains. As the land was wild and not surveyed, settlers were constantly encroaching upon it. His lordship was therefore desirous of having his property accurately measured and bounded. He accordingly chose Washington for the purpose, who readily undertook the enterprise, as it suited both his business and his tastes. The journey through the wilderness was rough and dangerous, but was accomplished spiritedly, and its object satisfactorily gained. Other engagements ensued, and the youthful surveyor passed three years busily and profitably in his profession.

The threatening troubles with the French and Indians on the frontiers, called out the militia of the province; and Washington, at the age of nineteen, received his first military appointment. He was made adjutant-general, with the rank of major, and the pay of a hundred and fifty pounds a year. His duty was to discipline the militia of one of the districts into which the province was divided.

This appointment revived his military tastes, and he devoted himself with great eagerness to his new pursuit. His brother Lawrence's experience was now of good service, as it enabled him to tutor the young officer in the military art; and he accordingly gave him daily lessons in the use of the sword, the manual exercise, and tactics. George at the same time read industriously all the books he could obtain, and mastered pretty thoroughly the theory of war.

These martial pursuits were now interrupted by the illness of Lawrence, who was in consequence advised to take a voyage to the West Indies. George accompanied him, and they sailed for Barbadoes in September, 1751. They had hardly arrived there, when the younger brother was taken sick with the smallpox; but, although the disease was severe, he so soon recovered in that tropical climate, that he was able to be out again in less than three weeks. Lawrence appeared in the meantime so greatly to have improved, that it was agreed that George, now entirely well, should return to Virginia and bring his brother's wife to Bermuda, where Lawrence proposed to proceed. Lawrence, however, on reaching this island, and finding that he grew weaker, hastened back to Mount Vernon, where he died soon after his arrival.

Of Washington's subsequent military campaigns against the Indians and the French we have already given a record, and the rest of his military history will be developed in the course of this narrative.

Mount Vernon fell to the possession of Washington, by the death of his brother's daughter; and there, in the intervals of his military career, he lived the life of a southern planter. On the 6th of January, 1759, he married Mrs. Martha Custis, a widow three months younger than himself, and the mother of a son and daughter by her former husband, John Parke Custis. She received one third of this gentleman's property, which consisted of several large estates and forty-five thousand pounds sterling in money. Washington thus became greatly enriched, for those early times, by his marriage. Although he had won fame in the wars of the province, and still continued, as a member of the house of burgesses in Virginia, to bear somewhat the character of a public man, Washington retired, soon after his marriage, to his estate on the banks of the Potomac, with the view of passing the remainder of his days in the privacy and simplicity of a country gentleman.

His country now had called him; and he did not hesitate to give up the ease and happiness of his home for the leadership of a cause whose trials and dangers were immediate, while its triumphs, however certain in the future, were yet too indefinite greatly to tempt the desires of the most ambitious.

1775. Washington set out from Philadelphia, on the 21st of June, to take command of the troops at Cambridge, now adopted as the army of the twelve confederated colonies. He was accompanied by Generals Lee and Schuyler, and all three started on horseback,

24

escorted by a troop of gentlemen of Philadelphia. The newly-appointed general was received everywhere on the journey with great distinction. Each town and village was on the alert, and welcomed Washington and his cavalcade with every possible exhibition of respect. Deputations of the principal gentlemen rode out to meet him, and, escorting him to the places whence they came, addressed him in highly-eulogistic terms, expressive of their joy at his appointment.

Washington, even at this late moment, still hopeful of a reconciliation with the mother-country which he so warmly loved, declared to the committee of the provincial Congress of New York, who had addressed him, that "every exertion of my worthy colleagues and myself will be extended to the re-establishment of peace and harmony between the mother-country and these colonies."

It was at New York that the news of the battle of Bunker's hill was first announced to Washington, when he anxiously inquired whether the militia had stood their ground against the British regulars. Upon being told that they had, he answered in these memorable words: "The liberties of the country are safe." He was now more anxious than ever to reach the camp at Cambridge, and sped on with unusual haste. As he entered Massachusetts, he was met by a cavalcade of New-England gentlemen and a committee of the provincial Congress, who addressed him in the usual congratulatory terms, to which the general suitably responded.

Washington's personal appearance produced an impression, upon all who now beheld him for the first time, in every respect corresponding to the reputation which preceded him. His figure was tall and commanding, and the sedate dignity of his demeanor secured respect, while his refined courtesy of manners invited approach. His excellent horsemanship, perfected in the chase, of which he was so fond, added much to the popular effect of his manly appearance. He had, moreover, the true martial bearing: his service in the provincial campaigns, and as an aid-de-camp under that military martinet Braddock, had given him the air of a veteran; for, young as he was, being little over forty, he always appeared older than his years. The nice fastidiousness he exhibited in his dress, which was in character with the systematic regularity of all his personal habits, served still more to distinguish him in the public eye. All the particularities of military costume were seen to be rigidly observed in his personal adornment, and thus a contemporary describes "his blue coat with buff-colored facings, a rich epaulette on each shoulder, a buff under-dress, an elegant small-sword, and a black cockade in his hat." The chastened severity of his countenance, and his formal and somewhat paternal manners, did not even prevent the softer sex from warming in admiration of the new general. "I was struck," writes Mrs. Adams to her husband, "with General Washington. You had prepared me to entertain a favorable opinion of him, but I thought the half was not told me. Dignity, with ease and complacency, the gentleman and soldier, look agreeably blended in him. Modesty marks every line and feature of his face...."

Though "much too *old* a young man" to please the Mrs. Mountains of the cavalier times of Virginia, this sedateness of anticipated age was but an additional claim to the admiration of the prim and pious New-England ladies, who, in the calm sobriety of Washington's manners, saw with no disappointment the absence of any proof of "early wild oats," but looked with satisfaction upon the signs of a well-ordered youth, and anticipated with confidence the hopes they gave of a manhood endowed with a strength of virtue equal to its highest and gravest duties. The young southern aids-de-camp — the Mifflins and Randolphs — doubtless found more favor in the eyes of the Mrs. Mountains of those days, than the rigidly-virtuous Washington.

On reaching Cambridge, Washington was received by the whole army, drawn up to do honor to the occasion. **July 3.** The firing of the artillery, and the loud shouts of the patriots, echoed the welcome with which his presence was hailed. Washington was now escorted to the handsome quarters provided for him, where he and his suite, having alighted and tarried awhile, they returned on foot to the Cambridge common. The general, having stepped forward out of the group of the chief officers who surrounded him, spoke a few words to the assembled troops, and with drawn sword formally assumed command of the continental army. General Greene, of Rhode Island, testified for himself and his officers

in a few well-spoken and dignified words, the satisfaction they should feel in serving under Washington as their commander, and that commander had never a more faithful subordinate.

Washington, with his quick sense of duty, lost no time, but at once set about learning what he had to do and how it was to be done, and doing it. His presence was immediately felt everywhere in the camp by the change effected by his orders. "There is a great overturning in the camp as to order and regularity," writes a contemporary. "'New lords, new laws.' The generals Washington and Lee are upon the lines every day. New orders from his excellency are read to the respective regiments every morning after prayers. The strictest government is taking place, and great distinction is made between officers and soldiers. Every one is made to know his place, and keep in it, or be tied up and receive thirty or forty lashes, according to his crime. Thousands are at work every day from four till eleven o'clock in the morning. It is surprising how much work has been done. The lines are extended almost from Cambridge to Mystic river, so that very soon it will be morally impossible for the enemy to get between the works, except in one place, which is supposed to be left purposely unfortified, to entice the enemy out of their fortresses. Who would have thought, twelve months past, that all Cambridge and Charlestown would be covered over with American camps, and cut up into forts and intrenchments, and all the lands, fields, orchards, laid common — horses and cattle feeding in the choicest mowing-land, whole fields of corn eaten down to the ground, and large parks of well-regulated locusts cut down for firewood and other public uses? This, I must say, looks a little melancholy. My quarters are at the foot of the famous Prospect hill, where such great preparations are made for the reception of the enemy....

"It is very diverting to walk among the camps. They are as different in form as the owners are in their dress; and every tent is a portraiture of the temper and taste of the persons who encamp in it. Some are made of boards, and some of sail-cloth; some partly of one and partly of the other. Again, others are made of stone and turf, brick or bush. Some are thrown up in a hurry; others curiously wrought with doors and windows, done with wreaths and withes, in the manner of a basket. Some are your proper tents and marquees, looking like the regular camp of the enemy. In these are the Rhode-Islanders, who are furnished with tent-equipages, and everything in the most exact English style. However, I think this great variety is rather a beauty than a blemish in the army."[*]

Soon after his arrival at Cambridge, Washington summoned the major and brigadier generals to a council of war. The military appointments by the general Congress, it will be recollected, were, in addition to Washington as commander-in-chief, four major-generals, in the rank and order named, viz.: 1. Artemas Ward.

* Letter of Reverend William Emerson, quoted by Sparks in his Life of Washington.

2. Charles Lee. 3. Philip Schuyler. 4. Israel Putnam; and eight brigadier-generals, viz.: 1. Seth Pomeroy. 2. Richard Montgomery. 3. David Wooster. 4. William Heath. 5. Joseph Spencer. 6. John Thomas. 7. John Sullivan. 8. Nathaniel Greene. The precedence which this established was not altogether satisfactory. Spencer grumbled at the advancement of General Putnam over his head; and Thomas was dissatisfied with the superior rank given to Pomeroy. General Spencer, in fact, took what he considered his relative degradation in such high dudgeon as to leave the army, without having paid his respects to Washington; but he was induced to return, on being promoted to the first rank after Putnam. Pomeroy's resignation gave Thomas a chance of advancement, and the urgent advice of his friends induced him to remain and take the benefit of it. These were some of the minor difficulties which thronged in upon Washington, and embarrassed his action. He continued, however, in the calm and resolute performance of his duty, and went systematically about the organization into an army of the miscellaneous crowd of patriots under his command.

At the council of war, an inquiry was instituted in regard to the numbers and condition of the two armies. Eleven thousand five hundred regulars were given as the estimate of the British force; while the Americans had seventeen thousand men enrolled, of whom only fourteen thousand five hundred were considered capable of duty. The patriot force was deemed inadequate, and it was resolved to make an effort to increase it to twenty-two thousand.

The position of the two opposing camps at this time is best described in a letter written by Washington himself: "I found the British," he says, "strongly intrenching on Bunker's hill, **July 10.** about a mile from Charlestown, and advanced about half a mile from the place of the late action, with their sentries extended about one hundred and fifty yards on this side of the narrowest part of the Neck, leading from this place [Cambridge] to Charlestown. Three floating batteries lie in Mystic river, near their camp, and one twenty-gun ship below the ferry-place, between Boston and Charlestown. They have also a battery on Copp's hill, on the Boston side, which much annoyed our troops in the late attack. Upon Roxbury neck they are also deeply intrenched and strongly fortified. Their advance-guards, till last Saturday, occupied Brown's houses, about a mile from Roxbury meetinghouse, and twenty rods from their lines; but, at that time, a party from General Thomas's camp surprised the guard, drove them in, and burned the houses. The bulk of their army, commanded by General Howe, lies on Bunker's hill, and the remainder on Roxbury neck, except the light-horse, and a few men in the town of Boston.

"On our side we have thrown up intrenchments on Winter and Prospect hills—the enemy's camp in full view, at the distance of little more than a mile. Such intermediate points as would admit a landing, I have, since my arrival, taken care to strengthen, down to Sewall's farm, where a strong intrenchment has been thrown up. At Roxbury, Thomas has thrown up a strong work on the hill, about two hundred yards above the meeting-house; which, with the brokenness of the ground, and a great number of rocks, has made that pass very secure. The troops raised in New Hampshire, with a regiment from Rhode Island, occupy Winter hill; a part of those of Connecticut, under General Putnam, are on Prospect hill. The troops in this town (Cambridge) are entirely of the Massachusetts; the remainder of the Rhode-Island men are at Sewall's farm. Two regiments of Connecticut, and nine of the Massachusetts, are at Roxbury. The residue of the army, to the number of about seven hundred, are posted in several small towns along the coast, to prevent the depredations of the enemy."

Washington arranged the army in three great divisions. The centre, at Cambridge, was under the command of Major-General Putnam; the right, at Roxbury, under Major-General Ward; and the left under Major-General Lee, part of which was at Prospect hill, and the rest at Winter hill. The country, once so beautiful at this season (July), was now sadly changed. The landscape described as so charming with its hills and valleys, rocks and woods, interspersed with straggling villages, with here and there a spire peeping over the trees, and with everywhere fields of the most charming green that delighted eyes ever gazed on, presented now a universal scene of preparation for war. The wide-spread camp covered a surface of several miles in extent;

farmhouses were turned into barracks, and pastures into parade-grounds; and the quiet of the country was disturbed by the daily beatings to arms of the assembled troops.

Washington found a disorderly crowd of followers, whom it required all his generalship to drill into the shape of soldiers; "a mixed multitude of people," he said, "who are under very little discipline, order, or government." Disrespect to officers and unsoldierlike conduct were the chief vices of his irregular forces; and Washington did his best, by means of fines, the pillory, the wooden horse, whipping, and drumming out of camp, to inculcate among his independent militia lessons of respect and subordination. The chief's military eye was greatly offended at the ragged and miscellaneously-assorted dresses of his men. One of his first efforts was to get a supply of ten thousand hunting-shirts, to clothe the nakedness and to give some uniformity of appearance to the troops.

There was a meagerness of supply, in another respect, more serious than any scantiness of clothing. The American army was short of powder. Washington found his " situation in the article of powder much more alarming than he had the most distant idea of." — "We reckoned upon three hundred quarter-casks," wrote his secretary, Reed, " and had but thirty-two barrels." The scarcity, in fact, had become so great, that an order was issued, forbidding any one to waste it in shooting birds, or in any kind of sport. This deficiency became very alarming, as the enemy seemed to threaten an attack, and were daily keeping up a brisk cannonade at the American lines, though fortunately with but little effect, except when the imprudence of the raw militia exposed them to danger. "Two were killed," writes Reed, "at the lines last week, by running after cannon-shot. We scarcely lie down or rise up, but with the expectation that the night or the day must produce some important event." The want of ammunition was not only alarming, but exceedingly vexatious, as it forced Washington to "bear with the rascals on Bunker's hill, when a few shot, now and then, in return, would keep the men attentive to their business, and give the enemy alarms."

Nor were these the only wants which Washington required to be supplied. He was in need of money, being much embarrassed, as he wrote to the president of Congress, for want of a military chest. He also solicited the appointment of a commissary-general, a quartermaster-general, a commissary of musters, and a commissary of artillery. With all these disadvantages of want of discipline, want of ammunition, and want of the means of organization, the American troops were not distrustful of their powers to cope with the enemy, and, in frequent skirmishes with the British, showed no lack of spirit, but often "played the man and beat them."

CHAPTER VI.

Rumors of a Sortie of the British from Boston.—Gage discouraged.—The Ill Condition of the British Force.—The Sufferings of the Patriots at Boston.—Forced Gayety of the Tories.—The American Prisoners.—Ill Treatment.—Sharp Correspondence between Washington and Gage.—Long Inaction.—A Bombardment.—Arrival of Ammunition.—Expedition to Canada determined upon.

1775. RUMORS now began to circulate in the American camp, of an intended sally of the British from Boston. Gage, however, was not much in the humor for active operations against the besiegers. Although reinforced by some troops originally intended for New York, **July.** he began to think, and so wrote to the government at home, that his position was the most disadvantageous possible for action. He now felt himself to be on the defensive, and talked of what he would do in case "the rebels presumed

to make an attack." The troops suffered severely from their fatiguing duties, being kept constantly on the alert by the "audacity" of the provincials, who were continually advancing near to the British lines ever since the "arrival of Generals Washington and Lee to command them." The men, unaccustomed to an American climate, suffered greatly from the heat, to which they were much exposed in their encampments. Their food, too, was so scanty, that even the sick and wounded had often nothing to eat but "salt pork and fish." Strong drink, however, they had in abundance, from which it was impossible to keep the soldiers, for a sixpence would buy a quart of West-India and fourpence the same quantity of New-England rum. With the excessive thirst engendered by the heat of the summer sun, and by their hard work, the men freely indulged in the liquor which was so cheaply obtained, and destroyed their vigor and health. Fevers and dysentery prevailed in the camp, attributed to "the fatigue of duty, bad accommodation, and the use of too much spirits." An occasional supply of fresh provisions would be obtained by a lucky capture, by the British men-of-war, of some stray coaster, when the bells of Boston were rung, as if in honor of a triumph, so greatly overjoyed were the half-starved soldiers at the prospect of a mess of fresh beef or mutton:—

> "Britons, with grief your bosoms strike;
> Your faded laurels loudly weep;
> Behold your heroes, Quixote-like,
> Driving a timid flock of—sheep!"

Thus, with less heart than truth, sneered a whiggish wag of London, on the announcement that General Gage had succeeded in capturing "eighteen hundred sheep and above some one hundred head of oxen, which will be some relief to the troops in general, and of great benefit to the hospitals."

The few patriots left in Boston were subjected to all kinds of annoyances and injury. Now one was clapped into the guardhouse, for seditious conversation; again, another was thrown into prison on suspicion of being a spy, and signalling the enemy from the church-steeple; and all were daily exposed to insult from the soldiers and wrong from the authorities. It was not until food became scarce, that Gage would allow the patriots to leave the city, and thus escape his persecutions. Even then they were not permitted to carry away with them their valuables or any money, beyond a few pounds each. Many, however, succeeded in eluding the vigilance of the guards; and women were known to have carried out their silver spoons, sewed in the lining of their petticoats.

The tory citizens suffered, in common with all, from the scant supply of the luxuries and even the necessities of life, but kept up their hearts with the confident hope that a better time was soon coming, and, as one wrote, that "Boston will be this winter the emporium of America for plenty and pleasure." These loyal folks rather pitied the patriots, and in their letters to those of their friends engaged in the American cause, "heartily wished" they were as safe as they themselves were. They kept up a forced gayety within the besieged town, by an occasional concert and farce, at the playhouse in Faneuil hall, during the week; and managed on Sundays to form a "genteel audience" to listen to the "excellent discourse" of the tory parson, who had "received a call to the elegant new church" vacated by the flight of its patriotic rector.

There were certain sufferers within the besieged city, whose position awakened especially the sympathy of the patriots: these were the prisoners who had been taken at Bunker's hill. Washington, having learned that they were treated with severity, and that, no distinction being made between officers and soldiers, both were thrown into a common jail, determined to write to the British general, and demand redress. His letter was calm and dignified.

The British general sent an answer, which was unnecessarily irritating and impolitic. Gage must have recalled the old times when he and Washington were comrades in Braddock's campaign; and, although the lapse of twenty years had brought the great change which placed them in antagonism as enemies, nothing had ever occurred to ruffle the relations which the two bore to each other as gentlemen. Gage might therefore have forborne the use of those expressions of contumely in which he indulged.

Washington rejoined in severe but well-merited terms, and, true to his word, treated his British prisoners as Gage had treated the Americans. He ordered those who had enjoyed comparative liberty at Watertown and Cape Ann, to be thrust into jail at Northampton. His humanity, however, soon revolted at this severity, and in a few days he countermanded those orders. The correspondence with Gage here closed for ever, as Washington had thought probable.

It was now two months since the arrival of Washington; and, although he had been active in strengthening his defences and in organizing the army—with such a success, that he flattered himself that in a little time he should work up the "raw materials into a good manufacture"—yet little had been done in the way of active hostility. The British were so hemmed in, and so depressed, that they showed even less than the Americans any disposition toward beginning an attack. A battery, however, which in the course of a night had risen under the busy hands of a thousand patriots, on the top of Ploughed hill, excited the enemy to action, and they began a brisk cannonade from Bunker's hill upon the new American works. At one time the British were seen to move, and it was thought that they were preparing for an attack. Washington, accordingly, with hopes of an engagement, sent down five thousand men on the Charlestown road to meet the enemy, and be prepared to give battle. The British, however, did not come out; and, as a contemporary chronicler records, "the most awful silence was observed on both sides." The next day the bombardment was resumed, which the Americans, careful of their ammunition, did not return, except by firing a single pounder, with which they succeeded in sinking a floating battery.

Aug. 26.

The American camp was greatly encouraged by the timely arrival of a supply of ammunition from Rhode Island. It was said to have been got from the various British posts on the coast of Africa, by means of the New-England coasters, which went laden with native rum, and brought back a "fiery commodity of a different quality." So successful was this venture, that every garrison visited on the African coast was supposed to have given up its last ounce of powder, in exchange for the highly-marketable Yankee liquor. The British, however, still kept within Boston, and would give Washington no opportunity to use with effect his fresh supply of ammunition. But while thus condemned to a forced inactivity at Cambridge, he found an occasion Sept. 12. for the employment of a portion of his troops in active service. He had resolved upon sending an expedition to Canada.

CHAPTER VII.

Allen and Arnold disputing for the Command at Ticonderoga.—Arnold called to Account by the Massachusetts Legislature.—Throws up his Commission in High Dudgeon.—Returns to Cambridge.—Is pacified by the Prospect of a Command in the Expedition to Canada.—Appointed to co-operate with Schuyler.—Daniel Morgan and his Rifle-Corps.—Arnold sets out for Canada.—Schuyler sets out also.—Illness of Schuyler.—Montgomery succeeds to the Command.—His Life and Character.—Siege of St. Johns.—Allen succeeded in Command of the Green-Mountain Boys by Seth Warner.—Allen goes on an Expedition on his own Account.—Is defeated and taken Prisoner.—Sir Guy Carleton defeated.—St. Johns surrendered.

1775. WITH the successes of Ethan Allen and Benedict Arnold at Ticonderoga and Crown Point, there began a strife between these adventurous leaders for the command of the forts, which was, as has been already related, temporarily decided by the Connecticut committee, which had accompanied the expedition, in favor of Allen. He therefore remained with his "Green-mountain boys," as commandant of Ticonderoga and its dependencies. Arnold was forced to yield, but did it with an ill grace, while still declaring that his rights had been usurped. "Colonel Allen," he wrote, in a statement of his grievances sent to the Massachusetts committee of safety, "is a proper man to head his own wild people, but entirely unacquainted with military affairs; and, as I am the only person who has been legally authorized to take possession of this place, I am determined to insist upon my right." Allen and his friends

of course had their own views upon the subject, and took care to make them known to the authorities.

In the meantime, the restless Arnold found work for his busy activities. Having armed the sloop, schooner, and the batteaux he had captured at Skenesborough and St. Johns, he appointed his captains, and hoisted his flag as the self-constituted admiral of this Lilliputian squadron. Crown Point was his naval station; and when he heard rumors of the approach of a British force of four hundred from Montreal, he valiantly resolved with his armed vessels and his hundred and fifty men to defend his post, and remain master of the waters of Lake Champlain, upon which his adventurous flag floated so defiantly.

Arnold was enabled to gather valuable information of the proceedings of the British in Canada. He had, during former trading-enterprises, made acquaintances in both Montreal and Quebec, with whom he now, by means of a trusty messenger, held confidential communication. The result Arnold reported to the continental Congress. In his statement he said that there were certain persons in Montreal who had agreed to open the gates to an American force; and that General Guy Carleton, the Canadian governor, had only five hundred and fifty effective men, scattered at different posts, to oppose an attack. He, moreover, expressed his belief that a successful expedition against all Canada could be undertaken with two thousand men; and, offering to lead it, pledged himself for its success.

Arnold was waiting impatiently at Crown Point for an answer to his proposition laid before the Congress, when he was disagreeably surprised and his ardent hopes dashed by the arrival of a "committee of three" from the Massachusetts legislature, empowered to make certain inquiries in regard to his "spirit, capacity, and conduct." The impetuous Arnold could not brook any interference, and he was greatly indignant when the committee laid their instructions before him. There were no charges specified; and, without them, he declared, and with seeming justice, that an inquiry into his "conduct" was against all law and precedent. As for the investigation into his "capacity and spirit," this he in a great rage denounced as an insult. As for the account of expenses which was required of him, all he had to say was, that he had already paid a hundred pounds out of his own pocket, and had incurred debts in behalf of his forces which must be paid,

or he himself would be personally dishonored. Connecticut, to which province Massachusetts had left the decision of the question between Arnold and Allen, had settled it by the appointment of Colonel Hinman as commandant of the forts on Lake Champlain. This so enraged Arnold, that he swore he never would submit to the degradation of being superseded by a junior officer. Full of wrath and disappointment, he resolved upon throwing up his commission, and wrote a letter of resignation. His men were discharged by Arnold, and, as they were unpaid, they became as unruly and resistant as their discontented leader. They were, however, soon pacified by the liberal promises of the committee, and most of the soldiers were induced to re-enlist. Arnold himself hurried back to the army at Cambridge, where he continued violent in his complaints of wrong, and restlessly discontented, until Washington — conscious of the daring and capacity of the man — found in the proposed expedition against Canada a suitable scope for the exercise of that turbulent spirit which seemed only calm in difficulty and danger.

Congress was naturally distrustful of the propositions which it had received from such men as Allen and Arnold. When the former was writing in such a "Bombastes" vein of what he could and would do; and when the plans of the latter, however rational they might seem, came from one whose conduct was a subject at least of question, it was right that no hasty act of legislative concurrence should commit the Congress to plans coming from such apparently doubtful sources. Both Arnold's and Allen's letters were characteristic of the men. Those of the former were arrogant and self-seeking, and those of the latter exaggerated and incoherent. Allen writes to the provincial Congress of New York: —

"I wish to God America would, at this critical juncture, exert herself agreeably to the indignity offered her by a tyrannical ministry. She might rise on eagles' wings and mount up to glory, freedom, and immortal honor, if she did but know and exert her strength. Fame is now hovering over her head. A vast continent must now sink to slavery, poverty, horror, and bondage, or rise to unconquerable freedom, immense wealth, inexpressible felicity, and immortal fame.

"I will lay my life on it, that, with fifteen hundred men and a proper train of artillery, I will take Montreal. Provided I could be thus furnished, and if an army could command the field, it would be no insuperable difficulty to take Quebec."

Arnold, after stating the plan he proposed, which we have already mentioned, writes to the continental Congress at Philadelphia: —

"I beg leave to add that, if no person appears who will undertake to carry the plan into execution, I will undertake, and with the smiles of Heaven answer for the success, provided I am supplied with men, to carry it into execution without loss of time.....

"In order to give satisfaction to the different colonies, I propose that Colonel Hinman's regiment, now on their march from Connecticut to Ticonderoga, should form part of the army — say one thousand men — five hundred men to be sent from New York, five hundred of General Arnold's regiment, including the seamen and marines on board the vessels (no Green-mountain boys)."

The "no Green-mountain boys," in the parenthesis, was a vindictive thrust at Allen, whom Arnold hated as a rival, and feared, from his adventurous spirit and his popularity among the wild settlers of the "New-Hampshire grants," as a competitor in his own line of daring enterprise. The services of both Allen and Arnold, however, were too valuable to be disregarded; and both, as we shall see, were to be again availed of.

Schuyler, of New York, who had been appointed one of the major-generals of the army, was, after some hesitation and delay, directed by the continental Congress to attempt, by the way of the forts on Lake Champlain, an **June 17.** invasion of Canada. The time was now supposed to be favorable, as the governor, Guy Carleton, was strengthening the Canadian fortifications, and awaiting reinforcements, to retake Ticonderoga and Crown Point. It was believed that the French-Canadians, averse to British dominion, were ready to welcome any prospect of deliverance from their English masters, and that they would be ready to enroll themselves under the banner of the first continental force that should present itself. Schuyler was accordingly urged to advance as rapidly as possible into Canada, that he might avail himself of the present favorable disposition of the people, and anticipate the preparations for defence which had been made by the British authorities.

Washington saw Arnold often at head-quarters, and was so struck with the undaunted spirit of the man, and his evident familiarity with the ground and position of affairs in Canada, that he did not hesitate to confide to him the command of the force he had resolved upon sending, to co-operate with Schuyler. Eleven hundred men were detached for this service. They were for the most part picked New-England troops, to which were added three companies of riflemen from Pennsylvania and Virginia. At the head of this rifle-corps was Captain DANIEL MORGAN, who, on his arrival in the camp with his band of sharpshooters a few weeks before, had greatly excited the curiosity of the whole army. Morgan himself was a remarkable man in appearance, with his great, stalwart frame; and his followers were no less conspicuous for their size and strength. Many of them were gaunt Irishmen, and their leathern huntsmen's dress added to their wildness of aspect. Each wore upon his breast the motto "Liberty or death!"—and, what with their fierce look and unrestrained manners, Daniel Morgan and his men were regarded by the prim New-Englanders very much as if they were so many savages. The camp was not averse to their departure, as, apart from their somewhat rude bearing, the fact of so many of them being Irishmen was no recommendation in those early days to popular favor.

Arnold, having been appointed colonel by Washington, set out, on the 13th of September, with his eleven hundred men, for Canada. The expedition was one full of danger and difficulty, and was thus peculiarly attractive to its bold and adventurous leader, as it was to other youthful and ardent spirits, who fretted impatiently against the inactivity of the camp at Cambridge. Aaron Burr, then only twenty years of age, was at that time serving in a New-Jersey regiment, but, when he heard of Arnold's expedition, offered himself as a volunteer, and was accepted, much to the satisfaction of his martial longings. The chief officers under Arnold as the colonel, were Lieutenant-Colonel Christopher Greene, Lieutenant-Colonel Roger Enos, and Majors Bigelow and Meigs.

The route to be taken by the expedition was by the Kennebec river, through a wilderness, to Canada, and was known only through the reports of some rare traveller or the vague accounts of the Indians. Two explorers were sent in advance, to make their way secretly to Quebec, and to return to Arnold on his march with what information they could obtain. Washington had made every possible provision for the success of the enterprise. Transports were provided at Newburyport, and carpenters sent from Cambridge to construct two hundred batteaux on the banks of the Kennebec for the conveyance of the troops up that river. Arnold marched to Newburyport, and thence, after taking care to send out several small boats, to look if the coast was clear of British cruisers, embarked his force in the eleven vessels which had been provided, and sailed on the 19th of

September for the mouth of the Kennebec river.

General Schuyler had in the meanwhile, in accordance with the orders of Congress, left New York for the north, reaching Ticonderoga on the 18th of July, where he was long delayed in fortifying that post. Having placed the fort under the command of General Richard Montgomery, Schuyler returned to Albany, to meet with the chiefs of the Caughnawagas and of the Six Nations, assembled to confer with him, with the view of a treaty. While here, he received a despatch from Washington at Cambridge, informing him of the project he had devised of sending a detachment of his troops to Canada. This intelligence was joyfully received by Schuyler, as it fell in very opportunely with the expedition which he himself had just resolved — in consequence of some information he had received of the position of affairs in Canada — to send against that province. He answered Washington's despatch, with a very hopeful expression of the probable success of the proposed enterprises, and immediately prepared to perform his share of the undertaking.

From Albany Schuyler pushed on to Ticonderoga, but, on arriving there, found Montgomery had gone, leaving word for his superior to follow him at once in a whale-boat. Montgomery had heard of a proposed movement of Sir Guy Carleton, by which that British officer intended, with a fleet of armed vessels, which were nearly ready, to sail from St. Johns through the Sorel river into Lake Champlain. To anticipate this manœuvre, Mont-

gomery embarked in haste with a thousand men and two fieldpieces, and sailed from Ticonderoga to the Isle aux Noix, with the view of taking possession and fortifying that island, at the entrance of the Sorel river, and thus preventing the approach of the enemy.

Schuyler, on his arrival at Ticonderoga in the night, was so ill with fever, that he was unable to follow Montgomery until the next morning, and then by the slow conveyance of a batteau instead of a whale-boat, as he was too weak to proceed except on a bed, which could only be spread in the larger craft. It was several days before he overtook Montgomery; and then, assuming the command, the force proceeded to the Isle aux Noix, which they reached on the 4th of September. Trusting to the report of very formidable preparations by the enemy, Schuyler, after sailing down the Sorel to within a mile and a half of St. Johns, and receiving a few shots from the garrison, determined to return to the Isle aux Noix. Upon reaching this place, Schuyler yielded up the command to Montgomery, and returned himself to Ticonderoga, to recruit his broken health, and do what he could in furthering the objects of the expedition, by forwarding men and supplies.

Aug. 30.

RICHARD MONTGOMERY was perhaps as ardent and hasty as Schuyler was cool and cautious. Quick blood was characteristic of the Irish descent of the former, and torpid phlegm was not unnatural in one of Dutch origin. Montgomery, although born in Ireland, came early to America, as a young subaltern in a British regiment, but won a commission as lieutenant by his bravery at Louisburg. Subsequently serving with Amherst, he was promoted to a captaincy; and at the close of the French War, he retired to England. His visit to America, however, had attached him to the land and its people. He accordingly sold his commission, and, purchasing an estate on the banks of the Hudson, retired there with a wife whom he had married in New York: here he desired to live a quiet life, in domestic happiness and the peaceful pursuit of husbandry. His repose, however, lasted but three years. The disturbances with the mother-country having broken out, he joined the popular cause, and was, from his earnest attachment to the principles of liberty, and his military experience, elected by the continental Congress second in rank of the brigadier-generals. He was still a young man, not having reached his fortieth year, but had the reputation of prudence in counsel, although known to be impetuous in spirit. His personal appearance was all in his favor, having a frank, handsome face, and a well-proportioned, manly figure. He was a great favorite with his men, and in action they did not hesitate to follow willingly wherever their gallant commander led them.

Montgomery, now in command, was eager to be at work: so he prepared at once to invest St. Johns. He first sent forward a force of five hundred men, to command the junction of the two roads which lead to Chambly and Montreal, and thus cut off supplies and reinforcements from that direction. Montgomery then,

having thrown across the entrance to Sorel river a quantity of trees and brushwood, to stop the progress of the enemy's vessels into the lake, advanced his forces and artillery to within a short distance of St. Johns. Here, while exposed to a brisk fire, he commenced his operations for a siege, constructing batteries and other covers for his attack. His means, however, proved miserably scanty. His artillery was deficient in guns, and not of sufficient weight; his ammunition was small in quantity, and his men were not sufficiently skilled in the management of the cannon. The ground, too, on which he had taken his position was swampy, and so crowded with trees and undergrowth as to interfere greatly with the works. To add still more to his misfortunes, disease broke out among the troops, who, finally losing spirit, began to grow disaffected. Montgomery now proposed to change his position to a spot at the northwest, where some heights would give him more suitable ground, and a better chance at the enemy. This plan, after some opposition on the part of the men and officers, was finally adopted; and the troops shifted their position, and began to throw up anew some works on the fresh place selected.

While Montgomery was at the Isle aux Noix, Ethan Allen and Major Brown had been sent with a few men on a secret enterprise into Canada, to **Sept. 5.** endeavor to obtain recruits among the inhabitants of that province, who were reported to be favorably disposed toward the patriot cause. Allen had been obliged to yield the command of his beloved

"Green-mountain boys" to Seth Warner. In his own account of his loss he said: "Notwithstanding my zeal and success in my country's cause, the old farmers on the New-Hampshire grants, who do not incline to go to war, have met in a committee meeting, and, in their nomination of officers for the regiment of Green-mountain boys, have wholly omitted me. I find myself in the favor of the officers of the army and the young Green-mountain boys. How the old men came to reject me I can not conceive, inasmuch as I saved them from the encroachments of New York."—"The old men," says Irving, who quotes this letter, "probably doubted his discretion."

Allen, thus deprived of his command, was so desirous of having a share in the expected glories of the northern expedition, that he solicited employment from Schuyler, and was accordingly attached to the army. That so *harum-scarum* a character should be intrusted with the delicate service upon which he was now engaged, seems very remarkable; but his success was still more astounding, if we can take his own word:—

"I am now," Allen writes to Montgomery, "at the parish of St. Ours, four leagues from Sorel, to the south. I have two hundred and fifty Canadians under arms. As I march, they gather fast. You may rely on it, that I shall join you in about three days, with five hundred or more Canadian volunteers. I could raise one or two thousand in a week's time; but I will first visit the army with a less number, and, if necessary, go again recruiting. Those that used to be enemies to our cause, come cap in hand to me; and I swear by the Lord, I can raise three times the number of our army in Canada provided you continue the siege. The eyes of all America, nay, of Europe, are or will be on the economy of this army and the consequences attending it."

Brown and Allen, who had separated in the course of their recruiting-duties in Canada, now met between Longueuil and La Prairie. Brown, declaring that the garrison at Montreal was composed only of some thirty men, suggested that the occasion was favorable for an attack upon that city. Allen's adventurous spirit was up in a moment, and he eagerly seized the opportunity of distinguishing himself. It was then agreed between the two, that the enterprise should be undertaken by them jointly; and it was arranged that Allen should return with his force to Longueuil, and cross the St. Lawrence to the opposite bank a little below Montreal, while Brown should proceed farther up the river with his two hundred men and land above the city. The two forces were then to march from their several positions, and attack Montreal simultaneously from two opposite points.

The two men separated, and Allen led his eighty Canadians and thirty Americans—for this was the whole extent of his force, notwithstanding the grandiloquent account he had sent to Montgomery of the success of his recruiting-service—back to Longueuil. On arriving at this place, which is nearly opposite to Montreal, he was disappointed in **Sept. 24.** not finding a sufficient number of canoes to take all his men over the river at once.

He succeeded, however, in getting them all across in the course of the night, and in safety, notwithstanding that the weather was boisterous, and the stream so disturbed by the blustering wind, that it was with difficulty the canoes were kept from being overset. Sending out guards on the road to Montreal, to prevent a surprise, Allen anxiously awaited to hear of Brown's landing. The night was fast passing, and no word came from Brown; day dawned, and still nothing was heard of the impatiently-waited-for Brown.

In the meanwhile, the enemy had got the alarm, and sent out forty regulars and a considerable number of Canadians and Indians, to drive away the invaders. Allen could not retreat, as there were not enough canoes to take his men back to the opposite side of the river, and he accordingly prepared to give battle. A severe struggle ensued, which lasted for nearly two hours; but most of Allen's raw Canadian recruits having given way, he was left with only twenty-eight Americans, seven of whom were wounded. There was no alternative now for Allen but surrender, and he accordingly yielded himself up to the British major and his force, with the condition, however, of honorable terms for himself and his men. He was then led into the city, and brought before General Prescott, the commandant, when—

"He asked me," writes Allen, "my name, which I told him. He then asked me whether I was that Colonel Allen who took Ticonderoga. I told him I was the very man. Then he shook his cane over my head, calling me many hard names,

among which he frequently used the word 'rebel,' and put himself in a great rage." The wild appearance of Allen and his men, with their rough huntsmen's shirts, had certainly nothing of the military "regulation" character, and it was not surprising that a general of the "regular army" should look at his prisoners as so many freebooters. "Their leader," says Irving, "albeit a colonel, must have seemed worthy of the band; for Allen was arrayed in rough, frontier style—a deerskin jacket, a vest and breeches of coarse serge, worsted stockings, stout shoes, and a red woollen cap."

Ethan was treated without regard to his rank as colonel, and he and his men were indiscriminately handcuffed, shackled, and sent away to be thrust into the hold of the Gaspée schooner-of-war, and thus carried to England; the British commandant of the fort swearing at Allen as he was led off, and telling him he deserved a halter.

Allen, before the schooner sailed, took occasion to write to General Prescott, in his usual rhetorical vein, and then reluctantly yielded to his fate. The Gaspée schooner was his prison for five weeks, and then he was transferred at Quebec to another British vessel, which carried him to Falmouth, in England, where he was confined in Pendennis castle. Subsequently he was sent back to America, and, after an imprisonment of a year and a half at New York while in possession of the British forces, he was exchanged for an English officer, when he retired to his home in Vermont, and lived there to a good age, to talk and write copiously about his wonderful exploits and adventures.

While poor Ethan Allen's ambitious flights were thus suddenly clipped at Montreal, a great triumph awaited his old band of "Green-mountain boys," under the command of Seth Warner, with the aid of Brown, who, for some reason or other which has never been explained, instead of fulfilling his agreement with Allen, had returned to the main body under Montgomery. General Guy Carleton, having finished his boats, and gathering a large but miscellaneous force of British, Canadians, and Indians, embarked them at Montreal, with the view of proceeding to the relief of St. Johns, invested by Montgomery. Carleton, however, in attempting to cross the St. Lawrence, met with an unexpected opposition from Seth Warner, who with his "Green-mountain boys" posted on the bank of the river near Longueuil, opened such a brisk fire upon the enemy, that they were forced in great confusion to fall back again into Montreal. This, together with Brown's success at Chambly, and his defeat of a band of Highlanders on their march to co-operate with Carleton, decided the fate of St. Johns. Montgomery, as soon as he received word of the defeat of Carleton, summoned the garrison to surrender, informing the commandant that his expected reinforcement had been cut off. The brave Preston, the British commandant, doubted the truth of the report, and declared that he would still hold out for four days; but, provided the aid he anticipated did not come in the course of that time, he would give up the fort. The aid of course did not come. St. Johns was then surrendered. Montgomery now advanced upon Montreal, the gates of which were opened without Nov. 12. resistance, and the Americans entered in triumph.

CHAPTER VIII.

1775. ARNOLD entered the Kennebec on the 20th of September, and sailed up to Gardiner without difficulty, save the grounding of one or two of his transports, which were, however, finally got off. At Pittston, opposite to Gardiner, he found in readiness the two hundred batteaux which had been constructed by the

26

carpenters sent by Washington from the camp at Cambridge; and he accordingly transhipped his men and provisions into these boats, and continued his route to Fort Western. On reaching this point, Arnold found an Indian messenger, with news from the two pioneers he had sent on in advance to obtain information of the proposed route of the expedition. There was little, however, that was satisfactory in the communication received, as the pioneers had only penetrated as far as the head-waters of the Dead river, and sent back such discouraging accounts of the dangers and difficulties of the wilderness, that it was presumed they had given ear to the exaggerated tales of the Indians, who, although professing to be friendly to the Americans, were suspected to be in the interest of the British in Canada.

Arnold, however, was not the man to be swerved from his purpose by any reports of danger, nor in fact by danger itself. He accordingly persisted in his plan of forcing his way through the wilderness, in spite of its terrors. The course he marked out for himself was along the western branch of the Kennebec, called the Dead river, and through Lake Megantic into the Chaudiére. Arnold, having sent in advance two parties of half a dozen men each, to survey the route and obtain what information they could, began to move his whole force. The army was divided into four parts, each of which set out on separate days, that there might be always a day's distance between the divisions. Morgan, with his riflemen, led the van; on the next day went Greene and Bigelow, with three companies; on the third, Meigs with four; and finally, on the fourth, Enos with the remainder.

Arnold having, with great personal effort, succeeded in starting his forces, now set out himself in a birch-canoe, and pushed his way so rapidly along the Kennebec, that on the third day he reached the van of his little army under Morgan, who had got as far as the falls of Norridgewock. Here there was a portage, and it became necessary to land and carry the boats around the falls, to the part of the stream above, where it was navigable. As the banks of the river were composed chiefly of irregular rocks, the labor of the men was immense; but Arnold, always active, and personally overseeing all the details of the work, succeeded in getting each division, as it came up, in safety around the falls. They were not able to set out again on their route for nearly a week, in consequence of the condition of the batteaux, which, being new and hastily constructed, leaked so badly, that much of the provision was damaged. They had their carpenters, however, with them, who set to work making the necessary repairs, and all the boats were again launched and pushing on their course.

Arnold remained until the last batteau had shoved off, and then betook himself again to his birchen canoe, with his Indian guide, and paddled swiftly on, passing all the boats, until he reached the "Great Carrying-place," between the Kennebec and its western branch, or Dead river. The first two divisions of his force had already arrived at this place, and here awaited them a labor more toilsome than even what they had already undergone. The men thus far had successfully overcome all the difficulties of their arduous voyage. They had forced their course against the rapid current by often jumping into the stream up to their waists, and shoving their boats along by main strength. "You would have taken the men," wrote Arnold to Washington, "for amphibious animals, as they were great part of the time under water." They had been obliged to drag or carry their boats already over no less than four portages. The men, however, had borne the labor and exposure so far without much suffering; for, although the effective force was reduced, by illness and desertion, from eleven hundred to nine hundred and fifty, there had been but one death. Arnold was, as usual, full of hope, and sanguinely held out to his men that he would take them to the Chaudière river in little more than a week.

But the "Great Portage" was now before them, and its obstacles proved more formidable than was anticipated by Arnold. The batteaux were to be alternately carried by the men, dragged by oxen, and floated, through a space of some fifteen miles of rugged territory, with precipitous granite rocks, morasses, ponds, and other rude features, of what was then a remote wilderness, and is still a wildly-picturesque country. Arnold, however, undertook the work, and accomplished it. His men were able to obtain a welcome refreshment in the large quantities of salmon and trout which they caught in the lakes and streams; and Arnold judiciously built a log-house on the route, where

he left the sick and disabled, and thus disembarrassed himself of those who only encumbered his progress. On reaching the Dead river, and launching their batteaux upon its waters, the men, as they moved easily on its smooth surface, with hardly a resistance from the gentle current, were cheered with the hope that their greatest trials were over. They continued their course in fine spirits, and looked with delighted wonder upon the solemn beauties of the scenery, where great mountains, topped with snow, rose high and clear above the forest wilderness.

On reaching the base of one of the highest of the mountain-range, Arnold hoisted the American flag, and encamped his men, for several days' repose. There seems to have been still a superfluity of animal spirits in the army, for one of the officers took occasion to mount to the top of the peak which is now called "Mount Bigelow," from the adventurous major of that name who accomplished the ascent.

Arnold now began to fear that his provisions would fall short; so he sent back a party of ninety men for supplies: but, directing them to make the utmost speed, so as not to detain him, he continued to pursue his route. The riflemen he sent on in advance, and followed himself with the second division a day subsequently. He had no sooner started, than it began to rain, and did not cease for three days, pouring down a perfect deluge, drenching the men to the skin, and wetting the baggage through and through. The river now began to swell from the effects of the constant rain, and the current became so rapid, that it was with the utmost difficulty the boats could stem the torrent. Worn out with fatigue, the men landed and encamped at the close of a day of hard work, upon some low ground on the margin of the stream, and had hardly laid down for a night's repose, when the river, which had overflowed its banks, came rushing in upon them so rapidly, that they barely succeeded in reaching their boats. Embarked again, they found themselves bewildered in their attempts to keep their course, and were constantly wandering out of their way into the smaller branches of the river, which had been swollen into great streams by the deluge. The waters, too, were so thick with driftwood and so turbulent, that there was danger every moment of the whole fleet of boats being swamped; and finally seven of the batteaux were upset, and everything in them swept away in the torrent.

The men now became so disheartened by this accident, which greatly diminished their supplies, that Arnold thought it expedient to land and consult with his officers upon what should be done in the emergency. By the advice of their leader, who was never despondent, it was resolved to persevere, after the force should be relieved of those who were too ill or faint-hearted to proceed. A number were accordingly sent back, and with them orders to Greene of the third, and Colonel Enos who had command of the last division, at some distance still in the rear, to select their strongest men, and, hurrying forward with them, to leave the rest to

return along with Arnold's own invalided party to Norridgewock. Greene did as he was bid; but Enos, instead of obeying his orders, retreated with his whole force to Cambridge, where he was tried by a court-martial, and acquitted on the plea of a want of provisions.

Washington, on hearing of Enos's abandonment of his leader, was greatly grieved, though he did not seem to doubt but that Arnold would ultimately overcome every obstacle. "Notwithstanding this great defection," wrote the commander-in-chief, "I do not despair of Colonel Arnold's success." Arnold showed himself in every respect worthy of this confidence in his resolute energies, and continued, under increasing trials to his patience and courage, to strive on as manfully as ever.

The weather continued to get worse, for the rain changed to a heavy fall of snow, and the men suffered now from excessive cold as well as from the dripping wet; while, to add to their discomforts, ice formed upon the water, through which they had to break when wading and dragging their boats along. Arnold, unwilling to force his army through difficulties which seemed too much for their powers of endurance, now determined to push on with a small party in advance, with the hope of being soon able to reach the river Chaudiére, and to send back, from the settlement on its banks, provisions of which they stood greatly in need to reinvigorate those left behind, and thus enable them to continue their arduous progress. He accordingly set out with sixty men, along a route which was but a repetition of the same difficulties and obstructions which he had already experienced. The weather continued bad, the portages did not diminish in number, and the men were constantly exposed to the severe cold, and kept hard at work dragging their boats through the river while up to their waists in the water, or carrying them for miles together over the rugged land, past fall after fall.

On entering Lake Megantic, Arnold overtook the pioneers who had been sent in advance to cut away the wood with the hatchet, and otherwise clear the way, and was met by one of his messengers, who brought back most favorable accounts of the friendly disposition of the Canadians toward the expedition. This was encouraging; but what was more particularly required now by the half-famished men was, something to satisfy their hunger. So scarce had food become, that they were obliged to kill their dogs and eat the flesh; and when this supply was exhausted, they were reduced to the necessity of making a soup out of their mooseskin moccasins! Arnold now felt the urgent necessity of an immediate effort for relief; and, accordingly, landing his main force on the bank of the lake, with orders to move leisurely on by land, he hastily equipped half a dozen boats, and, taking sixteen men with him, pushed on up the lake. They quickly reached the northern extremity of Lake Megantic, and entered the Chaudiére. Without guides they began the dangerous navigation of this turbulent stream, and, getting among the rapids, three of the boats were overturned, and six of the men had a hard struggle for life. They were, however, saved from drowning, and conveyed to the land, where, after drying their clothes, they took to their remaining boats, and prepared to hurry forward. At this moment, one of the party, having proceeded for some distance in advance, cried out, "A fall ahead!" And, sure enough, they were just on the verge of a cataract, and barely had time to save themselves from being swept over, with the result of certain death to every man of them. They were now obliged to carry their boats around this dangerous fall; and, starting again, they finally succeeded, without further accident, in reaching the French settlement of Sertigan, near the Chaudiére and Des Loups rivers. **Oct. 30.** Arnold found abundance of provisions here, and immediately sent back a supply to his famished troops. The relief proved timely, for they had been reduced almost to starvation. They were found coming slowly and disconsolately along the banks of the river, having lost all their boats, with most of the baggage, in the turbulent waters of the Chaudiére. Refreshed with abundance of food, they hurried their march, and soon began, in straggling detachments, to enter Sertigan, where they all finally arrived in a few days.

Arnold now, as he was approaching the Canadian capital, was anxious that Schuyler, with whom he was to co-operate, should be made aware of his movements. He therefore, with an imprudent confidence, intrusted a chance Indian with a despatch to the American general, which was enclosed in a letter to one of Arnold's friends in Quebec. Arnold was encouraged by the reception which he met with among the inhabitants of the valley of the Chaudiére. He had followed the directions of Washington, who had urged upon him to treat the Canadian people with great kindness, to avoid offending in any respect their religious prejudices, and strictly to regard their rights of property. Arnold had been provided with printed manifestoes, setting forth the cause of the provincials, and appealing to the Canadians for active sympathy. These were diligently distributed, and appeared to produce everywhere a favorable effect. After a delay of a few days in the enjoyment of the abounding hospitality of the generous and simple-minded French inhabitants of that sequestered valley, Arnold moved on with all his force, and arrived at Point Levi, opposite to Quebec, on the 13th of November.

1775.

Arnold was disappointed, on reaching the shore, to find that there were no boats to take his force across the St. Lawrence. The enemy, in fact, had learned the particulars of his march through the despatch to Schuyler, which had been intrusted to the Indian messenger, and who had treacherously delivered it up to the British officer in command at Quebec. The boats were accordingly all withdrawn to the Quebec side of the river, a frigate and a sloop-of-war stationed in the St. Lawrence to intercept the invaders, and additional troops from Sorel and Newfoundland hurried in to reinforce the garrison. Arnold's impetuosity, however, was not to be checked; and getting together, through the agency of the Indians and Canadians who had joined him, a number of birchen canoes, he succeeded, in the course of a night, in setting all but a hundred and fifty of his men on the Plains of Abraham, having landed at "Wolfe's cove," and clambered with his men the same rugged path up which that brave general had led the British troops.

The American commander, conscious of the increased strength of the garrison, could have had little hope of a successful assault; but, as he had reason to believe that the inhabitants of Quebec were disaffected toward their rulers and favorably disposed toward his own enterprise, he was determined to try the temper of the people. Arnold accordingly marched his force close to the walls of the city, and ordered them to send up three loud huzzas, with the hope that the troops would be provoked to make a sally, and that the gates being thus opened, the Canadians would take the occasion of co-operating with him. He was, however, disappointed in the effects of his bravado, for the garrison only answered it by a salute from their guns. Arnold next tried the lieutenant-governor, with a pompous demand, in the name of the American Congress, to surrender. This, of course, the British officer, confident in his superior force, and the humble means of his enemy, contemptuously disregarded.

Arnold was now fain to depart, particularly as he heard from some of his old friends in Quebec that the British were about coming out to attack him with a large force, and knew that his own troops were so deficient in numbers and in supplies of ammunition—for they had but five rounds of cartridge to a man—that it would be folly to attempt a resistance. He acordingly marched up the banks of the St. Lawrence, and took post at Point aux Trembles, to await the approach of Montgomery.

CHAPTER IX.

Montgomery enters Montreal without Opposition.—Sir Guy Carleton enclosed between two American Forces.—Escapes in Disguise, but loses his Flotilla.—Montgomery worried by the Disobedience of his Troops.—Many refuse to follow Him.—He marches, however, with a Few, and joins Arnold.—Montgomery assumes the General Command, and marches to the Plains of Abraham.—Quebec summoned to surrender.—A Siege.—Vain Attempts to communicate with the Disaffected Inhabitants of Quebec.—An Ice-Battery.—An Assault determined upon.—Trouble among the American Troops.—The Assault begins.—Its Progress.—Death of Montgomery.—Morgan's Desperate Struggle, and Final Capture.—Failure of the Assault.—Arnold succeeds to the Chief Command, and is promoted to the Rank of Brigadier-General.—Retires to a Short Distance from Quebec, and prepares to receive an Expected Attack from the British.

1775. As Montgomery entered Montreal without opposition, on the 12th of November, Sir Guy Carleton, the governor of Canada, passed hurriedly out with his officers and small force, and, embarking in a half-dozen river-craft, sailed down the St. Lawrence with the view of reaching Quebec. The Americans, however, under the command of Major Brown, after their success at Chambly, and the defeat of the Highlanders sent to reinforce Carleton, had taken possession of a post at the mouth of the Sorel, which they fortified, so placing their guns as to command the passage of the St. Lawrence between Montreal and Quebec. Carleton attempted to pass this resistance, and was driven back, with his small flotilla. He now found himself imprisoned between Montgomery above, at Montreal, and the American batteries at the mouth of the Sorel below, with hardly a hope of escape.

Montgomery was eager to get hold of Carleton—as his capture, he believed, might settle the fate of Canada. Carleton was equally anxious to save himself, but was perplexed to discover the means, and remained fixed, with his vessels anchored in the St. Lawrence, with the enemy above and below. Montgomery now made a move which appeared decisive. He came down from Montreal with a fleet of batteaux, mounted with guns, determined to crowd Carleton down upon the American battery at the mouth of the Sorel, and so close in upon him as to make sure of his capture. Carleton, seeing the approaching danger, gave up all hope of the safety of his flotilla, but resolved upon making an effort to secure himself from capture. He accordingly disguised himself as a Canadian *voyageur*, and taking a boat, with six men to pull it, set off in the midst of a dark night, and silently floated down the St. Lawrence with muffled oars, passed all the dangers of the mouth of the Sorel, and getting on board a vessel below, reached in safety the city of Quebec at the very moment Arnold took his departure. In the meanwhile, Montgomery had reached the British vessels, which at once surrendered, with all on board, among whom was General Prescott, the former commander at Montreal, of whose rough treatment Ethan Allen had reason to make so much complaint.

Montgomery had met with great success in his efforts toward conciliating the people of Montreal. His courtesy, and careful regard of their rights and privileges, proved to them that he was no military adventurer, and they became favorably disposed toward a cause sustained by a man so peaceful in his bearing and so just in his conduct. His own troops, however, gave him great trouble, and so worried him by their disobedience and importunate demands to be sent home, that he quite sickened of his command, and wrote to Schuyler, expressing the hope that his health would soon allow of his resuming a position of which he himself wearied and disgusted. "I must go home," he added, "if I walk by the side of the lake. I am weary of power, and totally want that patience and temper so requisite for such a command."

Montgomery had received intelligence of the arrival of Arnold at Point aux Trembles, and was anxious to march with his troops and co-operate with him in an attack on Quebec. He was trying "to prevail on the troops to accompany" him, but was met with all kinds of objections. Some were too ill to go; some declared that their time was out; others openly refused; and a few only were disposed to obey orders, or rather to yield to persuasion, for in those days the militia were mostly inclined to enjoy their independence before they had won it. Montgomery was, however, determined to go, notwithstanding the reluctance of most of his army, and accordingly embarked with some three hundred men, who were all that were willing to follow him, and sailed down to Point aux Trembles, where he formed a junction with Arnold, and took command of the whole force, which amounted to nine hundred in all. Montgomery seems to have been struck with admiration by the soldierly appearance of Arnold's troops, and by the character of their leader. "There is a style of discipline among them," he wrote to Schuyler, "much superior to what I have been used to see in this campaign. He [Arnold] himself is active, intelligent, and enterprising." Favorably impressed as he was with what he saw of Arnold's troops — who were well-disciplined, had been refreshed, and comfortably clad with a supply of woollens from Montreal — Montgomery became sanguine of success in the contemplated attack upon Quebec. Arnold, however, was less hopeful, and wrote to Washington that it would require five thousand men to reduce that stronghold.

Montgomery calculated upon the disaffection of the inhabitants of Quebec; the miscellaneous character of the British troops, made up of sailors, raw recruits, and a few regulars; and the great extent of the fortifications, which seemed to require a larger number for their defence than Carleton possessed. The latter, however, though unpopular from the reserve of his aristocratic manners, was a man full of vigorous energy in an emergency, and he accordingly prepared to meet with spirit the expected assault. To assure loyalty, he turned out all suspected persons from official position, and even sent "trooping out of the town" all those inhabitants who showed any unwillingness to put forth their might in its defence. He had, by this thinning out, so far diminished his numbers within Quebec, as to leave only fifteen hundred men, nearly double that of the American force; but although Carleton was not conscious of this disparity, he confidently awaited the coming of his enemy.

As soon as the junction of the American forces had been formed, Montgomery Dec. 1. marched to the Plains of Abraham. Immediately on his arrival, he attempted to send a summons to the British commander to surrender; but Carleton would not allow any flag to approach the walls, and all communication was refused. Montgomery then began to play with his artillery upon the town and its suburbs, but with no effect beyond the occasional burning of a house, and the killing of a man or two. After this ill success, a *ruse* was tried, with the hope of communicating with some of the inhabitants supposed to be favorably disposed toward the American cause. A woman was induced to carry letters into the city, addressed to some of the merchants, who were promised every possible favor in case of co-operation with Montgomery. With these letters there was a summons to surrender, with an exaggerated state-

ment of the American force, intended for the eye of Carleton. This was handed him; but the British commander, nothing daunted, merely imprisoned the messenger in petticoats, withheld all answer to the communication of the American general, and steadily persevered in strengthening his defences.

Montgomery, disappointed in not producing, by summons and letters, any impression upon Carleton, or apparently upon the inhabitants of Quebec, now began a systematic attack. Approaching within four hundred yards of the centre of the walls, opposite to one of the gates, he commenced the construction of a breastwork. The army had but a poor supply of intrenching-tools to work with; and the ground, moreover, was so hardened by the severe frost, that it was only with the greatest labor that pick or spade could make any impression upon it. A snowstorm had set in as soon as Montgomery left Montreal, and was still in full blast, so that the men were much incommoded by the weather. The snow, however, which now in great depth covered the ground, was turned to advantage, for it was used to fill in the space behind the trees and brushwood which formed the frame of the breastwork. After being well packed, and covered with water—which froze immediately in those cold December days—the snow became a mass of solid ice. Half a dozen small fieldpieces were here planted, and kept firing bombs into the city, with the hope of frightening the inhabitants, and inducing them to force Carleton into submission. No such result, however, ensued; and then Montgomery tried the expedient of attaching letters to arrows, and ordering the Indians to shoot them into the town, that the citizens might pick them up, and, reading them, be advised to insist upon a surrender, which was the purport of what was written. This also failed in its effect.

After the "ice-battery" had been for five days ineffectually trying its artillery upon the walls, and its powers of persuasion upon the people within, the general took occasion one night to pay a visit to the captain in command — Lamb was his name. Montgomery had hardly arrived, when a ball came plump from the enemy's guns against the walls of ice, shattering them like so much glass, overturning the light fieldpieces, and wounding several of the men. "This is warm work, sir," said the general to Lamb. "It is, indeed, and certainly no place for you, sir."—"Why so, captain?"—"Because there are enough of us here to be killed, without the loss of you, which would be irreparable."[*] This was the end of the brittle ice-battery; for Montgomery, seeing its entire inefficiency and danger, immediately ordered Lamb and his brave men to abandon it.

Three weeks had been spent in these vain attempts to influence the inhabitants, when it was finally decided to make a general assault upon the city. Montgomery was distrustful of his means for a successful attempt; but, as his troops were growing dissatisfied with the long delay, and discouraged by labors and sufferings undergone without any compensating advantage, he felt it necessary,

either to strike a blow, or retire. He could not submit to the latter alternative, for he knew that his country expected much of him, and his own brave spirit prompted him to deeds of daring. Montgomery was, indeed, conscious that his men were hardly in a condition to undertake so hazardous an enterprise; for they had suffered (ill clothed and ill provided as they were with food) from the severity of the weather, and they not only murmured loudly, but even refused to obey orders. The commander, however, hoped that their martial ardor, warming with the prospect of action, would melt away disaffection, and soon reunite the hearts of all in common sympathy.

The plan of operations being settled, the various divisions of the troops were ordered to be drawn up, to prepare for their separate duties. At this moment word was brought to the general that three companies of Arnold's detachment refused obedience, declaring that they would no longer serve, unless placed under a different command. Montgomery might well be discouraged by such an occurrence at such a moment; but he mastered his feelings, and promptly presenting himself to the disorderly troops, succeeded by his firmness in bringing them back to their duty.

The whole force was now mustered, and it was found that disease—for the small-pox had broken out among them — and desertion had reduced the troops to the small number of seven hundred and fifty. These were then detailed for duty. One division, under Montgomery, was to descend the cliffs, and, proceeding along

---

[*] Life of John Lamb, p. 125, quoted by Irving.

the river around Cape Diamond, attack the town in that quarter; another, under Arnold, was to advance on the other side by the suburb of St. Roque, and the two were to fight their way from these opposite directions until they met. The third division, under Brown and Livingston, was to advance from the Plains of Abraham, set fire to St. John's gate, and make a show of assault against the walls of the fortress on the heights, in order to divert the enemy from the movements of the main body below. It was arranged that these various attacks should be simultaneous, on the letting off of some signal-rockets.

It was two o'clock in the morning, in **Dec. 31.** the midst of a heavy snowstorm, when the movement began. Montgomery led his men down the rugged path to Wolfe's cove below, and along the shore of the river, without opposition, until he reached a narrow point below the slate-crags of Cape Diamond. Here he found a fence of pickets, which the carpenters soon cut away with their saws, the general helping to pull them down with his own hands. Montgomery was the first to enter, followed by his aid-de-camp. The men hesitated and lingered. About fifty yards before them, with the river on one side and a precipitous rock on the other, stood a blockhouse or redoubt, strongly fortified, mounted with some heavy guns, and garrisoned with fifty of the enemy. Montgomery fancied his approach was unperceived, and confidently advanced along the narrow and irregular path, doubly insecure from the accumulated ice, urging his New-York regiment

to follow, saying: "Men of New York, you will not fear to follow where your general leads! Push on, brave boys, and Quebec is ours!" Montgomery, with sword in hand, then hurried in advance, and had hardly made a dash at the redoubt, when a sudden light flashed upon the darkness, and a volley of cannon-shot swept the American column, killing the general, his two aids, and many of the rank and file, at the first discharge. The rest of the men were driven back in confusion to Wolfe's cove, where they were rallied by Colonel Campbell, who, however, did not attempt to bring them up again to the attack.

The signal-rockets had been by some accident let off too soon, and the diversion which was to have been made by the division on the Plains of Abraham had failed: so the enemy within the city was on the alert, prepared to receive Arnold and his detachment, in their attack through the suburb of St. Roque. Arnold, at the head of an advanced guard of a lieutenant and thirty men, led the van; next went the artillery-company, under Captain Lamb, with a single fieldpiece on a sledge; Morgan and his riflemen, together with a company in charge of scaling-ladders, brought up the rear. They proceed along the bank of the St. Charles, floundering in the depths of the drifted snow, and go groping in the dark into the lower town. Here, with the narrow, irregular streets, the crowded houses, the stores, boats, and wharves, all seems inextricable confusion; but Arnold continues to lead on his advance-guard in single file, each man making his way as best he can after him. He now comes upon a two-gun battery stretched across the street, and halts momentarily for his fieldpiece; but, finding that it can not be dragged up through the deep snowdrifts, Arnold begins the attack: he is, however, so severely wounded in the knee on the first advance, that he has to be carried back to the rear, and is obliged to leave the assault to Morgan, the next in command, who hurries up with his riflemen, and after a severe struggle, which lasts nearly an hour, carries the battery. The enemy, although they fired their muskets briskly, and even a discharge of grapeshot, did but little mischief beyond wounding Arnold and killing one man. Morgan was so rapid in his approach, and came so close to the battery, that his riflemen were enabled to shoot through the embrasures and drive the men from their guns; and thus give free scope for the use of the scaling-ladders, which were at once planted against the pickets. The Americans now clambered over and took the captain and his thirty men captive.

Pushing on immediately along the street, Morgan finds himself obstructed by another and more formidable battery. The citizens, too, are now everywhere on the alert, and keep firing from their windows upon the Americans, who, though sorely galled, continue to advance. Morgan leads his men as before right up to the barrier, which, strongly fortified with pickets, and planted with heavy guns, stretched from the precipice which overhangs the lower town down to the river. The riflemen, getting close under the enemy's cannon, fire away, aiming through the embrasures, and succeed in making room for the ladders. The men, however, are driven back with their scaling-implements; they are planted again and again, but without success. The Americans, with a fire now concentrated upon them from every point of the city fortifications, are obliged to withdraw, and protect themselves in the narrow alleys and the neighboring houses, where they continue, however, to keep up a brave struggle against the enemy. Rallying again for another attack upon the battery, they finally succeed in carrying it, but not without a severe loss of life. Lamb, the captain of the artillery, was struck at the last moment by a grapeshot, which tore away a part of his jawbone. As the gunners were about retreating from the barrier, one of them determined to have one more shot, when Lamb, observing his purpose, levelled a musket at the fellow, but missed his fire, and received in full face the discharge of grape which so terribly mutilated him.

The battery taken, Morgan and his men prepared for a rush into the town; and they issued out for the purpose, but were forced by overwhelming numbers to take refuge in a stone building, whence they kept up a severe fire upon the enemy thronging the street below. Morgan now heard of the death of Montgomery, and that a large detachment from the garrison had come down, and, suddenly bursting through the gates upon the American rearguard under Captain Dearborn, forced it to surrender. He was thus so completely hemmed in, and cut off from all reinforcement, that he offered no further resistance, and yielded himself up with his men to the enemy.

Arnold now resumed the command, and determined, in spite of the severity of a Canadian winter, and the mere handful of troops left him, to blockade the city, and await reinforcements. He was encouraged in this resolution by the apparent distrust in which Carleton, the British commander, seemed to hold his own strength; for, after his success within the town, he did not even attempt to pursue the remnant of Americans beyond the walls. Arnold, however, anticipating a pursuit, had withdrawn his men to a distance of three miles from Quebec, and there, hastily fortifying himself, awaited an expected attack.

The loss of the Americans in this unsuccessful attack was heavy, being about one hundred and sixty killed and wounded, while that of the enemy amounted to only twenty. The patriots mourned, in the death of Montgomery, one of the bravest and purest of the defenders of their cause. The enemy respected his character; and Carleton eulogized his worth, and reverently ordered his remains to be buried with military honors in a soldier's grave. M'Pherson and Cheesman, his two aids-de-camp, who had fallen with their commander, were men of spirit, whose loss was grieved, as is always that of the young and the brave. Cheesman is supposed to have had a presentiment of approaching death, and on the day of the fatal struggle had dressed himself with even more than the usual care of the youthful officer. As he prepared to go out, he thrust some gold pieces into his pocket, saying laughingly, " This will insure me a decent burial."

The continental Congress rewarded Arnold for his persevering courage and skill while leading his troops through the wilderness, and his gallantry at Quebec, by promoting him to the rank of a brigadier-general. The other officers proved their merit by their conduct during that night's struggle at Quebec; and there was hardly one whose name we shall not afterward find memorable in the subsequent history of the battles of the Revolution. They need no tribute but the record of their names: Morgan, Dearborn, Meigs, Greene, Lamb, Oswald, Thayer, and Potsfield.

CHAPTER X.

Inactivity of the American Camp at Cambridge.—Washington's Anxieties.—Gage summoned to England.—Succeeded in Command by Howe.—Howe's Plans for Incursions on the Coasts.—The Burning of Falmouth.—American Privateers.—Howe increases his Fortifications.—Churches turned into Barracks and Stables.—Harsh Proceedings of Howe against the Patriots.—Retaliation.—A Committee of Congress visits the American Camp.—Benjamin Franklin.—An Attack upon Boston considered in Council.—Franklin takes Occasion to collect a Debt.—Treason in the American Camp.—Washington *laughs.*—Doctor Church's Trial.—His Condemnation and Subsequent Fate.—A Small American Fleet fitted out.—The Various Fortunes of the Vessels.—Sickness in the American Camp.—A Visit from some Indian Gentlemen.—Comparison with some of the New-England Gentry.

1775. WASHINGTON, in the movement against Canada, in which he took a great interest, found some relief for his forced inactivity at Cambridge. Here, however, in his camp, although desirous by "some decisive stroke" to drive the enemy from Boston, he could do nothing, as the condition of his troops was such as not to justify any offensive operations. Still, he had been so importuned to activity, that he determined to call a council of war, and consult upon the expediency of making an immediate attack on Boston. It was, however, unanimously agreed "that it was not expedient to make the attempt at present." The state of the army was certainly not very encouraging. The time of service of many of the troops would soon expire, and they already anticipated their liberty by a free indulgence in their own caprices, and a general disobedience of orders. "My situation," wrote Washington, "is inexpressibly distressing; to see the win-
Sept. 21. ter fast approaching upon a naked army, the time of their service within a few weeks of expiring, and no provision yet made for such important wants. Added to these, the military chest is to-

tally exhausted; the paymaster has not a single dollar in hand. The commissary-general assures me he has strained his credit for the subsistence of the army to the utmost. The quartermaster-general is precisely in the same situation; and the greater part of the troops are in a state not far from mutiny, upon the deduction from their stated allowance."

Nor were these the only troubles against which Washington had to contend. All New England was disaffected toward him, because he refused to send out detachments from his army to protect the towns along the coast from the marauding parties of the enemy. "I would like to extend protection to all," he said, "but the numerous detachments necessary to remedy the evil would amount to a dissolution of the army, or make the most important operations of the campaign depend upon the piratical expeditions of two or three men-of-war and transports." The British, in the meantime, with their small cruisers, were doing a good deal of mischief by sailing into the harbors and helping themselves to supplies, of which they stood greatly in need. The local militia, however, soon became watchful, and so well able to defend themselves, that the enemy were often disappointed, and seldom succeeded in their object without a hard and bloody struggle.

The British troops in Boston were not more actively occupied than the besiegers without. A change, however, in the chief command was an event which excited no little interest. Governor Gage was recalled, and sailed for England on **1775.** the 10th of October, leaving General Howe as his successor. Howe was in favor (as Gage had been) of an evacuation of Boston, and in his despatches to the government advised large reinforcements, and a transfer of military operations to New York. In the meantime, he prepared to "distress the rebels by incursions along the coast." With this view, one of his first acts was, to send out a small armed squadron, under a Lieutenant Mowatt, against Falmouth (now Portland), the authorities of which had given great offence by preventing the sailing of a ship loaded with some tories and their property. Mowatt appeared before the town in the night, and, sending word to the inhabitants that he would allow them two hours to remove themselves, determined to burn it. A committee of citizens was immediately appointed to confer with the lieutenant, who told them, on their arrival on board his ship, that his orders were to fire every town on the coast between Boston and Halifax, and that he had no alternative but obedience.

A respite was, however, at the earnest solicitation of the citizens, granted until the next morning, when the committee again made their appearance, and prayed that their town might be spared. Mowatt offered to do so, provided they would send him off four carriage-guns, deliver up all their arms and ammunition, and four prominent citizens as hostages. These conditions were, however, considered too dishonorable to comply with. The committee then returned on shore, and the lieutenant hoisted his signal for the attack to commence. The squadron now began to throw its bombs into the town, and the firing continued until the close of the day, when most of the houses were destroyed. The burning of Falmouth spread an alarm all over the New-England coast, but produced no disposition to submit to British arms. The indignation it excited, in fact, only served to give greater intensity to the resistance of the patriots. "Oh," wrote General Greene, "could the Congress behold the distresses and wretched condition of the poor inhabitants driven from the seaport towns, it would kindle a blaze of indignation against the commissioned pirates and licensed robbers .... People," he adds, "begin heartily to wish a declaration of independence."

Howe, in his despatch to the government, "hoped Portsmouth, in New Hampshire, would feel the weight of his majesty's arms;" and the inhabitants of that place, as well as of Newport, in Rhode Island, were in daily expectation of being served as had been the people of Falmouth. The patriots now began, under an act of the general court of Massachusetts, to fit out privateers for the defence of the seacoast, and were soon able to take revenge upon the British cruisers for their cruel devastations.

Although Howe had resolved upon keeping quiet at present within Boston, he took care to find work for his men. He strengthened his fortifications on Bunker's and Breed's hills, where General Clinton had now the command, and added to those on Charlestown neck, where he set six hundred men to labor. Within the city, houses were pulled down to clear space for the exercise of the troops; redoubts were built on the common; and the meetinghouse "where sedition had been often preached" was made "a riding-house for the light dragoons."

Howe did not confine himself to insulting those of the patriots still left in Boston, but persecuted them with all the rigor of martial law. In his proclamations he spoke of some who had escaped to Cambridge as those who had "lately absconded to join his majesty's enemies, assembled in open rebellion," and declared his determination to punish with "military execution" any who should attempt to follow their example. Those who succeeded he pronounced traitors, who were to be treated accordingly by a "seizure of their goods and effects." These harsh proceedings led to retaliation on the part of the patriots; and, by a general order from Washington, those officers of government known to be devoted to the throne were seized and imprisoned.

Congress having appointed a committee to visit the camp at Cambridge, and confer with Washington and the various delegates from the provinces of New England in regard to the reorganization of the army, the three gentlemen who composed it now arrived. **Oct. 15.** These were, Benjamin Franklin, of Pennsylvania; Thomas Lynch, of South Carolina; and Colonel Benjamin Harrison, of Virginia. Franklin was regarded by all as an example of prudence and an oracle of wisdom. "I had the honor," says General Greene, of Rhode Island, "to be introduced to that very great man Doctor Franklin, whom I viewed with silent admiration during the whole evening," and adds, in his enthusiastic rhetoric, "Attention watched his lips and conviction closed his periods." The conference committee immediately began their sessions, with Washington as president, and Joseph Reed as secretary. The first question was, the new organization of the army; and the satisfactory result was, the adoption of a plan for the enlistment, for one year, of twenty-six regiments, of eight companies each, besides riflemen and artillery, based upon the respective capacities of the colonies as stated by the delegates. This would give an effective force of twenty-two thousand, two hundred and seventy-two men and officers, whom it was proposed, as far as possible, to recruit from those already in service, that the army might not be altogether composed of undisciplined and inexperienced troops.

The subject of the inactivity of the present army now came up, and the propriety of an immediate attack on Boston was discussed. Washington formally put the question as to whether he should attack the British, at the expense of the destruction of the city. The delegates preferred that so important a matter should be left to the decision of Congress. A council of his officers had been previously held, at which Washington declared he had summoned them in consequence of having learned that Congress desired an attack upon Boston, if practicable. Their opinions are best given in their own words:—

GENERAL GATES.—" That under present circumstances it is improper to attempt it."

GENERAL GREENE.—" That it is not practicable, under all circumstances; but, if ten thousand men could be landed at Boston, thinks it is."

GENERAL SULLIVAN.—" That at this time it is improper. The winter gives a more favorable opportunity."

GENERAL HEATH.—" Impracticable at present."

GENERAL THOMAS.—" Of the same opinion."

GENERAL PUTNAM.—" Disapproves of it at present."

GENERAL LEE.—" Is not sufficiently acquainted with the men, to judge; therefore thinks it too great a risk."

GENERAL WARD.—" Against it."

Such were the opinions of the generals, with whom Washington also agreed; but the delegates, although hesitating to decide upon the question, were for the most part in favor of an attack. Doctor Belknap dined with a party of general officers and gentlemen belonging to the various committees, when the absorbing topic naturally became the subject of after-dinner conversation. The doctor tells us that Lynch, Harrison, and Wales, wished to see Boston in flames. Lee told

28

them it was impossible to burn it unless they sent men in with bundles of straw on their backs to do it. He said it could not be done with carcass and hot shot; and instanced the Isle Royal, in St. Lawrence river, " which was fired at in 1760 a long time, with a fine train of artillery, hot shot, and carcasses, without effect."

The delegates now returned home. Their presence had given increased encouragement to the patriots in arms. Franklin's devotion to the public interests was especially appreciated, as his comprehensive policy and systematic business-habits enabled him to suggest plans that were not only grand, but feasible. He had an opportunity, moreover, of attending to a little private business, and succeeded in obtaining from the Massachusetts general court the sum of eighteen hundred and fifty-four pounds sterling, as payment in full of his services while acting as agent in England for the colony. " The doctor might," says a contemporary, " have liked specie, at the time such grants were made, better than the present paper-money; but his foresight will undoubtedly transform the latter into some solid substance!" Franklin, however, had to make, from the handsome sum which he was paid, a deduction of one hundred pounds in favor of a committee " appointed to wait upon him within a day or two, being the amount of a sum sent by several persons in England, for the relief of those Americans who were wounded in the battle of Lexington, and of the widows and children of those who were there slain."

The greatest consternation was created

in the camp at Cambridge, by the supposed discovery of a treasonable correspondence of a hitherto unsuspected patriot with the enemy. Early in July, a woman presented herself at Newport, to a Mr. Wainwood, with a letter, which she wished him to aid her in conveying to Captain Wallace, the British officer in command of the man-of-war off the harbor. Wainwood, who was a patriot, was suspicious of any correspondence with the enemy; but, concealing his thoughts, he prevailed upon the woman to leave the letter with him. She was induced to do so, and Wainwood immediately advised with a friend, upon whose recommendation the letter was broken open, and found to be written in characters entirely unintelligible. Thus the matter remained until Wainwood, having received a note from the woman, inquiring about the disposition of the letter, had his suspicions reawakened, and it was then determined to send it to Washington.

Oct. 15.

The woman, on again presenting herself in the camp, was arrested. "Tradition," says Irving, "gives us a graphic scene connected with her arrest. Washington was in his chamber at headquarters, when he beheld from his window General Putnam approaching on horseback, with a stout woman *en croupe* behind him. He had pounced upon the culprit. The group presented by the old general and his prize, overpowered even Washington's gravity. It was the only occasion throughout the whole campaign on which he was known to laugh heartily. He had recovered his gravity by the time the delinquent was brought to the foot of the broad staircase in headquarters, and assured her, in a severe tone from the head of it, that unless she confessed everything before the next morning, a halter would be in readiness for her."

The woman for a long time resisted every attempt to extort the truth from her; but finally she confessed that the letter had been given to her by Doctor Church, of whom, in fact, she was said to be the "kept mistress." Church was a prominent man among the patriots, being a member of the Massachusetts house of representatives, and surgeon-general of the army-hospitals. On being arrested, and confronted with the charge of treasonable correspondence with the enemy, he was greatly agitated, and showed every mark of guilt. The letter having been successfully deciphered, and found to contain little beyond an exaggerated account of the American force, the doctor wrote to Washington a vindication of himself, stating that his object was merely to use his efforts in bringing about an accommodation of the dispute with the mother-country, and that he was entirely innocent of any traitorous design. He was now brought before a council of war, which, unable to satisfy itself of his innocence, unanimously decided upon referring the matter to the Congress.

Oct. 23.

The legislature of Massachusetts then summoned Church before the bar of the house, and the doctor made a long speech in his defence. He endeavored to evade the censure of the house, by insisting that

Oct. 27. as the affair would be before another court, where the matter must have a final issue, should the house proceed to expel him, it would have a fatal effect whenever a final judgment was to be given on his conduct. He made the most solemn appeal to Heaven that the letter was written with the design of procuring some important intelligence. He observed that there was not a single paragraph in it which contained information that could hurt the Americans; and that the exaggerated accounts of their force, strength, and unanimity, tended to dishearten the enemy and keep them quiet, at a time when the Americans, for want of powder, were poorly able to have withstood a vigorous attack. "If the force of rhetoric and the powers of language," says a contemporary, "if the most pathetic arts of persuasion, enforced by all the ingenuity, sense, and spirit of the doctor, could have made him innocent, he would have appeared spotless as an angel of light." The house, however, was not convinced, and expelled him. Congress inflicted the punishment, resolving "that he be close confined in some secure jail in Connecticut, without the use of pen, ink, and paper, and that no person be allowed to converse with him, except in the presence and hearing of a magistrate or the sheriff of the county." The doctor was accordingly clapped into the jail at Norwich, whence he was subsequently released, on the plea of ill health, and removed to Boston, where his personal liberty was given him on his parole, backed by a surety of one thousand pounds, that he would hold no correspondence with the enemy, or leave the colony without permission. He was eventually allowed to depart for the West Indies, but the vessel in which he sailed was never heard of afterward.

The legislative assemblies of the various New-England provinces had authorized at an early period the fitting out of small armed vessels; and several were now in commission, doing effective service in protecting the coasts against the British cruisers. Washington, having received instructions from Congress to endeavor to capture the transports laden with supplies for the army at Boston, and especially "two north country built ships with military stores," began to fit out a small fleet, and succeeded toward the end of October in having six schooners in commission. These were the Lynch, Captain Broughton, and the Franklin, Captain Sellman, which were ordered to the St. Lawrence; the Lee, Captain Manly, the Warren, Captain Adams, the Washington, Captain Martindale, and the Harrison, Captain Coit, sent to cruise about the coast. Washington felt a great interest in this humble naval movement as a means of obtaining supplies, for he writes, "I am in very great want of powder, lead, mortars—indeed, of most sorts of military stores." Efforts had been made, and not without success, to supply the army with ammunition, but still the quantity fell short of what would be needed in a protracted campaign. The manufacture of saltpetre had been commenced in every colony, and powder-mills had been erected at Philadelphia and New York. A hundred barrels of gunpowder had also been received from Bermuda, by a couple of coasting-schooners, the crews of which had succeeded in landing on that island in the night, and rifling the magazine, at some distance from the town, of its contents. Some of the inhabitants, with a favorable disposition toward the American patriots, were supposed to have connived at or aided in the proceeding; and Congress responded to their friendliness by this grateful resolve: "That the inhabitants of Bermuda appear friendly to the cause of America, and ought to be supplied with such a quantity of the produce of these colonies as may be necessary for their subsistence and home consumption."

Washington's little fleet was not entirely successful. One or two were lost, from the inexperience of the officers; and another was taken by the enemy, and the captain and crew sent to England. The Lee, however, under Captain Manly, vindicated the "pine-tree flag"—for this, which was composed of a white ground, a pine-tree in the middle, and the motto "We appeal to Heaven," was the standard hoisted upon the floating batteries, and adopted by the colonial fleet. We shall see, in the progress of events, the fortunate result of Manly's cruise.

There was a good deal of suffering in the camp at Cambridge, from sickness, which a chronicler of the times quaintly accounts for: "Many of the Americans," says he, "have sickened and died of the dysentery, brought upon them, in a great measure, through an inattention to cleanliness. When at home, their female relations put them upon washing their hands and faces, and keeping themselves neat and clean; but, being absent from such monitors, through an indolent, heedless turn of mind, they have neglected the means of health, have grown filthy, and poisoned their constitution by nastiness." The weather, too, was becoming very cold; and the soldiers, with insufficient barracks, and a want of wood, were greatly exposed. Several regiments were obliged to keep the field, and some were tented in bleak positions upon the high tops of hills, where it was difficult to drag up what supplies of fuel they could get.

The camp, however, with all this suffering of the soldiers, and their by no means presentable condition, if we are to believe the chronicler just quoted, was cheered by the presence of "gentlemen, ladies, and others, from neighboring and distant colonies, attracted by curiosity." A number of native gentlemen, too, arrived: these were Indian chiefs, who had come to see and judge for themselves how far the stories which they had heard in their own wigwams of the quarrel of the Americans with King George were true. Washington received them at headquarters with great consideration, and they were entertained by him and his officers with a banquet and a ball. Two of the Indians had with them their squaws, who were remarkably well-looking women, making all allowance for their very dark complexions. They both joined their husbands at the ball at headquarters, and were much admired, although one seemed rather low-spirited, from having recently lost a papoose. When the Indians danced in company with the American gentlemen and ladies, both the chiefs and their squaws kept time with the greatest precision, and showed an example of grace and dignity by which Washington and his Virginian friends thought that some of their New-England associates might benefit.

At that time, in fact, in the early days of anticipated independence, there was great room for improvement in the manners of even the officers. Many of them, elected by their own troops, allowed themselves to be treated too much as equals by the men; and the captain or the lieutenant carried his ideas of behavior from the ranks, where they were naturally popular, to headquarters, where, under the strict *régime* of the formal Washington, they were not by any means so attractive.

Many of the higher officers felt as Montgomery wrote, from Canada: "I wish some method could be fallen upon for engaging *gentlemen* to serve. A point of honor, and more knowledge of the world, to be found in that class of men, would greatly reform discipline, and render the troops much more tractable." There were worse faults, however, than bad manners. Gordon says: "It is a mortifying truth that some of the Massachusetts officers disgrace the colony by practising the meanest arts of speculation. Every subtlety that avarice can invent, or rascality carry on, are used to cheat the public, by men who procured commissions, not to fight for the liberty of their country, but to prey upon its distresses. The army about to be enlisted will undoubtedly be better officered."

CHAPTER XI.

Want of Officers and Men.—Washington's Troubles.—The Tailors set to work in the Army.—A Spirited Affair.—The British in search of Beef.—The Schooner Lee and Captain Manly.—A Capture.—Its Welcome in Congress.—Anecdote.—"Old Put" acting Godfather to a Big Gun.—The Difficulties of Enlistment.—The Desertion of the Connecticut and Massachusetts Men.—Arrival of Mrs. Washington.—Its Effect at Headquarters.—Indian Guests.—"Bows and Scrapes."—Ground broken at Lechmere's Point.—A Sanguine Colonel.—The American Camp unusually prosperous. —Plenty to eat.—An American Fleet organized.—The Brutal Wallace.—His Raids upon the American Coast.—His Conduct at Newport.—General Lee sent to Rhode Island.—Lee's Conduct.—Life and Character of Lee.—His Profanity.

1775. WASHINGTON was in hopes that his forces might be "better officered," and strove to effect so desirable an object, now that he was engaged in reorganizing the army, in accordance with the decision of Congress. He was, however, perplexed not only how to get "better," but any officers at all, or even men. As the number of regiments was to be reduced under the new arrangement, and the officers necessarily diminished, Washington was desirous of selecting those that were best qualified. He found great difficulty from both officers and men. The first were clamorous for high rank; and the latter were insisting upon being subjected only to the command of those whom they themselves should choose. After completing his list of officers, he had hoped to have succeeded readily in recruiting his new army out of his present forces, but was greatly disappointed in finding so few disposed to re-enlist.

Colonel Reed had resigned his post, and was now at Philadelphia; but Washington, strongly attached to him, kept up an intimate correspondence, in which he opened his heart to his former secretary. "Such dearth of public spirit," he emphatically writes to Reed, "and such **Nov. 28.** want of virtue; such stockjobbing, and fertility in all the low arts to obtain advantage of one kind or another in this great change of military arrangements, I never saw before, and I pray God's mercy that I may never be witness to again. What will be the end of these manœuvres is beyond my scan. I tremble at the prospect. We have been till this time enlisting about three thousand five hundred men. To engage these, I have been obliged to allow furloughs as far as fifty men to a regiment; and the officers, I am persuaded, indulge many more. The Connecticut troops will not be prevailed upon to stay longer than their term, saving those who have enlisted for the next campaign, and are mostly on furlough; and such a mercenary spirit pervades the whole, that I should not be surprised at any disaster that may happen..... Could I have foreseen what I have experienced and am likely to experience, no consideration upon earth should have induced me to accept this command."

General Greene was disposed to think the commander-in-chief somewhat inconsiderate in his judgment of the New-Englanders, and wrote: "His excellency has been taught to believe the people here a superior race of mortals; and finding them of the same temper and dispositions, passions and prejudices, virtues and vices of the common people of other governments, they sank in his esteem."

Washington, however, perplexed as he was, steadily resolved to overcome all obstacles, and reorganize an army. He was desirous, too, of giving his men more of the appearance of soldiers, and issued an order in which he recommended the non-commissioned officers and soldiers to lay out their money in shirts, shoes, stockings, and a good pair of leather breeches, and not in coats and waistcoats, as it was intended that the new army should be clothed in uniform; to effect which, the order declared that the Congress would lay in goods upon the best terms they could be obtained anywhere for ready money, and that they would be sold to the troops without any profit, and thus enable each soldier to get a uniform coat and waistcoat cheaper than any other kind. The written order then closed with the notice that "a number of tailors will be immediately set to work to make regimentals for those brave men who are willing at all hazards to defend their invaluable rights and privileges."

Notwithstanding Washington's complaints of the backwardness of his troops generally in re-enlisting, he had occasion to be gratified by the spirited conduct of some of them in a slight affair which occurred with the enemy. Some four hundred British soldiers, under Lieutenant-Colonel Clark, landed on Phipps's **Nov. 9.** farm, at Lechmere's point, with a view of making a raid upon the cattle there, for the benefit of the half-starved troops and people in Boston, where such was the scarcity of provisions, that beef, mutton, and pork, had risen to one shilling and a penny halfpenny sterling the pound; geese ten shillings and fowls five shillings apiece; while half a guinea was asked for a dozen of eggs. Owing to the high tide which overflowed the causeway that led from the camp, and prevented the Americans from crossing, the British were left for an hour or more without interference, when they employed themselves shooting the cattle, with the view of making off with the carcasses. Colonel Thompson, with a regiment of American riflemen, was ordered to displace the invaders. The tide was still high, but the Colonel ordered his troops to the attack; and the men for the most part (though some hesitated) plunged readily into the water breast-high, and waded a quarter of a mile in the face of a fire from a man-of-war and several floating batteries, which covered the British marauders. As the Americans advanced, the enemy hastened to their boats, with a booty of ten cows, but leaving two of their men killed by the fire of the riflemen, whose alacrity on the occasion was highly extolled by Washington, though he reprimanded the backwardness of others, and some of the officers for the unmilitary appearance and conduct of their regiments. A Major Mifflin, who "flew about as though he would have raised a whole army," came in for a large share of the honor of the day by his active gallantry.

The whole camp was now in a high tide of cheerful excitement, in consequence of the success of Captain **Nov. 30.** Manly with his armed schooner the Lee. Several British vessels had already been captured and taken safely into harbor, when, as he was cruising on the coast, Manly fell in with and took the brig Nancy, an ordnance-ship from Woolwich, full of everything in the greatest abundance that was necessary for camps and artillery. There was found on board a large brass mortar, of a new construction; two thousand muskets; several pieces of fine brass cannon; one hundred thousand flints; thirty thousand round shot; thirty tons and more of musket-shot; plenty of powder, and "all manner of tools, utensils, and machines."

This anecdote illustrates the welcome with which this capture was received. The naval committee of the Congress was in secret session, deliberating on the means of obtaining certain small articles which were indispensable to the equipment of vessels-of-war, but which were not to be had in the country, when a clamor for admittance at the door interrupted the proceedings. Admittance was denied, but the intruder insisted on entering. The door was finally opened, when a gentleman appeared, with an inventory of the stores found in the captured brig Nancy, and among which were the very articles wanted. When the fact was ascertained, Mr. Adams arose and exclaimed with his wonted earnestness: "We must succeed

—Providence is with us—we must succeed!"

The Nancy was carried into Cape Ann, and her cargo conveyed thence to the camp at Cambridge. Great was the exultation on its arrival. "Such universal joy," writes an officer, "ran through the whole camp as if each grasped victory in his hand. To crown the glorious scene, there intervened one truly ludicrous— which was, Old Put mounted on the large mortar, which was fixed in its bed for the occasion, with a bottle of rum in his hand, standing parson to christen, while Godfather Mifflin gave it the name of 'Congress.' The huzzas on the occasion, I dare say, were heard through all the territories of our most gracious sovereign in this province."

The "huzzas on the occasion" were at any rate heard in Boston, where the officers spitefully remarked that, "should their expected reinforcements arrive in time, the rebels would pay dear in the spring for all their petty triumphs." Manly continued his successes on the coast until he became a terror to every British vessel. A man-of-war was sent out in pursuit of him, but he escaped by running his vessel ashore in Gloucester harbor, where the enemy, after firing broadside after broadside at him, was obliged by the spirit of Manly's crew, aided by the inhabitants, to leave him, after the British ship had lost nearly one half of its men. Manly got his schooner afloat soon after, and again sailed on a cruise.

Washington was still greatly annoyed by the conduct of his troops in regard to re-enlistment. The Connecticut regiments refused to serve after their time, which would soon expire, unless they received a bounty. This was refused, and they became mutinous, declaring that they would quit the camp. Washington, to meet the emergency, determined to make a requisition upon the general court of Massachusetts for reinforcements. This body, in answer to the demand, promptly voted that three thousand of the minutemen of Massachusetts and two thousand of New-Hampshire should be called out and ordered to present themselves in the camp on the 10th of December. This was the period at which the service of most of the Connecticut troops would expire, and they were ordered to remain until then. Their officers confidently expressed their belief that not a man would disobey; but they were disappointed and greatly chagrined to find that the order had hardly been given out, when the men began to desert.

"Yesterday morning," writes Washington, "most of them resolved to leave the camp; many went off, **Dec. 2.** and the utmost vigilance and industry were used to apprehend them; several got away with their arms and ammunition." They had suffered greatly, it is true, from the intensity of the cold, and the want of necessities with which they ought to have been better supplied. The army, however, and the country were not disposed to justify, under any circumstances, the desertion of their cause in the time of its agony; and as the deserters made their straggling way to Connecticut, they were hooted and treated with other significant marks of opprobrium, in every town and village through which they passed. They were not secure from reproach even at their own firesides; and the scolding of wives, and the averted glances of sweethearts, drove and shamed many a deserter back again to duty.

That the Connecticut men were not alone in their reluctance to serve—although more recreant than others, by their open desertion—appears from the records of the time. "The Massachusetts people," says a chronicler, "show as much backwardness as the others. In short, they expect to be hired, and that at a very high price, to defend their own liberties; and choose to be slaves unless they can be bribed to be freemen. *Quid facit libertas, cum sola pecunia regnat?* How must it afflict General Washington to observe in the present crisis so little of that patriotic spirit which he was taught to believe was the characteristic of the Massachusetts people, and on which he relied greatly for support!....

"While burdened with an apprehension that he might possibly be deserted, he could recollect the severity of the season, and the distresses of his fellow-creatures at a distance, and wrote to the gentleman with whom he had intrusted the management of his concerns at Mount Vernon: 'Let the hospitality of the house be kept up with respect to the poor. Let no one go hungry away. If any of this kind of people should be in want of corn, supply their necessities, provided it does not encourage them in idleness. I have no objection to your giving my money in charity, when you think it will be well

29

bestowed. I mean it is my desire that that it should be done. You are to consider that neither myself nor wife are now in the way to do these good offices.'"

His wife, as this letter indicates, was now with Washington at headquarters, where she had arrived on the 11th of December, with her son John Parke Custis. The coming in of the "general's lady" was quite an event in the camp; and the plain New-England provincials did not fail to remark upon the grand style of the Virginian dame, who drove into Cambridge with a chariot-and-four, with negro postillions in scarlet-and-white liveries. Her presence greatly enlivened headquarters, and invitations to dinner with the general became more frequent after she began to rule the household. Her example, too, had a cheering influence upon others of the "best society" of the camp; and party succeeded party, night after night, during the gloomy month of December. Adjutant-General Mifflin, who, though bred up with the formalities of Quakerism, had received a dash of liveliness from a residence in France, was prominent among the gayest of the officers, and provoked the conviviality of the camp by frequent invitations to supper and dinner. "I dined," says John Adams, "at Colonel Mifflin's, with General Washington and lady, and a vast collection of other company, among whom were six or seven sachems and warriors of the French Caughnawaga Indians, with their wives and children. A savage feast they made of it, yet were very polite in the Indian style. I was introduced to them by the general as one of the

1775.

grand council at Philadelphia, which made them prick up their ears. They came and shook hands with me, and made many low bows and scrapes."*

Massachusetts and New Hampshire had come nobly to the rescue on the desertion of the Connecticut regiments, and the recruits came in rapidly from these provinces. Washington was quite inspirited, and wrote: "I have the satisfaction to tell you that things wear a better complexion here than they have done for some time past. The army is filling up. The barracks go on well. Firewood comes in. The soldiers are made comfortable and easy. Our privateers meet with success in bringing in vessels that were going to the relief of Boston." Washington, reinforced with new troops, and encouraged by the better spirit of the men, was enabled now to proceed vigorously with his defences.

Dec. 13.

The American general carried his approaches to within half a mile of Boston, and broke ground at Lechmere's point. The enemy did not attempt any hinderance, and allowed the Americans to proceed with their works for several days without firing a shot. This puzzled Washington, who could not understand their object, unless it was to lull him into a fatal security. He was, however, on the alert, for it only increased his vigilance, and induced him to fortify all the advances to the camp, and to guard any approaches upon the ice. He was in hourly expectation of an attack. The work continued, notwithstanding; and the men had succeeded in constructing a causeway over the marsh, nearly to Lechmere's point, when the enemy's ships and batteries at last began to fire. The Americans were driven away, with one man wounded, and did not renew their labors until the next morning, when the British man-of-war was forced by the artillery in the camp to shift its moorings. The British batteries, however, still played upon the spot; but the men, growing familiar with the bombs which were bursting and scattering the dirt over them, and learning how to dodge them as the sentinels cried out, "A shot!" continued their labors: so that, in spite of the snow, the frozen ground, and the dangerous proximity of the enemy, there were soon two redoubts built on Lechmere's point, with a causeway and a covered approach leading to them. "Give us powder and authority," says an enthusiastic colonel, "I say give us these, and Boston can be set in flames." So important did he, as in fact all his comrades, esteem these new works.

Everything seemed now unusually prosperous in the camp. The soldiers were supplied with abundant food—getting corned beef and pork four days, fresh beef two days, and salt fish one day, in the week; a quart of spruce-beer, or an equivalent in molasses daily, in the way of liquid refreshment; and fair proportions of such delicacies as rice, Indian meal, hog's lard, and butter, on stated occasions. A spectator describes the appearance of

* Irving, who quotes this extract, remarks upon the "bows and scrapes" with which Adams states the Indians received him, that it is a kind of homage never paid by an Indian warrior. If, however, Irving admits the "shaking of hands," he might concede to the savages the further progress in civilized politeness of "bows and scrapes," especially on calling to mind that the Indians were *French* Caughnawagas.

the American camp with enthusiasm: "About two months ago," he says, "I visited the camps at Roxbury and Cambridge. The lines of both are impregnable; with forts (many of which are bombproof) and the redoubts, supposing them to be all in a direction, are about twenty miles; the breastworks of a proper height, and in many places seventeen feet in thickness; the trenches wide and deep in proportion, before which lay forked impediments; and many of the forts, in every respect, are perfectly ready for battle. The whole, in a word, the admiration of every spectator; for verily their fortifications appear to be the works of seven years, instead of about as many months. At these camps are about twenty thousand men. The generals and other officers, in all their military undertakings, solid, discreet, and courageous; the men daily raving for action, and seemingly devoid of fear. There are many floating batteries, and batteaux in abundance; besides this strength, ten thousand militia are ordered in that government to appear on the first summons. Provisions and money there are very plenty, and the soldiers faithfully paid. The army in great order, and very healthy, and about six weeks ago lodged in comfortable barracks. Chaplains constantly attend the camps, morning and night; prayers are often offered up for peace and reconciliation, and the soldiers very attentive. The roads at the time I viewed the camps were almost lined with spectators, and thousands with me can declare the above respecting the camps to be a just description."

Congress had determined upon the organization of a fleet, and had ordered five ships of thirty-two guns, five of twenty-eight, and three of twenty-four, to be built; but while these were in process of construction, the coasts of New England suffered greatly from the British cruisers. The American privateers were on the alert, but being of small force and few in number, were (although some continued to give a good account of themselves) unable to effect much against the powerful English squadron, which continued its depredations along the coast from the St. Lawrence to the bay of New York. Rhode Island had been a great sufferer, and now called upon Washington for aid to protect her harbors from the severe exactions of a British naval captain, Wallace. **Dec. 13.**

Wallace was a brutal fellow, who had been long on the coast, and was notorious in America, even before the war, for his coarseness and insolence. Being asked once by the mistress of a boarding-house in Philadelphia, where he happened to be a lodger, if he would be helped to a dish before her, Wallace replied, "Damme, madam, it is to be supposed that at a public table every man has a right to help himself, and this I mean to do!" The poor woman, with tears in her eyes, begged the brute's pardon. On another occasion, Wallace got as much as he gave, from a cool Quaker with whom at dinner he had made very free, twitting him about his broad brim, and *theeing* and *thouing* him very familiarly. The Friend bore it very patiently until after dinner, when he at length ventured to say to his persecutor:

"Captain, thee has made very free with me, and asked me a great many questions, which I have endeavored to answer to thy satisfaction. Wilt thou now permit me to ask thee one in my turn?"— "Oh, by all means!" exclaimed the captain, "anything thee please, friend; what is it?"—"Why, then, I wish to be informed what makes thee drink so often: art thou really dry every time thou carriest the liquor to thy mouth?" The captain, drunk as he was, felt this home thrust, frowned savagely, and, swearing a loud curse, asked, "What! do you think I am like a hog, only to drink when I am dry?" The fellow was as cruel in disposition as he was coarse and violent in manner.

This Wallace had stationed his vessel-of-war off Newport, where he would land his sailors and marines, to make depredations upon the inhabitants. A party of these marauders had lately gone ashore, and, not satisfied with killing and carrying off the cattle, had broken into, plundered, and finally burned, some of the houses. It was also feared by the Rhode-Islanders that the British admiral at Boston was about sending a large naval force, with the view of subjecting, by the connivance of the tory residents, the whole island to British military rule.

The governor of Rhode Island, in soliciting the aid of Washington, had suggested that Lee might be sent; and he accordingly was ordered to Newport with several companies of riflemen, which were joined on the march by a considerable number of militia. Lee was the very man for the emergency; his usual faults of character became merits on the occa-

sion. His self-willed temper made him prompt in the execution of his measures. He entered Newport, and at once summoned before him all persons known or suspected of giving countenance to the enemy. He then forced them to take an oath by which they "religiously swore they would neither directly nor indirectly assist the wicked instruments of ministerial tyranny and villany commonly called the king's troops and navy, by furnishing them with provisions and refreshments;" and swore, moreover, to denounce "all traitors before the public authority, and to take arms in defence of American liberty, whenever required by Congress or the provincial authority." We may conceive of the terror infused into the hearts of the tories by the determined conduct of Lee, when he succeeded in extorting such an oath from all but three of those who were brought before him. He soon returned to Cambridge. As Lee will, from this moment, begin to appear more prominently upon the scene, we may here give a record of his history.

CHARLES LEE can almost be said to have been born a soldier. His father was a general in the British army, and the son received a commission at the early age of eleven years. Born in Wales, in 1731, young Lee had all the impulsive characteristics of the Welsh. He was ardent and brave, irascible and headstrong. In the army, where he began so early a career, his energetic courage was soon noticed, and led to his frequent employment in active service. In 1756, he first came to America, and won renown in the colonial battles as an officer in the royal army.

From his earliest days his disposition had been wayward, and his conduct socially irregular. He now gave signal proof of his eccentricity, by abandoning civilized life, and casting himself adrift among the roaming Indians. He was welcomed by the Mohawks, whom he had joined, and made by them a chief, with an Indian name, which signified "Boiling Water." This title, so characteristic of the restless disposition of the man, was a remarkable proof of the shrewd insight of his savage friends who conferred it. The capriciousness of Lee, which had led him to leave, induced him to return to civilization. A new whim took possession of his mind. He wished to take part in political strife. He had always been fond of books, and, having an ambition as a writer, often indulged in literary compositions, chiefly of a partisan character.

On his return to England, however, Lee was induced to take up arms again, and, having received a colonel's commission, served under General Burgoyne in Portugal, where he exhibited great daring, on one occasion swimming the Tagus at the head of his troops. After the war, he lived in London, where he made himself somewhat famous as a political writer and advocate of liberal principles. In a short time he wearied of this life, and sought promotion from the British authorities, who, however, would not listen to the appeal of a man who had been notoriously engaged in attacking them with all the bitterness of which he was capable. Indeed, such was the keenness and vigor of his pen, that some even attributed to him the authorship of the cele-

brated letters of "Junius." Lee now went abroad, and travelled for several years on the continent of Europe, where he acquired a knowledge of various languages, and succeeded in making the acquaintance of the great, with whom he so far ingratiated himself, that he was commended by them to Stanislaus Augustus, king of Poland, who made him his aid-de-camp. From Poland he repaired, in some official capacity, to Constantinople. After a short residence in Turkey, Lee threw off his allegiance to the Polish king, and went to Paris. In 1773, he returned to America, determined to make it his home for the rest of his life. By the advice of his old comrade and countryman Gates, he purchased an estate in Virginia, and was there living, with his books and his dogs, the easy life of a southern planter, when the struggle with Great Britain commenced. Lee, who was always a liberal, promptly declared for the Americans. His accession to the cause was gladly welcomed, and his experience as a military leader induced Congress to make him a brigadier-general.

Lee was an eccentric person, who, although possessed of the breeding of a gentleman, was fond of ruffling the formalities of society by personal irregularity of manners. He was slovenly in his dress, and not seldom careless in behavior. "Plain in person even to ugliness, and careless in his manners even to a degree of rudeness, his nose was so remarkably aquiline that it appeared as a real deformity. His voice was rough, his garb ordinary, his deportment morose. He was ambitious of fame, without the dignity to support it. In private life, he sank into the vulgarity of the clown." Such was the by no means flattering account given of Lee by an observant lady. He does not seem to have been a favorite with the gentle sex, of whom another is reported to have said that he was "a crabbed man ;" and Mrs. Adams declares that "the elegance of his pen far exceeds that of his person." He is supposed to have suffered in the good opinion of the ladies by his fondness for dogs, a pack of which always followed him wherever he went, to the manifest disorder of the good housekeeping of his female friends. "I was very politely entertained and noticed by the generals," writes Mrs. Adams— "more especially General Lee, who was very urgent for me to tarry in town and dine with him and the ladies present at 'Hobgoblin hall,' but I excused myself. The general was determined that I should not only be acquainted with him, but with his companions too ; and therefore placed a chair before me, into which he ordered Mr. Spada (his dog) to mount, and present his paw to me for a better acquaintance. I could not do otherwise than accept it."

The New-Englanders were dreadfully shocked by Lee's impiety. He "swore like a trooper," and did not fear to scoff openly at the ordinances of religion. When a day was appointed to invoke the aid of Heaven upon the American cause, Lee ridiculed it, and remarked, "Heaven is ever found favorable to strong battalions!" Tom Paine said of him that "he was above all monarchs, and below all scum."

CHAPTER XII.

1775. THE British in Boston had more than their share of the sufferings of the winter. The distress of the troops and inhabitants was spoken of as "great beyond all possible description. Neither vegetables, flour, nor pulse, for the inhabitants ; and the king's stores so very short, none can be spared from them ; no fuel, and the winter set in remarkably severe. The troops and inhabitants are absolutely and literally starving for want of provisions and fire. Even salt provision is fifteen pence sterling per pound." The small-pox, too, broke out in Boston, terribly alarming the people, whom even the thought that the disease was the best protection against the assault of the enemy did not reconcile to its infliction. The weather was so severe, with its freezing cold and drifting snows, that it was found necessary to order General Clinton and the larger portion of his troops to take refuge within the town from the exposed heights of Bunker's hill, where only a small garrison was left in three redoubts.

Wood, too, was as scarce in Boston as in the American camp; but Howe had less scruples than Washington in supplying his wants. The British general issued orders for pulling down the old North meetinghouse, containing a great deal of timber, and a hundred wooden dwelling-houses and other buildings to be used for fuel. The trees on the common were hewed down, and the celebrated Liberty-tree furnished fourteen cords of wood! Though they succeeded in thus supplying one want, they had much greater difficulty in satisfying others. An occasional coaster from Nova Scotia would escape the American privateers, and succeed in landing a cargo of beef, poultry, and hay; but such was the scarcity of these articles, that they were snatched up at once, at the most exorbitant prices, by the few who were rich enough to buy them. The great mass of the troops and people were forced to live exclusively upon salt provisions, and even upon meager supplies of those. The necessary result was, the prevalence of scurvy and fatal dysenteries.

The British officers, however, made a commendable effort to sustain the spirits of their men under these severe trials. They got up concerts, balls, and plays, in Faneuil hall, to enliven the people. In their dramatic performances they tried to serve the double purpose of making the audience, by provocatives to their cheerfulness, less discontented with themselves, and, by appeals to their sense of ridicule, more regardless of their enemies. The Americans were "taken off" by the military playwrights, and "shown up" to the manifest delight of a nightly concourse of tories and red-coats. The bills of the plays were, with a refined irony, frequently sent by some anonymous tories to Washington and his generals. The "Blockade of Boston," supposed to have been composed by Burgoyne himself, who was known even at that time to have a dramatic turn, having been written with the express purpose of ridiculing Washington and his troops, drew together on the night of its performance an unusually large audience.

"The Busy-body," the first piece on the bill, being over, the curtain drew up for the farce of "The Blockade of Boston." Washington was, of course, a prominent character, and appeared with a large wig on his head, a long, rusty sword by his side, and followed by his orderly sergeant, who had on his shoulder a rusty gun seven feet long, and was otherwise ludicrously equipped. These dramatic personages had hardly made their appearance, when a real character presented himself in the shape of a British sergeant, who came running on the stage, and, throwing down his musket, called out lustily, "The Yankees are attacking Bunker's hill!" The audience thought that this was a part of the play, until Howe, who was present, cried out, "*Officers, to your alarm-posts!*" when the military portion of the crowd made great haste away, leaving the ladies shrieking and fainting, and the rest of the audience in a state of great consternation.

The alarm had been caused by an attack of two hundred men, under Captain Knowlton, sent out by General Putnam, from his works on Cobble hill, to destroy some houses in Charlestown: these houses, about fourteen in number, were all that were left after the general fire, and were occupied by the British. The Americans started out at night, and, crossing the ice at the dam, succeeded in burning eight or ten of the houses, killing one man, and taking captive the guard, with their arms. The British garrison on Bunker's hill were alarmed by the flames, and commenced a brisk fire, doing no damage to the Americans, but greatly disturbing the equanimity, as we have seen, of the troops and people within Boston.

1776. The opening of the year in the American camp was a time of great anxiety. The period of service of most of the regiments had expired; and the old troops were in such a hurry to get away, and the new were so slow in coming in, that during the early days of January there were hardly ten thousand men before Boston. Washington was not only full of care, from the great interests at stake, but annoyed exceedingly by the resistance with which his orders were met by the disbanding troops. Many of the fresh men had come in unprovided with arms, and it became necessary to insist that those who were leaving the ranks should sell their guns, at a price fixed by inspectors appointed for the purpose. This caused dissatisfaction, and much grumbling. Washington, observing the dissatisfied spirit of his forces, appealed to their patriotism in a general order, in which, after reminding them that "an army without order, regularity, or discipline, is no better than a commissioned mob," he entreated them to conduct themselves like true soldiers, as "everything dear to freemen was at stake," and could only be secured by the faithful performance of their military duties.

The care which weighed upon Washington's mind at this time was known then only to his most intimate friends, to whom in the confidence of his letters he unburdened his heart. To his former secretary (Reed) he writes: "Search the volumes of history through, and **Jan. 4.** I much question whether a case similar to ours is to be found: namely, to maintain a post against the flower of the British troops for six months together, without powder; and then to have one army disbanded, and another to be raised, within the same distance of a reinforced army. What may be the issue of the last manœuvre, time only can unfold. I wish this month were well over our heads."

Again he writes, a few days later: "The reflection upon my situation, and that of this army, produces many an uneasy hour, when all around me are wrapped in sleep. Few people know the predicament we are in, on a thousand accounts; fewer still will believe, if any disaster happens to these lines, from what cause it flows. I have often thought how much happier I should have been, if, instead of accepting of a command under such circumstances, I had taken my musket on my shoulder and entered the ranks; or, if I could have justified the measure to posterity and my own conscience, had retired to the back country, and lived in a wigwam. If I shall be able to rise superior to these, and many other difficulties which might be enumerated, I shall most religiously believe that the finger of Providence is in it, to blind the eyes of our enemies; for surely if we get well through this month, it must be for the want of their knowing the disadvantages we labor under."

With all this discouragement, the patriotic feeling in the camp does not seem to have flagged. When for the first time, on New-Year's day, the flag with thirteen stripes, symbolical of the union of the thirteen colonies, was hoisted, there was apparently great enthusiasm, which found vent in loud hurrahs. On the same day, the British commander sent in with a flag of truce a "volume" of the king's speech at the opening of Parliament. This, however, only served to fire the patriotic ardor of the troops—although, singularly enough, the hoisting of the new flag, and the loud rejoicings of the American camp, were "received in Boston as a token of the deep impression which the speech had made," and as "a signal of submission."—"By this time" (January 4th), writes Washington, "I presume they begin to think it strange that we have not made a formal surrender of our lines."

30

The king's speech, on the contrary, was received with a feeling the very reverse of that which might lead to the hoisting of "a signal of submission." The patriots now talked of absolute independence, and looked forward with hope to raising in America "an empire of permanent duration, supported upon the grand pillars of truth, freedom, and religion, based upon justice, and defended by her own patriotic sons." The obstinate resolve expressed by George III., not to give up the colonies at any expense of blood and treasure, and the proof he gave of his determination (by the fact of his recommendation that the navy and army of Great Britain should be increased, and the mercenary aid of the Hessians hired, for the purpose of suppressing the "rebellious war"), did not shake the firmness of the Americans, but greatly excited their patriotic rage.

The Congress, after a long debate, having passed a resolution authorizing Washington to make an assault upon the enemy, "in any manner he might think expedient, notwithstanding the town and property in it might be destroyed," he began seriously to contemplate an attack. In his anxiety to do something, he went so far as to declare to the council of war called to deliberate upon the question, that "it is indispensably necessary to make a bold attempt to conquer the ministerial troops in Boston before they can be reinforced in the spring, if the means," he cautiously added, however, "shall be provided, and a favorable opportunity shall offer."

How great his desire for an assault,

and how inadequate his means, may be learned from this letter to the Congress at Philadelphia: "No man upon earth wishes more ardently to destroy the nest in Boston than I do; no person would be willing to go greater lengths than I shall to accomplish it, if it shall be thought advisable. But if we have neither powder to bombard with, nor ice to pass on, we shall be in no better situation than we have been in all the year; we shall be worse, because their works are stronger."

Jan. 24.

To strengthen his force, Washington had proposed to call out the New-England militia; and accordingly a requisition was made on Massachusetts, New Hampshire, and Connecticut, for thirteen regiments, to assemble at Cambridge on the first of February. While this plan was in operation, Washington felt more keenly than ever the inadequacy of his forces, for he had heard of the defeat and death of the gallant Montgomery, and would have desired to send reinforcements at once to the aid of Arnold. He could not, however, spare a man from his own camp; and his only alternative was to order three of the new regiments of militia, when filled, to proceed to Quebec.

Washington was thus, as it were, fastened in his camp, unable to move in consequence of the want of troops and ammunition, although other circumstances seemed favorable to action. How keenly he felt his position is told in every letter he wrote. To Congress he writes: "To have the eyes of a whole continent fixed with anxious expectation of seeing some great event, and to be restrained in every military operation for want of the necessary means to carry it on, is not very pleasing, especially as the means used to conceal my weakness from the enemy, conceal it also from our friends, and add to their wonder." Washington, however, had some diversion for his pent-up energies, in the prospect of activity in another quarter, where, if his personal presence was not required, the exercise of his judgment became necessary.

Information had been brought to headquarters, by a trustworthy person from Boston, of great activity in the British fleet. Admiral Shuldham, appointed to supersede Graves, had arrived in the harbor with a squadron and considerable reinforcements. On his arrival, a busy movement began: troops were detailed off for service, baggage packed, provisions inspected, biscuit baked, and ammunition taken out of store, with the evident purpose of making ready for sea, preparatory to an attack against some place or other. Finally, five transports loaded with troops under the command of Sir Henry Clinton, with munitions of war, two bomb-vessels, and a number of flat-bottomed boats, sailed away from Boston under the convoy of the Scarborough and Fowey men-of-war. It was supposed that Long island was the destination of this force, and Washington accordingly was anxious to provide a resistance to meet it. He had written to Congress, urging them to have some of the New-Jersey troops thrown into New York; but, not getting much satisfaction in that quarter, he determined to act for himself.

General Lee, who was at that time in Connecticut, had written a letter to Washington, in which, with his usual emphatic earnestness, he said : " New York must be secured, but it will never, I am afraid, be secured by direct order of Congress, for obvious reasons. You must step in to their relief. I am sensible no man can be spared from the lines under present circumstances ; but I would propose that you should detach me into Connecticut, and lend your name for collecting a body of volunteers." Lee was especially anxious to lay his hands upon the "dangerous banditti of tories" in New York, who were giving great countenance and aid to the enemy. "Not to crush," said he, "these serpents before their rattles are grown, would be ruinous."

Lee's proposition accorded with Washington's views, but he was anxious not to overstep his authority, and therefore hesitated to act until he had consulted with John Adams, who highly approved of the plan, "as practicable, expedient, and as properly lying within his excellency's authority without further directions from Congress." Washington accordingly ordered Lee to raise a volunteer force in Connecticut, to march to New York, and, with the aid of the New-Jersey troops, under Lord Sterling, to put the city and its immediate neighborhood in a posture of defence. Lee was, moreover, authorized to disarm or secure that "dangerous banditti of tories" whom he so cordially hated.

With the aid of Governor Trumbull, Lee soon gathered together the respectable force of twelve hundred men, and marched to Stamford. There he was met by a communication from the New-York committee of safety, who expressed a very decided aversion to his entering the city, lest it might provoke hostility on the part of the British ships-of-war in the harbor. Lee replied with unusual suavity, which was the more remarkable, as he was at the time suffering from a fit of the gout. Toward the end of his letter, however, there is a very perceptible spasm of disease or temper. "If the ships-of-war," growls he, "are quiet, I shall be quiet ; but I declare solemnly, that if they make a pretext of my presence to fire on the town, the first house set on flames by their guns shall be the funeral-pile of some of their best friends !"

Lee got to New York as soon as his gout would permit him, arriving there just two hours after Sir Henry Clinton had come to anchor in **Feb. 4.** the lower bay with the Mercury and a transport-brig. The inhabitants were in a state of great alarm, in consequence of two such belligerent arrivals. Though it was Sunday, they began moving away their effects, and continued to do so the whole night. The town seemed in a state of convulsion with the confusion of the hurried exodus : carts were going, boats loading, women and children crying, and distressed voices were even heard along the roads in the dead of night. Clinton, however, soon relieved the city's fears, by giving out that his object was merely a visit to his friend Governor Tryon, who at that time held state in the secure quarters of a British man-of-war anchored in the North river. In a few days, Sir Henry sailed away to North Carolina, and left Lee to deal with the tories.

Lee began his administration with an emphatic menace, by declaring, "If the men-of-war set one house on fire in consequence of my coming, I will chain a hundred of their friends together by the neck, and make the house their funeral-pile!"—"He would," says Gordon, "in all likelihood, have retaliated in some manner."

The American commander busied himself in removing the cannon on the Battery, and those in the king's store, to a place of safety, notwithstanding the "perdition to the city" threatened by the British men-of-war. They, however, withheld their fire; the naval authorities publishing a "pleasant reason" for their reserve, saying that as it was evidently Lee's purpose to bring destruction on the town, they were determined not to indulge him. Lee, laughing at them and their reasons, continued his work, and, after removing the cannon, made good use of them by planting them in the redoubts and breastworks which he erected in various places about New York. Besides, he ferreted out his old enemies the tories, and administered to them one of his "tremendous oaths," which led Congress to resolve "That no oath by way of test be imposed upon, exacted, or required, of any of the inhabitants of these colonies, by any military officer." Lee's martial law was not seldom in conflict with legislative enactment, and his measures were too often laid with gunpowder not to startle the timid counsels of the prudent. He wished to pursue a very high-handed course with all in opposition to the patriot cause; and, justly suspecting that the friends of the enemy were especially strong in New York, he was particularly anxious to make them feel the weight of his blow. Governor Tryon, in consequence of his influence upon many of the "respectable" inhabitants of New York, was extremely odious to Lee. "The propensity, or rather rage, for paying court to this great man," he writes, "is inconceivable. They can not be weaned from him. We must put wormwood on his paps, or they will cry to suck, as they are in their second childhood!" Lee's energetic measures, however, were soon checked by a call to duty elsewhere.

The tories were not confined to the city; in the interior of the province they had gathered in strong force at the call of Sir John Johnson, the son of Sir William, renowned in the French War. Sir John had succeeded to his father's estate on the Mohawk, and his baronial influence over the Highland tenants and Indian retainers. Fortifying Johnson hall, he was preparing, it was believed, to set out with his clansmen and savages along the valley of the Mohawk, with the view of forcing submission to the king's authority. General Schuyler, having kept watch of his movements, sent word to Congress, which, in answer, committed to him the business of checking Sir John's proposed enterprise. There being no troops at Albany, Schuyler was obliged to have recourse to the sub-committee of the county with whose aid he succeeded in raising some seven hundred militia. With this force he commenced his march, and was gratified to find that such was the enthusiasm in behalf of the patriot cause, that he had not gone far before his troops were increased by volunteers to the number of three thousand. Even Tryon county, supposed to be the stronghold of the tories, supplied him nine hundred men.

As Schuyler proceeded with this augmented force to Johnstown, he was met by a deputation from the Mohawks, which addressed him in magniloquent Indian rhetoric, and haughtily forbade him to advance against their "father," Sir John. Schuyler replied that he had full proof that many people in Johnstown and the neighborhood thereof had for a considerable time past made preparations to carry into execution the wicked design of the king's evil counsellors. "We have no objection," said Schuyler in conclusion, "nay we wish, that you and your warriors should be present to hear what we shall propose to Sir John and the people in and about Johnstown, who are our enemies. But we beg of you to tell your warriors that, although we have no quarrel with them, yet if we should be under the disagreeable necessity of fighting with our enemies, and your warriors should join them and fight against us, that we will repel force by force."

The Indian chiefs had occasion, on entering the American camp, and casting their wary eyes upon the large number of soldiers, to become convinced of the force of Schuyler's last argument, and accordingly when they replied, meekly said: "Brother Schuyler, the great man, attend! Everything that has been said to us, brother, has been perfectly agreeable to us."

Schuyler now sent a letter to Sir John Johnson, requesting a meeting with him next day, and assuring him that he and such persons as he might choose to attend him should pass safe and unmolested to and from the place appointed for the rendezvous. Sir John accordingly met the general about sixteen miles from Schenectady, when Schuyler's proposal having been submitted, Johnson asked until the following day for time to answer. Schuyler consented, and in the meantime advanced his troops on the frozen Mohawk to within four miles of Johnstown. Sir John's response now came, but, not being satisfactory, Schuyler resolved that he would march against the Johnson stronghold, at the same time informing the baronet that he would give him until twelve o'clock at night to reconsider his answer. Sir John, true to time, sent in precisely at that hour a satisfactory reply. He agreed to deliver up all the arms and military stores in his possession, with the exception of a few favorite family arms which Sir John was allowed, at his own request, to retain. He pledged himself besides, on his parole of honor, neither to take up arms against America, nor to move in the county beyond certain specified limits. His followers were, of course, bound by similar obligations.

The next day Schuyler proceeded to Johnstown, and drew up his men in the street, when Sir John's Highlanders, some two or three hundred in number, marched to the front of the lines and grounded their arms. Schuyler then dismissed them with an exhorta-

Jan. 20.

tion strictly to observe the terms of their agreement, and to refrain from all acts of hostility. The conduct of the American general, throughout this whole transaction, was highly approved by Congress, and applauded by the patriots.

CHAPTER XIII.

Patrick Henry in the Legislature of Virginia.—The Virginian Volunteers.—The Culpepper Corps.—The Rattlesnake Device.—Lord Dunmore's Proceedings.—The Fight at Great Bridge.—Lord Dunmore retires from Norfolk.—The City burned.—Description of Norfolk.—Plantations laid waste.—North Carolina.—The Manœuvres of the Tories.—M'Donald and M'Leod.—Their Highland Followers.—General Moore and the Patriots.—M'Donald retreats.—Moore pursues.—The Battle at Moore's-Creek Bridge.—M'Leod falls.—The Enemy put to Flight.—The Spirit in South Carolina and Georgia.

1775. "THERE is no longer any room for hope. If we wish to be free; if we wish to preserve inviolate those inestimable privileges for which we have been so long contending; if we mean not basely to abandon the noble struggle in which we have been so long engaged, and which we have pledged ourselves never to abandon until the glorious object of our contest shall be obtained, we must fight! I repeat it, sir, we must fight! An appeal to arms and the God .of hosts is all that is left us." These were the words uttered by Patrick Henry, in the course of his eloquent speech in support of the resolutions he introduced in the Virginia legislature, recommending a levy of volunteer troops: the resolutions were passed by a large majority. The appointment of a committee of safety followed, which at once proceeded to raise an armed force, of which Patrick Henry was made commander-in-chief. Volunteers came in readily, among whom was a corps of men from the county of Culpepper, whose appearance gave promise of doughty service.

Dressed in green hunting-shirts, like so many Robin-Hood foresters, with bucks' tails in their slouched hats, and with tomahawks and scalping-knives bristling from their belts, their very looks frightened the people.* Their flag, with the device of a coiled rattlesnake, and the motto, "Don't tread on me !" and the inscription on the bosom of each man's shirt, of "Liberty or death," taken from Henry's speech, were no less alarming. These Culpepper men proved themselves no less formidable than they looked.

Lord Dunmore, the governor of Virginia, had been frightened away from Williamsburg, the seat of government, by

* " Companies were raised in nearly every county ; among the rest, in Culpepper, adjoining Fauquier. This troop, which was three hundred and fifty strong, assembled near an old oak, which is still standing ; and Colonel Thomas Marshall was elected major. His son John was made lieutenant. The flag of the troop presented a coiled rattlesnake — the head for Virginia, and the twelve rattles for the other states : the mottoes, ' DON'T TREAD ON ME !' and ' LIBERTY OR DEATH !' These latter words were also painted upon the breasts of the green hunting-shirts of the company. The men were armed with rifles, tomahawks, and knives. Such was the warlike guise in which the afterward famous chief justice appeared at the head of his ardent troop."—JOHN ESTEN COOKE.

the energetic conduct of the patriots, and taken refuge on board of a ship-of-war. Arming several vessels, and collecting .together a number of tories and negroes, he determined to inflict punishment upon the " rebels." He sailed with this force along the coast, doing all the damage in his power, seizing here and there a patriot, destroying plantations, carrying off negroes, and burning houses. Having received a reinforcement of soldiers, he prepared to make an attempt on Hampton. His vessels, in the course of the night, warped in close to the town, and in the morning began a furious cannonade. A company of the Culpepper riflemen had in the meantime reached Hampton, and, being properly dispersed and hid, commenced firing at the ships, and with such effect, that the enemy were forced to haul off precipitately, for no man who ventured to show himself on deck was secure from the deadly aim of the Virginia marksmen.

Dunmore was terribly vexed at being thus repulsed by a few raw militiamen, and took his revenge by proclaiming martial law, requiring all persons capable of bearing arms to resort to his majesty's standard, or to be looked upon as traitors ; and declaring all indentured servants, negroes, or others (appertaining to " rebels"), who were able and willing to bear arms, free, upon serving with the royal troops. Dunmore was at this time at Norfolk, where there were a goodly number of tories, and his proclamation brought some hundreds of them, both black and white, to his standard. With this miscellaneous rabble added to his

two hundred regulars, he prepared to meet a force of Virginian patriots who were rapidly advancing to drive him from Norfolk.

His lordship's first operation was, to take possession and remove the planks of the Great bridge, which was the only approach to the town ; and then, with the utmost expedition, he began building a redoubt on the Norfolk side. He had not made much progress when the Virginians arrived, under the command of Captain Woodford, who took up a position at the other end of the bridge, at cannon-shot distance from Dunmore, and began throwing up intrenchments. The two parties thus remained for several days, busy at their works, without firing a shot, when the Virginians, becoming impatient, resolved to provoke an attack. For this purpose they availed themselves of a *ruse*. A servant belonging to one of the Virginian officers was directed to join Dunmore's force, as a pretended deserter, and report that the patriots only numbered three hundred "shirtmen" (so the riflemen were called from their hunting-dress) in all. The negro performed his part admirably ; and the enemy, swallowing the bait, determined to attack the patriots in their intrenchments.

The British regulars, under Captain Leslie, were accordingly detailed for the service, together with about three hundred "white and black slaves." The party set out at three o'clock in the morning, in order to take the Virginians by surprise before dawn. Leslie, having replaced the planks of the Great bridge, marched his men across, with Captain Fordyce, at the head of his grenadiers, leading the van. The regulars, with fixed bayonets, advanced steadily along the causeway directly up to the American intrenchments. The Virginian riflemen, however, were on the alert, and, waiting until the enemy were close to them, began a murderous fire, by which Fordyce and several of his men were at once killed. The grenadiers held their ground with a coolness and intrepidity that excited the admiration of all; and such was their discipline, that they continued to advance until not one of them escaped either death or capture. Leslie, who was in the rear with the main body, now ordered a retreat, when the whole of the British force retired to their fort under the cover of its guns, having lost sixty-two men killed and wounded. The Virginians did not lose a single man, and had only one slightly wounded. Captain Fordyce was buried with the honors due to his rank and gallantry; and all the prisoners, with the exception of the American royalists, who were rigorously dealt with, were treated kindly by their captors. The British forces retired during the next night within Norfolk. Leslie now refused to serve any longer on shore, until assured of a better support from the tory inhabitants; and the loyalists, both white and black, on their part declined to serve, unless aided by a stronger reinforcement of regulars. Under these discouraging circumstances, Lord Dunmore determined to abandon his position at Norfolk.

Dec. 14. The Virginians entered the city as the British withdrew, and found that the tory inhabitants had gone on board the English ships, with the exception of the poor negroes, who had been left to shift for themselves. Colonel Woodfood now resigned the command of the provincials to Colonel Howe, who remained in possession of Norfolk until the beginning of the ensuing year.

1776. Lord Dunmore was still with his ships in Hampton roads, unable to effect anything until the arrival, on the first of January, of the British frigate Liverpool. A flag of truce was then immediately sent into the town, with a demand for supplies. These being positively refused, Dunmore determined to bombard and set fire to Norfolk, where the Virginia riflemen, under cover of the warehouses by Elizabeth river, were continuing greatly to harass the ships by their sharpshooting. Notice having been given to the inhabitants, that they might have an opportunity of removing the women and children from danger, the British vessels began their cannonade, while parties of sailors and marines were sent ashore to set fire to the buildings by the water's edge. The whole town, which was built of wood, was soon in flames and reduced to ashes, notwithstanding every exertion made by Howe and his men to extinguish the fire.

Norfolk at that time was a place of great importance, having a population of six thousand, and a thriving commerce. It was thought to be "an odious business for a governor to be himself a principal actor in burning and destroying the best town in his government," and great indignation was excited in consequence throughout the province. The patriots were able greatly to harass his lordship, in revenge for his cruelty, by cutting off supplies from the ships. The plantations along the Norfolk shore were laid waste; and their proprietors, who were chiefly loyalists, were forced to retire into the interior with their stock and stores of provisions, so that they might not have it in their power to supply the necessities of the British. Dunmore was thus driven away from Norfolk; and, after continuing his depredations upon the banks of the southern rivers and coast and carrying off some thousand negroes, he betook himself with his piratical fleet to St. Augustine, in the then Spanish province of Florida.

In North Carolina, the patriots were emulating the spirit of their Virginian brethren. The British governor, Martin, had been early forced, like Lord Dunmore, to seek refuge on board a man-of-war, where for the most part he had been obliged to content himself with the proclamation, without the exercise, of his authority. Learning, however, that Sir Henry Clinton had sailed for North Carolina, and that an expedition was to be sent out from Great Britain probably for the same destination, Martin took courage, and began to intrigue with the Scotch settlers in the western districts of the province, who were known to be favorably disposed to the crown. Among these were a large number of Highlanders, and Martin selected two gentlemen among them, who had been British officers, of the names of M‘Donald and M‘Leod, and gave them commissions, with authority to raise a body of troops. These two per-

sons had not been long in the country, but their names were enough to excite all the clannish predilections of the Highlanders, who gathered as if rallying about their chieftains among their native hills, and enrolled themselves to the number of sixteen hundred under the royal standard, which they regarded little, except as unfurled by a M‘Donald and a M‘Leod.

The North Carolina patriots were on the alert; and General Moore, assembling some eleven hundred militiamen, marched to meet the enemy. Coming up within seven miles of the "Regulators," as they were called, and the Highlanders, who were encamped in the neighborhood of Cross creek (now Fayetteville), which was in the midst of those Scotch settlers who were favorably disposed toward the king, Moore halted in a strong position. The enemy then advanced within four miles, and sent in to the patriots with a flag of truce one of the governor's manifestoes, and a letter to their general, summoning him to join the royal standard or be treated as an enemy. Moore, in his answer, declined the proposition for the present, but promised a more specific reply on the next day. M‘Donald, in command of the royalist force, received accordingly, the following morning, Moore's promised letter, in which the American general, as a significant offset to the Scotchman's summons, called upon him to sign the patriotic association of the province.

While Moore was expecting a rejoinder to his communication, he learned that M‘Donald, without waiting to indite a reply, had crossed the river in the night, and pushed on rapidly toward the coast.

Moore, after ordering off a detachment to join the approaching reinforcements of eight hundred militia which were coming from Newbern, under the command of Colonel Caswell, and another party to secure the ford of Cross creek, marched himself in pursuit. The Newbern militia fortunately reached Moore's-creek bridge in time to take possession of it, and oppose the retreat of the royalist force.

The Americans, however, had held possession only a few hours, during which time they had destroyed a portion of the

Feb. 27. bridge, and raised a small breastwork, when the enemy came up. M'Leod, who was now in command, in consequence of the illness of M'Donald, no sooner saw that his progress was opposed, than he led his men at once against the American works. They marched up within thirty paces, when they were met by a well-served fire from the American breastwork. Captain M'Leod fell at the first volley, pierced with twenty bullets,

and his troops immediately took to flight. Even M'Donald's influence could not succeed in rallying them; and he, completely abandoned, was forced to surrender himself a prisoner. General Moore, coming up soon after, confronted the fugitives, and took nearly nine hundred of them captive. The royalists lost about seventy killed and wounded; the patriots only two wounded. A good supply of arms also fell into the possession of the conquerors.

In South Carolina and Georgia, little was done in the way of active hostility as yet by the patriots, beyond the seizure of an occasional vessel. There was, however, sufficient evidence of a resolute spirit of resistance; and in the course of this narrative we shall have occasion to record abundant proofs that the southern no less than the northern provinces were willing and able to strike a blow for the liberties of the country. We must now return to Washington and his camp at Cambridge.

CHAPTER XIV.

Everything thaws but "Old Put."—An Assault on Boston proposed, but rejected by the Council of War.—Arrival of Knox from Ticonderoga, with an Abundant Supply of Ammunition, &c.—The taking Possession of Dorchester Heights proposed.—Morals of the Camp protected.—Bombardment of Boston.—Expedition for Dorchester sets out.—The Enemy oppose, and are defeated.—Great Preparations of Lord Howe.—A Storm.—The Attack postponed.—A New Missile invented.—Howe at last acknowledges the Position on Dorchester Heights too formidable for him.—He prepares to evacuate Boston.—A Flag of Truce.—A Communication from the Selectmen of Boston.—Attempt on Nook's Hill.—A Terrible Cannonade.

1776. "THE bay is open. Everything thaws here except 'Old Put.' He is still as hard as ever, crying out for 'powder, powder! ye gods, give us pow-

der!'" wrote an officer. And Washington, too, had his complaints to make on the same score. "The weather," he writes, "turns out exceedingly mild, insomuch as to promise nothing favorable from ice. ...And no appearance of powder." Toward the middle of February, however, some "freezing weather" having formed "some pretty strong ice," which afforded a wider and consequently less dangerous approach to Boston, Washington was in favor of an assault, notwithstanding the militia were not all come in, and there was little or no powder for a regular cannonade or bombardment. A council of war was accordingly summoned, **Feb. 16.** but the enterprise being thought too dangerous, it was abandoned for the present.

A few days subsequently, Colonel Knox arrived in the camp with a welcome supply of cannon, mortars, and howitzers, which that spirited officer had succeeded, in the depth of a northern winter, in bringing from Crown Point and Ticonderoga. By means of sleds, and with the utmost labor, Knox dragged for hundreds of miles through the drifted snows and over the frozen lakes an armament of immense weight, "a noble train of artillery," as he called it, and safely deposited it at Cambridge, where he received, as he well merited, the praises of the commander-in-chief and the applause of the whole army. Simultaneously with this acquisition came a supply of shells and powder, captured from the enemy. The militia had come in, too, in considerable force. Under these prosperous circumstances, the council of war was at last so far inspirited as to decide upon action. It was resolved that Dorchester heights should be taken possession of as soon as possible, with the view of drawing the enemy out.

"How far," wrote Washington, who had suggested this movement, "our expectations may be answered, time only can determine; but I should think, if anything will induce them to hazard an engagement, it will be our attempt to fortify these heights [Dorchester]; as, that event's taking place, we shall be able to command a great part of the town and almost the whole harbor." Great activity and animation now pervaded the camp. Carts loaded with intrenching-tools, carts with fascines and huge bundles of hay, went by the hundreds lumbering along the roads, flanked by guards and followed by detachment after detachment of working-parties; the surgeons and surgeons' mates throughout the army were busy in preparing lint and bandages; of the latter two thousand had been ordered, although a sanguine member of the medical department expresses the hope that "not one quarter of the number will be required, whatever may be the nature of the occasion." To add to the seriousness of the approaching events, the soldiers were reminded of their duty by these severely earnest orders, which could only have been addressed with effect to men like those of Washington, fighting for conscience sake:—

"All officers," rigidly declares the order, "non-commissioned officers, and soldiers, are positively forbid playing at cards, and other games of chance. At this time of public distress, men may find enough to do in the service of their God and their country, without abandoning themselves to vice and immorality.

"As the season is now fast approaching

when every man must expect to be drawn into the field of action, it is highly important that he should prepare his mind, as well as everything necessary for it. It is a noble cause we are engaged in; it is the cause of virtue and mankind; every temporal advantage and comfort to us and our posterity depends upon the vigor of our exertions; in short, freedom or slavery must be the result of our conduct. There can, therefore, be no greater inducement to men to behave well. But it may not be amiss for the troops to know that, if any man in action shall presume to skulk, hide himself, or retreat from the enemy without the orders of his commanding officer, he will be instantly shot down as an example of cowardice; cowards having too frequently disconcerted the best-formed troops by their dastardly behavior."

A night was now appointed for the attempt on Dorchester heights. The time, at the suggestion of the New-England officers, was the 4th of March; the next day, which probably would be the day of action, being the anniversary of the "massacre of Boston," which, it was believed, would stimulate by its memories the courage of the Massachusetts troops.

For two days previously, the Americans bombarded Boston, but with no effect on the enemy, beyond splintering a few of their wooden buildings and wounding a soldier or two. The Americans themselves, however, met with a serious loss in the bursting of two heavy mortars, one of which was the big gun the "Congress," Old Put's christling. The bombardment, notwithstanding, had the effect

intended, of concealing from the enemy the preparations for taking possession of Dorchester heights. General Howe, not suspicious of anything more serious, contended himself with responding to the American fire, and threw a shower of bombs, but fortunately without serious damage.

All things being ready, the expedition sets out for Dorchester on the night appointed. The covering-party of **March 4.** eight hundred men lead the way; then go the carts with the intrenching-tools, followed by the working-detachment of twelve hundred men, under General Thomas; while the rear of the procession is closed by a long train of more than three hundred carts laden with fascines and bundles of hay, and dragged by oxen. The bundles of hay are designed for Dorchester neck, which is very low, and exposed to be raked by the enemy on one side, where accordingly they are to be laid to cover the Americans in passing and repassing. "Every man," says Gordon, who describes the whole affair quaintly yet graphically, "knows his place and business. The covering-party, when upon the ground, divides; half goes to the point nearest to Boston, the other to that next to the castle. All possible silence is observed. But there is no occasion to order the whips to be taken from the wagoners, lest their impatience and the difficulty of the roads should induce them to make use of them, and occasion an alarm. The whips used by the drivers of these ox-carts are not formed for making much noise, and can give no alarm at a distance. The men in driving their oxen commonly make most noise with their voices; and now a regard to their own safety dictates to them to speak to their cattle, as they move on, in a whispering note.

"There are no bad roads to require an exertion; for the frost having been of long continuance, they are so hard frozen as to be quite good. The wind lies to carry what noise can not be avoided in driving the stakes, and picking against the ground (still frozen above eighteen inches deep in many places), into the harbor between the town and the castle, so that it can not be heard and regarded by any who do not suspect what is going on, especially as there is a continued cannonade on both sides. Many of the carts make three trips, some four; for a vast quantity of materials has been collected, especially chandeliers and fascines.

"By ten o'clock at night the troops have raised two forts, one upon each hill, sufficient to defend them from small-arms and grape-shot. The night is remarkably mild; a finer for working could not have been selected out of the three hundred and sixty-five. They continue working with the utmost diligence until relieved at three o'clock next morning. It is so hazy below the heights, that the men can not be seen, though it is a bright moonlight night above on the hills.

"It is some time after daybreak before the ministerialists in Boston can clearly discern the new-erected forts. They loom to great advantage, and are thought to be much larger than is really the case. General Howe is astonished upon seeing what has been done; scratches his head, and is heard to say: 'I know not what I shall do; the rebels have done more in one night than my whole army would have done in months!'"

Washington felt confident that this movement of his troops would bring on an attack from the enemy; and he prepared in case of this event—which he not only supposed probable, but eagerly hoped for—to make an assault, while the British should be engaged in the direction of Dorchester heights, on another part of Boston to the west. He had accordingly ordered four thousand picked troops to be in readiness to embark on forty-five batteaux which had been prepared for the purpose, and were moored at the mouth of Charles river, under the cover of two floating batteries. These troops were formed in two divisions: General Sullivan leads the first, General Greene the second; and all are under the general command of Putnam.

The whole plan of defence and offence has been settled by Washington. Every movement of the enemy is watched: from the hills, which command a view of Boston, the officers can observe with their glasses everything that takes place in the city which lies below them. Proper signals are arranged, by which intelligence can be rapidly communicated from height to height—from Dorchester to Roxbury, and from Roxbury to Cambridge. The boats being prepared, and the troops in readiness to embark, Washington is on the alert, when the enemy attack the American position on Dorchester heights, and are defeated, to signalize to Putnam to send his four thousand men across from

Cambridge to assault the city, while the British are in a state of confusion from their expected repulse.

All is hurry and bustle in Boston. General Howe is collecting all the ladders in town, and having them cut to the proper length for scaling. A large body of troops is drawn up by the water-side; and the transport-vessels are weighing their anchors, in readiness to receive them. The men finally embark; an observer reports that most look pale and dejected, and some are heard to say, with a sad presentiment, " It will be another Bunker's-hill affair, or worse !" while others, in a spirit of bravado, talk of how they intend " to serve the rebels." The gallant Lord Percy commands the force, and all seems ready for the attack.

The Americans, as they behold this movement of the British troops, clap their hands for joy, and " wish them to come on." Washington is on the heights, and says to those about him, " Remember it is the 5th of March, and avenge the death of your brethren !" —" What says the general ?" eagerly inquire those who had not distinctly heard his words. " Remember it is the 5th of March, and avenge the death of your brethren !" is repeated in answer, and passed rapidly from man to man, until the whole body of troops is aroused to martial excitement, as by an electric flash.

March 5.

Crowds of people gather upon the surrounding hills, and with hushed lips and beating hearts fearfully await the coming struggle. They wait and wait until the evening, straining their eyes to catch if possible, through the gathering darkness, the approach of the enemy. Night closes; the tide ebbs; the struggle is put off until another day; the spectators go homeward, with sad expectations of the morrow. Mrs. Adams is among these anxious beholders, and on returning home, before retiring for the night, writes a hurried note to her absent husband : " I have just returned," she says, " from Penn's hill, where I have been sitting to hear the amazing roar of cannon, and from whence I could see every shell which was thrown. The sound, I think, is one of the grandest in nature, and is of the true species of the sublime. 'Tis now an incessant roar; but oh, the fatal ideas which are connected with the sound ! How many of our dear countrymen must fall !" She goes to bed, but not to sleep, for she writes on the following morning : " I went to bed about twelve, and rose again a little after one. I could no more sleep than if I had been in the engagement; the rattling of the windows, the jar of the house, the continual roar of twenty-four pounders, and the bursting of shells, give us such ideas, and realize a scene to us of which we could scarcely form any conception."

The troops continue their work, while the whole camp is on the alert for the call of duty at any moment. The bombardment goes on from both sides during the whole night. The British transports and floating batteries are hauled out in the night, to be in readiness for the debarkation of the troops on the next day; but, in attempting to make their way to Castle William, their rendezvous, the wind proves unfavorable, and blows with such a gale, that three of the vessels are driven ashore, and the rest are obliged to return. The gale increases to a storm, which rages all the night and next day, while torrents of rain keep pouring down. The attack is postponed once more ; for, with the violence of the wind, and the heavy surf beating against the shore, it is in vain to attempt to land the troops.

In the meantime, the Americans continued to strengthen their fortifications. The quartermaster-general, Mifflin, who had the supervision of the work, was indefatigable in his exertions. Having brought upon the ground the buildings already framed, he had the men in three days under the cover of fairly comfortable barracks. Moreover, he ingeniously devised a new species of arms, which promised to prove of great effect. These were barrels filled with stones, gravel, and sand, and placed round the works in readiness to be rolled down against the enemy, in order to break their ranks and legs, if they should venture to attempt to advance up the hill.

March 6. Another day passes, and the weather continuing unfavorable the British still hold back ; and, finally, giving up all hopes of dislodging the patriots from their now formidable position on Dorchester heights, they determine to evacuate Boston. Howe had no other alternative. The last spirited and effectual movement of the Americans, favored by the weather, so propitious to them and so fatal to their enemy, had made the town untenable. The admiral had told Howe that, if the Americans contin-

ued in possession of the heights of Dorchester, not one of his majesty's ships could be kept in the harbor ; and Howe was now forced to admit that his enemy was too formidable to be dislodged. The British army, thus hemmed in, was useless for offence, and would soon be incapable of defence ; the fleet, thus exposed, was in hourly danger, and could only save itself by sailing away.

Howe had long been in favor of removing the scene of hostilities from Boston to New York, but had never expressed a doubt of the safety of his army in its present position. He had, in fact, in his despatch to the British government, declared, " We are not under the least apprehension of an attack upon this place from the rebels, by surprise or otherwise." So far was he from having any fears on that score, that he expresses the wish that " they would attempt so rash a step, and quit those strong intrenchments to which they may attribute their present safety." He had felt perfectly secure, and had determined to take his own good time, when the spring had fairly advanced, and reinforcements had come in from Great Britain, in shifting the scene of war from Massachusetts to a southern province. On the morning when those works on Dorchester heights—which had been raised in a single night, " with an expedition," as a British officer wrote, " equal to that of the genii belonging to Aladdin's wonderful lamp"—struck the astonished eyes of Howe, he felt for the first some " apprehension" of the "rebels." When, moreover, Nature herself seemed to join the Americans, and he was baffled by the winds and storms in his only hope of triumph, he wisely submitted to his misfortune, and judiciously giving up all thought of victory, sought only a means of escape.

Great preparations were now made in Boston, evidently for departure. The transports were preparing for sea with the utmost expedition. There was the greatest movement and confusion among the troops. Night and day they were hurrying down their cannon, ammunition, and stores, to the wharves. Such was the haste with which they were loading the vessels, that no time was taken to make even a memorandum of what was put on board. The carpenters were hard at work on the transports, fitting up bunks for the soldiers and cabins for the officers, and there was everywhere proof of an early intention on the part of the British to escape from Boston.

Intelligence of Howe's resolution was now conveyed to the American camp, in a manner which, although not directly official, could leave no doubt of the fact. A flag of truce came out from the enemy, with a letter, which was received by Colonel Learned, in command of the advance post at Roxbury. This communication, being taken to headquarters, was there opened by Washington, for whom it was evidently intended, although not so addressed. Here is the letter:—

"BOSTON, 8th March, 1776.

"As his excellency General Howe is determined to leave the town, with the troops under his command, a number of the respectable inhabitants, being very anxious for its preservation and safety, have applied to General Robertson for this purpose, who at their request has communicated the same to his excellency General Howe, who has assured him that he has no intention of destroying the town, unless the troops under his command are molested during their embarkation, or at their departure, by the armed force without; which declaration he gave General Robertson leave to communicate to the inhabitants. If such an opposition should take place, we have the greatest reason to expect the town will be exposed to entire destruction. Our fears are quieted with regard to General Howe's intentions. We beg we may have some assurance that so dreadful a calamity may not be brought on by any measures without. As a testimony of the truth above, we have signed our names to this paper, carried out by Messrs. Thomas and Jonathan Amory and Peter Johannot, who have, at the earnest entreaties of the inhabitants, through the lieutenant-governor, solicited a flag of truce for the purpose.   "JOHN SCOLLAY,
                "TIMOTHY NEWELL,
                "THOMAS MARSHALL,
                "SAMUEL AUSTIN."

Howe had succeeded in frightening the inhabitants by his threat to burn the town in case of his being assaulted by Washington's troops, and effected the object he is said to have intended. His pride is supposed to have revolted at making terms of capitulation directly with the "rebel" leader; and at the same time, being conscious how much he was at the mercy of his enemy, he was desirous of securing conditions of safety to his army. The citizens of Boston, as was expected, took the alarm, and, by writing the letter, did as was hoped and probably suggested.

Washington, on receiving the communication, called together such of the general officers as he could immediately assemble, and with their advice determined not to answer it, as it was not addressed to him, nor signed or authenticated by General Howe. It was, however, thought proper to direct Colonel Learned, to whom the letter had been first presented, to answer it thus:—

"ROXBURY, *March* 9, 1776.

"GENTLEMEN: Agreeably to a promise made to you at the lines yesterday, I waited upon his excellency General Washington, and presented to him the paper handed to me by you, from the selectmen of Boston. The answer I received from him was to this effect: 'That as it was an unauthenticated paper, without an address, and not obligatory upon General Howe, he would take no notice of it.' I am, with esteem and respect, gentlemen, your most obedient servant,

"EBENEZER LEARNED.

"To MESSRS. AMORY AND JOHANNOT."

Somehow or other, the object of the letter was obtained, through a tacit understanding between the two generals, although each dodged the responsibility of committing himself to a written agreement. "General Washington," writes a chronicler of the time, "brought himself under no obligation; but expressed himself in words which admitted of a favorable construction, and intimated his good wishes for the towns-people." General Howe probably never thought seriously of burning the city. His preparations for

32

departure were such as to indicate no such intention. Washington himself had come to that conclusion; for he infers, "from the destruction they are making of sundry pieces of furniture, of many of their wagons, carts, &c., which they can not take with them," that there is no design to burn the city, for in that case the whole might have been destroyed together. At any rate, Washington did not attack, and Howe did not burn.

The Americans, however, went on with their works, and now attempted to take possession of Nook's hill, which was still nearer Boston than Dorchester heights, and completely commanded the town. Washington sent out during the night a strong force to raise a **March 8.** redoubt, and establish a position there. On reaching the height, however, some of the men imprudently lighted a fire, which alarmed the British, and drew from their ships a heavy cannonade, which, although well returned by the American batteries, was so severe, that the patriots were forced to retire. The camp and the whole country round were kept in a state of anxious excitement by the incessant firing throughout the night. Mrs. Adams is again on the alert with her ever-ready pen, and writes to her husband on Sunday evening, March 10: "A most terrible and incessant cannonade from half-after eight till six this morning. I hear we lost four men killed, and some wounded, in attempting to take the hill nearest to the town, called Nook's hill. We did some work, but the fire from the ships beat off our men, so that they did not secure it, but retired to the fort on the other hill."

CHAPTER XV.

General Howe's Proclamation.—Crean Brush, Esquire.—His Proceedings.—Impatience of Howe to depart.—The License of Sailors and Soldiers.—Howe threatens.—Offers Rewards.—Washington hastens the Departure of the British by another and Successful Attempt on Nook's Hill.—The Result.—The British depart.—The Inhabitants of Boston.—Alarms of Fire.—The Precipitate Hurry of the Enemy.—The Tories anxious to get away.—Many of them unable to escape.—The Patriot Army enters Boston.—Appearance of the City.—Washington's Letters to his Brother and John Hancock.—The Small-Pox.—General Heath sent with a Detachment to New York.—The Puzzling Movements of the British Fleet.—It sails at last.—The Joy of the Enemy at getting away.—Tribute of Honor to Washington.—The Evacuation of Boston.—How received in England.

1776. THE attempt on Nook's hill, although temporarily unsuccessful, served to hasten the preparations for departure of the British. General Howe **Mar. 10.** issued a proclamation, which was addressed to Crean Brush, Esquire, an inveterate tory of New York, who had become notorious as an importunate adviser and an active and insolent agent of British tyranny. The proclamation was printed in the form of a handbill, and was circulated throughout the city. These are its words:—

"SIR: I am informed there are large quantities of goods in the town of Boston, which, if in possession of the rebels, would enable them to carry on war. And whereas I have given notice to all loyal inhabitants to remove such goods from hence, and that all who do not remove them, or deliver them to your care, will be considered as abettors of rebels, You are hereby authorized and required to take into your possession all such goods as answer this description, and give certificates to the owners that you have received them for their use, and will deliver them to the owners' order, unavoidable accidents excepted. And you are to make inquiry if any such goods be secreted or left in stores; and you are to seize all such and put them on board the Minerva ship or the brigantine Elizabeth.

"Given under my hand, at headquarters, Boston, this 10th day of March, 1776.

"W. HOWE, *Com. Chief.*

"To CREAN BRUSH, Esquire."

This order was interpreted by Crean Brush, Esquire, with all the liberality of insolence for which he was notorious. Various shops, belonging to persons in the country, were broken open, and all goods of whatever sort or kind (although Howe had more particularly specified, in one of his orders, linens and woollens) were taken out and put on board ship, to be carried away. Brush was not content with despoiling the absent, but, growing more audacious, in the confusion of the approaching departure of the troops, he began to strip the shops of all their goods, in the very face of the owners who were in town! Under this apparent official sanction, the soldiers and sailors went about plundering and committing depredations. Shops, stores, and dwelling-houses, were entered by these ruthless robbers, who destroyed what they could

not carry away. Howe strove to check the villains by proclamations and orders; but, although he threatened the guilty with death, they continued their pillage.

The British commander was now evidently impatient to depart. The streets were barricaded in different parts of the town, and proclamation was made by the **Mar. 15.** crier for every inhabitant to keep to his house from eleven o'clock in the morning till night, that there might be no interference with the troops, who were now disposed in readiness for embarkation. The wind, however, being unfavorable for the ships, the departure was postponed, and the troops sent back to their quarters. The soldiers thus detained were thrown loose from their ordinary discipline, and had "little else to study but mischief, which they practised to a great degree, by breaking open stores and tossing the contents, being private property, into the dock; destroying the furniture of every house they could get into, and otherwise committing every kind of wantonness which disappointed malice could suggest." The naval department acted in ready concert of licentiousness with the military, and sailors landed in gangs from the ships-of-war (led, it was said, by officers), and went about the city, rifling and destroying everything within their reach. Howe continued by proclamation to threaten the rogues with hanging, but with little or no effect. He proved his anxious loyalty by securing safety to its appurtenances, by the more effective system of pecuniary awards: he offered fifty pounds sterling for the conviction of any one found cutting or defacing the king's or queen's picture hanging in the townhouse, which had already been entered and somewhat damaged by his lawless soldiers.

These delays of the British in evacuating Boston were a disappointment to Washington, as he fully expected that he would have got rid of them **Mar. 13.** before. He was now well persuaded of their intention of going, as all their movements indicated it; but he felt that it was necessary to continue on his guard, lest after all it should prove a feint to deceive him. He resolved, with the advice of his council, to precipitate Howe's movements, by making another attempt on Nook's hill. A strong force was accordingly detached for this purpose; **Mar. 16.** and it succeeded in taking possession, erecting a breastwork, and holding that important post, in spite of a sharp cannonade from the enemy.

This successful movement of the Americans was what "the king's troops had most fearfully dreaded," as Nook's hill gave Washington the entire command of Boston neck and the south end of the town. The British commander now no longer hesitated, and began to embark his troops as early as two o'clock on the next morning (Sunday), and had **Mar. 17.** every man on board and the ships under sail before ten. The whole number of soldiers thus hastily shipped amounted to seven thousand five hundred and seventy-five. These, with the sailors and marines, made up the entire available force of the British, to the number of about ten thousand.

So soon as the last red-coat disappeared, the inhabitants hurried out of their dwellings and began anxiously to seek for any lurking evidences of fire. Combustibles, so placed as to indicate a design of burning the town, were found in some of the houses. These preparations had probably been made to carry out the threat of Howe, in case of being fired upon during embarkation. The Americans, however, did not fire a shot. "Our troops," wrote an English officer, "did not receive the smallest molestation, though the rebels were all night at work on the near hill ...and we kept a constant fire upon them from a battery of twenty-four pounders. They did not return a single shot. It was lucky for the inhabitants now left in Boston they did not; for I am informed everything was prepared to set the town in a blaze, had they fired one cannon."

The hurry of the retreat is shown by this graphic letter of another British officer: "Our not being burdened with provisions, permitted us to save some stores and ammunition, the light fieldpieces and such things as were most convenient of carriage. The rest, I am sorry to say, we were obliged to leave behind; such of the guns as, by dismounting, we could throw into the sea, was so done. The carriages were disabled, and every precaution taken that our circumstances would permit; for our retreat was by agreement. The people of the town who were friends to government, took care of nothing but their merchandise, and found means to employ the men belonging to the transports in embarking their goods, so that several of the vessels were entirely filled with private property, instead of the king's stores. By some unaccountable accident, the medicines, surgeons' chests, instruments, and necessaries, were left in the hospital. The confusion unavoidable to such a disaster will make you conceive how much must be forgot, where every man had a private concern. The necessary care and distress of the women, children, sick, and wounded, required every assistance that could be given. It was not like breaking up a camp, where every man knows his duty; it was like departing your country with your wives, your servants, your household furniture, and all your encumbrances. The officers, who felt the disgrace of their retreat, did their utmost to keep up appearances. The men, who thought they were changing for the better, strove to take advantage of the present times, and were kept from plunder and drink with difficulty."[*]

The departure of the British from Boston had been so sudden and unexpected, that there had not been provided a sufficient number of vessels, properly appointed, for carrying away the fugitives. In addition to the troops, there were nearly a thousand of the inhabitants who were either so attached to the royal cause that they preferred to go, or who were so far suspected of tory principles that they did not think it prudent to remain. These greatly encumbered the transports with their numbers, and their plunder and effects. The ships, too, had been hurried away so quickly, that many of them were quite unfit for sea. Some had hauled out even before their yards, booms, and bow-

---

[*] Remembrancer, vol. iii., p. 108; quoted by Irving.

sprits, had been bent; and the fleet was now supposed to be delaying, in the Nantasket roads, where it had come to anchor, in consequence of not being in a fit condition to sail, particularly at a season when the equinoctial gale was hourly to be expected.

As soon as the British troops had left Bunker's hill, and were observed passing in crowds to the ships at anchor below the castle, the continental forces were drawn out in parade. Several regiments, under the command of Putnam, then embarked immediately in boats, and went down the river; while two men were sent in advance to Bunker's hill, to reconnoitre that position and report upon its condition. As the latter approached, they were surprised to find the British sentries still at their posts; but, advancing cautiously till they came close to the works, they discovered that the supposed soldiers on guard were merely wooden men, with muskets on their shoulders, which the enemy had put up there, to conceal the moment of their departure, and thus guard themselves against an attack during their flight. The two Americans, finding the fort entirely deserted, made a signal to the camp, and a detachment of soldiers was immediately ordered to take possession.

The troops which sailed down the river had in the meantime landed at Sewall's point, where, learning that all the British had left Boston, a portion of them entered to take possession, and the main body returned to Cambridge. At the same time, General Ward, with about five hundred troops, under the immediate command of Colonel Learned — who unbarred and opened the gates — entered Boston from the Roxbury quarter. On their way over the Neck, the men picked up numbers of crowfeet, which had been scattered there by the enemy. The "crowfoot" is an iron instrument, consisting of a round ball with spikes, so arranged that it will wound the step of horse or man in whatever manner it may be thrown.

Everything in Boston showed the precipitation with which the British had departed. Their barracks and other works on Bunker's hill, although of wood, were all left standing, while but a small part of their lines was destroyed. Some two hundred and fifty cannon, among them a very large iron mortar, had been left behind, and one piece of artillery was thrown into the water from the end of the wharf. Some thirty thousand pounds of powder, twenty-five hundred chaldrons of sea-coal, twenty-five thousand bushels of wheat, twenty-three hundred bushels of barley, six hundred bushels of oats, a hundred jars of oil, and a hundred and fifty horses, were among the stores left by the British in their haste to get away.

Washington, in a letter to his brother, says: "The enemy left all their works standing in Boston and on Bunker's hill; and formidable they are. The town has shared a much better fate than was expected, the damage done to the houses being nothing equal to report. But the inhabitants have suffered a good deal in being plundered by the soldiery at their departure. All those who took upon themselves the style and title of government-men in Boston, in short all those who have acted an unfriendly part in this great contest, have shipped themselves off in the same hurry, but under still greater disadvantage than the king's troops, being obliged to man their own vessels, as seamen enough could not be had for the king's transports, and submit to every hardship that can be conceived. One or two have done, what a great number ought to have done long ago, committed suicide. By all accounts, there never existed a more miserable set of beings than these wretched creatures now are: taught to believe that the power of Great Britain was superior to all opposition, and, if not, that foreign aid was at hand, they were even higher and more insulting in their opposition than the regulars. When the order issued, therefore, for the embarking the troops in Boston, no electric shock, no sudden explosion of thunder, in a word, not the last trump, could have struck them with greater consternation. They were at their wits' end, and, conscious of their black ingratitude, they chose to commit themselves, in the manner I have above described, to the mercy of the waves at a tempestuous season, rather than meet their offended countrymen."

Washington, in his letter to John Hancock, the president of Congress, was enabled to say : " I have a particular pleasure in being able to inform you, sir, that your house has received no damage worth mentioning. Your furniture is in tolerable order, and the family pictures are all left entire and untouched." This was a fortunate result, which Hancock well merited for his patriotic readiness of self-sacrifice, when, in communicating the resolve of Congress (December 22), authorizing Washington to make an assault upon the enemy, "notwithstanding the town and property in it might be destroyed," he had written : " May God crown your attempt with success! I most heartily wish it, though I may be the greatest sufferer."

The small-pox was prevailing with severity in several parts of Boston, and accordingly Washington, to prevent the spread of the infection, forbade any one to enter the town without a pass, which was given but to few, except those who had had the disease, or been protected by inoculation. A great many, however, who were from inland places, and had never been in a seaport, were so far excited by the natural curiosity of rustics to see " the great town of Boston," that they did not hesitate to resort to tricks and fraud in order to gain admission. " The thought of being liable to catch the distemper would have terrified them in the highest degree a little while back; but to gratify a different passion they suppressed their fears, which might operate for the preventing of their taking the infection. The works of the enemy naturally engaged their attention. These, by judicious persons who have surveyed them, are acknowledged to be excellent, and every one is convinced that it would have been a most hazardous attempt to have endeavored forcing them."

Washington, believing the scene of war was to be shifted to New York, sent five regiments and some artillery there, under the command of **April 18.**

General Heath, and moved his main body into Boston. On the next day he issued **April 20.** a proclamation, enjoining mutual good feeling and treatment on the part of the soldiers and citizens; and soon a concourse of people from the country came crowding into the town, "full of friendly solicitude." Then were witnessed "the tender interviews and fond embraces of those who had been long separated under circumstances so peculiarly distressing."

The British fleet, after having, by fire and powder, destroyed the works on Castle William, dropped down, and lingered for ten days in Nantasket roads. In the meantime, Washington was kept quite anxious by its movements. "The enemy," he says, "have the best knack at puzzling people I ever met with in my life. They have blown up, burnt, and demolished the castle totally, and are now all in Nantasket road. They have been there ever since Wednesday. What they are doing, the Lord knows." After speculating upon various supposed causes of the enemy's delay, Washington adds: "My opinion of the matter is, that they want to retrieve their disgrace before they go off, and I think a favorable opportunity presents itself to them. They have now got their whole force into one collected body, and no posts to guard. We have detached six regiments to New York, and have many points to look to; and, on Monday next, ten regiments of militia, which were brought in to serve till the first of April, will be disengaged. From former experience, we have found it as practicable to stop a torrent as these

people, when their time is up. If this should be the case now, what more favorable opening can the enemy wish for, to make a push upon our lines, nay upon the back of our lines at Roxbury, as they can land two miles from there, and pass behind? I am under more apprehension from them now than ever, and am taking every precaution I can to guard against the evil; but we have a kind of people to deal with who will not fear danger till the bayonet is at their breast, and then they are susceptible enough of it."

Washington went on preparing for the worst, by fortifying; and when he had made considerable progress with his works on the commanding position of Fort hill, he had the satisfaction of finding the enemy gone. The fleet finally sailed, with the exception of a few cruisers, **Mar. 27.** which were left for the protection of any British vessels which might arrive off the New-England coast with supplies for the British troops. The delay in the harbor seemed to have greatly vexed the patience of some of the English officers: "We were," writes one, "cannonaded fourteen days by the provincial army, and, at last, after many losses, embarked on board several vessels, and are got thus far. We do not know where we are going, but are in great distress.... I wish I was with you."—"Our men have suffered," writes another, who, better informed, knew where he was going. "We have one consolation left. You know the proverbial expression, 'Neither Hell, Hull, nor Halifax,' can afford worse shelter than Boston. To fresh provision I have, for many months, been an utter stranger.

An egg was a rarity. Yet I submit. A soldier may mention grievances, though he should scorn to repine when he suffers them. The next letter from Halifax." Halifax, in fact, was the destination of the fleet, and not New York, as Washington supposed.

The evacuation of Boston by the British was hailed throughout the colonies as a great triumph for the American cause, and Washington received congratulations from all quarters on his success, and flattering testimonials to his skilful conduct of the siege. First came the selectmen of Boston, with an address; then a long and flattering testimonial from the council and house of representatives of Massachusetts; and finally from Congress a vote of thanks moved by John Adams, and this letter, drawn up by him, John Jay, and Stephen Hopkins:—

PHILADELPHIA, *April* 2, 1776.

"Sir: It gives me the most sensible pleasure to convey to you, by order of Congress, the only tribute which a free people will ever consent to pay—the tribute of thanks and gratitude to their friends and benefactors.

"The disinterested and patriotic principles which led you to the field have also led you to glory; and it affords no little consolation to your countrymen to reflect that, as a peculiar greatness of mind induced you to decline any compensation for serving them, except the pleasure of promoting their happiness, they may, without your permission, bestow upon you the largest share of their affection and esteem.

"Those pages in the annals of America will record your title to a conspicuous place in the temple of fame, which shall inform posterity that, under your directions, an undisciplined band of husbandmen, in the course of a few months, became soldiers; and that the desolation meditated against the country by a brave army of veterans, commanded by the most experienced generals, but employed by bad men, in the worst of causes, was, by the fortitude of your troops, and the address of their officers, next to the kind interposition of Providence, confined for near a year within such narrow limits as scarcely to admit more room than was necessary for the encampments and fortifications they lately abandoned.

"Accept, therefore, sir, the thanks of the united colonies, unanimously declared by their delegates to be due to you, and the brave officers and troops under your command; and be pleased to communicate to them this distinguished mark of the approbation of their country.

"The Congress have ordered a golden medal,* adapted to the occasion, to be struck, and when finished to be presented to you.

"I have the honor to be, with every sentiment of esteem, sir, your most obedient and very humble servant,

"JOHN HANCOCK, *President.*"

---

* "The medal which was struck in Paris, contains on the obverse a head of Washington in profile, exhibiting an excellent likeness, and around it the inscription: Georgio Washington supremo duci exercituum udsertori libertatis comitia Americana. On the reverse is the town of Boston in the distance, with a fleet in view under sail. Washington and his officers are on horseback in the foreground, and he is pointing to the ships as they depart from the harbor. The inscription is: Hostibus primo fugatis Bostonium recuperatum xvii. Martii, MDCCLXXVI." SPARKS.

Private individuals no less than public bodies took occasion to congratulate and compliment Washington upon his triumph. "I congratulate you," wrote John Adams, "as well as all the friends of mankind, on the reduction of Boston; an event which appeared to me of so great and decisive importance, that, the next morning after the arrival of the news, I did myself the honor to move for the thanks of Congress to your excellency, and that a medal of gold should be struck in commemoration of it." Eldridge Gerry declared, "I am at a loss to know how Great Britain will reconcile all this to her military glory."

The intelligence of the evacuation of Boston was received in England with a feeling of such surprise that few would believe it true. There were those, however, who were well aware of the fact, and the duke of Manchester, in a remarkable speech in the house of lords, showed that he was not only fully informed of the circumstances of the flight from Boston, but conscious how much they lessened the prestige of Great Britain and brightened the fame and hopes of the colonies. "To come now, my lords," said the duke, "to that which has cast the deepest stain on the glory of the British arms, to that which must rouse the indignation of all who feel for her disgrace; the army of Britain, equipped with every possible essential of war, a chosen army, with chosen officers, backed by the power of a mighty fleet, sent to correct revolted subjects, sent to chastise a resisting city, sent to assert Britain's authority, has for many tedious months been imprisoned within that town by the provincial army, who, their watchful guards, permitted them no inlet to the country, who braved all their efforts, and defied all that their skill and abilities in war could ever attempt. One way, indeed, of escape is left; the fleet is still respected; to the fleet the army has recourse; and British generals, whose names never met with a blot of dishonor, are forced to quit that town, which was the first object of the war, the immediate cause of hostilities, the place of arms, which has cost this nation more than a million to defend. We are informed of this extraordinary event by a gazette, published by authority from government, in which it is related that General Howe had quitted Boston; no circumstances mentioned to palliate the event, no veil but that of silence to cast over the disgrace. But, my lords, though the government account is short and uncircumstantial, yet private intelligence and public report, on which, till it is with authenticity denied, I must rely, informs us that General Howe quitted not Boston of his own free will; but that a superior enemy by repeated efforts, by extraordinary works, by the fire of their batteries, rendered the place untenable."

33

CHAPTER XVI.

Washington still perplexed about the Enemy's Movements.—Another Command proposed for Lee.—Canada first proposed.—Finally the South.—Lee goes to Virginia.—Lord Stirling left in Command at New York.—His Life and Character.—Sterling continues the Works at New York and on Long Island.—Washington resolves upon going to New York.—General Thomas appointed to the Command of the American Troops in Canada.—Arnold before Quebec.—General Wooster arrives at last.—The Small-Pox among the Troops.—Thomas, anxious to do something, sends down the St. Lawrence a Fire-Ship.—Failure.—Retreat.—Carleton sallies out.—His Success.—Death of Thomas.—The Canadians less favorably disposed toward the Cause of the Patriots.—Washington's Solicitations about Canada.—Schuyler censured.—His Character.—Unpopular with the New Englanders.—Why ?—Defended by Washington.—Schuyler justifies himself.—His life.

WASHINGTON was perplexed about the destination of the British fleet. "Whither they are bound and where they will next pitch their tents I know not," he says, but believing that New York was to be the place he ordered the main body of his army there, and determined soon to follow himself. General Lee, it **Mar. 27.** will be remembered, had with his usual energy repressed the mischievous machinations of the tories, and driven by his military operations, Governor Tryon and the enemy's ships from the North river to the safer distance of the bay, where they were now moored off Staten island. Congress had other occupation in view for Lee, and ordered him to take the command in Canada. These orders were hardly given, however, when they were changed, and it was resolved to send Lee to the South. He would have preferred the Canadian command, as he thought himself, from the fact that he was the only general officer on the continent who could speak or think in French, the best adapted for that quarter. Washington seemed to be of the same opinion, and wrote to Lee, saying: "I was just about to congratulate you on your appointment to the command in Canada, when I received the account that your destination was altered. As a Virginian, I must rejoice at the change; but as an American, I think you would have done more essential service to the common cause in Canada. For, besides the advantage of speaking and thinking in French, an officer who is acquainted with their manners and customs, and has travelled in their country, must certainly take the strongest hold of their affection and confidence." Washington had a high opinion of Lee's capacity, but was not unconscious of his irritable and capricious temper. To his brother John Augustine, who remained at Mount Vernon, Washington writes: "General Lee, I suppose, is with you before this. He is the first officer, in military knowledge and experience, we have in the whole army. He is zealously attached to the cause, honest and well-meaning, but rather fickle and violent, I fear, in his temper. However, as he possesses an uncommon share of good sense and spirit, I congratulate my countrymen (Virginians) upon his appointment to that department."

Lee accordingly proceeded to Virginia,
and soon after his arrival, in answer to a letter he had received
from Washington at Boston, giving an
account of his success there, wrote: "I
must sincerely congratulate you, I congratulate the public on the great and
glorious event, your possession of Boston.
It will be a most bright page in the annals of America, and a most abominably
black one in those of the beldam Britain.
Go on, my dear general, crown yourself
with glory, and establish the liberties and
lustre of your country on a foundation
more permanent than the capitol rock."
What he says of himself in the same letter, does not seem so satisfactory, and is
stated in his usual half-humorous, half-
discontented tone: "My situation is just
as I expected. I am afraid I shall make
a shabby figure, without any real demerits
of my own. I am like a dog in a dancing
school. I know not where to turn myself, where to fix myself. The circumstances of the country intersected by
navigable rivers, the uncertainty of the
enemy's designs and motions, who can fly
in an instant to any spot they choose with
their canvass wings, throw me, and would
throw Julius Cesar, into this inevitable
dilemma. I may possibly be in the north,
when, as Richard says, I should serve my
sovereign in the west. I can only act
from surmise, and I have a very good
chance of surmising wrong. I am sorry
to grate your ears with a truth, but must
at all events assure you, that the provincial Congress of New York are angels of
decision when compared with your countrymen, the committee of safety assem-

April 5.

bled at Williamsburgh. Page, Lee, Mercer, and Payne are indeed exceptions;
but from Pendleton, Bland, the treasurer
and Company, *libera nos domine.*"

When Lee departed for the South, Lord
Stirling was left in command of the troops
at New York. William Alexander was
the genuine name of his "lordship," but
he was always called Lord Stirling by the
Americans, probably to compensate him
for the obstinate resistance to his claim
in Great Britain, where he had made an
unsuccessful effort for a recognition of
his title as earl. He was a great stickler
for *the lordship.* On one occasion being
present at the execution of a soldier for
desertion, the criminal repeatedly cried
out, "the Lord have mercy on me;" his
lordship, with warmth, exclaimed, "I wont,
you rascal, I wont have mercy on you."[*]
His father was a Scotchman who had gone
to America to escape the consequences
of having engaged in the unsuccessful
rebellion in behalf of the Pretender in
1715. He settled in New York where
he married the daughter of a fortunate
speculator called "Ready-money Provost,"
and where his son William was born in
1726. The youth had an early inclination for war, and volunteering for the
French and Indian campaign, served as
aid-de-camp to General Shirley. Subsequently, visiting England, he laid his claim
to the earldom of Stirling before the
house of lords, and upon its not being
allowed, he returned to America, where
his rights to the "lordship" were always
afterward recognised by courtesy. He
now married the daughter of Philip Liv-

[*] Thacher.

ingston, the "second lord of the manor," and building "a fine mansion" in New Jersey, went to live there. On the breaking out of the difficulties with Great Britain, Lord Stirling joined the popular cause, and after being appointed colonel of the first battalion of New Jersey militia, was finally promoted by Congress to the rank of brigadier-general. Lee spoke of him as *"Alexander pas le grand, mais le gros."*

Stirling being now in command of some twenty-five hundred men, and continuing to carry into execution the plans of defence for New York and Long island which had been formed by General Lee, awaited the arrival of the main body of the army. Washington having sent most of his troops in two large detachments, the first under the immediate command of Brigadier-General Heath, and the second under Brigadier-General Sullivan, ordered General Putnam to New York, to assume the **Mar. 29.** general command, and to proceed "to execute the plan proposed by Major-General Lee for fortifying the city and securing the passes of the East and North rivers." Washington himself did not propose yet to set out for a week or more.

While Washington had determined to proceed to New York, and Lee had been sent to Virginia to meet the expected operations of the enemy in those quarters, Congress was not unmindful of the important interests at risk in the North. General Thomas was accordingly appointed to take command of the American troops in Canada, where we left them, as will be recollected, after the repulse of their assault upon Quebec, encamped within three miles of the walls of the city, apparently for the winter.

Arnold's small force having received some additions from a few straggling soldiers who, in spite of the severity of the season and the hardships of a long journey through the snow and over the frozen rivers, had succeeded in making their way to the camp, the Americans were enabled to hold their ground, and do something, by means of their ice-batteries, in keeping up the show of a siege. Sir Guy Carleton kept within his walls and showed a degree of caution that could only be attributed to the distrust of his own people, whose loyalty was somewhat dubious, and not to any dread of his enemy, whose aspect was by no means formidable. He seemed more desirous of exercising benevolence than hostility toward his opponents. He treated his prisoners with a kindness and generosity, so great, that no chronicler of the events of those days has failed to give his testimony to the humanity of Governor Carleton. He sent out to the American camp for the clothes of those held captive in Quebec, and allowed their friends to send them money and such necessaries and luxuries as they might require.

General Wooster passed the whole winter in inactivity at Montreal, while Arnold was encamped before Quebec. **April 1.** He came at last as the spring opened, and brought such an addition to the American force as raised it to the apparently respectable number of two thousand eight hundred and fifty-five; but one third at least of these, were prostrate with small-pox. A girl, who was a nurse in the hospital at Quebec, had some friends in the American camp, whom she came out to visit, and was supposed thus to have brought the infection among the troops. The disease soon after broke out and began to spread, when many of the men inoculated themselves, and thus became disabled for duty. On the arrival, however, of Wooster, in spite of the condition of the troops, something was attempted in the way of action, by cannonading the enemy, and more vigorous measures, doubtless, would have followed, had not Arnold been disabled by an injury to his wounded leg from the fall of his horse. This accident, which kept him in bed for a fortnight, was a serious matter for the Americans, for without Arnold the soul of the enterprise was gone. With this misfortune, and with his spirit chafed at the conduct of Wooster who, being his superior in command, did not yield as readily to Arnold's imperiousness as he would have wished, Arnold asked leave of absence, which was granted, and he retired to Montreal. Wooster did nothing until the arrival of General Thomas to whom he yielded up the command.

Thomas, on his arrival, was anxious to attempt something, and he therefore, as **May 1.** the St. Lawrence was free of ice, prepared a fire-ship. At the same time making ready his scaling-ladders, he drew up his forces with the view of making an assault. The fire-ship was sent adrift at night, and floating with the flood-tide toward Quebec was supposed by the enemy at first to be a friendly vessel. As she neared, however, the shipping, her true character was discovered, and the batteries began to fire upon her. The crew on board finding that their purpose was discovered, lighted the train and took to their boats. The ship was soon in a blaze, but the sails taking fire, she lost her headway, and the tide beginning to ebb, she was carried down the river and the whole attempt failed.

Next day, General Thomas, disappointed by the failure of his plan, and finding from the condition of his troops and the scarcity of provisions that it was useless to make an assault or to continue the siege, determined to retreat. When making preparations to carry out this purpose, the enemy received a reinforcement by the arrival of a squadron from Great Britain with several hundred troops on board. Carleton, with this addition to his troops, sallied out and made an attack upon the Americans who, in the confusion of their retreat which had already begun, and being pressed by the enemy, were forced to fly precipitately and abandon their baggage, artillery, and stores. There were a great number of sick among the provincials, some of whom, with the small-pox full upon them, strove, ill as they were, to escape, while others gave themselves up at once to the assailants, and were treated by Carleton with his usual considerate kindness.

The British did not continue the pursuit far, or they might have totally destroyed the provincials. These, however, continued their flight, night and day, for a distance of forty-five miles. On reaching the mouth of the Sorel they halted, and being reinforced by the arrival of several regiments, encamped there for several days, during which period General Thomas, who had sickened with the small-pox, died. As he had forbidden his troops, that they might not be disabled by their temporary illness, to be inoculated, he refused himself to take advantage of the only means then known of protection against the fatal disease, and thus became a sacrifice to the severity of military discipline. General Sullivan now succeeded to the command, superseding Wooster.

Affairs in Canada were a source of great anxiety to all engaged in the American cause. The friendly disposition at one time evinced by the Canadians seems greatly to have changed. When General Montgomery first penetrated into the country, he readily obtained men, wagons, and provisions; and when he was before Quebec, offers of service were made to him from a number of parishes, in the neighboring country. His death, however, added to other occurrences, had caused such a change in the disposition of the people, that, as an American officer wrote, "we no longer look upon them as friends, but, on the contrary, as waiting an opportunity to join our enemies." The clergy and landed proprietors had not been properly conciliated, and they became unanimously opposed to the American cause, and even while Montreal was held by our troops, many of the inhabitants of consequence were supposed to be carrying on a correspondence with Carleton at Quebec. "With respect to the better sort of people, both French and English," wrote the same officer just quoted, "seven eights are tories, who would wish to see our throats cut, and

perhaps would readily assist in doing it." The Americans were to blame greatly for this result, for they not only neglected to conciliate the better classes, but had ill-used the peasantry. The inhabitants had been "dragooned at the point of the bayonet to supply wood for the garrison at a lower rate than the current price. For carriages and many other articles furnished, certificates had been given that were either not legible or without a signature, and the consequence was that on being presented they were rejected by the quartermaster-general." The people thus deceived became importunate in their claims, which being only met by vague promises, they concluded that their labor and property had been expended in vain, and had no longer faith in the united colonies, which they believed bankrupt.

Washington shared in this solicitude about Canada, and wrote **Apr. 19.** to Schuyler: "The commotions among the Canadians are alarming. I am afraid proper measures have not been taken to conciliate their affections; but rather that they have been insulted and injured, than which nothing could have a greater tendency to ruin our cause in that country. For human nature is such, that it will adhere to the side from whence the best treatment is received. I therefore conjure you, sir, to recommend the officers and soldiers in the strongest terms to treat all the inhabitants, Canadians, English, and savages, with tenderness and respect, paying them punctually for what they receive, or giving them such certificates as will enable them to receive their pay."

Congress, too, was so far impressed with the unfortunate state of affairs in Canada, and the necessity of a remedy, that it appointed Dr. Franklin, Samuel Chase, Charles Carroll of Carrollton, and the Rev. John Carroll, a Roman catholic priest, as commissioners to proceed to the North, with the view of investigating and removing grievances, and conciliating the Canadian people. Everything seemed to be in such an ill condition, in regard to the military operations in Canada, as almost to justify the sweeping remark of a traveller of those days, who, after descanting freely upon men and things in that quarter, declared over his bottle to some American officers who were his chance companions at an inn in Albany : " In short, gentlemen, we have commissioners there without provisions; quartermasters without stores ; generals without troops ; and troops without discipline, by G—d."

General Schuyler was held responsible by many of the New Englanders for the disastrous condition of things at the North. " In a time of adversity," says Irving, who never fails to say a good word for Schuyler, " it relieves the public mind to have some individual upon whom to charge its disasters. General Schuyler, at present, was to be the victim." He was charged with having neglected to send forward supplies and reinforcements to the troops in Canada, and even treason was hinted at by some of his enemies, in the bitterness of their hostility. Schuyler was not a popular man with the New England officers, many of whom were of too coarse a mould to please his somewhat fastidious tastes. His own associations were aristocratic, while theirs were of the true democratic stamp. He was a stickler for the respect due to *rank ;* they, with a disposition to yield to popular majorities, made common cause with the *ranks.* He was reserved and formal toward his inferiors; they, free and " hail fellows" with all, as they acknowledged no superiority. Schuyler had the incidental circumstances of distinguished birth, and of refinement and wealth, to give him personal and social importance ; the New England officers were, for the most part, men of humble origin, of little education, and, when drawn from the field or the bench, had nothing but their military pay. He was a conventional gentleman; they made no pretensions to anything beyond the rude simplicity of honest manners.

Graydon, in his gossiping memoirs, gives us, probably, a better insight than more dignified historians, into the true cause of Schuyler's unpopularity with the New Englanders. Graydon, then a young officer of a Pennsylvania regiment, had been appointed by Congress to carry a sum of money in specie to Schuyler. He arrives at Lake George, and gives this account of his visit to the general : " Though General Schuyler has been charged with such haughtiness of demeanor, as to have induced the troops of New England to decline serving under his command, the reception we met with, was not merely courteous but kind. His quarters being contracted, a bed was prepared for us in his own apartment, and we experienced civilities that were flattering from an officer of his high rank. Though thoroughly the man of business, he was also a gentleman and a man of the world; and well calculated to sustain the reputation of our army in the eyes of the British officers (disposed to depreciate it), as is evidenced by the account given by General Burgoyne of the manner in which he was entertained by him at Albany. But that he should have been displeasing to the *Yankees*, I am not at all surprised: he certainly was at no pains to conceal the extreme contempt he felt for a set of officers, who were both a disgrace to their stations and the cause in which they acted! Being yet a stranger to the character of these men, and the constitution of that part of our military force which in Pennsylvania was considered as the bulwark of the nation, I must confess my surprise at an incident which took place while at dinner. Beside the general, the members of his family, and ourselves, there were at table a lady and gentleman from Montreal. A New England captain came in upon some business, with that abject servility of manner which belongs to persons of the meanest rank: he was neither asked to sit or take a glass of wine, and after announcing his message, was dismissed with that peevishness of tone we apply to a low and vexatious intruder. This man, in his proper sphere, might have been entitled to better treatment; but when presuming to thrust himself into a situation, in which far other qualifications than his were required, and upon an occasion, too, which involved some of the most important of human interests, I am scarcely prepared to say it was unmerited."

Schuyler, however, found a nobler advocate in Washington, who, on sending to him a letter containing charges against his conduct, accompanied by documents which had been received at headquarters from a committee of Kings county, wrote: "From these you will readily discover the diabolical and insiduous acts and schemes carrying on by the tories and friends of government, to raise distrust, dissensions, and divisions among us. Having the utmost confidence in your integrity, and the most incontestable proof of your great attachment to our common country and its interests, I could not but look upon the charge against you with an eye of disbelief, and sentiments of detestation and abhorrence; nor should I have troubled you with the matter, had I not been informed that copies were sent to different committees and to Governor Trumbull, which I conceived would get abroad, and that you, should you find that I had been furnished with them, would consider my suppressing them as an evidence of my belief, or at best of my doubts, of the charges."

On receiving this letter, Schuyler wrote to Washington, insisting upon a court of inquiry, and in the meantime some who had been ready to give credence to the charges, frankly acknowledged their suspicions unfounded, although there were others in whom the feeling against the New York general continued to rankle.

General Philip Schuyler, of whom we have said so much, and of whom we shall have occasion to say more, was born in Albany, on the 22d of November, 1733. His family was of colonial distinction. His grandfather was mayor of Albany, and proprietor of one of the Dutch manors, which descended by the law of primogeniture to John Schuyler his son, and the father of Philip who, being the eldest son, inherited the estate, and with unexampled generosity divided it with his brothers and sisters. His mother was Cornelia Van Cortlandt, a woman of great force of character, and remarkable for the graceful dignity of her manners.

Philip Schuyler served during the French campaign, and won the friendship of the gallant and young Lord Howe, who fell at Ticonderoga. He was a prominent man in the colonial assembly, and an early advocate of the American cause. In 1775 he was a delegate to the continental Congress, and in the same year was appointed third major-general of the American army.

CHAPTER XVII.

General Putnam at New York.—His Cousin.—The Appearance of the Troops.—The Officers.—Colonel Putnam coming Home from Market.—Alexander Hamilton.—His Life.—Personal Appearance.—His first Acquaintance with General Greene.—Washington at New York.—The Provincial Navy.—Commodore Hopkins.—His Exploits.—The Engagement between the Alfred and Glasson.—The American Squadron puts into New London.—Hopkins censured by Congress.—Washington's Despair of Reconciliation with Great Britain.—Perplexities of Business.—Uncertainty of the Enemy's Movements.

1776. GENERAL PUTNAM had arrived at New York and went busily to work at once, carrying out the plans of Lee in fortifying the exposed points of the island, and disciplining the troops. His cousin, Colonel Rufus Putnam, had been, in want of a better, appointed to the head of the engineer department, and though, like the general, an illiterate man, seemed, as Washington said, "tolerably well qualified for conducting that business." Graydon says, " Mr. Putnam might have been a good practical artist, though misterming the *Gorge* the *George*." The same vivacious writer gives us an account of the troops gathered in New York at that time. "They were," he says, "chiefly from the eastern provinces. The appearance of things was not much calculated

to excite sanguine expectations in the mind of a sober observer. Great numbers of people were indeed to be seen, and those who are not accustomed to the sight of bodies under arms are always prone to exaggerate them. But this propensity to swell the mass had not an equal tendency to convert it into soldiery; and the irregularity, want of discipline, bad arms, and defective equipment in all respects, of this multitudinous assemblage, gave no favorable impression of its prowess."

The eastern battalions, especially, seemed to have offended the eye of the young military aspirant. The ranks were unpromising, and particularly the officers, "who were in no single respect distinguishable from their men, other than in

34

the colored cockades, which, for this very purpose, had been prescribed in general orders; a different color being assigned to the officers of each grade." So far from aiming at a deportment which might raise them above their privates, and thence prompt them to due respect and obedience to their commands, the object was by humility, to preserve the existing blessing of equality: an illustrious instance of which was given by Colonel Putnam, the chief engineer of the army, and no less a personage than the cousin of the major-general of that name. "What," says a person meeting him one day with a piece of meat in his hand, "carrying home your rations yourself, colonel!"—"Yes," says he, "and I do it to set the officers a good example."

There were, however, other officers who better pleased the fastidiousness of our annalist; those of New York, for example, among whom was Alexander Hamilton. Hamilton at that time was barely twenty years of age, and had not only shown that ardor of youthful spirit and genius which always excites a sympathetic glow of appreciation among the young, but had won, by the premature manliness of his character and judgment, the respect of the old. Hamilton was born on the West Indian island of Nevis. His father was a Scotch trading captain of the name of Hamilton. His mother, a creole woman, of Spanish or French origin. The child, not over carefully watched by parental solicitude, was left to wander very much at his will. On one occasion he had strayed into the counting-house of a distinguished merchant, who was so much struck by the lively and precocious parts of the boy, that he proposed to "make his fortune for him." The benevolence of the merchant met with no resistance from his natural guardians, and young Hamilton was accordingly taken by him into his counting-house. Child as he was, he made such rapid progress in the knowledge of business, that in the temporary absence of the "head of the firm," he was left sole manager of its concerns, at the age of fourteen. From the West Indies he was sent to assume a more important station in the New York branch of his patron's establishment. His remarkable talents and the great zeal he had shown for study induced his generous friends to give him the benefit of a classical education. He was accordingly put to school at Elizabethtown, and thence, in 1773, admitted into King's, now Columbia college, with the view of preparing for a medical education. Young Hamilton had an early taste for literature, and, by frequent clever articles, sometimes lively and sometimes severe, written on the exciting political topics of the day, showed a natural power and acquired great facility as a writer.

Yet a student, he had an occasion to prove that he could speak as well as write. A meeting of the New York whig citizens had been called together to express their indignation at the new blow of British tyranny which had fallen upon the New Englanders in the shape of the Boston port-bill. Naturally self-reliant and with his confidence in his own powers, stimulated by the warmth of his interest in the popular cause, young Hamilton, then hardly seventeen years of age, ventured to address the meeting, and spoke with a force of eloquence which, from so juvenile an orator, surprised every listener. He now took an active part in the political movements of the times, both as a speaker and writer. On the war breaking out he formed a company of artillery and was chosen the captain. He was thus serving, when Graydon seems to have marked him out as an exceptional officer for his gentlemanlike air and bearing.*

Irving gives this account of the impression the youthful captain made upon another more acute military observer: "As General Greene one day, on his way to Washington's headquarters, was passing through a field—then on the outskirts of the city, now in the heart of its busiest quarter, and known as "the park" —he paused to notice a provincial company of artillery, and was struck with its able performances, and with the tact and talent of its commander. He was a mere youth, apparently about twenty years of age; small in person and stature, but remarkable for his alert and manly bearing. It was Alexander Hamilton.

"Greene was an able tactician and quick to appreciate any display of military science; a little conversation sufficed to convince him that the youth before him had a mind of no ordinary grasp and quickness. He invited him to his quarters, and from that time cultivated his friendship."

Washington followed the army to New York, where he arrived on Saturday, the thirteenth of April, having passed through Providence, Norwich, and New London. While at the latter place, Commodore Hopkins put into the harbor after a cruise which was not supposed to redound much to the fame of the embryo provincial navy. It will be recollected that Congress had in December established the basis, however humble, of a naval force. The following were the resolutions passed at that time (December 22d, 1775.)

"Resolved that the following naval officers be appointed: Ezek Hopkins, Esquire, commander-in-chief; Dudley Salterstall, captain of the Alfred; Abraham Whipple, captain of the Columbus; Nicholas Biddle, captain of the Andrea Dora; John B. Hopkins, captain of the Cabot. First

* At a later period in life he is described by another observer as being "under middle size, thin in person, but remarkably erect and dignified in his deportment. His hair was turned back from his forehead, powdered, and collected in a club behind. His complexion was exceedingly fair, and varying from this only by the almost feminine rosiness of his cheeks. His might be considered, as to figure and color, a very handsome face. When at rest it had rather a severe and thoughtful expression; but when engaged in conversation it easily assumed an attractive smile. He was expected one day [the writer is speaking of as late a period as 1795] at dinner, and was the last who came. When he entered the room it was apparent from the respectful attention of the company that he was a distinguished individual. He was dressed in a blue coat with bright buttons; the skirts of his coat were unusually long. He wore a white waistcoat, black silk small clothes, white silk stockings. The gentleman who received him as a guest, introduced him to such of the company as were strangers to him; to each he made a formal bow, bending very low, the ceremony of shaking hands not being observed. The fame of Hamilton had reached every one who knew anything of public men. His appearance and deportment accorded with the dignified distinction to which he had attained in public opinion. At dinner, whenever he engaged in the conversation, every one listened attentively. His mode of speaking was deliberate and serious; and his voice engagingly pleasant. In the evening of the same, he was in a mixed assembly of both sexes; and the tranquil reserve, noticed at the dinner table, had given place to a social and playful manner, as though in this alone he was ambitious to excel."—Familiar Letters on Public Characters and Public Events, from the Peace of 1783 to the Peace of 1815. Boston, 1834.

Lieutenants, John Paul Jones, Rhodes Arnold,——— Stansbury, Heysted Hacker, and Jonathan Pitcher. Second lieutenants, Benjamin Seabury, Joseph Olney, Elisha Warner, Thomas Weaver, and ——— McDougal. Third lieutenants, John Fanning, Ezekiel Burroughs, and Daniel Vaughan.

Most of the vessels were purchased, and ill adapted for the purpose intended. There was not a tolerable sailer in the whole fleet. The Alfred was the largest of them all, and she had only a main-deck battery of twenty, and quarter-deck and forecastle guns, varying from two to ten. It was on board this vessel that the first American man-of-war ensign was ever hoisted, and it was done by John Paul Jones, then a lieutenant, of some of whose future more important deeds we shall have occasion to speak. The device of that flag is supposed to have been the Massachusetts one of a pine tree, with the addition borrowed from Virginia of a coiled rattlesnake about to strike, and the motto, "Don't tread on me." The squadron, consisting of the Alfred twenty-four guns, Columbus twenty, Dora fourteen, and Cabot fourteen, having been got ready for sea, rendezvoused under Cape Henlopen early in February. Soon after they were joined by the Hornet ten, Wasp eight, and Fly, three small vessels which had been equipped at Baltimore. Hopkins, who had received from Congress the title of commander-in-chief, was generally spoken of by the sailors as commodore, although not seldom styled admiral. The commodore, as we shall call him, having received orders to cruise to the southward, in order to try to fall in with Lord Dunmore's fleet, and stop its ravages on the coast, sailed in that direction on the seventeenth of February. He was on the third night out, going before the wind with a stiff breeze, when the Hornet and Fly parted company and were not again seen during the cruise.

Abaco, in the Bahamas, was the place of rendezvous appointed, which was reached in fifteen days, without any occurrence of moment. The island of New Providence being but a short distance and known to contain a supply of military stores, Hopkins determined to make a descent upon it. Accordingly, setting sail one night, he landed on the island early the next morning some three hundred marines, who met with no resistance until a fort was reached at some distance from the place where they had debarked. Here, as they approached, the garrison fired a volley at them, and then spiking the guns retired. The Americans taking possession of the fort tarried there until next day, when they marched into the town without interruption. The officer in command went straightway to the governor and demanding the keys, which were given up at once, entered the fort within the town, where was found a good supply of cannon and mortars. There was, however, no powder, for the governor, having taken the alarm, had sent it all off the night before. After having shipped their plunder, and taken on board the governor, his lieutenant, and a counsellor, the squadron put to sea again on a cruise.

Hopkins' course was now to the north,

and on reaching the east end of Long island he captured a British schooner, and on the day after a bomb brig of eight guns in command of a son of the Wallace who had rendered himself so notorious on the New England coast by his brutal violence. As the American squadron, somewhat scattered, was moving on during the night-watch, with a light breeze and smooth sea, an enemy's ship was observed bearing down apparently for the Alfred. Shortly, however, she went on another track, which brought her in the direction of the Cabot, when the younger Hopkins, who commanded the latter, closed in with his little vessel and fired a broadside though with not much effect, as his metal was too light to do much damage to his formidable opponent. The enemy returned the fire with much greater force, and cannonaded the Cabot so heavily that she was obliged to haul off, with her captain severely wounded, her master and several of the crew killed, and her hull and rigging badly damaged. The Alfred now bore up and ranged alongside of the British ship, which proved to be the Glasgow of twenty guns, Captain Tyringham Howe. The two were at once engaged as hot as possible, broadside to broadside, and both were delivering their fires with great spirit when the Providence came up under the stern of the enemy, and the Dora approached near enough to give some effect to her guns. For nearly an hour they were thus briskly keeping up the fight, when a shot from the Glasgow unfortunately carried away the block and wheel rope of the Alfred, which made

April 4.

her unmanageable, and she broached to. This gave the British ship an opportunity to rake her effectually. The day was now beginning to dawn, and Howe could see, as the several vessels of the American squadron bore up, the strength of his antagonist. He accordingly found it prudent to give up the battle, and making all sail he could crowd upon his ship stood in for Newport.

The squadron did its best to overtake him, and kept up a running fire in pursuit, but the Glasgow proved the better sailer and distanced the American vessels which were so deep with the stores with which they had been laden at New Providence, and not very fast goers at their best, that they could not keep up. Hopkins, as they approached Newport, fearing that the British fleet off that harbor might come out, gave up the chase, and, contenting himself with the capture of the Glasgow's tender, took his vessels into New London.

The enemy was a ship of twenty guns, with a crew of a hundred and twenty souls, and was well appointed in every respect, as she was well handled by her commander. Her loss was slight, however, having had only one man killed and three wounded. The Alfred had six men killed and six wounded. The Cabot had four killed and seven wounded, and one man on board the Columbus lost his arm from a shot from the enemy during the chase. The hull and rigging on both sides were well cut up, and showed the severity of the encounter.

Hopkins' conduct was so much disapproved that he was summoned to answer for it before Congress. He was charged with disobedience of orders for having returned northward after his descent upon New Providence, as that action was deemed a poor compensation for the expense of fitting out a fleet, and by no means an heroic beginning to the history of the American navy. Hopkins, **May 15.** on reaching Philadelphia, did not succeed in satisfying Congress as to the propriety of his conduct, and he consequently received the censure of the house.

Washington preceded the arrival of some of his troops, which had set out on the same day with him from Cambridge. Although on his journey he had done everything in his power to expedite the march, he found, from the badness of the roads and the difficulty of procuring teams for bringing the stores and baggage, that his army would be still delayed for a week or more in reaching New York.

Washington, being now, after the triumph of Boston, relieved from the duties of conducting a special military operation, began to be more conscious of the scope of the cause of which he had been chosen leader. He had given up all hopes of reconciliation with the mother-country, and confessed freely his conviction that he was engaged in a struggle not only for freedom but independence. He gave but little heed to what he heard of the plans of the British for negotiation with the view to bring back the colonies to their loyalty. He was told that the English government was about to send over a large number of commissioners to America, and that they were to make advances to the colonies separately. Mark how

he scouts the idea! "The account given of the business of the commissioners from England seems to be of a piece with Lord North's conciliatory motion last year, built upon the same foundation, and, if true, that they are to be divided among the colonies to offer terms of pardon, it is as insulting as that nation; and only designed, after stopping all intercourse with us, to set us up to view in Great Britain as a people that will not hearken to any propositions of peace. Was there ever anything more absurd than to repeal the very acts which have introduced all this confusion and bloodshed, and at the same enact a law to restrain all intercourse with the colonies for opposing them? The drift and designs are obvious; but is it possible that any sensible nation upon earth can be imposed upon by such a cobweb scheme or gauze covering? But enough."

This was written while he was at Cambridge, and although emphatic in denunciation of British policy, it still shows from the very fact of arguing the question, that there was in Washington's heart a lurking hope of accommodation. Again, still in Cambridge, he writes: "If the commissioners do not come over with full and ample powers to treat with Congress, I sincerely wish they may never put their feet on American ground, as it must be self-evident, in the other case, that they will come over with insidious intentions, to distract, divide, and create as much confusion as possible. How, then, can any man, let his passion for reconciliation be ever so strong, be so blinded and misled as to embrace a measure evidently designed for his destruction? No man does, no man can wish the restoration of peace more fervently than I do; but I hope, whenever made, it will be on such terms as will reflect honor upon the councils and wisdom of America." This, too, is emphatic language, but it does not express such a decided hopelessness of England as that which, only a fortnight later, he uses in writing to John Adams. **Apr. 15.** It is true Washington begins, "I have *ever* thought," but he has not before given such a definite form to his views. "I have ever thought," he says, "and am still of opinion, that no terms of accommodation will be offered by the British ministry, but such as can not be accepted by America. We have nothing, my dear sir, to depend upon but the protection of a kind Providence, and unanimity among ourselves."

While Washington became thus convinced of the greatness and probable length of the struggle in which he was engaged, he found himself plunged deeper and deeper, from day to day, in the perplexities, troubles, dissensions, and complications of business, his military leadership of the patriot cause necessarily involved him. The recruiting went on slowly, and when troops were got it was hard to find equipments for them. There was equal difficulty in obtaining arms and men. Provision was not only to be made for the defence of New York and Long island, but reinforcements were to be sent to Canada. Officers were complaining for want of pay, and militia-men were insisting upon returning home. The tories of New York were exciting anxiety by their relations with Governor Tryon and the enemy's ships in the harbor, and news had arrived of the great preparations made by the British ministers to crush, as they believed, the "rebels."

With these cares and labors we can well understand how Washington should be so devoted to business as to declare, "I give in to no kind of amusement myself; and consequently those about me can have none, but are confined from morning till evening, hearing and answering the applications and letters of one and another." To his brother Augustine, too, he gives "the hurry and multiplicity of business in which I am constantly engaged from the time I rise out of my bed until I go into it again" as the true cause for not writing oftener.

Washington, however, struggled bravely with all these cares and embarrassments. He sent as many troops as he could spare to Canada. He checked the tories by putting a stop to their correspondence with the enemy, by his own decided measures, and a firm and dignified appeal to the New York committee of safety. He only succeeded after much difficulty in gathering together an army of ten thousand men, and while disciplining them and keeping them busy at the works of defence, strove, by every effort, to prepare himself for the enemy.

Washington was perplexed about the intentions of Howe, who, with his army strongly reinforced by troops from Great Britain, might be daily expected to arrive and begin the campaign. The whole American army was so small as yet that to make it effective it was necessary to concentrate the forces. When Congress, therefore, requested the opinion of Washington as to whether it was necessary to send more troops to Canada, he answered them in these dubious words: "With

April 26. respect to sending more troops to that country, I am really at a loss what to advise, as it is impossible at present to know the designs of the enemy. Should they send the whole force under General Howe up the river St.

Lawrence to relieve Quebec and recover Canada, the troops gone and now going will be insufficient to stop their progress; and should they think proper to send that or an equal force this way from Great Britain, for the purpose of possessing this city and securing the navigation of Hudson's river, the troops left here will not be sufficient to oppose them; and yet for anything we know, I think it not improbable they may attempt both."

CHAPTER XVIII.

1776. AFTER Arnold had, in consequence of his accident and his dissatisfaction with the bearing of General Wooster, his superior in command, retired to Montreal, he remained there for several weeks with little inclination, in consequence of illness, for service, and without any especial work to do. He was now, however, aroused to activity by the disaster at the "Cedars," which he determined to make an effort to repair. Before tracing Arnold's movements, however, let us describe the affair which prompted them.

Early in May three hundred and ninety Americans were posted, under Colonel Beadle, in a small fort at a place called

the Cedars, situated on the St. Lawrence about forty miles above Montreal. Captain Forster, a British officer with forty regulars, a hundred Canadians, and five hundred Indians, descended from the mouth of the Oswegatchie, and approached the fort. The American colonel in command, as soon as he became aware of this approach, cowardly hurried off to Montreal, under the plea of seeking reinforcements, and left the command of the garrison to Major Butterfield, who, emulating the faintheartedness of his superior, surrendered the fort to Forster without a blow.

Major Henry Sherbourne was immediately, on the arrival of Beadle at Montreal, although that discreet colonel refused himself to return, despatched with one hundred and forty men to reinforce the garrison at the Cedars. Sherbourne, however, was too late, for the garrison had surrendered the day before he had got across Lake St. Louis. He, however, was not aware of the fact, and leaving forty of his men as a rear guard, pushed on with the hundred others, and had reached within five miles of the fort, when he was set upon by five hundred Canadians and Indians from under the cover of a thick wood. The Americans defended themselves as best they could for more than an hour and a half against the fire of the enemy, but were finally completely overwhelmed by the Indians, who rushed upon and disarmed them. They had already lost in action twenty-eight killed and wounded, when many more were massacred in cold blood by the savages, and the rest, being stripped almost naked, were driven to the fort and delivered up to Captain Forster, from whom the Americans now learned, for the first time, that Butterfield had surrendered himself and garrison. The enemy had but some twenty-two killed, among whom was a chief of the Senecas, whose death greatly excited the ferocity of the savages.

This was the affair at the Cedars which had stirred Arnold to revenge, and he hastened with about eight hundred men to inflict it. On setting out, he sent forward some Caghnawaga Indians in his interest, to demand of the hostile savages to deliver up the American prisoners at once, or in case they refused, to declare

35

to them that he would sacrifice every Indian who should fall into his hands, and burn their villages.

On reaching St. Annes, at the western extremity of the island **May 26.** upon which Montreal is built, Arnold and his men could see the American prisoners, as they were being taken off by the enemy in their batteaux from an island about a league distant, and conveyed to the opposite shore of the St. Lawrence. Arnold was now impatient for the arrival of his batteaux which were coming down the river, but which he and most of his men, having reached by land, had preceded. The batteaux were delayed until sunset, and in the meantime Arnold's Caghnewagas came back with an answer to his demand and a threat from the hostile Indians, who sent word that they had five hundred American prisoners in their power, whom they would put to death if any attempt was made to rescue them, and give no quarter to any others they might capture.

Arnold was perplexed. "Torn," he says, "by the conflicting passions of revenge and humanity; a sufficient force to take ample revenge, raging for action, urged me on one hand: and humanity for five hundred unhappy wretches, who were on the point of being sacrificed if our vengeance was not delayed, pleaded equally strong on the other." He, however, decided not to turn back, and crowding his men into the batteaux, rowed to the island whence he had seen the prisoners taken off. He found there five Americans still left, who were almost bare of clothes and nearly famished. From these he learned that all the others had been carried off to Quinze Chiens, with the exception of two who, being too ill to move, had been killed. Arnold now crossed with his boats toward Quinze Chiens, which was about four miles below on the opposite shore. When within less than a mile of the shore, the enemy began firing at him with their field-pieces and musketry. As the day was closing, and Arnold, not knowing the ground, feared to expose his men to the risks of a night attack, he returned.

On reaching St. Annes in the evening, a council-of-war was immediately called, when it was determined by all the officers that an attack should be made on the next morning. The whole force was astir with busy preparations until past midnight, when a flag of truce was observed coming from the enemy. It was borne by Lieutenant Park, who came to submit to Arnold a copy of the articles which had been agreed to between Major Sherbourne and Captain Forster for the exchange of prisoners—Sherbourne having been informed by Forster that the prisoners who were crowded together in the church at Quinze Chiens would certainly fall a prey to the savages, whose ferocity that British officer professed to be unable to control, unless the Americans submitted to the terms proposed. Sherbourne, under these circumstances, was forced to sign them, and Arnold was now expected to confirm the act of his subordinate in command. Arnold was greatly vexed that he should be thus balked of his purpose by this ungenerous advantage taken by the enemy, and, though he longed to have his revenge

upon "these savages and still more savage British troops," could not but give heed to the proposition, as Captain Forster declared positively, that the fate of the American prisoners depended upon his confirmation of Sherbourne's capitulation.

There was one condition which Arnold rejected at once without hesitation. By this it was insisted that the American prisoners should not again take up arms, and that they should pledge themselves not to give any information, by word of mouth, or writing, or by signs, which might be prejudicial to his majesty's service. The other terms, having been modified by Arnold and consented to by Forster, were finally agreed to. By these it was arranged that the Americans should be released on parole, in exchange for British prisoners of equal rank, and reparation made for all property which had been destroyed by the continental troops. It was moreover added, that four American captains should be sent to Quebec, and remain as hostages until the exchange should be effected, while six days were allowed to the British for the delivery of the prisoners at St. Johns. Congress refused to ratify these terms, although Washington expressed strongly the opinion that it was a military convention, which, although extorted by a barbarous threat, was sufficiently regular to be binding. Arnold returned to Montreal, full of fierce rage at being thwarted in his revenge, and burned for a more favorable occasion to give it vent.

General John Sullivan, it will be recollected, had arrived at the mouth of the Sorel with reinforcements, and assumed the command of the troops, immediately after the death of Thomas. Sullivan was a New-England man, having been born at Berwick, Maine, in 1740. He was now in the vigor of life, and although originally a farmer, and subsequently a lawyer, he had already, in addition to the usual military training of his fellow-provincials, acquired some military experience. After retiring from the continental Congress, of which he had been a member, he made his first essay in warfare as a joint leader, with Langdon, the speaker of the New Hampshire Congress, of a small party of continentals in an attack on Fort William and Mary at Portsmouth, and succeeded in carrying off all the cannon. On the organization of the American army, in 1775, Sullivan was appointed one of the eight brigadier-generals, and in '76, a major-general. Having served under Washington at the siege of Boston, he now, so rapid was the experience of those days, presented himself with almost the claims of a military veteran.

Affairs in Canada seemed to have been in the worst possible condition just previous to the arrival of Sullivan, for the commissioners sent there by Congress give this doleful account: "You will have," **May 27.** they say, writing from Montreal, "a faint idea of our situation, if you figure to yourself an army, broken and disheartened, half of it under inoculation and other diseases, soldiers without pay, without discipline, and altogether reduced to live from hand to mouth, depending on the scanty and precarious supplies of a few half-starved cattle, and trifling quantities of flour, which have hitherto been picked up in different parts of the country." Sullivan's presence, according to his own letters, which generally gave a more rose-colored view of things than was justified by reality, produced a most encouraging effect upon the hitherto suffering and disheartened troops.

"It was," he writes, "really affecting to see the banks of the Sorel lined with men, women, and children, leaping and clapping their hands for joy, to see me arrive; it gave no less joy to General Thompson, who seemed to be wholly forsaken, and left to fight against an unequal force or retreat before them." He continued to write in the same strain, and while every one else was down with despair, he was exalted with confident hope. "I venture to assure you," he writes to Washington, "and the Congress, that I can, in a few days, reduce the army to order, and with the assistance of a kind Providence, put a new face to our affairs here, which, a few days since, seemed almost impossible." It was no wonder, then, that with such an expression of sanguine self-confidence from Sullivan, that Washington himself, in spite of the cool calculations of the Congressional commissioners, and the melancholy forebodings of the saturnine Schuyler, should grow more hopeful.

"Before it [the letter from Sullivan just quoted] came to hand," writes Washington, "I almost dreaded to hear from Canada, as my advices seemed to promise nothing favorable, but rather further misfortunes. But I now hope that our affairs, from the confused, distracted, and almost forlorn state, in which you found them, will emerge and assume an aspect of order and success." In a postscript, however, Washington apparently becomes somewhat dubious of Sullivan's glowing account of affairs, and puts him on his guard against the dangers of deception. "Knowing your great zeal," says Washington, "for the cause of your country, and your desire to render her every possible service, I must caution you not to put too much to the hazard in your exertions to establish her rights, and to receive with a proper degree of caution the professions which the Canadians may make. They have the character of an ingenious, artful people, and very capable of finesse and cunning. Therefore, my advice is, that you put not too much in their power; but seem to trust them, rather than actually do it too far. I would also have you keep all your posts as you go, well secured, to guard against any treacherous conduct."

Washington knew Sullivan very well, and the next day after writing the postscript just quoted, he had occasion to give an opinion of him, apropos to a private letter which he had received, and from which he inferred that Sullivan was aiming at the command in Canada. "Whether he wants it or not," Washington writes, "is a matter to be considered; and that it may be considered with propriety, I think it my duty to observe, as of my own knowledge, that he is active, spirited, and zealously attached to the cause. That he does not want abilities, many members of Congress can testify; but he has his wants, and he has his foibles. The latter are manifested in his little tincture of vanity, and in an over desire of being popular, which now and then lead him into embarrassments."

Sullivan was eager to realize his sanguine expectations, and accordingly he sent out a force of eighteen hundred men under General Thompson, to attack the British at Three Rivers, while he **June 4.** himself remained at the mouth of the Sorel, engaged in constructing works for the defence of that post. Thompson in the meantime having embarked his men in fifty boats, coasted along the south side of that wide part of the St. Lawrence called Lake St. Peter, until he reached Nicolet, whence, waiting until night, he floated down the river and passed to the left bank, within a few miles of Three Rivers. It was intended to have reached this place at night, in order to take the enemy by surprise. There had been, however, an unexpected delay, so that it was near daylight when the troops landed.

In order to make up for the loss of time, a forced march had to be made, and the men were hurried on to a run; and when they had thus gone for several miles, and were greatly fatigued, it was discovered that the wrong road had been taken through the ignorance or the deception of the Canadian guide. They were obliged to turn back, and as they hurriedly retraced their steps the day began to break, and all hope of a night attack was gone. They, however, succeeded in finding the proper route, and continued to move on briskly, until, by a turn in the road, they came in sight of the enemy's shipping lying off Three

Rivers. Thompson knew that it was useless to attempt to conceal his approach, and therefore ordering his drums to beat and fifes to play, marched on until he came within range of the men-of-war's guns, when he turned off from the road by the river, to another at a right angle with it, and thus avoided exposure to the fire of the enemy. The Americans had, however, got so close to the ships, that the orders to land, resounding through the speaking-trumpets of the deck-officers, were distinctly heard.

Thompson having been obliged to leave the route by the river, prepared to enter the town by the rear. When within about two miles, there was found a great morass, through which the men had to flounder up to their waists. They, however, succeeded in struggling through, and reached some solid ground, where Thompson was enabled to form his men. The enemy were ready, with a large force under General Fraser, to receive them, and as soon as the Americans began to advance, they were met by so severe a fire that they were staggered at once and thrown into confusion. Thompson tried to rally his men, but in vain; on they fled, each man looking out for himself, straggling back again through the morass, and making his way as rapidly as possible along the road by which he had come. Hearing from the Canadians they met that the enemy had sent a detachment with artillery to seize their boats and cut off their retreat, and knowing that there was a large body in hot pursuit of them, the straggling fugitives were brought to a halt, but

entirely bewildered how to act. At this moment, Colonel Maxwell, taking advantage of the pause in the flight, called together the officers about him, and asked, " What shall we do ? Shall we fight those in the front or in the rear ? or shall we tamely submit ? or shall we turn off into the woods, and let each man shift for himself ?"

The last question was the only one they were prepared to answer, and with an affirmative reply to it, the fugitives, without more ado, scattered off down the hill, and through the woods to the river. As they fled, the enemy in their rear fired at them, but fortunately without much effect. The boats had been removed out of harm's way, by those left in the care of them, and thus a great number of the Americans succeeded in escaping, by straggling parties, after wandering during the night in the covert of the forest. General Thompson and Colonel Irvine, the second in command, several other officers, and some two hundred of the men, were left in the hands of the enemy, while nearly thirty were killed. The king's troops lost hardly a man. While this complete rout of Thompson's force was taking place under the hot cannonade of the British, Sullivan, at the mouth of the Sorel was triumphing over an imaginary victory, and writing a despatch full of sanguine anticipations of Thompson's success. " He has proceeded," writes the confident Sullivan, " in the manner proposed, and made his attack at daylight, for at that time a very heavy cannonading began, which continued with some intervals to twelve o'clock. It is now near one P. M., the firing has ceased, except some irregular firing with cannon, at a considerable distance of time one from the other. At eight o'clock a very heavy firing of small arms was heard even here, at the distance of forty-five miles. I am almost certain that victory has declared in our favor, as the irregular firing of the cannon for such a length of time after the small arms ceased, shows that our men are in possession of the ground."

Sullivan's bright anticipations were destined to be soon dispersed, by the arrival of the shattered remains of his force, with a sad account of their misfortunes, which supplied the general with a less jubilant subject for his next despatch. He triumphed no longer in imaginary victories. He had the sad fact to communicate of the total defeat and discouragement of his officers and men. He spoke, however, of his own manful spirit, and declared his determination to hold his ground as long as any person would "stick by" him. He seemed, in fact, resolved to keep the post at the mouth of the Sorel, and went on strengthening its fortifications. This, however, was but the desperation of an unfortunate general, struggling against inevitable fate. It was clear to all that there was no alternative but retreat, and retreat was determined upon. The Americans had less than three thousand men, discouraged by defeat, surrounded by a hostile people, and threatened by an overwhelming British force. Flight afforded the only hope of escape from total destruction.

Carleton, strengthened by several regiments from England under Burgoyne, and by a body of mercenary troops from Brunswick under Baron Reidesel, had now at his command nearly thirteen thousand men. When Wooster was driven from before Quebec, Carleton moved on a large force by land under General Fraser, and another by water under General Nesbitt, to Three Rivers. These two had just made a junction when the Americans began their attack, unconscious of the overwhelming numbers prepared to receive it. The result was necessarily fatal. Carleton now determined to pursue the advantage the large numbers of his troops gave him; and accordingly, moving on his reinforcements as they arrived at Quebec, he sent Burgoyne with a strong advance-column to drive the Americans out of Canada.

Sullivan, now persuaded of the necessity of retreat, abandoned his post, but not until the enemy **June 14.** were at his heels; for the fleet of transports arrived, and Burgoyne took possession of the works at the mouth of the Sorel, only a few hours after the rear of the Americans had left. Sir Guy Carleton had over-cautiously ordered Burgoyne not to pursue his enemy farther up the river than St. Johns. This saved the Americans, who had got but little start of their pursuers. Sullivan having embarked his men, sailed off with them up the river in advance, leaving Major Fuller to follow with the baggage. The wind proved favorable and good progress was made for several hours, when the breeze lulled, and the vessels were becalmed. In the meantime the British were gaining upon them, and had advanced so near to Fuller that he sent to Sullivan in advance, asking for orders what to do, in the probable emergency of being overtaken. The general promptly sent a hundred batteaux to bring off the men and baggage, and orders to burn the large vessels. The major had hardly time to accomplish this duty, before the enemy could reach him. He succeeded, however.

Arnold was determined to hold Montreal until the last moment; but hearing of the disaster at Three Rivers, and aware of the approach of the large force of the enemy, he found that nothing was left him but to retreat, and form a junction with Sullivan. He accordingly crossed from Montreal to Longueil on the mainland, and pushed forward to St. Johns, "making a very prudent and judicious retreat, with an enemy close at his heels," for Carleton, with a large detachment, was striving to intercept him. While Arnold was marching to St. Johns, the fleet with Burgoyne's troops were sailing up the river to the same place, and would have arrived at the same moment, probably, had not the wind failed. Joining Sullivan at St. Johns, preparations were made at once for embarking the troops. "To this work," says Sparks, "Arnold applied himself with his usual ability and vigilance, remaining behind till he had seen every boat leave the shore but his own. He then mounted his horse, attended by Wilkinson, his aid-de-camp, and rode back two miles, when he discovered the enemy's advanced division in full march under General Burgoyne. They gazed at it, or, in military phrase, reconnoitred it, for a short time, and then hastened back to St. Johns. A boat being in readiness to receive them, the horses were stripped and shot, the men were ordered on board, and Arnold, refusing all assistance, pushed off the boat with his own hand; thus, says Wilkinson, "indulging the vanity of being the last man who embarked from the shores of the enemy." The sun was now down and darkness followed, but the boat overtook the army in the night at "Isle aux Noix."

The retreat was full of hardship and danger, but yet it was considered creditable to Sullivan. Though worked to the utmost extent of endurance by the severity of their labors, in the course of which they had to drag their batteaux, heavily laden with cannon and baggage, up the rapids, and though threatened constantly by the approach of an overwhelming force in their rear, they succeeded in bringing off all their boats and baggage, destroying everything that might be of aid to the enemy, and escaping with the loss only of a single man. After a short delay at the Isle aux Noix, Sullivan continued his course along Lake Champlain, until he reached Crown Point. Thus closed the campaign of the northern army, which left Canada, as John Adams expressed it, "disgraced, defeated, discontented, dispirited, diseased, and undisciplined; eaten up with vermin, no clothes, beds, blankets, or medicines, and no victuals but salt pork and flour."

CHAPTER XIX.

General Ward at Boston.—A Naval Success.—"One Mugford."—Capture of the Hope.—Mugford gives the Enemy a Broadside of Oaths and forces him to strike.—Exultation on a Boston Fast-Day.—Mugford has another Struggle with the Enemy.—Falls.—Victory.—General Lincoln's Plan for driving the British Cruisers away.—Its Success.—Arrival of English Vessels in the Harbor of Boston.—Obstinate Resistance.—Capture.—Lieutenant-Colonel Campbell taken Prisoner.—Generals Ward and Frye Resign.—Gates promoted to a Major-Generalship.—His Life, Character, and Personal Appearance.—His Letter to Lee.—The "Traveller's Rest."—Gates appointed to the Command of the Northern Army.—Counter-claims of Schuyler.—The Question between them settled in Favor of Schuyler.—Gates and Schuyler in Harmony.—Resolution to abandon Crown Point.—Opposed by the Subordinate Officers.—Extraordinary Proceedings.—Washington rebukes the Conduct of the Officers but favors their Views.—The Enemy greatly reinforced.—Washington called to Philadelphia by Congress.—General Putnam in Command at New York.—Fortifications in New York.—General Greene on Long Island.—Tryon's Plan for seizing Washington.—A Traitor discovered among Washington's Guard.—The Traitor hung.—Concourse of Spectators.

1776. WHEN Washington set out for New York, he left five regiments under General Ward to complete the works at Boston, and provide, by new **April 4.** fortifications, against the return of Howe, which seemed greatly to have been feared by the New-Englanders. A few British vessels-of-war still lingered in Nantasket roads, much to the annoyance of the Bostonians, who were bent upon driving them away at the earliest moment. Nothing, however, was done for two months. In the meantime, there was a naval success in the very sight of the English ships which served to encourage the patriots of Boston to further effort.

One Mugford, as Gordon calls him, who was a trading skipper, applied for the command of the Franklin, a continental cruiser then unemployed. His request being granted, Mugford made all haste, got possession of the vessel, put on board a supply of powder and ball, shipped a crew of twenty men, and hauled off into the bay. Ward, in the meantime, had been beset by some of his religious New England friends, who gave him such a bad account of the morals of Mugford, that he sent off an express to withdraw his orders. It was, however, too late, the enterprising skipper had sailed, and already, before he had got well out of the harbor, pounced upon a prize. This was the ship Hope, last from Cork, a vessel of two hundred and seventy tons, four guns and seventeen men, and laden with fifteen hundred barrels of gunpowder, and a large supply of arms, implements, and other necessaries, intended for Howe's army supposed to be still at Boston. As soon as Mugford got a sight of her, he ran his little schooner alongside and ordered her to strike, which she did at once without resistance, although her captain, seeing that the British men-of-war were so near that they would be able to come shortly to his aid, ordered his men to cut the top-sail, halliards, and ties. Mugford heard the order, and knew that if it was executed he would certainly lose his prize, for it would give time to the British men-of-war to send their boats to the relief of the Hope, before she could be manageable. Mugford's impiety, which had nearly lost him his command, now appeared to serve him a good purpose, for he opened, says Gordon, upon the Hope's captain with vollies of oaths and execrations; and in the most horrid manner threatened him and every one on board with immediate death, if the order was executed, upon which the captain was so terrified as to desist.

It was fast-day in Boston, and its good people were just returning from church, but, notwithstanding the seriousness becoming such a religious occasion, they could not contain their manifestations of delight as Mugford came into the harbor with his prize. Our skipper, encouraged by the success of his first attempt, soon started out for another cruise with the Franklin and the Lady Wash-

May 19. ington, but in going down the bay the former got aground, and the two dropped their anchors. While thus anchored, they were observed by the British admiral who sent off at midnight thirteen boats to attack them. The men on both sides struggled manfully, and Mugford succeeded in sinking two of the boats. While foremost in the fight, however, he was mortally wounded, but continued to cheer on his men, shouting out with his last breath, as he fell, "Do not give up the ship—you will beat them off." And the men, without the loss of a single life but that of their gallant commander, did beat the enemy off.

36

The Bostonians, exceedingly anxious as they were to get rid of the British war-vessels, which, numbering some ten sail in all, presented a threatening aspect, readily concurred in General Lincoln's plans for driving them away. Everything being in readiness, the cit-

June 13. izens of Boston were made aware by beat of drum that the expedition was to set out. One detachment of soldiers, amounting to nearly six hundred men, was accordingly embarked and sent to Petlock's island and hill, another detachment took post on Morn island, Holk's neck, and Point Olderton, while a third with artillery sailed for Long island. The troops did not arrive at their several places of destination until near morning, but were active and alert for action. The cannon were soon planted, and a single shot fired as an announcement to the enemy of their intention. The commodore immediately hoisted a signal for the fleet to get under way, but in the meantime returned the Americans' fire, and did not succeed in getting under sail until a shot from Long island had damaged, somewhat, his upper rigging. Thus, on the very anniversary of the day on which, two years before, the British government had prohibited the sailing of any vessel from Boston, was its harbor made free.

No sooner had the British admiral gone than several English vessels arrived off the harbor of Boston, and as they supposed Howe still in possession, they came in without suspicion, and were thus captured. Among these were the George and Anabella, transports, which arrived after a passage of seven weeks from Scotland, in the course of which they had no opportunity of speaking a single vessel which could inform them of the evacuation of Boston. When off the coast, they were attacked by four privateers, with whom they fought until evening, when the latter bore away and the transports sought protection, as they supposed, by sailing for the harbor of Boston. They stood in and were passing up Nantasket roads, when an American battery opened upon them, and gave them the first proof that they had got among enemies instead of friends, as they had anticipated. The wind had died away, and the tide being still on the flood, there was no chance for them to get out again. The privateers, which had had a brush with them outside, now came up and prepared to renew the fight, the transports being hailed to strike the British flag. The sailors were ready to yield at once, but the lieutenant-colonel in command of the troops on board persisted in resistance, and was readily obeyed by his soldiers. The fight now began, and was continued for an hour and a half, when all their ammunition being expended, the British vessels surrendered, after losing one officer, and some twenty-five others killed or wounded. The troops which were captured amounted to over three hundred men, and with them was taken also as a prisoner Lieutenant-Colonel Campbell, a man of rank and an officer of distinction.

Major-General Ward and Brigadier-General Frye had sent in their resignations, which were accepted by Congress on the twenty-third of April, but they continued to serve until the operations at Boston we have just narrated were brought to a close, when they were relieved by new appointments. Through the New England influence, which watched with great jealousy the advancement of the military leaders who belonged to the middle and southern provinces, Congress now made another promotion which caused no little trouble in New York. Gates, having been sent by Washington to Philadelphia to confer with Congress in regard to the disastrous state of affairs in Canada, succeeded in obtaining promotion to a major-generalship and the command of the northern army, **June 18.** principally through the influence of the New-Englanders, with whom he had greatly ingratiated himself, during his service before Boston.

Horatio Gates was born in England. "He was," says Horace Walpole, "the son of a housekeeper of the second duke of Leeds, who marrying a young husband had this son by him. That duke of Leeds had been saved of a Jacobite plot by my father, Sir Robert Walpole, and the duke was very grateful and took notice of me when quite a boy. My mother's woman was intimate with that housekeeper, and thence I was God-father to her son, though I believe not then ten years old myself. This God-son, Horatio Gates, was protected by General Cornwallis when governor of Halifax, but being afterward disappointed of preferment in the army, he joined the Americans." He first came to America as an officer in an expedition against the French in Nova Scotia. On his return to London, he was consulted by the British ministry in regard to the proposed campaign under Braddock, but modestly pleading his youth, declined to give any advice. He, however, served in that famous expedition which resulted so fatally, and showed himself a brave and efficient officer. It was then that he became acquainted with Washington, and formed a warm friendship for him. Through this alliance he became familiar with colonial life in Virginia, and so strongly attached to the country, that he determined to settle there. This resolution was strengthened by his marriage to an American woman. Accordingly, selling out his commission in the British army, he bought a plantation in Virginia. Here he retired within his "Traveller's Rest," as he fondly called his estate, apparently resolving no longer to mingle in the busy world without.

To General Charles Lee, who was an old comrade, and whom he desired to become his neighbor and participator with him in the delights of his rural retreat, he writes:—

"I know not how you find it; but the older I grow, I become less and less inclined to new acquaintance. Selfishness and sycophancy possess so generally the minds of men, that I think the many are best avoided, and the few only, who are liberal and sincere, to be sought for and caressed. I therefore stick steadily to the cultivation of my farm, am intimate with few, read when I have time, and content myself with such domestic comforts as my circumstances and fortune afford me. I wish, therefore, most anxiously, you would come to my retreat, and there let us philosophize on the vices and virtues of this busy world, the follies and the vanities of the great vulgar and the small.

"'Laugh when we please, be candid when we can,
    And justify the ways of God to man.'

"Mrs. Gates is earnest in desiring to see you under her roof, where a good bed is provided for you, two or three slaves to supply all your wants, and space enough about us for you to exercise away all your spleen and gloomy moods, whensoever they distress you. In my neighborhood there is this moment as fine a farm-mill and tract of land to be sold as any in America, and provided it is convenient to you to pay down half the price, I am convinced you may have it a very great bargain. It is altogether two thousand four hundred acres, at thirty shillings sterling an acre. I am satisfied you might have it so. By paying down about one thousand eight hundred pounds sterling, you may be put in possession of an estate that ten years hence will be worth seven thousand pounds sterling; and I take it for granted that you may have the payment of the rest of the purchase-money at easy installments, and that, too, without interest; so, by laying out a thousand pounds sterling more in stocking and improvements, your produce will yield you a fine living, and wherewithal to pay your annual installment bargained for in the purchase."

Lee was tempted by the supposed attractions of rural life, and, in common with Gates and Washington, retired to cultivate his own acres, but was soon called to exchange the ploughshare for the sword; and not reluctantly, we would believe, apart from his devotion to a cause which would have prompted him to make every sacrifice of personal ease and comfort. All three were soldiers by nature, and would not have been long content with harvests of corn and tobacco, while there were laurels to reap on the field of battle. When the troubles with the mother-country began to agitate the provinces, Lee, Gates, and Washington were often together, and warming with indignation, as they talked over the oppressive acts of English tyranny, began already to think of taking down their hanging swords, and girding them on for the coming campaign. "I am ready to resign my life to preserve the liberty of the western world," says Gates at the close of the very letter just quoted, in which he philosophizes on the charms of the retirement of his "Traveller's Rest."

Together with Lee, he accompanied Washington to Cambridge, to whose influence he was chiefly indebted for his appointment as adjutant-general. Washington was so conscious of the military deficiencies of the militia leaders, that he was greatly anxious to secure the soldierly attainments of his friends Lee and Gates, whom he knew to be accomplished officers. In the beginning of the struggle they were almost indispensable. Time revealed, and experience perfected the military talents of some American officers upon whose skill Washington could equally trust, and in whose disinterested patriotism he had more faith.

Gates was now at the height of popu-larity. He was personally always a favorite from his courteous manners and kindliness of heart; but he was misled by vanity to an undue appreciation of his capacity. He was not a man of brilliant qualities; and though his ambition prompted him to aspire to the loftiest military position, he was not possessed of the genius of a great commander.

At the beginning of the Revolutionary war, Gates was between fifty and sixty years old; with his scant gray hair and "spectacles on nose," he looked fully his age. He had a brisk, good-natured manner, and was of a cheerful and social humor.

Being appointed to the command in Canada, Gates proceeded to the North, but found on his arrival in Albany that there was no longer, in consequence of the retreat to Crown Point we have already described, any force *in Canada* to command. Gates would seem, therefore, to have been very much in the position of Sancho Panza, in his imaginary Barataria, a governor without a government. He, however, was not disposed to rest contented with this impersonal condition, and laid claim to the command of the northern army wherever it might be. In this he seems to have been instigated not only by his own ambitious longings, but by the officious provocatives of his zealous New England friends. "I find," writes Joseph Trumbull to Gates, "you are in a cursed situation, your authority at an end, and commanded by a person who will be willing to have you knocked in the head, as General Montgomery was, if he can have the money-chest in his power."

Schuyler resisted Gates's claims; and as they could not agree upon the matter between themselves, they referred it to Congress, while in the meantime they resolved to act as harmoniously as possible with each other, until an authoritative decision should be received. General Sullivan, too, thought himself entitled to grumble at the appointment of Gates, who certainly superseded him in rank, however Schuyler's position might be affected. Sullivan accordingly obtained leave of absence from Washington, and made his way to Philadelphia, where he laid his grievances and his resignation before Congress, but being soothed by compliments upon the judiciousness of his late retreat from Canada, was induced to recall his resignation and return to his duty.

The question between Gates and Schuyler was soon settled by the decision of Congress in favor of the pretensions of the latter. Washington had been much harassed by these bickerings among his officers, whose example had been very extensively followed even by the soldiers, who were in a constant state of irritability from sectional feeling. He incloses a copy of the Congressional decision to Schuyler, and takes occasion to say, in regard to his dispute with Gates: "I hope that harmony and a good agreement will subsist between you, as the most likely means of advancing the interests of the cause which you both wish to promote." A few days subsequently, in another letter, he writes: "I am extremely sorry to have such unfavorable accounts of the condition of the army. Sickness of itself is sufficiently bad; but when discord and disorder are added, greater misfortunes can not befall it, except that of a defeat. I must entreat your attention to these matters, and your exertions to introduce more discipline, and to do away the unhappy and pernicious distinctions and jealousies between the troops of different governments."

Sufficient harmony seems finally to have been established between Schuyler and Gates for co-operation, after receiving the decision of Congress; and the two proceeded together to the American army at Crown Point, accompanied by Arnold, who had gone **July 6** to Albany to report the state of the troops after the retreat, and the threatening progress of the enemy. Upon reaching Crown Point, a council of war was held, and it was resolved unanimously that that post should be abandoned and the army removed to Ticonderoga. This was opposed by many of the subordinate officers, who resorted to the unmilitary proceeding of preparing and signing a remonstrance against the decision of their superiors. Washington himself, on receiving this extraordinary paper, although he condemned the signers of it, seems to have been impressed with the views they held in regard to the abandonment of Crown Point. "I doubt not," he writes, "that the measure was duly weighed by the general officers in council, and seemed to them best calculated to secure the colonies, and prevent the enemy from penetrating into them. However, I can not but observe—though I do not mean to encourage in the smallest degree, or to give the least sanction to inferior officers to set up their opinions against the proceedings and councils of their superiors, knowing the dangerous tendency of such a practice—that the reasons assigned by the officers in their remonstrance appear to me forcible and of great weight." The subject was subsequently greatly discussed, and finally the opinion of all military men concurred in justifying the expediency of the removal of the army to Ticonderoga.

Washington, troubled by the unfortunate result in Canada, could get but little consolation from the state of things in New York. Howe was hourly expected, with his army greatly increased by large reinforcements of British regulars, and mercenary troops composed of Hessians, Brunswickers, and other Germans; and Washington knew that his own force was neither in such numbers nor condition as to resist successfully a vigorous attack. Called to Philadelphia by Congress, to aid them with his counsels in this emergency, he succeeded in prevailing upon them to vote a reinforcement to the army of thirteen thousand eight hundred militia, the formation of a flying camp to consist of ten thousand men, and the construction of as many fire rafts, gondolas and floating batteries as might be deemed necessary by Washington for the defence of the bay and rivers surrounding New York. During his absence, General Putnam succeeded to the temporary command, and continued to push vigorously the various works at New York, while Greene was no less active on Long Island.

Washington, on his return, as he thought that the enemy would probably soon after their arrival, attempt to force their way up the North river, determined to erect new, and strengthen the old fortifications on its banks, with the view of preventing the passage of the British vessels. He accordingly ordered Colonel James Clinton, a New York officer, to take the command, and complete the construction of Fort Montgomery, near the Highlands, and Fort Constitution on an island opposite to West Point. Other works were also begun under the supervision of the chief engineer, Colonel Rufus Putnam, at King's Bridge and on the neighboring heights. There were a breastwork to defend the bridge, a redoubt on a hill overlooking the Hudson river, where, by means of the Spuyten Duyvil creek, it joins the Harlem river, and forms the northern water-boundary of the island of New York, and a strong fortification called Fort Washington, also on the Hudson, but several miles nearer New York. This last work was directly opposite to Fort Lee, which was on the west side, and it was supposed that the two together could command the passage.

Washington, while thus providing defences against the open enemies of the country, was beset by the machinations of some secret plotters against him and his army. By the disclosure of one of Washington's own guard, who had been tampered with, a conspiracy was discovered, which was supposed to have for its object the capture of Washington, a general massacre of his principal officers, the spiking of the guns, the blowing up of the forts and magazines, and the securing of the passes of the city, in order that New York and the patriot army might be at the mercy of Howe on the day of his arrival.

An investigation having taken place, the plot was traced through the dirty sources of various pot-houses, tavern-keepers, gunsmiths, negro servants, drummers, fifers, and the mayor, Matthews, to the arch-conspirator Tryon himself. This tory governor, it seems, had, from his safe refuge on board a man-of-war off Sandy Hook, where the British ships were at anchor, devised the scheme, and tempted the worthless to co-operate with him by the offer of five pounds and two hundred acres of land to each man who should enter the king's service, one hundred acres to his wife, and fifty to each child, with the understanding that he should remain in New York and lend his aid secretly to the royal cause. The mayor, in conjunction with many of his fellow tory citizens, readily concurred in and gave their aid to Tryon's plot. A large number of worthless fellows, who were in the habit of resorting to the low pot-houses of the town, were easily won over by the governor's bribe, and among these were some of the most dissolute of the soldiers. Washington's own guard even supplied two of the villains. **June 28.**

One of the name of Thomas Hickey, an Irish deserter from the British army, a stout, dark-faced fellow, was tried by court-martial, and, being found guilty of mutiny and treason, was led out by a strong military guard, and hung in a field, now forming a part of the Bowery, before a crowd of twenty thousand spectators.

CHAPTER XX.

Sir Henry Clinton on the Move.—The South his Object.—The Provincials timely informed.—Arrival of British Fleet and Troops off the Coast of South Carolina.—Clinton's Life and Character.—Charleston on the Alert.—Preparations to receive the Enemy.—General Lee on the Ground.—Assumes the Command.—Lee suggests to swear the Militia in.—Governor Rutledge opposes.—Lee's emphatic Appeal.—The Provincial Deficiencies.—Lee's Anxiety.—The English Fleet taking Position.—Lee lectures his Men.—The Attack on Fort Sullivan begins.—The Response from the American Batteries.—The unsuccessful Attempt of the British to land.—Lee encouraged by the Good Conduct of the Militia.—The British beaten off.—The Havoc.—Sir Peter's "Honor gone."—Wounded in the Breech.—The heroic Sergeant Jasper.—MacDonald.—The Actæn in Flames.—Moultrie's Gallantry.—Fort Sullivan receives the Name of Moultrie.—The beaten British sail for New York.

1776. It will be recollected that Sir Henry Clinton, as has been already recorded, left Boston with a small fleet in the month of January. New York was at that time supposed to be the object of the expedition, and in fact Clin- ton called in there with a single vessel, where Lee, having been sent by Washington to oppose his landing, happened to arrive on the same day, and wrote thus of the occurrence: " He [Clinton] brought no troops with him, and pledges his honor none are coming. He says it is merely a visit to his friend Tryon. If it is really so, it is the most whimsical piece of civility I ever heard of." Whatever might be Clinton's purpose in his visit to New York, an attack on that city was certainly not the object of his expedition.

Howe had received a despatch from the British government, in which it was stated that assurances had been received that the inhabitants of the southern colonies were so loyally disposed that they were ready to join the king's army on the least show of force there. Clinton was accordingly to be sent with a respectable display of British power, in order to encourage the manifestations of the cautious loyalty of the South. If, however, these expectations of tory concurrence should prove unfounded, he was to gain possession "of some respectable post to the southward, from which the rebels might be annoyed by sudden and unexpected attacks on their towns upon the sea-coast during open winter," and Clinton was positively ordered to destroy any towns which would not submit to the king's authority.

Clinton had sailed from Boston with orders from Howe, based on this despatch. The Americans became aware of the object of his expedition, by the fortunate capture of a British vessel, on board of which was found this letter addressed by the British government to Governor Eden of Maryland :—

"WHITEHALL, *December 23, 1775.*

"Sir: An armament of seven regiments, with a fleet of frigates and small ships, is now in readiness to proceed to the southern colonies, in order to attempt the restoration of legal government in that part of America. It will proceed in the first place to North Carolina, and from thence either to South Carolina or Virginia, as circumstances shall point out."

This fleet of men-of-war and transports was under the command of Admiral Sir Peter Parker, and reached the rendezvous at Cape Fear in May, where they joined the small squadron which had brought Sir Henry Clinton and his troops from Boston. Nothing could be done in Virginia, as Lord Dunmore's ill success proved ; and nothing in North Carolina, as was equally clear from the mishap of Governor Martin, with his Highlanders and Regulators in that colony. It was therefore determined to try South Carolina, and begin by making an attempt on Charleston. Confident in their large naval armament under Parker, and their numerous troops which amounted in all to three thousand men under Cornwallis and Clinton, who now assumed the command of all the land forces, they sailed down the coast, in full anticipation of an easy victory. The admiral's well-known dash and courage gave spirit to his men, and the soldiers obeyed with alacrity their general, who, although still young, had served with honor in the wars of Europe.

Henry Clinton was of distinguished family. His grandfather was the earl of Lincoln, and his father was appointed, through the influence of his aristocratic connections, governor of New York in 1743. The son entered the army at an early age, and had served in a European campaign, when he was raised to the rank of major-general, and ordered to Boston with General Howe in 1775. He showed his martial spirit and courage while there by dashing across the river to the aid of Howe during his struggle with the patriots on Bunker's hill, although without a command on that day. He had now been chosen for a service of moment, not only on account of his prominent military rank, but also for his well-known skill and daring. Clinton was not popular with the multitude, but his friendship was cherished by the few. He looked the Englishman with his "short and fat" body, "his full face and prominent nose;" and had that cold reserve of manner, with casual acquaintances, which is supposed to characterize his countrymen.

South Carolina was not unprepared for the formidable force now sailing down its coast, and threatening destruction to its chief city. Throughout the province the patriots had been diligent, and particularly at Charleston, which, from its importance as a commercial town, the excellence of its harbor, and the command it gave of the interior country and the southern coast, presented a desirable capture to the enemy. To secure the town against such a misfortune, the patriots busied themselves in fortifying it, and principally the islands which command the approach to the harbor. The chief works were erected on the southwestern extremity of Sullivan's and on James's islands, in order to defend the passage between the two, which leads from the sea to the harbor. On the former was

37

built a strong fort of palmetto, which is peculiarly serviceable for the purpose of defence, since, from its spongy texture, a ball on striking it sinks into it, without splitting the wood or shattering the structure. Colonel Moultrie had constructed this fort, and, mounting it with twenty-six heavy cannon, now garrisoned it with three hundred and seventy-five South-Carolina regulars and some few militiamen. The work on James's island, which was called Fort Johnson, was in charge of Colonel Gadsden, commanding a single regiment. Cannon, with breastworks, were also placed on the northeastern end of Sullivan's island; at Waddell's point, on the mainland to the north; and along the wharves in front of the town.

When the intelligence reached Charleston that the British fleet had anchored off the coast about eighteen miles from Sullivan's island, the whole country around was aroused into activity by the firing of the alarm-guns from the forts. The militia were everywhere called out, and hurried to the defence of the capital. Some, on their arrival, were distributed among the several garrisons; while others joined the inhabitants, in strengthening the immediate defences of the city. Stores on the wharves were pulled down to make way for breastworks; barricades were thrown across, and cannon planted in, the streets. Some seven hundred negroes were ordered down from the country, to assist in the labor; and so universal was the interest, "that hoes and spades were in the hands of every citizen" day and night, and men willingly exchanged their beds and home

June 1.

comforts for the ground and open air, with nothing but "blankets and knapsacks."

General Lee had arrived, to assume the chief command; and "the great opinion which was everywhere entertained of his ability and experience, added to the spirits of the troops and inhabitants." With his usual fondness for swearing, Lee inaugurated his command by a proposition to bind the militia by an oath. Governor Rutledge had scruples about the legality of the measure; but the men themselves were so ardent at that time, that they all came forward, with the exception of two, and volunteered to swear in accordance with Lee's desire.

The orders of the general are characteristic. Each word in the following snaps like a firelock:—

"As it now appears almost a certainty (from the intelligence of some deserters) that the enemy's intention is to make an attack on the city; and as the general is confident that the numbers and spirit of the garrison will prevent their landing, it only remains to guard against the injury which the city may receive from their cannon.

"The continental troops, provincials, and militia, are therefore most earnestly conjured to work with no less alacrity, than fight with courage. Courage alone will not suffice in war; true soldiers and magnanimous citizens must brandish the pickaxe and spade, as well as the sword, in defence of their country: one or two days' labor, at this critical juncture, may not only save many worthy families from ruin, but many worthy individuals from loss of limbs and life. On this principle the general does not, simply in his capacity of commanding officer, order, but entreat the whole garrison (those on the necessary duties excepted) to exert themselves in forwarding the requisite works of protection.

"The colonels, or commanding officers of the corps, are to review their men's arms this evening at roll-calling; to take care they are in as good order as possible, and that they are furnished with good flints. The officers commanding the different guards are to do the same with their respective guards.

"For the future it must be observed, as an established rule, that no artillery-officer fires a single cannon without previously acquainting the general."

All seemed to be actuated by a very determined spirit of resistance at Charleston, and the preparations to meet the enemy were made with great energy, and with as much skill as could be commanded. The resources of the patriots, however, were in some respects very deficient. Powder was so scarce, that each soldier in the forts was allowed only a limited number of rounds; and lead so scanty, that it became necessary to strip the windows of the dwelling-houses in the town of their weights, to melt and run into bullets.

Lee was very anxious about the result, for he had little faith in the steadiness and discipline of the American troops, most of whom were either raw recruits or militiamen. He was particularly desirous to strengthen the works on Fort Sullivan, which to his experienced eye appeared by no means to satisfy the demands of military art. He accordingly, after making a thorough personal inspection, points out the deficiencies, and orders that " the screen behind the aperture of the traverse be immediately begun and finished with all possible expedition; that a breastwork of timber, six feet high, be raised on the rampart; and that a banquet be raised behind the traverse, so as to enable the musquetry to fire over; the parapet to be made higher, the ditch deeper and wider, a screen to be thrown up behind the entrance, and a façade of fascines or old timber to be constructed, as necessary to keep up the light sand of which the breastwork of the rear-guard is composed." Lee was all astir, going from fort to fort, and issuing these emphatic orders.

Thirty-six of the English transports finally came up, and all crossed the bar in safety, with the exception of two, **June 7.** one of which was got off, but the other went to pieces. The vessels then anchored off Long island, which is situated to the northeast of Sullivan's, from which it is only separated by a narrow channel or creek. Sir Henry Clinton here landed two thousand of his troops and about five hundred sailors, with the intention of passing over to Sullivan's island, but was prevented by the depth of the creek, which was no longer fordable, in consequence of the large quantity of water driven into it by the strong and long-continued easterly winds. Clinton was accordingly forced to raise two batteries to secure his position upon Long island, and to cover a proposed landing with his boats (to which he would now be obliged to resort) upon the eastern end of Sullivan's, where the Americans— principally riflemen, under the command of Colonel Thompson — had posted themselves behind a breastwork.

General Lee was especially anxious about this position, and says to Thompson, in a characteristic order for the day: " It is a certain truth that the enemy entertain a most fortunate apprehension of American riflemen. It is equally certain that nothing can diminish this apprehension so infallibly as a frequent ineffectual fire. It is with some concern, therefore, that I am informed that your men have been suffered to fire at a most preposterous distance. Upon this principle I must entreat and insist that you consider it as a standing order, that not a man under your command is to fire at a greater distance than one hundred and fifty yards, at the utmost; in short, that they never fire without almost a moral certainty of hitting their object. Distant firing has a doubly bad effect: it encourages the enemy, and adds to the pernicious persuasion of the American soldiers, viz., *that they are no match for their antagonists at close fighting.* To speak plainly, it is almost a sure method of making them cowards. Once more, I must request that a stop be put to this childish, vicious, and scandalous practice. I extend the rule to those who have the care of the field-pieces; four hundred yards is the greatest distance they should be allowed to fire at. A transgression of this rule will be considered as the effect of flurry and want of courage."

Some of Thompson's men, from foolhardiness or curiosity, had crossed the creek to Long island; whereat Lee is greatly inflamed, and asks, in a postscript to his order: "Is this wise? Is it soldierlike? Is it to show the enemy where our weakness is?"

Sir Henry, while busy with his works on Long island, took occasion in the meantime to issue a proclamation, appealing to the loyalty of the people of Charleston; but it only served to inflame them to greater patriotism and to more active efforts for defence. The British commander seemed in no haste to attempt to cross over to Sullivan's island; and in the meantime his troops suffered greatly, while laboring at the works, from the sweltering summer heat, from which there was no relief of shade on the sandy, desert island upon which they had landed. Some of them became sun-struck, many ill with dysentery, and all more or less affected by the severe heat and the brackish water with which they were forced to satisfy their burning thirst.

The admiral was less patient than Clinton, and hastened to take his position off Sullivan's island, which he proposed to make the object of his attack. He had, soon after his arrival, moved the Bristol, **June 10.** his own ship, a fifty-gun vessel, opposite to the large fort on the western extremity of the island. He experienced some difficulty in crossing the bar, but, by lighting the ship of some of her cannon, finally succeeded in anchoring her in position. It was not until the 28th of June (when he was joined by a large man-of-war of fifty guns, the arrival of which he had been awaiting) that he determined to make his attack. On that day accordingly, at eleven o'clock in the morning, he began to move his ships. He brought the Experiment of fifty, the Active of twenty-eight, and the Solebay of the same number of guns, in line with his own ship the Bristol, and moved them all in close to the front of the fort; and ordered the Actæon, Siren, and Sphinx, each twenty-eights, to try to get inside, within the western extremity of the island, where the fort was known to be incomplete. These vessels, however, in attempting to get into position, got aground upon a shoal called the Middle Ground. The Actæon stuck fast, and all efforts to move her proved ineffectual. The other two got afoul of each other, and the Sphinx lost her bowsprit in consequence; but they finally succeeded, in the course of several hours, in getting off, although in the meantime they were exposed to a severe fire from the fort.

As the vessels were getting into position, the Thunder (bomb) was throwing her shells upon the island, but not with much effect, for most of them fell into a morass, where the fuses were soon extinguished. The Active was the first to haul in and anchor in front of the fort. As she approached, the Americans fired a shot or two at her, to try, as it were, the range of their guns. She was soon followed by the other ships; and when they had fairly let go their anchors, they began to pour in their broadsides, which were returned by a deadly fire from the forts. The vessels kept up an incessant and well-directed cannonade; but their balls, although well aimed, did but little mischief, as they sank into the spongy palmetto-wood without causing injury to the works. The American riflemen, in consequence of their small allowance of powder, did not fire rapidly, but always with effect. Thus the struggle was kept up, from noon till night. There was a pause for a long time in the fire of the fort, from a want of ammunition, and the enemy began to think they had won the day; but Lee, who was stationed at Haddrell's point, on the mainland, took care to send a supply, and soon the riflemen were enabled to renew their deadly shots.

Clinton in the meantime made an attempt to land from Long island with a flotilla of small boats; but Thompson and his men, bearing in mind Lee's orders, took care to wait till they reached within musket-shot, and then poured upon them such a volley, that Clinton was forced to retire. The struggle still continued between the ships and Fort Sullivan.

Lee was full of anxiety during this prolonged contest. He knew that the garrison was composed entirely of raw troops; he knew that their ammunition was short; and as the bridge of boats, which he had begun to construct between the island and the mainland, was not yet completed, by which he might send reinforcements, he was fearful that all would be lost. He attempted to reach the island; but his boat, carried adrift by the wind and the tide, could not make the place. His aid-de-camp was more fortunate, and came back from his visit with the most inspiriting accounts of the temper of the garrison. Lee was for awhile doubtful of the prudence of continuing the conflict; but, on hearing of the spirit of those in the fort, "I determined," he says, "to support it at all hazards. On this principle I thought it my duty to cross over to the island, to encourage the garrison by my presence; but I might have saved myself that trouble; for I found, on my arrival, they had no occasion for any sort of encouragement: I found them determined and cool to the last degree: their behavior would, in fact, have done honor to the oldest troops." Another witness tells us that so little confusion and disorder existed in the fort when General Lee visited it, in the height of the action, that the "officers laid aside their pipes in order to receive him with proper respect."

The fight was continued from noon until eleven o'clock at night, when Sir Peter Parker was forced to slip his cables and draw off his ships. The havoc upon his decks had been terrible. The fight has been eloquently described by no less a person than Edmund Burke, who at that time edited the "Annual Register," of Dublin: "Whilst the continued thunder from the ships seemed sufficient to shake the firmness of the bravest enemy, and daunt the courage of the most veteran soldier, the return made by the fort could not fail of calling for the respect, as well as of highly incommoding, the brave seamen of Britain. In the midst of that dreadful roar of artillery, they stuck with the greatest constancy and firmness to their guns; fired deliberately and slowly, and took a cool and effective aim. The ships suffered accordingly; they were torn to pieces, and the slaughter was dreadful. Never did British valor shine more conspicuous, nor never did our marine, in an engagement of the same nature with any foreign enemy, experience as rude an encounter. The springs of the Bristol's cable being cut by the shot, she lay for some time exposed in such a manner to the enemy's fire, as to be most dreadfully raked. The brave Captain Morris, after receiving a number of wounds, which would have sufficiently justified a gallant man in retiring from his station, still with a noble obstinacy disdained to quit his duty, until, his arm being at length shot off, he was carried away in a condition which did not afford a possibility of recovery.

"It is said that the quarter-deck of the Bristol was at one time cleared of every person but the commodore, who stood alone, a spectacle of intrepidity and firmness which has seldom been equalled, never exceeded. The others on that deck were either killed or carried down to have their wounds dressed. Nor did Captain Scott, of the Experiment, miss his share of the danger or glory, who, besides the loss of an arm, received so many other wounds, that his life was at first despaired of."

Lord William Campbell, a brother of the duke of Argyle, and the royal governor of the province of South Carolina, served as a volunteer, and was mortally wounded while directing a gun on the lower deck of the Bristol. Sir Peter Parker exposed himself during the whole fight with great courage, and continued, although bleeding from a wound, to give his orders calmly and discreetly. The wags of Carolina amused themselves subsequently with writing verses on Sir Peter's mishap, for the shot which struck him had taken a direction which naturally provoked the humorous if it did not inspire the poetical. Thus trolled one of the newspaper versifiers of the day:

> "If honor in the breech is lodged,
>   As Hudibras hath shown,
> It may from hence be fairly judged
>   Sir Peter's honor's gone!"

The loss of the British was very heavy, being nearly two hundred men in all, killed and wounded. The vessels were greatly damaged, particularly the two fifty-gun ships, the Bristol and the Experiment, at which the fire of the garrison was chiefly aimed. On the former, in addition to the commodore, Lord Campbell, and Captain Morris, the two latter mortally, sixty-nine men were wounded and forty killed. On the Experiment, her commander and seventy-nine of her officers and men were among the killed and wounded. This terrible havoc proves how greatly these two vessels were exposed. Their masts and rigging were cut up and riddled with shot, the Bristol having had over seventy balls put into her; their hulls were so battered and broken, that several of the ports were knocked into one. Moultrie, in the beginning of the engagement, had shouted to his men, "Mind the commodore and the fifty-gun ships!" We have seen how well they obeyed the word.

The Americans lost only thirty-five in killed and wounded; but the soft palmetto-wood of the fort was studded with balls as full as a birthday-pudding with plums. Almost every tree and hut on the island was levelled to the ground; and no less than twelve hundred balls of different weights, with a large number of shells, were picked up next day in and about the fort. All the Americans behaved themselves with admirable steadiness throughout, and some of them showed great daring. In the beginning of the action, the flagstaff was shot away; when Sergeant Jasper, of the grenadiers, immediately leaped over the parapet, and, picking up the flag, which had fallen on the outside upon the beach, fastened it to a sponge staff. He then mounted the merlon, and, while the balls from the ships were falling fast about him, coolly fixed the staff in its place. Sergeant M'Donald was mortally wounded, but, as he fell, exhorted with his last words his comrades to continue steady in the cause of liberty and their country.

Next morning, all the men-of-war had hauled off and anchored about two miles from the island, with the exception of the Actæon, which remained where she first struck. The garrison began to fire at her, and she returned several shots; but finally her crew set fire to her, and took to their boats, leaving her colors flying, guns loaded, and all the ammunition and stores aboard. A party of Americans then put off from the shore, and boarded her. These daring fellows, having hauled down the flag, taken possession of the ship's bell, and filled their boats with as many sails and stores as they could hold, prepared to return. They,

however, though the flames were already bursting through the deck and sides of the burning ship, stopped to have a shot at the commodore: so they pointed three of her guns at the Bristol, and fired them, before they took to their boats. They had not been half an hour away, when the fire reaching her magazine, the Actæon was blown up, and nothing left of her but a shattered remnant of her hull.

The British admiral made no further attempt upon the island. Clinton, however, strove again, early in the morning, to land, but was repulsed.

Colonel Moultrie came in for the chief share of the honors of the victory. Lee, in his despatch, awards great credit to him, and all the officers and men. "I beg leave," he says, "to recommend in the strongest terms, to the Congress, the commanding officer, Colonel Moultrie, and his whole garrison, as brave soldiers and excellent citizens; nor must I omit at the same time mentioning Colonel Thompson, who, with the South-Carolina rangers and a detachment of the North-Carolina regulars, repulsed the enemy in two several attempts to make a lodgment at the other extremity of the island.

"Our loss, considering the heat and duration of the fire, was inconsiderable; we had only ten men killed on the spot and twenty-two wounded; seven of whom lost their limbs, but with their limbs they did not lose their spirits, for they enthusiastically encouraged their comrades never to abandon the standard of liberty and their country."

Lee had never, from his distrust of the raw American troops, been very sanguine of success. He wrote that Charleston was "utterly defenceless," and he had been very anxious to secure a retreat from Sullivan's island, by means of a bridge of boats connecting it with the mainland at Haddrell's point. During the whole action he kept his men busy at this work; but he could not get boats enough, and was forced to resort to the expedient of fastening planks upon empty hogsheads. This, however, proved ineffectual, and the bridge was never made practicable for the purpose intended. Colonel Moultrie had more confidence in his men, and he knew them better than Lee. "For my part," says Moultrie, "I never was uneasy in not having a retreat, because I never imagined that the enemy could force me to that necessity."

Moultrie did not over-estimate the steady courage and endurance of his men; but all their good conduct would probably have proved vain, if the three vessels-of-war which Parker had ordered around the western extremity of the island had succeeded in getting into position, for they would have poured their broadsides upon a part of the fort which, being unfinished, could not have withstood the first cannonade.

The American colonel was fitly honored by an act of the legislature of Carolina, changing the name of Fort Sullivan to that of Fort Moultrie. Congress, too, voted him, as well as Lee and Thompson, the thanks of the country. The brave Sergeant Jasper was rewarded on the day after the victory, by Governor Rutledge, who presented him with the sword from his own side. He offered him, moreover, a lieutenant's commission; but the humble Jasper, who could neither read nor write, refused, saying: "I am not fit to keep officers' company; I am but a sergeant."[*]

The British vessels anchored off Long island to refit; and such was the damaged condition of the larger ships, that they were detained a long time in getting ready again for sea. General Clinton and Lord Cornwallis, in the mean- June 30. while, sailed with the troops, in a fleet of transports, under the escort of the Solebay frigate, bearing the flag of Commodore Parker, and bound for New York.

* Lossing.

CHAPTER XXI.

Washington's Troops busy with the Pickaxe and Spade on Long Island.—The Bustling Mifflin.—His Character.—A Military Dandy's Sneer at the Provincials.—Takes the "Measure" of the Outward Man.—Provincial Jealousies and Quarrels.—Washington rebukes the Quarrelsome.—Is anxious about the Approach of the Enemy.—The British arrive at Sandy Hook.—Washington on the Lookout.—Strengthens the Posts on the Hudson.—Sir William Howe awaits his Brother's Arrival.—Washington expects a Struggle, and appeals to the Patriotism of his Army.

1776. "TRUE soldiers and magnanimous citizens must brandish the pickaxe and spade as well as the sword," said Lee; and the army under Washington at New York was now in full appreciation of this military truth. The men were kept busily at work digging, ditching, and intrenching, on Long island, under Greene, and at Kingsbridge, under the ever-active Mifflin. The latter was a "bustler" who, as one of the sufferers reports, "harassed us unnecessarily, and, considering the unavoidable severity of our duty, to the real injury of the health of the troops." The manners of Mifflin "were better adapted to attract popularity than to preserve it. Highly animated in his appearance, and possessing in an eminent degree the talent of haranguing a multitude, his services in giving motion to the militia" were acknowledged. "He assumed a little of the veteran from having lain before Boston," and was very fond of telling his men that he would bring them into "a scrape." "He was a man of education, ready apprehension, and brilliancy; had spent some time in Europe, particularly in France, and was very easy of access, with the manners of genteel life, though occasionally evolving those of the Quaker."

General THOMAS MIFFLIN, with all his eccentricities, was undoubtedly one of the most useful men of the Revolution. After serving, as we have seen him, at the siege of Boston, as quartermaster-general, with unsparing energy and inexhaustible ingenuity of resource, he was appointed by Congress a brigadier-general, and now, at the early age of thirty-two, has command of the forces engaged in the construction of the works at Fort Washington and Kingsbridge.

The gentlemanly qualifications, and his ease "of access, with the manners of genteel life," if not the higher virtues of Mifflin, were appreciated by the military coxcombs of the day, one of whom[*] has been very free in his revelations of the graces and want of graces of his comrades while with them engaged in brandishing "the pickaxe and spade" about Fort Washington, a duty certainly not very favorable to over-nice appearances; for, as our authority acknowledges, it gave them all the look of "scavengers." He tells us how Colonel Putnam carried home from mar-

* Graydon.

38

ket his own meat, by the way of showing a good example to his officers, and remarks: "But if any aristocratic tendencies had been really discovered by the colonel among his countrymen, requiring this wholesome example, they must have been of recent origin, and the effect of southern contamination." This fastidious gentleman is especially shocked by the want of nice social discrimination on the part of the New-England officers, and, although rather unnecessarily delicate in his genteel sensibility, he seems justified in his sneers when colonels were known to make drummers and fifers of their sons, in order to put their pittance of pay into the family purse, and when other New-England officers turned their children into waiters.*

The ridicule of our fine gentleman was greatly moved by the arrival in camp of a body of Connecticut light-horse: "These consisted of a considerable number of old-fashioned men—probably farmers and heads of families, as they were generally middle-aged, and many of them apparently beyond the meridian of life. They were truly irregulars; and whether their clothing, their equipments, or caparisons, were regarded, it would have been difficult to have discovered any circumstance of uniformity; though in the features derived from 'local habitation' they were one and the same.

"Instead of carbines and sabres, they generally carried fowling-pieces; some of them very long, and such as in Pennsylvania are used for shooting ducks. Here and there one, 'his youthful gar-

* Thacher.

ments well saved,' appeared in a dingy regimental of scarlet, with a triangular, tarnished, laced hat. In short, so little were they like modern soldiers, in air or costume, that, dropping the necessary number of years, they might have been supposed the identical men who had in part composed Pepperell's army at the taking of Louisburg."

These men were volunteers, and might have proved fair soldiers, notwithstanding their "dingy regimentals" and "sorry jades," had they been a little more tractable. Washington discharged them—not, however, because they did not look like regular soldiers, but because they were not very ready to submit to become such. "The Connecticut light-horse," says Washington, in his despatch to Congress, "mentioned in my letter of the 11th, notwithstanding their **July 17.** then promise to continue here for the defence of this place, are now discharged, and about to return home, having peremptorily refused all kind of fatigue-duty, or even to mount guard, claiming an exemption as troopers. Though their assistance is much needed, and might be of essential service in case of an attack, yet I judged it advisable, on their application and claim of such indulgences, to discharge them; as granting them would set an example to others, and might produce many ill consequences."

A more sober authority is no less free in his revelations of the manners and conduct of the New-England officers than the fine gentleman we have already quoted. "It was the case," says Gordon, "in divers instances, that, when a company was forming, the men would choose those for officers who consented to throw their pay into a joint stock with the privates, from which captains, lieutenants, ensigns, sergeants, corporals, with drummers and privates, drew equal shares. Can it then be wondered at, however mortifying it may prove, that a captain should be tried and broken for stealing his soldiers' blankets, or that another officer should be found shaving his men in the face of distinguished characters ?"

There is a single exception "to these miserably-constituted bands from New England" made in favor of the regiment of Glover, from Marblehead "There was," says our fastidious military critic, "an appearance of discipline in this corps; the officers seemed to have mixed with the world, and to understand what belonged to their stations. Though deficient, perhaps, in polish, it possessed an apparent aptitude for the purpose of its institution, and gave a confidence that myriads of its meek and lowly brethren were incompetent to inspire." But even Glover's seems, in the nice eyes of Graydon, to have a blot; for in his regiment "there were a number of negroes, which, to persons unaccustomed to such associations, had a disagreeable, degrading effect."

Even aristocratic Virginia failed to come up to the high standard of our genteel annalist.* "Neither," he says, "did the fighting department appear to be fashionable among the gentry of Virginia. It must be admitted that she furnished some gentlemen aids-de-camp and volun-

*Graydon.

teers, and afterward corps of cavalry, respectably officered; but the serious, drudging business of war devolves on the infantry; and, in this description of force, she evinced but little brilliancy." He then tells us of a Virginian commander whom he knew, who had "the appearance of a reputable planter," and concedes that "he might have been both patriotic and brave," but adds, "neither himself nor his officers were of the kind that bespoke the *élite* of their country."

The general officers even did not escape the tailor-like scrutiny of Graydon, who says, "The celebrated General Putnam, riding with a hanger belted across his brawny shoulders, over a waistcoat without sleeves (his summer costume), was deemed much fitter to head a band of sicklemen or ditchers than musketeers." General Greene, too, did not "shine with all the *éclat*" that might have been desired by the army coxcombs. He also doubtless stripped his "brawny shoulders" to the work along with "Old Put."

The "city-bred Marylander," however, seems to have been faultless, for "he was distinguished by the most fashionably-cut coat, the most *macaroni* cocked hat, and hottest blood in the Union." One battalion, that of Smallwood, appears to have been particularly worthy of admiration, for "its officers exhibited a martial appearance, by a uniform of scarlet and buff."

There was something, however, more serious than these small distinctions of dress and manners between the various officers and men. Provincial jealousies often arose; and, although starting from the most trifling causes, led to the most serious results. "A singular kind of riot," says Thacher, "took place in our barracks last evening, attended by some unpleasant consequences. Colonel A—— W——, of Massachusetts, made choice of his two sons, who were soldiers in his regiment, to discharge the menial duties of waiters; and one of them, having been brought up a shoemaker, the colonel was so inconsiderate as to allow to work on his bench in the same room with himself. The ridiculous conduct has for some time drawn on the good old man the contemptuous sneers of the gentlemen-officers, especially those from Pennsylvania. Lieutenant-Colonel C——, of Wayne's regiment, being warmed with wine, took on himself the task of reprehending the 'Yankee' colonel for thus degrading his rank. With this view, he rushed into the room in the evening, and soon despatched the shoemaker's bench; after which he made an assault on the colonel's person, and bruised him severely. The noise and confusion soon collected a number of officers and soldiers, and it was a considerable time before the rioters could be quelled. Some of the soldiers actually took to their arms and dared the *Yankees,* and then proceeded to the extremity of firing their guns. About thirty or forty rounds were aimed at the soldiers of our regiment, who were driven from their huts and barracks, and several of them were seriously wounded." A reconciliation ensued, but it only added to the disreputableness of the affair.

"It was in the power of Colonel W——," adds Thacher, "and in fact it was his duty, to bring the audacious offenders to exemplary punishment; but, as if to complete the disgrace of the transaction, Colonel C—— sent some soldiers into the woods to shoot a fat bear, with which he made an entertainment, and invited Colonel W—— and his officers to partake of it; this effected a reconciliation, and Colonel W—— was induced to overlook the high-handed assault on his own person and on the lives of his soldiers." At the close, Thacher puts in a good word for his commander and fellow-provincial, saying, "Our colonel is a serious, good man, but is more conversant with the economy of domestic life than the etiquette practised in camp." This occurred in Gates's army, at the North.

In New York, the troops seem to have been no less jealous of, and quarrelsome with, each other; for Washington finds it necessary to issue this order: **August 1.** "It is with great concern that the general understands that jealousies have arisen among the troops from the different provinces, and reflections are frequently thrown out, which can only tend to irritate each other, and injure the noble cause in which we are engaged, and which we ought to support with one hand and one heart.

"The general most earnestly entreats the officers and soldiers to consider the consequences; that they can no way assist our enemies more effectually, than by making divisions among ourselves; that the honor and success of the army, and the safety of our bleeding country, depend upon harmony and good agreement with each other; that the provinces are all united to oppose the common enemy, and all distinctions sunk in the name of an 'American.' To make this name honorable, and to preserve the liberty of our country, ought to be our only emulation; and he will be the best soldier and the best patriot who contributes most to this glorious work, whatever his station or from whatever part of the continent he may come.

"Let all distinctions of nations, countries, and provinces, therefore be lost in the generous contest who shall behave with the most courage against the enemy, and the most kindness and good humor to each other.

"If there be any officers or soldiers so lost to virtue and love of their country as to continue in such practices after this order, the general assures them, and is authorized by Congress to declare to the whole army, that such persons shall be severely punished and dismissed from the service with disgrace."

Washington was naturally anxious, with his army as yet only reinforced by a small portion of the militia levied by Congress, and with considerable distrust of the good conduct of some of his troops, whose occasional disorderly behavior may be inferred from the facts which we have already stated. Although we have somewhat anticipated events for the sake of illustration, whatever we have said, in regard to the conduct of both officers and men, will apply to the earlier as well as the later period.

When, therefore, Washington learns, on the 28th of June, that General Howe had, on the 9th, left Halifax with a fleet of one hundred and thirty sail, bound to Sandy Hook, it is not surprising that he should write: "I could wish General Howe and his armament not to arrive yet, as no more than a thousand militia have come in, and our whole force, including the troops at all the detached posts, and on board the armed vessels, which are comprehended in our returns, is but small and inconsiderable, when compared with the extensive lines they are to defend, and most probably the army that he brings."

Washington, seldom perturbed, and never more calm than in danger, was still fully conscious of the difficulties of his position. "We expect a bloody summer in New York," he wrote to his brother, "and I am sorry to say that we are not, either in men or arms, prepared for it. However, it is to be hoped that, if our cause is just, as I most religiously believe it, the same Providence which has in many instances appeared for us, will still go on to afford its aid." Again Washington writes to Schuyler: "Our most vigorous exertions will be required in every instance. I am convinced our enemies will strain every nerve against us this campaign, and try to injure us wherever we may be unprovided." June 28.

On that day (28th of June) four British ships—on one of which, the Greyhound, was General Howe—came to anchor in the bay of New York. On the 29th, the officer appointed to keep a lookout on Staten island sent an express to Washington, with the word that forty-five more vessels had arrived off Sandy

Hook. "I am hopeful," writes Washington on the occasion, "before they are prepared to attack, that I shall get some reinforcements.... Be that as it may," he resolutely adds, "I shall attempt to make the best disposition I can of our troops, in order to give them a proper reception, and prevent the ruin and destruction they are meditating against us."

It was supposed that Howe would immediately begin an attack. Washington accordingly was active in preparation, and strenuously urged on the arrival of the expected militia from the neighboring provinces. His old Virginia friend, Doctor (now General) Mercer, was appointed to the command of the "flying camp," and kept busy at Amboy, in conjunction with General Livingston, of New Jersey, in recruiting and keeping a watch upon the enemy. As it was thought probable that the British would force their way up the Hudson, with the view of opening a communication with Carleton's victorious forces at the North, Washington directed his attention especially to the strengthening of his posts along the banks of that river.

Great vigilance was urged upon the commanders of all the forts, and Mifflin "the bustler" was especially on the alert at Kingsbridge and Fort Washington. His lines were manned every morning before daylight, and his ranks formed for action. The men were led to believe, by the confident assertions of their commander, that the enemy had already landed in the neighborhood. One of the officers, harassed by these early risings and frequent calls to duty, finally came to the conclusion that the general was merely crying "Wolf!" and that it was a contrivance of that "bustler" Mifflin to inure his troops to alarms and render them alert.

Although at the head of ten thousand men, General Howe was not yet prepared to make a demonstration. He was awaiting the arrival of his brother, Admiral Lord Howe, with a formidable fleet, having on board a large reinforcement of those hated Hessians. Washington became aware of Howe's purpose, and, as the admiral was hourly expected, strove to prepare his army for the formidable encounter which awaited them. He issued the following order, which in earnestness of patriotic feeling and force of expression has never been surpassed by the most ardent appeals to men to fight for their freedom:—

"The time is now near at hand, which must probably determine whether Americans are to be freemen or slaves; whether they are to have any property they can call their own; **July 2.** whether their houses and farms are to be pillaged and destroyed, and they consigned to a state of wretchedness, from which no human efforts will probably deliver them.

"The fate of unborn millions will now depend, under God, on the courage and conduct of this army. Our cruel and unrelenting enemy leaves us no choice but a brave resistance or the most abject submission. This is all that we can expect. We have, therefore, to resolve to conquer or die. Our own country's honor calls upon us for a vigorous and manly exertion; and if we now shamefully fail, we shall become infamous to the whole world.

"Let us rely upon the goodness of the cause, and the aid of the Supreme Being, in whose hands victory is, to animate and encourage us to great and noble actions. The eyes of all our countrymen are now upon us, and we shall have their blessings and praises, if happily we are the instruments of saving them from the tyranny meditated against them. Let us animate and encourage each other, and show the whole world that a freeman contending for liberty on his own ground is superior to any slavish mercenary on earth.

"The general recommends to the officers great coolness in time of action, and to the soldiers a strict attention and obedience, with a becoming firmness and spirit. Any officer or soldier, or any particular corps, distinguishing itself by any acts of bravery and courage, will assuredly meet with notice and rewards; and on the other hand, those who behave ill will as certainly be exposed and punished; the general being resolved, as well for the honor and safety of the country as of the army, to show no favor to such as refuse or neglect to do their duty at so important a crisis."

CHAPTER XXII.

Declaration of Independence.—The Sentiment of the Country.—"Common Sense."—Thomas Paine.—His Life, Character, and Services.—The Reception of the "Declaration" at Philadelphia.—In the Army.—By the Citizens of New York.—Destruction of the Statue of George III.—Washington rebukes the Riotous Inhabitants of New York.—General Howe in High Spirits.—The Rose and Phœnix again up the Hudson.—Arrival of Lord Howe.—His Life and Character.—Commissioners to treat.—Proclamation.—Franklin and Lord Howe.—Proof against Seduction.—A Flag. —"George Washington, *Esquire*, &c., &c., &c."—The Superscription not acknowledged.—The British General, taught better, writes "*General Washington.*"

1776. "THE greatest question ever debated in America, and as great as ever was or ever will be debated among men," as John Adams called it, was decided by this resolution of Congress on the 2d day of July, 1776: "THAT THESE UNITED COLONIES ARE, AND OF RIGHT OUGHT TO BE, FREE AND INDEPENDENT STATES."

The Declaration of Independence was not, however, adopted until the 4th of July, an event which is now so wrought into the heart of every American, that it is superfluous for the historian to record the day or the year of its occurrence.

This is an historical fact which requires no book for its record; it is so early learned by every child of America, that his knowledge of it seems an instinct of his nature.

When this momentous act was passed, the people were not unprepared for it. Many of the provinces had already, by vote in their assemblies, resolved upon independence from Great Britain; and North Carolina, we believe, claims not only to have anticipated the act, but even the words of the declaration.

By the thoughtful men of the country

the possibility and even the necessity and desirableness of separation from Great Britain, had long been considered. As early as November, 1774, Josiah Quincy wrote: "Doctor Franklin is an American in heart and soul. His ideas are not contracted within the narrow limits of exemption from taxes, but are extended on the broad scale of total emancipation. He is explicit and bold on the subject." Others capable of comprehensive views of national policy had undoubtedly seen at an early period, in common with Benjamin Franklin, the ultimate result of the difficulties between the colonies and the mother-country.

It was long, however, before the sentiment of the country was fully moulded to the definite idea of independence. This was a result which might have crowned with honor the noble endeavors of the highest: it was, however, reserved as a triumph for the humble staymaker of Thetford. All agree in attributing to Thomas Paine the preparation of the popular mind for independent government. "Common Sense," as its title promised, was a direct appeal to the general intelligence of the people. Clear, forcible, and familiar in style, straightforward in argument, and free from all theoretical abstractions and subtleties, this famous work was read and understood by all. "That celebrated pamphlet," Burke called it, "which prepared the minds of the people for independence."

"Common Sense" circulated everywhere throughout the provinces. It was read by the Virginian planter while lounging beneath his portico on the banks of the Potomac, and by the New-England farmer at his fireside during the long nights of winter. The soldier fired anew with martial spirit as, amid the stir and noise of war, he glanced at its pages of stirring eloquence; and the statesman learned wisdom from its clear exposition of political rights and principles.

THOMAS PAINE was born at Thetford, in the county of Norfolk, England, in the year 1737. His parents, who were Quakers, were reputable townspeople, and brought up their son in accordance with their own position. He was apprenticed to a staymaker in his own town, but, with a fondness for books, and some early success as a writer, he tired of his trade, and became subsequently a schoolmaster. By means of some small patronage, Paine succeeded in getting the appointment of an exciseman, and while thus occupied wrote a pamphlet upon a subject connected with his business. It was this early effort which is said to have first attracted the notice of Franklin, then in London, to the author. Paine was poor, and desirous of bettering his condition; and was thus induced by Franklin to try his fortune in America. He settled, on his arrival, in Philadelphia, where he became the editor of a journal, and soon attracted notice by the vigor of his political articles. In January, 1776, he published his "Common Sense;" and its influence was so great, that it almost justified the remark that "Paine did as much for the American cause by his pen as Washington by his sword."

The announcement of the DECLARATION OF INDEPENDENCE was received everywhere by the patriots with exulting joy. In Philadelphia, thousands of the citizens, expectant of the event, gathered in the streets, and thronged about the entrance of the Hall of Independence. The bell-man was posted in the tower above, and a messenger at the doors of the hall within which the representatives of America were assembled. The vote passed; the result was declared; a shout of enthusiasm followed; the bell rang vigorously; and the crowds without caught up the joyful sounds, and re-echoed them with loud hurrahs. That bell, which first proclaimed the news to the people of Philadelphia, had been wrought in London twenty-three years before, and upon it prophetically inscribed these words from the Bible : "Proclaim liberty throughout all the land, unto all the inhabitants thereof."

Washington, on receiving from Congress the "Declaration," ordered it to be proclaimed before all the army, **July 9.** accompanying his order with the expression of the hope "that this important event will serve as a fresh incentive to every officer and soldier to act with fidelity and courage, as knowing that now the peace and safety of his country depend, under God, solely on the success of our arms; and that he is now in the service of a state possessed of sufficient power to reward his merit and advance him to the highest honors of a free country."

Washington, accompanied by his staff, was present himself at the reading of the declaration to the brigade encamped on the common, or the park, as it is now called, in New York. The ranks were formed into a hollow square, and Washington placed himself in the centre on horseback, while one of his aids read out with a full voice each word of the famous document. The soldiers, and people gathered about, shouted at the conclusion with great spirit.

Graydon, who added to his other artificial accomplishments that of showing a genteel contempt for a sensation, acknowledges that, "If it [the declaration] was not embraced with all the enthusiasm that has been ascribed to the event, it was at least hailed with acclamations, as no doubt any other act of Congress, not flagrantly improper, would at that time have been.... The propriety of the measure," he adds, "had been little canvassed among us; and perhaps it was to our honor that we were so little of politicians. A predilection for republicanism, it is true, had not reached the army, at least the Pennsylvania line [to which Graydon himself belonged]; but as an attempt to negotiate, in our unorganized situation, would probably have divided and ruined us, the step was considered wise, although a passage of the Rubicon, and calculated to close the door to accommodation. Being looked upon as unavoidable, if resistance was to be persisted in, it was approved; and produced no resignation among the officers that I am aware of, except that of Lieutenant-Colonel William Allen. He called at our camp, on his way to Philadelphia, where he appeared somewhat surprised and mortified that his example had no followers."

The citizen-patriots of New York did

not receive the "Declaration" as coolly as Graydon's comrades. The crowd, after hearing the document read on the common, rushed tumultuously to the "Bowling-Green," and pulled down the equestrian statue of King George III., which stood there. The royal effigy was of lead, but had a coating of gilt. When it was torn down, it was broken into pieces; and a faithful annalist records that most of them were sent to Weathersfield, in Connecticut, where Governor Wolcott's family of two daughters and a son patriotically melted them into "forty-two thousand bullets."*

Washington, finding that some of his soldiers had taken part in this act, which partook too much of a riotous character to accord with his views of discipline, censured his men in the order of the day, and, while commending the newly-appointed chaplain to their reverential regard, concluded with this general advice to the army in regard to their conduct: "The blessing and protection of Heaven are at all times necessary, but especially so in times of public distress and danger. The general hopes and trusts that every officer and man will endeavor so to live and act as becomes a Christian soldier, defending the dearest rights and liberties of his country."

General Howe seems to have been much encouraged on his arrival at Staten island, by the cheering aspect and liberal promises of his tory friends. "I have the satisfaction," he writes to Lord George Germain, "to inform your lordship that

there is great reason to expect **July 7.** a numerous body of the inhabitants to join the army from the provinces of New York, the Jerseys, and Connecticut, who in this time of universal apprehension only wait for opportunities to give proofs of their loyalty and zeal for government. Sixty men came over a few days ago with a few arms from the neighborhood of Shrewsbury, in Jersey, who are all desirous to serve; and I understand there are five hundred more in that quarter ready to follow their example. This disposition among the people makes me impatient for the arrival of Lord Howe, concluding the powers with which he is furnished will have the best effect at this critical time; but I am still of the opinion that peace will not be restored in America until the rebel army is defeated."

The provincial Congress of New York, having changed its name, in accordance with the Declaration of Independence, to that of the "Convention of the Representatives of the STATE of New York," had appointed a secret committee to sit in the city and counteract the machinations of the royalists, upon which Howe was so confidently relying. Persons of known disaffection and enmity to the cause of America were thus ferreted out and sent away to the jail at Litchfield, Connecticut, and elsewhere. These measures forced such men as the Robertsons and Delanceys to join the enemy openly, and compelled some more timid partisans either to forego all active hostility or to give in their adhesion to the American cause.

The enemy's force continued to gather

---

* After the destruction of the statue of George III., he was called in New York, says Walpole, "the late king."

daily. On the 11th of July, Washington writes: "General Howe's fleet from Halifax has arrived, in number about one hundred and thirty sail. His army is between nine and ten thousand, being joined by some of the regiments from the West Indies, and having fallen in with part of the Highland troops in his passage. He has landed his men on Staten island, which they mean to secure, and is in daily expectation of the arrival of Lord Howe, with one hundred and fifty ships, and a large and powerful reinforcement. This we have from four prisoners who fell into our hands, and some deserters. They add that nothing will be attempted until his arrival."

July 12. Next day, however, the enemy did something, which, although trifling in itself, produced a great commotion. Early in the afternoon, two of the British ships-of-war, the Rose and the Phœnix (one of forty and the other of twenty guns), with three tenders, weighed anchor, and with a brisk and favorable breeze sailed up the North river with the flood-tide. The American batteries along the city and the Jersey shore, and the forts on the banks of the Hudson, kept up a heavy and incessant cannonade, which was returned by the ships as they passed by, but without much effect on either side. Even Fort Washington, with all its formidable preparation, proved of no avail. It seems to have been so placed, that it could neither do nor receive an injury. "We were too high for their guns," says an officer who was present, "to be brought to bear upon us with any certainty, though one ball was thrown into the fort. Our elevated situation was nearly as unfavorable for the success of our fire upon them."

The men-of-war, it is true, had been guarded by sand-bags spread over the decks and raised along the bulwarks, so as to protect them against the American riflemen; while they glided by so rapidly, with the wind and tide in their favor, that it was difficult to point a cannon at them with precision. Their rigging, however, was somewhat damaged, and several shots touched their hulls. Having run the gauntlet of all the batteries and forts, the ships finally came to anchor about forty miles up the river, in the middle of that broad part of the Hudson called Haverstraw bay, where they were out of reach of any shot from either bank.

Washington expected that this movement of the two ships would be immediately followed by others, with the view of landing and seizing the passes in the Highlands. He accordingly sent an express at once to Brigadier-General George Clinton, who commanded the New-York militia on Hudson river, with orders to him to call out instantly as many men as he could, and post them in such a way as to prevent, if possible, the supposed object of the enemy.

Clinton, however, had anticipated these orders, having been notified of the approach of danger by a signal-gun from his brother, who, as colonel, was in command of Fort Constitution below, and by the exaggerated reports of the captains of some sloops who came up the river with the story that New York was attacked. They had seen and heard the firing in the distance between the forts and the Rose and Phœnix, and, putting on all sail, had hastened away with the alarming intelligence of a general attack. Clinton accordingly had ordered out three regiments of militia, one of which he stationed at Fort Constitution, opposite West Point; another at Fort Montgomery below, under his own immediate command; and the third at Newburg, beyond these points. He also had sent word to the masters of all the river-craft which could be reached, to bring their vessels and anchor them off Fort Montgomery, that they might be ready to stretch across the narrowest part of the Hudson there, as a barrier, and to be set fire to in case the enemy's ships attempted to break through them.

The Rose and Phœnix were not immediately followed by any other ships, and, having anchored, remained quietly, while their boats were sent out daily to take soundings. The people, however, on the Hudson, fretted greatly at their presence, and watched every opportunity to harass and to drive them from the river.

July 12. Toward evening, on the same day that the Rose and Phœnix sailed up, several ships arrived from sea and entered the narrows. One of these had a St. George's flag flying from her foretopmast-head, and was saluted as she came in with full volleys from the vessels and the batteries at Staten island. This was the Eagle, which bore the admiral, Lord Howe.

RICHARD (Earl) HOWE was born in 1725, and entered the navy as a midshipman at the age of fourteen. By merit, aided by a powerful patronage, he passed rapidly through the grades of lieutenant, captain, and rear-admiral; and now, on being sent to America, was promoted to the rank of vice-admiral of the blue. On the death of his brother, Lord Howe (who fell at Ticonderoga in 1758), he succeeded to the peerage. The admiral, like the general, had a tall and well-proportioned figure, but his face was dark and stern in expression. His manners, too, were reserved, and he was thought to be somewhat haughty in disposition. He was a brave and skilful officer, and, unlike the general, active and indefatigable in business.

The two brothers had been appointed by Parliament commissioners for restoring peace; and accordingly, as soon as Lord Howe arrived, he drew up, jointly with the general, a proclamation. This document promised pardon to those who, having forsaken their allegiance to the crown in the time of excitement and trouble, would return to their duty. It also offered rewards to those who should aid in the restoration of public tranquillity. The paper was then sent to Franklin, the colonial governor of New Jersey, with the request to circulate it as freely as possible among the people. A copy was obtained by General Mercer, in command of the flying camp at Amboy, and forwarded by him to Washington, who thus spoke of it in his despatch to the president of Congress:—

"When the letter and declaration, from Lord Howe to Mr. Franklin and **July 22.** the other late governors, come to be published, I should suppose the warmest advocate for dependence on the British crown must be silent, and be convinced, beyond all possibility of doubt, that all that has been said about the commissioners was illusory, and calculated expressly to deceive and put off their guard not only the good people of our own country, but those of the English nation that were averse to the proceedings of the king and ministry."

Lord Howe is supposed to have sincerely desired peace, and greatly to have regretted that his arrival had been delayed until after the Declaration of Independence. He is known to have been early interested in the difficulties between the home government and the colonies; and it is related that, when Franklin was in London, he was invited by his lordship to dinner, with the view of extorting from him some information in reference to the probable measures of the American leaders. Lord Howe was ably seconded on this occasion by the diplomacy of his sister. While the former freely circulated the Madeira, the latter brought to play upon the philosopher all the enticements of her seductive graces. But Franklin's sober reason was proof against the intoxication of either the one or the other; and the domestic conspiracy of Lord and Miss Howe was defeated by the strength of head and steadiness of principle of the American patriot.

July 14. On the second day of Lord Howe's arrival in the bay, about three o'clock in the afternoon, word was brought to Washington that a flag had come up from his lordship, and was now detained by two of the American whale-boats on guard a few miles from the city. Washington immediately convened such of the general officers as were not upon other duty, and asked their opinion as to whether he ought to receive any letter directed to him as a private gentleman. Finding that they agreed with his own view, that he should not, he sent Colonel Reed (his former secretary, now adjutant-general) down to meet the flag, and to act accordingly. Reed went down as ordered; and, after passing the usual civilities, the British officer informed him that he had a letter from Lord Howe to Mr. Washington, which he showed, with the address, "*To George Washington, Esquire.*" Colonel Reed replied that there was no such person in the army, and that a letter intended for the general could not be received under such a direction.

The officer expressed great concern, and, stating that it was a letter rather of a civil than a military nature, declared that Lord Howe regretted that he had not arrived sooner, since he had great powers. The anxiety on the part of the officer to have the letter received was very apparent, although he disclaimed all knowledge of its contents. Colonel Reed, however, had received positive orders, and accordingly took his leave. After the two had separated and got some distance away from each other, the officer with the flag put about again with his boat, and asked how *General*—but, catching himself, *Mr.* Washington, would wish to be addressed.* Colonel Reed answered that the general's station was well known, and they could not be at a loss how to

* Irving.

direct to him. He added, moreover, that a proper address would obviate all difficulty of communication, as Lord Howe himself must be aware, since this matter had already been discussed in the course of the previous year.

"I would not," says Washington, commenting upon this affair, "upon any occasion sacrifice essentials to punctilio; but in this instance, the opinion of others concurring with my own, I deemed it a duty to my country and my appointment to insist upon that respect which, in any other than a public view, I would willingly have waved." Congress showed its approval of his conduct in this matter by the resolution "That General Washington, in refusing to receive a letter said to be sent from Lord Howe, and addressed to ‘ *George Washington, Esquire*,' acted with a dignity becoming his station."

Notwithstanding Lord Howe's want of success, his brother the general attempted the same manœuvre, and sent a flag addressed to " *George Washington, Esquire*," with the addition of " *&c., &c., &c*." It was, of course, not received. A few days subsequently, Howe accordingly hit upon another expedient. He sent Lieutenant-Colonel Patterson, the British adjutant-general, with a flag.

July 20. This dignified messenger was met with the usual formalities, and, as he was sent officially by General Howe to the American commander-in-chief, was by the order of Washington conducted ashore and admitted into his presence. The usual preliminary compliments having passed, during which the British colonel addressed Washington by the title of excellency, as he did throughout the interview, business began.

Colonel Patterson commenced by saying that General Howe much regretted the difficulties which had arisen in respect to the letter. He then justified the propriety of the address, on the ground that it was usual with embassadors and plenipotentiaries, when disputes or difficulties of rank arose. The colonel then reminded Washington that he had, during the previous summer, sent a letter to General Howe with the address, " *To the Honorable William Howe, Esquire*." Lord Howe and General Howe, he continued, did not mean to derogate from the respect or rank of General Washington, whose person and character they held in the highest esteem; and, as for the address upon the letter, the " &c., &c., &c.," implied everything which ought to follow. The colonel here produced a letter, which, however, he did not directly offer to General Washington, but, remarking that it was the same as had been already presented, laid it upon the table, where the address, " To George Washington, Esquire, &c., &c., &c.," could be readily seen.

Washington declined to receive it, and remarked that a communication directed to a person in his public character should have some indication of his station, otherwise it would appear a mere private letter. As for the " &c., &c., &c.," Washington said it was true they implied everything, but they also implied anything. In regard to the letter which had been addressed to General Howe without mention of his rank, that had been sent, Washington explained, in answer to one simi-

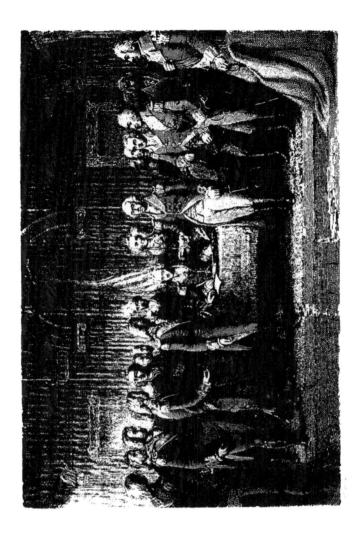

larly addressed to himself, and which had only been received because the officer on duty had not refused it when first presented. Washington now having firmly declared that he should decline to receive any letter directed to him as a private person, when it related to his public station, Colonel Patterson said that General Howe would not urge his delicacy further, and repeated his assertion that no failure of respect was intended.

Patterson then, saying that he would endeavor as well as he could to recollect General Howe's views, briefly gave them, and on finishing took a paper out of his pocket, and, having glanced over it for a moment, remarked that he had expressed nearly the words. A conversation now ensued in regard to the treatment of prisoners; and finally Colonel Patterson alluded to the object of the mission of Lord and General Howe, stating that the goodness and benevolence of the king had induced him to appoint these two gentlemen his commissioners to accommodate the unhappy dispute with the colonies; that they had great powers, and would derive the greatest pleasure from effecting an accommodation; and that he (Colonel Patterson) wished to have his visit considered as making the first advance toward this object.

Washington replied that he was not vested with any powers on this subject by those from whom he derived his authority; but, from what had appeared, Lord and General Howe were only to grant pardons, and that those who had committed no fault wanted no pardon. "We are only defending," added Washington, "what we deem our indisputable rights." To which Colonel Patterson answered, "That would open a very wide field for argument."

The greatest courtesy prevailed during the conference, and at its close Colonel Patterson strongly expressed his acknowledgments that the usual practice of blindfolding had been dispensed with in his case. Washington pressed him to partake of a collation which had been provided, but "he politely declined, alleging his late breakfast." After staying a few moments to be introduced to the general officers, he took leave. Colonel Reed and one of Washington's aids-de-camp accompanied him in the president's barge to his own boat, which awaited him some four miles below the city, where they separated in the best good nature, after a lively chat during their short fellowship.

"This interview," wrote General Howe to Lord George Germain, "was more polite than interesting. However, it induced me to change my superscription for the attainment of an end so desirable; and in this view I flatter myself it will not be disapproved." Washington was subsequently always addressed by the title of "general." Lord Howe, however, though evidently desirous from the beginning of being courteous in this particular, hesitated for fear of disapproval on the part of the British ministry, whose insolent tyranny hesitated at no insult, however gross. An interview with Lord Howe, ten days after the visit of Colonel Patterson, showed that his lordship was still haggling about this matter of titles.

Colonel Palfrey, paymaster-general of

July 30. the army, was sent, together with another officer, on board the Eagle, Lord Howe's ship, to negotiate an exchange of prisoners. The colonel gave this account of his visit, in a letter to Congress: "We were treated with the utmost politeness and civility by Lord Howe. He spoke with the highest respect of General Washington, and lamented the nice distinctions which, he said, prevented his addressing him by letter; and said he wished to convey his sentiments to him in any mode of address that might prevent his being blamed by the king his master.

"In all his discourse he called him *General* Washington, and frequently said the *states* of America. He said the Congress had greatly hurt his feelings by reminding him, in one of their publications, of the esteem and respect they had for the memory of his brother, and drawing by manifest inference a contrast between the survivors and the deceased; that no man could feel more sensibly the respect shown to their family than his lordship and the general; that they should always esteem America for it, and particularly Massachusetts Bay; and added, 'I hope America will one day or other be convinced that, in our affection for that country, we also are HOWES.' His lordship, when speaking of his brother, was greatly affected, and I could perceive a tear standing in his eye.

"He hinted an inclination that I should take the letter to General Washington, with the addition of ' &c., &c., &c.,' which he said would imply everything that we could desire, and at the same time save him from censure. I gave him to understand that, as it had been before refused under the same circumstances, I could not with propriety receive it, especially as it was against the express direction of Congress. When we parted, he desired his compliments to General Washington."[*] This closed the chapter of "&c., &c., &c."

CHAPTER XXIII.

The Phœnix and Rose up the Hudson.—The Inefficacy of the Forts.—A Chain put across the River.—Anderson's Fire-Ships.—Old Put's Pet Project.—Chevaux-de-Frise, Chains, Booms, &c.—The "American Turtle."—Washington rejoices over the Victory at Charleston.—The Ten Thousand British on Staten Island.—Washington determines to remain on the Defensive.—The British Thirty Thousand strong.—The Americans about half the Number.—The Fire-Galleys put in Operation on the Hudson.—The Rose and Phœnix forced to shift their Quarters.—The Fate of Anderson, the American Turtle, &c.

1776. THE Americans were greatly disturbed by those two British ships, the Phœnix and Rose, quietly lying at their anchors up the Hudson. There they were, only forty miles above New York, cutting off all communication by water between the city and Albany, and between Washington's army and that of Schuyler upon the lakes. It was true

* Sparks's Life of Washington.

they were watched so closely by Clinton and his militiamen stationed on the banks of the river, that they were prevented from making a landing, or from having communication with the tories who, with " the most diabolical dispositions and intentions," abounded in those quarters.

Washington was aware of the inefficacy of the American forts; and when the two ships ran by them, it exhibited a proof, he says, " of what I had long most religiously believed, and that is, that a vessel with a brisk wind and strong tide can not, unless by a chance shot, be stopped by a battery, unless you can place some obstruction in the water to impede her motion within reach of your guns."

The ingenuity of all was now being exercised to destroy or drive away these impudent intruders. Clinton was busy above, and particularly active when he discovered that the ships had one night moved still farther up the river, and anchored within six miles of Fort Montgomery, where he himself was stationed. He was anxious lest they might " take advantage of a dark night and slip by him in the deep shadows of the mountains." He accordingly determined to be on the alert. Guards were sent below, and preparations made with combustibles to light alarmfires, so soon as the ships should move. Fire-rafts were constructed at Poughkeepsie, and sloops filled with inflammable materials of all kinds, and kept ready to be lashed together and sent down against the Rose and Phœnix; while an iron chain was forged, to stretch across from Fort Montgomery to Anthony's Nose, in order to put a stop to their progress should they attempt to sail up.

Washington, too, was vexing himself with all sorts of contrivances to do something effective from below against the audacious tars. Governor Trumbull, of Connecticut, had sent him two row-galleys, fitted out by the whalemen of New London, and promised him a third; while Cooke, the governor of Rhode Island, had been urged to do something with the nautical resources of his province in the emergency. One " Mr. Anderson" had been received into the confidence of the commander-in-chief, to whom he had been especially commended by the president of Congress. He had laid before that body a plan for the destruction of the British fleet in the harbor of New York, which had been received with such favor, that he was sent to Washington, with the request that he would facilitate his proposed operations. Anderson himself was so sanguine, that he declared he was willing to risk his life in the experiment. He was confirmed in his self-confidence by a previous trial of his plan against the British vessels off Quebec, which would have succeeded, as he believed, " had it not been defeated by the accident of his being burnt himself" instead of the ships, " and by the enemy's getting intelligence of his plan and taking measures to counteract it." He was now at work under the eye of Washington, **July 27.** who writes that " the fire-ships are going on under Mr. Anderson's direction, but rather slowly."

Anderson himself, with the usual enthusiasm of projectors, gives a more en-

40

couraging account of his progress. "I have been," he writes to the president of Congress, "for some time past very assiduous in the preparation of fire-ships. Two are already complete, and hauled off into the stream; two more will be off to-morrow, and the residue in a very short time. In my next, I hope to give you a particular account of a general conflagration, as everything in my power shall be exerted for the demolition of the enemy's fleet. I expect to take an active part, and be an instrument for that purpose. I am determined (God willing) to make a conspicuous figure among them, by being 'a burning and a shining light,' and thereby serve my country, and have the honor of meeting the approbation of Congress."

July 31.

"I am preparing," writes Washington, "some obstructions for the channel nearly opposite the works at the upper end of the island." And a few days later he says: "The hulks and three *chevaux-de-frise*, that had been preparing to obstruct the channel, have got up to the place they are intended for, and will be sunk as soon as possible." This contrivance was due to the Yankee ingenuity of "Old Put," who was as full of enthusiasm for his pet project as Anderson, whose darling invention, it would seem from the following letter, that Putnam had adopted with all the affection as if it had been his own offspring :—

"The enemy's fleet," he writes to General Gates, "now lies in the bay very safe, close under Staten island. Their troops possess no land here but the island. Is it not very strange

July 26.

that these invincible troops, who were to destroy and lay waste all this country with their fleets and army, are so fond of islands and peninsulas, and dare not put their feet on the main? But I hope, by the blessing of God and good friends, we shall pay them a visit on their island. For that end we are preparing fourteen fire-ships to go into their fleet, some of which are ready charged and fitted to sail, and I hope soon to have them all fixed.

"We are preparing *chevaux-de-frise*, at which we make great despatch by the help of ships, which are to be sunk; a scheme of mine, which you may be assured is very simple, a plan of which I send you. The two ships' sterns lie toward each other, about seventy feet apart. Three large logs, which reach from ship to ship, are fastened to them. The two ships and logs stop the river two hundred and eighty feet. The ships are to be sunk, and, when hauled down on one side, the picks will be raised to a proper height, and they must inevitably stop the river if the enemy will let us sink them."

Nor was this the last of the projects. A mechanician of Connecticut, of the name of Bushnell, had invented a boat, so contrived as to be rowed and steered, and raised and sunk under water, at the will of the operator within. To a part of this submarine craft was attached a moveable magazine of powder, which was to be exploded by means of a clocklike piece of mechanism. It was proposed to get a bold navigator to start with this machine, dive down into the bay, and bring up under an enemy's vessel; and then, detaching the magazine, and boring through the ship's copper, to fasten it like a barnacle to the bottom. This being done, the magazine was to be wound up, and its going off so timed, that the adventurous submarine navigator might have an opportunity of making good progress homeward bound when the "American Turtle," as the machine was called, should begin its infernal operations.

"Old Put" likewise took kindly to the "American Turtle." "Major-General Putnam," says Thacher, "was decidedly of opinion that its operations might be attended with the desired success; accordingly, he encouraged the inventor, and resolved to be himself a spectator of the experiment on the British shipping in New-York harbor." While these schemes of destruction were plotting, an attempt was made against the enemy, according to the principles of more regular warfare.

Ship after ship continued to add its strength to the formidable fleet in the bay. Crowded transports had come and landed their thousands; and now came **August 1.** Sir Henry Clinton and Earl Cornwallis, after their defeat before Charleston. Washington, cheered by the intelligence which he had received some few days before the arrival of the British from the South, of the American success, concludes his letter full of anxious business, addressed to Schuyler, with the unusually lively remark for the sedate commander-in-chief: "Sir Peter Parker and his fleet got a severe drubbing in an attack made upon our works on Sullivan's island."

To his army Washington announces the southern victory with a decorous gravity, and makes it an occasion for the encouragement of the martial spirit and patriotic emulation of his soldiers: "The general has great pleasure," are the words of the order of the day, "in communicating to the officers and soldiers of this army the signal success of the American arms, under General Lee, in South Carolina. This glorious example of our troops, under the like circumstances with us, the general hopes, will animate every officer and soldier to imitate and even outdo them, when the enemy shall make the same attempt on us. With such a bright example before us of what can be done by brave and spirited men fighting in defence of their country, we shall be loaded with a double share of shame and infamy if we do not acquit ourselves with courage, or a determined resolution to conquer or die."

Washington had but little hope of acting offensively with advantage against the enemy. The British had a much superior army in numbers, discipline, and condition. General Howe had already landed ten thousand troops on Staten island; and his army, with those afloat in the transports in the bay, and those hourly expected, would amount soon, it was supposed, to twenty-five thousand men all told. The Americans could only count on about ten thousand men fit for duty; while the whole of Washington's army, including the sick and others, did not number much more than seventeen thousand. "Our situation at present," says Washington, "both in regard to men and other matters, is such as not to make it advisable to attempt anything against them, surrounded as they are by water, and covered with ships, lest a miscarriage should be productive of unhappy and fatal consequences. It is provoking, nevertheless, to have them so near, without being able to give them any disturbance."

There was little to be done but to remain on the defensive, and await the operations of the enemy. Washington, however, was not much more sanguine of his means of defence than of his powers of offence. "What kind of opposition we shall be able to make," he says, "time only can show. I can only say that the men appear to be in good spirits, and, if they will stand by me, the place shall not be carried without some loss, notwithstanding we are not yet in such a posture of defence as I could wish."

Washington, nevertheless, determined to make "some efforts to annoy the enemy," but not to put "too much to hazard, or in any manner to risk." It was accordingly proposed to begin at Staten island. It was found "impracticable to do anything upon a large scale," and it was therefore resolved merely to make an humble attempt from the Jersey shore. Major Knowlton, who was stationed at Bergen, New Jersey, and General Mercer, in command of the flying camp at Amboy, were directed to concoct a plan and carry it into execution. These two accordingly got ready a small force and some boats, and, marching down to the shore in the evening, prepared to embark when it should become sufficiently dark. The night, however, proved so stormy, and the waters of the "Kill" were in such a

state of agitation, that it was thought advisable to postpone the enterprise. On a subsequent occasion it was proposed to make another attempt, and a formidable force of nearly four thousand men was ordered out for the purpose; but it was found to be impossible to procure boats enough to carry more than half of the troops across to the island. All such attempts were therefore abandoned, and the attention of the whole army was now being concentrated upon the probable movement of the enemy.

Two deserters having come in, are taken to headquarters, and from them Washington learns "that **August 7.** General Clinton and Lord Cornwallis, with the whole southern army, have arrived on Staten island from South Carolina, in number about three or four thousand; that the fleet which came in a few days since, are the Hessians and Scotch Highlanders, part of twelve thousand who were left off Newfoundland, in the whole making about thirty thousand men; and that it is said by the officers of the army and navy, they are to attack New York and Long island in the course of a week."

"When," says Washington to Governor Trumbull, of Connecticut, "I consider the weakness of our army by sickness, the great extent of ground we have to defend, and the amazing slowness with which the levies come forward, I think it is absolutely necessary that the neighboring militia should be immediately sent to our assistance."

Washington's anxiety may be inferred from what he adds in the same letter: "The disgrace of the British arms to the southward, and the season being far advanced, will make them exert every nerve against us in this quarter. To trust altogether in the justice of our cause, without our own utmost exertions, would be tempting Providence; and, that you may judge of our situation, I give you the present state of our army. (Present fit for duty, 10,514; sick present, 3,039; sick absent, 629; on command, 2,946; on furlough, 97: total, 17,225.) By this you will see we are to oppose an army of thirty thousand experienced veterans with about one third the number of raw troops, and these scattered some fifteen miles apart."

There was now an opportunity of testing the various means of mischief so ingeniously devised against the Rose and Phœnix. Six of the row-galleys were soon got ready, and, being sent up the river, were manned by crews of doughty fresh-water men, principally belonging to Tarrytown, and commanded by Colonel Tupper. This little fleet boldly pushed out into the "Tappan sea," and began an attack upon the two British cruisers. The fight was gallantly maintained for nearly two hours, in the course of which the big ships were repeatedly hulled; but the little fleet, being badly damaged in return, was finally obliged to "haul off." "Never," says a writer quoted by Irving, "did men behave with more firm, determined spirit, than our little crews. One of our tars, being mortally wounded, cried to his companions: 'I am a dying man; revenge my blood, my boys, and carry me alongside my gun, that I may die there.' We were so preserved by a gracious Providence, that in all our galleys

we had but two men killed and fourteen wounded, two of which are thought dangerous. We hope to have another brush with these pirates before they leave our river; which God prosper."

The fire-ships, too, were brought into play, and not without effect. Two of them were sent up the river, in order to set fire to the British **Aug. 16.** vessels. One got alongside of the Phœnix and grappled with her for some minutes, but she succeeded in clearing herself. The other made an attempt upon the Rose, but, failing to reach her, fell afoul of one of the tenders, and soon had her in a blaze. The crews behaved with great resolution and intrepidity; and one of the captains stuck so long to his fire-ship, that he was finally obliged to make his escape by plunging into the water and swimming for his life.

Next morning the Rose and Phœnix, evidently very much discomposed by the dangerous encounter of the day before, made ready to shift their quarters. While the ships were weighing anchor, a bold militia lieutenant and two men pushed off in a boat from the shore, and towed in the hulk of the burnt tender, in spite of the enemy's guns, which kept up a brisk fire. The Phœnix and Rose, now taking advantage of a fresh and fair wind and an ebbing tide, hoisted all sail and hurried away, after a sojourn of five weeks. The American riflemen along the banks of the river were on the alert, and did not fail to shoot with their usual skill at the flying vessels; but most of the men were kept so close below, and those on duty upon deck were so well guarded by the thick ramparts of sandbags, that the rifles failed to do much execution. The forts, too, were busy, and their cannon were so well pointed, that the Phœnix was three times hulled and a tender once by the shots from Fort Washington; while the Rose did not escape without a ball from the opposite side of the river. They finally succeeded in passing without much damage, and were not stopped even by the *chevaux-de-frise* upon which " Old Put" had expended so much ingenuity and labor, and so greatly calculated. By some oversight or other, his famous obstruction had not been completed, and the vessels passed through the opening left unclosed.

Of Anderson's project and extensive preparations nothing more was heard; and he failed to prove " a burning and a shining light" of as mighty an illumination and conflagration as he had promised. His fellow-projector Bushnell, the Connecticut mechanician, also disappointed the expectations of his enthusiastic friends. Though it is somewhat in anticipation of events, it may be as well to finish here the history of these famous projects, by recording the end of the " American Turtle." It was determined to make the first experiment upon Lord Howe's own ship, the Eagle, of sixty-four guns. Accordingly, the machine was got ready, and a night appointed. A number of officers collected together on the wharf at Whitehall, among whom General Putnam, as the chief patron of the scheme, was in a high state of active enthusiasm on the occasion. At the very beginning, however, there was a serious disappoint-

ment. Bushnell's brother, having been well drilled for the purpose, was to navigate the machine; but unfortunately, just as he was about to make his adventurous voyage, he was suddenly taken ill.

" Old Put," however, was not to be thus put off; so he selected a sergeant out of his own Connecticut regiment, in whose native ingenuity he had naturally great faith, and appointed him to the command of the "American Turtle." The sergeant readily consented to take charge, and, being installed, strove at once to make himself acquainted with the mysteries of the machine. All being ready, the "American Turtle" was started on its adventurous voyage. " Old Put" and his fellow-officers, having bid a God-speed to the bold sergeant, remained upon the wharf, anxiously awaiting the result. The night passed slowly, the day began to break, and still the great ship of the admiral reposed quietly in her smooth berth off Governor's island. The Eagle was evidently there; but the "American Turtle" —where was it? The waters of the bay were undisturbed; the bell-watches of the ship were striking with their usual regularity; the island had still the apparent solidity of *terra firma*; and the sun appeared to be rising as orderly and in as good time as ever!

At last, the officers from the wharf at Whitehall see a movement on Governor's island. A barge filled with men shoves off and rapidly approaches the admiral's ship. It is seen suddenly to stop, and then to return in great haste, as if frightened by a dark object which can now be discerned floating quietly upon the surface of the bay. In a moment after, a loud noise is heard, "like thunder," and a great column of water rushes up with the force of a waterspout just alongside the Eagle. Instantly her cables are cut, and she drifts down the bay with the ebbing tide.

The adventurous Connecticut sergeant in the meantime pops up from below, in his submarine boat; but, finding that he is within range of the sentries on Governor's island, he dives down again, and does not make his appearance upon the surface of the water until within hailing distance of his patron, "Old Put," on the Whitehall wharf. He is now towed in by a small boat, and on his arrival gives an account of his voyage. It seems he had reached in safety the place whither he was bound, under the bottom of the Eagle; but, finding that her copper was too thick to penetrate, for the purpose of attaching his magazine of powder, he had visited some of the other vessels: meeting, however, the same difficulty under them, he finally let off his infernal machine, which produced, as we have seen, the commotion in the water and the agitation in the fleet. The officers on the Eagle reported afterward that they had been aware of something under the bottom of their ship, but, supposing it was nothing but a floating log, they took no further thought of the matter.

CHAPTER XXIV.

General Greene on the Alert at Long Island.—The British Plan of Attack—The Tories on Long Island ferreted out, and dealt with vigorously.—Washington touched with the Sufferings and Dangers of the People of New York.—Rumors of Peace.—Greene falls ill.—Putnam succeeds to the Command on Long Island.—The Enemy cross, land, and beat back the Provincial Outposts.—The Excitement in New York.—Washington's Preparations for the Worst.—The Provincial Defences.—The Struggle.

1776. GENERAL GREENE, in command of the American troops and works on Long island, was on the alert, watching **August 9.** every movement of the enemy. Now he sends word to Washington, at New York, that his lookouts had reported that on the previous evening a hundred boats were seen bringing troops from Staten island to the transports, and that three of the men-of-war had moved down toward the narrows. A general embarkation, it was supposed, had begun, and an attack might be hourly expected. Deserters came in, and confirmed these reports. The plans of the Howes were even openly discussed. Ships were to sail up the North and East rivers, and land the British troops on both sides of the island of New York, and, forming a junction, to hem in the Americans and hold them at their mercy.

Washington was active, and hurried to bring all his resources to bear on the emergency. He writes to General Mercer, in New Jersey, to send him two thousand men from his flying camp, but confesses that he knows not where they are to come from, for, according to the "general's last return, not more than three or four hundred of the new levies had come in." Smallwood's battalion of Marylanders had, however, already been sent. The convention of New York was emphatically urged to do its best, and responded by a call upon the militia of the state, to join the encampment above Kingsbridge. The summons was urgent, and all were to come, however accoutred, it being ordered " that each man who shall not have arms shall bring with him a shovel, spade, pickaxe, or a scythe straightened and fixed on a pole." Even all the disarmed and disaffected, from sixteen to fifty years of age, were to be brought forcibly along, that they might serve as fatigue-men to the respective regiments.

The recreant were to be severely dealt with; and when, for example, it was discovered that the inhabitants of Kings county, on Long island, did not intend to oppose the enemy, a committee was appointed to visit them, and, if they found them still in that temper, was authorized to disarm and secure the disaffected persons, remove or destroy the stock of grain, and if they should judge it necessary, to lay the whole county waste. Some of these Long-islanders did not appear very formidable, as may be judged from the account of a party of tories by General Greene, who was actively engaged in ferreting them out:—

"I have examined the prisoners," says Greene, "and find them to be a poor parcel of ignorant, cowardly fellows. Two are tailors and the other two common laborers. They candidly confess that they set off with an intention of going to Staten island; not with any intention of joining the enemy, but only to get out of the way of fighting here. There has been a draft amongst the militia to fill the new levies, and it was rumored that these persons were drawn. It was also reported that they were to go to the northern army, and that almost all that went there either died or were killed. The prospect was so shocking to them, and to their grandmothers and aunts, that I believe they were persuaded to run away. Never did I see fellows more frightened. They wept like children, and were exceedingly sorrowful. I beg your excellency's direction how to dispose of them. They do not appear to be acquainted with one public matter. They have been *toryish;* I fancy not from principle, but from its being the prevailing sentiment in the country."

The tories, however, were not by any means all of this character. New York was full of men of wealth and position who were lending their aid and encouragement to the enemy. Washington was very solicitous to have them removed; and suspected persons were being daily arrested and sent off to Connecticut, where they were confided to the safe keeping of the patriotic Governor Trumbull. "There are but few of them," says Washington, "who will not defray their own expenses," and they were promised every indulgence consistent with the public safety. They expressed "a very earnest desire to be permitted to choose their own lodgings and accommodations," to which Washington, with his usual gentlemanly consideration, says, " I see no objection."

Washington's good heart was touched and his gentle humanity called into exercise by the condition of the helpless in New York. He writes to the New-York convention : " When I consider that the city of New York will in all human probability very soon be the scene of a bloody conflict, I can not but view the great numbers of women, children, and infirm persons, remaining in it, with the most melancholy concern. When the men-of-war passed up the river, the shrieks and cries of these poor creatures, running every way with their children, were truly distressing ; and I fear they will have an unhappy effect on the ears and minds of our young and inexperienced soldiery. Can no method be devised for their removal ?"

General Howe still lingered in his purpose, and had so long delayed his attack, that the American soldiers, at the suggestion of artful emissaries from the enemy, began to discuss the probability of peace. This became so general, that Washington thought it necessary to allude to it in the order of the day : " The general being informed, to his great surprise, that a report prevails, and is industriously spread far and wide, that Lord Howe has made propositions of peace, calculated by designing persons probably to lull us into a fatal security ; his duty obliges him to declare that no such offer has been made by Lord Howe, but, on the contrary, from the best intelligence

Aug. 20.

41

he can procure, the army may expect an attack as soon as the wind and tide shall prove favorable. He hopes, therefore, that every man's mind and arms will be prepared for action, and, when called to it, show our enemies and the whole world that freemen contending on their own land are superior to any mercenaries."

While artful gossips were distracting the minds of his soldiers with rumors of peace, the American chief was awaiting the " bloody conflict" which he knew was inevitable. He expected the enemy each moment. The signals and alarms were ready : two cannon were to be discharged from Fort George, at the lowest part of the city ; a flag in the daytime, or a light at night, was to be raised on Bayard's hill, and three guns of its battery fired quickly but distinctly, to signify to the troops to proceed to their alarm-posts and prepare for action ; while the drums were to beat to arms at the first sound of the alarm-cannon.

The position of the Americans was not very encouraging, and, to add to their disadvantages, General Greene unfortunately fell ill. " I am very sorry," he writes to Washington, " to be under the necessity of acquainting you that I am confined to my bed with a raging fever. The critical situation of affairs makes me the more anxious ; but I hope, through the assistance of Providence, to be able to ride, before the presence of the enemy may make it absolutely necessary." This was a serious misfortune, as Greene had the command on Long island, and, having directed the construction of the works there, and thor-

Aug. 15.

oughly studied the topography, he alone probably was capable of a judicious defence.

Washington, aware of Greene's efficiency, anxiously awaited his return to duty, and hesitated to appoint a successor. The threatening aspect of the enemy, however, forbade any further delay, and the chief finally ordered Putnam to the general command on Long island, and General Sullivan to the special charge of the troops without the lines. The loss of Greene at this moment was especially felt, as it appeared probable that the enemy would first move against Long island. Washington, it is true, knew that it was impossible to prevent Howe from landing on the island, as its great extent afforded "a variety of places favorable for that purpose," and the whole of the American works were "at the end opposite to the city." With Greene in command, he had hopes, no doubt, of holding the position at Brooklyn. Now, however, he seems less sanguine, and says, "We shall attempt to harass them as much as possible, which will be all that we can do."

Aug. 20.

The long-expected movement of the enemy at last began. The men-of-war had been anchored at the narrows, to cover the landing; and, as soon as the day dawned, the tents on Staten island were struck, and the troops embarked. Soldiers, too, principally Hessians, crowded the decks of the fleet of transports, and thronged over the ships' sides into the boats. Boat followed boat in quick succession, and, passing rapidly to the shore, and making for Gravesend

Aug. 22.

bay, landed the men near Gravesend and New Utrecht, on Long island. As the troops debarked, and crowded up in thousands toward the high ground, Colonel Hand retired with his riflemen from his post on the hill, burning the wheat and destroying whatever else might fall into the hands of the British.

"Nine thousand men have landed and approached within three miles of the American lines," is the intelligence brought by a hurried messenger to Washington. He immediately sends six battalions to reinforce the troops at Brooklyn, and is ready to detach five more in case that this movement of the enemy does not prove a feint, and that the fleet should not move up with the remainder of the army and make an attack upon New York. While in this state of uncertainty about the precise manœuvres of Howe, Washington is well persuaded that, whatever they may be, "a little time will produce some important events.... I hope," he says, "they will be happy." He is encouraged somewhat by the temper of his men. The reinforcement sent off had gone in "high spirits," and "the whole of the army, that are effective and capable of duty, discover the same and great cheerfulness."

Still further to encourage the good spirit of his soldiers, and to remind them of their high duties, Washington addresses them in these ardent words: "The enemy have now landed on Long island, and the hour is fast approaching on which the honor and success of this army, and the safety of our bleeding country, will depend. Remember, officers and soldiers, that you are

Aug. 23.

freemen, fighting for the blessings of liberty; that slavery will be your portion, and that of your posterity, if you do not acquit yourselves like men. Remember how your courage and spirit have been despised and traduced by your cruel invaders; though they have found by dear experience at Boston, Charleston, and other places, what a few brave men, contending in their own land, and in the best of causes, can do against hirelings and mercenaries.

"Be cool, but determined; do not fire at a distance, but wait for orders from your officers. It is the general's express orders that if any man attempt to skulk, lie down, or retreat without orders, he be instantly shot down as an example. He hopes no such will be found in this army; but, on the contrary, that every one for himself resolving to conquer or die, and trusting in the smiles of Heaven upon so just a cause, will behave with bravery and resolution. Those who are distinguished for their gallantry and good conduct, may depend upon being honorably noticed, and suitably rewarded; and if this army will but emulate and imitate their brave countrymen in other parts of America, he has no doubt they will, by a glorious victory, save their country, and acquire to themselves immortal honor."

The inhabitants of New York were in the meantime in a state of great excitement. The struggle was now almost at their doors, and they hourly, as they listened with trembling to the sound of the cannon's roar, expected that the enemy would be in their midst. To the certain horrors of the sword were added the terrors of fire, which they feared was about to desolate their homes. It was rumored throughout the town that, in case the American army should be obliged to retreat, the city would be burned. The New-York convention wrote with anxious alarm to Washington, who replied: "I can assure you, gentlemen, that this report is not founded upon the least authority from me; on the contrary, I am so sensible of the value of such a city, and the consequences of its destruction to many worthy citizens and their families, that nothing but the last necessity, and that such as should justify me to the whole world, would induce me to give orders for that purpose."

Washington, with his usual caution and systematic regard to business, had placed all the papers he held "respecting the affairs of the state" in a large box, nailed them up, and committed them to the care of Lieutenant-Colonel Reed, brother of his old secretary (now adjutant-general), to be delivered to Congress. "I hope," he says, "the event will show the caution unnecessary; but yet prudence required that it should be done, lest by any accident they might fall into their hands." Mrs. Washington had left New York some time previously, and was now on her way to Mount Vernon; while the rest of the wives and families of the general officers had also gone for security to their homes, or into the interior of the country. All were evidently preparing for the worst.

The British continued to land on Long island without opposition. On the first day eight thousand came, and in two days more the whole   Aug. 22.

invading force, amounting to ten thousand men and forty cannon, reached the ground. Forming as they arrived, they marched inland for several miles and then encamped.

General Putnam was now in command of the American troops within the lines. The works, consisting of redoubts and intrenchments, stretched from Wallabout bay on the north to Gowanus on the south —across the neck of that peninsula over which a city now expands, but within which at that time there were only a few scattered houses, forming the village of Brooklyn. Opposite, to the northwest, stands New York, separated from Brooklyn by the East river, nearly a mile broad at that point. To the west lies Governor's island, where the Americans had erected a fort; and at Red Hook, on the southwest corner of the peninsula, was a strong battery.

Beginning about two and a half miles to the east of the American lines, there was a ridge of hills, which, covered with thick wood, extended for three miles toward Jamaica on the northeast, and to the narrows for the same distance on the southwest. Through this natural barrier across the island, there were three narrow roads, bounded on each side by acclivities. One passed along the shore, from Gowanus to the narrows; a second led directly east to Jamaica, through Bedford; and the third, which was between the two, passed through the hills to Flatbush on the south. There were, however, by-paths and a narrow causeway, which, clearing the ridge, passed well to the east, and by which the passes through the hills

near their termination on the Jamaica road could be reached. Two of these passes through the hills were guarded by outposts of eight hundred men each, and hastily-constructed breastworks of trunks of trees and brushwood; the third, leading through Bedford, seems to have been overlooked. Colonel Miles was, however, posted beyond the hills, to the south of Bedford, to watch the advance of the enemy in that quarter, and to reconnoitre the approaches toward the Jamaica road. The chief command of all the forces outside the lines was intrusted to General Sullivan, who had arrived on the ground but a few days before the engagement, and was now posted in person with a considerable force, defended by a redoubt, within the mountain-pass on the road to Flatbush.

General Howe, well informed by his tory confederates on Long island, had arranged his plan of attack with skilful adaptation to the nature of the country. His army was separated into three divisions: the centre, composed chiefly of the Hessians, under De Heister; the left wing, of a small force of British, under General Grant; and the right, which constituted the chief body of troops, under General Clinton, aided by Earls Cornwallis and Percy, and accompanied by Howe himself.

Soon after landing, the army began its march. Grant led his force with slow deliberation along the road overlooking the river, and leading toward the right of the Americans. De Heister marched his centre from New Utrecht direct to Flatbush; while Howe and Clinton hurried with their right, composed of the main force, to Flatlands, and thence toward the Jamaica road.

Howe's plan was, by means of this circuitous route, to turn the left of the Americans, and thus taking them by surprise, to hem them in between his right coming from behind, and the left and centre advancing in front. Grant and De Heister were accordingly ordered to move deliberately, and not to precipitate an attack until signal-guns from Clinton, who had the chief active command, should announce to them the success of his manœuvre.

De Heister, finding the central pass occupied by Colonel Hand and his riflemen, who had retired there upon the landing of the British at New Utrecht, did not give immediate battle, but retired, in accordance with his orders, to Flatbush, where he posted his men for the night.

Grant in the meantime advanced along the road by the shore, driving before him the Americans, who fled without firing a gun. He continues his march unopposed during the night, and at break of day has got through the pass in the hills, and is marching toward the American lines beyond. General Parsons, in command of the outpost, now succeeds in rallying some of the fugitives, and, posting them advantageously on a hill, checks the British advance within about two miles of the American camp, until the arrival of Lord Stirling, who is sent by Putnam to his aid with fifteen hundred men.

Washington meanwhile crosses over to Brooklyn, and anxiously strives to discover the manœuvres of the enemy. He remains the whole day with Putnam in his camp, and counsels **Aug. 26.** him in the emergency. He observes "a scattering, unmeaning, and wasteful fire" from his undisciplined soldiery, and he therefore desires Putnam "to call the colonels and commanding officers without loss of time" before him, and to "let them afterward do the same by their respective officers, and charge them in express and positive terms to stop these irregularities, as they value the good of the service, their own honor, and the safety of the army, which, under God, depends wholly upon the good order and government that is observed in it." Proper lines of defence were ordered to be formed around the encampment, and works raised on the most advantageous ground. The guards were to be strictly instructed in their duties, and a brigadier of the day was to remain constantly upon the lines, that he might be on the spot to command and see that orders were executed. Field-officers were also to be appointed, to go the rounds and report the situation of the guards; and no person was to be allowed to pass beyond without special order in writing. The woods were to be secured by abattis; the wood next to Red Hook was to be well attended to, and some of "the most disorderly riflemen" posted in it; while the militia who "have seen least service" were to be kept within the interior works, and the "best men" were to do their utmost to prevent the approach of the enemy.

Foreseeing a general attack, Washington returns to the city at night, full of anxious expectation of what the morrow may bring forth.

Aug. 27. Lord Stirling arrived early in the morning with his fifteen hundred men, composed of the reinforcements sent by Washington, which were the choicest of his troops. These were Atlee's, Haslet's, and Smallwood's regiments, of Pennsylvania, Delaware, and Maryland. Stirling posted most of his force on the acclivity of what is now called "Battle hill," in Greenwood; and the rest, under Atlee, in a neighboring wood, some little distance in advance. Grant continued to approach until he reached an orchard, within a hundred yards or so of Stirling, when the latter briskly attacked him.

The right wing of the British, having reached Flatbush, began their silent march at nine o'clock in the evening. General Clinton led the van; then came Earl Percy, with the artillery and dragoons; while Earl Cornwallis, accompanied by Howe, the commander-in-chief, followed in the rear with the reserve. Guided by a tory Long-islander through by-paths and over a causeway raised above a swamp, the van continues to march without disturbance. On arriving within a half-mile of the Jamaica road, Clinton brings his men to a halt, and sends out a reconnoitring-party. They soon return, bringing back a mounted patrol of American officers whom they have captured, and the word that the road is unoccupied. Clinton immediately sends forward a body of light-infantry to secure it, and following at the break of day, with the rest of his force, takes possession of the hill through which the road passes.

The defence of this pass had been overlooked; and, moreover, the outposts had been apparently neglectful in watching and reporting in time the progress of Clinton's force. Colonel Miles, whose duty it was to guard this quarter, was not aware, until too late, of the enemy's approach; and General Sullivan himself seems to have been remiss in not sending out fresh patrols when he found those previously sent were so long in returning, as they well might be, since they had, as we have related, fallen into the hands of the enemy.

CHAPTER XXV.

The Struggle continued.—Success of General Howe's Plan.—Assisted by his Brother, Lord Howe.—The Firmness of the Delawares and Marylanders.—Lord Stirling hemmed in.—Tries to escape.—Is forced to surrender.—De Heister and the Hessians.—Sullivan retreats.—The Hessians show no Mercy.—Sullivan taken Prisoner.—The Loss on Both Sides.—The Americans withdraw within their Line of Defence.—Sullivan excuses Himself.—The Americans reinforced.—The Movement of the British.—Washington resolves to retreat.

1776. CLINTON, possessed of the Jamaica road, passed rapidly on with his van through the pass in the Bedford hills. His light-infantry then pushed on in the direction of the American lines; and finding no opposition but here and there a small post, which was attacked and speedily forced, they continued their march. The artillery coming up, Clinton ordered two signal-guns to be fired, to signify to Grant and De Heister that his manœuvre had succeeded, and that they were now to begin a vigorous attack. The design of Howe had been successful. The attention of the Americans had been diverted from Clinton's fatal movement on their left by Grant's leisurely advance on the right. Lord Howe, too, had aided in furthering the deceit by bringing up some of his ships from the narrows, and opening a noisy cannonade upon Governor's island and the battery at Red Hook. Putnam and Sullivan were induced to believe that the chief danger was on the right of their lines, and they had accordingly concentrated all their force in that direction.

Grant had coquetted for several hours with Lord Stirling and his force: now advancing his light troops within a hundred yards or so, and exchanging fires with the American riflemen, then ordering them back to his main body; and, again, commencing a desultory cannonade with his two fieldpieces, and thus appearing to fear a general engagement. Colonel Haslet, in command of the southern troops, who was unconscious of the enemy's purpose, says: "The Delawares and Marylanders stood firm to the last; and, after a variety of skirmishing, the Delawares drew up on the side of a hill, and stood upward of four hours, with a firm, determined countenance, in close array, their colors flying, the enemy's artillery playing on them all the while, not *daring to advance and attack them, though six times their number, and nearly surrounding them*." The Delawares and Marylanders were undoubtedly as brave men as ever fought; but Grant, in holding off, was merely obeying orders.

The firing of Clinton's troops in his rear now first awakens Stirling to the consciousness that he is hemmed in between them and Grant in front. The earl's only thought at this moment is of escape; while Grant, catching the sound of the guns, knows that it is a signal for action, and pushes on his advance. The Americans nearest at hand are dispersed, and Atlee their colonel taken prisoner.

Lord Stirling strives to make his way back to the American lines by a circuitous route toward the shore, in course of which he would be obliged to ford a creek at Yellow Mills. He reaches this place, and finds himself opposed by Lord Cornwallis, who has been detached from the British right with a strong force, and, having taken a position at the creek, defends its passage. Stirling had with him but a small remnant of his troops, principally composed of the brave "Delawares and Marylanders."

Washington and a group of officers were on the heights, watching with anxiety the movements of Stirling, who was only separated from the American lines by the creek which emptied into Gowanus cove, the southern boundary of the Brooklyn peninsula. "The earl will surely surrender," thought Washington and each of his officers, as they observed his desperate position. Stirling, however, was evidently bent on an attempt to reach the lines. He prepares to attack Lord Cornwallis, strongly posted as he is without and within the mill, which commands the passage of the creek. Sending most of his men to make the best of their way through the water, he leads about half of Smallwood's brave regiment against the enemy. Washington, surprised at this daring movement, exclaims to the officers at his side, "Good God! what brave fellows I must lose this day!"*

The attack began: Stirling was driven back, but, rallying on his men, the assault is renewed. He is again and again, for five or six times, repulsed; but, bringing

up his handful of brave troops once more to the charge, he is "on the point of driving Lord Cornwallis from his station; but, large reinforcements arriving, rendered it impossible to do more than provide for safety." The slaughter was terrific. Colonel Smallwood's regiment of Marylanders suffered extremely, and was almost cut to pieces. It lost two hundred and fifty-nine. "This loss was much regretted, on account of their being young men of the best families in the country."

While the struggle was going on, some succeeded in crossing the creek; one man, however, was drowned. The rest came into the American lines drenched, bemired, and covered with blood, but bringing in with them twenty-three prisoners. "Twenty-seven of the Delawares," writes Colonel Haslet, "next morning were missing. In that number were Lieutenants Stewart and Harney, the latter a prisoner, the other not yet heard of. Major M'Donough was wounded in the knee; a ball passed through the sleeve of his coat, without wounding the arm or his body. Lieutenant Anderson had a ball lodged in his throat; Lieutenant Corn a ball still in his back. The standard was torn with grapeshot in Ensign Stephen's hand, who is now in his element, and a most excellent officer. Such is our fate. The Delaware battalion, officers and men, are respected throughout this army."*

Lord Stirling tried still to reach the lines; but, in attempting to escape, he found that in front he was met by a considerable body of troops, and was pursued by others on his right and left, and all

* Irving.

* Sparks.

pouring a hot fire upon him and his few remaining brave Marylanders. His lordship now gave up all hopes of escape, and, falling back behind a hill in his rear, determined to seek out General De Heister, and surrender himself.

De Heister, too, had strictly obeyed orders, and awaited the signal of Clinton before he made a serious attempt. His troops, after sleeping on their arms at Flatbush during the night, were early aroused, and marched along the road. As soon as the signal-guns of Clinton were heard, De Heister sent forward Count Donop with his regiment to storm the redoubt which protected Sullivan and defended the pass through the hills, while he himself led forward the rest of his Hessians to the attack. A bloody struggle was the consequence. The Americans, however, did not long continue their resistance; as Sullivan, becoming conscious of Clinton's manœuvre, ordered a retreat, with the view of preventing himself from being shut out from the American lines. He was, however, too late; for Clinton was ready to intercept him, and, meeting the American troops on the road, drove them back upon the Hessians. De Heister and his soldiers showed no mercy, and pitilessly bayoneted every man within their reach. Driven thus backward and forward between Clinton in front and De Heister in the rear, the Americans, with hardly a chance of escape, suffered terribly. The ferocity of the Hessian soldiers was such as to give countenance to the rumor, which was generally circulated, that General Howe had said to De Heister on his arrival, "The

Americans will give the foreigners no quarter;" and that De Heister had answered, "Well, as I know it, I am ready to fight on these terms." The soldiers' ears, too, were said to have been industriously filled with the most terrific accounts of the cruelty of the Americans, who were represented as more than half savages, and would, if they caught a Hessian alive, stick his body "full with pieces of pine-wood," and burn him to death! The Hessians, it must be confessed, if such was their belief, proved themselves on that day fit to cope with the most barbarous enemies.

A few of the Americans succeeded, under the cover of the woods, in making their escape to Brooklyn, but most were either killed or taken prisoners. Sullivan surrendered himself, together with a number of his officers.

General Howe now closed in with his separate divisions, and pursued the scattered remnants of Stirling's and Sullivan's forces to within a few hundred yards of the American lines. The British soldiers, exulting in their success, would have rushed at once against the works, but Howe cautiously withdrew them out of the reach of the American guns, to the cover of a wood, and, encamping his army, prepared to make an assault upon the fortifications of Brooklyn by deliberate approaches. The enemy had suffered little comparatively, their loss being only three hundred and eighty in all; while that of the Americans was over two thousand in killed, wounded, and captured, among whom were the two generals, Sullivan and Lord Stirling, and a large number of other officers. Sullivan was anxious to exonerate himself from all responsibility for the loss of the day, and wrote to the president of Congress a letter which shows a care to redeem his own character, at all hazards to the fame of others. He says:—

"I know it has been generally reported that I commanded on Long island when the action happened there. This is by no means true. General Putnam had taken the command from me four days before the action. Lord Stirling commanded the main body without the lines. I was uneasy about a road, through which I had often foretold that the enemy would come, but could not persuade others to be of my opinion. I went to the hill near Flatbush to reconnoitre, and with a picket of four hundred men was surrounded by the enemy, who had advanced by the very road I had foretold, and which I had paid horsemen fifty dollars for patrolling by night, while I had the command, as I had no foot for the purpose.

"What resistance I made with these four hundred men against the British army, I leave to the officers who were with me to declare. Let it suffice for me to say, that the opposition of the small party lasted from half-past nine to twelve o'clock.

"The reason of so few troops being on Long island was because it was generally supposed that the enemy's landing there was a feint to draw our troops thither, that they might the more easily possess themselves of New York. I often urged, both by word and writing, that, as the enemy had doubtless both these objects in view, they would first try for Long island, which commanded the other; and then New York, which was completely commanded by it, would fall of course. But in this I was unhappy enough to differ from almost every officer in the army, till the event proved my conjectures were just."

The night after the engagement on Long island was one of gloomy anxiety to the Americans. Prostrated by defeat, and doubtful of the security of their position, they passed a sleepless night, full of ill forebodings of the future. The morning came, but with it no bright summer sun, and no hope to cheer the spirits of the troops. A dull mist overhung land and water, and so darkened the day, that every visible object had lost its summer glow, and seemed dimmed, like the hearts of the patriots, with a breath of sadness. The enemy, with an overwhelming force, were within a few hundred yards; and the guards could see their working-parties turning out, with the spade and the pick, to begin their approaches.

Aug. 28.

The Americans were, however, momentarily cheered by the arrival in the early forenoon of the orderly battalions of Shee, Magaw, and Glover. "The faces that had been saddened by the disasters of yesterday, assumed a gleam of animation" as they approached; while "a murmur of approbation" was heard among "the spectators, occasionally greeting each other with the remark, 'These were the lads that might do something!'" Comparatively well dressed, well armed, and well disciplined—soldiers, in fact, of whom

Washington himself had said, " They had been trained with more than common attention," their appearance in that moment of danger, naturally won the admiration and aroused the hopes of their less-happily-conditioned comrades. The misfortunes of the previous day had taught even the most self-confident of the militia of the disadvantages of a want of order and martial training. They now exhibited no rude contempt for " fine feathers and fine airs," but heartily welcomed the very looks of a soldier.

General Mifflin had been ordered, on the previous afternoon, to bring down from Kingsbridge the battalions of Shee, Magaw, and Glover, forming in all some fifteen hundred men, and the next morning they were sent from the city, where they had passed the night, to take post in Brooklyn near Wallabout bay. The men cheerfully took their position on the ground. It was low and unfavorable for defence, and, with nothing but a *fraised* ditch in front, gave little promise of security; while the enemy, within a few hundred paces, were rapidly constructing batteries upon the heights which commanded Mifflin's position. The drizzling mist of the morning had closed in a heavy rain, and the men, unprovided with tents, were drenched to the skin. Each soldier had drawn his rations, but without the ordinary camp conveniences he was forced to eat " his pickled pork" without the preliminary boiling which, although generally considered " desirable," was found " not absolutely necessary" by these self-denying patriots, who, as one of them tells us, discovered in the course of their hard experience that " the article was esculent without culinary preparation." It is comforting to know, however, that there was occasionally a more savory morsel for a lucky mouth than the " esculent without culinary preparation ;" for, says the same military annalist we have quoted, " I remember, however, on one of the days we were in this joyless place, getting a slice of a barbecued pig, which some of our soldiers had dressed at a deserted house which bounded our lines."

During the day the enemy were driven from their works by the drenching rain to their tents. There was, however, a constant skirmishing between their outposts and the Americans. Those within the lines continued to suffer greatly from exposure to the weather. " Yesterday," says Washington, writing on the 29th of August, " it rained severely the whole afternoon, which distressed our people much, not having a sufficiency of tents to cover them, and what we have not being got over yet. I am in hopes they will be all got to-day, and that they will be more completely provided for, though the great scarcity of these articles distresses us beyond measure, not having anything like a sufficient number to protect our people from the inclemency of the weather; which has occasioned much sickness, and the men to be almost broken down."

In the evening the rain ceased to fall, and the British resumed their advances toward the American lines. Washington was with the army at Brooklyn, and remained in anxious suspense, undetermined about the future, which, from the ill condition and discouragement of the troops, was not very cheering. The night was passing, and still he and his aids were on horseback, riding from post to post, throughout the whole extent of the lines, examining the defences, consulting with the officers, and encouraging the men.

Aug. 29. With the morning came a heavy fog, which so covered the land and water, that nothing could be seen of the enemy's troops or fleet. General Mifflin, however, accompanied by Adjutant-General Reed and Colonel Grayson, one of Washington's aids, rode to Red Hook, at the farthest end of the American lines toward the bay, to strive to catch a glimpse of the British fleet, and discover its movements. While straining their eyes in vain to see through the shroud of mist, a light breeze suddenly sprang up, and so dispersed the fog, that the ships at the narrows could be distinctly seen. Lord Howe was evidently making ready for a movement. All were astir. The yards were manned, anchors were being weighed, and boats were passing from ship to ship. Reed galloped back to Washington, to report what had been seen. Mifflin and Grayson followed. So impressed were they all with the idea that Lord Howe was preparing to advance with his ships up the East river, with the view of hemming in the Americans at Brooklyn, and so persuaded were they of the necessity of an immediate retreat, that Reed was authorized by his companions to suggest it to Washington.

The commander-in-chief immediately called a council of war in an old stone church, standing near the centre of the village. There was no difference of opinion. It was now apparent to all that a retreat was necessary. Some had from the earliest moment thought it advisable. As soon as Mifflin arrived from New York, and had examined the relative condition and position of the two opposing forces, he said to Washington: "You must either fight or retreat immediately. What is your strength?"—"Nine thousand," was the answer. "It is not sufficient—we must therefore retreat," rejoined Mifflin.

When the council was consulting, Mifflin undertook to propose the retreat; but lest, in making such a proposition, he might incur the suspicion of a want of spirit, he stipulated that, in case it was determined upon, he should command the rear, but, if action was the resolve, the van.[*]

Immediate retreat was, however, unanimously determined upon by the officers of the council, for these cogent reasons: the great loss sustained, by death and capture, in the late action; the injury which the arms and ammunition had received from the heavy rains; the probability that the enemy would succeed in getting their ships up the East river, and thus cut off the communication between Long island and New York; the divided condition of the troops, having so many points to defend; and the expectation that the enemy's ships, now in Flushing bay, would transport across the sound a part of the British army, who would form an encampment above Kingsbridge, and thus command New-York island.

* Gordon.

CHAPTER XXVI.

Preparations for the Retreat.—The Retreat begins.—The Night.—Crossing the East River.—Glover and his Marblehead Men.—A Change of Wind.—A Dreadful Mistake.—The Providential Fog.—The Quick Steps of the Rear.—The Last Boat.—The Next Morning.—General Howe's Matutinal Surprise.—The Unbelief of the British.—A Harmless Cannonade.—General Sullivan a Messenger from Lord Howe to Congress.—Washington does not approve.—Lord Howe moves his Fleet nearer New York.—Washington doubtful of his Power to hold the City.—The "Weakness within" more feared than the "Strength without."

1776. "This day passed off like the last, in watching, skirmishing, and rain. After dark, orders were received and communicated to us," says the lively annalist whom we have so often quoted, "to hold ourselves in readiness for an attack upon the enemy—to take place in the course of the night. This excited **Aug. 29.** much speculation among the officers, by whom it was considered a truly daring undertaking, rendered doubly so from the bad condition of our arms, so long exposed to the rain; and, although we had bayonets, this was not the case with the whole of our force, upon whom we must depend for support. It was not for us, however, to object to the measure: we were soldiers, and bound to obey. Several nuncupative wills were made upon the occasion, uncertain as it was whether the persons to whom they were communicated would survive, either to prove or to execute them." Graydon, who thus reports the rumors of the camp, was soon relieved from his anxieties about the attack. "There was a deep murmur," he says, "which indicated some movement, and the direction of the decaying sounds was evidently toward the river. About two o'clock, a cannon went off with a tremendous roar. If the explosion was within our lines, the gun was probably discharged in the act of spiking it." The retreat had begun; and the Pennsylvania battalion, in which Graydon was an officer, had been appointed to cover the movement.

Eight o'clock in the evening was the hour when the troops were ordered to be drawn out, in readiness to be moved toward the river. The soldiers were kept in ignorance of Washington's purpose, and they were not conscious of it until they began to embark. The preparations had been made with the utmost secrecy and despatch. Early in the day, craft of all kinds—sloops and *periaguas*, flat-bottomed scows and row-boats—had been collected from the wharves, the stream, up and down the rivers, and gathered at Brooklyn. Colonel Glover, with his men of Marblehead (each one skilled, from his experience in the fisheries, in the management of the sail and the oar), had charge of the boats. The colonel was active from an early hour, passing frequently from Brooklyn to New York and back again, in collecting and fitting out his flotilla for the perilous passage of the night.

A delay occurred in moving the troops, and it was nine o'clock before the militia had reached the river, ready for embarkation. The boats were hauled close in shore; Glover and his men were on duty, showing, in their skilful handling of the craft, their Marblehead experience. The tide was at the flood, and swept along the shore in a rapid current; the wind, too, began to blow freshly from the northeast. The "old sailors" shook their heads, and declared that, with wind and water against them, it would not do to attempt the passage under sail. The small boats, however, were filled with troops, and began to cross. Still, with the row-boats only, it seemed impracticable to convey nine thousand men across a river three quarters of a mile in breadth; and General M'Dougall, who was stationed on the Brooklyn shore to superintend the embarkation, was so discouraged, that he sent word by Colonel Grayson to Washington, that he thought it impracticable to accomplish the retreat that night. Grayson went and returned without finding the commander-in-chief, and the slow operation of the crossing and recrossing of the small boats was continued.

Now, however, a fortunate change occurred: the wind sprang up from the opposite quarter, and, blowing freshly from the southwest, would carry the sailing-craft straight to New York. The nautical skill of the Marblehead men was at once put into requisition; and, with sails all set, they were soon, with their fleet of sloops, *periaguas*, and sail-boats (although loaded with men deep down to the gunwales), dashing across to the city.

The delay had been long, and morning was approaching, when the enemy would be on the alert to dash the hopes of all by an attack, the result of which was too terrible to contemplate. "Providence interposed in favor of the retreating army, by sending a thick fog about two o'clock, which hung over Long island, while on the New-York side it was clear." This fog proved no less a merciful interposition for those still in the American camp. Washington had despatched an aid-de-camp, Colonel Scammel, to General Mifflin, with orders to hasten down all the troops on their march. Scammel hurried away, but soon returned, followed by Mifflin and all the covering-party! "Good God! General Mifflin," exclaimed Washington, as soon as he saw him, "I am afraid you have ruined us, by so unseasonably withdrawing the troops from the lines."—"I did so by your order," quickly answered Mifflin. "It can not be," emphatically replied Washington. "By G–d I did!" as resolutely rejoined the other, and asked, "Did Scammel act as aid-de-camp for the day, or did he not?"— "He did," answered Washington. "Then," replied Mifflin, "I had orders through him." Washington then calmly said: "It is a dreadful mistake; and, unless the troops can regain the lines before their absence is discovered by the enemy, the most disastrous consequences are to be apprehended."[*]

The fog was here again their salvation. Mifflin succeeded in leading his troops back without the British having discovered that they had been absent. "This

_____
[*] Irving.

was a trying business for young soldiers," reports one of them, and particularly so in this case; for, on their march to the ferry, there had already been a cry that the British light-horse were at their heels, and the battalion had halted and formed, while the front rank, kneeling, had presented pikes "to receive the charge of the supposed assailants." When ordered to return to the lines, the men willingly obeyed. "Whoever," says another military annalist, "has seen troops in a similar situation, or duly contemplates the human heart in such trials, well knows how to appreciate the conduct of these brave men on this occasion."

It is not surprising, when a genuine order did come, that they "did not linger;" and, though they naturally "moved with celerity," it is no more than we expect of such true soldiers that they "guarded against confusion." They were the last of the troops to leave the lines; and, succeeding in reaching the place of embarkation without annoyance from the enemy, took to the boats in readiness for them, and crossed to New York in safety. "I found," says Graydon, "a boat prepared for my company, which immediately embarked, and, taking the helm myself, I so luckily directed the prow, no object being discernible in the fog, that we touched near the centre of the city."

The whole manœuvre was a great success, and, although much aided by the "providential" fog, reflected no little credit upon Washington's military skill. The cannon and stores were, for the most part, brought off without loss or damage. A few heavy pieces of artillery were, how-ever, left behind, which it was found impossible to drag away, in consequence of the wheels of the carriages sinking up to the hubs in the earth which had been saturated with the severe and long-continued rains. A few heads of cattle, also, which had been driven within the lines, were abandoned, after various attempts to force them across the water. Washington himself and his staff, though often entreated, would not leave the shore of Brooklyn until the last body of troops had embarked. At about eight o'clock, the fog cleared away. Four boats were still on the river: three half way over, filled with troops; the fourth, containing three fellows who had tarried behind to plunder, was so near the shore, that the enemy, who at this moment thronged into the lines deserted by the Americans, commanded it with their guns and forced it to return.

Howe had only been aroused to the fact of the retreat at early dawn of day. "The high-feeding English general," says a compatriot of his own, "slept on; and his brother the admiral, not so apt to doze, did not move a single ship or boat, and was to all appearance unconscious of what was going on." The first intelligence brought to General Howe was by a negro-servant of a Mrs. Rapelye, of Brooklyn. This lady's husband, suspected of tory proclivities, had fallen under General Greene's scrutiny, in the course of his raid against the disaffected, and been duly secured. His wife, however, had tory inclinations of her own, which were now sharpened by revenge from the forced absence of her

Aug. 30.

husband. Remaining in Brooklyn, she became aware, in the evening, of the retreat of the Americans, and sent her negro, with information of the fact, to the British camp. The first man into whose hands he fell chanced to be a Hessian, who could not understand a word of the poor African's English splutter; so he was clapped into the guardhouse for the night, and only brought before the British general next morning, by whom his message was understood, when it was too late to be of service.

Even now the story was hardly believed; and it was only when Captain Montressor, fortified by the presence of an armed party, had cautiously approached the lines, and, climbing up the embankment, had peeped over and found the place abandoned, that Howe was fully persuaded of the mortifying fact that the American army had escaped from his clutches. The drums now beat the morning *réveille*; and, while the British troops were striking their tents and preparing to move, small bodies of light-horse galloped to various points toward the shore to reconnoitre; and some fieldpieces were hurried into Brooklyn, and began to pour a harmless cannonade at the retreating boats.

On the succeeding night, the Americans also brought away their artillery, stores, and tents, from Governor's island. One man, however, lost his arm by a shot from a British man-of-war, while engaged in this dangerous enterprise. During the whole of this perilous time, Washington was personally so active, that for forty-eight hours previous

Aug. 30.

to the completion of the retreat from Long island, he had hardly been off his horse, or closed his eyes; "so that I was quite unfit," he says on the next day, " to write or dictate till this morning."

General Sullivan, when taken prisoner during the battle of Long island, was immediately sent on board the admiral's ship. Here Lord Howe had frequent interviews with Sullivan, and took occasion to tell him how desirous he was of accommodation with the colonies, and of fulfilling the purpose of his appointment by the British government as a commissioner to treat with the Americans. With this object in view, his lordship expressed the wish of seeing some of the members of Congress. The American general was so far impressed by the admiral's earnest desire, that he consented to go (on his parole) to Philadelphia with a verbal message, the purport of which was, that, although Lord Howe could not treat with Congress as such, he was desirous of conferring with some of its members as private gentlemen only, whom he would meet at any place they would appoint; that in conjunction with General Howe, his brother, he had full powers to compromise the dispute with America, on terms advantageous and honorable to both the colonies and the mother-country; that he wished a compact might be settled at this time, when no decisive blow was struck, and neither party could allege being compelled to enter into such agreement; and that in case Congress were disposed to treat in the manner suggested, many things not yet asked might be granted them; and if, upon the conference being held, there should arise good ground for the accommodation, this might lead to an acknowledgment of its authority, as otherwise the compact could not be completed.

Sullivan was put ashore at New York on the day after the retreat from Long island, and immediately presented himself to Washington, with a statement of his desire to lay before Congress the message which he had received from Lord Howe. Washington urges no objection. "I have consented," he says, "to his going to Philadelphia, as I do not mean, or conceive it right, to withhold or prevent him from giving such information as he possesses in this instance." Washington evidently did not sympathize very warmly with this diplomatic movement, the issue of which we shall have occasion to record in the course of our narrative.

General Howe now took possession of the American works at Brooklyn, and, garrisoning them with a force principally of Hessians, distributed the rest of his troops along the shores of Long island which overlooked the East river; posting them at Bushwick, Hellgate, Flushing, and Newtown. The admiral, too, now began to close with his fleet toward the city, and, anchoring most of his ships off Governor's island, sent on the night after the battle a forty-gun frigate up the East river. She succeeded in passing up between Governor's and Long islands, and, although fired upon by the American batteries, was enabled to reach an anchorage in Turtle bay without damage. The next morning, however, Washington despatched Major Crane, of the artillery, with two twelve-

pounders and a howitzer, which, hulling her several times, forced her to take shelter behind Blackwell's island, where she remained. Several other British ships-of-war, with a whole fleet of store and transport vessels, which had come round Long island, were also stationed in the sound above.

As the enemy were thus closing about him, Washington began to be doubtful of the possibility of continuing to hold the city of New York. He felt the need of disciplined troops, and ordered General Mercer to send the thousand men intended for the flying camp to the city; while a corresponding number of the militia were to be detached to take their place in New Jersey, and try to make a diversion, if practicable, upon Staten island. "Till of late," says Washington, in unusually despairing words for him, "I had no doubt in my own mind of defending this place; nor should I have yet, if the men would do their duty; but this I despair of." He was already contemplating an evacuation, and writes to the president of Congress, asking —"If we should be obliged to abandon the town, ought it to stand as winter-quarters for the enemy? .....They would," he continues, "derive great conveniences from it, on the one hand; and much property would be destroyed on the other. It is an important question, but will admit of but little time for deliberation. At present, I dare say the enemy mean to preserve it, if they can. If Congress, therefore, should resolve upon the destruction of it, the resolution should be a profound secret, as the knowledge of it will make a capital change

43

in their plans." Washington's great difficulty was, however, with his troops, which,
since the defeat on Long island, were so
disheartened and disorganized, that no reliance could be placed upon them as an
army, either for offence or defence. The
American commander-in-chief was thus
placed almost *hors de combat*, not so much
by the strength without as by the weakness within.

CHAPTER XXVII.

Discouragement of the American Troops.—Desertion.—Villany and Rascality.—Washington calls loudly for Reform.—
Low Fellows in High Places.—Fort Constitution garrisoned and strengthened.—Removal of Stores from the City of
New York.—The Enemy threaten to cross the East River and cut off the Communication with the Country.—New
York to be burned, or not?—Opinions on the Subject.—The New Disposition of the American Army.—The Howes
pause for a Reply from Congress.

1776. WASHINGTON would be particularly happy, he writes to Congress, if
he could transmit to them information
that would be agreeable to their wishes;
but " unfortunately for me, unfortunately
for them," it is not in his power. " Our
Sept. 2. situation," he declares, " is truly
distressing. The check our de-
tachment sustained on the 27th ultimo
has dispirited too great a proportion of
our troops, and filled their minds with
apprehension and despair. The militia,
instead of calling forth their utmost efforts to a brave and manly opposition, in
order to repair our losses, are dismayed, in-
tractable, and impatient to return. Great
numbers of them have gone off; in some
instances, almost by whole regiments, by
half ones, and by companies, at a time.
This circumstance, of itself, independent
of others, when fronted by a well-appoint-
ed enemy superior in number to our whole
collected force, would be sufficiently disagreeable; but, when their example has
infected another part of the army, when
their want of discipline and refusal of almost every kind of restraint and government have produced a like conduct but
too common to the whole, and an entire
disregard of that order and subordination
necessary to the well-doing of an army,
and which had been inculcated before, as
well as the nature of our military establishment would admit of—our condition
becomes still more alarming; and with
the deepest concern I am obliged to confess my *want of confidence in the generality
of the troops.*"

These were strong words, which, however, seemed unfortunately too well justified by the conduct of the army, and especially of the militia. "Almost every
villany and rascality are daily practised;
so many of our officers want honor, and
so many of our soldiers want virtue, civil, social, and military, that nothing but
the severest punishments can keep them
from ruining the American cause"—was

the testimony of others besides Washington. A contemporary declares, "I have heard some tales of wo, occasioned by the robberies of our army, which would extort sighs from the hearts of tigers." Another emphatically asserts: "Unless some speedy and effectual measures are adopted by Congress, our cause will be lost. The few who act upon principles of disinterestedness are, comparatively speaking, no more than a drop in the ocean. As the war must be carried on systematically, you must establish your army upon a permanent footing, and give your officers good pay, that they may be and support the character of gentlemen, and not be driven, by a scanty allowance, to the low and dirty arts which many of them practise, to filch the public of more than the difference of pay would amount to. The men must be engaged by a good bounty, for the continuance of the war. To depend upon militia is assuredly resting on a broken staff. They can not brook subordination. It would be cheaper to keep fifty or a hundred thousand in constant pay, than depend upon half the number, and supply the other half occasionally by militia. If I was to declare, upon oath, whether the militia have been most serviceable or hurtful, upon the whole, I should subscribe to the latter. No man who regards order, regularity, or economy, or who has any regard for his own honor, character, or peace of mind, will risk them upon militia."

The system of choosing their own officers, in the militia-companies, seemed destructive of all order and discipline. The men would select those only who consented to throw their pay into a joint stock, from which captains, lieutenants, ensigns, sergeants, corporals, drummers, and privates, drew equal shares. With this system, low fellows naturally were found in high places; and accordingly it was not surprising that a captain should be proved guilty of stealing his soldiers' blankets; that another officer should be found shaving his men "in the face of distinguished characters;" and that many of the regimental surgeons made a practice of selling recommendations to furloughs and discharges at a less sum than a shilling a man.[*]

Washington finds that affairs were not changing for the better, and the militia were daily so diminishing, that "in a little time I am persuaded," he writes, "their number will be very inconsiderable." He found it impossible to check the desire of these men to return to their homes. Although he refused to give them their discharge, they insisted upon going, and did go, so fast, that in a few days the Connecticut militia were reduced from six to less than two thousand! Washington was forced to acquiesce in these shameful desertions, which, however, greatly harassed him.

In the meantime, little could be done, either for offence or defence. General Mercer was, however, ordered to detach a force from Amboy, where he was stationed, to take possession of and strengthen the works on the Jersey bank of the Hudson, called Fort Constitution, and subsequently Fort Lee, opposite Fort Washington, on the New-York side. Wash-

---

[*] Gordon.

ington, moreover, as he thought it "expedient to guard against every contingency," and that he might have resources left if obliged to abandon New York, began to remove all the stores, not immediately wanted, above Kingsbridge. The evacuation of the city was now, in fact, a subject of constant talk and consideration. The probability of such an event, and the possibility of the destruction of New York, had been discussed in Congress, which hurried to pass and send to the commander-in-chief this resolution: "*Resolved*, That General Washington be acquainted that Congress would have special care taken, in case he should find it necessary to quit New York, that no damage be done to the said city by his troops on their leaving it; the Congress having no doubt of their being able to recover the same, though the enemy should for a time obtain possession of it."

As the British were closing in with their ships, and extending their encampments along the Long-island shore of the East river, there was reason to suppose that they intended to make a landing above or below Kingsbridge, in order to hem in the American army, and cut off its communication with the country. This called for prompt action; and Washington immediately summoned a council of war, to fix upon some system of conduct to be pursued, in order to baffle the efforts and counteract the schemes of General Howe, and also to determine as to the expediency of evacuating or attempting to maintain the city and the several posts on the island of New York.

The council of general officers met, ac-

cording to the summons.[*] There was a division of opinion. But **Sept. 7.** all agreed that New-York city would not be tenable if the enemy resolved to bombard and cannonade it. Some, however (not a little influenced in their opinion by the supposition that Congress desired it to be maintained at every hazard), were opposed to the evacuation. Others strongly advocated the immediate and total abandonment of the town. This was the opinion of General Greene, who strenuously presented it in a letter to the commander-in-chief two days before the assembling of the council. "The object under consideration is," he writes, "whether a general and speedy retreat from the island is necessary or not. To me it appears the only eligible plan to oppose the enemy successfully and secure ourselves from disgrace. I think we have no object on this side of Kingsbridge. Our troops are now so scattered, that one part may be cut off before the others can come to their support. In this situation, suppose the enemy should send up the North river several ships of force, and a number of transports at the same time, and effect a landing between the town and the middle division of the army; that another party from Long island should land directly opposite; and that these two parties should form a line across the island and intrench themselves. The two flanks of this line could be easily supported by the shipping. The centre, fortified with the redoubts, would ren-

[*] Among them were some of those lately promoted: for Congress had appointed Heath, Spencer, Greene, and Sullivan, major-generals; and James Reed, Nixon, St. Clair, M'Dougall, Parsons, and James Clinton, brigadier-generals.

der it very difficult, if not impossible, to cut our way through. At the time the enemy are executing this movement, they will be able to make sufficient diversions, if not real lodgments, to render it impossible for the centre and upper divisions of the army to afford any assistance here. Should this event take place—and, by-the-by, I do not think it very improbable—your excellency will be reduced to that situation, which every prudent general would wish to avoid; that is, of being obliged to fight the enemy at a disadvantage, or submit." Greene went even further, and advised the destruction of New York. "I would burn the city and its suburbs," he says, and thinks that they should not be put into competition with the general interests of America, for "two thirds of the property of the city and the suburbs belong to the tories."

Putnam, too, agreed with Greene, while Mercer, Spencer, Heath, and Clinton, were of the opposite opinion. Washington himself was evidently in favor of evacuation. "It is now extremely obvious," he says, "from all intelligence, from their movements, and every other circumstance, that having landed their whole army on Long island, except about four thousand on Staten island, they mean to enclose us on the island of New York, by taking post in our rear, while the shipping effectually secures the front; and thus, either by cutting off our communication with the country, oblige us to fight them on their own terms, or surrender at discretion; or by a brilliant stroke endeavor to cut this army in pieces, and secure the collection of arms and stores which they well know

we shall not be able soon to replace." With this view of the enemy's tactics, Washington, while considering the best means of opposing them, says it is "impossible to forget that history, our own experience, the advice of our ablest friends in Europe, the fears of the enemy, and even the declarations of Congress, demonstrate that on our side the war should be defensive (it has even been called a war of posts); that we should on all occasions avoid a general action; not put anything to risk, unless compelled by a necessity into which we ought never to be drawn. .... With these views," he continues, "and being fully persuaded that it would be presumption to draw out our young troops into open ground against their superiors both in number and discipline, I have never spared the spade and pickaxe."

A compromise was finally agreed upon between these extreme opinions, and it was determined by the council to arrange the army under three divisions: five thousand to remain for the defence of the city; nine thousand to be stationed at Kingsbridge and its neighborhood, in order not only to secure the posts there, but to be ready to attack the enemy, who were moving eastward on Long island, if they should attempt to land; and the rest of the army to occupy the intermediate space, in readiness to support either division above or below.

Washington immediately proceeded to put into execution these plans. He made preparation to shift his own headquarters to Kingsbridge. Rough wooden structures were ordered to be built there for the troops, and the sick removed from

New York to Orangetown, in New Jersey. The enemy, although hourly and anxiously expected to begin their manoeuvres, seemed to hesitate, probably awaiting the issue of the interview just about to take place between Lord Howe and the committee appointed by Congress to meet him on Staten island.

CHAPTER XXVIII.

1776. GENERAL SULLIVAN had arrived at Philadelphia, in his capacity of embassador from Lord Howe, and, having laid before Congress the verbal message of his lordship, was requested to reduce it to writing. This having been done, Congress, after a long discussion, resolved that they could not send any of their members in a private capacity; but were willing, as they were desirous of an honorable peace, to appoint a committee to wait upon his lordship, who might receive them in whatever character he pleased. Benjamin Franklin of Pennsylvania, John Adams of Massachusetts, and John Rutledge of South Carolina, were accordingly chosen in fulfilment of these resolutions. They immediately set out to meet Lord Howe on Staten island.

A private letter had already been written to Franklin by his lordship, who had stated the object of his mission, and expressed to his "old acquaintance and worthy friend," whom he had known in London, his earnest desire to have it successfully accomplished. Franklin's answer was somewhat pungent, but seemed justified by the apparent desire of Lord Howe to obtain his concurrence in a movement which no American patriot could believe was favorable to the interests of his country:—

"Directing pardons," writes Franklin, "to be offered to the colonies, who are the very parties injured, expresses indeed that opinion of our ignorance, baseness, and insensibility, which your uninformed and proud nation has long been pleased to entertain of us; but it can have no other effect than that of increasing our resentments. It is impossible we should think of submission to a government that has, with the most wanton barbarity and cruelty, burnt our defenceless towns in the midst of winter; excited the savages to massacre our peaceful farmers, and our slaves to murder their masters; and is even now bringing foreign mercenaries to deluge our settlements with blood. These atrocious injuries have extinguished every spark of affection for that parent-country we once held so dear. But were it possible for us to forget and forgive them, it is not possible for *you* (I mean the British nation) to forgive the people you have so heavily injured....

"Your lordship may possibly remember the tears of joy that wet my cheek, when, at your good sister's in London, you once gave expectations that a reconciliation might soon take place. I had the misfortune to find these expectations disappointed, and to be treated as the cause of the mischief I was laboring to prevent. My consolation under that groundless and malevolent treatment was, that I retained the friendship of many wise and good men in that country; and, among the rest, some share in the regard of Lord Howe.

"The well-founded esteem, and permit me to say affection, which I shall always have for your lordship, make it painful to me to see you engaged in conducting a war, the great ground of which, as described in your letter, is 'the necessity of preventing American *trade* from passing into foreign channels.' To me it seems neither the obtaining nor retaining any trade, how valuable soever, is an object for which men may justly spill each other's blood; that the true and sure means of extending and securing commerce are the goodness and cheapness of commodities; and that the profits of no trade can be ever equal to the expense of compelling and holding it by fleets and armies. I consider this war against us, therefore,

as both unjust and unwise; and I am persuaded that cool and dispassionate posterity will condemn to infamy those who advised it; and that even success will not save from some degree of dishonor those who have voluntarily engaged to conduct it.

"I know your great motive in coming hither, was the hope of being instrumental in a reconciliation; and I believe, when you find that to be impossible, on any terms given you to propose, you will then relinquish so odious a command, and return to a more honorable private station."

With such preliminaries, his lordship could not have much hope of a successful negotiation with Franklin. We shall find that his associates, Adams and Rutledge, were no less inflexible in their spirit of patriotic independence.

The committee finally set out on their journey, Franklin and Rutledge driving in a "chair," and Adams **Sept. 9.** riding on horseback. On the first night they reached Brunswick, in New Jersey, where they lodged at an inn. They had now an opportunity of seeing something of the soldiery, about whom they had lately received so many complaints while in Congress. There were numbers, both of officers and men, straggling about the roads and loitering in the public houses, whose conduct and condition were such as not to inspire very sanguine hopes of the country's cause intrusted to such defenders. The three patriotic legislators, however, consoled themselves with the expectation that the disorderly military characters which they had thus encountered would be "chastised into order in time."

The taverns at Brunswick were so full of rollicking troopers, that it was difficult to find entertainment. Finally, a single bed was obtained for the joint occupancy of Franklin and Adams, in a chamber little larger than the bed, without a chimney, and with only one small window. Here they turned in for the night. The window was open; and Adams, who was an invalid, and afraid of the night air, shut it close.

"Oh!" cried out Franklin, "don't shut the window: we shall be suffocated!"

"I am afraid of the night air," replied Adams.

Doctor Franklin rejoined: "The air within this chamber will soon be, and indeed is now, worse than that without doors. Come! open the window, and come to bed, and I will convince you. I believe you are not acquainted with my theory of colds."

Whereupon, Adams opened the window, and, leaping into bed, began a discussion with his philosophical bedfellow upon his theory of colds. He had read, Adams said, Franklin's letters to Doctor Cooper, in which he had advanced the opinion that nobody ever got cold by going into a cold church or any other cold air; but he declared it was so inconsistent with his experience, that he thought it a paradox. Notwithstanding, Adams added that he was so curious to have Franklin's views, that he would be glad to hear them, even at the risk of a cold.

The doctor then began a harangue up-on air and cold, and respiration and perspiration, and with so much profundity of science, that he soon put his bedfellow asleep. "I soon," says Adams, "left him and his philosophy together, but I believe they were equally sound and insensible within a few minutes after me, for the last words I heard were pronounced as if he was more than half asleep."

The next morning, Rutledge, who probably had slept alone, or at any rate had not enjoyed the honor or suffered from the theory of a "philosophical bedfellow," joined Franklin and Adams, and the three continued their journey to Amboy. On reaching this place, Lord Howe's barge was in waiting to take them over to the opposite shore of Staten island. A British officer had also arrived, who was to give himself up to the Americans as a hostage for the security of the committee. Adams, however, as soon as he saw him, told his colleagues that he thought it would be childish to depend upon such a pledge; and, they agreeing, the three accordingly insisted upon taking the hostage back again to the island. The officer, declaring that he was at their disposition, could not, of course, refuse to comply, and crossed with the committee.

As they approached the shore, Lord Howe (having been on the lookout from his house, which stood not far from the water) observed the barge, and immediately went down to the water's edge to receive his congressional visiters. On their landing, his lordship, looking at the returned hostage, remarked, "Gentlemen, you make me a very high compliment,

Sept. 10.

and you may depend upon it I will consider it as the most sacred of things."

They then walked up together to the house "between lines of guards of grenadiers, looking fierce as ten furies, and making grimaces and gestures, and motions of their muskets," which were supposed to be in accordance with military etiquette, "but which we neither understood nor regarded," says the inflexible republican Adams; who, however, must have been struck with the difference between the "grimaces" of the British grenadiers and the "straggling and loitering" of his own undisciplined countrymen on the roads and about the doors of the public houses.

The house occupied by Lord Howe still stands, a solid stone structure, upon Ward's point. It is a simple farmhouse. Cattle feed peacefully upon the meadow, which stretches from the door to the water's edge. Well-cultivated fields extend back to the road; on the right there is a grove, where school-children in the summer-time come from the stifling streets of the great city, to enjoy within the shade of the cedars the innocent gayeties of the pic-nic, and to breathe the pure air which blows fresh from sea and land; beyond, on the opposite shore, crowded town succeeds town; on the water in front, sail-boats and steamers pass and repass in busy but peaceful activity; while everywhere upon the island is a calm landscape, varied with hill and wooded vale, and dotted with low cottage-roofs of plain farmers and imposing villas belonging to the opulent merchants of New York.

44

The house on Ward's point was then, when visited by the congressional committee, the headquarters of Lord Howe. It had been the habitation of military guards, and was as dirty as a stable. His lordship, however, had prepared to do honor to his distinguished guests, and had accordingly got ready a large, handsome room, by spreading a carpet of moss and green sprigs, from bushes and shrubs in the neighborhood, till he made it not only wholesome, but romantically elegant, and entertained his visiters with "good claret, good bread, cold ham, tongues, and mutton."

While thus sharing Lord Howe's hospitality, a lively conversation took place, in the course of which his lordship, looking toward Mr. Adams, expressed in warm terms his gratitude to the state of Massachusetts for erecting a marble monument in Westminster abbey to his elder brother, Lord Edward Howe, who fell at Ticonderoga during the French War. " He esteemed, said he, that honor to his family *above all things in this world;* and that such was his gratitude and affection to this country, on that account, that he felt for America as for a brother; and if America should fall, he should feel and lament it like the loss of a brother." Doctor Franklin, "with an easy air and a collected countenance, a bow, a smile, and all that *naiveté* which sometimes appeared in his conversation," replied, "My lord, we will do our utmost endeavors to save your lordship that mortification." The earl's sensibility was not a little wounded by this unexpected and rather rude shock; but he merely remarked, with his usual courtesy, "I suppose you will endeavor to give us employment in Europe."

Lord Howe now turned the conversation toward business, and began by saying that he could confer with his visiters not as members of Congress, but only as private gentlemen and British subjects. Hereupon Mr. Adams quickly rejoined: "Your lordship may consider me in what light you please; and indeed I should be willing to consider myself, for a few moments, in any character which would be agreeable to your lordship, *except that of a British subject!*" At these words, Lord Howe turned to Doctor Franklin and Mr. Rutledge, and said, with a grave and solemn air, "Mr. Adams is a decided character."

It must be conceded that his lordship was in a fair way of being roughly handled by these knotty republicans. He, however, now took care to confine himself to business, and not expose his soft compliments to any further chance of hard usage. The earl then repeated, in a more serious tone, that he could not receive the committee as delegates from Congress; but that, as his powers enabled him to confer and consult with any private gentlemen of influence in the colonies, on the means of restoring peace between the two countries, he was glad of the opportunity of conferring with those present on that subject, if they thought themselves at liberty to enter into a conference with him.

The committee replied that their business was to hear, and that his lordship might consider them in what light he pleased, and communicate such propositions as he was authorized to make; but that they could consider themselves in no other character than that in which they were placed by order of Congress.

His lordship then spoke at considerable length, but in all he said there was nothing but this which could be regarded as an explicit proposition of peace, namely, that the colonies should return to their allegiance and obedience to the government of Great Britain. The rest of the earl's remarks were simply assurances that there was an exceedingly good disposition on the part of the king and his ministers to make the government easy to its American subjects; and that, in case of their submission, the offensive acts of Parliament should be revised, and the instructions to the governors of the several provinces be reconsidered, in order that, if any just causes of complaint should be found, they might be removed.

To this the committee replied that in their opinion a return to the domination of Great Britain was not now to be expected, as the colonies had declared themselves independent states, and it was not in the power of Congress to agree for them to return to their former condition of dependence. There was no doubt, however, they said, an inclination to peace, and a willingness to enter into a treaty with Great Britain, which might be advantageous to both countries. As his lordship had at present no power to treat with them as independent states, he might (if there was the same good disposition on the part of the British government) much sooner obtain fresh powers for such a purpose, than could be obtained by Congress from the several states, to consent to a submission.

Lord Howe, then remarking that he was sorry to find no accommodation was likely to take place, put an end to the conference. The committee, therefore, took leave of his lordship, and, having passed over by barge to Amboy, returned through New Jersey, to their duties in Congress.

Sullivan's mission was generally considered a "fool's errand." Adams expresses himself emphatically upon this point. He says: "The conduct of General Sullivan, in consenting to come to Philadelphia, upon so confused an errand from Lord Howe—though his situation, as a prisoner, was a temptation, and may be considered some apology—appeared to me to betray such a want of penetration and fortitude, and there was so little precision in the information he communicated, that I felt much resentment, and more contempt, on the occasion, than was perhaps just. The time was extremely critical. The attention of Congress, the army, the states, and the people, ought to have been wholly directed to the defence of the country. To have it diverted and relaxed, by such a poor artifice and confused tale, appeared very reprehensible."

Washington says briefly of the whole affair, "The mode of negotiation pursued by Lord Howe I did not approve of."

CHAPTER XXIX.

Evacuation of New York resolved upon.—Hale, the American Spy.—His Life, Character, and Fate.—The Movement of the British Ships up the East River.—The Americans on the March out of New York.—Washington's Headquarters.—The Morris Home.—The Landing of the Enemy.—The Flight of the Provincials.—Washington's Indignation.—Putnam and the Rear-Guard in Danger.—Aaron Burr comes to the Rescue.—The Enemy too late.—Escape of Putnam and his Force.—The British arrive in Full Strength.—An Agreeable but Expensive Visit.—"Mrs. Murray saves the American Army."—The British take Possession of New York.—The Action on the Plains of Harlem.—Death of Knowlton and Leitch.

1776. GENERAL WASHINGTON, having received a despatch on the 12th of September from President Hancock, stating that it was by no means the sense of Congress that the army or any part of it should remain in the city of New York a moment longer than he should think it proper for the public service, was left to act according to his own judgment. His opinion, as we have seen, was evidently in favor of evacuating the town; and he was now confirmed in his views by a petition, signed by seven of his general officers, headed by General Greene, who urged the calling of a council of war, to decide upon such action as the circumstances seemed to require. A council was accordingly summoned; and it was

Sept. 12. determined, by a majority of ten out of the thirteen present, that the removal of the army was not only prudent, but absolutely necessary, as they were entirely convinced, from a full and minute inquiry into their situation, that it was extremely perilous : for it appeared from every movement of the enemy, and the intelligence received, that their plan of operations was to get in the rear of the Americans, and, by cutting off the communication with the mainland, oblige them to force a passage through the British lines, or to become prisoners in some short time, for want of necessary supplies of provisions.

Anxious to have more explicit information of the condition and the intended movements of the enemy, it was determined to send a spy into the British camp on Long island. Colonel Knowlton was requested by Washington to obtain some one from his regiment, which had a high character for its daring, to undertake this perilous duty. Captain NATHAN HALE, a young Connecticut officer, immediately volunteered his services, and, being provided by Washington with an order to the commanders of all American vessels to convey him wherever he desired to go, set out. Crossing the sound, Hale reached Huntington, on Long island, and thence proceeded to the British camp, where, by skilfully avoiding suspicion, he gathered such information as he had sought. He now returned to Huntington, and was about recrossing to New York, when he was arrested by a British guard, and, being taken before General Howe and examined, condemned to die. When Howe

removed his headquarters to New York, Hale was brought over from Long island and confined in the greenhouse attached to the Beekman mansion, on the East river, of which the British commander-in-chief had taken possession in the absence of its patriotic owner. Hale was treated with great severity. Pronounced guilty without the form of a trial, he was not even allowed the usual privileges of a condemned criminal. His bible was taken from him, the presence of a clergyman denied him, and his last written words to his mother and sisters were destroyed. He was led out to be hanged, and, as he stood beneath the fatal tree,* he said, "I only lament that I have but one life to lose for my country." Hale was young, and full of patriotic enthusiasm. He had left Yale college but three years before, and had, by his zeal for study, given great promise of distinction in the higher walks of civil life. His ardent temperament was, however, greatly inflamed by the wrongs of his country ; and when the Revolutionary struggle began, he threw aside his books, and took up the sword with the patriotic resoluteness of a young Brutus.

Four ships-of-war, two of forty and two of twenty-eight guns, had moved up the East river, and anchored about **Sept. 13.** a mile above the city. The fort at Governor's island, now in possession of the British, kept up a brisk cannonade, and the ships were pouring broadside after broadside upon the works at New

* "He was hanged upon an apple-tree in Rutgers' orchard, near the present intersection of East Broadway and Market streets."—LOSSING.

York, as they sailed with a gentle breeze slowly up the river. The Americans returned the fire, and Washington was riding on horseback from point to point, encouraging the cannonade. As he was entering one of the forts, a ball fell within six feet of his horse ; and another struck down and killed with one blow three citizens who were looking with idle curiosity upon the scene. General Howe had also landed a considerable body of his troops upon Buchanan's and Montressor's (now Ward's and Randall's) islands, in the East river, off the mouth of the Harlem river.

Six more of the enemy's ships, transports, and men-of-war, now joined the other British vessels in the East river. Soon an express came hurriedly to Washington at his headquarters, with word from Colonel Sargent at Horen's Hook, that the enemy had crossed with large reinforcements to the encampment on Montressor's island ; and again, immediately after, another messenger rode in, with a despatch from General Mifflin, stating that he discovered "uncommon and formidable movements" among the British troops. Washington at once galloped to Harlem and Morrisania, where he supposed the principal attempt to land would be made. Nothing, however, was done until next day.

In the meantime, the measures determined upon by the council of war were being carried out with all possible despatch. The first movement was, to get the sick, the ordnance, the stores, and the provisions, safely away from the city. Colonel Glover and his ready-handed Marblehead fishermen were especially employed for that service. The work was begun late at night. An attack from the enemy was expected every moment. Some five hundred sick were, however, safely carried over the river to New Jersey, without interruption, before sunrise next morning. On the following day, Glover with his active brigade was back again to the city, at work from morning until late at night, in striking the tents and carrying the heavy stores and ordnance to the water's side, ready to be transported by boats up the North river ; while wagons were loaded with the light baggage, prepared to start by land. The commander-in-chief was anxiously awaiting the result of Glover's labors. "I fully expected," he writes on the 14th of September, "that an attack somewhere would be made last night. In that I was disappointed ; and happy shall I be, if my apprehensions of one to-night, or in a day or two, are not confirmed by the event. If it is deferred a little while longer, I flatter myself all will be got away, and our force be more concentrated, and of course more likely to resist them with success."

Washington had already moved the main body of his army, which had been principally stationed **Sept. 13.** along Turtle and Kip's bays (leaving, however, a force of militia to guard the works at those points), to the upper part of the island. General Putnam had been left with four thousand men within the city, as a rear-guard to protect the removal of the stores, and with orders to close up with the rest of the army whenever he should find it necessary, from any movement of the British.

The chief himself took possession of the mansion of Colonel Roger Morris, his old companion-in-arms under Braddock, and his successful rival for the hand of the rich Mary Philipse. Morris had, since his marriage, made America his home, and had retired to his beautiful country-seat, in the enjoyment, as he hoped, of a secure retreat for life. On the possession of the island of New York by the American army, however, he was obliged to abandon his home, and seek safety at the house of his brother-in-law, Beverly Robinson, in the Highlands.

The Morris mansion still stands, upon the high ground which rises from the marshy margin of Harlem river; and, notwithstanding the ambitious city already claims it as its own, and fixes it with numerical precision in "one hundred and sixty-ninth street," it yet retains in its situation much of its former picturesque beauty. Standing upon the heights of Harlem, it commands an extensive view of land and water. At the base of the hill upon which the house is built, flows the Harlem river, where it is spanned by the High-bridge aqueduct, through which runs a stream (drunk up by the daily thirst of the great city) more copious than the whole river below! Toward New York are the plains of Harlem, upon which houses now are crowded, but which then were green meadows and not seldom bloody battle-fields. Beyond, to the east, is the sound, now enlivened by steamboats and the peaceful sails of commerce, but then gloomy with threatening men-of-war. The Morris mansion was then all astir with the busy activity of a commander-in-chief's headquarters: it is now the solitary dwelling of an eccentric Frenchwoman,* the widow of Aaron Burr.

The American chief's apprehensions of an attack were proved to be well founded. Early in the morning which succeeded the night when he had been hastily summoned to Harlem, the enemy began their operations. Three ships-of-war sailed up the North river as high as Bloomingdale, and thus put a total stop to the removal (which Colonel Glover from an early hour had begun) of the heavy baggage by water. As the day advanced, the fleet in the East river began also with a most severe and heavy cannonade to "scour the country," and thus cover the landing of a large body of British troops.

As soon as he caught the sound of the firing, Washington hurried to the breastworks between Turtle bay and Kip's bay, where some militia had been left to guard them, and where the enemy were now landing. He found to his "great surprise and mortification" the troops which had been posted in the lines retreating with the utmost precipitation; and Parsons' and Fellows' Connecticut brigades, which had been ordered to support them, flying in every direction and in the greatest confusion, notwithstanding the exertions of their generals to form them. Washington rode up, and, finding his own attempts to stop the fugitives fruitless, was so indignant at their cowardice, that he drew his sword, threatened to run them through, and cocked and snapped his pistols at

* Madame Jumel.

the "scoundrels." He used every means in his power to rally them, but his efforts proved ineffectual ; and when a small party of the enemy, not more than sixty or seventy, made their appearance, the disorder of the cravens increased, and they continued to run away, without firing a single shot, leaving Washington himself in so hazardous a situation, that his attendants, to extricate him, caught the bridle of his horse and gave him a different direction. There he was, within eighty yards of the enemy, "so vexed," wrote General Greene, "at the infamous conduct of his troops, that he sought death rather than life." Washington dashed his hat upon the ground, and cried out, almost in despair, as he beheld the flight of his soldiers, "Are these the men with whom I am to defend America !"

The cowardly militia continued their headlong scamper across the island until they were met by Colonel Glover with his spirited Marblehead men and other troops, who had been suddenly called away from their works, to come to the defence of the posts on the eastern part of the city. The fugitives, encouraged or shamed by the presence of these steady brigades of Glover, now halted, and, being formed in rank, marched on along the Bloomingdale road, and took post on the heights of Harlem.

Cheered by the presence of the more regular troops, the militia seemed eager to redeem their tarnished valor, and would have faced about at once to attack the approaching British, who now appeared, coming up in large force. Washington at first encouraged this newly-awakened zeal, and ordered them to give battle to the enemy ; but, after a moment's reflection upon their late conduct, he naturally distrusted their courage, and countermanded the order.

The chief's great anxiety was now for Putnam and his rear-guard, who were still within New York, and in imminent danger of being hemmed in by the enemy, as they thronged upon the shore, and prepared to stretch their lines across the island. Washington immediately sent an express to Putnam, ordering him to hasten away from his perilous position ; and, fearful lest the British might pass over from the East river to Harlem plains, and cut off the retreat of that part of the army still in the city, he ordered the heights of Harlem to be secured in the best manner by the troops which were stationed on or near them.

Putnam, finding that the enemy had landed and taken possession of the main roads which led from the city to the upper part of the island where Washington had extended his lines, was greatly perplexed to discover a means of escape. His aid-de-camp, Major Aaron Burr, observing the perplexity of Putnam and his general officers, and being well acquainted with the ground, suggested a road which led along the North river from Greenwich to Bloomingdale. Putnam now hurriedly abandoned the city, leaving in his necessary haste most of the heavy cannon and a part of the stores and provisions which had been got ready for removal. Taking the road suggested by Burr, the troops were urged on to a rapid march. Putnam would allow of no flagging; and he himself was flying about on his horse, covered with foam, and stirring up the energies of the whole column. The day was stifling hot; the road was in a continued cloud of dust; a large number of women and children, who had followed the troops out of the city, embarrassed the march, and the men suffered greatly; but "Old Put," by his own personal exertions, infused such a spirit of activity into his men, that they moved on rapidly in spite of every obstacle.

They were just turning into a cross-path which led from Bloomingdale to Harlem, when an aid-de-camp rode up to Putnam in full speed, to inform him that a column of British infantry was coming up against his right flank. The order for the troops to file to the right with all speed was hardly given, when the enemy came within firing distance of Putnam's rear and opened a volley. One of the colonels fell at the first shot. Some seventeen men were killed and three hundred taken prisoners. With no other loss, the troops succeeded just at nightfall in reaching the American lines at Harlem heights.

Putnam's escape was, however, due to a fortunate incident, which shows how great events may often be traced to the most trifling causes. The British troops had landed in large force, and to the number of some eight thousand were stretching across the island. Having put to flight the militia who had so ignominiously deserted their posts at Turtle and Kip's bays, the enemy halted temporarily before extending their lines as they designed, and by which they would have certainly cut off Putnam's retreat. The day, as before observed, was hot, and the British generals were thirsty : so Governor Tryon, well acquainted with the ground, volunteered to guide them to a place where good refreshments might be secured. He accordingly took them to the country-house of a Mr. Robert Murray, a patriotic Quaker, who lived on Murray hill, near by. On entering, they were met, in the absence of her husband, by the wife, who courteously received her visiters, and offered them the best cheer she had. Wine and cake were served up in abundance; and the thirsty and gallant British officers, gratified with the good Madeira, and charmed with the courtesies of their hostess, were disposed to linger. Tryon was in the most jovial humor, as the morning's work so far had been a great success; and he was particularly pleasant when bantering Mrs. Murray, who was a devoted patriot, upon the conduct of her American friends.

Hour after hour was passed delightfully. While Mrs. Murray was thus successful in entertaining her British guests, she was saving her American friends; for while Tryon was joking the hostess, and Clinton and his officers were drinking her wine, their troops were resting on their arms, and giving Putnam and his men — who were only a mile from them — an opportunity of escape. It was ever after the remark in the patriot camp that "Mrs. Murray saved the American army."

The British now took possession of the city with a large detachment of troops under General Robertson; while the main body of the army, under General Howe, encamped on the outskirts of the town. The line which bounded the British camp at the north extended from Horen's Hook on the East river, across the island to Bloomingdale on the Hudson, and was at once protected by breastworks and batteries. Behind were posted a strong body of Hessians, under De Heister, and another of British, under Earl Percy; while each flank, on the right and the left of this large body of troops, was protected by the English men-of-war, at anchor in both rivers which bound the island. Harlem plains spread for more than a mile in width between the British and the encampment of Washington's army. The former numbered nearly twenty-five thousand, while the latter had not more than fourteen thousand fit for duty, so reduced were the American troops by sickness and desertion.

The front line of the Americans embraced the heights of Harlem, which extend from the river of that name to the Hudson. About a quarter of a mile beyond, to the north, was another line; and about the same distance still beyond was Washington's headquarters at the Morris mansion. Again, at the distance of a mile farther to the north, stood Fort Washington, on the North river, held by a strong garrison of Americans. King's bridge, which crossed the Harlem river at the most northern part of the island, some eight miles from the city, and was the only communication with the mainland, was also defended by a detachment of Washington's troops.

The Americans, however, had posted two advanced guards of considerable force between their front and that of the British — one at M'Gowan's pass, and the other at Harlem. The former was commanded by Putnam and the latter by Spencer.

The enemy were not long in making a demonstration. Washington was expecting an attack, and wrote these words: "We are now encamped **Sept. 16.** with the main body of the army on the heights of Harlem, where I should hope the enemy would meet with a defeat in case of an attack, if the generality of our troops could behave with tolerable bravery. But experience, to my extreme affliction, has convinced me that this is rather to be wished for than expected. However, I trust that there are many who will act like men, and show themselves worthy of the blessings of freedom." The letter which contained this sentence had just been despatched by the post, when word was brought that the enemy had appeared in several large bodies upon the plains of Harlem. Washington immediately galloped from his headquarters to the advanced posts, a distance of about two and a half miles, and discovered that a small company of Connecticut rangers, under the brave Colonel Knowlton, were already engaged with an advanced party of the enemy, who were reported to be only three hundred strong.

Washington now ordered Major Leitch, with three companies of Weedon's Virginia regiment, to advance to the aid of Knowlton; and directed that they should try to get in the rear of the enemy, while they made a feint of attacking them in front. The last part of the order was faithfully obeyed; and the British, seeing

45

the Americans in considerable force coming directly upon them as they supposed, ran down the hill and took possession of some fences and bushes, under the cover of which they stood and began a smart fire, but with little execution, as they were at such a distance. The Americans now made a circuit as they advanced, but commenced their attack too soon, and thus made it rather in flank than in rear. A severe engagement ensued, and Major Leitch fell almost immediately, severely wounded with three balls in his side, and was carried off the field. He was soon followed by Colonel Knowlton, who had been shot through the head.

The men, however, persevered, and continued the engagement with the greatest resolution. Washington, finding that they wanted a support, advanced some of the Maryland and New-England troops at hand to their aid. These charged the enemy with great intrepidity, and drove them from the wood where they had sought a cover, into the plain; and had succeeded in nearly silencing their fire, when Washington, expecting that large reinforcements would be sent to the aid of the British, withdrew his troops.

Colonel Knowlton died of his wounds soon after the engagement; and, "when gasping in the agonies of death, all his inquiry was whether we had driven in the enemy." He was "a brave and a good officer," said Washington in one of his letters; and in the order of the day he did not forget to do public honor to his gallantry, as well as to that of Major Leitch and all their brave soldiers: "The general most heartily thanks the troops commanded yesterday by **Sept. 17.** Major Leitch, who first advanced upon the enemy, and the others who so resolutely supported them. The behavior of yesterday was such a contrast to that of some troops the day before, as must show what may be done where officers and soldiers exert themselves. Once more, therefore, the general calls upon officers and men to act up to the noble cause in which they are engaged, and to support the honor and liberties of their country. The gallant and brave Colonel Knowlton, who would have been an honor to any country, having fallen yesterday while gloriously fighting, Captain Brown is to take the command of the party lately led by Colonel Knowlton."

The name of Leitch was given as the parole for the next day;* but the hero who bore it only lived for a short time to enjoy the good fame he had acquired by his gallant conduct.

* Irving.

CHAPTER XXX.

New York on Fire.—Who were the Incendiaries ?—The British Accounts.—The Ravage.—"Our General."—His own Account of the Enterprise against Montressor's Island.—A Failure.—Reorganization of the American Army.—Washington urges the Enactment of more Rigorous Laws.—Congress slowly consents.—Inactivity of General Howe.—The Abounding Tories.—Oliver Delancey.—His Life and Character.—His Influence.—Plans to counteract it.—Major Rogers and his Rangers.—His Career.—His Cunning.—The Americans eager to catch Him.

1776. In the middle of the night of the 20th of September, the guards on the advanced pickets of the American line beheld a great light in the direction of the city, apparently rising at a distance of nine miles. Soon it became so intense and wide spread, that "for a considerable extent the heavens appeared in flames."* It was thought that New York was on fire. This supposition was confirmed on the arrival in camp next day of one of the aid-de-camps of General Howe, with a flag, and a letter to Washington in regard to the exchange which was about being arranged for General Sullivan, Lord Stirling, and Daniel Morgan, then held as prisoners by the British. The aid-de-camp spoke of the great extent of the conflagration in the city, and stated that several Americans had been punished with death as incendiaries, some by hanging, and others by burning on the spot, who were caught in the act.

A number of incendiaries, according to the British accounts, had stayed behind, on the evacuation of New York by Washington, and concealed themselves in the houses. Combustibles had been carefully prepared; and, taking advantage of a

* Graydon.

brisk gale of wind, these desperadoes began their work about midnight, when most of the citizens and troops were buried in sleep. But when the spreading flames gave the alarm, the soldiers were beat to quarters, detachments of sailors from the fleet were landed, and, after a hard struggle, the fire was stayed, though not before it had reduced nearly a third part of the fair city to ruins. It was then that some of the incendiaries were "caught in the act," and were either despatched by the sword or bayonet, or thrown into the flames which "they had kindled" by the "infuriated soldiery." Infuriated soldiers are not apt to be very calm investigators of a charge of crime, when the suspected persons chance to belong to the enemy. Fortunately, there were other less partial observers, whose testimony is much more satisfactory and convincing. They all agree in attributing the conflagration to accident.

The fire was discovered about midnight, first breaking out at the lower end of the city, near the wharf of Whitehall, in a small wooden building, a miserable pot-house and brothel, resorted to by sailors. Most of the houses were either of wood or of brick covered with shingles; the weather had been dry for a long time, and on the night of the fire a brisk south wind was blowing. Few citizens had been left in town; and the fire-engines, pumps, and leathern buckets, were either out of order from neglect, or not readily to be got at or worked from the absence of those who knew where to find or how to use them. The flames spread rapidly, licking up house after house along the narrow streets, and, stirred by the blast of the strong southerly wind, went on ravaging in every direction. Whitehall and Broad streets were soon in ruins, and then Beaver; finally Broadway was swept from left to right; the old church of Trinity,* erected at the beginning of the century, caught, and was left in a short time a gutted ruin from the pinnacle of its tall spire to the lowest step of its porch; the fire raged on, and the "new" church of St. Paul was in peril. Now, however, the sailors from Lord Howe's fleet and the soldiers from the camp, turning out at beat of drum from their night-quarters, came to the rescue. The fire at length was stayed, but not before nearly five hundred houses were laid in ashes. Washington, in speaking of the fire, says, "By what means it happened we do not know." Even if it were the act of American incendiaries, it is clear that it was without authority, for it had been resolved by the council of war to leave the city uninjured.

The American army had been much

* "Among the buildings consumed," says an English authority, "was the old English church. When the Americans stationed at Paulus' Hook [now Jersey City] saw the steeple fall, they gave three cheers, probably rejoicing in a double sense, and more as Presbyterians than as patriots."

encouraged by the spirited conduct and partial success of their comrades under the gallant leadership of Knowlton and Leitch. The soldiers found it required only "resolution and good officers to make an enemy they stood too much in dread of" give way.

Thus inspirited, the Americans began to be eager for an opportunity to distinguish themselves. General Heath, who boasted himself quite a tactician, found an occasion for the vent of some of the abounding martial spirit of his troops. We shall let "our general," as he calls himself, describe the occurrence: "Two seamen, belonging to the La Brune, a British ship-of-war, which lay near Montressor's [Randall's] island, deserted and came to our general's [Heath's] quarters, and informed him up- **Sept. 22.** on examination that the British had then but a few men on the island, stating the number; that the piece of cannon, which had been put on the island, was taken back again on board the La Brune; that there were a number of officers at the house, in which there was a considerable quantity of baggage deposited, &c.

"Our general [Heath] supposed that these troops might be easily taken; and having called the general officers of his division together, took their opinion, who all coincided with him in sentiment. He then communicated his intention to the commander-in-chief, who gave it his approbation. Two hundred and forty men were destined for this enterprise. The command was given to Lieutenant-Colonel Michael Jackson, of the Massachusetts line, with Majors Logan and ——

(whose name can not be recollected),* of the New-York troops. They were to embark on board three flat-boats, covered by a fourth with a detachment of artillery, with a light three-pounder, in case it should be found necessary in retreating from the island. The mode of attack was settled, and every circumstance seemed to promise success. They were to fall down Harlem creek with the ebb. The time was so calculated, that the young flood was to be so much made at the break of day as to cover the flats at the island sufficiently for the boats to float.

"Matters being thus settled, our general ordered the two sailors to be brought in. He then told them that, in consequence of their information, an enterprise against the British troops on Montressor's island was to take place that night; that he had ordered them to be kept in safe custody until the next morning, when, if their declarations respecting the state of the British on the island proved to be true, he would give them a passport to the back country, whither they wished to go; but, in case their information was false, he would order them hanged immediately as spies; that he gave them the opportunity, if they had made a wrong statement to him, then to correct it. They both answered, with perfect composure, that they would cheerfully submit to the condition.

"Major Thomas Henley was now one of our general's aids-de-camp. He importuned that he might go with the detachment. He was refused, and told that he had no business there; that he could ex-

* Such is fame!

ercise no command. He grew quite impatient, returned again to the general's room, and addressed him: 'Pray, sir, consent to my going with the party; let me have the pleasure of introducing the prisoners to you to-morrow.' All his friends present advised him not to go. The general finally consented.

"The troops, at the hour assigned, embarked. Our general informed them that he, with others, would be spectators of the scene, from a certain point near Harlem creek. Notice had been given to the guards and pickets on the *York-island* side, not to hail the party as they went down. Unfortunately, the lower sentinel had not been so instructed.* He was nearly opposite to the point where our general was to be; and just at the instant when he arrived, had challenged the boats, and ordered them to come to the shore. From the boats they answered, 'Lo! we are friends.' The challenge was repeated. The answer was, 'We tell you we are friends — hold your tongue!' A bounce into the water was heard; and instantly Major Henley came wading to the shore, stepped up to our general, catched him by the hand, and said, 'Sir, will it do?' Our general, holding him by the hand, replied, 'I see nothing to the contrary;' to which Henley concluded by saying, '*Then it shall do.*' He waded back to his boat, and got in. The sentinel called again: 'If you don't come to the shore, I tell you I'll fire!' A voice from some one in the boats was, '*Pull away!*'

* It is well for history, that an occasional simple-minded and truthful chronicler like Heath presents himself, who not only tells us what he did, but what he ought to have done.

"The boats went on, and the sentinel fired his piece. The boats reached the island almost at the moment intended, just as the glimmer of the dawn was discoverable. The three field-officers were in the first boat. Their intention, on the moment of landing, was, for the two seconds in command to spring, the one to the right and the other to the left, and lead on the troops from the other two boats, which were to land on each side of the first boat. The field-officers landed, and the men from the boat. The enemy's guard charged them, but were instantly driven back. The men in the other two boats, instead of landing, lay upon their oars! The British, seeing this, returned warmly to the charge. The Americans, finding themselves thus deserted, returned to their boat; but not until Lieutenant-Colonel Jackson received a musket-ball in his leg, and Major Henley, as he was getting into the boat, one through his heart, which put an instant end to his life. The boat joined the others, and they all returned, having in the whole about fourteen killed, wounded, and missing; Major Henley deeply regretted."[*]

Washington was fully convinced, notwithstanding an occasional spirt of spirit, that an entire reorganization of the army was necessary, in order to give it that efficiency required to sustain a struggle with disciplined troops. The term of service of almost every man was to close in about three months, and Washington believed that it would be impossible to induce them to re-enlist without higher pay. "We

[*] Heath's Memoirs, pp. 63–66.

are now," he writes to Congress, "as it were upon the eve of another dissolution of our army. The remembrance of the difficulties which happened upon the occasion last year, and the consequences which might have followed the change if proper advantages had been taken by the enemy, added to a knowledge of the present temper and situation of the troops, afford but a very gloomy prospect in the appearance of things now, and satisfy me, beyond the possibility of doubt, that unless some speedy and effectual measures are adopted by Congress, our cause will be lost." **Sept. 24.**

It was useless, thought Washington, to rely upon patriotism for the recruiting of an army. When men are irritated, and their passions are inflamed, they hastily and cheerfully fly to arms; but when the first ebullition of feeling has subsided, to "expect among such people as compose the bulk of an army, that they are influenced by any other principles than those of interest, is to look for what never did and I fear never will happen."

The army should be established upon a permanent footing, and the officers be well paid, in order to induce gentlemen and men of character to engage in the service. "They ought to have such allowances," continues Washington, "as will enable them to live like and support the character of gentlemen, and not be driven by a scanty pittance to the low and dirty arts which many of them practise." He also contends that nothing but a good bounty (as, for example, a hundred acres of land, with a suit of clothes, &c., to each man) can secure permanent soldiers.

The officers, too, should stand by character and social position in such a relation toward the privates as to secure their respect and obedience. "But while," emphatically writes Washington, "the only merit an officer possesses is his ability to raise men — while those men consider and treat him as an equal, and, in the character of an officer, regard him no more than a broomstick, being mixed together as one common herd — no order nor discipline can prevail."

As for placing any dependence upon militia, it is "assuredly resting upon a broken staff. Men just dragged from the tender scenes of domestic life, unaccustomed to the din of arms, totally unacquainted with every kind of military skill, are timid, and ready to fly from their own shadows."

Some more severe laws for the government of the army are necessary, or else "but for the name," says Washington, "it might as well be abandoned.... The infamous practice of plundering" began to prevail to the most alarming extent. "Under the idea of tory property, or property that may fall into the hands of the enemy, no man is secure in his effects, and scarcely in his person." The lawless soldiers would frighten quiet citizens out of their houses, under pretence that it had been ordered to burn them, and then enter and seize the goods! Washington strove to stop these horrid practices, but with "the lust after plunder, and the want of laws to punish offenders," he might, he declares, "almost as well attempt to move Mount Atlas." To illustrate the difficulty of checking these crimes, he sends to Congress the proceedings of a court-martial which had acquitted an officer who with a party of men had robbed a house, a little beyond the American lines, of a quantity of valuable property. This consisted, among other things, of four large pier looking-glasses, some women's clothes, and a variety of articles which could be of no possible use to officer or soldier, certainly, in their military capacity. A major of brigade, meeting the rogues, loaded down with their booty, ordered the officer at the head of the party to return the property; whereupon that military vagabond drew up his men for a fight, and swore that he would defend his possession of pier-glasses, women's petticoats, and all, at the hazard of his life! Though this fellow escaped on his first trial, Washington, by ordering a reconsideration of the matter, and obtaining fresh evidence, made a shift finally to cashier him.

These views of the commander-in-chief, when laid before Congress, made a strong impression. So great, however, was the dread of a standing army, that it was only after a long debate, during more than a fortnight, that the resolution was passed to reform the army into eighty-eight battalions, "to be enlisted as soon as possible, and to serve during the war." Washington's suggestions, too, in regard to the appointment of officers, their pay, and that of the soldiers, were, for the most part, adopted.*

* To encourage enlistments, a bounty of twenty dollars and of one hundred acres of land was offered to each non-commissioned officer and soldier. The commissioned officers were also to receive bounties of land in the following proportions: a colonel, five hundred acres; lieutenant-colo-

Washington, thoroughly conscious of his weakness from the disorganized condition of his army, which must be known to the enemy, was surprised at the inactivity of Howe. That general, however, remained within his lines, without making a movement for nearly three weeks. The American commander, in the meantime, was strengthening his position by means of redoubts, breastworks, and abattis, and presented a front which the British evidently deemed formidable; for General Howe (now Sir William, as he had been created a knight for his Long-island victory) wrote to the ministry in England: "The enemy is too strongly posted to be attacked in front, and immeasurable difficulties are in our way of turning him on either side, though his army is much dispirited from the late success of his majesty's arms; yet have I not the smallest prospect of finishing the combat this campaign, nor until the rebels see preparations in the spring that may preclude all thoughts of further resistance. To this end I would propose eight or ten line-of-battle ships to be with us in February, with a number of supernumerary seamen for manning boats, having fully experienced the want of them in every movement we have made. We must also have

nel, four hundred and fifty; major, four hundred; captain, three hundred; lieutenant, two hundred; ensign, one hundred and fifty. A certain number of the eighty-eight battalions voted by Congress was assigned to each state, as its quota. The states were to appoint all officers as high as colonels, and to fill up vacancies; and also to provide arms and clothing for their respective quotas — the expense of clothing to be deducted, as usual, from the soldiers' pay. All officers were to be commissioned by Congress. Articles of war were also passed, better suited to the requirements of the army, and more calculated to secure discipline.

SPARKS.

recruits from Europe, not finding the Americans disposed to serve with arms, notwithstanding the hopes held out to me upon my arrival in this port."

Tories by profession abounded since the British success on Long island. Staten island, New York, and Long island, were now filled with those who were profuse in their expressions of loyal attachment, but by no means as free in giving their services as they were bountiful in professions of good will. There was one, however, who, now that he was embarked in the cause, was evidently doing his best to aid Howe. This was OLIVER DELANCEY, the son of a Huguenot colonist, who had early come to America, and, having received an extensive grant of land in Westchester county, became wealthy, and the founder of an influential family. Oliver, like his brother James, the lieutenant-governor of New York, reached a position of high influence in the province. When the French War began, and he was solicited to accept the command of the New-York regiment, he said that, if he did, he could in ten days raise the whole quota of troops required of that colony. Nor was this the mere boast of a braggadocio. He was strongly attached to his country, and boldly advocated its rights; but when the question came of separation, he opposed it, and, so soon as the Revolutionary struggle began, he staked his all on the side of the British throne. On Howe's arrival at Staten island, Delancey was the first American loyalist to be made a brigadier-general in the royal army.

Great hopes were entertained of his

influence in obtaining recruits in New York and its neighborhood. He, however, although only required to obtain fifteen hundred men in all, was more than a year in getting six hundred to join his standard, and during the whole war they never amounted to eight hundred. He was now at work on Long island, tempting the Americans by offers of the same pay and treatment as English soldiers, and Washington supposed with such success, that he thought it necessary, if possible, to counteract his manœuvres. General George Clinton was accordingly sent from his station on the Hudson, beyond Kingsbridge, to meet General Lincoln, just appointed to the command of the new levies of troops from Massachusetts. Clinton was to proceed to Fairfield, in Connecticut, and there concoct with Lincoln a plan to make a descent upon Long island, and try to check Delancey's "pernicious practices." The expedition was, however, finally abandoned, for want of the necessary boats.

The tories, too, seemed to be very active at this moment in Westchester and Dutchess counties. Washington had been informed that there were several companies of men preparing to go off and join the king's army. Accordingly, he ordered the guard-boats and the sentries at the works on Mount Washington to keep a strict lookout, in case these American recruits for the British army should attempt to come down the North river. General Heath also, then in command at Kingsbridge, was urged to do his utmost, by means of his troops, to intercept any coming down the East river, with the purpose of joining the enemy's forces on Long island. Washington was determined to use every precaution in his power "to prevent these parricides from accomplishing their designs."

On Long island there was another man, of a different stamp from Delancey, one Major Rogers, who was all the more formidable as he was entirely unscrupulous. ROBERT ROGERS was born in New Hampshire, where his father emigrated from Scotland. During the French War, he entered the British service, and commanded a corps of New-England riflemen, who became renowned for their exploits, under the name of Rogers' Rangers. When peace with France was declared, Rogers retired, on half-pay, to his native town. He did not, however, long remain at rest, but soon took up arms in the campaign against the Cherokee Indians. He was rewarded for his services by being appointed governor of Michillimackinac in 1766; but his artfulness of character, and want of directness of conduct, exposed him to the suspicion of laying a plot to plunder his own fort and join the French. He was accordingly put in irons, and sent to Montreal for trial. He escaped condemnation, however, and went to England, where he contrived to establish himself on such a respectable footing, that he was presented to the king. But his good fortune soon failed him, and he was clapped into prison for debt.

When the difficulties between Great Britain and her colonies were fast approaching the crisis of war, Rogers again made his appearance in America. So little scrupulous was he supposed to be,

46

that it was the opinion of all who knew him, that he was ready to join either the British or the Americans, as his personal interest might prompt, or chance direct. When the Revolutionary War began, Rogers kept wandering about the country, and haunting the quarters of Americans in authority, civil or military, with the view of either selling his services, or fulfilling his duties as a spy, in which character he was suspected to have been already employed by the British.

In the course of his wanderings, he fell in with Doctor Wheelock, of Dartmouth college, who wrote: "The famous Major Rogers came to my house, from a tavern in the neighborhood, where he called for refreshment. I had never before seen him. He was in but an ordinary habit for one of his character." He treated the doctor with great respect, and gave him an account of his travels. He spoke of his visit to London, where the doctor's college, he said, was in great repute, and that Lord Dartmouth and many other noblemen had spoken of it in his hearing with "expressions of the highest esteem and respect." He told of his deeds in foreign lands, and how he had fought two battles in Algiers, under the dey; and, with the apparent desire to live thereafter in peace and innocence, he declared that he had now returned to his native country "to take care of some large grants of lands made to him," and to visit his sister and his wife, whom he had not seen since his return from England. He had been, however, according to his own account, very deliberate in performing his conjugal duties; for he had already spent twenty days with the Congress at Philadelphia, and as many more in New York. He had been offered and urged, he said, to take a commission in favor of the colonies; but, with a scrupulous delicacy, as he was on half-pay from the crown, he thought it proper not to accept it. The major wound up his interview with the doctor by declaring that he was a great friend to his college, and volunteered to assist in obtaining a large grant of land for it.

Rogers, as we have seen, had been in Philadelphia, where he had been arrested; but having "solemnly promised and engaged, on the honor of a gentleman and soldier, that he would not bear arms against the American united colonies, in any manner whatsoever, during the American contest with Great Britain," he was set free, and provided with a passport by the Pennsylvania committee of safety. Thus fortified, Rogers proceeded (about a month after his visit to Doctor Wheelock) to the American camp before Boston, and wrote Washington a letter, requesting his signature to his Philadelphia certificate, and making this emphatic profession of patriotism: "I love America; it is my native country, and that of my family, and I intend to spend the evening of my days in it."

About the same time that Washington received this letter, Doctor Wheelock also wrote him that "two soldiers, returning from Montreal, informed him that our officers were assured by a Frenchman (a captain of the artillery, whom they had taken captive) that Major Rogers was second in command under General Carleton; and that he had been, in an Indian habit, through our encampment at St. Johns." Washington sent General Sullivan to have an interview with Rogers, who was then within a few miles of Cambridge. Sullivan confronted the major with this statement of Doctor Wheelock about his service in Canada. Rogers denied his having been there, but confessed that he had gone to the westward of Albany. As Washington did not care to see the major, and could not know of any reason why he should be haunting the American camp, Sullivan was directed to tell him that he could neither be received at headquarters nor get his passport signed; but that he might depart, and enjoy such security as the papers with which he was already provided might give him.

The next event in the history of the major was his arrest, by the order of Washington, at South Amboy, where he was prowling about the American camp, and in the neighborhood of the British on Staten island, under suspicious circumstances. Washington sent him to Philadelphia, under the care of an officer, as Rogers had declared that he was on his way to make a secret offer to serve Congress — a body which, however, the commander-in-chief took care to put on its guard, by suggesting to President Hancock "whether it would not be dangerous to accept the offer of his services." Congress would have nothing to do with the major, but handed him over to the provincial legislative assembly of New Hampshire.

Rogers now appeared in his true character, as a colonel in the British army, engaged in recruiting his famous corps, called the Queen's Rangers. By an offer to recruits "of their proportion of all rebel lands," he was filling his ranks with a set of desperate adventurers, who made themselves notorious, throughout the war, as among the most audacious and unscrupulous of the enemy.

He was now on Long island, getting men, out of the abounding tories there. He had made his headquarters at Huntington; and Connecticut seemed greatly alarmed lest he should carry out his threat of landing at Norwalk, taking the continental stores, and laying waste the town. Governor Trumbull says: "I hope we shall be able to frustrate his designs. I have no need to apprize you [he is writing to Livingston] of the art of this Rogers. He has been a famous scouter, or woods-hunter, skilled in waylaying, ambuscade, and sudden attack."[*] Rogers was a dangerous fellow, as cunning as an Indian, and as unscrupulous as a highwayman. His tricks were a constant topic of conversation in the American camp, and all the officers and soldiers of spirit were anxious, if possible, to catch the wily colonel.

[*] Sparks's Life of Washington.

CHAPTER XXXI.

The Americans at Ticonderoga.—The Ill Condition of the Troops.—Their Sufferings.—Reinforcements.—Boat-Building at Skenesborough.—Arnold and his Fleet.—Arnold again in Trouble.—Condemned by the Court.—Gates comes to his Rescue, and dissolves the Court.—Activity of Sir Guy Carleton.—Arnold sets sail.—Prepares to fight the Enemy.—The Action.—Victorious Result.—Arnold's Escape.—Humanity of Carleton.—Carleton takes Crown Point.—Reconnoitres Ticonderoga.—Gates makes a Great Show of Defence.—Carleton frightened away.—Retires into Canada.

1776. Soon after the arrival at Crown Point of Generals Schuyler, Gates, and Arnold, who had met at Albany and set out together to join the northern army, the troops, it will be recollected, were withdrawn to Ticonderoga. General Sir Guy Carleton, the governor of Canada, was at St. Johns (on the Sorel river, near the northern extremity of Lake Champlain), and might be expected, so soon as he could construct proper vessels for the purpose, to sail up the lake and attack the Americans. The latter began to prepare, in all haste, to defend themselves. The old French fort was strengthened by new defences, and the neighboring hills and grounds cleared of their forest-wood, and fortified with redoubts and batteries.

The American troops, when they had reached Crown Point, after their retreat under General Sullivan, were in a state of extreme misery. "I found them," said Adjutant-General Trumbull, "dispersed, some few in tents, some in sheds, and more under the shelter of miserable bush huts, so totally disorganized by the death or sickness of officers, that the distinction of regiments and corps was in a great degree lost; so that I was driven to the necessity of great personal examination: and I can truly say that I did not look into tent or hut in which I did not find either a dead or dying man. I found the whole number of officers and men to be five thousand two hundred, and the sick who required the attentions of a hospital were two thousand eight hundred; so that when they were sent off, with the number of men necessary to row them to the hospital, which had been established at the south end of Lake George, a distance of fifty miles, there would remain but the shadow of the army."

With this "shadow of the army," however, the Americans began their operations at Ticonderoga, and with their new duties their old sufferings did not end. As the forest was cleared for the encampment, the exhalations from the earth, thus exposed for the first time to the rays of a midsummer sun, together with the miasm from the lake, soon produced a fever, which not seldom carried off the strongest men in two or three days after an attack.

Reinforcements, however, soon arrived from New England and Pennsylvania, so that the post at Ticonderoga began to assume the aspect of military strength and activity. Ship-carpenters had also arrived from Boston and New London, and were at once set to work at Skenesborough, building the hulls of boats and galleys. These as soon as launched were towed down the lake to Ticonderoga, where they were equipped and armed. General Gates had appointed Arnold, from his well-known activity and his experience as a sailor, to superintend the fitting out of this little fleet, and promised him the command. The difficulty of obtaining proper materials for ship-building, and the distance to which they had to send for skilful workmen, interfered greatly with the work; but Arnold's energy so overcame every obstacle, that by the middle of August he had a squadron of one sloop and one schooner of twelve guns, two schooners of eight, and five gondolas with each three.

Arnold, however, with his usual facility of quarrel, had just now a difficulty on hand, which nearly led to the loss of his command. When about leaving Quebec, he lawlessly ordered some goods to be seized belonging to merchants in Montreal, but gave receipts to the owners, who were promised payment on presenting them to Congress. They had made their claims, and Arnold was now called upon to account for his disposition of the goods. All he had to say was, that they had been damaged and plundered, and that Colonel Hazen was responsible, for he had disobeyed orders in not taking proper charge of them. Hazen accordingly was arrested, and tried by court-martial. Arnold brought forward, as his principal witness, a Major Scott. His testimony, however, was rejected by the court, on the ground that, as he had seized the goods, though under the orders of Arnold, he was a party concerned. Arnold became so enraged at this, that he completely lost all self-control, and addressed an insulting communication to the court. They insisted upon an apology, in vindication of their wounded dignity. This only made Arnold still more intemperate in his rage; and, insultingly refusing to apologize, he hinted so broadly that he was ready to give each member personal satisfaction, that the whole court considered themselves as being challenged! This was, of course, too outrageous a contempt of their dignity to be passed over without rebuke and punishment; and General Gates was accordingly appealed to, to interpose the severity of his executive power. Gates, however, was not disposed to spare his admiral of the lake-fleet, and therefore acted "dictatorially," as he himself calls it, and dissolved the court-martial. To Congress, Gates justified his conduct, saying, "The United States must not be deprived of that excellent officer's [Arnold's] services at this important moment."[*]

The vessels being equipped, and Arnold in command, the flotilla rendezvoused at Crown Point. Here floated the Royal Savage, the Enterprise, the Revenge, and the Liberty, the four larger craft, together with the half-dozen gondolas and several new galleys. Sir Guy Carleton was not less busy and active than Arnold. Bringing a large force of shipwrights, riggers, and sailors, from Quebec, together with frames of vessels, sup-

* Sparks's Life of Arnold.

plies of timber, cordage, guns, and everything that was necessary for constructing and fitting out ships-of-war, the Canadian governor was soon enabled to launch at St. Johns a formidable fleet.

Toward the end of September, Arnold was prepared for a cruise, and set sail down the lake. General Gates had ordered him not to advance beyond the Isle-aux-Têtes (near what is now called Rouse's point), at the northern part of Lake Champlain, where its waters are narrowed toward the outlet of the Sorel river. When Arnold had reached Windmill point, within four miles of the Isle-aux-Têtes, observing that that island and the neighboring shores were in possession of the British, he came to anchor, moving his flotilla across the lake. Having occasion to land his men, in order to cut some timber and brushwood for the purpose of raising the bulwarks of his little vessels, and thus prevent them from being so accessible to boarders, he found that his position was not yet secure from annoyance by the enemy. A party that he had sent ashore had, in fact, been set upon by an ambuscade of Indians, and driven to their boats, with the loss of several killed and wounded. Arnold now weighed anchor, and sailed back some eight or ten miles, until he reached Isle-la-Motte.

From this point scouts were sent along the banks of the lake, and guard-boats stationed in advance along its waters, in order to watch the approach of the enemy, and obtain information of their movements. From what was thus learned, Arnold thought it advisable to move still farther down, and accordingly sailed back and took a position with his flotilla in the narrowest part of the channel between Valcour island and the western bank of the lake. Here he stretched his little vessels in line across and toward the upper part of the strait. While thus moored, awaiting the approach of the enemy, he was reinforced, from Crown Point, by the cutter Lee, of four guns; the three galleys Congress, Washington, and Trumbull, each of ten guns; and several additional gondolas. His whole force in guns now amounted to ninety; in metal, six hundred and forty-seven pounds; and in men, most of whom were soldiers, to six hundred.

The advance guard-boats were constantly on the lookout, as the approach of the British was hourly expected. At break of day, accordingly, Carleton's fleet hove in sight off Cumberland head to the north, and its approach was duly reported. As vessel after vessel bore down, the appearance of the enemy was truly formidable. There was the ship Inflexible, of sixteen guns; the schooner Maria, of fourteen; the schooner Carleton, of twelve; the razee Thunderer, of fourteen; the gondola Royal Consort, of six; together with a score of gun-boats, four long-boats, each armed with a gun, and four-and-twenty other small craft.

Carleton had almost proved himself a match in activity for even the energetic Arnold. The ship Inflexible had been got ready to sail within twenty-eight days after her keel had been laid; and between July and October, so great had been the despatch of the enemy, that no less than

Oct. 11.

"thirty fighting-vessels of different sorts and sizes, and all carrying cannon," had been equipped. Carleton, however, had all the resources of the British fleet, then at Quebec, at his command. British men-of-war supplied abundant materials, educated naval officers to superintend the work, skilful artificers to execute it, and all the possible requirements for building and equipping vessels-of-war. The preparations had all been conducted by Captain Douglas, of the Isis; and, when the fleet was ready to sail, seamen to the number of more than seven hundred were drafted from the naval ships at Quebec, to man the squadron of the lake; while each vessel was officered by lieutenants and midshipmen, and the whole were commanded by the British naval captain Pringle, of the Lord Howe. Carleton himself, though yielding the direction of the fleet to the nautical experience of Pringle, could not restrain his ardor to be a witness of the struggle, and accordingly went on board the flag-ship, the Inflexible, determined to share the common danger. The young officers, some of them now for the first time in separate command, were full of eager desire to distinguish themselves. Among the midshipmen was the youthful Pellew (already noticed for his gallantry), afterward famous as Lord Exmouth.

The British fleet bore for the southern point of Valcour island, with the view of rounding it, and bringing the whole force against Arnold's line stretched across the strait to the north. The wind, however, was unfavorable for this manœuvre, and only the smaller craft were able to enter the channel, as the larger vessels had not room to beat up, and could not sail sufficiently close hauled.

Arnold, observing the difficulty, and seeing the British force thus divided, ordered three of his galleys and his schooner the Royal Savage to get under way. He himself took the lead, on board the Congress galley, and sailed, followed by the rest, to attack those of the enemy in advance, which consisted of all their small craft and the schooner Carleton of twelve guns, commanded by Lieutenant Dacres.

The engagement soon began, hot and heavy, and continued from eleven o'clock in the morning till five in the afternoon. The American boats suffered greatly, and none more than the Congress, which Arnold took care to keep in the hottest of the struggle. He was constantly on deck, pointing the guns with his own hands; and, when the enemy retired from the fight, Arnold's galley was almost a wreck, with her hull riddled with shot, her mast barely standing, her rigging torn into shreds, and a large proportion of her men killed or wounded. The Washington galley, commanded by Waterbury, had hardly suffered less, her captain being wounded, her lieutenant with many of her men killed, and the vessel itself well shattered. One gondola lost every officer but her captain, and another sank immediately after the engagement. No less than sixty in all were either killed or wounded.

The Royal Savage, in attempting to reach the line, got aground, when she was set on fire by her crew, and abandoned. The larger British vessels, which were unable to take part in the action, strove, by landing their men and some Indians on Valcour island, to harass the Americans with musketry; but, although they kept up a constant fire, they only added to the confusion and excitement of the scene, and failed to do much damage.

Arnold, upon retiring to his former anchorage, called a council of his officers, when it was unanimously resolved that, with the superiority in ships, men, and armament, of the British, it was impossible to cope with them, and that the only resource left was to attempt to escape back to Crown Point. How to accomplish this was, however, the great difficulty, as the enemy had stretched their vessels across the strait, within only a few hundred yards of the American line. As the night was dark, and the wind blew favorably from the north, Arnold determined upon the bold expedient of passing through the British fleet. The attempt was made, and with perfect success. The Trumbull galley, commanded by Colonel Wigglesworth, of the Massachusetts militia, led the retreat, with barely enough sail set to give her steerageway, and a lantern under her stern, so masked as not to be seen except by those directly in her wake. The rest of the squadron (each with a lantern hung at her stern in the same manner) followed in succession, at intervals of two or three hundred yards. The night was profoundly dark, and a heavy fog hung over the lake. Strict silence was enjoined, and thus each vessel sailed, in the dead of night, through the enemy's line, Arnold bringing up the rear with his usual disregard or rather love of danger. The British were so completely kept in the dark, that they were unconscious of his escape until next morning, when he had reached Schuyler's island, some ten miles up the lake.

Arnold was now brought to a stop by the ill condition of his vessels, which had been so damaged in the fight, that all of them were either leaking or required to have new sails bent. Two of the gondolas were such complete wrecks, that they were abandoned and sunk. The necessary repairs detained him for half a day at Schuyler's island, and Arnold was not enabled to get under way again until the evening.

The wind proving favorable, Arnold made good progress during the night. In the morning, however, a fresh breeze sprang up from the south, **Oct. 13.** dead ahead; and, although it was unfavorable for both the pursued and the pursuing, the enemy succeeded in gaining upon the rear of the American flotilla. The two galleys, the Washington and Congress, and four of the gondolas—all of which were in bad sailing-condition, from the damages they had suffered—were soon overtaken by the leading British vessels, which crowded all sail in chase. The Washington was the first to suffer, and, having received a broadside or two, was forced to strike. The enemy now bore up against Arnold's galley, the Congress. Arnold did not refuse the fight, notwithstanding the odds against him of a ship and two schooners. Unequal as was the struggle, he resolutely engaged in it, and with such a brave and skilful resistance, that it was prolonged for four hours; and Arnold did not withdraw his galley until she was nearly a wreck, and the enemy had been reinforced by four additional vessels, and thus with seven of their larger craft were preparing to surround him on all sides.

Arnold, finding himself in this extremity, ran the Congress and the four gondolas ashore. He then ordered all the boats, with their flags flying, to be set on fire, and his men to spring overboard with their muskets in hand, and, having waded to the land, to draw up and keep off the enemy's small boats should they attempt an attack. Arnold himself was the last man to leave the galley; and, on reaching the shore, he stood his guard until the flames had so enveloped the whole flotilla, that hardly a plank was left to fall into the hands of the enemy.

Arnold then pushed on by land through the forest to Ticonderoga, where on his arrival he found the remnant of his flotilla—the two schooners, two galleys, one sloop, and the gondola—which, by being in advance, and in fair sailing-condition, had succeeded in escaping Carleton's fleet. Every one awarded to Arnold great credit for his daring and the skill with which he managed his little flotilla in so unequal a struggle, although some have doubted his prudence in engaging with the enemy under such disadvantages.

Sir Guy Carleton treated the prisoners with his usual humanity and chivalrous courtesy. He ordered his army-surgeons to take the same care of the American wounded as they did of his own men. The others he sent for on board his own ship, where "he first treated them to a drink of grog," and then praised their courage; and, after expressing a regret that it had not been displayed in the service of their lawful sovereign, offered to send them home to their friends, on their giving their parole that they would not again bear arms against Great Britain until they should be exchanged.

General Waterbury, who had commanded the Washington, was invited by Carleton into his cabin below, and asked for his commission. When it was shown, and observed to be signed by Governor Trumbull, of Connecticut, the courteous Sir Guy gave his prisoner his hand, saying: "General Waterbury, I am happy to take you by the hand, now that I see that you are not serving under a commission and orders of the rebel Congress, but of Governor Trumbull. You are acting under a legitimate and acknowledged authority. He is responsible for the abuse he has made of that authority. That which is a high crime in him, is but an error in you: it was your duty to obey him, your legitimate authority."[*]

In a few days after Arnold's defeat, a number of row-boats pulled up the lake, and lay upon their oars off the advanced posts of the Americans. The boats bore a flag of truce, and contained General Waterbury and one hundred and ten prisoners, who were now returned on parole by Sir Guy Carleton. This noble-hearted Englishman had treated those who had fallen into his hands by the chances of war with so much humanity and even gentle courtesy, and each man who returned was so full of gratitude and ex-

[*] Autobiography, &c., by John Trumbull.

47

pressions of good feeling toward Sir Guy, that he was thought to "have made a very dangerous impression." The boats, therefore, which contained the prisoners were placed under the guns of a battery, and orders given that not a man should be allowed to land, lest by intercourse with the American troops he might affect them with a dangerous good will toward the enemy. The prisoners were accordingly, immediately after their arrival was reported to General Gates, ordered to proceed to Skenesborough, on their way to their homes; and they went forward the same night, without being permitted to land. We know of no such illustration as this fact exhibits, of the humanity of a chivalrous enemy, as well as of the policy of such conduct. Many such British officers might have proved fatal to the American cause.

Sir Guy meanwhile did not neglect the more positive duties of his command. He advanced with his whole force, and took possession of Crown Point; and thence sent out a reconnoitring-party to observe the condition of the Americans at Ticonderoga. Gates was prepared to make an effective display of his powers of resistance. He had been largely reinforced, and now mustered nearly thirteen thousand men, who by proper care and timely supplies of food and clothing, were in a tolerably effective condition. So soon as Carleton's boats appeared off a point within three miles of Ticonderoga, Gates ordered his whole force under arms, and each man to his post. The American lines must have made an imposing show to those on the lake. The summits of the rising ground on both sides of the water were crowned with redoubts and batteries, bristling with cannon, and full manned with soldiers, while above all floated the new flag of the United States.

The enemy's boats retired, but Gates did not neglect to continue to prepare for an attack. The works were manned at daylight each morning, and the troops kept busy the whole day in strengthening the defences. Poles of twelve feet in length were cut in the neighboring forests, armed with sharp iron points, and kept in readiness within the breastworks to thrust back the assailants in case of an assault. Carleton, however, did not advance, whether owing to the formidable appearance of his antagonists at Ticonderoga, or to the strong southerly wind which had continued to blow in his teeth ever since his arrival at Crown Point, and prevented the advance of his vessels. Finally, Gates, growing impatient, ordered a detachment of troops to march toward Crown Point, to reconnoitre. They soon returned, with the information **Nov. 1.** that Sir Guy with his whole fleet and army had abandoned that post, and withdrawn into Canada. The enemy gone, there was less occasion for the American army to remain. A small force, under General St. Clair, having been left to garrison the post at Ticonderoga, the remainder of the troops were ordered to other service. Gates proceeded to Albany, and Arnold to join Washington's army.

CHAPTER XXXII.

1776. SIR WILLIAM HOWE, after his long inactivity, began at last to show some disposition to move. Early one morning the British men-of-war, the Roebuck, Phœnix, a frigate of twenty guns, and several tenders, which had been stationed off Bloomingdale, taking advantage of a fair southerly breeze, got under way and sailed up the Hudson.

Oct. 9. The batteries and forts on both sides of the river kept up a heavy fire, but the ships sailed by them without much damage. The famous *chevaux-de-frise*, that had been stretched across the stream under the auspices of "Old Put," proved still less an obstruction, notwithstanding the old gap in it had been filled in. The ships, borne by a strong flood-tide and a fair wind, came with head on, and broke through the barrier with hardly a check to their way, chasing before them the two vessels laden down with stones, ready to be sunk, to add to the strength of the *chevaux-de-frise*, the four armed galleys stationed to protect it, an American vessel from the West Indies, with a cargo of rum and molasses, anchored for safety under the cover of the guns of the fort, and a small schooner containing Bushnell's "American Turtle." The two ships were driven ashore by their pursuers; two of the galleys secured a retreat; two were run aground and fell into the enemy's hands, although their crews saved themselves by swimming; the West-India skipper was forced to strike his flag; and a well-aimed shot sent the small schooner, with Bushnell's submarine exploder, to the bottom — meeting a fate, as General Heath remarks, "finely in contrast with its design;" for the purpose of the "American Turtle" was to destroy, and not to be destroyed.

Washington saw in this movement of the enemy's ships an intention to stop the navigation of the Hudson, and thus cut off his communication and supplies by that river. He immediately sent an express to General James Clinton, who commanded at the Highlands, to put him on his guard, in case there should be any attempt upon the posts and forts above. He also ordered a detachment of troops from his camp to hurry along the eastern bank of the river, to oppose the enemy in case they should land. As Putnam was still sanguine of the efficacy of his favorite *chevaux-de-frise*, Washington was induced to send a party to try and get off the two stone-laden ships which had got aground, and in the meantime to order some old hulks to be filled up and towed down to close the break in the obstruction across the river, and thus prevent, if possible, the return of the ships to their anchorage in the bay.

The convention of the state of New York were greatly agitated by the advance of the enemy's ships up their main river. They had great distrust of many of the population, and believed that this movement was in co-operation with the disaffected, with the view of seizing such passes as would cut off the communication between the interior and Washington's army, and thus prevent supplies. They therefore strenuously urged upon the commander-in-chief the propriety of sending a body of men to the Highlands or to Peekskill, to " secure the passes, prevent insurrection, and overawe the disaffected."

Washington was induced by these apprehensions which the convention were under, on account of the disaffected whom they had reason to suppose were plotting so much mischief, to order up a part of the militia which had lately come in from Massachusetts, under the new general, Lincoln, to prevent if possible the consequences which might happen, and which it was believed the conspirators had in contemplation. " I am persuaded," says Washington, " that they are upon the eve of breaking out, and that they will leave nothing unessayed that will distress us and favor the designs of the enemy, as soon as their schemes are rife for it."

The attention of the commander-in-chief was, however, soon called to a more pressing danger near at hand. The enemy had landed on " Trog's" point (Throgg's it is now always called, though Washington writes Trog's) in large force. Nine ships and a great number of transports and store-vessels, " full of men," had been observed to pass up the sound the night before, and it was believed that the greatest part of Howe's army had moved upward with the view of getting in the rear of Washington's lines and cutting off his communication with the country. " Our situation here," writes Washington, " is not exactly the same as it was at New York. It is rather better." He had some hope, by extending his force, now consisting of some nineteen thousand, toward East and West Chester, to oppose the enemy, and prevent the accomplishment of their plans.

Oct. 12.

General Howe, after landing, did not seem to be very impatient to begin operations. He was waiting (he afterward said, in explanation) for the arrival of reinforcements and stores, while the Americans believed that he was forced to hold back in consequence of the state of the causeway, which had been broken up, and which was necessary for the conveyance of his troops and artillery from Throgg's point to the mainland. His landing, moreover, was opposed by some vigorous manifestations on the part of the American forces. Howe finally re-embarked, and landed at Pell's point, whence he began to move his troops toward New Rochelle.

The arrival of General Lee at this anxious time, on his return from the South, was welcomed by the whole American army. " The troops,"

Oct. 14.

says a contemporary, "were mightily elated with his presence, and felt themselves stronger by one thousand men upon the occasion; for they had great confidence in his abilities, and expected much from him, because of the success which had attended him at Charleston." Washington at once gave him the command of the division stationed above Kingsbridge. The other three divisions were under Generals Heath, Sullivan, and Lincoln. Greene had command of the post on the Jersey shore, opposite to Fort Washington, previously called "Fort Constitution," now changed to "Fort Lee," in honor of the general whose arrival seemed so greatly to be welcomed by all.

Lee's success in the South had greatly added to his reputation; and when Washington's army was apparently in such a strait at New York, Congress despatched an express to Georgia, ordering him to repair immediately to Philadelphia. He at once obeyed the summons; and, having waited on Congress, and consulted with that body, it was resolved that he should proceed to Washington's camp without delay, although leave was granted to him to visit the American posts in New Jersey. Lee accordingly, before presenting himself at Washington's headquarters, visited the camp at Amboy, just previous to crossing to New York. While there, he took occasion to make a survey of the enemy's position and movements on Staten island. Here, on the day of his arrival, Lee beheld a great encampment of Hessians, and on the next morning discovered that every tent was struck, and the whole force had disappeared.

Thereupon he writes to Congress, and in his usual emphatic style says: **Oct. 12.** "I am confident they will not attack General Washington's lines; such a measure is too absurd for a man of Mr. Howe's genius; and unless they have received flattering accounts from Burgoyne that he will be able to effectuate a junction (which I conceive they have not), they will no longer remain kicking their heels at New York. They will put the place in a respectable state of defence, which, with their command of the waters, may be easily done, leave four or five thousand men, and direct their operations to a more decisive object.

"They will infallibly proceed either immediately up the river Delaware with their whole troops; or, what is more probable, land somewhere about South Amboy or Shrewsbury, and march straight to Trenton or Burlington. On the supposition that this will be the case, what are we to do? What force have we? What means have we to prevent their possessing themselves of Philadelphia? General Washington's army can not possibly keep pace with them. The length of his route is not only infinitely greater, but his obstructions almost insuperable. In short, before he could cross Hudson river, they might be lodged and strongly fortified on both banks of the Delaware. ...For Heaven's sake, arouse yourselves! For Heaven's sake, let ten thousand men be immediately assembled and stationed somewhere about Trenton! In my opinion, your whole cause depends upon it. I set out immediately for headquarters, where I shall communicate my apprehension that such will be the next operation of the enemy, and urge the expediency of sparing a part of his army (if he has any to spare) for this object."*

A few days after writing this letter, General Lee had an opportunity of making known his views and sustaining his opinions before a council of war called by Washington. A warm discussion took place, and Lee was among the foremost in the debate, strenuously urging the necessity of extending the American lines toward East and West Chester, in order to outflank the enemy, whose purpose evidently was to hem in Washington by drawing a line in his rear. There was considerable opposition to his views, it being contended that the island of New York, as it was well defended by strong posts, and difficult of access, might be held, and that it was there that the army should remain and await the attack of the enemy. Lee asked what they meant by thinking of holding their position, while Howe had the command of the water on each side of them, and was so strong both in front and rear, and there was but a single communication with the mainland held by themselves, and that only a bridge (King's bridge), over which they must pass to escape being enclosed. He declared that it was fallacious to suppose a position was good merely because its approaches were difficult, and stoutly argued against the policy of having anything to do with the islands, adding that for his part he "would give Mr. Howe a fee simple in them."

Oct. 16.

* American Archives, fifth series, 11, 1008, quoted by Irving.

These opinions, emphatically expressed, evidently had their effect; so that when the question was put—"Whether, it having appeared that the obstructions in the North river have proved insufficient, and that the enemy's whole force is in our rear at Throgg's point, it is now deemed possible in our present situation to prevent the enemy from cutting off the communication with the country, and compelling us to fight them at all disadvantages or surrender prisoners at discretion?"—it was agreed, with the single dissenting voice of General Clinton, that it was not possible to prevent the communication from being cut off, and that one of the consequences mentioned must certainly follow.

Lee was equally emphatic in denouncing the attempt to hold Fort Washington, but not equally successful in impressing the council with his views. The generals were probably influenced by a late resolution of Congress, desiring Washington, "by every art and at whatever expense, to obstruct effectually the navigation of the river between Fort Washington and Mount Constitution, as well to prevent the regress of the enemy's frigates lately gone up, as to hinder them from receiving succor." Apart from this, there were some who believed that the fort should be held at all risks. Among them was General Greene, who was stationed at Fort Lee. He contended that the possession of Fort Washington would divert a large body of the enemy, and thus divide the force of Howe; and that it, in conjunction with Fort Lee opposite, would serve to cover the transportation of provisions and other articles up the North river for the service of the American troops. He moreover held that, at the worst, the garrison would be safe, as they could be conveyed away at any moment by boats from the Jersey side of the river. It was finally agreed by the council of war that Fort Washington be retained as long as possible. More than two thousand men were accordingly assigned for that purpose; and Colonel Magaw, to whom the command was given, was urged to defend the position to the last.

Sir William Howe, reinforced by a large body of Hessians under General Knyphausen, just arrived from Germany, continued to gather his forces on the New-York border of the sound, and to extend them northward.

Oct. 22.

Washington, in the meantime, having stationed Lee on Valentine's hill, beyond Kingsbridge, with one of the four divisions of the army, the rest followed and formed a line of detached camps along the western side of the river Bronx, extending from Lee's position to White Plains, a distance of thirteen miles. The chief himself abandoned the Morris mansion, on Harlem heights, and, after remaining a few days with Lee at Valentine's hill, established his headquarters near White Plains. General Heath, who had the command of the division of the army toward Long-island sound, was directed to watch and harass the enemy as much as possible in that quarter, while landing and marching into the interior.

WILLIAM HEATH, a native of Roxbury, in Massachusetts, like many of the New-England officers, was a farmer, and had left the plough to gird on the sword. He had, however, according to his own account, a very early proclivity toward a martial life, and read every book which fell in his way on military tactics, until he became, as he tells us, quite a proficient in the theory of war. He was commissioned by the Congress of his own province, in 1775. During the siege of Boston, he was present as a general officer, but when offered the command of a division, "he declined the hazardous service."* Having been appointed a few months before by Congress a major-general in the continental army, he was now in command of one of its divisions. Heath was in person corpulent and bald-headed, and seemed flattered by being reminded that he resembled the marquis of Granby. He had little opportunity of playing the hero, but proved himself an officer who was always faithful to duty; and, though of an easy temper, he was not without spirit when called upon to sustain his own dignity or the honor of his country.

Howe did not succeed in marching into position without some stout resistance. Glover's brigade was on the alert, and disputed the ground with the advancing parties; and battalions of American riflemen, stationed behind the stone-fences, succeeded in greatly annoying them. Twice the British were repulsed, and it was not until they came up for the third time, and in solid columns, that they were able to force their way. The right and centre of Howe's army now moved two miles

* Thacher.

to the northward of New Rochelle, on the road to White Plains.

The two armies, in the course of this simultaneous movement, were for some distance in a line with each other from north to south, and several skirmishes ensued between the outposts. The great desire of the Americans to get hold of that slippery rogue, Colonel Rogers, was very nearly being gratified. Howe, when encamped beyond New Rochelle, ordered Rogers with his Queen's Rangers to take possession of Mamaroneck, and there establish an outpost. Lord Stirling, who had now rejoined the army (having been lately exchanged), heard of the whereabouts of Rogers, and determined, if possible, to entrap him. A detachment of Colonel Haslet's "Delawares and Marylanders" were selected for the purpose, **Oct. 21.** and the night was chosen, in order that darkness might increase the chances of a successful surprise. Everything was conducted with great caution, and the Americans succeeded in coming upon the "Rangers" and taking them unawares. The guard and an officer were put to the sword, thirty-six were taken prisoners, and a pair of colors, sixty stand of arms, and a supply of clothing and provisions, captured. Rogers, however, succeeded in making his escape, having skulked off in the dark.

These skirmishes became quite frequent, and the spirit with which the Americans conducted them forced Howe to extreme vigilance, and checked the confidence and rapidity of his movements. Washington thus, together with Howe's delay in landing, was enabled to outflank him. The whole movement of the Americans was well conducted. By keeping the Bronx river on his right, and presenting a constant front of well-protected posts to the enemy, Washington was enabled to remove his stores and baggage, and rapidly to extend his line so far into the country, as to defeat the enemy's intention of getting in his rear and hemming him in.

At White Plains, where Washington had proceeded with the advanced division, he chose and fortified his position in such a manner as to afford a cover for his whole army. He defended the front of his camp, which was situated on high ground, by a double line of intrenchments. The right wing, as well as part of the rear, was protected by a bend of the river Bronx, while the left was secured by a deep lake. As the British continued to advance, and after Washington had succeeded in bringing up all his baggage and stores, he ordered the detached posts to be abandoned, and withdrew all his army, with the exception of the garrison at Fort Washington, within his fortified camp at White Plains.

Lee, of course, came in with his division, and none was more conspicuous than he, looked up to as he was by all for his supposed military skill, and made not the less remarkable by his whims and oddities. He lodged in a small house near the road by which General Washington and his officers frequently passed when out reconnoitring. On returning, they would occasionally stop and take a dinner with Lee — not, perhaps, so much on account of the good fare of the house, as for the amusing characteristics of the host. Lee, however, affected to be annoyed by these frequent visits, and said one day to his aids : " You must look me out another place, for I shall have Washington and all his puppies continually calling upon me, and they will eat me up !"   The next morning, seeing Washington, surrounded by a suite of officers, coming up the road, the eccentric Lee, expecting another visit, ordered his servant to chalk upon the door of his house, " No victuals dressed here to-day."   When the cavalcade of the chief passed by and read the obvious hint, they spurred on their horses, and laughingly returned to dine that day at their own quarters.

Lee, notwithstanding, was one of the most frequent companions of Washington on these reconnoitring expeditions, and, with no modest reserve, was always of his opinions very free in criticising the disposition of the army.   Washington had a deservedly great opinion of Lee's mili-

tary talents, and always listened to his suggestions with marked attention.   On one occasion, the two rode out together, in company with some officers, when Lee objected to the ground occupied by the army, and, pointing to some heights in the distance, said, " Yonder is the ground we ought to occupy."—" Let us, then, go and view it," answered Washington. He had, however, hardly turned his steed in that direction, when a light-horseman rode up in haste, and quickly exclaimed, " The British are in the camp, sir !"— " Then, gentlemen, we have now other business than reconnoitring," said Washington ; and he galloped with all speed back to the camp, followed by his companions.   On reaching his headquarters, he was informed that the advance-guards had been driven in, and that the enemy were advancing.   Washington then dismissed his officers, saying, " Gentlemen, you will repair to your respective posts, and do the best you can."[*]

CHAPTER XXXIII.

1776.   Though the intelligence of the advance of the enemy came somewhat suddenly to Washington and his reconnoitring-party, the army had already

been posted in order of battle, and was not unprepared to meet the threatened attack.   Washington, however, rode along

the lines to take a final survey, to encourage his men, and make such changes
in the disposition of his troops as the circumstances of the moment might suggest.
On the right, within a short distance of
the camp, there was a height called Chatterton's hill. This was an advantageous
position, as it commanded the right wing,
which, however, was somewhat protected
by the river Bronx, which enclosed by its
windings that part of the camp within an
elbow. Some militia had already been
posted upon the hill; but Washington
now sent Colonel Haslet, with his spirited Delawares and Marylanders, and two
pieces of artillery under Captain Alexander Hamilton, to reinforce the position,
while General M'Dougall was ordered to
take the command of the whole.

Oct. 28. The enemy now showed themselves, advancing in great force
along the acclivities of the heights upon
which they had been encamped. They
came on in two columns, their right under the command of Sir Henry Clinton,
and their left under the Hessian De Heister. It was a fine October noon, and the
arms and gay accoutrements of the well-
appointed army glistening in the mid-day
sun, appeared to the eyes of the Americans " a brilliant but a formidable sight."

The solid British columns moved steadily on, bearing directly for Washington's
front, apparently with the view of driving
everything before them by main strength.
As they approach the village of White
Plains, and toward the American breastworks, there is a sudden pause in the
march, as if momentarily hesitating in
their purpose. The general officers ride

up and gather together in the middle of
a wheatfield, and hold council. Soon the
result is apparent: Howe changes his purpose. His right and centre are still mo-
tionless, but there is a great stir on his
left. The artillery is rapidly drawn into
position and pointed toward Chatterton
hill, on Washington's right ; and working-
parties hurry forward to the Bronx river,
followed by a large detachment of British and Hessian troops, commanded by
General Leslie. At the same moment, a
Hessian brigade, under Colonel Rahl, falls
back to some distance from the left wing,
and covers the Bronx below.

General Leslie, under the cover of the
artillery, which keeps up a constant and
heavy fire, passes over with his whole detachment, and, leaving his cavalry to skirt
the base, pushes directly up the hill with
his body of grenadiers and light-infantry.
His troops are thinned by the two fieldpieces under the skilful handling of the
young Hamilton, and severely galled by
the musketry of the Marylanders. Rahl
has in the meantime crossed the river below, and is ascending the hill toward the
right flank of the Americans. The two
detachments now form a junction and
throng up the heights together, filling
every ravine and covering every acclivity with their numbers.

The American militia soon disposed of
themselves. A shot from the enemy's
artillery at the beginning of the engagement had carried away one man's thigh,
and so frightened the others, that General M'Dougall had great difficulty in keeping them from running away. He finally
posted them, however, behind some stone-

walls, and had got them in a fair way of doing some service, when the sight of about two hundred and fifty British light-horse, dashing about the base of the hill, so alarmed them, that they at once took to their heels!

The combined force of Leslie and Rahl did not gain the summit of the hill without a hard fight. M'Dougall, by the cowardice of the militia, had been left with only six hundred men, but these were the brave troops of Haslet, Smallwood, and Ritzema, and they clung to the ground with such resolution, and resisted the enemy so spiritedly, that the British were twice driven back, and did not finally win the position until after a hard struggle, which lasted for nearly an hour. General M'Dougall brought off the remnant of his men in good order, who disputed every inch of ground with the enemy, as the latter pursued them down the hill, until they were met by General Putnam and a detachment of troops to cover their retreat to the camp. Young Hamilton succeeded in securing his two effective fieldpieces, and nothing was left behind but the bare breastworks upon the hill. Even the wounded were carefully carried off the field. The loss on both sides was about equal, amounting to some three hundred each in killed, wounded, and taken prisoners.

The British, in possession of Chatterton hill, busied themselves in strengthening the position by additional intrenchments and breastworks. General Howe contented himself for the rest of the day with the success of the morning, and toward evening merely moved his right wing closer to the American camp, so that his whole front presented a semicircle. The British troops, resting on their arms during the night, waited for further action until the coming of the next day.

The American militiamen, who had been so frightened by the sight of the English cavalry, gradually in scattered groups found their way back to the lines from the neighboring hills to which they had fled. The undisciplined provincial troops seem to have had as great a dread of a horse with a trooper on his back as the ancient Mexicans when they beheld the mounted warriors of Cortez. Washington, perceiving that this absurd fear of cavalry was creating a great deal of mischief, found it necessary to issue an order, in which he says: "Observing that the army seems unacquainted with the enemy's horse, and that when any parties meet with them they do not oppose them with the same alacrity which they show in other cases, thinks it necessary to inform the officers and soldiers that, in such a broken country, full of stone-walls, no enemy is more to be despised, as they can not leave the road." Washington then tells his militiamen that they can at any time attack a body of horse to advantage by taking post in the woods by the roads, or along the stone-walls, where mounted troops will not venture to follow them. Moreover, "as an encouragement to any brave parties who will endeavor to surprise some of them," the general "offers one hundred dollars for every trooper, with his horse and accoutrements, who shall be brought in, and so in proportion for any part, to be divided according to the rank and the pay of the party."

General Howe was no less disposed to take advantage of this terror of cavalry than Washington was to remove it. Having early observed how apt the militia were to be scared away by a show of mounted troops brandishing their swords, Howe took care to collect throughout the country all the horses he could, in order to keep up his cavalry regiments, which had been greatly thinned by the losses at sea in the course of the long voyages of the transports. He also wrote to the British government for an additional supply; and, whenever occasion offered, he was sure to send out his mounted troopers, to make as clattering and brilliant a dash as possible, in order to frighten the weak nerves of the uninitiated.

Washington was expecting an attack at any moment. His lines were accordingly manned during the whole night, and the men kept at work at the redoubts and breastworks, with but rare intervals of repose, when they were forced to lie down in the "cold trenches." So much exposed, so hard-worked, and in such a wretched condition (from want of proper food and clothing), were the American troops, that some of the officers began to believe that if the enemy did not destroy the American army, it would perish of itself without fighting. The British officers looked on all this misery with undisguised contempt, and spoke mockingly of "the tatterdemalions who have but a few coats among them but what are out of elbows," and of "whole regiments in which there is scarce a pair of breech-

es."[*] We shall find, however, that these "tatterdemalion," ragged and shirtless as they were, succeeded under Washington in checking and outmanœuvring all the brilliant and haughty battalions marshalled by Sir William Howe and his proud staff of officers.

Meager as Washington's resources were, he made the most of them; and in justice to his troops it may be stated that however poor a military show they might make in battle array, they were indefatigable in their labors with the pick and the spade. They worked well and long during that night of anxious expectation, and, before morning, had doubled the intrenchments and raised three re- **Oct. 29.** doubts. The breastworks were rudely made of the best material at hand. Cornstalks were plucked from the neighboring fields, and served, with the earth clinging to their roots, the purpose of sods and fascines.

General Howe, when he observed the result of one night's work upon Washington's line, seemed in no disposition to begin a general attack; and, waiting for reinforcements, he limited himself to an occasional skirmish with the more advanced American posts. Early in the morning, however, he moved his right wing still closer to the left of the Americans. Washington supposed that Howe's design was to get to his rear, according to his original plan. Every measure was taken, therefore, to prevent this movement. The stores and baggage were hurried toward the rear as fast as possible, and the left of the army fell some dis-

[*] Quoted by Irving.

tance back, to prevent being outflanked by Howe's advancing right wing. When this manœuvre of the enemy began, Washington's secretary was writing to Congress thus: "Our post, from its situation, is not so advantageous as could be wished, and was only intended as temporary and occasional, till the stores belonging to the army, which had been deposited here, could be removed. The enemy coming on so suddenly has distressed us much. They are now close at hand, and most probably will in a little time commence their second attack; we expect it every hour; perhaps it is beginning. I have just heard the report of some cannon."

The firing which was heard by the secretary came from a hot skirmish between a detachment of Hessians and Colonel Glover's brigade. The colonel held possession of a height in advance of the American camp, where he had posted his troops behind a breastwork mounted with one brass twenty-four, a six and a three pounder, and three iron twelve-pounders. As the British closed in with their columns, in order to approach nearer to the American camp, Glover determined to harass them. Their line extends from right to left, with the cavalry and artillery in front, as far as can be seen, and no less a number than twelve thousand men appear to be under arms. They approach Glover's position, but he withholds his fire until some of the troops have entered a valley and are about to ascend the heights which bound it. He then begins with his three-pounder, next with his six, and finally with his twenty-four. The British are much confused by this brisk cannonade, but persevere in trying to mount the high ground with their light-horse and artillery. After firing a few rounds, however, they are obliged to retire, and content themselves with a position farther back, and out of reach of Glover's cannon.

Howe evidently was not disposed to risk a general engagement; and, having encamped his army within "long cannon-shot" of the American lines, he awaited the arrival of reinforcements under Earl Percy, who had been ordered up from Harlem, where he was stationed. **Oct. 29.**

While the two armies lay opposite to each other, an incident occurred which a diligent annalist has not thought too frivolous to record, in the absence, during that night of expectation, of more important events. It happened that a garden of a widow woman, which lay between the two hostile camps, had been repeatedly robbed. Her son, a mere boy, and "little of his age," asked permission to try to find out and secure the thief, in case he should return. His mother having consented, the lad, armed with a gun, concealed himself at night among the overgrown weeds of the garden. Soon a great strapping Highlander came groping his way among the cabbages, and, having filled a large bag he carried, prepared to decamp. The lad stole softly after him, and, coming close to the fellow, cocked his gun and called out: "You are my prisoner. If you attempt to throw your bag down. I'll shoot you dead! Go forward in that road." The man did not venture to turn around, but went on as he was bid, with the boy and his gun close after him, and was thus driven into the American camp, where he was secured. The strapping grenadier was now permitted to come to a halt, whereupon he threw down his bag, and turned to look at his captor. When he discovered that he was a mere boy, and "little of his age," he gave vent to his indignant vexation, exclaiming, "A British grenadier made prisoner by such a d——d brat —by such a d——d brat!"*

Oct. 30. Another day passed without any show of active hostility. The British general, however, kept his troops at work in entrenching his camp. In the evening Earl Percy arrived, and the next morning was appointed for the attack upon the American lines. But at midnight, a heavy storm with wind and rain began, and continued during the whole of the following day, so that the British commander was again forced to remain inactive.

Washington, having learned from a deserter, of the arrival of Earl Percy, and of Howe's intended movements, determined to shift his position. Accordingly, in the course of the night, he **Oct. 31.** withdrew his army from White Plains, for a distance of five miles, to the higher ground toward Newcastle and the Croton river, leaving a strong rear-guard on the heights and in the woods of White

* Gordon.

Plains. Washington's ground was admirably chosen; and with the breastworks which he threw up, extending from hill to hill, he could bid defiance to the enemy. Howe, becoming aware in the early morning of this movement, discovered that, with all his brilliant advantages, he had been outmanœuvred, and that it was hopeless to attempt by an assault to dislodge the Americans from their new position. He therefore contented himself with making a demonstration against Washington's rear-guard on the heights of White Plains; but, before his troops could advance to the attack, they were driven back again into camp, to take shelter from the heavy rain.

During the night while the Americans were evacuating White Plains, the village church, the courthouse, and other buildings, were set on fire and burnt by the order of a major in the command of the guards and sentries, while "heated with liquor." Washington was indignant at this act, and warmly expressed himself upon the subject, saying in the general order of the next day: "It is with the utmost astonishment and abhorrence that the general is informed that some base and cowardly wretches last night set fire to the courthouse and other buildings, which the enemy had left. The army may rely on it that they shall be brought to justice, and meet with the punishment they deserve."

CHAPTER XXXIV.

The Enemy decamp.—Puzzling Conduct.—Washington still worried about the Army.—Rebellion among the Troops.—The Americans abandon Fort Independence, &c., on the Approach of the Enemy.—Fort Washington strengthened.—Doubts about holding it.—Washington opposed, Greene in favor, and carries the Day.—Washington at Peekskill.—The Great Preparations of the Enemy against Fort Washington.—Description of the Fort.—The Fort invested.—Summons to surrender.—Magaw's Spirited Response.—The Defences.—Operations of the Assailants.

1776. THE British, after remaining several days in front of the American lines without attempting anything, finally broke up their encampments on the 4th of November, and marched toward the North river and Kingsbridge. Their purpose was a matter of anxious speculation in Washington's camp. Some supposed that they were going into winter-quarters, and would sit down in New York, content with doing nothing more than investing Fort Washington. The general himself wrote: "I can not subscribe wholly to this opinion myself. That they will invest Fort Washington is a matter of which there can be no doubt; and I think there is a strong probability that General Howe will detach a part of his force to make an incursion into the Jerseys, provided he is going to New York. He must attempt something on account of his reputation; for what has he done as yet with his great army?" Governor Livingston, of New Jersey, to whom this letter was written, was then urged by Washington to place the militia of his state on the best possible footing, and recommended to see that the inhabitants contiguous to the water should be prepared to remove their stock, grains, effects, and carriages, upon the earliest notice. Washington believed that New Jersey was to be the scene of the coming campaign, and declared that, as soon as he was satisfied that the movement just made by the enemy was a real retreat, and not a feint, he would, with the utmost expedition, throw over into Jersey a body of troops, to assist in checking Howe's progress.

Washington was still anxious lest he should be left almost without troops. The dissolution of the army was fast approaching, and there seemed but little prospect of levying a new one. "The situation of our affairs," he says, "is critical and alarming." He wrote to the assembly of Massachusetts to raise at once four thousand men properly accoutred and equipped, to supply the place of those under General Lincoln, who it was feared would not be prevailed upon to stay a moment longer than the time they first engaged for.

The New-York militia were in a state of mutiny, and, refusing to do duty, declared that General Howe had promised them *peace, liberty,* and *safety,* and that was all they wanted. "What is to be done with them?" writes General Greene, who had come over from Fort Lee, and found the New-Yorkers stationed at Kingsbridge in this condition of almost open revolt. "This spirit," he declares, "should be checked in its infancy....I propose," he adds, "to send to the colonel about fifty men, and I have directed him to acquaint the militia that if they refuse to do duty, agreeably to the orders of the state, I will send up a regiment and order them to Fort Lee, to do duty there."

Knyphausen had been despatched by General Howe, previous to his own movement in that direction, with six battalions of Hessians and Waldeckers, to take possession of Kingsbridge. He started from New Rochelle, and marched across the country to the west, and, after crossing the Harlem river at Dykeman's bridge, took up his post on a plain near King's bridge. The Americans, deserting Fort Independence and all the works in that neighborhood on his approach, retired to Fort Washington.

General Howe had now reached the North river with his main body, and was encamped at Dobbs's ferry. A **Nov. 6.** frigate and two transports were immediately despatched by his brother, Lord Howe, from the fleet in New-York harbor, to carry supplies to the general. They succeeded without difficulty in passing through the *chevaux-de-frise* and the forts again, and anchored safely in the river. As the main purpose of holding Fort Washington seemed to be thus entirely frustrated, the commander-in-chief had doubts about the expediency of defending that post. He accord- **Nov. 8.** ingly writes to General Greene: "The late passage of three vessels up the North river, of which we have just re-

ceived advice, is so plain a proof of the inefficacy of all the obstructions we have thrown into it, that I can not but think it will justify a change in the disposition which has been made. If we can not prevent vessels from passing up, and the enemy are possessed of the surrounding country, what valuable purpose can it answer to attempt to hold a post from which the expected benefit can not be had? I am therefore inclined to think that it will not be prudent to hazard the men and stores at Mount Washington; but as you are on the spot, I leave it to you to give such orders as to evacuating Mount Washington as you may judge best, and so far revoking the order given to Colonel Magaw to defend it to the last." The opinion of Washington is here very explicitly declared against holding the post, but he modestly waived his own views, and, as he had great confidence in Greene's judgment, he left more to his discretion than he otherwise probably would have done.

The defence of Fort Washington was a pet measure with Greene; and, in spite of the opposition of the commander-in-chief, of General Lee, Colonel Reed, and the most skilful of the officers, he advocated it with resolute pertinacity. General Greene answers Washington's letter, saying: "The passing of the ships up the river is, to be sure, a full proof of the insufficiency of the obstructions to stop the ships from going up; but that garrison employs double the number of men to invest it that we have to occupy it. They must keep troops to Kingsbridge, to prevent a communication with the country; and they dare not leave a very small number, for fear our people should attack them. Upon the whole, I can not help thinking that the garrison is of advantage; and I can not conceive it to be in any great danger."

Greene was confirmed in his view of the strength of the position by the confident declaration of Colonel Magaw, in command of the garrison, that it would take the enemy, to get it, at least until the end of December. Moreover, Greene held that if matters should grow desperate, the men could be brought off at any time; and even the stores, though not so easily removed, might be got away. Finally, he concludes, "if the enemy do not find the fort an object of importance, they will not trouble themselves about it; if they do, it is a full proof that they feel an injury from our possessing it. Our giving it up will open a free communication with the country by the way of Kingsbridge. That must be a great advantage to them, and injury to us."

The enemy now prepared to invest Fort Washington; and the garrison, in command of the brave Colonel Magaw, to defend it.

Washington, believing that Howe was preparing for an expedition to New Jersey, disposed his troops accordingly. The Maryland and Virginia regiments, under Lord Stirling, were the first sent across, and the commander-in-chief himself prepared soon to follow them. The posts in the Highlands, including the passes on both sides of the Hudson, and the upper forts, Constitution, Montgomery, and Independence, were placed under the command of the faithful Heath, with his Con-

49

necticut and Massachusetts troops, and a brigade of New-York militia under General George Clinton. Washington followed this division to Peekskill, in order to examine the passes in the Highlands, and direct the construction of such works as might be necessary.

Nov. 11.

General Lee was left in command of the troops remaining at the old encampment at Newcastle. The confidence of the commander-in-chief in Lee's capacity, as well as Washington's own modest appreciation of himself in comparison with his high esteem of his subordinate, may be inferred from the nature of his "instructions."

"The late movement of the enemy," says Washington, "and the probability of their having designs upon the Jerseys, confirmed by sundry accounts from deserters and prisoners, rendering it necessary to throw a body of troops over the North river, I shall immediately follow, and the command of the army which remains, after General Heath's division marches to Peekskill, will devolve upon you.

"A little time now must manifest the enemy's designs, and point out to you the measures proper to be pursued by that part of the army under your command. I shall give no directions, therefore, on this head, having the most entire confidence in your judgment and military exertions. One thing, however, I will suggest, namely, that the appearance of embarking troops for the Jerseys may be intended as a feint to weaken us, and render the strong post we now hold more vulnerable; or the enemy may find that troops are assembled with more expedition and in greater numbers than they expected, on the Jersey shore, to oppose them; and as it is possible, from one or the other of these motives, that they may yet pay the army under your command a visit, it will be unnecessary, I am persuaded, to recommend to you the propriety of putting this post, if you stay at it, into a proper posture of defence, and of guarding against surprises. But I would recommend it to your consideration, whether, should the above conjectures be realized, your retiring to Croton bridge, and some strong post still more easterly, covering the other passes through the Highlands, may not be more advisable than to run the hazard of an attack with unequal numbers."

The troops under Lee now numbered about eight thousand men. Among these there were, however, over four thousand militia from Massachusetts and Connecticut, whose term of service was about expiring. General Lee strove to induce them to remain, and made one of his usual stirring appeals to their patriotism, reminding them of the sacred cause in which they were engaged. His eloquence, however, proved of no avail, and the homesick militiamen could not be persuaded to remain even a single day beyond their term. The governors of Connecticut and Massachusetts were, nevertheless, doing their best to fill their places by new levies of militia.

Washington, after his arrival at Peekskill, passed a day in inspecting the posts and forts in the Highlands. He then, by a circuitous march of about sixty miles (which he was obliged to take in consequence of the British ships which opposed the passage at the lower ferries of the Hudson), repaired with five thousand men to Hackensack, in New Jersey, where he formed an encampment. Fort Lee, on the river, where Greene commanded, was in front of him, and this was his daily post of observation. The movements and intentions of the enemy were still perplexing. Sir William Howe had moved his main force from Dobbs's ferry in the direction of Kingsbridge; "and it seems," says Washington, "to be generally believed on all hands that the investing of Fort Washington is one object they have in view; but that can employ but a small part of their force." He thought that a southern expedition was intended, which opinion seemed to be confirmed by the fact that many transports were "wooding and watering."

Nov. 13.

Fort Washington was, however, at this moment, the great object of all the enemy's preparations. On the night of the 14th of November, thirty flat-boats had been sent up from the British fleet in the bay of New York, and, having passed up the Hudson between the forts unobserved —in spite of all the watchfulness of the American guards—got safely into Spuyten-Devil creek, and thence into the Harlem river. At this point the boats were kept in readiness for the use of General Howe's army, now brought down and encamped on Fordham heights, preparatory to the investment of Fort Washington. By means of this water-conveyance, the British commander was enabled to throw across the Harlem river at any point on New-York island, above or below, those troops which might be required to aid his operations.

Mount Washington, which was destined to be the scene of the coming conflict, presents a good site for a defensive work. The hill, with a height of some six hundred feet above the Hudson, is protected on all sides, except toward the south, by steep acclivities. Upon the summit is a stretch of table-land, of several acres in extent, which always affords some point for the command of each approach. Here was built the fort, which had been hastily thrown up by Colonel Rufus Putnam soon after the march of Washington's army from Boston to New York. The design was, to give a pentagonal form to the citadel, and surround it with five bastions. However, from want of engineering skill, of time, or of care, the works remained incomplete, as may be gathered from this description by one who was doing duty in its defence : "There were no barracks, or casemates, or fuel, or water, within the body of the place. It was an open, earthen construction, with ground at a short distance on the back of it equally high, if not higher ; without a ditch of any consequence, if there was a ditch at all ; no outworks (an incipient one on the north, not deserving the appellation), or any of those exterior, multiplied obstacles and defences, that could entitle it to the name of a fortress, in any degree capable of sustaining a siege. It required no parallels to approach it: the citadel was at once within reach of the assailants."*

* Graydon.

It was garrisoned at first by only about two thousand men, to which were added, however, some troops from the flying camp, sent over by General Greene from Fort Lee, making the whole number nearly three thousand, under the several commands of Colonels Magaw, Cadwallader, Baxter, and Rawlings. Magaw, as the senior of these officers, was commander-in-chief of the post. He was a spirited fellow, and spoke confidently of his ability to hold the place. The original purpose of the fort (which was, to command the entrance of the Hudson) had been so often defeated by the enemy's ships and boats defiantly passing it, that its defence was by many considered unnecessary and impolitic. The matter, however, had been left to the discretion of General Greene, and he encouraged Magaw in bravely resisting to the last.

The enemy now made such a disposition of their troops, that they were enabled to environ the whole fortress. General Knyphausen was near Kingsbridge, at the north, with five hundred Hessians and Waldeckers, in two divisions, the right one of which was commanded by Colonel Rahl. To the east was General Mathew, at the head of the first and second battalions of guards, supported by Lord Cornwallis with the thirty-third regiment and a body of British grenadiers. These were on the east side of the Harlem river, which they were ready to cross, under the cover of two redoubts raised there for that purpose. Lord Percy had been ordered down to the neighborhood of Harlem plains, whence he was prepared with a large force of English and Hessian troops to attack the American position from the south. A third division, composed principally of the forty-second regiment, was under Lieutenant-Colonel Stirling, who was directed to be in readiness to embark on board the flat-boats, and drop down the Harlem, with the view of making a feint of landing, or such an attack as circumstances would justify. General Howe, being thus prepared, summoned Magaw to surrender, threatening extremities in case of refusal. To this summons Magaw unhesitatingly answered :—

Nov. 15.

"Sir: If I rightly understand the purport of your message from General Howe, communicated to Colonel Swoope, this post is to be immediately surrendered, or put to the sword. I think it rather a mistake than a settled purpose of General Howe, to act a part so unworthy of himself and the British nation. But give me leave to assure his excellency that, actuated by the most glorious cause that mankind ever fought in, I am determined to defend this post to the very last extremity.

"Robert Magaw."

A copy of this spirited answer of Magaw was handed to General Greene, who was then at Fort Washington, and by him despatched immediately to the commander-in-chief at Hackensack. Washington at once hurried to Fort Lee, and, taking a boat, began to push across the river. He had got partly over, when he was met by Generals Putnam and Greene, on their return from Fort Washington. They informed him that the troops were in high

spirits, and would make a good defence. Washington, after this satisfactory intelligence, and it being late at night, was induced to return.

Magaw now prepared to defend his position. Early next morning, he posted his troops, partly in the lines which had been thrown up by the army in the neighborhood of Mount Washington on evacuating New York, and partly on a commanding hill lying toward the north. Magaw seemed conscious of the inadequacy of the defences of the fort, and therefore preferred, instead of cooping up his troops where they would be ill able to resist an assault, to extend them in such a way as to command, if possible, the approaches to Mount Washington, upon the summit of which stood the ill-conditioned fortress. The lines thus occupied by the American troops embraced a circuit of some four or five miles; and when we recollect that the whole number amounted to only about three thousand men, it may be easily conceived that there could be at no single point any great concentration of strength. An attacking force of nearly eight thousand men at its command could therefore outnumber greatly its opponents in every direction.

Nov. 16.

On a hill to the northward of the fort there was a redoubt, called Fort George. Here Colonel Rawlings was posted, with most of his troops, principally Maryland riflemen. He held, however, with a few men, an outpost called Cock-hill fort, situated beyond, just at the entrance of Spuyten-Devil creek; and another, called Fort Tryon, in the same direction, but nearer Mount Washington. Colonel Rawlings presented a front to oppose Knyphausen and his Hessians, stationed before him on the plain reaching to Kingsbridge.

On the wooded and hilly banks of the Harlem river, eastward of the fort, was Colonel Baxter, with a body, chiefly of militia, detached from the flying camp, and sent by Greene at the last moment, from New Jersey. These troops were not very efficient, and so few in numbers in proportion to the long extent of ground to be guarded, that for a distance of a mile or more the heights on the east, along the Harlem river, were in reality without defence. Baxter was to watch the movements of the enemy on the opposite side of the river, where General Mathew was posted, in readiness to cross and attempt to make a landing in front of the fort, under cover of the redoubts which had been raised by the British for that purpose.

Colonel Lambert Cadwallader, of Philadelphia, with about eight hundred men, chiefly the Pennsylvania regiment of Magaw, was posted about two and a half miles to the southward of the fort, to defend the American works in that quarter. These were composed of two lines, each about a mile in length, nearly parallel, which extended from near the Harlem river, across the island, to the Hudson. The first line, toward New York, was " a slight intrenchment, with a few weak bastions, without platforms for cannon, and furnished with no other ordnance than a few old iron pieces of small calibre, scarcely fit for use, and an iron six-pounder mounted on trucks. The second and inner line was stronger, both from the nature of the ground, which afforded small eminences for bastions closed in the rear, and from having the intervals between the bastions strongly picketed. The first line seemed calculated rather for retarding the approach of the enemy, than as a seriously defensive work ; it being nothing more (with the exception of the bastions) than a shallow ditch, with the earth thrown outward. The second line was formed at a proper distance from the first, so as to protect the latter by musketry as well as cannon, and to drive out the enemy, should he get possession of it: but this second line, on the day of the attack of Fort Washington, was from necessity wholly without defence, either of troops or artillery of any description."* Earl Percy, with his fifteen hundred British and Hessians, threatened the fort on the south. Colonel Cadwallader and his eight hundred men were posted to defend the outer lines, and if possible to prevent his lordship's approach in that direction. Colonel Magaw himself remained within the fort.

* Graydon.

CHAPTER XXXV.

Fort Washington.—The Attack of the Enemy.—The Separate Divisions.—Rahl with the Right of the Hessians.—Knyphausen with the Left.—Their Reception by the Provincials.—Mathew and the British Guards.—Their Success.—Death of Baxter.—Flight of his Men.—Earl Percy and his Force.—Spirited Resistance of Cadwallader.—Dropping down the Harlem River.—The Enemy secure a Landing.—The Marylanders forced to retire.—The Hard Struggle.—Capture of Forts George, Cock-Hill, and Tryon.—Concentration of the Hessians.—Successful Retreat of Cadwallader.—Washington watching the Movement.—His Company.—His Tenderness.—The Americans driven within the Fort, and summoned to surrender.—Washington sends a Messenger, to advise holding out.—Too late.—Surrender of Fort Washington.—Lee's Emotions.—" A Cursed Affair."—Washington's Grief.—Greene consoles Himself.—The Policy of holding Fort Washington considered.—The Loss.—Fort Lee abandoned to the Enemy.—The Retreat of Washington in New Jersey.—Critical State of Affairs.—A Strong Call for Reinforcements.—General Discouragement.

1776. At noon, on the 16th of November, the enemy, under the cover of a powerful artillery, began their attack upon Fort Washington simultaneously from all points. From the north, Knyphausen and Rahl approached with their separate divisions of Hessians. On the east, the British redoubts from the opposite side of the Harlem river began a heavy cannonade, under cover of which General Mathew embarked his "British Guards," and pushed across the stream. On the south, Earl Percy marched with his force from the plains of Harlem, and approached the American lines; while Lieutenant-Colonel Stirling began to float down the Harlem river with another division of British troops.

Colonel Rahl, who commanded the right of the Hessians, pushed on for the Cock-hill fort, and began to clamber up the woody height, in the face of a sharp fire from the small party which defended that post. General Knyphausen at the same moment moved with his left against Fort George. He soon got entangled in a woody defile, which led to the rugged heights he was attempting to ascend, and was thus exposed to a murderous fire from Colonel Rawlings's riflemen, as well as from the guns of the redoubt above.

Mathew, with his British guards, under the cover of a fire from the redoubts, soon crossed the river, in front and to the east of the fort. Colonel Baxter, posted with his militiamen on the heights, was only able to offer a short and ineffectual resistance to the landing of the enemy. Baxter, while cheering on his men, was killed by a British officer; and the American troops, overpowered by numbers, fled to the fort: while the British, taking a redoubt and two hundred prisoners on their way, inclined toward the left, and began to skirt the southern border of Mount Washington, apparently with the view of cutting off Colonel Cadwallader's force stationed within the outer line below.

In the meantime, Earl Percy, having marched across the plains of Harlem, approached the American lines from the south, under the cover of a wood, where he began to form his troops for an assault, and at the same time to fire with his artillery upon the American breastworks. Cadwallader's Pennsylvanians kept firmly to their ground, and spiritedly resisted the enemy as they approached. Cadwallader, now learning that the British were dropping down the Harlem river in large force, apparently with the view of getting between him and the fort, detached a hundred and fifty men, with an eighteen-pounder, to dispute their landing. The detachment arrived in time to open a fire upon the assailants before they reached the shore, and it was well directed and deadly. Nevertheless, the superiority of the enemy's strength in men and artillery enabled them to force a landing, and, by extending themselves, to gain the heights upon the bank of the river. Here there was a sharp contest; but, with the odds of eight hundred British against one hundred and fifty Americans, the latter were so outnumbered, that they were obliged to retreat toward the fort. The British troops which had thus made good their landing were those under Lieutenant-Colonel Stirling, and they now marched unopposed toward the southern acclivity of Mount Washington, and, together with Mathew's division, were endeavoring to interpose themselves between Cadwallader and the fort.

The Marylanders, under Rawlings, at the north, had made a brave defence, but they were finally obliged to retire to the fort. Knyphausen, however, did not win the position until after a long and hard struggle. The American riflemen continued their fire until their arms became so fouled from repeated use as to be of no

longer service, and only gave way when overpowered by the numbers of the enemy. Knyphausen having carried Fort George, and Rahl the outposts of Cock-hill and Fort Tryon, the two combined their forces and marched up Mount Washington to within a short distance of the fortress, and took post behind a large stone-house.

Cadwallader, finding himself about to be caught between two fires, called off his troops from the right and left of the line, and ordered a retreat. He supposed that Mathew and Stirling would take possession of the second and inner line; but, as they suspected that the enclosed bastions concealed a number of men, they seemed to hesitate. Cadwallader took advantage of this pause, and pushed rapidly for the fort, in a direction toward the North river. He made good his retreat, and, though attacked upon his flank by Stirling, and pursued in the rear by Lord Percy, succeeded in gaining the fort with but a small loss.

Washington, with Greene, Putnam, and Thomas Paine, watched from Fort Lee every movement during this engagement with anxious interest; and when he saw the Hessians in pursuit of the brave troops of Rawlings, bayoneting them even when asking for quarter, "he cried with the tenderness of a child, and exclaimed at the barbarity that was practised."

When the American troops had been driven into the fort, and the enemy had thronged up the hill from all sides within a few hundred yards of the fortress, Colonel Rahl, who was first on the ground with his column, sent in a summons to

Magaw to surrender. Washington, seeing from Fort Lee a flag of truce going into the fortress, understood the object, and immediately wrote a note to Colonel Magaw, directing him to hold out, and he would endeavor in the evening to bring off the garrison. A Captain Gooch bravely volunteered to be the bearer of the message, and, hurrying down to the river, jumped into a small boat, pushed across, landed on the shore, ran up to the fort, delivered Washington's letter, and hurried back, dodging the Hessian guards by the way, who attempted to bayonet him as he passed. He reached the shore, and, leaping into his boat, returned in safety to Fort Lee.

The letter was, however, too late: Magaw had already entered too far into a treaty to retract, and now delivered up the fort, and surrendered the garrison as prisoners-of-war, as he could "obtain no other terms;" but the men were allowed to keep possession of their baggage, and the officers of their swords. The arms, ammunition, and stores, however, were all given up.

"When General Lee," says Gordon, "read the letter, sent by express, giving an account of Fort Washington being taken, resentment and vexation led him, unfeeling as he was in common, to weep plentifully." He wrote to Washington: "Oh, general, why would you be over-persuaded by men of inferior judgment to your own? It was a cursed affair!"

Washington himself grieved at it no less than Lee. He writes to his brother Augustine: "This is a most unfortunate affair, and has given me great mortification; as we have lost not only two thousand men that were there, but a good deal of artillery, and some of the best arms we had. And what adds to my mortification is, that this post, after the last ships went past it, was held contrary to my wishes and opinions, as I conceived it to be a hazardous one; but it having been determined on by a full council of general officers, and a resolution of Congress having been received strongly expressive of their desire that the channel of the river, which we had been laboring to stop for a long time at that place, might be obstructed if possible, and knowing that this could not be done unless there were batteries to protect the obstruction, I did not care to give an absolute order for withdrawing the garrison, till I could get round and see the situation of things, and then it became too late, as the fort was invested. Upon the passing of the last ships, I had given it as my opinion to General Greene, under whose care it was, that it would be best to evacuate the place; but as the order was discretionary, and his opinion differed from mine, it unhappily was delayed too long, to my great grief; as I think General Howe, considering his army and ours, would have have had a poor tale to tell without it, and would have found it difficult, unless some southern expedition may prove successful, to reconcile the people of England to the conquest of a few pitiful islands, none of which were defensible, considering the great number of their ships, and the power they have by sea to surround and render them unapproachable."

The whole letter is pervaded by a tone of melancholy. Washington, after mourning over the difficulties in levying proper troops, says that he is almost compelled "to bid adieu to every hope of getting an army from which any services are to be expected; the different states, without regard to the qualifications of an officer, quarrelling about the appointments, and nominating such as are not fit to be shoe-blacks, from the local attachments of this or that member of assembly. I am wearied almost to death with the retrograde motion of things, and I solemnly protest," he declares, "that a pecuniary reward of twenty thousand pounds a year would not induce me to undergo what I do; and after all, perhaps, to lose my character, as it is impossible, under such a variety of distressing circumstances, to conduct matters agreeably to public expectation or even to the expectation of those who employ me, as they will not make proper allowance for the difficulties their own errors have occasioned."

General Greene consoled himself, for the loss of his pet fortress, by the reflection that the enemy had "suffered greatly on the north side of Fort Washington," where Colonel Rawlings's regiment was posted, and had "behaved with great spirit." He moreover persisted that the fort would not have been given up could Colonel Magaw have got the men to man the lines. He continued to declare that Fort Washington was tenable, and, when reproached for having attempted to hold it, exclaimed, "I would to God we had had ten thousand men there!"* The

holding of Fort Washington, however, was almost universally considered an error on the part of Greene; but we shall find that he amply redeemed it by his glorious successes in the future.

When the British hoisted their flag at the fort, its name was changed to Knyphausen, and that general was left in command of it, with a garrison of his Hessians. By the surrender, two thousand eight hundred Americans, according to Sir William Howe's return, became his prisoners; and these were marched, the very midnight after their capture, to the city of New York. It has been estimated that the enemy lost, in English and Hessians, over a thousand men. This is probably an exaggeration.* The British acknowledged a loss of only eight hundred.

The next object of the enemy, after the capture of Fort Washington, was Fort Lee, on the Jersey shore opposite. Cornwallis, with six thousand troops, **Nov. 20.** crossed the Hudson from the encampment near Yonkers, and landed on the Jersey shore at a place called Closter, about a mile and a half from the English Neighborhood. The flat-boats which had been brought up from the bay of New York, and stationed in Spuyten-Devil creek, afforded him the means of transport, and he was thus enabled to carry his men rapidly across the river, while the ships-of-war protected their passage. Cornwallis, on debarking, immediately formed his men, and marched along the Jersey shore toward the object of attack.

* Memoirs of our Own Times, by General J. Wilkinson.

50

* Gordon says, "It is imagined on good grounds that the royal army lost in the attack full twelve hundred men, in killed and wounded."

As Fort Lee was not tenable, and of no possible advantage after the loss of Fort Washington, it had been determined to evacuate it. The ammunition and some of the stores had already been removed, when intelligence was brought early in the morning, while General Greene was in bed, of the approach of the enemy. He immediately ordered the garrison out and marched them to join the commander-in-chief at Hackensack. The British were on the banks of the North river, only six miles above the fort; and their evident intention was, to draw a line from that point to the bridge across the Hackensack, and thus hem in Washington's force between the two rivers. The American commander, however, was too quick for his lordship, and gained the bridge before him: he thus secured a retreat for all his men, but was forced to leave behind him some hundred barrels of flour, most of the cannon, and "a considerable parcel of tents and baggage." Finding himself still enclosed between two rivers, the Hackensack and the Passaic, and in the same danger of being pent up as before, should the enemy continue to advance, Washington was obliged to cross the Passaic and retreat to Newark. Even here he did not propose to make a stand. The level and open nature of the country forbade it; and his force, which was now only about thirty-five hundred men, did not admit of the possibility of a pitched battle with the army of Cornwallis. He encamped at Newark, as the British did not seem in a hurry to molest him. Washington, however, was prepared at a moment's notice to retreat to Brunswick, in order to form a junction with the troops at that place under the command of Lord Stirling.

Washington was fully conscious of his danger. Flying, with a dispirited remnant of troops (amounting in all to little more than three thousand men), before the triumphant army of the enemy, he might well say, " The situation of our affairs is truly critical, and such as requires uncommon exertions on our part." In order that Congress might be fully apprized of the weakness of his position, and of the necessity of obtaining early succor, it was determined by the commander-in-chief, with the advice of all his general officers, to send General Mifflin to Philadelphia, to the end that he might make known personally the severe straits in which the American army was placed. Washington used every exertion to obtain reinforcements. He wrote to Livingston, governor of New Jersey, to give all the aid in his power, and try to induce that state to do more than it had done; for Washington found that, instead of meeting with "many of the militia," as he had expected on his arrival, there were not more than from four to five hundred at the different posts. General Schuyler was also written to, and directed to send down from the army in the northern department the New-Jersey and Pennsylvania troops. General Lee had been repeatedly urged to come over from his encampment at Newcastle, with the regiments under his command. The flying camp, which was on the point of dissolving, Washington was anxious to retain in service; and in his letter to Congress he suggests that an "early and immediate supply of money" should be sent to pay them, as it "might have a happy effect."

With the smallness and wretched condition of his force, and the difficulty with which his efforts to increase the one and improve the other were opposed, it was not surprising that Washington should have almost despaired of bringing an army into the field capable of meeting the enemy. It was under such a feeling of discouragement in his emergency at Newark that he asked Colonel Reed, "Should we retreat to the back parts of Pennsyl-

vania, will the Pennsylvanians support us?"—"If the lower counties are subdued and give up, the back counties will do the same," was the discouraging answer. Washington then passed his hand across his throat, and said with a manner half serious and half playful : "My neck does not feel as though it was made for a halter. We must retire to Augusta county, in Virginia. Numbers will be obliged to repair to us for safety ; and we must try what we can do in carrying on a predatory war ; and, if overpowered, we must cross the Alleghany mountains."

CHAPTER XXXVI.

General Lee urged by Washington to join him in New Jersey.—Lee's Answer.—His Proposition to General Heath.—Refusal of Heath to accede.—Lee's Procrastination in obeying Washington's Orders.—His Excuses.—The Correspondence.—The Motive of Lee's Conduct.—His Vanity.—His Partisans.—Joseph Reed.—His Life and Character.—His Intimacy with Washington.—His Infidelity to his Friend.—Proof of the Fact.—Letter from Reed to Lee.—Lee's Conduct accounted for.—Washington by an Accident discovers the Infidelity of Reed.—Lee's Letter to Reed.—A Rebuke.—Severely polite.—"Dear Sir."—Lee still recreant.—Complains of Heath.—The Latter justifies Himself.—"Our General's" Account of his Interview with Lee.—Lee crosses the Hudson.—Still disobedient of Orders.—More tender of Horse than of Man.

1776. WASHINGTON, as we have said, had repeatedly urged General Lee to break up his encampment at Newcastle, and come with his troops to his aid in New Jersey. After Lord Cornwallis had crossed the Hudson, Washington wrote to Lee from Hackensack : "I am of opinion, **Nov. 21.** and the gentlemen about me concur in it, that the public interest requires your coming over to this side of the Hudson, with the continental troops, leaving Fellows's and Wadsworth's brigades to take care of the stores during

their short stay, at the expiration of which I suppose they will set out for home.

"My reasons for this measure, which I think must have weight with you, are, that the enemy is evidently changing the seat of war to this side of the North river. Unless some new event should occur, therefore, or some more cogent reason present itself to the contrary, I would have you move over by the easiest and best passage."

This was explicit as regards Washington's opinion, but it is expressed rather as a suggestion than as an order—a not unusual thing at that time with the commander-in-chief when addressing Lee, to whose military experience he was disposed to defer.

General Lee, in answer, wrote to Washington, saying that he had received his orders, and would "endeavor to **Nov. 24.** put them into execution;" but alleged that he would not be able to take with him any considerable number of troops, "not so much from a want of zeal in the men, as from their wretched condition with respect to shoes, stockings, and blankets, which the present bad weather renders more intolerable." In the meantime he had sent orders to General Heath, who was stationed at Peekskill, to transport two thousand men across the river. Heath refused. "That great man," as Lee sarcastically writes in his letter to Washington, "(as I might have expected,) intrenched himself within the letter of his instruction, and refused to part with a single file, though I undertook to replace them with a part of my own." At the conclusion of his letter, Lee declares: "I should march this day with Glover's brigade, but have just received intelligence that Rogers's corps, a part of the light-horse, and another brigade, lie in so exposed a situation as to present us the fairest opportunity of carrying them off. If we succeed, it will have a great effect, and amply compensate for two days' delay."

Washington was surprised, on receiving this letter, that Lee had not yet set **Nov. 27.** out, and wrote at once: "My former letters were so full and ex-

plicit, as to the necessity of your marching as early as possible, that it is unnecessary to add more on that head. I confess I expected you would have been sooner in motion."

"You complain," writes Lee in reply to Washington, "of my not being in motion sooner. I do assure you **Nov. 30.** that I have done all in my power, and shall explain my difficulties when we both have leisure. I did not succeed with Rogers, and merely owing to the timidity or caution of the enemy, who contracted themselves into a compact body very suddenly. I am in hopes I shall be able to render you more service than if I had moved sooner. I think I shall enter the province of Jersey with four thousand firm and willing troops, who will make a very important diversion; had I started sooner, I should have only had an inferior number of unwilling."

Washington himself was so sincere in his friendship and so loyal to duty, that he did not suspect those about him to be capable of infidelity to either. He was, therefore, though puzzled by the conduct of Lee, not disposed to attribute it to that love of self-aggrandizement which facts, then unknown to Washington, now prove to have been the motive. Lee had been spoiled by the welcome he had received on his arrival at New York after his success at Charleston. He was regarded by the army as a military oracle. Washington himself always listened to his opinions with deference; and the officers, particularly the younger ones, while observing this marked respect on the part of

their commander-in-chief, warmed naturally into admiration of the military qualities of Lee. They were disposed to attribute every successful manœuvre since
his arrival in the camp to action suggested by his advice. His well-known opposition to General Greene's pertinacious
resolve to hold Fort Washington, now
served to increase his reputation as a general. From the apparently desperate condition in which the disastrous loss of that
fort had left the American army, there
were doubtless many who believed that
in Lee's military capacity was the only
hope of extrication.

Among those who were the especial
admirers of Lee at this time, and believed
that he was the only military saviour of
the country in its sad trial, was General
Reed. JOSEPH REED was now thirty years
of age. Born in New Jersey, and educated at Princeton college, he had commenced the study of law, and for awhile
was entered at the Temple in London.
On his return to his native land, he early
sided with the patriots in their struggle
for liberty, and was chosen president of
the first popular convention in Philadelphia. When Washington was in that city
and received his appointment as commander-in-chief, he formed an acquaintance with Reed, which soon warmed into
a sincere friendship, and ripened into the
most intimate confidence. Washington
appointed him his private secretary, and
took him with him to Cambridge, where
he remained until nearly the close of the
siege of Boston, when he was called home
to Philadelphia, to attend to some private
affairs. He was subsequently appointed

adjutant-general of the American army,
and was now serving in that capacity with
the forces in New Jersey. Washington
had a high regard for Reed's abilities, and
frequently took counsel with him in respect to the conduct of affairs. A still
stronger attachment than that which was
to be traced to their mutual relations as
honest co-workers in behalf of the public
cause, sprung up between them. They
became friends; and Washington, as his
letters show, unburdened himself to Reed
with a freedom of revelation that can not
be found even in his communications to
his own family.

The adjutant-general may possibly never have swerved in his affection for Washington as his private friend; but he undoubtedly wavered in his opinion of him
as a public leader. The following letter,
which Reed wrote, proves that at that
time he thought Lee, and not Washington, was the man for the occasion:—

"HACKENSACK, *November* 21, 1776.

"DEAR GENERAL: The letter you will
receive with this contains my sentiments
with respect to your present station; but
besides this, I have some additional reasons for most earnestly wishing to have
you where the principal scene of action
is laid. I do not mean to flatter nor
praise you at the expense of any other,
but I confess I do think that it is entirely owing to you that this army and the
liberties of America, so far as they are
dependent on it, are not totally cut off.
You have decision, a quality often wanting in minds otherwise valuable; and I
ascribe to this our escape from York isl-
and, from Kingsbridge, and the Plains;

and I have no doubt, had you been here, the garrison of Mount Washington would now have composed a part of this army: and, from all these circumstances, I confess I ardently wish to see you removed from a place where I think there will be little call for your judgment and experience, to the place where they are likely to be so necessary. Nor am I singular in my opinion. Every gentleman of the family, the officers and soldiers, generally have a confidence: the enemy constantly inquire where you are, and seem to me to be less confident when you are present.

"Colonel Cadwallader, through a special indulgence, on account of some civilities shown by his family to General Prescott, has been liberated from New York without any parole. He informs, that the enemy have a southern expedition in view; that they hold us very cheap in consequence of the late affair at Mount Washington, where both the plan of defence and execution were contemptible. If the real defence of the lines was intended, the number was too few; if the fort only, the garrison was too numerous by half. General Washington's own judgment, seconded by representations from us, would, I believe, have saved the men and their arms; but, unluckily, General Greene's judgment was contrary. This kept the general's mind in a state of suspense till the stroke was struck. O general! an indecisive mind is one of the greatest misfortunes that can befall an army: how often have I lamented it this campaign!

"All circumstances considered, we are in a very awful, alarming state; one that requires the utmost wisdom and firmness of mind.

"As soon as the season will admit, I think yourself and some others should go to Congress, and form the plan of the new army, point out their defects to them, and, if possible, prevail on them to bend their whole attention to this great object, even to the exclusion of every other. If they will not or can not do this, I fear all our exertions will be vain in this part of the world. Foreign assistance is soliciting, but we can not expect they will fight the whole battle.

"I intended to have said more, but the express is waiting; and I must conclude, with my clear and explicit opinion that your presence is of the last importance.

"I am, with much affection and regard, your very affectionate, humble servant,

"JOSEPH REED, *Adjutant-General.*
"MAJOR-GENERAL LEE,
    "At the White Plains."

Such a letter, from such a source — the most intimate friend of Washington — was surely calculated to increase the vanity and stir the ambitious longings of a man like Lee, among whose virtues no one has ever ranked modesty and contentment. There were others like Reed, not only officers, but men high in civil authority, who were writing to Lee in the same strain of praise of his own military capacity, and in depreciation of that of the commander-in-chief. Lee yielded to this influence, and doubtless thought that the star of Washington was setting, and that his was the bright luminary which was on its rise and might shine in its place. These aspirations will account for Lee's conduct in not obeying Washington's orders. He was only too willing, by withholding his aid, to allow the commander-in-chief to be sacrificed, while he himself, by acting independently, might have a chance of striking a blow against the enemy, which would establish his superiority and secure him the chief command.

Lee, therefore, while excusing himself on various pretences for not joining his chief in New Jersey, was purposely delaying, and trying to increase his force by obtaining a reinforcement from General Heath, that he might have an opportunity of attacking the enemy in the rear or the flank, while in pursuit of Washington's meager remnant of troops, and thus gaining a triumph which would give such an *éclat* to his military fame as could not fail to make him as prominent as his vaulting ambition aspired to be.

Washington hitherto had been apparently unsuspicious of Lee's true motives in continuing to delay, although repeatedly urged to hasten to form a junction with him in New Jersey. The enemy continued to advance and Washington to retreat. The American force was infinitely inferior in numbers, and such as could not "give or promise the least successful opposition." It was greatly reduced by the departure of the Maryland flying camp, and by sundry other causes.

Dec. 1.   Washington had now retreated as far as Brunswick, from which place he writes to Lee, "I must entreat you to hasten your march as much as possible, or your arrival may be too late to answer any valuable service." When Washington wrote this, which has a more peremptory character than his previous communications, he had accidentally discovered a correspondence which must have greatly weakened his confidence in Lee, as it certainly did in one in whom his orginal faith was much stronger.

We have read Reed's letter to General Lee. Washington never did, but he saw Lee's answer, and in this way: Reed was absent, and in the meantime a letter came to his address in the camp, which Washington opened and read. Here it is:—

"CAMP, 24 *November*, 1776.

"MY DEAR REED: I received your most obliging, flattering letter. I lament, with you, that fatal indecision of mind, which, in war, is a much greater disqualification than stupidity or even want of personal courage. Accident may put a decisive blunderer in the right, but eternal defeat and miscarriage must attend the man of the best parts, if cursed with indecision.

"The general commands in so pressing a manner as almost to amount to an order, to bring over the continental troops under my command; which recommendation, or order, throws me into the greatest dilemma, from several considerations. Part of the troops are so ill furnished with shoes and stockings, blankets, &c., that they must inevitably perish in this wretched weather. Part of them are to be dismissed on Saturday next, and this part is the best accoutred for service.

"What shelter we are to find on the other side of the river is a serious consideration; but these considerations should not sway me. My reason for not having marched already is, that we have just received intelligence that Rogers's corps, the light-horse, part of the Highlanders, and another brigade, lie in so exposed a situation as to give the fairest opportunity of being carried off. I should have attempted it last night, but the rain was too violent; and when our pieces are wet,' you know our troops are *hors du combat.* This night I hope will be better. If we succeed, we shall be well compensated for the delay. We shall likewise be able in our return to clear the country of all the articles wanted by the enemy. In every view, therefore, the expedition must answer.

"I have just received a most flattering letter from the governor of New Orleans. He gives me the title of '*General de los Estados Unidos Americanos,*' which is a tolerable step toward declaring himself our ally in positive terms. The substance is, that he is sensible of the vast advantages which must result from the separation to his master and nation; that he can not positively enter into a regular system of commerce without consulting his master; but, in the meantime, he will render us all the service in his power. I only wait myself for this business I mention of Rogers and Company being over. I shall then fly to you; for, to confess a truth, I really think our chief will do better with me than without me. I am, &c.,

"CHARLES LEE."

Washington could not feel flattered by this epistle, and must have been greatly grieved to find that his friend, whom he had trusted above all, was carrying on a correspondence, the whole purport of which was his own depreciation and the elevation of Lee. Washington, having opened the letter unsuspiciously, immediately enclosed it to Reed, with the following explanation:—

"BRUNSWICK, 30 *November,* 1776.
"DEAR SIR: The enclosed was put into my hands by an express from White Plains. Having no idea of its being a private letter, much less suspecting the tendency of the correspondence, I opened it, as I had done all other letters to you, from the same place and Peekskill, upon the business of your office, as I conceived and found them to be. This, as it is the truth, must be my excuse for seeing the contents of a letter which neither inclination nor intention would have prompted me to.

"I thank you for the trouble and fatigue you have undergone in your journey to Burlington, and sincerely wish that your labors may be crowned with the desired success. With best respects to Mrs. Reed, I am, dear sir, &c.,
"GEORGE WASHINGTON."

The formal politeness of this letter—where the "Dear sir" stands in place of the former "Dear Reed"—shows that the heart of Washington's friendship for Reed was paralyzed by this secret and unsuspected blow. From that moment there was no longer the same cordiality between the two, though there were the most courteous relations, and finally, in subsequent years, some return to former intimacy.

While Washington believed that, in accordance with his orders, Lee was on his route to join him, he received from that recreant general a letter dated "Peekskill, 30th November," in which he says: "The day after to-morrow we shall pass the river, when I should be glad to receive your instructions; but I could wish you would bind me as little as possible; not from any opinion, I do assure you, of my own parts, but from a persuasion that detached generals can not have too great latitude, unless they are very incompetent indeed."

Lee also complained of General Heath's resolute adherence to his instructions. This faithful officer had refused Lee's repeated solicitations to send two thousand men across the Hudson. Lest, however, he might thus be depriving the commander-in-chief of aid that was necessary, he wrote to him, asking him whether his conduct was approved. Washington, in his answer, justified Heath in his refusal, and ordered him to persist in it. Thus fortified, Heath adhered with continued pertinacity to his orders. Lee, notwithstanding, was still urgent, and went so far as to assume the responsibility of ordering out two of Heath's regiments. We shall, however, let General Heath narrate this occurrence in his own words, which he uses freely, speaking of himself always in the third person, as "our general."

Nov. 30. "Just before dinner, General Sullivan arrived at our general's [Heath's] quarters; and, in the afternoon, General Lee arrived. He called at the door; when our general, waiting upon him, requested him to alight, he asked if he could have a cup of tea, and was answered that he should have a good one.

Upon coming into the house, before he sat down he wished to speak in private, which being instantly granted, he told our general that, in a military view—or, to use his own words exactly—'In *point of law*, you are right; but, in point of policy, I think you are wrong. I am going into the Jerseys for the salvation of America; I wish to take with me a larger force than I now have, and request you to order two thousand of your men to march with me.' Our general answered that he could not spare that number. He was then asked to order one thousand; to which he replied that the business might as well be brought to a point at once—that not a single man should march from the post by *his* order.

"General Lee replied that he would then order them himself. He was answered that there was a wide difference between the two; that General Lee was acknowledged by our general to be his senior; but, as he had received positive written instructions from him who was superior to both, he would not *himself* break those orders. If General Lee was disposed to counteract them, its being done by him could not be imputed to any other person; and that he knew the commander-in-chief did not intend any of the troops should be removed from that post—having expressed it not only in his instructions, but also in a letter just received from him.

"On the letter being shown to General Lee, he observed, 'The commander-in-chief is now at a distance, and does not know what is necessary here as well as I do'—asked if he might be favored with

51

the return-book of the division. Major Huntington, the deputy adjutant-general, was directed to hand it. General Lee ran his eye over it, and said, 'I will take Prescott's and Wyllis's regiments;' and, turning to Major Huntington, said, 'You will order those two regiments to march early to-morrow morning to join me.' Our general, turning to the major, said, 'Issue such orders at your peril!'—and then, turning to General Lee, addressed him: 'Sir, if you come to this post, and mean to issue orders here which will break those positive ones which I have received, I pray you to do it completely yourself, and through your own deputy adjutant-general, who is present, and not draw me, or any of my family, in as partners in the guilt. General Lee replied: 'It is right. Colonel Scammel, do you issue the order;' which he did, and Huntington communicated it to the regiments, who were now posted at the gorge of the mountains, near Robinson's bridge, afterward called the Continental village.

"Matters carried thus far, our general turned to General Lee again: 'Sir, I have one more request to make, and that is, that you will be pleased to give me a certificate that you *exercise command* at this post, and do order from it Prescott's and Wyllis's regiments.' Lee replied, 'I do not know that I will comply with your request.' General Clinton, who was present, observed, 'General Lee, you can not refuse a request so reasonable.' Upon which General Lee wrote as follows:—

"'Peekskill, *December* 1, 1776.

"'For the satisfaction of General Heath, and at his request, I do certify that I am commanding officer, at this present writing, in this post; and that I have, in that capacity, ordered Prescott's and Wyllis's regiments to march.

"'(Signed),

"'Charles Lee, *Maj. Gen.*'

"General Lee, stepping out on the piazza, observed to an officer, 'General Heath is right.' Early the next morning, the regiments moved from their cantonment toward Peekskill; but, before they had reached it, General Lee, now ready to pass into the Jerseys, rode up to our general's door, and, calling him, observed: 'Upon further consideration, I have concluded not to take the two regiments with me. You may order them to return to their former post.' This conduct of General Lee's appeared not a little extraordinary, and one is almost at a loss to account for it."[*]

Lee finally crossed the Hudson with his troops, and, having taken two days (the 2d and 3d of December) for the passage, began a slow, lingering march. The commander-in-chief still continued to retreat before the enemy, and, having arrived at Trenton, writes again to Lee, saying, "The sooner you **Dec. 3.** can join me with your division, the sooner the service will be benefited." In regard to Lee's complaints of Heath's tenacity of his instructions, and of his refusal to allow any of his troops to cross the river, Washington says, very peremptorily, "As to bringing any of the troops under General Heath, I can not consent to it."

Lee, in his next letter to his superior, fairly discloses his purpose of acting in-

* Heath's Memoirs, pp. 94-96.

dependently, although he strives to conceal it beneath the shallow pretence that, since Washington had quitted Brunswick, it was impossible for him to know where to join him! "But although," continues Lee, "*I should not be able to join you at all,* the service which I can render you will, I hope, be full as efficacious." The northern army, it will be recollected, had been ordered by Washington to join *him.* Lee, it appears from his letter, had resolved that the junction should be with his own troops, and not with those of the commander-in-chief. "The northern army has already advanced nearer to Morristown than I am, and," grandly adds the ambitious Lee, "I shall put myself at their head to-morrow." He not only thus acknowledges that he is about to assume a command to which he is not entitled, but even alludes to the tactics which he proposes to pursue. "We shall," he says, "upon the whole, compose an army of five thousand good troops, in spirits. I should imagine, dear general, that it may be of service to communicate this to the troops immediately under your command. It may encourage them, and startle the enemy. In fact, their confidence must be risen to a prodigious height, if they pursue you, *with so formidable a body hanging on their flank and rear."*

Here we leave General Lee, lagging on his march from Haverstraw to Morristown, where he hoped to receive the reinforcements from the North, and watch his opportunity of marching and inflicting that triumphant blow upon the flank or rear of the enemy. Lee's only anxiety about Washington's hazardous position seems to be lest it should endanger the safety of his horse, for he writes, "I entreat you [General Washington] to order some of your suite to take out of the way of danger my favorite mare, which is at that Wilson's, three miles beyond Princeton." He truly remarks, however, previously, that "it is paltry to think of our personal affairs, when the whole is at stake."

CHAPTER XXXVII.

Washington quits Newark.—Cornwallis enters.—Washington at Brunswick.—He strives to obtain Reinforcements.—British Interests in the Ascendant in New Jersey.—The Persuasiveness of the Howes' Proclamation.—Mercy promised.—"Lord, deliver us from his Mercy!"—The Tory Disposition of the Magnates.—Washington hopeless of making a Stand in New Jersey.—He continues his Retreat.—Alexander Hamilton keeps the Enemy in Check.—Destruction of the Bridge at Brunswick.—The March to Princeton.—Washington crosses the Delaware.—Retreat of Lord Stirling from Princeton.—Putnam ordered to Philadelphia, to fortify.—Lee still recreant.—His Cool Impudence.—Washington entreats.—Letter upon Letter.—Lee intercepts the Forces from the North.—Gates ordered to the Rescue.—Capture of Lee.—Wilkinson's Account of it.—The Secret of the Capture disclosed.

1776. WASHINGTON was not enabled to linger on his march. After a week at Newark, it became necessary to move on again. "It was the wish of all," says Washington, "to have remained there longer, and to have halted before we came thus far; but, upon due consideration of our strength, the circumstances attending the enlistment of a great part of our little force, and the frequent advices. that the enemy were embarking or about to embark another detachment from Staten island, with a view of landing at Amboy," it was judged necessary to proceed. The advance-guards of Cornwallis entered the town as the American rear left. Bruns- **Nov. 29.** wick was the next point which Washington reached. Here the flying camp continued to dissolve. Not only did those whose services had expired go away, but even those who were engaged for a month longer departed also, so that the army was "reduced to a mere handful."

Washington made an urgent appeal to the governor of New Jersey to "fall upon the proper means to draw forth the strength" of his province to his support. Livingston was earnestly patriotic, but he could do little at that time toward getting recruits for service in the good cause. The British interests were in the ascendant. A miserable remnant of troops in retreat represented the one; a triumphant army supported the other. Under these circumstances, the proclamation of the two Howes proved wondrously persuasive. On the 30th of November, the two brothers, his lordship and Sir William, industriously circulated throughout the Jerseys a document, by which pardon was offered to all such as had opposed the king's authority; and who should, within sixty days, subscribe a declaration that they would remain in peaceable obedience to his majesty, neither taking up arms themselves nor encouraging others to take up arms against him. Washington reports that a clergyman, "who was a staunch friend to the cause," in allusion to the latitude of pardon extended by Lord Howe, said, "No one man in the continent is to be denied his mercy," but added, "The Lord deliver us from his mercy!" Numbers, who had been provincial congressmen, committee-men, justices, and the like, though out of the way of immediate danger, ran to take advantage of the proclamation. Many of the whigs shifted about. Only a few of fortune stood firm to the cause. It was the middle rank of people in general that remained steadfast in this day of trial. The success of the royal army extended its influence also to Pennsylvania. Mr. Galloway, the family of the Allens, with some others, repaired to the commissioners, to claim the benefits of the general pardon.*

Washington had little hope of being able to make a stand in New Jersey in resistance to his pursuers and their accumulating allies. He therefore began to forward a part of his stores to Philadelphia, even while at Brunswick. The enemy were close behind him, and, now showing themselves on the opposite bank of the Raritan, the American general Dec. 2. quitted Brunswick, taking care to destroy the bridge which crossed the river at that town, Captain Alexander Hamilton keeping the British in check with his artillery. Princeton was the next point at which the retreating army halted, where, in order that the country might in some measure be covered, Washington left two brigades (consisting of the five Virginia regiments and that of Delaware, containing in the whole about twelve hundred men fit for duty), under the command of Lord Stirling and his old Virginia comrade in the French War, Stephen, who had been lately appointed a brigadier-general. This detachment was set about transporting the baggage and stores over the Delaware, while Washington moved on with the rest of his troops to Trenton.

He now proposed to reinforce Lord

* Gordon.

Stirling, whom he had left at Princeton, with twelve hundred men; but while preparing to march in that direction, he received an express from his lordship, who informed him that he was retreating to Trenton. The earl gave as his reasons for this movement, the advance of the enemy by different routes—by one of which they were attempting to get in his rear; and the indefensibility of Princeton, from the nature of the place, and the small number of Americans to hold it.

The British were again close at hand; and one of the two divisions of Cornwallis reached the Delaware at midnight, just as the rear-guard of Dec. 8. Washington's army gained the opposite bank. The American troops had dwindled away to the scant number of about three thousand. All the boats along the river were secured; and Washington, although trying his utmost to check the progress of the enemy, thought it impossible with his small force to give them any considerable opposition in the passage of the Delaware, should they attempt it.

Under these circumstances, the security of Philadelphia was Washington's next object. He thought that a communication of lines and redoubts might soon be formed from the Delaware to the Schuylkill, on the northern entrance of the city; the lines to begin on the Schuylkill side about the heights of Springatebay, and run eastward to the Delaware, upon the highest and most advantageous grounds. If something of the kind should not be done, he believed that the British might march directly in and take possession.

"We have ever found," says Washington, "that lines, however slight, are very formidable to them. They would at least give a check till the people could recover from the fright and consternation that naturally attend the first appearance of an enemy."

Washington acted promptly, in accordance with these views. General Mifflin had just arrived and informed him that all the military stores yet remained in Philadelphia. He therefore thought there was no time to be lost in fortifying that city; and he accordingly despatched Major-General Putnam to superintend the works and give the necessary directions, and ordered Mifflin back again to take charge of the stores.

In the meantime, General Lee was so absorbed in his own magnificent schemes, that he did not seem to trouble himself about the commander-in-chief and his repeated summons. "I have no certain intelligence of General Lee," writes Washington on the 8th of December, "although I have sent frequent expresses to him, and lately Colonel Hampton, to bring me some accurate accounts of his situation. I last night despatched another gentleman to him, Major Hoops, desiring he would hasten his march to the Delaware, in which I would provide boats, near a place called Alexandria, for the transportation of his troops. I can not account for the slowness of his march."

Lee had only got as far as Morristown, having taken three weeks to reach that place, when Colonel Hampton arrived. What that officer could have reported in regard to the condition of Washington's army, we can not say; but if he confined himself strictly to the truth, the following seems a marvel of cool impudence on the part of Lee, when he writes to the commander-in-chief: "If I was not taught to think that your army was considerably reinforced, I should immediately join you; but, as I am assured you are very strong, I should imagine we can make a better impression by hanging on their rear, for which purpose a good post at Chatham seems the best calculated. It is at a happy distance from Newark, Elizabethtown, Woodbridge, and Boundbrook; it will annoy, distract, and consequently weaken them." **Dec. 8.**

Lee seems to have met with more success in recruiting than Washington, and estimates that, with the militia, added to the twenty-seven hundred troops which he brought with him across the Hudson, his army amounts to about four thousand men. Washington suggested the idea of surprising Brunswick. Lee, however, in those days of self-exaltation, was little disposed either to listen to the suggestions or obey the orders of his superior. "The post I propose taking," he replies, "offers the greatest probability of success; but we are so ill shod, and destitute of light-horse, that this desultory war is hard upon the poor soldiers. But I must do them the justice to say, that they have noble spirits, and will, I have no doubt, render great service to their country." The recreant Lee concludes this impudent self-assertion of authority with a "God bless you, general!"

Washington received this communication by Colonel Hampton on his return,

Dec. 10. and immediately despatched another summons. Taking care to inform Lee that his situation was directly the opposite of what he (Lee) supposed it to be, and that General Howe was pressing forward with the whole of his army to possess himself of Philadelphia, Washington continues: "I can not but request and entreat you, and this too by the advice of all the general officers with me, to march and join me with your whole force with all possible expedition. The utmost exertions that can be made, will not be more than sufficient to save Philadelphia. Without the aid of your force I think there is but little, if any, prospect of doing it.... Do come on; your arrival may be fortunate, and, if it can be effected without delay, it may be the means of preserving a city, whose loss must prove of the most fatal consequence to the cause of America."

Previous to the receipt of this communication, Major Hoops had arrived at Lee's quarters with a letter from the commander-in-chief, in which the smallness of his force was stated. Lee, in answer, as if suddenly startled by the fact, describes himself "shocked to hear" that **Dec. 8.** Washington's force was so inadequate to the necessity of his situation, as he had been "taught to think" that he had been considerably reinforced. Lee can not persuade himself that Philadelphia is the object of the enemy; and, having posted himself at Chatham, he seemed determined not to budge, let Washington beg, entreat, and order, as he might. "I have put myself in position," writes Lee to the chief, "the most convenient to co-operate with you, by attacking their rear." And, again: "It will be difficult, I am afraid, to join you; but can not I do you more service by attacking their rear?"

Three days subsequently, Lee writes again to Washington, and would seem to be in a more compliant **Dec. 11.** humor, for he talks of crossing the Delaware; but, as he also alludes to taking a route by the road toward Burlington, he evidently clings to his old idea of a separate attack upon the enemy, with a view of cutting their cordon, contrary to Washington's views and commands. General Howe, it must be understood, held the banks of the Delaware at that point, and as far north as Pennington; and Lee was directed to take a northerly route through Pittstown to Tinicum ferry, at Alexandria, by which he might avoid the British, and join Washington's enfeebled force at Trenton.

Orders, it will be recollected, had been sent by Washington to General Schuyler to despatch the northern troops as rapidly as possible to the aid of the army in New Jersey. These orders were communicated to General Gates, then at Albany, who despatched a detachment of three regiments, under General St. Clair, to descend the North river to New Windsor, and then march to reinforce the army in New Jersey. Lee, however, intercepted all that remained of these troops, with an order to join him! Gates himself, accompanied by General Arnold, led the remnant of the northern army, consisting of four regiments, and, having sailed down the North river, landed at Esopus, whence he proposed to join Washington in New

Jersey. The latter, aware of his approach,
sent a despatch, with the hope
Dec. 14. of its meeting him on his route.
In this, Gates was entreated not to delay
a moment in hastening to Pittstown. "I
expect General Lee will be there," says
Washington, "this evening or to-morrow."
At the moment this was written, Lee was,
however, unknown to Washington, in the
hands of the enemy. The lofty flights of
that ambitious general had been suddenly
checked, on the morning of the 13th, by
his capture, the particulars of which we
now give in the words of one who was
present.

Wilkinson (then a major), whose story
we relate, presented himself to General
Gates on the 5th of December, having
been temporarily absent from his command
in consequence of ill health. Gates,
says he, " had at that time heard of General
Washington's crossing the North river,
and the loss of Fort Washington, but
had received no satisfactory information
of posterior incidents and movements,
though a thousand vague reports were in
circulation. Thus circumstanced, his instructions
led him to take the back route
from Esopus, by the Delaware and the
Minisink, and we reached Van Kempt's,
near the Wallpeck, in very intemperate
weather. In this sequestered valley we
were thrown out of the ordinary current
of intelligence, and cut off from all authentic
information respecting the adverse
armies. The winter had set in with
severity; our troops were bare of clothing;
numbers barefoot, and without tents,
provisions, or transport of any kind. The
men and officers sought shelter wherever

they could find it in that thinly-settled
tract. We were halted on the 11th [of
December] by a heavy fall of snow, which
increased the general's anxiety for information
from General Washington, and, to
relieve his solicitude, I volunteered my
services to find him. The proposition
was adopted, and a letter (to Washington)
prepared, with which I was despatched
on the morning of the 12th of December.

" I crossed the hills to Sussex courthouse,
where I received advice that General
Washington had passed the Delaware
several days before, and that the
enemy had reached Trenton. In consequence
of this information, I employed a
guide, and proceeded down the country.
On the road I casually met an officer of
my acquaintance, who informed me that
the boats had been removed from the ferries,
and that I should find some difficulty
in getting across the Delaware, and that
Major-General Lee was at Morristown.

" Finding such obstacles in my way to
the commander-in-chief, I determined to
seek his second, and to ask orders from
him for General Gates; and, although
dark, I continued my journey without
halt. About midnight, passing a house
by the wayside, I discovered a glimmering
light, and, on application to my guide,
was informed it issued from a tavern. I
dismounted, and, after a short parley at
the door, gained admittance, and found
the women on the watch over the embers
of an expiring fire; for I perceived the
whole country to be in terror and alarm.
These women knew nothing of General
Lee; but, after some whispering, informed

me two strange officers were in bed above me, on which I desired one of the party to awaken and inform them an express desired to speak with them. The maid proceeded with a candle to execute my orders, and soon after I heard a loud shriek.

"I instantly mounted the stairs, and, guided by the light, entered the chamber, when a momentary scene of some interest took place. Two gentlemen were sitting up in the same bed, and the maid standing at a distance from them, in an apparent agony, with the candle in her hand. The shriek had been caused by the conduct of one of the gentlemen, whom the girl had awoke; but his wanton levity was in a moment changed into painful apprehensions. Awaking out of a sound sleep in the dead of night, the unexpected and menacing appearance of an officer, with a Canadian *capot*, a scarlet under-coat, and a gold-laced hat, with a pistol in each hand, was sufficient to dissipate all sense of an amorous nature, and to excite those frigid sensations which can not be realized so sensibly as when an unarmed man believes himself in the power of an enemy. For a moment the gentlemen were struck dumb with alarm; literally naked and defenceless, and believing me to be a British officer, their situation appeared hopeless, and it was several seconds before they demanded, 'Who are you?'"

The major soon relieved their fright, and, after making himself known, and receiving their names and quality in return, a greeting ensued, which was, however, so emphatic in expression—proving indubitably that "our army swore terribly" in the Jerseys—that we prefer to omit the verbal relation of Wilkinson. The gentlemen thus suddenly aroused were Colonel Gibson and a Mr. Nourse. They "had parted from General Lee the evening before, and were absent on furlough; and Mr. Nourse being General Lee's private secretary," continues Major Wilkinson, " they could of course direct me with precision where to find him. Taking leave of them, I pursued my journey, and about four o'clock in the morning reached his quarters at White's tavern, on Basking ridge.

"I was presented to the general as he lay in bed, and delivered into his hands the letter of General Gates. He examined the superscription, and observed it was addressed to General Washington, and declined opening it, until I apprized him of the contents, and the motives of my visit; he then broke the seal and read it, after which he desired me to take repose. I lay down on my blanket before a comfortable fire, amidst the officers of his suite; for we were not in those days encumbered with beds or baggage.

"I arose at the dawn, but could not see the general, with whom I had been previously acquainted, before eight o'clock. After some inquiries respecting the conduct of the campaign on the northern frontier, he gave me a brief account of the operations of the grand army, which he condemned in strong terms. He observed that our siege of Boston had led us into great errors; that the attempt to defend islands against a superior land and naval force was madness; that Sir William Howe could have given us *check-mate* at his discretion; and that we owed our salvation to his indolence, or disinclination to terminate the war. 'When I reached the army on York island,' said Lee, 'all hands were busily employed in collecting materials and erecting barracks; and I found little Mifflin exulting in the prospect of fine winter-quarters at Kingsbridge. I replied to him : " *Winter-quarters here, sir !* and the British army still in the field! Go, set fire to those you have built, and get away by the light, or Sir William Howe will find quarters for you !" ' . . . . .

" General Lee wasted the morning in altercation with certain militia-corps who were of his command, particularly the Connecticut light-horse, several of whom appeared in large, full-bottomed perukes, and were treated very irreverently. One wanted forage, another his horse shod, another his pay, a fourth provisions; to which the general replied : ' Your wants are numerous; but you have not mentioned the last : you want to go home, and shall be indulged, for, d—n you, you do no good here !' The call of the adjutant-general for orders also occupied some of his time, and we did not sit down to breakfast before ten o'clock.

" General Lee was engaged in answering General Gates's letter, and I had risen from the table, and was looking out an end-window, down a lane about one hundred yards in length, which led to the house from the main road, when I discovered a party of British dragoons turn a corner of the avenue at full charge. Startled at this unexpected spectacle, I ex-

claimed, ' Here, sir, are the British cavalry !'—' *Where ?*' replied the general, who had signed his letter in the instant.— 'Around the house !' for they had opened files, and encompassed the building. General Lee appeared alarmed, yet collected, and his second observation marked his self-possession : ' Where is the guard ?— d—n the guard ! why don't they fire ?' And, after a momentary pause, he turned to me and said, ' Do, sir, see what has become of the guard.'

" The women of the house at this moment entered the room, and proposed to him to conceal himself in a bed, which he rejected with evident disgust. I caught up my pistols, which lay on the table, thrust the letter he had been writing into my pocket, and passed into a room at the opposite end of the house, where I had seen the guard in the morning. Here I discovered their arms; but the men were absent. I stepped out of the door, and perceived the dragoons chasing them in different directions; and, receiving a very uncivil salutation, I returned into the house.

" Too inexperienced immediately to penetrate the motives of this enterprise, I considered the *rencontre* accidental; and, from the terrific tales spread over the country, of the violence and barbarity of the enemy, I believed it to be a wanton, murdering party, and determined not to die without company. I accordingly sought a position where I could not be approached by more than one person at a time, and with a pistol in each hand I awaited the expected search, resolved to shoot the first and the second person who might appear, and then to appeal to my sword.

"I did not remain long in this unpleasant situation, but was apprized of the object of the incursion by the very audible declaration—'*If the general does not surrender in five minutes, I will set fire to the house!*' which, after a short pause, was repeated, with a solemn oath; and within two minutes I heard it proclaimed, '*Here is the general—he has surrendered.*' A general shout ensued; the trumpet sounded the assembly; and the unfortunate Lee, mounted on my horse, which stood ready at the door, was hurried off in triumph, bareheaded, in his slippers and blanket-coat, his collar open, and his shirt very much soiled from several days' use."

It seems that a New-Jersey tory—"a domestic traitor," as Major Wilkinson calls him—who had passed Lee's quarters that morning, fell in on the road with Colonel Harcourt, at the head of a troop of British dragoons, out reconnoitring, and gave information of the general's whereabouts. Harcourt, however, might not have been in time, had not Lee lingered so long in bed, and spun out the morning chatting with his visiter, scolding at his militia-officers, and writing his letter to General Gates. If it had not been for this untimely delay, he would probably not have been caught at White's tavern, but have reached his camp at Vealtown. The guard were as careless as the general. The morning being cold and the sun bright, the men had stacked their guns, left their station, crossed the main road, and were sunning themselves on the south side of a house about two hundred yards from the tavern, when the British colonel rode up and cut them off from their arms.

CHAPTER XXXVIII.

1776. GENERAL LEE, at the time of his capture, was evidently not disposed to cross the Delaware, as he had repeatedly and most urgently been ordered to do by Washington. After lingering at Morristown for several days, he left it on the 12th of December; but, when taken, his army had only marched twelve miles, to Vealtown. Major Wilkinson, moreover, tells us that "when Colonel Scammel, the adjutant-general, called on him from General Sullivan, who was encamped with the troops, for orders of march on the morning of his capture, after musing a minute or two, he asked the colonel if he had with him the manuscript map of the country, which was produced and spread on a table. It attracted my attention, and I observed General Lee trace with his finger the route from Vealtown to Pluckimen, thence to Somerset courthouse, and on by Rocky hill to Princeton; he then returned to Pluckamin, and traced the route in the same manner, by Boundbrook to Brunswick, and, after a close inspection, carelessly said to Scammel, 'Tell General Sullivan to move down toward Pluckimen—that I will be soon with him.'"

The order to Sullivan to march to Pluckimen was not inconsistent with an intention to obey the command of Washington to cross the Delaware at Alexandria; but if the tracing of his finger on the map, so closely observed by the vigilant eye of Wilkinson, is to be taken as an indication of Lee's intended march, he clearly at the last moment was preparing to strike a blow against the enemy, at the risk of his fair fame. He was ready to hazard all on the chance of success. A victory, he thought, would raise such a flood of popular applause as to drown all inquiry. A defeat, he knew, could only result in disgrace and punishment for disobedience of orders. Lee was not, however, apparently very confident of winning in the hazardous game he was playing. His letter to Gates, which Wilkinson hurriedly thrust into his pocket be-

fore it was folded, is desponding, although it confirms the suspicion that he was about to act independently of Washington, and in disobedience to his orders. Here it is:—

"BASKING RIDGE, *December* 13, 1776.

"MY DEAR GATES: The ingenious manœuvre of Fort Washington has unhinged the goodly fabric we had been building. There never was so d——d a stroke. *Entre nous*, a certain great man is most damnably deficient. He has thrown me into a situation where I have my choice of difficulties: if I stay in this province, I risk myself and army; and, if I do not stay, the province is lost for ever. I have neither guides, cavalry, medicines, money, shoes, or stockings. I must act with the greatest circumspection. Tories are in my front, rear, and on my flanks; the mass of the people is strangely contaminated; in short, unless something, which I do not expect, turns up, we are lost: our counsels have been weak to the last degree. As to what relates to yourself, if you think you can be in time to aid the general, I would have you by all means go; you will at least save your army. It is said that the whigs are determined to set fire to Philadelphia: if they strike this decisive stroke, the day will be our own; but unless it is done, all chance of liberty in any part of the globe is for ever vanished. Adieu, my dear friend! God bless you! "CHARLES LEE."

General Lee's capture was suspected by many at the time to have been made by collusion with the enemy. The letter just read, however, proves that the senti ment at least of that eccentric commander was at the last moment true to liberty; and his rude treatment by his British captors is unquestionable evidence that Lee was not considered by them as their friend. They exulted greatly, however, in his capture, declaring, "We have taken the American palladium!" Some of the Americans thought no less, and seemed to imagine that, with the loss of Lee, had passed away all hopes of the salvation of the country. Washington spoke calmly of the event thus, in a letter to his brother Augustine: "Before you receive this letter, you will undoubtedly have heard of the captivity of General Lee. This is an additional misfortune, and the more vexatious, as it was by his own folly and imprudence, and without a view to effect any good, that he was taken."

Let us, however, return to Major Wilkinson, and learn from his own account how he escaped from the dilemma in which he found himself on the capture of Lee. "So soon," says Wilkinson, "as Lieutenant-Colonel Harcourt retreated with his prize, I repaired to the stable, mounted the first horse I could find, and rode full speed to General Sullivan, whom I found under march toward Pluckimen. I had not examined General Lee's letter, but believing a knowledge of the contents might be useful to General Sullivan, who succeeded him in command, I handed it to him, who, after the perusal, returned it with his thanks, and advised me to rejoin General Gates without delay, which I did the next morning at Sussex courthouse, whither he had led the troops from Van Kempt's."

Gates seems to have been greatly affected by the capture of his old comrade and friend, and no doubt sympathized fully with the views expressed in Lee's letter. Immediately after Wilkinson's arrival, the troops were put in motion. Brigadier-General Arnold led them directly to Easton, in Pennsylvania. Gates and his suite, with a light-guard of horse, took a more circuitous route, and, having reached the Delaware river some distance above Easton, in the night, lodged at "one Levy's." Gates had a predilection for his host, for he said that the Jews were whigs. Levy, however, in the course of the first interview, let drop certain remarks "a little mysterious," which made his guests somewhat suspicious of their host's patriotism. Gates accordingly desired those who accompanied him to conceal his name and rank, as well as those of Colonel John Trumbull, then adjutant-general, and afterward the patriotic panel-painter. The general presented himself as "Captain Smith, of Berkeley, Virginia." Levy's sharp eyes seemed to recognise an old acquaintance in Trumbull, and he observed that "he thought he had seen the colonel in Connecticut." General Gates, however, quickly answered, "No! he is a neighbor's son in Berkeley." The scrutinizing observation of Levy so alarmed his guests, that it was thought more prudent to shorten their stay; and accordingly the general, although the night was very inclement, ordered the horses to be saddled, "and," says Wilkinson, "we made a perilous passage of the river, through floating ice, and marched until midnight, before we lay down, in a dirty store-room, which almost suffocated me." The next morning they reached Nazareth in good time, and then pushed on for Bethlehem, where they overtook Arnold with the troops from the North, and Lee's army, with General Sullivan, who had changed his route the moment he found himself in command, and hurried forward to join Washington. While Gates was at Bethlehem, he received that letter from Washington which, as we have seen, was written on the 14th of December, and contained an account of the "melancholy situation" of affairs in New Jersey. The troops were now hurried on, and joined

Dec. 16. the commander-in-chief in the neighborhood of Coryell's ferry.

Washington's forces were considerably increased by the addition of Sullivan's and Gates's divisions, but his difficulties were "not sensibly diminished." His army was rapidly dissolving, and in ten days there would be (in consequence of the expiration of the time of service of many) only fourteen hundred men left, and "miserably provided in all things." Washington was deeply sensible of the dangers of the country. "I saw him," says Wilkinson, "in that gloomy period, dined with him, and attentively marked his aspect; always grave and thoughtful, he appeared at that time pensive and solemn in the extreme." Perplexed as he was, however, Washington did not despair. To his brother he writes, "Under a full persuasion of the justice of our cause, I can not entertain an idea that it will finally sink, though it may remain for some time under a cloud."

Such was the imminency of the approach of the British to Philadelphia, that it was thought advisable by Congress on its adjournment to choose Balti-

Dec. 12. more as the next place of meeting. Before adjourning, however, it was "resolved, that, until Congress shall otherwise order, General Washington be possessed of full power to order and direct all things relative to the department and to the operations of war." This was a wide extension of authority; but Washington, always so scrupulous in the exercise of his delegated powers, does not assume it without an explanation, which seems almost like an apology to the state. He orders three battalions of artillery to be recruited. He promises officers and men that their pay shall be increased twenty-five per cent. This was obviously not transcending the authority conferred upon him by the resolution of Congress, but Washington fears that what he has done may appear "premature and unwarrantable." In the same letter to

Dec. 20. Congress, however, he can not refrain (urged as he is by the emergencies of his position) from declaring the necessity of acting occasionally on his own responsibility. If, in the short interval in which great and arduous preparations must be made against the enemy, "every matter that in its nature is self-evident is to be referred to Congress, at the distance of a hundred and thirty or forty miles, so much time must elapse," he says, "as to defeat the end in view.....

"It may be said," continues the scrupulous and disinterested Washington, "that this is an application for powers that are too dangerous to be intrusted. I can only add that desperate diseases require desperate remedies; and I with truth declare that I have no lust after power, but I wish with as much fervency as any man upon this wide-extended continent for an opportunity of turning the sword into the ploughshare. But my feelings, as an officer and a man, have been such as to force me to say that no person ever had a greater choice of difficulties to contend with than I have. It is needless to add that short enlistments, and a mistaken dependence upon militia, have been the origin of all our misfortunes, and the great accumulation of our debt. We find, sir, that the enemy are daily gathering strength from the disaffected. This strength, like a snowball by rolling, will increase, unless some means can be devised to check effectually the progress of the enemy's arms. Militia may possibly do it for a little while; but in a little while also, and the militia of those states, which have been frequently called upon, will not turn out at all; or, if they do, it will be with so much reluctance and sloth as to amount to the same thing. Instance New Jersey! Witness Pennsylvania! Could anything but the river Delaware have saved Philadelphia?"

With no confidence in a militia, "who come in you can not tell how, go you can not tell when, and act you can not tell where, consume your provisions, exhaust your stores, and leave you at last at a critical moment," Washington ventures to advise the establishment of "a large standing army sufficient of itself to oppose the enemy." Not less than a hundred and ten battalions, he declares, should at once

be raised, as the eighty-eight proposed by Congress are by no means equal to the opposition that must be made. "It is not a time," says he, "to stand upon expense." Emboldened by the necessities of the occasion, Washington declares he shall encourage those officers who offer to raise men upon continental pay and establishment, and "regiment them when they have done it." His scrupulous sense of his responsibility to the state, however, here again shows itself in these remarkable words: "If Congress disapprove of this proceeding, they will please to signify it, as I mean it for the best. It may be thought I am going a good deal out of the line of my duty, to adopt these measures, or to advise thus freely. A character to lose, an estate to forfeit, the inestimable blessings of liberty at stake, and a life devoted, must be my excuse."

"What a wretched spectacle did our troops present in retreating through the Jerseys!" exclaims an American officer, "without cavalry; but partially provided with artillery; deficient in transport for the little we had to carry; without tents, tools, or camp-equipage; without magazines of any kind; half clothed; badly armed; debilitated by disease, disheartened by misfortunes, and worn out with fatigues." The very steps of the soldiers during that toilsome retreat could be traced upon the snow by stains of the blood which had dropped from their naked feet!

Crippled and exhausted as the army was, Washington could not make a show of offensive operations, and resorted to the only means in his power of saving

Philadelphia, which Congress had resolved should be defended to the last extremity. He did what he could to prevent the British from crossing the Delaware. For thirty miles along the western bank of that river (from Dunk's ferry, below Trenton, to Coryell's ferry above), at the ferries and fords, he distributed his force into patrolling-parties and stationary guards. The craft on the Delaware were secured, and the larger vessels formed into a chain of guard-ships. With the advantage of after-sight, which is the privilege of historians, we now discover that the enemy's design was not to march upon Philadelphia. General Lee's conjecture was correct. Sir William Howe did not intend to cross the Delaware during that winter's campaign. The British general, as appears from his despatch, was satisfied with establishing himself in New Jersey, and thus securing shelter, forage, and provisions, for his army, till the spring should open, and reinforcements arrive for carrying out other and more extensive designs.

Washington's army, reinforced by the division of Lee, the regiments from the northern army under Gates, and the militia from Pennsylvania, drawn out by the spirited exertions of the ever-active Mifflin, now numbered nearly six thousand effective men. With this addition to his force, the commander-in-chief resolved upon commencing offensive operations. How far he was actuated in this determination by a letter received from the adjutant-general, Colonel Reed, it is difficult to decide. It detracts nothing from the character of Washington **Dec. 22.** to concede that he acted from the suggestions of those in whose capacity and character he trusted. One of the most striking characteristics of the great man was the readiness with which he adopted any measure, come from what source it might, which he believed to be conducive to the welfare of the great cause in which he was engaged. No obstinate self-esteem ever interrupted the course of his generous love of country.

Reed was at the time with Colonel Cadwallader and a body of Pennsylvania militia, stationed at Bristol, when **Dec. 22.** he wrote this letter to Washington : " If we could possess ourselves again of New Jersey, or any considerable part, the effect would be greater than if we had not left it. Allow me to hope that you will consult your own good judgment and spirit, and let not the goodness of your heart subject you to the influence of the opinions of men in every respect your inferiors. Something must be attempted before the sixty days expire which the commissioners have allowed ; for, however many may affect to despise it, it is evident a very serious attention is paid to it: and I am confident that, unless some more favorable appearance attends our arms and cause before that time, a very great number of the militia-officers here will follow the example of Jersey, and take benefit from it. Our cause is desperate and hopeless if we do not strike some stroke. Our affairs are hastening apace to ruin, if we do not retrieve them by some happy event. Delay with us is near equal to a total defeat. We must not suffer ourselves to be lulled into security and inactivity, because the enemy does not cross the river. The love of my country, a wife and four children in the enemy's hands, the respect and attachment I have to you, the ruin and poverty that must attend me and thousands of others, will plead my excuse for so much freedom."

Washington, influenced or not by this outspoken letter, had so far carried out his purpose of offensive operations as to appoint the time for an attack; for he writes to Reed that "Christmas-day, at night, one hour before day, is the time fixed upon for our attempt at Trenton. For Heaven's sake, keep this to yourself, as the discovery of it may prove fatal to us—our numbers, sorry am I to say, being less than I had any conception of; but necessity, dire necessity, will, nay must, justify an attack. ..... I have ordered our men to be provided with three days' provisions, ready cooked, with which and their blankets they are to march; for if we are successful, which Heaven grant, and the circumstances favor, we may push on."

Dec. 23.

Washington at this moment naturally expected the cordial co-operation of General Gates, but that officer unfortunately was "unwell, and had applied for leave to go to Philadelphia." He was, however, desired by his superior, "if his health would permit him," to call and stay two or three days at Bristol, on his way, to give his aid in settling some probable disputes about rank; for "the colonels of the continental regiments," says Washington, "might kick up some dust about command." But Gates was not then in the humor to co-operate with the commander-in-chief. He had probably aims of his own, which he was more anxious to direct, than to aid in furthering those of Washington and of the country. Major Wilkinson rode with Gates to Philadelphia. They set out together on the 24th of December. On the road the general appeared much depressed in mind, and frequently expressed the opinion that while General Washington was watching the enemy above Trenton, they would privately construct batteaux, cross the Delaware in his rear, and take possession of Philadelphia, before he was aware of the movement; and that, instead of vainly attempting to stop Sir William Howe at the Delaware, General Washington ought to retire to the south of the Susquehanna river, and there form an army. Gates, moreover, declared that it was his intention to proceed to Baltimore, and there lay this plan before Congress. Wilkinson was entreated to accompany him, but refused. At night, Gates wrote a letter to Washington, with which he charged Wilkinson, who then took leave of him, and prepared to return to the army.

"I was on horseback early the next morning (Christmas-day)," says Wilkinson, "and reached Newtown about two o'clock. On my arrival there I discovered, to my surprise, that General Washington had transferred his quarters to that place, and had himself marched with the troops in that neighborhood. From Colonel Harrison, the general's secretary, who had been left in charge of his papers, I received the necessary directions, and proceeded in quest of the troops, whose

53

route was easily traced, as there was a little snow on the ground, which was tinged here and there with blood, from the feet of the men who wore broken shoes.

"I got up with my brigade near M'Conkey's ferry about dusk, and, inquiring for the commander-in-chief, was directed to his quarters. I found him alone, with his whip in his hand, prepared to mount his horse, which I perceived as I entered. When I presented the letter of General Gates to him, before receiving it, he exclaimed, with solemnity—

" ' What a time is this to hand me letters !'

"I answered that I had been charged with it by General Gates.

" ' By General Gates ! Where is he ?'

" ' I left him this morning in Philadelphia.'

" ' What was he doing there ?'

" ' I understood him that he was on his way to Congress.'

"Washington then earnestly repeated—

" ' On his way to Congress ! on his way to Congress !'" and broke the seal ; whereupon Wilkinson made his bow, took his leave, and, joining his brigade, prepared to bear his part in the eventful enterprise of that stormy Christmas-night.

CHAPTER XXXIX.

The British Troops in New Jersey.—Their Confidence in Themselves, and Contempt of their Enemy.—Colonel Rahl at Trenton.—His Military Character.—Daring and reckless.—A Warning unheeded.—A Christmas-Dinner.—A Hand at Cards.—Another Warning disregarded.—The Approach of Washington.—Disposition of his Force.—Crossing of the Delaware.—The Storm.—Squibbing.—The Advance and Charge.—The Attack on the Hessians at Princeton.—Personal Exposure of Washington.—The Assault led by Stark.—The Enemy driven from the Town.—The Brave Rahl.—He rallies and returns to the Charge.—He falls.—Flight of his Hessians.—They are overtaken and surrounded.—Their Surrender.—The Loss on Both Sides.—The March of Cadwallader.—Its Delays and Failure.—Reinforcement from Putnam at Philadelphia.—Count Donop left in the Lurch.—The Dying Rahl visited and consoled by Washington.—No Pursuit.—Washington recrosses the Delaware.

1776. The British troops in New Jersey were stretched in a line of cantonments across from Brunswick to the river Delaware, and along its banks to Burlington. The main body was at Brunswick, and the rest were so widely scattered as to leave but small forces at the various other posts. Confident in the possession of the country, and despising the meager and ill-conditioned army of Washington, Lord Cornwallis believed himself so secure, that he was no longer vigilant. He himself, in fact, had requested leave of absence, and had gone to New York, to prepare to embark for England. His sense of security was shared by the officers and the army which he left behind, and none doubted their immunity from attack.

Trenton was held by Colonel Rahl with three regiments of Hessians (those of Anspach, Knyphausen, and Rahl), numbering fifteen hundred men, and a troop of British light-horse. Rahl was a brave and active executive officer, but careless of danger even to recklessness. He was a bustling disciplinarian, and was ever harassing his men by his minute attention to the formalities of dress and parade. He was, however, no tactician, and could neither foresee danger nor provide against it. He had, moreover, a great contempt for his enemy; and when it was suggested that an assault was possible, and that he should fortify his position, he made a jest of it, exclaiming, "Works!—pooh! pooh! An assault by the rebels? Let them come: we'll at them with the bayonet!"[*] He had given proofs of his dashing qualities as a spirited officer in the attack on the lines at Fort Washington, and was placed in command at Trenton as a compliment to his bravery. Notwithstanding his general want of forecaste, he is said to have been aroused to a temporary apprehension for the security of his frontier post, and to have applied for a reinforcement from General Grant, who replied: "Tell the colonel he is very safe. I will undertake to keep the peace in New Jersey with a corporal's guard." He was soon lulled into his habitual confidence, which remained undisturbed, although he was warned that the Americans threatened an attack.

On the afternoon of Christmas-day the whole garrison was suddenly aroused to arms by a firing at one of the outposts. Colonel Rahl hastened to the point, and found that a picket-guard had been fired upon, and six men wounded. The ene-

my, however, had retired. So the colonel, thinking all was over, hurried back to his dinner and his bottle, to which he was devotedly attached. It was Christmas, and of course a high festival with the German soldiers. Rahl himself was a guest on the occasion, at the house of one Abraham Hunt,[*] who was a trader, and made no nice distinctions between whigs and tories, provided they were his customers. The Christmas-dinner was eaten, the wine circulated freely, and finally cards were proposed. The convivial colonel was as fond of play as of his bottle, and soon became deeply absorbed in both. Thus the afternoon and night passed gayly. "Just at dawn a messenger came in haste with a note to Colonel Rahl, sent by a tory on the Pennington road, who had discovered the approach of the Americans." There was a negro-servant at the door, and he refused admittance to the messenger, telling him that "the gemmen can't be disturbed." The bearer of the note, however, aware of its pressing importance, insisted upon the negro carrying it in. He did as he was bidden, and handed it to Rahl. The hilarious colonel carelessly thrust the note into his pocket without reading it, and continued his game. The men, like their master, were revelling, and forgetting all sense of danger and duty in drunken frolic.

Washington had chosen this night of Christmas for his attack with the expectation that his Hessian enemy, thus yielding to the festivities of the day, would be more exposed to a surprise. His plan was, to cross the Delaware with three di-

* Irving.   * Lossing.

visions of his army. One, under Cadwallader and Reed, was to pass the river at Bristol; another, under Ewing, at the ferry a little below Trenton; and the main body, consisting of twenty-five hundred men, Washington proposed to lead himself (in conjunction with Sullivan, Stirling, Greene, and Colonel Knox of the artillery) across M‘Conkey's ferry, nine miles above Trenton. The British posts at Mount Holly, Burlington, Black Horse, and Bordentown, were the points of attack set down for the first two divisions. Trenton itself was reserved for the commander-in-chief.

Boats having been got in readiness, Washington ordered the troops to be paraded early in the evening "back

Dec. 25. of M‘Conkey's ferry," and began to embark them as soon as it grew dark. He hoped to be able to throw them all over, with the artillery, by midnight, and thus arrive at Trenton by five o'clock in the morning, the distance from the point of landing on the opposite side being about nine miles. The darkness of the night, however; the frost, by which ice was rapidly made; the severity of the cold, so great that two or three men froze to death; and the force of the current, rendered still more violent by a high wind, impeded the passage of the boats so much, that it was three o'clock before all the artillery could be got over, and nearly four when the troops took up their line of march. Washington, thus delayed, despaired of surprising the town, as he knew that he could not reach it before the day had fairly broken. He determined, nevertheless, to push on, as he

could not retire without being discovered, and harassed while recrossing the river.

On landing, Washington formed his detachment in two divisions. One, under the command of Sullivan, was ordered to march by the lower or river road, and enter Trenton to the south. The other, Washington was to lead himself by a circuitous route to the Pennington road, and thus into the town at the north. In order that the two divisions might be ready to attack simultaneously, the general-in-chief, as he had a circuit to make, ordered Sullivan to halt for a few minutes at a cross-road, to give him time to come up. The final order being issued, that the troops, having first forced the outguards, should push directly into the town, and thus charge the enemy before they had time to form, each division took up its march.

When the division on the lower road halted, in accordance with Washington's order, it was discovered that the snowstorm which was beating violently in the soldiers' faces, had so wetted the best-secured arms, that they were not in firing condition. The fact was announced to Sullivan. He cast a look at General St. Clair, who was at his side, and observed, "What is to be done?"—"You have nothing for it but to push on and charge," was St. Clair's immediate answer. The march was then continued, the troops being ordered to clear their muskets in the best manner they could as they moved along, and a great deal of "squibbing" ensued. In the meantime an officer was sent to Washington, to inform him of the condition of the arms. He returned for answer that the soldiers "must advance and charge."

It was now broad day, and both divisions having reached the outskirts of the town at the same moment, their fires were heard by each other, as they began their simultaneous attacks upon the enemy's pickets. As his column approached the town, Washington kept near the front, and, coming up with a man chopping wood by the roadside, he asked, "Which way is the Hessian picket?"—"I don't know," replied the fellow, with an air and tone as if he were concealing the truth. Captain Forrest, who was in command of the artillery, was on horseback at the side of the commander-in-chief, and, observing the reluctance of the man, said, "You may speak, for that is General Washington." The man was astonished at the discovery, and raising his hands to heaven, exclaimed, addressing the general: "God bless and prosper you, sir!—the picket is in that house, and the sentry stands near that tree." Captain Washington was immediately ordered to dislodge it, which he did with great promptness. The artillery was now unlimbered, and the column proceeded. As Forrest opened his battery, Washington kept on the left, and, advancing with it, directed the fire. He was thus so much exposed, that the officers repeatedly entreated him to fall back; but he continued on, notwithstanding their solicitude for his safety.

Colonel Stark commanded the advance-guard of Sullivan's division, and made quick work with the picket on his side. Having forced this, he pressed on into the town, dealing "death wherever he found resistance, and breaking down all opposition before him." The whole column followed close at the heels of the dauntless Stark. The enemy made a momentary show of resistance by a wild and aimless fire of musketry from the windows of the houses in which they were quartered, but were soon compelled to abandon their cover as the Americans advanced. A troop of British dragoons, with about five hundred infantry, took to flight across the Assumpink, and joined Count Donop at Bordentown.

Colonel Rahl seemed to have lost all but his courage in the confusion of the surprise. He was riding wildly about on his horse, endeavoring to rally his men, and crying, "Forward! march! advance! advance!" His troops, thus encouraged by the presence of their commander, made an attempt to form in the main street. Captain Forrest, however, opened his battery (with General Washington at his side, directing the fire) at the head of King street, and greatly confused the forming battalions; while Captain William Washington, who, seconded by Lieutenant James Monroe (afterward president), led the advance-guard of General Washington's column, perceiving that the Hessians were endeavoring to form a battery in the street, rushed forward, drove the artillerists from their guns, and took two pieces just as they were about being fired. Captain Washington and Lieutenant Monroe were both wounded in this perilous act, the former in his wrist and the latter in the fleshy part of his shoulder. This gallant conduct of the advance-guard was of great service; for, if the enemy had been able to serve their artillery in the narrow street, the Americans might have been checked.

Colonel Rahl succeeded, by a great effort, in withdrawing his troops from the town into a field near by. Here he formed his grenadiers, and, instead of retreating, as prudence would have suggested, he recklessly led them on against the town, now filled by the triumphant soldiers of his enemy. He madly pushed on, right in the teeth of the fire of the artillery sweeping the streets, and the brisk musketry of the American riflemen taking deliberate and sure aim from the doors and windows of the houses. At the first onset, the gallant Rahl was shot from his horse. His men, seeing their leader fall, turned by their right along the river Assumpink, which runs through the town, and endeavored to escape to Princeton. General Washington, observing their purpose, instantly threw Colonel Hand with his riflemen in their way, and ordered the Virginia troops under Colonels Scott and Lawson to take them on their left. Thus hemmed in on every side, the Hessians halted and formed in order of battle. At this moment General Washington ordered the guns of Forrest's battery to be turned on them, "with a discharge of canister."—"Sir, they have struck!" was Forrest's answer to the command. "Struck!" replied the general. "Yes," said Forrest, "their colors are down."—"So they are," observed Washington, and, putting spurs to his horse, he galloped toward them, followed by Forrest and his officers. The enemy having ordered their arms, Washington

summoned them to surrender, when they at once agreed to do so at discretion.

The wounded Rahl was now borne, by a file of sergeants, to present his sword to General Washington. At this moment, Wilkinson rode up, having been sent for orders. "On my approach," says he, "the commander-in-chief took me by the hand and observed, 'Major Wilkinson, this is a glorious day for our country!' his countenance beaming with complacency; while the unfortunate Rahl, who the day before would not have changed fortunes with him, now pale, bleeding, and covered with blood, in broken accents seemed to implore those attentions which the victor was well disposed to bestow on him."

The whole loss of the Americans was trifling, amounting in all to four men wounded, two killed, and two frozen to death. The enemy had their commander, six officers, and four men, killed; and surrendered to Washington twenty-three officers, nearly one thousand non-commissioned officers and privates, four stand of colors, twelve drums, six brass field-pieces, and a thousand stand of arms and accoutrements. The triumph was great, and it might have been much greater had Washington's plan been carried out in all its details. But General Cadwallader, who was to have crossed the Delaware at Bristol, and Ewing at Trenton ferry, had both failed him. General Putnam, too, who had been urged to lend his aid in the affair, had been prevented from carrying out fully the orders of Washington.

Ewing did everything in his power to cross; but the quantity of ice in the river was so great, that he could not possibly get over. Cadwallader was also hindered by the same difficulty in crossing above Bristol. He then made an attempt at Dunk's ferry, below. As soon as it was dark, he sent down all the boats that he could muster, and marched down about eight o'clock. A few men were first embarked, to line the river, and prevent any persons from escaping to give intelligence to the enemy; next followed a part of the first battalion of militia, and then two fieldpieces, with which Cadwallader himself crossed, in order to see if it was practicable to land them. Upon reaching the other side, and finding, in consequence of the thickness of the ice, that it was impossible to get the guns on shore, he called together his field-officers, and consulted as to whether it would be proper to march without the artillery. They all agreed that it would not. In the meantime, another battalion of troops had succeeded in crossing. They were, however, all taken back to the Pennsylvania side of the Delaware, where, in consequence of the ice and stormy weather, they did not arrive until four o'clock in the morning. Cadwallader then marched to Bristol. "I imagine," he said, in writing to Washington, and giving an account of his own unsuccessful operations, "the badness of the night must have prevented you from passing over as you intended."

General Putnam had answered Washington's solicitation for aid in the attack upon Trenton, by a statement that such was the insubordinate and defective condition of the militia, and the threatening aspect of affairs (foreboding an insurrection) in Philadelphia, that it was impossible for him to march in person, or be of any material aid. At the last moment, however, he sent off Colonel Griffin, with a meager detachment of Pennsylvania militia. This officer reached the Jerseys in time, but being indisposed himself, and his troops ill conditioned, he declined to join in the attack, and wrote to Cadwallader at Bristol, that he thought he could be of more service by diverting Count Donop at Bordentown, and thus draw him off from giving his aid to Colonel Rahl at Trenton. Griffin acted accordingly. He marched toward Donop's camp sufficiently near to be observed, and to provoke the enemy to come out. He then retired leisurely, skirmishing here and there, followed by a large body of the Hessians, until they reached Mount Holly, when Griffin rapidly retreated, leaving Donop in the lurch, who was left to find his way back to Bordentown.

If all the details of Washington's plan could have been successfully carried out, not a man would have escaped from Trenton; and, with the aid of Cadwallader, he would have been able, as he hoped, to drive the enemy from all their posts below that town. He was well satisfied, however, with the conduct of those troops who were with him and won the day. He pays this tribute to them in his letter to the president of Congress: "In justice to the officers and men, I must add that their behavior upon this occasion reflects the highest honor upon them. The difficulty of passing the river in a very severe night, and their march through a violent storm of snow and hail, did not in the least abate their ardor; but when they came to the charge, each seemed to vie with the other in pressing forward: and were I to give a preference to any particular corps, I should do great injustice to the others."

When the wounded Rahl had surrendered his sword, he was borne to a tavern, kept by a Quaker of the name of Stacey Potts. Rahl's wound was mortal, and, as he was dying, Washington, in company with General Greene, visited and consoled him with expressions of sympathy, and well-deserved praise for his heroic daring. The Hessian commander was soothed, but declared that he preferred rather to die than to outlive his honor.

General Greene and Colonel Knox (the latter of whom had been made a brigadier-general the next day by Congress, without a knowledge of the triumph at Trenton) were solicitous that Washington should push on and increase the alarm of the enemy by striking a succession of immediate blows. The general-in-chief himself was apparently inclined to this bold policy, but most of the officers were against it; and "his excellency did not then think he could answer going contrary to the judgment of the majority of a council of war."*

Washington, therefore, with inferior numbers to the enemy posted below, and with "a strong battalion of light-infantry" at Princeton above him, thought it most prudent to return; and accordingly, on the evening of his triumph, he recrossed the Delaware with the prisoners and artillery which he had taken.

Dec. 26.

CHAPTER XL.

The Americans greatly encouraged by the Triumph at Trenton.—Pennsylvania comes more readily to the Rescue.—New-Jersey Whigs more decided.—The Tories more vacillating.—The Insolence of the Hessians.—Conduct of the British Troops in New Jersey.—"Protections."—No Rights of Property.—Rapine, Ravage, and Rape.—New Jersey becomes more favorable to the Patriots.—Cadwallader crosses the Delaware, and marches to Burlington.—No Resistance.—"Down with the Red Rags!"—Panic of the Enemy.—Cadwallader at Bordentown.—Washington makes Great Preparations to attack.—Sir William Howe aroused.—Lord Cornwallis sent to take the Command in New Jersey.—Washington without Money.—Robert Morris called upon.—His "Ways and Means."—A Friend indeed.—Washington crosses the Delaware.—Reed sent out to reconnoitre.—His Capture of a Foraging-Party.—Riding double.—Washington's Position on the Assumpink.—The Arrival and Position of the Enemy.—Washington made Military Dictator.—His Dignified Acceptance of the Trust.—The Enemy postpone their Attack.—The Americans in Danger.—A Chance of Escape.

1776. THE triumph at Trenton was a great encouragement to the American cause. The troops were so much inspirited by their success, that all were more eager for the fight, and some whose term of service was about expiring were induced to re-enlist. Influences which before proved unavailing were now brought to bear with effect. When such as appeared determined to go off and return to their homes were harangued, artfully

* Gordon.

reminded that they would be called cowards should they leave, and promised a bounty of ten dollars each man, more than half agreed to remain six weeks longer. The militia more promptly answered to the call upon them. Pennsylvania was now roused, and General Mifflin was enabled in the course of a few days to send a reinforcement of upward of a thousand men to Washington's army. The vacillating whigs of New Jersey became more decided, and no longer feared to declare and act for the American cause; while even many of the tories clung less tenaciously to British interests. The insolence and violent outrages of the royal troops, and especially of the Hessians, had increased the virulence of their original foes, and even provoked some of their former friends to hostility.

When the royal army entered the Jerseys, most of the inhabitants remained in their houses, and many thousands received printed "protections," signed by Sir William Howe. But these saved their holders neither from insult nor robbery: their property was taken or destroyed, without distinction of persons. They might show their "protections:" the Hessians could not or would not understand them, and the English took care to have their share of the plunder. The officers, both Hessian and British, were no less ready to violate the rights of property than their soldiers. The carriages of gentlemen "of the first rank" were seized, their arms defaced, while the commissioned plunderers blazoned their own on the panels, and thus insolently paraded throughout town and country.

"Discontents and murmurs increased every hour at the licentious ravages of the soldiery, both British and foreign, who were shamefully permitted, with unrelenting hand, to pillage friend and foe in the Jerseys. Neither age nor sex was spared. Indiscriminate ruin attended every person they met with. Infants, children, old men and women, were left in their shirts, without a blanket to cover them, under the inclemency of winter. Every kind of furniture was destroyed and burnt; windows and doors were broken to pieces: in short, the houses were left uninhabitable, and the people without provisions; for every horse, cow, ox, and fowl, was carried off.

"Horrid depredations and abuses were committed by that part of the army which was stationed at or near Pennytown. Sixteen young women fled to the woods, to avoid the brutality of the soldiers, and were there seized and carried off. One man had the cruel mortification[*] to have his wife and only daughter (a child of ten years of age) ravished. Another girl of thirteen was taken from her father's house, carried to a barn about a mile off, there dishonored and abused by five others. A most respectable gentleman, in the neighborhood of Woodbridge, was alarmed with the cries and shrieks of a most lovely daughter: he found a British officer in the act of violating her, and instantly put him to death. Two other officers rushed in with their fusees, and fired two balls into the father, who was left languishing under his wounds."[†]

[*] Rather a mild term for so heinous a crime!
[†] Gordon.

54

Exasperated by such enormities, the people of New Jersey were ready, at the least show of strength on the part of Washington's army, to rally to his aid. The commander-in-chief, thus assisted, not only by reinforcements to his troops, but by an accession of feeling in his favor, determined to cross over into New Jersey again, and make another demonstration against the enemy.

General Cadwallader, having heard of Washington's successful attack upon the Hessians at Trenton, crossed into Jersey early the next morning, with fifteen hundred of the Pennsylvania militia. **Dec. 27.** He had no sooner landed most of his troops, when he learned that Washington had recrossed the Delaware the night before, and was then on the Pennsylvania side. As Cadwallader was thus defeated in his intention of forming a junction with the main body, he was much embarrassed which way to proceed. He himself thought it most prudent to retreat. Colonel Reed, who was with him, warmly advocated the bolder policy of marching to Burlington, lest the fluctuating militia, whose spirit was now up, should be discouraged by a second disappointment. It was soon discovered that there was little fear of immediate opposition from the enemy. Although Cadwallader crossed the river in open daylight, there was no show of resistance to his landing; notwithstanding, with the overpowering force of the enemy, they could have readily overcome him. They were, in fact, so panic-stricken by their defeat at Trenton, that they fled precipitately, as we shall see, abandoning their posts at Black Horse, Mount Holly, Burlington, and Bordentown, and were now retreating toward South Amboy.

General Cadwallader, meeting with no opposition, now did not hesitate to accede to Colonel Reed's views, and determined to push on, though cautiously. Reed, accompanied by two other officers, rode on in advance to reconnoitre. On approaching Burlington, the enemy's outposts were found abandoned; and, on entering the place, there were all the signs of a late and precipitate retreat. As Reed and his companions in their continental uniforms rode through the streets of the town, the inhabitants pulled down the "red rags," which had been nailed to their doors as a demonstration of loyalty to the British flag, and gladly welcomed the protection of another color. So Reed pushed on, from post to post, sending back intelligence from each point to Cadwallader, who followed with the troops. The country was found everywhere clear of the enemy as far as Bordentown; and here, when all arrived, they halted. Cadwallader immediately wrote to Washington, informing him of his arrival at that place with eighteen hundred men, and that five hundred more were advancing from below. Washington, in reply, ordered Cadwallader to remain at Bordentown until he himself should pass over the Delaware, which he proposed to do on the 29th of December, when the troops might be sufficiently refreshed for another movement.

The commander-in-chief was making extensive preparations for his enterprise. He wrote to Generals M'Dougall and Maxwell, who were at Morristown, to use their utmost efforts in collecting a body of militia, with which to harass the enemy on flank and rear, should they advance or retreat. They were informed that the continental regiments from the eastern provinces had agreed to stay six weeks beyond their term of enlistment, and that he had agreed to pay them for " this extraordinary mark of their attachment to their country" a bounty of ten dollars each man. "I hope," added Washington, "this noble example will be followed by the four regiments under your command. Promise them the same reward, and endeavor to work upon them by every means in your power." He also wrote to General Heath to cross the Hudson from Peekskill with the New-England militia, and advance southerly by way of Hackensack, in order that he might be ready, on receiving orders from his chief, to co-operate with him, as "I think," he wrote, "a fair opportunity is offered of driving the enemy entirely from Jersey, or at least to the extremity of the province." Every precaution in his power had been taken for subsisting the troops, and all other preparations made; and "I shall," says Washington, "without loss of time, and as soon as circumstances will admit of it, pursue the enemy in their retreat, try to beat up more of their quarters, and, in a word, adopt in every instance such measures as the exigency of our affairs requires and our situation will justify."

In the meantime, Sir William Howe heard with alarm of the defeat of the Hessians at Trenton, and of the panic of the troops. Earl Cornwallis was imme-

diately sent from New York (where he was preparing to embark for England) to resume the command in New Jersey. He accordingly hastened to Princeton, where he was followed by a large force from the British encampment at Brunswick.

Washington, by his liberal promise of a bounty of ten dollars to each man, had succeeded in keeping his army together, but was puzzled, with an empty military chest, to find means for the fulfilment of his word. The army treasury was so far exhausted, that the commander-in-chief, when requiring a small amount of money for secret service, had been obliged to write to ROBERT MORRIS, a wealthy banker at Philadelphia, in these terms: "If you could possibly collect a sum, if it were but one hundred or one hundred and fifty pounds, it would be of service." Morris, with his usual promptness, at once sent the sum. His financial resources, however, were now to be more severely tasked. Washington wanted a large sum to meet the payment of the promised bounty to the troops. The "patriot financier" was the only resource; but he himself, when written to, was, with all his facilities, momentarily puzzled to meet the demand.

Morris pondered over the ordinary ways and means of raising the money, but, discovering that none were available, sallied out from his counting-house almost in despair. He had not gone far when he met a Quaker fellow-citizen, who was known to be wealthy. Morris stopped him, and acquainted him with his wants. "Robert, what security wilt thou give?" asked the Quaker. "My note, and my honor," answered Morris. "Thou shalt have it," was the prompt rejoinder.* The next day, by the timely aid of his Quaker friend, Morris was enabled to write to Washington: "I am up very early this morning, to despatch a supply of fifty thousand dollars to your excellency. You will receive that sum with this letter; but it will not be got away so early as I could wish, for none concerned in this movement except myself are up. I shall rouse them immediately. It gives me great pleasure that you have engaged the troops to continue; and if further occasional supplies of money are necessary, you may depend on my exertions either in a public or private capacity."

Dec. 30. Washington, being now fully prepared, crossed the Delaware with the van of his troops. The river, however, was so full of drifting ice, and the passage so difficult, that it was impossible to get the entire army over until late on the following day. During this movement, Washington sent Colonel Reed out, at the head of twelve dragoons, to reconnoitre and try to discover if the enemy were approaching, about whose operations nothing certain was known. Reed, being well acquainted with the country, had no difficulty in scouring it pretty effectually. In the course of his ride, he discovered that a British commissary, with a foraging-party, was in a house on the road. Reed accordingly rode up with his dozen men and immediately surrounded the place. The party within, which amounted in numbers to the same as that of the Americans, was so taken by surprise, and panic-stricken, that it

* Lossing.

surrendered without a blow. Reed and his men galloped back to the American camp; and, as each trooper rode in with a prisoner mounted behind him, he was received with a loud shout of applause.

Washington could obtain no certain intelligence of the number and situation of the enemy; but, from the most reliable accounts, it appeared that they had collected the principal part of their force from Brunswick and the adjacent posts at Princeton, where they were throwing up some works. Their number was reported to be from five to six thousand. General Howe was also said to have landed at Amboy with a thousand light-troops, with which he was on his march.

As soon as he had crossed the Delaware, Washington took up his position on the high ground to the east of Trenton, along the bank of the Assumpink creek, and was thus separated from the town by this small stream. His delay in passing his troops over the Delaware had given the enemy an opportunity of drawing in their several cantonments and assembling their whole force at Princeton. They evidently meditating an attack, and had pushed forward strong advanced pickets toward Trenton.

Washington, with his small force, now felt himself to be in a most critical situation. He was embarrassed, as was frequently the case, by a want of reliance upon his militia. He could not act merely as the military tactician, and move his men as a general could a well-disciplined army. The American commander was forced to become the politician, and consult the caprices of his fluctuating and

irregular troops. He might, as a strate-
gist, have wished to retire; but "to remove immediately was again destroying
every dawn of hope which had begun to
revive in the breasts of the Jersey militia." He therefore determined to hold
his present position, dangerous as it was,
and strengthen himself by ordering the
troops lying at Crosswicks, under General Cadwallader, and those under General
Mifflin, to join him at Trenton, although
it was "to bring them to an exposed
place." They accordingly came, and, after a hard night's march, reached
the camp on the first day of the
new year.

1777.

Washington had now about five thousand men, encamped in a line of two
miles in length, along the Assumpink
creek. The bridge and the fords which
crossed that stream were strongly guarded with artillery, and General Greene was
sent out with a detachment to harass the
advance of the enemy. Greene, by provoking him to frequent skirmishes, succeeded in delaying the approach of Lord
Cornwallis. While Greene was spiritedly
holding the British in check on the road
from Princeton, within a short distance of
Trenton, Washington rode up, and, joining the advanced detachment, thanked
the troops, and particularly the artillery,
for the services of the day. Then, having given orders for them to make as obstinate a stand as they could where they
were without risking the safety of their
cannon, he rode back to marshal his troops
on the other side of the Assumpink. The
commander-in-chief "stood fairly committed to a general action if the enemy had

provoked it."* He was therefore particularly anxious to retard their march until nightfall. His orders were so well
obeyed, that the head of the British column did not reach Trenton un-
til four o'clock in the afternoon,
while their rear was as far back as Maidenhead. As soon as the enemy entered
the town, they made a rush for the bridge
and the fords across the Assumpink creek,
but finding them well guarded, and receiving a hot fire from the American artillery, they halted and kindled their fires.
Thus the two opposing forces remained
until dark, with the small stream between
them, and cannonading each other with
their fieldpieces.

Jan. 2.

On the day before only, Washington
had received intelligence of a resolution
of Congress, which, although it freed him
from accountability to others, must have
greatly added to the feeling of personal
responsibility which now weighed upon
him at this trying time. He had, by the
deliberate act of the representatives of
his country, been endowed with the powers of a dictator. The great cause of
achieving the independence of the combined states was confided to him alone.
With what a simple yet lofty calmness
does he accept the trust!

"Instead of thinking myself," Washington writes to the committee of Congress,
"freed from all *civil* obligations, by this
mark of their confidence, I shall constantly bear in mind that, as the sword was
the last resort for the preservation of our
liberties, so it ought to be the first thing

* Memoirs of our Own Times, by General James Wilkinson.

laid aside when those liberties are firmly established."*

* The following was the resolution of Congress, which was then in session at Baltimore :—

"December 27, 1776.—This Congress, having maturely considered the present; and having perfect reliance on the wisdom, vigor, and uprightness, of General WASHINGTON, do hereby

"Resolve, That General WASHINGTON shall be, and he is hereby, vested with full, ample, and complete powers, to raise and collect together, in the most speedy and effectual manner, from any or all of these United States, sixteen battalions of infantry, in addition to those already voted by Congress; to appoint officers for the said battalions of infantry; to raise, officer, and equip, three thousand light-horse, three regiments of artillery, and a corps of engineers, and to establish their pay; to apply to any of the states for such aid of the militia as he shall judge necessary ; to form such magazines of provisions, and in such places, as he shall think proper; to displace and appoint all officers under the rank of brigadier-general, and to fill up all vacancies in every other department in the American army ; to take, wherever he may be, whatever he may want for the use of the army, if the inhabitants will not sell it, allowing a reasonable price for the same; to arrest and confine persons who refuse to take the continental currency, or are otherwise disaffected to the American cause ; and return to the states of which they are citizens, their names, and the nature of their offences, together with the witnesses to prove them.

"That the foregoing powers be vested to General WASHINGTON for and during the term of six months from the date hereof, unless sooner determined by Congress."

A copy of these resolutions was sent to the governor of each state, together with the following letter :—

"BALTIMORE, December 30, 1776.

"SIR: Ever attentive to the security of civil liberty, Congress would not have consented to the vesting of such powers in the military department as those which the enclosed resolves convey to the continental commander-in-chief, if the situation of public affairs did not require at this crisis a decision and vigor which distance and numbers deny to assemblies far removed from each other, and from the immediate seat of war.

"The strength and progress of the enemy, joined to prospects of considerable reinforcements, have rendered it not only necessary that the American forces should be augmented beyond what Congress had heretofore designed, but that they should be brought into the field with all possible expedition. These considerations induce Congress to request, in the most earnest manner, that the fullest influence of your state may be exerted to aid such levies as the general shall direct, in consequence of the powers now given him ; and that your quota of battalions, formally fixed, may be completed and ordered to headquarters with all the despatch that an ardent desire to serve the public happiness can dictate.

"I have the honor to be, &c.   "JOHN HANCOCK, President."

Washington was only a thousand yards distant from the front of his enemy. It was true, there was the little stream of the Assumpink intervening, but this was fordable at almost every point. Cornwallis's columns were displayed in great force along the border of the town and the heights beyond. "Thirty minutes would have sufficed to bring the two armies into contact, and thirty more would have decided the combat." But it was growing dark, and the British troops were fatigued with the long march of that day "from sunrise to sunset." They had been under arms for twelve long hours ; they were consequently languid, and required rest. Moreover, Cornwallis thought he had "the enemy safe enough, and could dispose of them the next morning." He therefore ordered his men to make fires, refresh themselves, and take repose. The other British officers coincided with their chief, with the exception of Sir William Erskine, who could not control his vexation at this imprudent resolution, and exclaimed impetuously, "My lord, if you trust these people to-night, you will see nothing of them in the morning !" Sir William, however, was not heeded : the fires were lighted, the men ordered to supper, and the advanced sentries posted for the night.

Opposite was Washington's army, ap-

The committee of Congress, composed of Robert Morris and George Clymer of Pennsylvania, and George Walton of Georgia, who remained in Philadelphia, sent the resolutions of Congress to Washington, with these words : " We find, by these resolves, that your excellency's hands will be strengthened with very ample powers ; and a new reformation of the army seems to have its origin therein. Happy it is for the country that the general of their forces can safely be intrusted with the most unlimited power, and neither personal security, liberty, nor property, be in the least degree endangered thereby !"—SPARKS.

parently preparing, like the enemy, for repose; with fires blazing up here and there along the whole line, and the sentinels pacing the bank of the Assumpink stream, within a hundred and fifty yards of their antagonists. But the approach of night did not bring with it any suggestion of repose to the minds of Washington and his general officers. They were anxiously pondering upon the hazardous position of their army. With an enemy greatly superior in numbers and discipline before them, and with the Delaware river (clogged with floating ice) behind, there was certainly enough in the prospects of the dangers of the coming morning to disturb the slumbering influences of night.

Washington, fully conscious of all the hazards of his position, early in the evening called together his general officers in council. He had but a brief statement to make. The situation of the army was known to all: a battle was certain if his troops remained where they were until the morning, and a defeat hardly less sure, with the superior advantages of the enemy; if a defeat without means of retreating, the result would be disastrous, and perhaps fatal to the cause. What, then, was to be done, was the question submitted. Some were in favor of retreating at once; while others were disposed to await the chances of the morning, and risk a general engagement, with all its hazards to the troops and to the country.

In the course of the day, General St. Clair, when charged with the guarding of the fords of the Assumpink, and while examining the ground to his right, had discovered a circuitous route, which was called the "Quaker road," or that leading to the Quaker bridge and meetinghouse.[*] He, therefore, is said to have suggested this as a way by which Princeton might be reached, and the rear of the British (under the command of General Leslie, on the high-road) be avoided. Washington heartily welcomed this suggestion, and adopted it without hesitation. It was accordingly determined to march at once by this roundabout Quaker road to Princeton, where it was concluded, from the large force which Cornwallis had thrown into Trenton, that he could not have left many troops, and might have left stores. "One thing I was certain of," says Washington, "that it would avoid the appearance of a retreat (which was of consequence, or to run the hazard of the whole army being cut off), whilst we might, by a fortunate stroke, withdraw General Howe from Trenton, and give some reputation to our arms."

* Wilkinson.

CHAPTER XLI.

The Quaker Road.—Providential Change of Wind.—The Stolen March.—A Successful Ruse.—The Night.—The Route to Princeton.—General Mercer and the Advance.—Meeting with the Enemy.—A Surprise.—A Conflict.—The Provincials beaten back.—Washington to the Rescue.—His Personal Exposure and Danger.—The Enemy routed.—" The Day is our own !"—Turned out of College.—The Pursuit.—A Fine Fox-Chase.—Bayoneting of General Mercer.—Lord Cornwallis bewildered.—" Washington at Princeton !"—No Pursuit.—Loss on Both Sides.—Death of Mercer.—Biographical Sketch.—Washington retires from Princeton.—The Winter's Bivouac.—Alarm of Cornwallis, and his Rapid March to Brunswick.—The American Winter-Quarters at Morristown.—Movements of General Heath.—An Affair, and Heath's own Account of it.

1777. THERE was one serious difficulty in carrying out the plan proposed of a rapid movement that night (January 2d) along the rough and circuitous route called the " Quaker road." The weather for two days had been unusually mild, and the ground had become so soft, that it would be almost impracticable to get on with the cattle, carriages, and artillery. While the council of war, however, are pondering over this difficulty, it is providentially removed. The wind suddenly changes into the northwest; the weather becomes intensely cold; and the ground freezes so hard, that soon the road is like a solid pavement. There is now no obstacle to the manœuvre, and immediate preparations are made for its execution.

Great precautions are taken to prevent the suspicions of the enemy. Washington orders the guards to be doubled at the bridge and the fords of the Assumpink stream, sends a strong fatigue-party with their picks and spades to work on an intrenchment within hearing distance of the British sentries, and directs the camp-fires to be kept blazing by using the neighboring fences for fuel. The first movement is to send off the baggage to Burlington, which is done early in the night. The troops are not prepared to march until twelve o'clock.

The army was filed off silently by detachments. The night was exceedingly dark, although calm, **Jan. 2.** clear, and severely cold. The working-parties, guards, and those charged with keeping the fires blazing, were left behind, with orders not to retire until toward the break of day. The stratagem is entirely successful. The whole American army gets away without exciting the least suspicion on the part of Earl Cornwallis, who reposes for the night in the confident expectation of " catching the fox in the morning," as he himself declared to his officers.

The Quaker road, comparatively new, and not much used, was so scored with deep, frozen ruts, and studded with stumps of trees, that the march was greatly obstructed. Washington's purpose was, to have reached Princeton before daylight, with the expectation of taking the British troops there by surprise, and of then pushing on rapidly to Brunswick, and seizing the magazine and stores before the enemy should take the alarm. The march, however, was so long delayed, that the day broke before his van arrived at Princeton. Washington, crossing the lower bridge over the Stony brook, kept his main body on the "Quaker road" until he reached a thick wood, when he defiled to the right, with the view of taking a by-path toward the town. He ordered General Mercer, however, with three hundred and fifty men (composed of the fragments of Colonel Smallwood's brave Delawares and Marylanders, of the first Virginia regiment, and some few volunteers), together with two fieldpieces, to continue to the left on the Quaker road, which conducted along the Stony brook, until he reached the bridge over which passed the highway that led from Princeton to Trenton. Here he was to take possession of the bridge, for the double purpose of intercepting the fugitives from Princeton, and to guard against an attack from Cornwallis at Trenton.

Jan. 3.

The British had left three regiments at Princeton, under the command of Lieutenant-Colonel Mawhood, when the main body pushed on to Trenton. These were the seventeenth, fortieth, and fifty-fifth. They had been quartered during the previous night in the town; but, at early dawn, the first-named regiment (the seventeenth), with Mawhood at its head, had marched out by the main road, to join Cornwallis. Passing the bridge over Stony brook, they reached some high ground a little distance beyond, on their route, at the moment when Washington's troops

were emerging from behind the wood, around which they were defiling toward the town.

The morning was fine, and in the clear, frosty air every object could be distinctly seen. The British and Americans seemed at this moment to have caught a simultaneous view of each other. On looking across the country toward the Trenton road, some of Washington's officers saw the reflection of arms in the light of the rising sun, as the enemy were ascending the high ground. It was but for a moment, however, for the British had immediately shifted their position. That they had not been less observant was soon evident, for two of their horsemen were seen to leap a fence and advance through the fields for the purpose of reconnoitring. After a hurried glance, they galloped back; and soon the enemy, having faced about, were observed rapidly descending the hill and retracing their steps toward Princeton. They had succeeded in recrossing the bridge, when, without suspecting its approach, they suddenly came upon General Mercer's detachment, which was hurrying along the Quaker road toward its junction with the highway, for the purpose of securing, in accordance with Washington's orders, the crossing of Stony brook near that point. The two parties were within less than five hundred yards of each other when the mutual surprise took place—for Mercer, like Mawhood, was unconscious of the approach of his enemy.

The two hostile detachments now hurried to anticipate each other in getting possession of some rising ground, about

55

half a mile north of Stony brook, to the east of the main road, and on the western edge of the town. The Americans, manœuvring for this purpose, had got into the orchard behind the house of William Clark, when they observed the British, from an opposite point, making for the height. Mercer pushed on his detachment in all haste through the orchard, and succeeded in first gaining the ground beyond, and so disposing his men as to leave a "worm fence" stretching curvically across the acclivity between them and the enemy.

Mercer, in possession of the ground, began the attack, under the cover of the fence, with a volley from his riflemen. Mawhood returned the fire, and then ordered his men to charge. The Americans fired again and again, and with terrible effect; but, as they were only armed with rifles, they could not withstand the onset of the British troops thrusting home their formidable bayonets, and were obliged to retire. At the first volley from the enemy, Mercer's gray horse was shot in the knee, and that gallant officer was forced to dismount, and struggle with the foe hand to hand. The British continued to pursue, and the Americans to retreat, when Washington, hearing the fire, immediately summoned the Pennsylvania militia and Moulder's battery of two guns to the support of General Mercer, and led them in person against the enemy.

Colonel Mawhood, observing a large force coming up, is suddenly checked in in the midst of his hot pursuit, and, halting, brings up his artillery. The American militia hesitate to advance, waver be-

fore the shot, and are giving way, when Washington gallops forward and strives to press them on. He is thus, while brandishing his sword, and spurring his white charger in front of the lines, a conspicuous target for the enemy. His death appears inevitable. His aid-de-camp, Colonel Fitzgerald, a warm-hearted Irishman, is in a moment aware of the danger of his chief. He drops the reins upon his horse's neck, and draws his hat over his face, that he may not see him die—a fate which he believes that Washington at that moment can not possibly escape.

A shout of victory immediately succeeds, and Fitzgerald ventures to raise his eyes. Washington is safe: the militia have rallied, Moulder's battery has discharged a volley of grapeshot, and the British are flying in confused haste, over fields and fences, toward the road leading to Trenton, leaving their artillery behind them. Colonel Fitzgerald, who was "celebrated as one of the finest horsemen in the American army," digs his spurs into his steed, dashes forward, and, bringing up by the side of Washington, exclaims, "Thank God, your excellency is safe!" The sudden reaction from despair to joy was too much for the impulsive Irishman, and he "wept like a child." The chief grasped his hand with warmth, and only said: "Away, my dear colonel, and bring up the troops. The day is our own!"

While the enemy's seventeenth regiment was being hotly engaged, the fifty-fifth was marching to its aid; but, on discovering that their comrades had been put to flight, they returned to the college,

at the north of the town, where, being re-inforced by the fortieth, quartered there, they marched out again to encounter the American detachment under General St. Clair, which had been sent after them. A ravine separated the parties, which, although deep and precipitous, the Americans did not hesitate to cross. While ascending the acclivity on the opposite side, and when within sixty or eighty yards of them, the British wheeled about, and hurried back to the college. On reaching it, they began to knock out the windows, that they might have free scope for the use of their musketry. The Americans, as they came up, expected warm work; but they had hardly got within a quarter of a mile of the building, when the enemy rushed out at the front, and retreated by long and loose files to Rock hill, and thence to Brunswick. As St. Clair had no cavalry, he could not pursue the fugitives, although such was the disorder of their flight, that "two troops of dragoons would have picked up the two regiments."

While Colonel Mawhood was flying over the fields and fences toward the road to Trenton, Washington was encouraging his troops in pursuit, and, as his riflemen were charging them, he shouted, "It is a fine fox-chase, my boys!" The American general, no less spirited a sportsman than Lord Cornwallis, was evidently enjoying "the run" as much as that nobleman had anticipated for himself, when, on the preceding night, he so complacently talked of "catching the fox in the morning."

General Mercer's horse was crippled by a shot, as we have seen, in the beginning of the engagement, and he himself obliged to dismount. As he was in front of his men, trying ineffectually to rally them, he was left alone on the field, and the British soldiers, coming up, knocked him down, bayoneted him, and left him for dead. He was afterward found near the barn of William Clark, still alive, and conveyed to Clark's house, where he lingered for awhile under the effect of his fatal wounds.

The distant firing was heard in the British camp at Trenton. Some thought it was thunder; and Earl Cornwallis, with an expression of anxiety, asked his surrounding officers what it could be. Sir William Erskine (who had so earnestly recommended an attack on the evening before) immediately answered, "My lord, it is Washington at Princeton!"

While the American troops were gathering together in Princeton, there was great alarm felt for the safety of Washington, who had followed the enemy in pursuit several miles along the road to Trenton. He continued after the fugitives, and did not turn back until General Leslie, commanding the rear of the British at Maidenhead, discovering that Washington's army was behind and not before as he had supposed, changed his front, and, followed by Cornwallis and his main body, began to march toward Princeton, which he reached just as the rear-guard of the Americans was leaving — Washington, on his return, having ordered his troops to march immediately. The precaution was taken to break down the bridge over Stony brook; but the British commander, not waiting to replace it, ordered his men (he himself showing them the example) to plunge into the shallow stream and wade across. Thus thoroughly wetted, and then stiffened into ice by the frost, the troops hurried on into the town and thence along the road toward Brunswick, which, with its stores and magazines, was supposed to be Washington's next point of attack.

The Americans were not disposed to linger at Princeton, with the whole army of Cornwallis pressing by a forced march on their rear. Washington's original plan was, to have pushed on to Brunswick; but the harassed state of the troops, many of them having had no rest for two nights and a day, and the danger of losing the advantage he had gained by aiming at too much, induced him, "by the advice of his officers," to give it up. But "in my judgment," says Washington, "six or eight hundred fresh troops, upon a forced march, would have destroyed all their stores and magazines, taken their military chest containing seventy thousand pounds, and put an end to the war."

The result at Princeton was sufficiently successful to greatly encourage the Americans and dishearten the enemy. Washington had only lost about a hundred in all, fourteen of whom were buried on the field. The British, in killed, wounded, and prisoners, suffered a loss of nearly six hundred. Among the killed of the English officers was a Captain Leslie, son of the earl of Levin, who was so much beloved, that those who were taken prisoners besought the privilege of his being buried with the honors of war; and when it was granted, the men who had belonged to his company were observed to weep bitterly over the grave of their young commander. Washington, too, grieved over the death of some of the most able and spirited of his officers. These were, Colonels Haslet and Potter; Major Morris; Captains William Shippen, Fleming, and Neal; and, above all, General Mercer.

Mercer was at first supposed to have died on the field, or Washington would have endeavored to bring him away, although he believed, as he declared, "that it could not have been effected." When he heard that he was still lingering at Princeton, the commander-in-chief sent his nephew, Major Lewis, under a flag, to the enemy, to visit him. Mercer was dying; but with his aid-de-camp, Major Armstrong, constantly at his side, and the family of the Clarks (in whose house he was) ever at hand to administer to his wants, the last moments of the general, though his wounds gave him acute pain, were greatly soothed. He died in the fifty-sixth year of his age, in the arms of Major Lewis, on the 12th of January.

HUGH MERCER was a Scotchman by birth and a Jacobite, having served on the side of the Young Pretender, Prince Charles Edward, as a surgeon's mate, at the battle of Culloden, in 1746. When the cause of the Stuarts was extinguished for ever, and its friends dispersed, Mercer emigrated to Virginia. In the French border wars, he laid aside the scalpel for the sword, and became a military officer, serving in the campaigns of 1755 and 1756 as a comrade of Washington, by whom he was greatly beloved. Mercer was living in Fredericksburg, Virginia, when the

American Revolution began, and, though he was practising as a doctor with success, he gave up his profession, and volunteered to bear arms in the cause of the colonies. In 1775 and 1776, he organized and commanded large bodies of the Virginia militia; and on the 5th of June, of the latter year, he was appointed by Congress a brigadier-general. He was an intimate associate of Washington's mother and sister, who were his neighbors at Fredericksburg, and highly esteemed by Washington himself, who knew him as a faithful comrade and sincere friend. He spoke of him, while mourning his death, as "the brave and worthy General Mercer."

Having given up all thought of marching immediately upon Brunswick, Washington now retired from Princeton. He was not greatly encumbered with baggage, for that of his own army he had sent to Burlington, and there was nothing of the enemy's to take away but some blankets, shoes, and a few other trifling articles. The two fieldpieces which had been captured from the British could not be brought away for the want of horses. The hay and "other such things" as the shortness of the time would admit were destroyed, and then the army marched out. The Americans proceeded down the Millstone river, and halted for the first night at Somerset courthouse, where many of the militia on that January night were obliged to lie down in the open air without blankets, which with the rest of their baggage had been sent to Burlington.

Jan. 3.

Next morning, Washington marched to Pluckimen, where he halted for several days. The hardships of a winter campaign would, it was feared, discourage the militia, as well might be the case, when they were day after day and night after night in midwinter without "any cover," and many of the "poor soldiers quite barefoot and ill clad in other respects... They have undergone, however," says Washington, "more fatigue and hardship than I expected militia, especially citizens, could have done at this inclement season."

Jan. 4.

Earl Cornwallis was in a state of great alarm for the safety of his stores, magazines, and well-filled military chest, at Brunswick. He pushed on with his whole army, in the greatest speed, to save them. The camp at Trenton was broken up and totally abandoned. Princeton was entered, and, after a check from the battery of the American rear-guard which delayed him over an hour, Cornwallis hurried on again, and by forced marches (here and there retarded by the want of bridges, which Washington had taken care to destroy) reached Brunswick.

The enemy seemed to be panic-struck, and Washington was in "some hopes of driving them out of the Jerseys." In order to effect this, he wrote to General Putnam, then at Philadelphia, and also to General Heath at Peekskill, to co-operate with him in his design. To the former he says: "It is thought advisable for you to march the troops under your command to Crosswicks, and keep a strict watch upon the enemy in that quarter. If the enemy continue at Brunswick, you must act with great cir-

Jan. 5.

cumspection, lest you meet with a surprise. As we have made two successful attacks upon them by surprise, if there is any possibility of retaliating, they will attempt it. You will give out your strength to be twice as great as it is. Forward on all the baggage and scattered troops belonging to this division of the army, as soon as may be.

"You will keep as many spies out as you may see proper. A number of horsemen might be kept going backward and forward for this purpose; and if you discover any motion of the enemy which you can depend upon, and which you think of consequence, let me be informed thereof as soon as possible by express."

To General Heath Washington wrote: **Jan. 5.** "The enemy are in great consternation; and, as the panic affords us a favorable opportunity to drive them out of the Jerseys, it has been determined in council that you should move down toward New York with a considerable force, as if you had a design upon the city." It was hoped that, by such a diversion, the British would be obliged to draw a large part of their force from New Jersey, for the protection of New York. General Lincoln was ordered, after leaving four thousand of the New-England militia with Heath, to cross the Hudson with the remainder, and march them to **Jan. 6.** join the commander-in-chief at Morristown, where he had now moved his troops.

Washington had gone to Morristown, as the place best calculated in that quarter to accommodate and refresh his army. Its resources proving less than he expect-

ed, and his men becoming so impatient from the severity of the season and their consequent sufferings, that they left him in considerable numbers, he thought of removing. He finally determined, however, to take up his winter-quarters at the place, for he did not know where else to procure covering for his troops. Wilkinson says: "This position, little understood at the time, was afterward discovered to be a most safe one for the winter-quarters of an army of observation, and such was General Washington's. The approach to it from the seaboard is rendered difficult and dangerous by a chain of sharp hills, which extend from Pluckimen by Boundbrook and Springfield to the vicinity of the Passaic river; it is situate in the heart of a country abounding with forage and provisions, and is nearly equidistant from New York and Amboy, and also from Newark and New Brunswick, with defiles in rear to cover a retreat should circumstances render it necessary."

Washington, on arriving at Morristown, repeated his orders to General Heath in regard to advancing on the city of New York, but suggested that General Lincoln should remain with him, instead of accompanying the New-England detachment ordered to Morristown. Heath at once began to make his dispositions in accordance with Washington's orders. He moved his troops down from Peekskill, advancing them gradually toward New York. On one day a regiment is marched to Newcastle, and on another the militia is ordered to White Plains. Again, "our general," as he always designates himself, moves to the southward, and arrives at

Newcastle before sunset. Soon he is again on the march, and " our general" reaches the outposts of the enemy at Fort Independence and Kingsbridge, where his three divisions have also arrived : "General Lincoln's on the heights above Colonel Van Cortland's; Wooster's at Williams's; and Scott's on the back of Volentine's." Here occurred an engagement, which we shall allow Heath to describe in his own words :—

" Our general, who moved with the centre division, knew that Volentine's house was the quarters of one of the guards; he did not know but it might be defended. As he approached it, he ordered Captain Bryant to advance a fieldpiece to the advance-guard, and, if there was any opposition from the house, to cannonade it immediately. He then ordered two hundred and fifty men from the head of the column (as it was moving on) to incline to the right, and by a double step to push into the hollow, between the house and the fort, to cut off the guard who were at the house, in case they should run toward the latter. At this instant, two light-horsemen, who had been sent out by the enemy as the day broke to reconnoitre the vicinity, came unexpectedly, at the descent of a hill, plump upon the head of Wooster's column. They attempted to turn about, but, before it could be fully effected, a fieldpiece was discharged at them: one of them was pitched from his horse and taken prisoner; the other galloped back to the fort, hallooing as he passed, 'The rebels! the rebels!' This set all the outguards and pickets running to the fort, leaving in some places their arms, blankets, tools, provisions, &c., behind them. Those who fled from Volentine's and the *Negro fort* were fired at as they ran, but none were killed: one who could not run so fast as the rest was taken prisoner. Ten muskets were taken at Volentine's house. The guard above Van Cortland's was as completely surprised as the others, where General Lincoln took about forty arms, some blankets, &c., &c.

"The left and centre divisions moved into the hollow, between Volentine's house and the fort, from whence our general immediately sent a summons to the commanding officer of the fort to surrender." As " our general" modestly withholds the lofty words he used on that occasion, we here supply them : " Forty minutes only," said Heath, " can be allowed for the garrison to give their answer; and, should it be in the negative, they must abide the consequences." No answer was given; and the only consequence which followed was the firing of a gun at an outpost!

In a few days, General Heath, with all his usual skill in tactics, drew back his army up the Hudson—having learned from a *soi-disant* deserter that Governor Sir Guy Carleton's Canadian troops had lately arrived in New York by water, and that a detachment from Rhode Island, under Lord Percy, was about to land in Westchester county. Fearful of being thus surrounded, and threatened by " the appearance of a severe snowstorm coming on," Heath cautiously retired. " Our general," who prided himself upon being, above all things, a good tactician, could hardly have felt flattered by this criticism

from Washington on these late manœuvres: "This letter," he says, writing to
Heath, "is in addition to my public one
of this date. It is to hint to you, and I
do it with concern, that your conduct is
censured (and by men of sense and judgment, who have been with you on the
expedition to Fort Independence) as being fraught with too much caution, by
which the army has been disappointed,
and in some degree disgraced. Your
summons, as you did not attempt to fulfil your threats, was not only idle, but
farcical, and will not fail of turning the
laugh exceedingly upon us. These things
I mention to you as a friend, for you will
perceive that they have composed no part
of my public letter. Why you should be

so apprehensive of being surrounded, even
if Lord Percy had landed, I can not conceive. You know that landing men, and
procuring horses, are not the work of an
hour, a day, or even a week."

Heath had a word to say for himself:
"Every officer," he declares, "objected to
a storm, as they apprehended the militia
inadequate to such enterprise." In his
memoir, Heath says that his "success at
the outposts flew through the country,
and was soon magnified to a reduction of
the fort and capture of the garrison. It
reached General Washington long before
the official account, and he had communicated the report to Congress; hence a
double disappointment, when the true
state of facts was received."

CHAPTER XLII.

The Hessian Prisoners.—Their Reception.—Hootings and Revilings.—Interposition of Washington.—"A Very Good Rebel."—Treatment of American Prisoners.—Prison-Ships at New York.—Disease and Death, Famine and Filth, Robbery and Insult.—The Waste-House.—Otho Williams's Experiences.—Ethan Allen a Prisoner in New York.—His Emphatic Opinion of Loring and of Cunningham.—Washington writes to General Howe, on Behalf of the Ameri-can Prisoners at New York.—The Letter.—General Lee at New York.—Exchange proposed and refused.—Retaliation.—Lieutenant-Colonel Campbell the First Victim.—His own Account of his Sufferings.—Washington disapproves of the Treatment of Campbell.—He remonstrates with Congress.—The Reply of that Body.

1777. THE Hessian prisoners, who had
been taken after the successful surprise at Trenton, were carried across the
Delaware, and then sent through the interior of Pennsylvania to Winchester, in
Virginia. As they passed from place to
place, the exasperated common people of
the country, looking upon them with horror and detestation as so many hired robbers and murderers, hooted and reviled

them at every step. Washington, however, with a feeling of humanity and a
motive of policy, ordered notices to be
posted about the country, calling upon
the inhabitants to treat the Hessian soldiers with kindness, as they were not responsible for the war, but mere passive
instruments in the hands of a tyrannical
and cruel government. It was hoped that
many of the prisoners, while proceeding

through Pennsylvania, and mingling with the German population of that province, might, by kindness and association with those speaking their own language, be conciliated toward the American cause. Washington's interposition was not without its effect; for "from this time," confesses a Hessian officer, "things went better with us. Every day came many out of the towns, old and young, rich and poor, and brought us provisions, and treated us with kindness and humanity."* They felt grateful to Washington for a treatment which was so much beyond their expectations, and did not hesitate to style him "a very good rebel."†

The American prisoners in the hands of their British captors met with a very different fate. Those who had been taken at the surrender of Fort Washington were driven through the streets of New York, amid the hootings and revilings of soldiers' tribes and other vagabonds, male and female, who are always hanging, like so many screeching vultures, about an army, and living upon its plunder and corruption. "Which is Washington? which is Washington?" cried these ill-omened creatures, who believed that the war was at an end, and that the American leader himself was among those who were thus exposed to their foul aspersions.

The men were thrust in crowds into the prison-ships, churches, and sugar-houses. Here they were enclosed within bare walls, scantily supplied with provisions of bad quality, wretchedly clothed, and destitute of sufficient fuel, if indeed they had any. Disease was the inevita-

ble consequence, and the prisons where the American captives were immured soon became hospitals. A fatal malady was generated, and the mortality thence ensuing was enormous. Some fifteen hundred prisoners were supposed to have perished in the course of a few weeks in the city of New York! The dead, too, were treated with brutal dishonor; their bodies being allowed to lie in numbers uncoffined and exposed, to the horror of their living comrades, and to the jeers of the insulting enemy.

Some of the American officers had less to complain of, and were enabled to enjoy "the benefit of free air and the use of their limbs." Graydon, who was a prisoner in New York at that time, says: "I ventured to take boarding at four dollars per week. I knew that I had an excellent banker in Philadelphia, and that if specie was to be procured, my good mother would take care to get it and send it to me." But all had not, like Graydon, the specie of a banker, or the more sterling fund of a mother's affection, to draw upon. Graydon, too, with the clever tact of a man of the world, succeeded in conciliating the good will of the oppressors, by whom he was treated with exceptional indulgence, although not seldom "berebelled." The fate of others was more cruel.

Many of the American officers were plundered of their baggage, robbed of their side-arms, hats, and cockades, and otherwise grossly ill treated. A Major Otho Holland Williams, of Colonel Rawlings's rifle-regiment, was one of those who fell into the hands of the enemy

---

* Quoted by Irving.   † Thacher.

56

after the surrender of Fort Washington. He and three companies of the regiment were put on board the Baltic merchantman, used as a hospital-ship, and then lying in Long-island sound. Here he was placed upon such a small allowance of food, that he was only saved from famishing by "a pittance of pork and parsnips" which a good-natured sailor spared from his own mess. In a few days, Williams and his companions were taken ashore, and, having been put into one common dirt-cart, were dragged through the city of New York, amid the hootings of the crowd, to an old "waste-house," near the Bridewell. Here they were glad to find a rest from the insults and sufferings which they had endured, although it was in a place which, from its "openness and filthiness," had a few months before, while Washington was in possession of the city, been refused as barracks for the private soldiers. Such officers as had not the banking facilities or the maternal resources of Graydon, were obliged to take their board in the "waste-house," and content themselves with "six ounces of pork, one pound of biscuit, and some peas, per day, and two bushels and a half of sea-coal per week, for each." Such ill-conditioned quarters and meager fare soon had their natural effect upon the health of the officers.

Ethan Allen's great stalwart frame had lost its robustness; and his gay suit of blue-and-gold, which had been bestowed upon him by his admirers in Cork, hung loosely upon his body, collapsing under his meager prison-diet. After his capture in Canada, and a voyage to England and

thence back to Halifax, Allen had been conveyed to New York, where he was now a prisoner, startling both friend and foe with his emphatic denunciations and his stories of his strange adventures and doughty deeds. No doubt his British jailers congratulated themselves upon having caged so formidable a fellow. There must have been something to be dreaded in one who could growl so fiercely and bite so effectively. His captors he savagely denounced, and particularly Loring, the British commissary of prisoners, saying: "He is the most mean-spirited, cowardly, deceitful, and destructive animal, in God's creation below; and legions of infernal devils, with all their tremendous horrors, are impatiently ready to receive Howe and him, with all their detestable accomplices, into the most exquisite agonies of the hottest regions of hell-fire!"

Of Cunningham, the provost-marshal, he said that "he was as great a rascal as the army could boast of," and other testimony seems to confirm Allen's opinion; for this British official would stride about the prison, whip in hand, and send the prisoners to bed as if they had been so many hounds, with the cry — "Kennel, ye sons of bitches! kennel, G—d d—n ye!"* That Allen's persecutors might be made conscious that "his bite was as good as his bark," he used to show a fracture in one of his teeth, occasioned by his twisting off with it, in a fit of anger, the nail which fastened the bar of his handcuffs, while in irons on shipboard! "D—n him, can he eat iron?" was the exclamation of his astonished listeners.

* Graydon.

Washington, hearing of the treatment of the American prisoners at New York, immediately wrote to General Sir William Howe, denouncing it, and threatening retaliation in case it was not changed for the better. Those prisoners, who had recently been restored to liberty, "give the most shocking account," writes Washington, "of their barbarous usage, which their miserable, emaciated countenances confirm..... If you are determined," he says to Howe, "to make captivity as distressing as possible, let me know it, that we may be upon equal terms, for your conduct must and shall regulate mine." To the admiral, Lord Howe, Washington has also occasion to write, in consequence of the complaint of a Captain Sanble, of the ill treatment which he and other naval prisoners had suffered. In these words of dignified remonstrance his lordship is addressed: "From the opinion I have ever been taught to entertain of your lordship's humanity, I will not suppose that you are privy to proceedings of so cruel and unjustifiable a nature; and I hope that, upon making the proper inquiry, you will have the matter so regulated, that the unhappy persons whose lot is captivity may not in future have the miseries of cold, disease, and famine, added to their other misfortunes. You may call us rebels, and say that we deserve no better treatment; but remember, my lord, that, supposing us rebels, we still have feelings as keen and sensible as loyalists, and will, if forced to it, most assuredly retaliate upon those upon whom we look as the unjust invaders of our rights, liberties, and properties. I should not have said thus much, but my injured countrymen have long called upon me to endeavor to obtain a redress of their grievances; and I should think myself as culpable as those who inflict such severities, were I to continue silent."

General Lee, who had been at New York ever since his surprise and capture by the British, was kept a close prisoner, being considered by Sir William Howe as a deserter. Lee, however, was not brought to trial, as it was doubted whether, by his public resignation of his half-pay as lieutenant-colonel in the British service, previous to his acceptance of a commission in the American army, he was still amenable to military law for desertion. Howe informed the English ministry of his doubts, and received this peremptory answer: "As you have difficulties about bringing General Lee to trial in America, it is his majesty's pleasure that you send him to Great Britain by the first ship-of-war." In the meantime, however, Washington had refused to exchange the Hessian field-officers taken at Trenton, or Lieutenant-Colonel Campbell, unless General Lee was recognised as a prisoner-of-war. Howe, in consequence, fearing that his German troops might grow discontented if their officers should suffer from Washington retaliating upon them for the treatment of Lee, waited for further instructions from the home government before sending him away. The next despatch from the British minister was in these words: "His majesty consents that Lee (having been struck off the half-pay list) shall, though deserving the most exemplary punishment, be deemed as a prisoner-of-war, and may be exchanged as such, when you may think proper."

It is but just to state that both Lord Howe, the admiral, and Sir William Howe, the commander of the land-forces, indignantly repelled all responsibility for the ill treatment of the American prisoners in their hands. His lordship emphatically declared: "I abhor every imputation of wanton cruelty in multiplying the miseries of the wretched, or of treating them with needless severity." Sir William insisted that the prisoners were "provided with proper habitations, sufficient and wholesome food, and medicines." The illness and speedy death of many were, however, not denied. Those gentlemen were, no doubt, guiltless of the inhumanity of direct and intentional cruelty, although they were justly held responsible for the sufferings (probably somewhat exaggerated) caused by their agents.

During the early period of General Lee's imprisonment, Sir William Howe, while awaiting instructions from his government, resisted all appeals toward mitigating the severity of his captivity. Five Hessian officers were offered in exchange for Lee, but refused. Congress accordingly determined to retaliate, and Washington wrote to General Howe: "I must give you warning that Major-General Lee is looked upon as an officer belonging to and under the protection of the United Independent States of America; and that any violence you may commit upon his life or liberty will be severely retaliated upon the lives or liberties of the British officers, or those of their foreign allies, at present in our hands."

Lieutenant-Colonel Campbell, who had been taken prisoner on board a transport captured off Boston, was the first to suffer. He was lodged in the common jail of Concord, and there treated as if he had been a criminal condemned for the most atrocious crimes. His dungeon was but twelve or thirteen feet square, and shut out from the adjoining yard by two doors, with double locks and bolts. Although it was in the depth of winter, the window was barred only with iron, and unglazed. He had, however, an inner apartment, but this was described as "a loathsome, black hole, decorated with a pair of fixed chains," from which its former occupant, a felon, had just been removed, leaving his litter and filth behind him. "The attendance of a single servant," said Campbell, in a letter to General Howe, "is also denied me, and every visit from a friend positively refused. In short, sir, was a fire to happen in any chamber of the jail— which is all wood, the chimney-stacks excepted—I might perish in the flames before the jailer could go through the ceremony of unbolting the doors; although, to do him justice, in his station, I really think him a man of humanity: his house is so remote, that any call from within, especially if the wind was high, might be long of reaching him effectually."

This was certainly hard treatment for a colonel in the British army, and a member of Parliament, and one who had as yet been guiltless of American blood. Washington remonstrated with the council of Massachusetts for this excessive severity, reminding them that Campbell, according to the act of Congress, was to have exactly the same treatment as was received by General Lee; and, as that officer was "only confined to a commodious house, with genteel accommodations," there was no right or reason in being more severe upon Colonel Campbell, whom "I should wish," adds Washington, "should immediately upon the receipt of this [letter] be removed from his present situation, and put in a house where he may live comfortably."

To Congress Washington also wrote, strongly denouncing this treatment of Campbell, as a retaliation which had been prematurely begun. On the point of policy, apart from the inhumanity, he condemned it. "The balance of prisoners," he says, "is greatly against us; and a general regard to the happiness of the whole should mark our conduct. Can we imagine that our enemies will not mete the same punishments, the same indignities, the same cruelties, to those belonging to us, in their possession, that we impose on theirs in our power? Why should we suppose them to possess more humanity than we have ourselves? Or why should an ineffectual attempt to relieve the distresses of one brave, unfortunate man, involve many more in the same calamities? However disagreeable the fact may be, the enemy at this time [March 1] have in their power, and subject to their call, near three hundred officers belonging to the army of the United States. In this number there are some of high rank, and most of them are men of bravery and of merit. The quota of theirs in our hands bears no proportion, being not more than fifty at most. Under these circumstances, we should do no act to draw upon the gentlemen belonging to us, and who have already suffered a long captivity, greater punishments than they have experienced and now experience. If we should, what will their feelings be, and those of their numerous and extensive connections?

"Suppose the treatment of the Hessians should be pursued, will it not establish what the enemy have been aiming to effect by every artifice and the grossest misrepresentation—I mean an opinion of our enmity toward them, and of the cruel conduct they experience when they fall into our hands, a prejudice which we on our part have heretofore thought it politic to suppress and root out by every act of lenity and kindness? It certainly will. The Hessians would hear of the punishments with all the circumstances of heightened exaggeration; would feel the injury, without investigating the cause or reasoning upon the justice or necessity of it. The mischiefs, which may and must inevitably flow from the execution of the resolves, appear to be endless and innumerable." Thus was the judicious Washington always humane in his policy; and if politic in his humanity, it was only to avoid sacrificing the broad philanthropy of a patriot to the personal benevolence of the sentimentalist.

Congress, on the receipt of this letter, resolved "that General Washington be informed that Congress can not agree to any alteration in the resolve passed on the 6th of January." This resolve was, "that the board of war be directed immediately to order the five Hessian field-officers and Lieutenant-Colonel Campbell into safe and close custody, it being the unalterable resolution of Congress to retaliate on them the same punishment as may be inflicted on the person of General Lee." In regard, however, to the complaints of Colonel Campbell, Congress deigned to declare that it was never their intention that he should suffer any other hardship than such confinement as was necessary for his security, to carry out the object of their resolve.

CHAPTER XLIII.

Increased Popularity of the American Cause in New Jersey.—General Howe responsible for the Violation of the Rights of Property.—His Manifesto of Rapine.—American Scoundrels, too.—Washington checks and punishes them.—His Order against Disorder.—His Proclamation to the People of New Jersey.—Its Effect.—Nothing but Skirmishes.—Lord Cornwallis.—His Chain of Posts.—His Force.—The American Line and Posts.—Successful Skirmishes with the Enemy.—General Philemon Dickinson.—His Position and that of his Brother.—The Martial Brother.—His Engagement with the British Plunderers.—Communications between the Opposing Armies.—A Letter from General Lee.—His Proposition.—Refused by Congress.—Lee's Disappointment and Sombre Reflections.—Washington regrets the Refusal of Congress.—General Putnam's Ruse to magnify his Force in the Eyes of the Enemy.—A College Illumination.—The Effect.—The Meager American Force.—Fewer Men than Miles to guard.—Tardy Reinforcements.—Wants.—French Applicants for Commissions—General Arnold in Rhode Island.—An Abortive Plan.—New Regiments and New Officers.—Take none but Gentlemen.—Five New Major-Generals.

1777. THE American cause had greatly increased in popularity among the New-Jersey people. The Hessian and British troops spared neither friend nor foe in their cruel devastations; and, although Sir William Howe could scarcely have been such a monster of iniquity as to justify the brutalities practised by his soldiery upon the defenceless mothers, wives, and daughters, of the country, he clearly made himself responsible for the violation of the rights of property when he issued such orders as this:—

"All salted meat and provisions, which may be judged to exceed the quantity necessary for the subsistence of an ordinary family, shall be considered as a magazine of the enemy, and seized for the king, and given to the troops as a saving for the public."

This allowed a wide latitude to the propensities of a soldiery for plunder, whose only control was the word of command, and who looked for no principle of action beyond the order of the day. The American army had its brutal vagabonds, too, eager to rob and destroy; but in Washington their commander they ever found one who, with a scrupulous regard to the rights of person and property, was at all times prompt to punish with severity the least violation of them. It was this which greatly aided now in conciliating to the American cause the people of New Jersey, who, though afflicted by the horrors of war, triumph who might, could yet distinguish between a brutality licensed by authority and that which was emphatically denounced and threatened with punishment.

Washington, indignant at the conduct of some of his troops, issued the following emphatic order: "The general prohibits, in both the militia and continental troops, in the most positive terms, the infamous practice of plundering the inhabitants, under the specious pretence of their being tories. Let the persons of such as are known to be enemies to their country be seized and confined, and their property disposed of as the law of the state directs. It is our business to give protection and support to the poor, distressed inhabitants, not to multiply and increase their calamities. After the publication of this order, any officer, either militia or continental, found attempting to conceal the public stores, plundering the inhabitants under the pretence of their being tories, or selling at vendue plunder taken from the enemy, in any other manner than these orders direct, may expect to be punished in the severest manner." Copies of this order were then immediately circulated among all the troops.

Jan. 21.

Taking advantage of the favorable disposition of the people, Washington now issued a proclamation, in which he called upon all those who, while the British forces were in the ascendant in New Jersey, had signed declarations of fidelity to the king of Great Britain, to come forward and take an oath of allegiance to the United States of America. Those, however, who preferred " the

Jan. 25.

interest and protection of Great Britain to the freedom and happiness of their country," were told to withdraw themselves and their families forthwith within the enemy's lines. Many of the people gladly welcomed this opportunity of giving their names to a cause in which their hearts were already engaged; while others, who had only been able to secure British protection by swearing allegiance to the king, hesitated, not because they were less friendly, but more scrupulous. Some of the substantial farmers of the country had thus committed themselves; and now, although their hearts had been won over to Washington, they felt compelled to withhold their hands.

Beyond an occasional skirmish, in which the Americans not seldom got the advantage, there was little opportunity for action, as Sir William Howe, with his usual caution or indolence, was not disposed to move. Lord Cornwallis, with the main body of the army, was at New Brunswick, while his communication with the Hudson river and New York was kept up by means of a chain of small posts. His force was great—not less, it was supposed, than eight thousand. The Americans, with their fluctuating militia, were constantly varying in number; which, however, was never large, seldom over four thousand, and at times reduced as low as fifteen hundred. But the enemy thought them much more numerous; and, fortunately, they had been favorably impressed by their prowess in the occasional skirmishes which had occurred.

The whole line of Washington's army was widely extended; he himself being with the centre and main body at Morristown, while General Putnam commanded the right at Princeton, and General Heath the left in the Highlands. From these different points occasional small detachments (generally militia, for the sake of breaking them gradually into warfare) would be sent out to harass the enemy's outposts, and to pounce upon their foraging-parties. In these encounters, the Americans, with the advantage of a thorough knowledge of the country, and the sympathy of the inhabitants, were generally successful. On one Sunday morning, for example, some fifty Waldeckers were fallen in with by about the same number of militia, and so taken by surprise, that ten of the enemy were killed or wounded, and the rest taken prisoners, while the Americans came off without the least damage.

On another occasion, General Philemon Dickinson, by a gallant little action, won from the commander the praise—" His behavior reflects the highest honor upon him." Dickinson was a man of fortune and influence, belonging to New Jersey, and was now in command of the militia of that state. He was brother to John Dickinson, who, although an earnest political writer in behalf of the American cause, opposed (while a delegate to Congress from Pennsylvania) the Declaration of Independence, as premature. He, in consequence, lost his popularity, but never his patriotism. His spirit was not of the warlike stamp of that of his brother. " Where duty and honor require my presence," said John Dickinson, " there I shall be; but much, much rather would I choose

that these severe masters would give me up to my dear connections, my books, and my friends, an intercourse and employment for which my constitution is better formed, than for the toils of war, and to cultivate which my temper is more disposed, than to relish all the united glories, could I obtain them, of every heroic death from the Roman Curtius to the British Wolfe."

The martial brother had just now distinguished himself, though not in a way to rival a Curtius or a Wolfe, still in a manner worthy of all praise. General Dickinson had the command of the American outpost nearest to the enemy at New Brunswick, stationed on the west bank of Millstone river. On the opposite side was a mill, with a large stock of flour; and Cornwallis, covetous of the booty, had sent out a party to seize it, and take whatever other plunder they could lay their hands on. Dickinson was on the alert, and, heading four hundred New-Jersey militiamen, plunged into the river, and, pouncing upon the plunderers, put them to rout, and relieved them of forty wagons, upward of a hundred horses—" most of them of the English draught-breed"—and a number of sheep and cattle which they had collected. The enemy returned, with nothing to carry back to the camp of Cornwallis but " a good many dead and wounded in light wagons."

The ordinary communications between opposing armies were kept up during this period of inactive hostility. Now Lord Cornwallis has a convoy of money and stores to send to the Hessian

Jan. 8.

prisoners, and wishes a safe-conduct for it through New Jersey and Pennsylvania. Washington answers his lordship that no molestation will be offered by any part of the regular army under his command. "But I can not," he says, "answer for the militia who are resorting to arms in most part of this state, and who are exceedingly exasperated at the treatment they have met with, both from Hessian and British troops."

Again, flags are passing to and fro, and messengers and bearers of letters coming and going between the hostile camps. On one of these occasions a packet arrives from General Lee, containing a letter to Congress under cover of one to Washington, who is most earnestly entreated to despatch it immediately, and order that body to be as expeditious as possible. The letter to Congress contains the request from General Lee that two or three delegates may be sent immediately to New York, to whom he had to communicate something, as he avowed, of the greatest importance. What it was, Lee did not say; but it was evidently something concocted between him and the brothers Howe, for he declares that these commanders would grant a safe-conduct to the gentlemen sent. Congress, probably not anxious for the second time to play a part in such a frivolous negotiation as was the result of the swelling preliminaries arranged by General Sullivan and Lord Howe, resolved that it was inexpedient to send any of their members to confer with Lee. Notwithstanding, the imprisoned general reiterated his request, and was a second time answered

57.

with a refusal. Lee's captivity had given him an opportunity of reflecting upon the uncertainty of all human greatness; and his manner, if we may judge from his letter, had lost all its early flash, in the sombre shadow now cast over his thoughts. He writes to Washington in this subdued strain, expressive of his disappointment:

"It is a most unfortunate circumstance for myself, and I think not less so for the public, that the Congress have not thought proper to comply with my request. It could not possibly have been attended with any ill consequences, and might with good ones. At least, it was an indulgence which I thought my situation entitled me to. But I am unfortunate in everything, and this is the severest I have yet experienced. God send you a different fate!

"Adieu, my dear general. Yours most truly and affectionately,

"CHARLES LEE."

Washington appears to have sympathized with Lee, or, at any rate, not to have approved of the resolve of Congress, for he says, in a letter to Robert Morris: "I wish, with all my heart, that Congress had gratified General Lee in his request. If not too late, I wish they would do it still. I can see no possible evil that can result from it; some good I think might. The request to see a gentleman or two came from the *general*, not from the *commissioner*; there could have been no harm, therefore, in hearing what *he* had to say on *any* subject, especially as he had declared that his own personal interest was deeply concerned."

During these communications between

the British and the American lines, Washington was particularly anxious lest the meagerness of his force should be discovered by the enemy. He accordingly insisted that his officers should avail themselves of the ordinary military expedient authorized by such circumstances, and give out the strength of the army to be twice as great as it was. General Putnam, who was stationed at Princeton, now that he had been deserted by a large party of New-Jersey militia, and left with only a meager remnant of troops, had especial reason to bear in mind the order of his commander-in-chief. A British officer, who was lying mortally wounded in Putnam's camp, requested the privilege of a visit from a friend and comrade stationed at Brunswick, under Lord Cornwallis. The request was granted. A flag was sent, and returned with the wounded man's friend. He was, however, not allowed to enter Princeton until he was blindfolded, and the night had advanced. General Putnam, mindful of Washington's orders, and not indisposed to exercise his Yankee ingenuity in the execution of a *ruse*, took the occasion to produce an impression, the largeness of which it was hoped would compensate for the smallness of the American force. He accordingly had a light put in every room in the college-buildings, and of the empty houses in the town, and kept his handful of men so noisily parading about, that the British visiter returned to the camp of Earl Cornwallis with the report that the Americans at Princeton were at least five thousand strong !*

* Irving.

The Americans, indeed, had every reason to strengthen themselves in the eyes of the enemy with imaginary reinforcements, for the real troops came in but slowly to take the place of those rapidly departing. Putnam, at one time, had fewer men than miles of frontier to guard ! The militia were constantly in a state of fluctuation. " We have a full army one day," says Washington, " and scarce any the next ; and I am much afraid that the enemy, one day or the other, taking advantage of one of these temporary weaknesses, will make themselves masters of our magazines of stores, arms, and artillery. Nothing but their ignorance of our numbers protects us at this very **Jan. 24.** time ; when, on the contrary, had we six or eight thousand regular troops, or could the militia, who were with me a few days ago, have been prevailed upon to stay, we could have struck such a stroke as would have inevitably ruined the army of the enemy, in their divided state."

The reinforcements came in so extremely slow, there was at times actually danger (in the interval of the dissolution of the old and the organization of the new army) that Washington might be left entirely destitute of men ! Under these circumstances, he wrote in the most urgent manner to the governors of the several states to forward on their regiments with all possible expedition. Although, from the supineness of the enemy, there was a long cessation of active hostility, Washington was full of work. On one day, he is writing to Governor Trumbull, of Connecticut, entreating him to hasten and equip the lines from that state ; and to

Governor Livingston, suggesting a different organization of the militia of New Jersey, whose "officers are generally of the lowest class of the people, and instead of setting a good example to their men, are leading them into every kind of mischief, one species of which is plundering the inhabitants, under the pretence of their being tories."

On another day, the general-in-chief is writing to Congress about the destitution of the commissariat department, from the want of money or the want of clothing; or about the exchange of prisoners, the appointment of officers, and the proper place of the laboratories. Again, he is beset by a number of French officers who come to headquarters applying for commissions in the army. "This evil," says Washington, "is a growing one; for, from what I learn, they are coming in swarms from Old France and the islands. There will, therefore, be a necessity of providing for them, or discountenancing them. To do the first is difficult; and the last disagreeable and perhaps impolitic, if they are men of merit; and it is impossible to distinguish these from mere adventurers, of whom I am convinced there is the greater number."

Then, on yet another day, Washington is conferring by letter with General Arnold about his schemes on Rhode Island. The British were at Newport, to the number of six thousand, under the command of Earl Percy. Arnold, immediately after his arrival from the North at the camp of Washington, had been ordered, in conjunction with General Spencer, to take command of the American force sent to Rhode Island. This consisted of some four or five thousand militia, who were now encamped at Providence. As a detachment had been ordered away from the camp of the British, which had reduced their numbers to four thousand, Arnold and Spencer proposed an attack on Rhode island. Washington, upon being consulted, examines the map sent to him, together with the plan of the enterprise; and, after suggesting the difficulty of passing a body of water to attack an enemy, and of making a good retreat in case of repulse, advises that the assault should not be made, unless with a strong probability, amounting almost to a certainty, of success. The enterprise was finally given up.

The subject, however, which was uppermost in Washington's thoughts at this time, was the recruitment of the new army. To this he was directing all his energies. Eighty-eight battalions, according to a resolve of Congress, were to be enlisted. Colonel Hazen was sent to superintend this service in New York and the New-England states; and Lieutenant-Colonel Antill in New Jersey. Pennsylvania, Maryland, and Virginia. With these gentlemen the commander-in-chief was frequently communicating by letter, urging them to exert themselves as much as possible in filling the companies, and sending them forward with the utmost despatch. Over the appointment of the officers to these battalions Washington had but little control, each state choosing its own according to its quota of troops. There were, however, sixteen additional regiments, where the choice of the officers was left to the commander-in-chief. He generally contented himself with the appointment of the colonels, and left the subordinate commissions to be distributed by them, subject to his approval. Nathaniel Gist, John Patton, William Grayson, Thomas Hartley, Samuel B. Webb, David Henley, Ezekiel Cornell, Henry Sherburne, Alexander Scammel, and Henry Jackson, were the colonels appointed in January, and they were now busily engaged in obtaining men and officers for their regiments. Colonel Gist was authorized to raise four companies of rangers, and was instructed to proceed to the Cherokee or any other nation of Indians and attempt to procure a number of warriors, not exceeding five hundred, who were to be supplied with arms and blankets, and paid like the continental troops. There was, however, a good deal of reserve on the part of the Americans in availing themselves of the aid of the Indians; and during the whole war the British, with less scruple, always succeeded, by their profuse largesses, in obtaining a preponderance of savage auxiliaries.

While Washington gave his colonels the privilege of choosing their officers, he earnestly recommended them to be circumspect in their choice. "Take none," he says, "but gentlemen; let no local attachments influence you; do not suffer your good nature, when an application is made, to say 'Yes,' when you ought to say 'No;' remember that it is a public, not a private cause, that is to be injured or benefited by your choice; recollect, also, that no instance has yet happened of good or bad behavior in a corps in our service, that has not originated with the officers. Do not take old men, nor yet fill your corps with boys, especially for captains."

Washington had constantly urged upon Congress the necessity of hastening the appointment of the general officers. "We have very little time," he says, "to do a very great work in;" and tells them that, if they are withholding the commissions from parsimonious principles, they are mistaken. He, with a delicate reserve, did not pretend to direct the choice of Congress, but could not refrain from suggesting the names of two officers for the new appointments: General Cadwallader, whom he pronounces a man of ability, a good disciplinarian, firm in his principles, and of intrepid bravery; and Colonel Reed, whom he recommends for the command of the horse, as a person in every respect qualified.

Congress finally responded to these urgent appeals of the commander-in-chief, and appointed five major-generals. These were Stirling, Mifflin, St. Clair, Stephen, and Lincoln. Two days after, eighteen brigadier-generals were chosen, namely: Poor, Glover, Patterson, Learned, Varnum, Huntington, Clinton, Wayne, De Haas, Cadwallader, Hand, Reed, Weedon, Muhlenberg, Woodford, Scott, Nash, and Conway, the latter an Irishman. Cadwallader, however, did not accept the appointment. Even this act of Congress, as we shall find, served to add to the embarrassment and anxious cares of Washington. Jealousies were excited and disappointments created, which the chief was called upon to remove and allay.

Feb. 19.

CHAPTER XLIV.

Activity of the Enemy.—Lord Percy arrives at Amboy.—Sir William Howe in New Jersey.—" Some Push" intended.—
Its Purpose uncertain.—Washington persuaded that Philadelphia is the Object of the British.—More American Forces,
or " the Game at an End."—The Indolent Howe true to his Character.—The Americans on the Alert.—Skirmishes.—
Success of Nielson of Brunswick.—Washington's Skilful Management.—Lauded in Europe.—Botta's Opinion.—Gen-
eral Arnold's Non-Promotion.—Washington takes up his Cause.—Arnold's own Protestations.—He asks for a Court
of Inquiry.—Washington opposes, and gives Good Advice.—Not taken by Arnold, who persists.—Discontent of other
Officers, who are soothed by Washington.—Difficulties in Recruiting.—A Remarkable Letter.—The Small-Pox in the
Army.—Inoculation.—Its Mild Effects.—Want of Arms.—A Timely Arrival from France.—Resignation of Colonel
Joseph Reed.—General Gates offers his Services to Washington.—A Dilemma, from which Gates is relieved.—He is
appointed to the Command of the Forces at Ticonderoga.—Irascibility of General Schuyler.—He is rebuked by Con-
gress.—Alexander Hamilton appointed Secretary to Washington.

1777. THERE was now some appearance of activity on the part of the enemy. A detachment of their troops, under Lord Percy, with several pieces of heavy artillery, had moved from Newport, Rhode Island, and landed at Amboy. **Feb. 20.** Sir William Howe, too, had forsaken his snug quarters at New York, with its convivial delights, and come over the Hudson. It was now probable that, with a force of nearly eight thousand men in New Jersey, and the reinforcements just landed and marching to join them, General Howe was " on the point of making some push." Whether his object was to beat up the American quarters and extend his own, to make a large forage and collection of provender of which the enemy were in great want, or to cross the Delaware with the view of marching to Philadelphia, could not be determined.

Washington was on the alert, but naturally anxious, when he knew his force was so small as to be quite unequal to a successful opposition. Sir William Howe would surely move forward, thought the American general, with Philadelphia as his object. The British were at least ten thousand strong. The Americans were only four thousand. The former were well disciplined, well officered, and well appointed ; the latter raw militia, badly officered, and under no government. General Howe's numbers, it was true, could not in any short time be increased. As for Washington's, "they must be," he said, " very considerably, and by such troops as we can have reliance upon, or the game is at an end." With what propriety, then, can the enemy miss so favorable an opportunity of striking a heavy blow at Philadelphia, from which the Americans are deriving so many advantages, and the carrying of which would give such *éclat* to the British arms? " The longer it is delayed," wrote Washington, who believed the attack was almost certain, " the better for us, and happy shall I be if am deceived."

Sir William Howe did not, however, belie his reputation for indolence. He cantoned his reinforcements with the rest of his army at Brunswick and the adjacent posts, and sat down to contemplate his magnificent designs for a future campaign. The Americans, notwithstanding, were vigilant, and attentive at their several posts to guard against surprises; while every preparation for resistance was made that the feeble state of their little army admitted of. Small skirmishes continued; and, although in one week a militia-guard in Monmouth, near the Hook, is taken by a party of British troops, in the next full revenge is obtained by the success of Colonel Nielson, of Brunswick. This officer, with a small detachment of militia, sallies out and takes by surprise Major Stockton, of General Skinner's corps of New-Jersey royalists, whom he captures, together with fifty-nine of his men, and all their arms.

Thus was presented, during the whole winter, " the extraordinary spectacle of a powerful army, straitened within narrow limits by the phantom of a military force, and never permitted to transgress those limits with impunity, in which skill supplied the place of means, and disposition was the substitute for an army."[*] The conduct of Washington was everywhere greatly extolled. Botta, the Italian historian of America, expresses the admiration with which it was appreciated in Europe:—

" Achievements so astonishing gained for the American commander a very great reputation, and were regarded with wonder by all nations, as well as by the Americans. Every one applauded the prudence, the firmness, and the daring, of General Washington. All declared him the sav-

iour of his country; all proclaimed him equal to the most renowned commanders of antiquity, and especially distinguished him by the name of the *American Fabius*. His name was in the mouths of all men, and celebrated by the pens of the most eminent writers. The greatest personages in Europe bestowed upon him praise and congratulation. Thus the American general wanted neither a noble cause to defend, nor an opportunity for acquiring glory, nor the genius to avail himself of it, nor a whole generation of men competent and well disposed to render him homage."[*]

Horace Walpole wrote thus to Mann: " Washington, the dictator, has shown himself both a Fabius and a Camillus. His march through our lines is allowed to have been a prodigy of generalship."

In the list of the new major-generals chosen by Congress, the name of Arnold had been omitted, although those thus appointed were all his juniors in rank. This gave Washington great concern, and he wrote to Richard Henry Lee, a member of Congress from Virginia: " I am anxious to know whether General Arnold's non-promotion was owing to accident or design; and the cause of it. Surely a more active, a more spirited and sensible officer, fills no department in your army. Not seeing him, then, in the list of major-generals, and no mention made of him, has given me uneasiness; as it is not to be presumed, being the oldest brigadier, that he will continue in service under such a slight." Fearing the effect of this neglect upon the irascible temper of

* Alexander Hamilton.

* Quoted by Sparks.

Arnold, Washington wrote to entreat him not to take any hasty steps, and he would use his best endeavors to remedy any error that might have been committed.

Arnold, after courteously acknowledging Washington's interposition in his behalf, expresses his sense of the wrong he has suffered by a self-complacent statement of his fastidious conscientiousness, his sensibility to disgrace, and the claims he has upon his country for his patriotic services. "My commission," writes Arnold, "was conferred unsolicited, and received with pleasure only as a means of serving my country. With equal pleasure I resign it, when I can no longer serve my country with honor. The person who, void of the nice feelings of honor, will tamely condescend to give up his right, and retain a commission at the expense of his reputation, I hold as a disgrace to the army, and unworthy of the glorious cause in which we are engaged. When I entered the service of my country, my character was unimpeached. I have sacrificed my interest, ease, and happiness, in her cause. It is rather a misfortune, than a fault, that my exertions have not been crowned with success. I am conscious of the rectitude of my intentions. In justice, therefore, to my own character, and for the satisfaction of my friends, I must request a court of inquiry into my conduct; and, though I sensibly feel the ingratitude of my countrymen, yet every personal injury shall be buried in my zeal for the safety and happiness of my country, in whose cause I have repeatedly fought and bled, and am ready at all times to risk my life."

Washington, who was fully conscious of Arnold's ability, and had at that time no reason to doubt the sincerity of his professions of patriotism, was anxious to place him in the position to which he was thought to be entitled. The commander-in-chief continued to solicit his friends in Congress to repair the wrong supposed to have been done to that officer, and requested General Greene, who was then at Philadelphia, to investigate the causes which had influenced their action. The only satisfaction obtained was the professed motive, on the part of the members of Congress, of proportioning the general officers to the number of troops supplied by each state, and the explanation that, as Connecticut had already two major-generals, it was necessary to pass Arnold by. Washington, in answer to Arnold's demand for a court of inquiry, replied that he could not see upon what ground he could ask it, as no particular charge was alleged against him. Public bodies are not amenable for their actions. They place and displace at pleasure; and all the satisfaction that an individual can obtain, when he is overlooked, is, if innocent, a consciousness that he has not deserved such treatment for his honest exertions.

This was a kind of advice which came naturally from the upright mind of the commander-in-chief, but which was far from calming the perturbed spirit of Arnold. The purest air of heaven will only inflame an angry sore: an appeal to conscience gives no relief to a corrupt heart. Arnold was obliged to give up all hopes of a court of inquiry; but he determined to visit headquarters, and obtain permission from Washington to proceed to Philadelphia, and seek an investigation into the cause of the treatment which had so disappointed his ambition and stirred his anger.

There were others besides Arnold who had been wronged, as they supposed, by being passed over in the recent appointments by Congress. Washington strove to soothe the wounded sensibilities of these latter as he had those of the former. Brigadier-General Andrew Lewis had reason to expect promotion to a major-generalship. He had been disappointed. Washington writes to him: "Let me beseech you to reflect that the period is now arrived when our most vigorous exertions are wanted; when it is highly and indispensably necessary for gentlemen of abilities in any line, but more especially in the military, not to withhold themselves from public employment, or suffer any small punctilios to persuade them to retire from their country's service." General Lewis, however, did not yield to this patriotic appeal, but resigned his commission, which was accepted by Congress. Again, William Woodford, although promoted to the rank of brigadier-general, was named after two of his juniors. In this instance also, Washington, anticipating a wound to Woodford's feelings, endeavors to divert him from all personal considerations, by invoking the generosity of his patriotism. "Trifling punctilios," he says, "should have no influence upon a man's conduct in such a cause, and at such a time as this. If smaller matters do not yield to greater, if trifles

light as air in comparison with what we are contending for, can withdraw or withhold gentlemen from service, when our all is at stake, and a single cast of the die may turn the tables, what are we to expect?"

A remarkable letter, written about this time by Washington to General **Mar. 15.** Sullivan, shows the vexations to which he must have been subjected by the jealous rivalries and fancied slights of some of the officers under his command. "Do not, my dear General Sullivan," says Washington, "torment yourself any longer with imaginary slights, and involve others in the perplexities you feel on that score. No other officer of rank, in the whole army, has so often conceived himself neglected, slighted, and ill treated, as you have done; and none, I am sure, has had less cause than yourself to entertain such ideas. Mere accidents, things which have occurred in the common course of service, have been considered by you as designed affronts..... Why these unreasonable, these unjustifiable suspicions— suspicions which can answer no other end than to poison your own happiness, and add vexation to that of others?.... But I have not time to dwell upon a subject of this kind. I shall quit it with an earnest exhortation that you will not suffer yourself to be teased with evils that only exist in the imagination, and with slights that have no existence at all." Sullivan was vain, and sensitive, as all vain men are; but, as he was a sincere patriot and a faithful friend of Washington, it is not doubted but that he took this severe lesson in good part, and benefited by it.

In addition to these troubles on the score of the officers, Washington was much perturbed by the difficulties and obstructions which interfered with the recruiting of his new army. The spring had already opened; and yet such was the delay in the enlistments, that Washington expected to be left on the 15th of March with only the remains of five Virginia regiments, containing less than five hundred men; parts of two or three other continental battalions, "all very weak;" and some small parties of New-Jersey and Pennsylvania militia, on which but little dependence could be put, as they "come and go when they please.... The enemy must be ignorant of our numbers and situation, or they would never suffer us to remain unmolested, and," adds Washington, "I almost tax myself with imprudence in committing the secret to paper."

Nor were the recruits who came in so slowly and in such scant numbers immediately available. The small-pox hitherto had created terrible ravages among the American troops, and Washington was determined to use the only means then known to protect them from its fatality. All the officers and soldiers in the cantonment at Morristown were now inoculated, and each recruit as he came in was subjected to the same operation. Whole regiments were thus suffering under the disease at the same moment. Fortunately, little or no mortality ensued; and "the disorder was so slight," says an annalist, doubtless with some exaggeration, "that from the beginning to the end of it there was not a single day in which they could not, and if called upon would not, have

turned out and fought the British." If the inoculated had been able to take the field, they could not have brought against their enemy a more formidable power than the terrors of the dreadful disease which presented its horrid front in the American ranks.

When the new recruits presented themselves, Washington was perplexed to find means for equipping them. The old regiments, at the expiration of their term of service, returned home, taking their arms with them. How to provide the new army was now the question, which was so embarrassing, that all began to consider it with dismay, when it was fortunately solved by the arrival of a supply of arms from France. One ship, escaping all the vigilance of the British cruisers, had arrived at Portsmouth, in New Hampshire, laden with a cargo consisting of twelve thousand fusees, one thousand barrels of powder, and a good stock of blankets and military stores. Another French vessel had reached Philadelphia in safety, with six thousand fusees for the United States, and five thousand for sale on private account. The whole army could now be equipped, and there was no longer any anxiety on the score of arms.

Colonel Joseph Reed's resignation as adjutant-general, although it was welcomed by a large number of New-England men (with whom, in the course of the sectional jealousies in the army, he had incurred great unpopularity), was a serious loss to the service, and a source of perplexity to Washington. There was difficulty in finding for that important office a successor of equal efficiency with

58

its former active incumbent. President Hancock wrote to General Gates, proposing that he should again become the adjutant-general, a position to which he had been appointed on the organization of the first American army. Gates's aspirations had in the meanwhile risen to a greater height. He evidently was not flattered by Hancock's proposition. His vexation was ill concealed beneath a profession of willingness to serve, in a letter which he wrote to Washington: "I own," he writes, referring to the letter of the president of Congress, "I was surprised at the contents; and the more so, as it was not preceded by one on the same subject from your excellency. Unless it is your earnest desire that such a measure should directly take place, I could by no means consent to it."

Washington wrote to General Gates in answer: "Although I often wished in secret that you could be brought to resume the office of adjutant-general, I never even hinted it, because I thought it might be disagreeable to you, for the reason which you yourself mention—that you 'commanded last campaign at the second post upon this continent'—and that therefore it might be looked upon by you as a degradation. But you can not conceive the pleasure I feel when you tell me that, 'if it is my desire that you should resume your former office, you will with cheerfulness and alacrity proceed to Morristown.' Give me leave to return you my sincere thanks for this mark of your attention to a request of mine which, now you give me an opening, I make, and at the same time assure you that I look up-

on your resumption of the office of adjutant-general as the only means of giving form and regularity to our new army." The frank and direct manner in which Washington took Gates at his word might have been supposed to greatly embarrass that officer, who was not disposed to restrain his ambition within the narrow bounds of a subordinate position. The timely appointment of the command of the northern army at Ticonderoga, however, relieved him from the apparent dilemma in which his own professions, and Washington's sincere belief in them, had placed him. Still, there is reason to believe that General Gates had anticipated this means of escape from his unpleasant situation, and that he was eagerly awaiting the command which he now received when offering his services to Washington in the humbler position. Timothy Pickering, of Massachusetts, became the new adjutant-general.

Gates was indebted to the irascibility of General Schuyler for his new appointment. Schuyler had involved himself in a quarrel with Congress. His enemies had been industrious, and made various charges against him. He insisted upon resigning his commission, but Congress would not accept his resignation. The surgeon of his army, a Doctor Striger, had been removed from his office; whereat Schuyler is greatly angered, and writes to Congress: "As Doctor Striger had my recommendation to the office he had sustained, perhaps it was a compliment due to me that I should have been advised of the reason of his dismission." Colonel Joseph Trumbull had insinuated that General Schuyler had suppressed a commission intended for his brother, whereupon the angry commander writes to Congress, complaining of the base insinuation, and says: "I hope Congress will not entertain the least idea that I can tamely submit to such injurious treatment. I expect they will immediately do what is incumbent on them on the occasion. Until Mr. Trumbull and I are upon a footing, I can not do what the laws of honor and a regard to my own reputation render indispensably necessary. Congress can put us on a par by dismissing one or the other from the service."* Congress would not gratify this pugnacious desire of the general, whereupon he is vexed to exceeding wrath, and tells them—"I really feel myself deeply chagrined on the occasion. I am incapable of the meanness he [Colonel Trumbull] suspects me of; and I confidently expected that Congress would do me that justice which it was in their power to give, and which I humbly conceive they ought to have done."

For awhile Congress passed these communications over in silence, but finally its offended dignity vindicated itself by a resolution, in which certain passages in Schuyler's letters were pronounced "ill advised and highly indecent," and by the appointment of Gates to supersede Schuyler in the command of the northern army. The latter, however, lost none of his ardor in behalf of his country's cause; and, as a major-general of the army, he continued to serve with undiminished interest and energy. Stationed at Philadelphia, he was busily engaged in fortifying

* Quoted by Irving.

the southern bank of the Delaware, and in reorganizing the commissary department.

Early in the spring, while Washington was still at Morristown, young ALEXANDER HAMILTON became one of his aids-de-camp, and was received into what is technically called his "family." General Greene, as we have seen, had been early struck with the skill of the youthful captain of artillery, and had spoken of him with admiration to the commander-in-chief. Washington, too, at White Plains, and during the perilous retreat through New Jersey, had noticed the art with which, in the one instance, he had directed the construction of the works, and, in the other, the daring and skill with which he had brought his guns to bear upon the pursuing enemy. Young as he was, being only twenty years of age, Hamilton had already become a marked man. He had acquired a reputation as a writer, and Washington gladly availed himself of his fluent pen. Colonel Harrison ("the old secretary," as he was always termed) being now employed in other service, the new aid-de-camp took his place. As the commander-in-chief never allowed any idlers about him, he took care that the industry and capacity of his young secretary should be put thoroughly to the test; and that they were, and proved equal to the trial, no one has ever doubted. It was left, however, for an aspiring descendant and biographer, not content with the greatness of his distinguished parent, to claim for him that which belongs to Washington himself.

The two other members of the chief's

military family at this time were Colonels Meade and Tench Tilghman, both men of gallant spirit and gentlemanly bearing. Colonel Robert H. Harrison, the former secretary, although frequently employed in other service, was still a constant writer at headquarters. He looked with admiration upon his youthful successor, whom he styled "the little lion." Washington himself is said to have often indulged in the fond expression of "my boy" when speaking of Hamilton, to whom he became warmly attached, and whose great abilities and sterling integrity he did not fail fully to appreciate. Hamilton is described at this time as "a youth, a mere stripling, small, slender, almost delicate in frame." His vivacity made him the favorite companion of the young, while his ripe intelligence and great intellectual powers won for him the regard of the old.

CHAPTER XLV.

1777. It was thought probable that during the winter, the British forces in Canada, under Sir Guy Carleton and General Burgoyne, taking advantage of the frozen lakes, would make a vigorous attack upon Ticonderoga. To provide against it, the fifteen new battalions to be supplied by Massachusetts were ordered, as fast as they were raised, to be forwarded to the North. The spring was now opening, however; the attack by the British had not been made; and it was conjectured that, secure in the possession of the lakes, the greater part of the enemy's force would be drawn from Canada, by the St. Lawrence, and that Ticonderoga, at least for the present, would be disregarded. Washington and his general officers were persuaded that the determined resolution of the British was to take possession of Philadelphia as soon as the roads, after the spring thaw, became passable for their artillery and wagons.

Washington considered it a waste of power to send so many troops to Ticonderoga, and accordingly ordered eight of the battalions originally intended for that post to be sent to Peekskill, on the Hudson river. A concentration of force here would be advantageous, to give the required support to the army of the eastern or middle states. Should the enemy strive to penetrate the country up the North river, the troops at Peekskill would be well posted to resist them. Should the British attempt to march into New England, the troops at Peekskill would be well stationed for opposition; should they move westward, the eastern and southern forces would be enabled easily to form a junction; and, with a strong American force so near as Peekskill, Sir William Howe would be obliged to keep a powerful garrison in New York, and thus diminish his resources for active operations elsewhere. Even granting that the army in Canada had designs against Ticonderoga, the post at Peekskill would not be disadvantageously situated for despatching reinforcements to the north.

Washington was convinced that the army in Canada would be governed in a great degree by the operation of General Howe's, then in New Jersey. "If this is held at bay, curbed and confined," he said, "the northern army will not dare to penetrate." Washington would have greatly wished to give Howe some "capital stroke" in the early part of the season, that he might open the campaign with the *éclat* of a triumph. The aspirations of Congress, however, greatly transcended those of the commander-in-chief. They eagerly desired that the enemy might be confined in their present quarters, prevented from getting supplies from the country, and totally subdued before they were reinforced. "Could such grand objects be accomplished, I should be happy indeed," wrote Washington, in answer to the impracticable and rather importunate suggestions of Congress. His whole force was but "a handful," and the greater part of this was made up of militia. Under such circumstances, the commander-in-chief felt it necessary not only to curb his own heroic desires, but to extinguish the brilliant expectations of the national counsellors. "I confess, sir," writes Washington to President Hancock, "I feel the most painful anxiety when I reflect on our situation and that of the enemy. Unless the levies arrive soon, we must before long experience some interesting and melancholy event."

Mar. 14.

The swelling conceptions of General Howe were also destined to a collapse. He, while doing nothing during the long winter, had consoled himself with the hope of doing a great deal in the coming summer and autumn. He had magnificently resolved upon making an incursion into Rhode Island and Massachusetts, taking Boston; ascending the Hudson river to Albany; attacking Philadelphia; and invading Virginia! This grand scheme was concocted in the heat of his success in New Jersey. The subsequent defeat of the Hessians at Trenton, however, somewhat clipped the wings of his imagination, and confined its flights to the single state of Pennsylvania, which he proposed to reduce. He wanted, nevertheless, thirty thousand men to execute what had been so brilliantly conceived. These he was told by the prime minister he could not get, and Sir William was again forced to restrict still further his designs.

General Howe now gave up all hope of making an attempt upon New England, or any important movement up the North river. New Jersey being almost wrested from his possession, he was fain to change his purpose of marching through that state in order to reduce Pennsylvania. The latter he now proposed to invade by sea. This was to be the main object of the coming campaign. Governor Tryon, however, was to be left at New York with three thousand provincial troops, in order that he might be prepared to act on the Hudson or against Connecticut, as circumstances might direct. To Sir Guy Carleton, in Canada, no hopes were held out of co-operation, in the outset of the campaign, although General Howe thought he would be able to spare a sufficient force to open a communication through the Highlands on the North river for the passage of the men-of-war, and that these troops might co-operate with the British army in the North.

These designs of the enemy, although now fully known to the historian, could only be conjectured or learned by the Americans through the irregular and uncertain means of the spy or the deserter. That the British troops were preparing to move in some direction, was clear. At the camp at Brunswick, they were very busily employed in building a bridge, to be supported by flat-boats, which were to be transported by land on carriages. It was inferred by the Americans that this bridge was designed for crossing the Delaware, and that the British commander intended to march through New Jersey into Pennsylvania; while the transports which were getting ready at New York should bring troops thence by water to Philadelphia, in order to co-operate with the main body of the army, marched over land from Brunswick.

General Howe, before opening the campaign, and bringing his whole army into the field, inflicted several small blows, to try, as it were, the temper of his troops, and the powers of resistance of his antagonists.

General Heath, who was in command of the American forces at Peekskill, had obtained leave to visit his home in New England. Being subsequently appointed to the command of the garrison at Boston, he did not retire. General M‘Dougall, as his second, succeeded him, and was now in command at Peekskill.

Howe, tempted by the large amount of military stores and provisions collected at Peekskill, devised a scheme for taking or destroying them. To divert the Americans from his real purpose, an American officer, who was one of the prisoners taken at Fort Washington, was allowed to hear, with affected inadvertence, the conversation of some British officers. The American was then sent out with a flag to the outposts of General M‘Dougall, and there left, with the understanding that he had been exchanged. Getting among his countrymen, and suspecting nothing of the enemy's *ruse*, his first step was toward headquarters, to report himself and give all the information which he possessed. Accordingly, he communicated to General M‘Dougall all that he had gathered from the conversation to which he supposed he had been unintentionally made a party. The enemy, he said, talked of making an incursion into Westchester county, with the design of taking off the forage. With this view, they were about sending out three detachments: one to proceed up Long-island sound to Mamaroneck; another by the Hudson to Tarrytown; and the third to go by land, by way of Kingsbridge.

General M‘Dougall had only two hundred and fifty men, and could hardly venture to oppose so formidable an invasion, of which he had been thus fictitiously informed. He, however, did all he could: he began to send away the stores which were at Peekskill to Forts Montgomery and Constitution, that they might be more secure. While thus engaged, the **Mar. 22.** enemy made their appearance, with ten sail, in the North river, off Tarrytown; and, on the same evening, two of the vessels advanced to within twelve miles of Peekskill. By noon on the following day, the whole fleet (con- **Mar. 23.** sisting of the Boome frigate, two ships and two brigs, three galleys and four transports) rode at anchor in Peekskill bay. In an hour's time, five hundred men and four pieces of artillery, under the command of Colonel Bird, were landed at Lent's cove.

General M‘Dougall, finding the number of the enemy double that of his own, did not venture to oppose them, but retreated to the hills behind the town—having, however, first set fire to some of the storehouses situated by the river-side, and sent orders to Lieutenant-Colonel Marinus Willett to march with a detachment of troops from Fort Constitution to his aid.

The British were left undisturbed during a whole day, when they secured some of the stores, and burned the greater part, as the only wharf at which they could be shipped had been destroyed by the fire ordered by M‘Dougall as he retreated. In the meantime, Willett had come up with his reinforcement, and finding that a party of the British had the next morning detached themselves from the main body and taken possession of some high ground near the town, he attacked them with such spirit, that they were forced, after a loss of nine killed and wounded, to retire to their comrades in the town. The whole British force, having accomplished their purpose, now prepared to embark, setting fire, as they went, to the houses and the boats along the bay. Favored by a moonlight night, they were soon on board their transports, and sailing down the river.

"The loss of rum, molasses, flour, biscuit, pork, beef, wheat, oats, hay, tallow, iron pots, camp-kettles, canteens, bowls, nails, wagons and carts, barracks, storehouses, sloops and *pettiaugers* laden with provisons," says Gordon, "was very considerable, far beyond what was given out by the Americans, though not of that importance and magnitude as to answer the expectations of General Howe."

The enemy were evidently in a more lively disposition for attack, and their attempts became more frequent. They even showed a disposition **April 13.** to disturb the Americans in New Jersey. General Lincoln was posted with his division (in which there were only about five hundred effective men) at Boundbrook, who had to guard an extent of five or six miles. Lord Cornwallis determined to attack the post thus weakened. Lincoln was not unexpectant of such a manœuvre, and had put his men on their guard against a surprise. The patriots, however, became neglectful; and the enemy, numbering about a thousand men, led on by Lord Cornwallis and General Grant, succeeded in crossing the Raritan, a short distance above Lincoln's quarters, and were not discovered until they had advanced within two hundred yards of the American lines. While these were attempting to surround the general, two thousand more British troops marched along the banks of the Raritan to attack the Americans in front. Lincoln barely had a chance to escape, but succeeded, together with one of his aids, in getting off; but his other aid-de-camp, with all his papers, fell into the hands of the enemy. Lincoln immediately galloped to the front of his troops, while Earl Cornwallis threw a part of his force in the rear of his right, and attempted to pass another detachment on their left, with the purpose of surrounding and cutting off the retreat of the Americans. Lincoln saw the design, and, while these two detachments of the enemy were closing and about to hem him in, he with great promptness pushed his force through the passage between them, and thus effected his escape, with the loss only of sixty killed and wounded. Cornwallis was left in possession of Boundbrook; but, after destroying a score of barrels of flour, a few casks of rum, and

some miscellaneous stores, he evacuated the place.

Sir William Howe now struck another preliminary blow against the Americans Learning that Danbury, in Connecticut, had been made the dépôt of a large quantity of stores, he fitted out an expedition at New York to destroy them. Governor Tryon was given the command, and with him were associated General Agnew and Sir William Erskine. Two thousand troops were detailed for the **April 25.** service; and, being embarked on board twenty-six British men-of-war and transports, the whole expedition sailed up Long-island sound—exciting by its formidable appearance the greatest alarm along the shores of Westchester and Connecticut. As the fleet stood in toward the villages of Norwalk and Fairfield, the inhabitants hurried to their arms and prepared for resistance.

The vessels having come to anchor, the boats were lowered and the British troops landed on the low shore which stretches out from the base of the Compo hill, near the mouth of the Saugatuck river. Tryon, having planted his artillery, was enabled soon to disperse the miscellaneous throng of people which had gathered to oppose him, and take up his march, although his men were severely galled here and there by the American marksmen, who as they retired fired upon their invaders from under cover of the woods and stone-fences. The British, however, pushed their way for seven miles into the interior of the country, and halted for the night.

General Silliman, of the Connecticut

militia, who was at Fairfield, so soon as he was aware of the landing of the enemy, sent out expresses in every direction to call the inhabitants to arms. Early **April 26.** next morning, the militia, obedient to the summons, came in to the number of five hundred men, and Silliman marched them to Reading, in pursuit of the enemy. It happened that General Arnold, who was on his way from Providence to Philadelphia, to lay before Congress his complaints, was sojourning with his friends at New Haven when the intelligence arrived of the British invasion. Forgetting momentarily all his private troubles, his ardent spirit was roused to active sympathy with the public cause. He immediately mounted his horse, and, joining General Wooster, who was also at New Haven, rode with him in great haste to overtake Silliman, some thirty miles distant. Stirring up with their ardent appeals the people along the road, Wooster and Arnold succeeded in bringing in with them, when they reached Silliman at Reading, over a hundred men. The whole body now moved on toward Danbury, which was known to be the object of the enemy, but halted within four miles of that town, at Bethel, which they did not reach until midnight, in consequence of the heavy rain.

April 26. The British, after their nighthalt, were on the march again early the next morning, and proceeded with such despatch, that, with the aid of two native tories as guides, they reached Danbury at two o'clock in the afternoon. The inhabitants were not aware of their approach until some of the frightened country-people rode in with the intelligence that the enemy were but nine miles off, and were coming with all speed. The alarm was great in Danbury. Any attempt at resistance, with the scanty militia force of only a hundred and fifty men, which was the whole number in the place, was felt to be useless. Those who could leave, fled with their wives, children, and effects, to the woods and neighboring villages; for, with exaggerated fears of the cruelty of the British, they believed them capable of every outrage. The small militia force made their way out of Danbury at one extremity while the enemy marched in at the other, and succeeded in joining General Silliman at Bethel.

The British, as soon as they entered the town, began to destroy the public stores, and made great havoc, turning out of the episcopal church the barrels of flour and pork with which it was crammed to the galleries, and the contents of two other buildings, and then burning them. In this manner, eighteen hundred barrels of pork and beef, seven hundred of flour, two thousand bushels of wheat, rye, oats, and Indian corn, clothing for a whole regiment, and seventeen hundred tents, the greatest loss of all, were consumed.

Their object accomplished, the enemy did not seem disposed to commit any further outrage. They were, however, provoked to an act of revenge by the senseless conduct of four of the inhabitants, who, well charged with liquor, and armed with rifles, had posted themselves in one of the houses, and commenced to fire upon the troops. The British soldiers, thus irritated, rushed forward, and, seizing the four men, thrust them into the cellar, and burnt the house and the poor wretches with it! This was a signal for general riot, and the troops began to break open the casks of rum, and help themselves freely to their contents. The whole force was consequently in such a state of intoxication that night, that the men could have been readily mastered by the American militia, few as they were.

Generals Silliman, Wooster, and Arnold, however, had deemed it imprudent, with their small force, to risk an attack upon the enemy while at Danbury: they preferred to await their return, and try to cut them off from their ships. They soon had an opportunity of beginning operations. Tryon, finding that his men were fast losing all sense of discipline in their debauchery, and fearing that the Americans (whom he knew to be at Bethel) might come upon him in the midst of disorder, prudently determined to withdraw his troops from Danbury as soon as the drunkards had partially slept off the effects of their liquor, and the wearied their fatigue. Before the morning broke, therefore, Tryon began his march, having first set fire to all the buildings in the village, with the exception of those which had been previously marked with a cross, to indicate that they were in possession of his tory friends, and were to be spared. From the contrast of the darkness of the lingering dawn on that stormy morning, the blaze of Danbury on fire was visible throughout a wide extent of the adjacent country, and the inhabitants were inflamed to

April 27.

great indignation against these modern Vandals.

As Governor Tryon was conscious that the Americans would attempt to cut off his retreat to his ships lying in the sound, he took an indirect route, with the view of giving the impression that he was about returning to New York by land through Westchester, the county bordering on Connecticut. This led him to Ridgeway.

The veteran Wooster, who, as senior in rank, had taken the chief command of the militia, on discovering this movement of the enemy, sent Generals Arnold and Silliman, with four hundred men, to march and post themselves in front of Tryon, in order to oppose his advance, while he himself, with two hundred, prepared to hang upon his rear and do what he could to harass it. Arnold arrived at Ridgefield (which the enemy would be obliged to pass, on their way to Compo) about ten o'clock, and took a position in a narrow road where it entered the northern end of the village. Here he hastily gathered as many carts and logs as he could, and built them up, with earth, into a barricade across the road, between a house on one side and a ledge of rocks on the other; and with his force now increased to five hundred by the militiamen that he had picked up on his route, he awaited the approach of the enemy.

As Tryon hurried on, General Wooster, with his two hundred men, followed after, and came up with the rear-guard of the British within a few miles of Ridgefield. The Americans succeeded in picking up a score of stragglers, and then continued to push on, when the enemy turned, and, planting their artillery, discharged a volley of shot, which caused Wooster's little band of militia to falter. The old general, riding at their head, and full of spirit, though a veteran of nearly seventy years, strove to rally his troops, and cried out, "Come on, my boys! Never mind such random shots!" At this moment a ball struck him in the side, and he fell mortally wounded. His men gave up the pursuit, and bore their dying general to Danbury.

The enemy pushed on toward Ridgefield, sending their flanking-parties out on either side, and marching with their main body in solid array direct for Arnold's barricade. The Americans gave them a warm reception as they came up; but, as the British gained the ledge of rocks on his flank, and began to pour down upon his little band volley after volley of musketry, Arnold was forced to order a retreat. He himself, with his usual dare-devil spirit, was the last to leave the ground; and, when thus left in the rear of his men, he became a prominent target for the fire of the enemy. Just as he was turning his horse to follow, a shot struck the animal, which brought it down upon its knees. While Arnold was still in the saddle, trying to get his foot out, which had got entangled in the stirrup, a Connecticut tory rushed at him with his bayonet, crying out—

"Surrender! you are my prisoner!"

"Not yet!" answered Arnold, who at the moment, drawing a pistol from his holster, shot the man dead; and then, extricating himself from his wounded horse, he made for a swamp by the roadside and

escaped, although followed by the bullets of a whole platoon of the enemy. Tryon now entered Ridgefield, and allowed his troops, harassed by the day's hard work, the rest of a night.

At dawn next day, the British, having burnt four houses at Ridgefield, were again on the march, and **April 28.** continued their route for Compo, through Norwalk. The ever-active Arnold was on the alert. Again in the saddle, he had rallied his scattered militia, and posted them on the road leading to the bridge across the Saugatuck river, prepared once more to oppose Tryon's retreat; while at the bridge itself he had stationed Colonel Lamb and his corps, and planted three fieldpieces, under Lieutenant-Colonel Oswald. Tryon, finding his way thus opposed, turned his column toward a ford of the stream above, and ordered his men to get across with all possible expedition. His object was, to anticipate the Americans before they could pass over and be able to oppose his retreat. He partially succeeded, but did not escape without a severe struggle, as his rear came in collision with the van of his pursuers just crossing the bridge. Colonel Huntington, too, posted on the other side, with Wooster's men and the militia of Danbury, gave Tryon a good deal of annoyance on his flank.

The enemy, however, pushed on, with the whole body of the Americans close after them. On reaching Compo, Tryon took his position upon the hill, while the Americans came to a halt and waited till he should attempt to embark his troops, when they hoped greatly to harass him.

Sir William Erskine, observing the dangerous position of Tryon, immediately landed from the fleet lying off the shore a large body of sailors and marines, who drove back the pursuers, and thus succeeded in covering the embarkation of the whole British force, when the ships set all sail and moved down the sound.

In the struggle, Arnold, as usual, was foremost; and, although he himself escaped, his horse was shot in the neck. Colonel Lamb was dangerously wounded by a grapeshot while directing his battery, and gallantly standing his ground among the last.

The British, although they had effected their main purpose in the expedition, were much the greater losers in men, having lost in killed, wounded, and prisoners, at least three hundred, while the loss of the Americans was only one hundred. The death of the veteran Wooster, which occurred at Danbury on the 2d of May, was greatly regretted. Though sixty-seven years of age when he fell, he had all the spirit and gallantry of youth.

DAVID WOOSTER was one of the few leading military men of his day who, when the Revolutionary War began, brought into the field a practical knowledge of tactics derived from experience. He had served in the French War, fought under Sir William Pepperell at Louisburg, and commanded with honor as a colonel and subsequently a brigadier in the French and Indian campaign of 1763. Taking part with the revolutionists in 1775, he was appointed, on the organization of the continental army, the third in rank of the eight brigadier-generals then chosen. After a brief command in Canada in 1776, he returned to his native state of Connecticut, when he received the appointment of major-general, the first in rank, and thus became the chief in command when Governor Tryon attacked Danbury. His birth in Stratford, education at Yale college, his marriage with the daughter of the president of that institution, and his devotion to the interests of Connecticut, had greatly endeared him to the people of that state.

On hearing of the result of the invasion by Tryon, Washington wrote: "I regret our loss of stores at Danbury, and the misfortunes of our brave men who fell, and of those who were wounded. However, from these latter events we derive this consolation, that the sentiments of the people are still powerfully directed to liberty, and that no impression of the enemy, be it ever so sudden and unexpected, will pass with impunity." Washington was always confident in the uprightness of the American cause, and never despaired of its final triumph, while his countrymen remained true to it, however they might be temporarily overwhelmed by the profuse resources of a powerful enemy.

CHAPTER XLVI.

General Arnold's Gallantry.—Applause and Rewards.—Arnold made a Major-General.—He is still dissatisfied.—Seeks Satisfaction from Congress.—His Enemies and Friends.—Arrival at Headquarters.—Reception by Washington.—He is justified by the Board of War.—Unfavorable Aspect of Arnold's Accounts.—The Report of Congress intentionally postponed.—Washington and the Foreign Officers.—Rebuke to Monsieur Malmedy.—Monsieur Colerus.—Monsieur Ducoudray.—A Rebuke from Congress.—The End of Monsieur Ducoudray.—Colonel Conway.—He is made a Major-General.—First Impressions.—Kosciusko.—"Try me."—Appointed Aid-de-Camp by Washington.—His Early Life. —French Engineers.—"None but Natives."—The Washington Guard.—All Personal Aggrandizement sternly resisted.—Description of the Camp and Headquarters at Morristown.—General Wayne.—Dinner at Washington's Table.— The Company.—Alexander Hamilton.—Innocent Gayety encouraged.—Serious Thoughts.—Anxieties.—Peculation —The Provincial Attack on Sag Harbor.—Meigs's Gallantry.—Applauded by Washington.

GENERAL ARNOLD's gallantry was **1777.** highly applauded. Congress immediately raised him to the rank of a major-general, and voted him the gift of a horse "properly caparisoned, as a token of their admiration of his gallant conduct in the action against the enemy in their late enterprise to Danbury, in which General Arnold had one horse shot under him and another wounded." There was, however, even in these honors conferred by Congress, an implied censure, which the irritable temper of Arnold could not brook. The date of his commission still kept him below the five other major-generals whose elevation had so greatly stirred his angry spirit. Washington did his best to soothe the chafed feelings of the man. Conscious of his merits as a military officer, he gave him the command of the important post of guarding the North river at Peekskill. Arnold was flattered by this tribute to his worth, but was not appeased. He still impetuously insisted upon an examination into his conduct; and, declining for the present the command at Peekskill, he asked the permission of Washington to go to Philadelphia and confront Congress with a statement of his wrongs.

"I am exceedingly unhappy," wrote Arnold to Congress, "to find that, after having made every sacrifice of fortune, ease, and domestic happiness, to serve my country, I am publicly impeached of a catalogue of crimes, which, if true, ought to subject me to disgrace, infamy, and the just resentment of my countrymen. Conscious of the rectitude of my intentions, however I may have erred in judgment, I must request the favor of Congress to point out some mode by which my conduct and that of my accusers may be inquired into, and justice done to the innocent and injured."

If Arnold had bitter enemies in Congress, he also had strong friends. Among the latter was Richard Henry Lee, of Virginia, who warmly advocated his cause. In regard to the charges so industriously circulated against Arnold, Lee wrote: "One plan now in frequent use is, to assassinate the characters of the friends of America, in every place and by every means; at this moment they are reading in Congress a bold and audacious attempt of this kind against the brave General Arnold." When Arnold presented himself at headquarters at Morristown, on his way to Philadelphia, Washington received him with marked favor, and so far advocated his cause as to give him a letter to Congress, in which Arnold's claim to be heard in his own vindication was urged. Although Washington, with his usual reserve, withholds all expression of opinion in regard to a matter not within his own sphere of observation, he does not hesitate to say of Arnold's military **May 12.** character that "it is universally known that he has always distinguished himself as a judicious, brave officer, of great activity, enterprise, and perseverance."

The board of war, to whom the charges were referred, reported that they were entirely satisfied with Arnold's character and conduct, which had been "so cruelly and groundlessly aspersed." Congress confirmed the report, but did not go further and elevate Arnold to that priority of rank among the major-generals which he claimed as his right, and desired more than any unsubstantial testimonials of character. Congress acted with apparent inconsistency; but it must be recollected that, if all admired the military genius and personal daring of Arnold, there were also many who considered his moral character at the best equivocal, the tendencies of which it behooved them to check.

There was now a test of character by which Arnold was more severely tried. His accounts were submitted to Congress, and these not only presented the irregularity of outlay without vouchers, but extravagant expenditure in his own favor. Arnold was known to have been a poor man, and of no personal pecuniary credit; and, therefore, when he claimed an enormous balance for money spent from his private purse, it was naturally inferred that he was asking what was not his due. His enemies openly declared that a fraud was attempted, and his friends hesitated to defend a man so obviously guilty. The report of the committee was intentionally delayed; for Congress, in the emergency of the country, did not care to be deprived of the services of one to whom none denied the possession of the highest military qualities, though all deplored his destitution of moral principle.

Washington was perplexed by the sensitiveness of his officers in regard to rank, but particularly with that of the foreign gentlemen who came to headquarters in crowds, expecting to be provided for. "I take the liberty," he writes to Richard Henry Lee, "to ask you what Congress expect I am to do with the many foreigners they have at different times promoted to the rank of field-officers, and, by the last resolve, two to that of colonels."

There was a Monsieur Malmedy, who had, on the recommendation of General Lee, received the commission of brigadier-general of the state of Rhode Island. He was subsequently appointed a colonel in the continental service. This appeared to him such a descent in rank, that he was dissatisfied, and so pestered Washington with his complaints, that he was obliged to write to him: "Though I wish not to offend or wound, yet justice both to you and myself requires that I should plainly inform you that your scruples and difficulties, so often reiterated, and under a variety of shapes, are exceedingly perplexing to me, and that I wish them to cease."

A certain Monsieur Colerus, too, was somewhat importunate in his demands; and Washington, having made a major of him, lets him know that, if the appointment does not satisfy. he has no other in his power, and that if monsieur should take "a calm and dispassionate view of things," he would expect no more.

Then comes a Monsieur Ducoudray, who had been promised by Silas Deane, the American agent in Paris, the command of the artillery, with the rank of major-general. Washington, being well satisfied with the gallant and able Knox, is not disposed to oust him, in order to make way for the French gentleman, and says, moreover, that "it may be questioned, with much propriety, whether so important a command as that of the artillery should be vested in any but a native, or one attached by the ties of interest to these states." It having been reported that Ducoudray had been appointed a major-general in the army, with the command of the artillery, Generals Greene, Sullivan, and Knox. were so indignant, that each wrote a letter to Congress, desiring permission, if it were so, to resign at once. Congress had not acted as was rumored; and, when that body received the letters of the American generals, it rebuked them for an attempt to influence its decisions. Deane's treaty was not ratified, and Ducoudray was accepted only as a volunteer.

All further question about his rank was settled, a few months after, by a mishap which terminated his life. While crossing the Schuylkill in a flat-bottomed boat, his horse, an unruly young mare, could not be controlled by Ducoudray, and plunged with him into the river, where he was drowned.

A great difficulty with these French officers was, their want of knowledge of English. This objection could not be urged against Colonel Conway, who was an Irishman by birth, although an officer in the French army. He was therefore more readily provided for, and appointed a brigadier-general. He had presented himself to Washington, and seems to have made a not unfavorable impression upon him. "From what I can discover," says the commander-in-chief, "he appears to be a man of candor." We shall find that in this, as in many other cases, first appearances are often deceitful.

Though the feeling of Washington was naturally more favorably disposed toward his countrymen, who had everything at stake, than toward foreigners, who were for the most part merely military adventurers, seeking either the pay of the mercenary or the satisfaction of a restless ambition, he was ready to do justice to the claims of the worthy, come from where they might. Kosciusko, at the first interview, won Washington's confidence. The noble Pole came to headquarters, with no better title to consideration than a host of others, soliciting employment in the army.

"What do you seek here?" inquired Washington.

"I came to fight as a volunteer for American independence," replied Kosciusko.

"What can you do?"

"Try me," was the brief response of the Pole. Washington was pleased with his frank and self-reliant bearing, and at once made him one of his aids-de-camp.

THADDEUS KOSCIUSKO had been well educated at the military schools of his native country and of France, and his scientific acquirements were soon made available in the engineer department, in which he chiefly served. Of his early life the romantic story is told that, having eloped with a young and beautiful girl of a noble family, he was overtaken by the father, who drew his sword and attempted to wrest his daughter by violence. Kosciusko, finding that he must either kill the one or give up the other, saved the father and lost the daughter. On his departure for America, Doctor Franklin, who had known him in Paris, commended him by a letter to the notice of Washington, and his own personal qualities accomplished the rest.

Apart from those officers of note who afterward fought in the American cause, there was a number of engineers engaged in France by Deane, in accordance with an act of Congress. The services of these were of the greatest importance, for the country was naturally deficient in that particular class of officers.

Washington at this time had not much faith in foreign aid. "I profess myself," he says, "to be of that class who never built sanguinely upon the assistance of France, further than her winking at our supplies from thence for the benefits derived from our trade." His chief reliance was upon his own country and his countrymen. In all places of trust he greatly preferred Americans. When forming his guard, he wrote to the four colonels from whose regiments he was to receive the men, "Send me none but natives." He was, however, too discreet to offend the sensibilities of the foreigners, and guards his officers against any intimation of his preference of natives.

Washington was solicitous about this guard. He desired that it should be composed of men of undoubted integrity, for during the campaign his baggage, papers, and other matters of great public import, would probably be committed to their sole care. Always mindful, too, of a good soldierly effect, he wished that his guard "should look well and be nearly of a size," and therefore ordered that the men should neither exceed in stature five feet ten inches nor fall short of five feet nine inches, and be "sober, young, active, and well made." He wanted, he said, men of good character, and those "that possess the pride of appearing clean and soldierlike."

That this was not to gratify his own personal pride, or to increase his individual importance, was evident even at that early period, for Washington had rebuked with severity every tendency among his officers and men toward worship of himself, or any separate power or interest of the state. Two of the new regiments had been called "Congress's own" and "General Washington's Life-Guards;" and Congress had, with a quick sensibility to the danger of such distinctive appellations, passed a resolve by which they were condemned as improper, and ordered not to be kept in use. Washington's fastidious delicacy in the matter had, however, anticipated the action of that body. "I can assure Congress," he says, "the appellation given to the regiments officered by me was without my consent or privity. As soon as I heard it, I wrote to several of the officers in terms of severe reprehension, and expressly charged them to suppress the distinction."

We obtain a glimpse of the camp and headquarters of Washington at Morristown, about this time, in the lively account of a visit by Graydon, who during the winter had been a prisoner in New York and on Long island, and, having been released on parole, was now on his way to his native city of Philadelphia. While Graydon and his companions were rambling in a "coal-wagon" along the road within a few miles of Morristown, they met Washington on horseback, with three or four attendants. He recognised them, and after a salutation, a few words of courteous congratulation on their release from captivity, and saying he should return to the camp in a few hours, where he expected to see them, the general rode on. Accordingly, in the evening, Graydon and his friends went to pay their respects to Washington, at his marquee. The chief topic of conversation was naturally the probable objects of Sir William Howe in the coming campaign, and the American commander requested to hear from his visiters their opinion, as far as they could give it consistently with their parole. One of them answered that he

thought a co-operation with the northern army, by means of the Hudson river, was General Howe's purpose. Washington, however, although he allowed that indications seemed to point in that direction, was of the opinion that the enemy's object was Philadelphia.

Graydon spent two days in the camp at Morristown. He found everybody about headquarters in the most cheerful mood. The appearance of the army did not, however, seem to justify the good spirits of the officers. "I had been," says Graydon, "extremely anxious to see our army. Here it was, but I could see nothing which deserved the name. I was told, indeed, that it was much weakened by detachments; and I was glad to find that there was some cause for the present paucity of soldiers." The brave and daring General Wayne was apparently in a high state of exhilaration, and, notwithstanding the drooping of his feathers, and his faded appearance "in a dingy red coat, with a black, rusty cravat, and tarnished laced hat," he could yet crow exultingly. "He entertained," says Graydon, "the most sovereign contempt for the enemy. In his confident way, he affirmed that the two armies had interchanged their original modes of warfare: that, for our part, we had thrown away the shovel, and the British had taken it up, as they dared not face us without the cover of an intrenchment." The appearance of the soldiers brought to mind the answer of a gentleman when asked what was the uniform of the army. "In general," he said, "it is blue-and-buff, but by this time it must be all buff." The period of "all buff"

60

seemed to be rapidly approaching, from the "motley, shabby covering" of the soldiers—who, however, like the spirited Wayne, had not, it is presumed, lost their pluck with the tarnish of their regimentals.

There was apparently no want of social enjoyment. Graydon was dined at Washington's table, where there was a large company, among which there were several ladies, Mrs. Washington no doubt among the rest, for she was at that time at Morristown. Colonel Alexander Hamilton presided, "and he acquitted himself with an ease, propriety, and vivacity," says Graydon, "which gave me the most favorable impression of his talents and accomplishments." In the evening, escorted by Colonels Tilghman and Hamilton, both aids of Washington, Graydon was taken to "drink tea with some of the ladies of the village," where a part of the dinner-company was again assembled.

Washington, in fact, did all he could to encourage the cheerfulness of both officers and men. While, however, he promoted innocent pleasures, he was ever mindful of the seriousness of the cause in which he was engaged, and took care that his army should not lose sight of the moral influence which it was expected to exercise. In his instructions to the brigadier-generals, Washington says: "Let vice and immorality of every kind be discouraged as much as possible in your brigade; and, as a chaplain is allowed to each regiment, see that the men regularly attend divine worship. Gaming of every kind is expressly forbidden, as being the foundation of evil, and the cause of many a brave and gallant officer's ruin. Games of exercise for amusement may not only be permitted, but encouraged."

There were, however, at this time, notwithstanding the mood of apparent cheerfulness in the American camp, not a few sources of anxiety. The remissness in the appointment of general officers, the resignation of some of them, the non-acceptance of others, "and I might add," says Washington, "the unfitness of a few, joined to the amazing delay in assembling the troops, and the abuses which I am satisfied have been committed by the recruiting-officers, have distressed me and the service exceedingly." To the slow recruiting was to be added the further trouble of frequent desertions. The men were not regularly paid, and were going off to the enemy, where at least they were sure of their wages; and common soldiers are not, under such circumstances, very apt to discriminate between a good and a bad cause. The military chest was nearly exhausted. "But there is a cause," said Washington, "which I fear will be found on examination too true, and that is, that the officers have drawn large sums, under pretence of paying their men; but have been obliged, from extravagance and for other purposes, to appropriate this money to their own use."

With all these drawbacks, there were not wanting sterling men in the army to do their duty when called upon. The bold and successful enterprise of Lieutenant-Colonel Meigs gave such proof of gallantry and ability as to encourage the most despairing. The British had been

April 24.

gathering forage, grain, and other necessaries for the army, which were deposited in large quantities at Sag Harbor, on Long island. General Parsons, having become aware of the fact, proposed to make a descent and destroy the stores. Lieutenant-Colonel Meigs, a spirited officer, who had served under Arnold in Canada, was selected to conduct the enterprise. He accordingly left New Haven with two hundred and thirty-four men **May 21.** in thirteen whale-boats and sailed to Guilford. Here he was delayed, as the sound was so rough, that he could not venture to cross to Long island. On the 23d, however, early in the afternoon, he embarked one hundred and seventy of his men, and sailed from Guilford, accompanied by two armed sloops. On reaching Southold, in the evening, where he expected to meet some of the enemy, Meigs learned that the troops had left the place two days before and crossed over to New York. He was informed, however, that at Sag Harbor he would probably find a party. Meigs accordingly made all haste to come up with them. The distance was fifteen miles, with a stretch of land, over which the men were obliged to carry the whale-boats, before reaching the bay which separates the northern from the southern branch of the island on which Sag Harbor is situated.

At midnight, Meigs had reached, with all his men, the opposite side of the bay, about four miles from Sag Harbor. Here he secured his boats in a neighboring wood, and, leaving a party to guard them, marched on with the remainder of his force. At two o'clock in the morning, he arrived at the place, and at once began the attack. The guards **April 24.** having been bayoneted, Meigs led his men to the wharf, and commenced the work of destruction. An armed schooner of twelve guns, lying off some hundred and fifty yards or so, opened a fire, which was continued uninterruptedly for three quarters of an hour, but without the least effect.

Colonel Meigs never ceased till his purpose was fully accomplished, and only departed after he had destroyed twelve brigs and sloops, one of which was an armed vessel of twelve guns, a hundred and twenty tons of pressed hay, a considerable amount of corn and oats, ten hogsheads of rum, and a large quantity of merchandise. Moreover, after having killed six of the enemy, he brought off ninety prisoners, while he had not a man killed or even wounded. Meigs with all his men was back again at Guilford as early as two o'clock on the same afternoon, having been absent only twenty-five hours, during which time a distance of ninety miles of land and water had been traversed. Meigs's gallantry was publicly acknowledged by General Washington, and rewarded by Congress with the vote of a sword, as a token of their sense of the " prudence, activity, enterprise, and valor," with which he had conducted the enterprise.

CHAPTER XLVII.

1777. THE designs of the British were not yet clearly revealed, but it was believed that Philadelphia was their main object. They were still busy at work on the bridge; and Washington was so fully persuaded that it was to be used when finished to cross the Delaware, that he ordered the exact breadth of the river for a considerable distance to be obtained, in order to compare it with the length of the bridge, a knowledge of which he hoped to acquire through his spies, and thus discover the part of the stream intended to be traversed.

It was, however, believed that General Howe would also make an effort to secure the North river; and Washington was accordingly very anxious to resist any attempt in that direction. The British had anchored several transports at Dobbs's ferry on the Hudson, with the purpose, it was conjectured, of diverting the attention of Washington from their movements toward the Delaware. It was possible, moreover, that they might attempt from Brunswick to make an incursion into the country back of Morristown, in order to seize the passes through the mountains, and thus try to cut off the communication of the American army with the North river. The general-in-chief accordingly urged General M'Dougall, at Peekskill, to be on the alert, and George Clinton (recently appointed a brigadier-general) to post as large a body of troops in the passes of the Highlands as he could spare from the forts which he commanded on the Hudson.

Major-General Greene and General Knox, two of his officers in whose capacity and fidelity Washington had great trust, were sent by him to examine into the state of the defences on the Hudson and at the Highland passes. They proceeded to Peekskill, and, meeting there with Generals M'Dougall, Clinton, and Wayne, the five officers began their investigations. They inferred that the passes through the Highlands were so "exceedingly difficult," that the British would not attempt to operate by land, provided the river was effectually obstructed. For this purpose, they recommended in their report to Washington that a boom or chain should be stretched across the river at Fort Montgomery, with one or two iron cables in front to break the force of any vessel should it attempt to pass the barrier. These, with two armed ships and two row galleys stationed above, ready to fire upon the approach of the enemy, were believed to be sufficient to defeat any efforts they might make to sail up.

Washington approved of the views of Greene and his associates, and immediately sent the vigorous and laborious Putnam to superintend the work, while Congress was urged to supply without delay the necessary means. That body was advised by the commander-in-chief to purchase the iron cables at Philadelphia, as they could not be procured elsewhere, and which, as they were to be laid diagonally across the river of five hundred and forty yards in breadth, should not be less than four hundred and fifty fathoms long, and of the "largest size that can be had."

In the meantime, while Congress was deliberating about the cables, Old Put's ingenuity was put to the task in fixing a boom. Presuming upon his exhaustless activity, other work was also provided for the veteran general. Washington proposed that he should get up a secret expedition against the British at Kingsbridge, on the upper end of the island of New York. Two plans were suggested. A number of troops might be embarked in boats, under pretence of transporting them and their baggage across the river to Tappan, as if to join Washington's army in New Jersey. To give this purpose the appearance of greater plausibility, a number of wagons might be got ready at the landing on the Jersey side, as if waiting for the baggage. If this plan did not suit, there was the other of embarking the troops at Peekskill, under pretence of reinforcing the garrison on the Hudson, in order to expedite the works, and to set off as bound thither; and then, under the cover of the night, to turn and push down the river. The place proposed for the landing of the troops was the hollow between Fort Washington and Spuyten-Devil creek. Here was a good spot to land upon, and a passage into the road leading from the fort to Kingsbridge: this route, being deeply hidden, would enable Putnam to fall in upon the back of the British troops at Fort Independence, by which their surprise would be greater, and their retreat cut off. "Thence," says Washington, in his instructions, "your troops might, or might not, march up by land, and sweep the country before them of the enemy and provisions, as circumstances might justify."

Washington, now that his army was somewhat reinforced, determined to shift his encampment. His troops, however, even at this time, hardly numbered eight thousand, as most of the regiments were greatly scant of their full complement of men.* Forty-three regiments (those of New Jersey, Pennsylvania, Delaware, Maryland, and Virginia, together with Colonel Hazen's) composed the army in New Jersey, under the immediate orders of the commander-in-chief.

May 28.

* Sparks

These were divided into ten brigades, under Brigadier-Generals Muhlenberg, Weedon, Woodford, Scott, Smallwood, Wayne, Deborre, De Haas, Conway, and Maxwell. The divisions were five, of two brigades each, under Major-Generals Greene, Stirling, Sullivan, Stephen, and Lincoln: General Knox commanded the artillery. The New-York and New-England troops were chiefly at Ticonderoga, under Generals Gates and St. Clair; and at Peekskill, under Generals Putnam, M'Dougall, and Clinton.

The new position taken by Washington was a strong one on the high ground about Middlebrook, and several miles nearer than Morristown to the main body of the enemy at Brunswick. There was no attempt on the part of the British to oppose this movement, beyond sending out a body of light-horse, which, after skirmishing with the advance-guard, retired on finding a large detachment of the American army coming forward. Washington's purpose was to oppose the march of General Howe to the banks of the Delaware, which it was thought to be his design to cross on the way to Philadelphia. The American chief, however, was not sanguine of his power to check the enemy, in consequence of the meagerness of his force. **June 1.** "If," says he, "some effectual mode is not devised to fill the regiments, it is impossible, at least very unlikely, that any effectual opposition can be given to the British army with the troops we have, whose numbers diminish more by desertion than they increase by enlistments."

General Howe finally began to move.

Reinforced from New York and Rhode Island, he commenced his **June 13.** march in the evening, and in the course of the night his front had reached Somerset courthouse, where it halted, while his rear remained at Brunswick. It appeared to be his intention to push directly for the Delaware, although Washington did not know whether it was a real move toward Philadelphia or an endeavor to draw the Americans from the heights which they occupied along the whole front of the enemy. Howe's only object, as we now know, was to bring Washington to a general action, for he had determined to attack Philadelphia by sea. His plans then, however, could only be conjectured by the Americans, and they prepared to act in accordance with their surmises.

As the prospect of action approached, the militia began to turn out in a more spirited manner; and they, together with the continental troops, seemed determined to harass and oppose the enemy "upon their march through the country." General Howe would have great difficulty, thought Washington, in crossing the Delaware. Arnold (who had been ordered from Philadelphia) and Mifflin would be ready with a considerable force to meet him on the western side of the river, while Washington's army on the opposite bank would "hang heavily on his rear." The American troops were withdrawn from Peekskill, with the exception of a thousand men, who were supposed sufficient (now that the enemy had diminished their force by their drafts for New Jersey) to prevent any surprise from New York.

The hostile armies now confronted each other, mutually expectant.

The main body of the Americans was encamped upon the high ground at Middlebrook, while a considerable force under General Sullivan was posted on the lowland hills. The position at Middlebrook was naturally very strong, but was further strengthened by works. The passes in the mountains were too difficult to be attempted; and, although the right of the army was not so well defended, two or three redoubts were all that were necessary to secure it effectually. The enemy were also strongly posted. Well fortified on their right, with the river Raritan all along their front and the Millstone creek on their left, they were in a situation where an attack upon them was not warranted by a sufficient prospect of success, and might "be attended with the most ruinous consequences." Under these circumstances, Washington determined to collect all the force at Middlebrook that could be properly withdrawn from other quarters, so as to bring the security of his army to the greatest possible certainty, and be ready to take advantage of any fair opportunity of attack which might offer. In the meantime, he would send out light bodies of militia (accompanied by a few continental troops to keep them in countenance by their more soldierly bearing), to harass and weaken the enemy by frequent skirmishes.

Whatever might be the ulterior purpose of the British, it was conjectured by Washington that their first object was to destroy his army, and then get possession of Philadelphia. The risk would be too great for the enemy to attempt to cross the Delaware, when they must expect to meet a formidable opposition in front, and have the whole American army in their rear. "They might possibly be successful," writes Washington, "but the probability would be infinitely against them. Should they be imprudent enough to do it, I shall keep close upon their heels, and do everything in my power to make the project fatal to them." The British general, however, had apparently no design upon the Delaware at that time, or he would have made a secret, rapid march for it, and not have come out openly, and as light as possible, leaving all his baggage, provisions, boats, and bridges, at Brunswick. From the position he had taken, his purpose was, more probably, to prepare for an attack upon Washington's right, which was the weakest point. But whatever might be General Howe's object, the people were in a high state of animation, and apparently ready for the enemy.

Howe soon made another change, that gave rise to much speculation at headquarters. After having moved his main body from Brunswick, and extended his van to Somerset courthouse, encamping between these two posts, and beginning a line of redoubts, he suddenly marched back his whole army to the former place, burning the houses **June. 19.** and devastating the country along his route. Washington at this time was constantly in the saddle, reconnoitring and sending out his light-troops to hover as near as possible about the enemy, who, however, secured as they were on their flanks by the Raritan and Millstone rivers, had no great difficulty in reaching their former posts.

June 22. In three days more, the British camp was again all astir night and day. A movement was evidently in prospect. Washington accordingly sent an express to General Maxwell to lie below Brunswick and Amboy, in order to intercept any British parties which might be passing; and detached three brigades, under Major-General Greene, to fall upon the enemy's rear as soon as they should move; while the main body of the army was paraded upon the heights of Middlebrook, to support Greene if there should be occasion.

Sir William Howe began his march, and the Americans were on the alert to harass him. A party of Colonel Morgan's light-infantry pushed forward betimes and drove in the Hessian picket before the sun was up; while the rest of Morgan's regiment and General Wayne's brigade followed rapidly, and posted themselves opposite to Brunswick. The enemy, however, crossed the bridge, and took possession of the redoubts which they had constructed on the north side of the river. General Greene, now advancing his troops briskly toward them, they quitted their position and retired by the road to Amboy, with Morgan and his riflemen close at their heels, keeping up a sharp fire, which "did considerable execution."

Greene continued to pursue the enemy as far as Piscataway, but finding it impossible to overtake them, and fearful lest he might be drawn away too far from the main body, he returned to Brunswick, reporting with great praise the conduct and bravery of General Wayne and Colonel Morgan, and of their officers and men, who constantly advanced upon an enemy far superior to them in numbers, and well secured behind strong redoubts. General Maxwell, unfortunately, missed the express messenger, who had by accident or design fallen into the hands of the British; otherwise their rear-guard, as they themselves confessed, would have been cut off. Maxwell was now reinforced by Lord Stirling and his division.

General Howe, on reaching Amboy, despatched some of his troops across to Staten island; but he soon brought them back, and advanced toward Westfield with his whole army. Washington had moved the entire American force to Quibbletown, in order to be nearer the enemy **June 24.** after their evacuation of Brunswick, and ordered Lord Stirling to move his division still closer to Howe's lines. When the enemy began apparently to return, with the purpose of turning the American left, Washington marched his main army back to the secure position at Middlebrook, but continued to hang upon the British flank with a body of light-troops and Morgan's riflemen. After some slight skirmishing, General Howe again withdrew, plundering and burning all before him, to Amboy, and finally passed over to Staten island with his entire army, using the bridge which **June 30.** had been so laboriously constructed at Brunswick for the purpose of transporting his artillery and baggage. The Americans were thus left in complete possession of New Jersey. The next move of the enemy was now the object of anxious speculation.

A great stir among the shipping in New-York bay, the general striking of the tents, and the marching of the troops from that part of Staten island opposite to Amboy to the other side, in the neighborhood of the anchorage of the fleet, made it apparent that General Howe had in contemplation some movement by water. At this time, intelligence was received from General St. Clair, commanding at Ticonderoga, that the British army in Canada evidently had designs upon that fort. It was thence inferred that Howe's purpose might be to push immediately up the Hudson, in order to co-operate with the British troops marching from the North. In case this should be the enemy's design, Washington promptly ordered General Putnam, at Peekskill, to reinforce St. Clair with a portion of his eastern troops; but, while Howe's object was not clearly manifest, he was in great uncertainty how to direct his main body. His situation was " truly delicate and perplexing." Should he march his army to Peekskill, leaving the British commander on Staten island, there would be nothing to prevent his crossing to South Amboy, and pushing thence to Philadelphia. On the other hand, if the North river and the possession of the Highlands should be General Howe's object, the keeping of the army in New Jersey would give the enemy the opportunity of effecting their purpose without resistance in that quarter. " We shall attempt in this dilemma," says Washington, " to do the best we can." In the meanwhile, he wrote to

Generals Putnam and George Clinton, urging them to put forth every exertion in their power, and instantly to call out a " respectable" body of militia to aid in the defence of the important posts on the North river. Washington also advanced a division of his army, under General Sullivan, to Pompton, in order to be nearer the enemy should they attempt to ascend the Hudson.

Further intelligence from the North induced Washington to believe that the possession of the Hudson and the communication with Canada, by which the eastern and southern states might be separated, was probably the intention of the enemy; and he therefore moved his whole force to Morristown, **July 11.** and thence to Pompton, from which place he prepared to march still farther toward the Hudson. Let us now for a moment glance at the condition of affairs at the North.

General Gates, as we have seen, had superseded General Schuyler in the command of the northern army, but had only served from the 25th of March, when on the 22d of May he was obliged to give it up. Schuyler had obtained from Congress the investigation which he had sought so pertinaciously, and was rewarded for his perseverance by a reinstatement in his command; not, however, before he had addressed a memorial to Congress, in which an apologetic explanation was made of the expressions in his former letter which had given so much offence. New England resisted Schuyler's appointment to the last, and it was only secured by the absence of some of the delegates from that quarter. It was, however, generally conceded that his influence in the state of New York rendered him the most effective man for the position.

Gates was greatly vexed at the result, and, refusing to serve under Schuyler, who offered him the command at Ticonderoga, requested permission to proceed to Philadelphia. Here he arrived, and so lost all self-control, that he presented himself on the floor of Congress, and began to indulge in some personal reflections on one of the members, which excited the indignation of the house, and, after a noisy debate, led to a request that he would withdraw. There was a great deal of partisan feeling exhibited in the discussion of the relative commands of Schuyler and Gates, and the reinstatement of the former was considered to be a triumph of what was then termed the New-York party over that of New England.

As soon as Schuyler reached Albany from Philadelphia (where he had been stationed during the interval of his loss of the northern command), he ordered General St. Clair to Ticonderoga.

June 5. Both Schuyler and St. Clair believed that the enemy were preparing to come in great force from Canada by way of the lakes. A British spy, one Amesbury, had been taken and examined, who stated that the main body of the Canadian army was advancing by St. Johns, and that a detachment of English, Canadians, and Indians, was about penetrating to the south by the Mohawk river. Apart from the information which he was to gather, Amesbury was intrusted with a canteen by a Judge Levins, of Canada, with direc-

tions to deliver it to General Sullivan, and request him to remove a false bottom, within which he would find a letter. The canteen was obtained by Schuyler, the concealed letter found directed as had been stated by the spy, and at once forwarded, through the commander-in-chief. It proved to be an appeal to General Sullivan to betray the American cause. It is needless to say that against this subtle exhortation that officer was patriotically proof.

This information of the probable advance of the Canadian army by way of the lakes took Washington by surprise, as he, together with his chief officers and Congress, had entertained the opinion that the British troops at the North would have come round by the St. Lawrence and the sea, to reinforce General Howe at New York. Ticonderoga had consequently been neglected, and frequent demands for reinforcements of the American strength at Albany and beyond not responded to.

Washington had, moreover, received exaggerated accounts of the force at the command of Schuyler and St. Clair. Even as late as the 2d of July, he says: "I see no reason for apprehending that it [Ticonderoga] can possibly fall into the hands of the enemy in a short time." He was still perplexed about the designs of his antagonists. "If a co-operation is intended," he writes to Schuyler, "General Howe must speedily throw off the mask, and make his preparations for going up the North river; if he does not, I shall think that the fleet and a small force of Indians and light-troops are amusing you upon the lake, while the main body comes round and forms a junction by water. One reason operates strongly against this, in my opinion, and that is, a man of General Burgoyne's spirit and enterprise would never have returned from England merely to execute a plan from which no great credit or honor was to be derived."

CHAPTER XLVIII.

General Burgoyne.—His Life and Character.—His Parliamentary Career.—His Dramatic Works.—His Military Career.—Horace Walpole's Estimate of Him.—Commander-in-Chief of the British Forces in Canada.—Plan of the Campaign.—Sir Guy Carleton's Magnanimity.—A Sufferer for his Humanity.—Estimate of Burgoyne's Force.—His Officers.—Beginning of the Campaign.—Burgoyne meets the Indians in Council.—Swollen Rhetoric.—Pompous Proclamation.—General Schuyler at Ticonderoga.—He strengthens the Fortifications.—Goes to Albany.—Sends Stores and Men.—He is sanguine about the Security of Ticonderoga.—Washington entertains the Same Opinion.—General St. Clair in Command of the Fort.—The Defences.—The Weak Points.—Wasted Energies.

1777. GENERAL BURGOYNE is now about to act a more important part in the American War; and we shall here, as we meet him for the first time in the capacity of a commander-in-chief, give some account of his life and character. This was his third visit to America. He had served in Boston, under Governor Gage; in Canada, under Sir Guy Carleton; and had recently, after visiting England, returned to take command of the British forces in the North.

The time and place of the birth of JOHN BURGOYNE—a man who rose to no mean celebrity as a writer, a senator, and a military officer—are unknown. Even his parentage has not been ascertained with certainty, although he is generally supposed to have been the natural son of Lord Bingley, who died an old man in 1774. He was probably early destined for a military life. There is, however, no record of the dates of his grades in the army until 1758, when he was raised to the rank of lieutenant-colonel. He distinguished himself in Portugal, where he was a comrade of the eccentric Charles Lee, who, under the orders of Burgoyne, swam the Tagus at the head of three hundred and fifty British soldiers, and surprised the Spanish camp. After the campaign in Portugal, Burgoyne was rewarded with a colonelcy.

In 1761, he was elected a member of Parliament for Midhurst, a position for which he was no doubt indebted to some powerful patronage through his putative relationship to Lord Bingley. In 1768, Burgoyne was again returned to Parliament for the borough of Preston; and his election drew upon him the brilliant invective of "Junius," who, considering him a satellite of the duke of Grafton treated him with the same unsparing severity. Burgoyne was now appointed governor of Fort William, and in 1772 raised to the rank of general. As a member of Parliament he began to take a prominent share in its debates. In 1772, he took the lead in denouncing the corrupt conduct of the officials of the East-India Company, and introduced with a brilliant and effective speech the motion that a committee be appointed to "inquire into the nature, state, and condition of the East-India Company, and of the British affairs in the East Indies." The committee having been appointed, Burgoyne as its chairman was frequently called upon to defend the conduct and measures of himself and his colleagues, and never failed to do it with great tact and power.

While a dashing young subaltern, Burgoyne made the acquaintance of a daughter of the earl of Derby. The two became deeply enamored, and were married clandestinely, greatly to the indignation of his lordship of Derby, who declared that he would never admit them to his presence. Burgoyne, however, with his brilliant promise as a soldier, and a rising man in Parliament, aided by his gentlemanly tact, soon reconciled the earl of Derby to the alliance. With this recognised relationship, we find Burgoyne, in 1774, acting as master of ceremonies in the *fête* given at the seat of the family, "The Oaks," to celebrate the marriage of his brother-in-law, Lord Stanley, with Lady Betsey Hamilton, the daughter of the duke of Hamilton. It was on this occasion that Burgoyne first publicly displayed his talents as a dramatist. He wrote a "dramatic entertainment, in five acts," styled "*The Maid of the Oaks*," which was played at the marriage-festival, and afterward successfully brought out (un-der the auspices, and with some touches of the pen, of Garrick) at Drury Lane. The pen was, however, soon dropped for the sword, and it was not until after his several campaigns in America that he renewed his literary pursuits. He then wrote "*The Lord of the Manor*," a comic opera in three acts—a light, sparkling piece, which was acted, and welcomed with much applause. Writing verse with facility, he contributed two lively, satirical compositions, "*The Westminster Guide*" and a "*Probationary Ode*," to one of the cleverest political *jeu d'esprits* of the day. In 1786, he brought out on the stage the comedy of "*The Heiress*," and, soon after, the historical drama of "*Richard Cœur de Lion*." In all these, Burgoyne exhibits a knowledge of society and the world, a quick fancy, and a flexible hand. His temper was gay, and his disposition social. He loved pleasure, but was active in business. A thorough soldier, he never failed to do his duty, though he always strove to soften the severities of war by acts of generosity and humanity, to which his natural kindliness of heart prompted him. Horace Walpole says of him smartingly, that he had "a half-understanding that was worse than none;" that he was "a classic scholar who had more reading than parts;" that he "was fond of writing, and did not want eloquence, but judgment extremely;" and, again, that he was "the most verbose and bombastic boaster that ever bore a truncheon," though "he did not want spirit, not knowledge, not any zeal for serving his master."

We have seen Burgoyne at Boston, and subsequently in Canada; and now, for the third time, we find him in America as commander-in-chief of the British troops at the North. This appointment had been conferred upon him by the British government in order to carry out the proposed plan of penetrating toward Albany from Canada, and thus form a junction with a portion of Sir William Howe's army which was to advance up the Hudson, that the American communication might be cut off between the northern and eastern states. Burgoyne, when consulted, had declared that a force of eight thousand regulars, two thousand Canadians, and one thousand Indians, would be necessary to secure the success of the plan.

On arriving in Canada, General Burgoyne met with some disappointment in filling up the complement of his army, but was able, however, to commence operations with an effective force. Sir Guy Carleton had been superseded, and might have justly complained of neglect, and want of acknowledgment of his previous services; but, waiving all personal feeling, he magnanimously welcomed Burgoyne with great friendliness, and earnestly aided him in executing his plans. Carleton, in character with his usual benevolence, is supposed to have objected to the employment of the Indians, and therefore been supplanted by Burgoyne, who had fewer scruples on this point. Carleton sent his resignation to England as governor of Canada, but in the meantime tendered his services to the newly-appointed commander-in-chief; and, with his knowledge of and influence in the country, he proved of great advantage. By his means the Indian tribes were conciliated, and the native Canadians induced to remain faithful to British interests.

Burgoyne's European force amounted to seven thousand men, of whom nearly one half were hired mercenaries from the principality of Brunswick, in Germany. To these were added four hundred Indians and about a hundred and fifty Canadians. His artillery corps and train were of the most serviceable character, "probably the finest and the most excellently supplied as to officers and private men that had ever been allotted to second the operations of any army." His officers were men of great repute for skill and daring. General Phillips commanded the artillery; Generals Fraser, Hamilton, and Powell, the various British divisions; and Baron Reidesel and General Specht, the Brunswickers.

Having first detached Colonel St. Leger from St. Johns with a miscellaneous force, consisting of British, Germans, Sir John Johnson's New-York tory confederates, and savages (amounting in all to about eight hundred), in order to make a diversion on the Mohawk river, Burgoyne himself set out with his **June 14,** force. After proceeding some distance, he encamped his army at the river Bouquet, on the western side of Lake Champlain, near Crown Point. Here he met the Indians in council, and gave them a war-feast. Burgoyne was naturally solicitous about the conduct of his savage allies, and took care to impress upon them the humane requirements of civilized warfare. They were told that they should only kill those who opposed them in arms; that old men and women, children and prisoners, the wounded and the dying, should be spared the hatchet; and that none but those who had been slain in battle should be scalped. Burgoyne promised them rewards for prisoners, but declared that he would call them to strict account for every scalp they brought in.

Having swollen his rhetoric, in his address to the savages, in accordance with the supposed requirements of Indian oratory, Burgoyne, it would seem, found it difficult to bring his imagination within its ordinary range; for the proclamation which he immediately afterward issued to the people of the country was full of pompous declamation. There was something in it, however, worse than its style. It held out the threat of savage cruelty. "I have," said he, "but to give stretch to the Indian forces under my direction, and they amount to thousands, to overtake the hardened enemies of Great Britain and America. I consider them the same, wherever they may lurk."

Soon after sending St. Clair to Ticonderoga, General Schuyler him-

June 17. self went to examine into the condition of affairs there. They did not appear as satisfactory as he had anticipated. Instead of the force of five thousand, which Washington supposed to be the strength of the garrison at this post, it was found that there were less than twenty-five hundred effective men in all, to defend both the works at Ticonderoga, on the west side of the lake, and Mount Independence, on the east. Such a meager supply of troops, it was clear, was quite inadequate to defend the two posts. Without reinforcements, in case of an at-

tack from the enemy, one or the other would have to be abandoned. In such an event, Mount Independence was considered as the post at which it would be desirable to concentrate all the available force. Attention was accordingly directed chiefly to this point. All the cannon and stores, not immediately wanted on the Ticonderoga side, were taken over; and Kosciusko, who was the engineer-in-chief of the northern army, at once commenced repairing the old and adding new works, in order to strengthen the by-no-means strong fortifications of Mount Independence. There was such a deficiency of provisions, that it was inferred that the garrison, unless soon supplied, would not be able to hold out for many days. With all these drawbacks, it was still thought advisable to obtain reinforcements and supplies, and to maintain the two posts as long as possible. It was deemed prudent, however, to collect and repair the batteaux, in case a retreat should become necessary.

General Schuyler, thus made aware of the weaknesses and wants of Ticonderoga, hastened back to Fort George, and so bestirred himself, that he was soon able to send a good supply of provisions, and some working-men to aid in the construction of the works. He seemed, however, to be in very little anxiety about the post, for he writes to Congress: "I trust we shall still be able to put everything in such order as to give the enemy a good reception, and, I hope, a repulse, should they attempt a real attack, which I conjecture will not be soon, if at all."*

* Irving.

Washington, too, from the information he had obtained, which was unaccountably inexact, continued to believe that Ticonderoga was beyond the chance of danger. "As the garrison at Ticonderoga," he writes to Schuyler, "is sufficient to hold it against any attack, I do not think it politic, under your representation of the scarcity of provisions, to send up troops to consume what ought to be thrown into the fort." He soon received intelligence which placed it beyond any chance of doubt, that Burgoyne was advancing; but he was still confident of St. Clair's security until the last moment, when a letter from Schuyler appears to

July 1. have conveyed for the first time a truthful account of the condition of Ticonderoga. Washington thereupon immediately ordered General Putnam to despatch a brigade, under Nixon, to reinforce the northern army.

Schuyler, in the meantime, was diverting himself with the idea that Burgoyne would march his main body from St. Francis or St. Johns to the east and invade New England. "I am," he writes, "the more confirmed in this conjecture, as the enemy can not be ignorant how very difficult, if not impossible, it will be for them to penetrate to Albany, unless in losing Ticonderoga we should lose not only all our cannon, but most of the army designed for this [the northern] department."

St. Clair, even at Ticonderoga, was for a long time in a state of uncertainty about the strength and designs of the enemy. In the meanwhile he kept his men busily occupied in increasing the defences of the place. There were not wanting some among the officers who were doubtful of the policy of holding the post. The garrison were so few in numbers, and the labors of all so much increased by the works and the strong guards necessary on the threatened approach of the enemy, that the men became prostrated by fatigue and watching. "If fortitude," wrote an officer at that time, "if enterprise, if perseverance or temerity, could avail, I would not complain; but, in the name of Heaven, what can be expected from a naked, undisciplined, badly-armed, unaccoutred body of men, when opposed to a vast superiority of British troops?"

The American lines were greatly extended, from Mount Independence, on the east side of Lake Champlain, to Ticonderoga on the west. The two places were connected by a floating bridge, supported on twenty-two sunken piers of very large timber, and the spaces between filled with separate floats, each about fifty feet long and twelve wide, strongly fastened together by iron chains and rivets. On the northern side of this bridge was stretched a boom made of large timber, well secured by riveted bolts, and a double iron chain, with links of one and a half inches square. The length of this combined bridge, boom, and chain, was four hundred yards, and its construction had cost an immensity of labor and expense. The work was supposed, however, to be admirably adapted to the double purpose of a communication between Ticonderoga and Mount Independence, and of an impenetrable barrier to any approach of the enemy by way of the lake.

There were two hills which command-ed the works: one called Mount Hope, rising about half a mile in advance of the old French lines on the Ticonderoga or west side of the lake; and another, known as the Sugar-Loaf hill, or Mount Defiance. Mount Hope was the least important of the two hills, as it only commanded the left of the works at Ticonderoga, and was unprotected, probably in consequence of the meagerness of St. Clair's force, which, composed of less than three thousand men — of whom nine hundred were raw militia, but just come in — was not suffi-cient, when the troops were ordered to man the lines, to occupy their whole ex-tent.

The Sugar-Loaf hill was, however, en-tirely neglected, from the prevalent im-pression that it was inaccessible for artil-lery, and too distant, even if in possession of an enemy, for their balls to reach the fort. This hill, which is the northern ter-mination of the mountain-ridge dividing Lake George from Lake Champlain, rises precipitously to a height of six hundred feet, and completely commanded both the works at Ticonderoga, from which it was only separated by the outlet from Lake George, and those at Mount Independ-ence, from which it was divided by the narrowest part of Lake Champlain. A year before, John Trumbull (then Gen-eral Gates's adjutant at Ticonderoga, and subsequently the well-known painter) had been impressed with the importance of guarding the Sugar-Loaf hill. "I had for some time," he says, "regarded this emi-nence as completely overruling our en-tire position. It was said, indeed, to be

at too great a distance to be dangerous; but by repeated observations I had satis-fied my mind that the distance was by no means so great as was generally sup-posed: and at length, at the table of Gen-eral Gates, where the principal officers of the army were present, I ventured to ad-vance the new and heretical opinion that our position was bad and untenable, as being overlooked in all its parts by this hill. I was ridiculed for advancing such an extravagant idea. I persisted, how-ever; and, as the truth could not be as-certained by argument, by theory, or by ridicule, I requested and obtained the general's permission to ascertain it by experiment.

"General (then Major) Stevens was bu-sy at the north point of Mount Indepen-dence in examining and proving cannon. I went over to him on the following morn-ing, and selected a long, double-fortified French brass gun (a twelve-pounder), which was loaded with the proof-charge of best powder, and double shotted. When I desired him to elevate this gun so that it should point at the summit of Mount Defiance (Sugar-Loaf hill), he looked sur-prised, and gave his opinion that the shot would not cross the lake. 'That is what I wish to ascertain, major,' was my an-swer. 'I believe they will; and you will direct your men to look sharp, and we, too, will keep a good lookout. If the shot drop in the lake, their splash will be easi-ly seen; if, as I expect, they reach the hill, we shall know it by the dust of the im-pression which they will make upon its rocky face.'

"The gun was fired, and the shot was

plainly seen to strike at more than half the height of the hill. I returned to headquarters, and made my triumphant report, and after dinner requested the general and officers who were with him to walk out upon the *glacis* of the old French fort, where I had ordered a common six-pound field-gun to be placed in readiness. This was, in their presence, loaded with the ordinary charge, pointed at the top of the hill, and when fired it was seen that the shot struck near the summit.

"Thus, the truth of the new doctrine was demonstrated; but still it was insisted upon that this summit was inaccessible to an enemy. This also I denied, and again resorted to experiment. General Arnold, Colonel Wayne, and several other active officers, accompanied me in the general's barge, which landed us at the foot of the hill, where it was most precipitous and rocky, and we clambered to the summit in a short time. The ascent *was* difficult and laborious, but not impracticable; and when we looked down upon the outlet of Lake George, it was obvious to all that there could be no difficulty in driving up a loaded carriage."

Notwithstanding this demonstration of the importance of Mount Defiance a year before, no regard was paid toward securing it; and the engineers and the dispirited troops went on wasting their energies in ceaseless labors upon works which alone were useless for defence, unless the enemy should be equally heedless, and dash their force against them in an assault.

CHAPTER XLIX.

Stealthy Approach of the Enemy.—General St. Clair in Despair.—The Beginning of the Attack.—A Hasty and Ineffectual Fire.—A Jolly Hibernian.—St. Clair hopeful of an Assault.—General Burgoyne discovers the Weak Point.—He takes possession of Sugar-Loaf Hill.—St. Clair calls a Council of War.—A Retreat determined upon.—The Night's Silent March.—The Enemy aroused.—The Scene described.—The Provincials escape to Skenesborough.—They are overtaken by Burgoyne.—Burning of Galleys and Batteaux.—The Struggle on Land.—"The Indians at our Heels."—The Fight at Fort Anne.—Disasters and Adventures of the Fugitives.—The Lost St. Clair.—His Wanderings.—The Success of the British at Hubbardtown.—Unsuccessful Attempt of St. Clair to aid the Discomfited Provincials.—St. Clair turns up in Vermont.—A Royal Conqueror.

1777. THE occasional sight of the Indian warriors at the American outposts (some of General Burgoyne's savage allies), as they were prowling about the adjacent forests, indicated the approach of the enemy. General St. Clair, however, was yet in ignorance of their force and designs. All his efforts to obtain information had been in vain. Although the heights of Ticonderoga afforded an extended view of the country, the approaches were concealed by mountain headlands and dense woods. Reconnoitring-parties were sent out, but they were either cut up, captured, or driven in, by the Indian scouts of the enemy.

62

Burgoyne's force, however, was reveal- ing itself more clearly from day to day. On the 30th of June, a part of his fleet had sailed up the lake from Crown Point, and troops debarked on the west side, within three miles and in full view of Ti- conderoga. Another detachment, com- posed of Indians and Canadians, had land- ed on the opposite side, and, falling in with an American scouting-party, attacked and put it to the rout. St. Clair was anx- ious, but yet, as he was ignorant of the strength and purpose of the enemy, un- decided upon what he should do. Per- fectly aware, however, of the weakness of his own position, St. Clair wrote to Gen- eral Schuyler : " Should the enemy invest and blockade us, we are infallibly ruined ; we shall be obliged to abandon this side [the Ticonderoga side], and then they will soon force the other from us, nor do I see that a retreat will in any shape be prac- ticable. Everything, however, shall be done that is practicable to frustrate the enemy's designs ; but what can be expect- ed from troops ill armed, naked, and un- accoutred ?" He was in hopes, notwith- standing, that Burgoyne's force was too small for an investment of the posts on both sides of the lake, and that he would attempt an assault, in which case St. Clair encouraged himself with the belief that, by withdrawing all his troops within the works at Mount Independence, a success- ful resistance might possibly be made.

July 1. Burgoyne's whole army now began to move from Crown Point. On the western shore the British came marching forward, and on the left the German troops, while the fleet sailed up the lake in advance. The British imme- diately and without resistance took pos- session of Mount Hope, which command- ed the left of the works at Ticonderoga. Desiring to possess themselves of another piece of rising ground in advance, within only a thousand yards of the American lines, they sent forward Captain Frazer, with a detachment of riflemen and sev- eral hundred Indians, to clear the way. They came on so audaciously, that they ventured to attack an American picket of sixty men, within two hundred yards of a battery of eight guns, and, having dispersed this outguard, approached to within less than a hundred yards of the main work, where, scattering themselves along the front among the brushwood, they kept up a brisk fire.

General St. Clair, who had consoled himself with the hope of an assault, be- lieved that it was now about to take place, and that the detachment which had approached so boldly had been sent for- ward to draw his fire and create disorder, preliminary to the general attack. He accordingly ordered his troops to sit down on the banquet, with their backs to the parapet, to cover them from the shot of the enemy, and to prevent their throw- ing away their own fire. One of the offi- cers at this moment, as he leaned on the parapet, observed a British light-infantry- man, who, having crept within forty paces of the ditch, and taken a position on his knees behind a stump, was loading and firing. " I stepped," says Wilkinson (for he was the officer, and gives the account of the incident), " to a salient angle of the line, and ordered a sergeant to rise and shoot him. The order was obeyed, and at the discharge of the musket every man arose, mounted the banquet, and without command fired a volley; the artillery followed the example, as did many of the officers, from the colonels down to subalterns: and, notwithstanding the exertions of the general, his aids, and several other officers, three rounds were discharged before they could stop the firing." The whole result of this hurried fire and large consumption of powder was the wounding of a single lieutenant, and the fright of the rest of the party, who, when the smoke had dispersed, were observed at three hundred yards' distance, retreating helter-skelter to the British position on Mount Hope. One drunken fellow, however, was left upon the field, who, having been brought into the American lines, proved of some service.

St. Clair was still ignorant of the force of the enemy, and of their purpose. He now hit upon an expedient for obtaining the information he desired. The tipsy captive, who had been picked up in front of the works, was clapped into the guardhouse, and, as he was supposed to be in a social and communicative humor, it was proposed to get what he knew out of him. An Irishman, one Captain Johnson, of the American artillery, temporarily assuming the character of a tory (putting on a ragged suit, and concealing about his person a bottle), was thrust in with the prisoner. Johnson's brogue, rags, and whiskey, dispelled all doubts of his country, and he soon succeeded in commending himself to the fellowship of the captive, who was also a jolly Hibernian.

The prisoner proved to be not only communicative, but intelligent; and Johnson was enabled to draw from him the number and name of every corps under General Burgoyne, and an estimate of the strength of his whole force. It would appear, moreover, to have been pretty clearly ascertained that the enemy's object was to invest the place.

The American commander, however, still deluded himself with the hope that Burgoyne would hazard an assault. Accordingly, for several days, he held his ground; and, although the British were in possession of Mount Hope, and continued to make their approaches, he opened his batteries and kept up a brisk cannonade. St. Clair strove with all his might to animate his fatigued troops, and ordered every man at morning and evening roll-call to the alarm-posts; while the greatest vigilance and alertness were enjoined.

Burgoyne, in the meantime, having thoroughly examined the American position, discovered its weak point. This was the unoccupied Sugar-Loaf hill, on the south side of the outlet from Lake George into Lake Champlain. A party of light-infantry had already encamped at its base, and the question was soon started whether it were possible to scale the hill and establish upon its summit a force sufficient for operations against the forts. The directing engineer of the British, Lieutenant Twiss, having been ordered to reconnoitre, reported that the hill had the entire command of the works and buildings of both Ticonderoga and Mount Independence, at the distance of about fourteen hundred yards from the former and fifteen hundred from the latter; that the ground might be levelled so as to receive cannon, and that the road by which to convey them, although difficult, might be made practicable in twenty-four hours; that the hill also commanded in reverse the bridge of communication across the lake between Ticonderoga and Mount Independence; and that from the summit the exact situation of the vessels could be seen, while not a movement of the Americans could be made during the day without being discovered, and even having their numbers counted.

Burgoyne, after this report, immediately ordered General Phillips to take possession of Sugar-Loaf hill. It was not effected without difficulty; for such was the steepness of the ascent, that it became necessary to hoist the cannon from tree to tree.* The final success, however, was complete; and, on the 5th of July, the British were in full possession, and signalized *their* triumph by christening the hill anew, by the name of "Mount Defiance." When St. Clair beheld the English flag flying from the summit, and the bristling cannon threatening his doomed post, he turned to his officers, saying, "We must away from this, for our situation has become a desperate one." A council of war was immediately called.

July 5. General St. Clair, having stated to his officers that there was every reason to believe that the batteries of the enemy were ready to open on the Ticonderoga side, that the camp was very much exposed to their fire, and that a

* Thacher.

simultaneous attack would probably be made upon Ticonderoga and Mount Independence, requested their opinion as to whether the whole of the troops, artillery, and stores, should be drawn over to Mount Independence for the defence of that post. The council unanimously agreed that they should be, on that very night. The general then proposed the question whether, after this movement, Mount Independence itself could be defended; and, if not, whether a retreat into the country were practicable. They unanimously expressed the opinion that, "as the enemy have already nearly surrounded us, and there remains nothing more to invest us completely but their occupying the neck of land betwixt the lake and the East creek (which is not more than three quarters of a mile over), and possessing themselves of the narrows betwixt that and Skenesborough—and thereby cutting off all communication with the country—a retreat ought to be undertaken as soon as possible, and that we shall be very fortunate to effect it."

The retreat having been determined upon, everything was done to effect it, without arousing the suspicions of the enemy. A cannonade was kept up every half hour from the redoubt against the advanced battery of the British; and, previous to striking the tents, all the lights were put out. The cannon left behind were ordered to be spiked, but the trunnions not to be knocked off, lest the noise might arouse the enemy. The evacuation had been resolved upon at three o'clock in the afternoon, but night was waited for, that it might be carried into execution with greater secrecy. Accord-

July 5. ingly, in the middle of the night, the whole camp was aroused, and began to move from both Ticonderoga and Mount Independence, with the usual bustle and confusion of a hasty retreat. The sick, the wounded, and the women, were brought out to the shore, together with as many of the cannon and stores as could be collected in the hurry. They were then thrust aboard of two hundred batteaux and boats, which, at three o'clock **July 6.** in the morning, pushed up Lake Champlain for Skenesborough, followed by an escort of five armed galleys and a guard of six hundred men, under Colonel Long, of New Hampshire. The main body of the troops crossed over the bridge from Ticonderoga to Mount Independence; and St. Clair, taking an unfinished road through the wilderness, on the east or Vermont side of the lake, led them on toward Hubbardton and Castleton, with the view of reaching Skenesborough by a circuitous march.

The retreat had been begun with great caution in the silence and darkness of the night, and the enemy seemed to be quite unconscious of the movement. But, by some blunder or accident, the house of General De Fermoy had been set on fire, and suddenly a blaze of light arose from Mount Independence, by which the British from their lofty position on the hills could see the Americans in full retreat. At once the sentries gave the alarm; the drums beat to arms; and the enemy, flocking into the deserted forts, prepared to follow in immediate pursuit.

The party on the lake got safely off; and, though looking "back with regret and forward with apprehension," there were not wanting those who were awakened to the picturesque interests about them. "The night was moonlit and pleasant; the sun burst forth in the morning with uncommon lustre; the day was fine; the water's surface serene and unruffled. The shore on each side exhibited a variegated view of huge rocks, caverns, and clefts, and the whole was bounded by a thick, impenetrable wilderness."* There were, fortunately, other available means to keep up the spirits of those less sensible to the exhilarating influence of the beauties of Nature. The drum and the fife struck up their cheering music; and among the hospital-stores gathered in the haste of the retreat, there were found many "dozen bottles of choice wine," which, by "breaking off their necks," were made available for the enlivenment of the desponding.†

Thus they sailed on during the night and a part of the next day, until they reached Skenesborough at three **July 7.** o'clock in the afternoon, the farthest point of the lake navigable by the galleys. Having got thus far in safety, there was no suspicion of further danger. The boats were lying quietly at the wharf, and the people, having landed, were loitering without concern upon the shore, when suddenly the enemy's fleet hove in sight, and began to pour a broadside into the American galleys and batteaux.

General Burgoyne was on board the frigate Royal George, on the lake, when he first learned the retreat of the Americans. He immediately ordered General

* Thacher.　　　　　　　　　　　† Ib.

Fraser with his brigade, and Baron Reidesel with a detachment of Brunswickers, to follow St. Clair by land, while he himself promptly pursued with his fleet the fugitives on the lake. The famous bridge, chain, and boom, which had cost such an immensity of labor and money, and were deemed so impenetrable, were before him. This was the security in the faith of which the Americans were reposing so complacently at Skenesborough. Bridge, boom, and chain, however, all gave way before the " uncommon efforts and industry" of Burgoyne, and so rapidly, that his gun-boats reached Skenesborough only two hours after the arrival of the American flotilla. He had thus almost overtaken it on the lake ; and, if he had, " horridly disastrous indeed would have been our fate," exclaims one of the pursued. Nor were they yet safe. The galleys at the wharves resisted for some time ; but soon two struck their colors, and the rest were blown up.

While the British gun-boats advanced to Skenesborough, the frigates came to anchor a short distance to the north, and landed a body of British soldiers and Indians. Colonel Long strove to rally his guard, and with them to give battle ; but his efforts were useless. His men were panic-struck, and, having set fire to the fort, mills, and batteaux, scattered in every direction, each one seeking only his personal safety in flight. A number of them, however, soon gathered together for mutual safety, and fled through a narrow defile, so closely pursued by the enemy, that those in the rear were constantly calling out, " March on! the Indi-

ans are at our heels!" Thus the fugitives pushed on the whole of that night, and until five o'clock the next morning, when they reached Fort Anne. **July 8.** Some of the sick succeeded in arriving at the same post, having made their escape in the boats by Wood creek, a small, navigable stream, which branches off from the lake at Skenesborough. All the artillery, provision, most of the baggage, and some of the invalids, fell into the hands of the enemy.

General Schuyler, being at Fort Edward, and hearing of the disaster, sent a small reinforcement, which so encouraged the fugitives under Colonel Long, that they not only stood their ground at Fort Anne, but prepared to sally out against their pursuers.

Lieutenant-Colonel Hill, with the ninth regiment of British regulars, had followed the panic-struck fugitives from Skenesborough, and had posted **July 7.** himself under cover of the woods near Fort Anne. Early the next morning the Americans sallied out, and, while one party attacked him in front with great vigor, another crossed a creek in order to take him in the rear. Colonel Hill was forced to shift his ground for fear of being surrounded, and post himself upon the summit of a hill. Here he was pursued and attacked, when a hot struggle ensued, which lasted for nearly two hours. Victory was almost in the grasp of the Americans, when a number of savages—detached by Burgoyne from Skenesborough—rushed out of the neighboring forests, and sent up their terrible war-whoop, which was answered by three cheers from the British troops, and Colonel Long's men gave way. Retiring to Fort Anne, which was a small picket-fort of little importance, the Americans set fire to it, and then proceeded to Fort Edward, on the Hudson, some thirty miles distant. Here they found General Schuyler, who had come on with the small reinforcement **July 9.** sent from Peekskill, which he had been anxiously awaiting, for the purpose of marching to the aid of the post at Ticonderoga.

"I am here," writes Schuyler from Fort Edward, "at the head of a handful of men (not above fifteen hundred), with little ammunition (not above five rounds to a man), having neither balls nor lead to make any. The country is in the deepest consternation; no carriages to remove the stores from Fort George, which I expect every moment to hear is attacked; and what adds to my distress is, that a report prevails that I had given orders for the evacuation of Ticonderoga."

Schuyler could learn nothing of the fate of General St. Clair and the main body of the troops. The Americans who had escaped by the lake to Skenesborough, and arrived at Fort Edward, could not clear up the mystery. They merely reported the retreat from Ticonderoga, and their own disasters and adventures. Whether St. Clair had been cut off by the enemy, or had succeeded in making his escape, and was now wandering through the forest wildernesses, was a question the solution of which was anxiously looked for. In two days more the solution came, in the intelligence that St. Clair was safe, with a remnant of his troops, in Vermont.

Let us now trace his course from the moment of abandoning the posts at Ticonderoga and Mount Independence.

It was three o'clock in the morning before St. Clair had begun his retreat with his van, and his rear **July 7.** was still lingering not far from the forts, when the enemy took possession. General Fraser, a brave and active officer, had no sooner planted the British flag, than he was out in pursuit with his brigade. Baron Reidesel, with his Brunswickers, had been ordered to reinforce him; but the heavy, formal Germans did not move with the same celerity as Fraser's light-troops, which pushed on quickly in advance.

St. Clair, too, did not linger, but moved on the whole day through the forest wilderness with great speed, and did not halt his advanced troops until the afternoon, at Hubbardton. Here he remained a short time for his rear-guard and stragglers; but, learning that they were coming, St. Clair left Colonel Warner, with a hundred and fifty men, to await their arrival, and pushed on until night, when he reached Castleton, some thirty miles distant from Ticonderoga.

Warner had been ordered to join the rear-guard when it arrived at Hubbardton, and then advance with it toward Castleton. When, however, Colonel Francis, who commanded the rear-guard, came up, he and Warner, either confiding in their numbers, which amounted to over fifteen hundred men, or underrating the activity of their pursuers, determined to halt for the night at Hubbardton. Early the next morning they were **July 8.**

parading their troops, in readiness to follow St. Clair, when General Fraser suddenly marched into Hubbardton! This brave and expeditious officer had kept close upon the heels of Warner the whole day before; and, as his own force was small, amounting to only eight hundred and fifty men, and he knew that St. Clair could not be far in advance, he ordered his troops to lie on their arms for the night, waiting to attack the rear of the Americans when their van should be sufficiently distant. The occasion was now offered; and Fraser, although with an inferior force, being too impatient to await the coming up of the Germans, at once began an attack. The Americans generally bore the onset gallantly; but Colonel Hale, who is said to have been dispirited by a long illness, fled immediately with his whole regiment of militia in the direction of Castleton. This greatly diminished the force of the Americans; but those left bravely stood their ground, and at their very first fire made great havoc in the front ranks of the enemy, striking down twenty-one men, killing Major Grant, a distinguished British officer, and wounding the young earl of Balcarras, at the head of the light-infantry. Colonels Warner and Francis led on their men with great gallantry, and were themselves foremost in the fight. The Americans were apparently driving their opponents from the ground, when the drums were heard of the German troops coming up to reinforce Fraser. This dispirited the Americans and encouraged the Brit-

ish. The latter now made a vigorous charge with their bayonets, and remained masters of the field. The loss of the enemy was a hundred and eighty-three in killed and wounded; that of the Americans amounted to over three hundred, twelve of whom were officers, and among them Colonel Francis. The recreant Hale and his militia met with a characteristic fate: they surrendered to a small party of British troops, much inferior to themselves.

General St. Clair, at Castleton, hearing the firing, immediately sent his aid-de-camp to order two militia regiments—which were encamped three or four miles in his rear—to reinforce the troops at Hubbardton. They, however, refused to obey. St. Clair then prepared to march himself; but, finding that the Americans had been put to flight, he continued his retreat. Skenesborough had been his object, in the circuitous route which he had taken; but an officer of one of the American galleys having come in and reported that the British were pursuing in force toward that place, he changed his line of march, and struck the woods to his left, on the route to Bennington (in the New-Hampshire grants, now Vermont); and, while on his way thither, intelligence was first received by General Schuyler, at Fort Edward, of his safety.

"The king," says Horace Walpole, "on receiving the account of the taking of Ticonderoga, ran into the queen's room, crying, 'I have beat them—beat all the Americans!'"

CHAPTER L.

Washington incredulous of the Fall of Ticonderoga.—He does not doubt the Advance of General Burgoyne.—Prepares to give Him a Check.—Urges that General Arnold be sent North for the Purpose.—Moves his own Army nearer the Hudson.—Encamps at the Clove.—He disapproves of the Abandonment of Ticonderoga.—Disappointed, but not disheartened.—General St. Clair at Fort Edward.—The American Force at the North.—Its Sorry Condition.—Fortunate Delay of Burgoyne.—General Schuyler fortifies a Camp at Moses' Creek.—The Discouragement of the Country.—Schuyler slandered.—St. Clair assumes the Responsibility.—A Lost Post: a Saved State.—The American Troops disaffected.—Arnold arrives at Moses' Creek.—His Disinterested Conduct.—Burgoyne on the Move.—A Difficult March.—Proclamations and Counter-Proclamations.—The British caught napping in Rhode Island.—A Novel Battering-Ram.—Capture of General Prescott.

1777. WHEN the first rumor of the loss of Ticonderoga reached Washington, he was loath to believe it. General Schuyler had written him from Stillwater, **July 10.** while on his way to Fort Edward, what he had heard; but the entire account appeared so confused to the commander-in-chief, that he could not "establish any certain deduction from it," and hoped that it might prove "premature and groundless." Whether true or not, he was no longer in doubt that General Burgoyne had come up Lake Champlain, determined to push his way toward the Hudson, and that a check to his progress was absolutely necessary. The militia from New York and the New-England states must be instantly called out in full force, and an active, spirited officer appointed to conduct and lead them on. General Arnold was recommended as the man for this business. "He is active, judicious, and brave, and an officer in whom the militia will repose great confidence;" and, besides, "he is well acquainted with that country, and with the routes and most important passes and defiles in it,"

wrote Washington to Congress, advising that body to send Arnold at once from Philadelphia to the northern department.

Believing, too, that Sir William Howe would push against the Highland passes, in order to co-operate with General Burgoyne, Washington moved his own army toward the North river. From Morristown, where he had encamped after leaving Middlebrook, he marched to **July 13.** Pompton plains. He was now no longer in doubt concerning the fall of Ticonderoga, for General Schuyler had sent him more specific information from Fort Edward. Washington pronounced the evacuation of the posts upon Lake Champlain as "among the most unfortunate that could have befallen us." Schuyler, having written that he had not been able to learn anything about General St. Clair and the army under him, Washington writes in answer that he is **July 13.** astonished beyond expression. "I am totally at loss," he says, "to conceive what has become of them. The whole affair is so mysterious, that it even baffles conjecture." He was sufficiently

63

sanguine, however, to hope that they might have "changed their design of retreating from the forts, and returned to them," although he feared that they had all fallen into the hands of the enemy.

July 15. Washington, having marched his army still nearer to the Hudson, and encamped at the Clove, he here receives a despatch from General Schuyler, clearing up the mystery in regard to St. Clair. He expresses his chagrin and surprise that Ticonderoga and Mount Independence should have been evacuated—an event, he says, "not apprehended, nor within the compass of my reasoning." Even at this late moment, Washington, by some strange and inexplicable neglect on the part of Schuyler, had not been correctly informed of the condition of St. Clair and his troops previous to their retreat. He very naturally declares that he knows not upon what principle the evacuation was founded, and that it was difficult to be accounted for, "*if the garrison amounted to five thousand men, in high spirits, healthy, well supplied with provisions and ammunition,* and the eastern militia marching to their succor."

Washington, however, does not allow himself to indulge long in useless regrets. "This stroke," he writes, "is severe indeed, and has distressed us much." But, with his usual firm reliance upon the justice of his cause, he calmly says: "Notwithstanding things at present have a dark and gloomy aspect, I hope a spirited opposition will check the progress of General Burgoyne's army, and that the confidence derived from his success will hurry him into measures that will in their consequences be favorable to us. We should never despair. Our situation has before been unpromising, and has changed for the better: so I trust it will again. If new difficulties arise, we must only put forth new exertions, and proportion our efforts to the exigency of the times."

General St. Clair finally succeeded in reaching Schuyler, at Fort Edward, **July 12.** with the remnant of his jaded troops, after their long and painful march through a wild country of forest, mountain, and morass. The whole northern army, when thus concentrated, numbered only four thousand four hundred men, inclusive of the militia. They were deficient in almost every requirement: they had neither tents, houses, barns, boards, nor any shelter, except a little brushwood; their supply of ammunition was so scanty, that the inhabitants of Albany were obliged to strip the windows of the shops and houses of their leaden weights to melt into balls; provisions they had in tolerable abundance, but means to cook them were so scarce, that only one camp-kettle could be afforded to every twenty men. Under these circumstances disease increased, and the troops were so disheartened, that desertions began to prevail to an alarming extent.

Fortunately for the Americans, General Burgoyne lingered at Skenesborough and in its neighborhood, waiting for the arrival of tents, baggage, and provisions. This delay of the British general gave Schuyler an opportunity of making some efforts to strengthen himself and oppose the march of the enemy. A position was selected for a fortified camp at Moses' creek, on the Hudson, five miles below Fort Edward. Kosciusko, who was chief-engineer, had chosen the ground and superintended the works. Everything was done, by the destruction of bridges, and the felling of trees across the roads and passes, to obstruct the march of the enemy from the north. Schuyler, however, with all his activity, found that his exertions were of little avail. His troops were daily diminishing by disease and desertion, and the country failed to respond to his earnest appeals for aid. "Every letter I receive from the county of Tryon," he says, "advise me that the inhabitants of it will lay down their arms unless I support them with continental troops.... The district of Schoharie," he adds, "has also pointedly intimated that, unless continental troops are sent them, they will also submit to the enemy."

The country was, in fact, greatly disheartened by the loss of the northern posts, for which Generals Schuyler and St. Clair were unjustly held responsible. It was even believed that they had acted the part of traitors to their country, and absurdly rumored that they had been paid for their treason by Burgoyne in silver balls, which he had shot into the American camp! General St. Clair soon relieved Schuyler from all responsibility for the abandonment of Ticonderoga and Mount Independence. "He knew nothing of the matter until it was over," was St. Clair's public refutation of the slanders against Schuyler. "As to myself," he continues, "I was perfectly easy. I was conscious of the uprightness and propriety of my conduct, and despised the vague censure of an uninformed populace." More than this, St. Clair justified his act, not only on the ground of its necessity, but its policy. "Although I have lost a post," he exclaims, "I have eventually saved a state;" and, notwithstanding the slanders which for a time were visited upon him by the ignorant and uncharitable, it was not long before his proud boast was recognised as the statement of a fact.

These slanders against the generals, however, circulated so freely and with so much effect in the army, that the troops became widely disaffected, and either lost all spirit for the service or abandoned it altogether. Schuyler himself gives this discouraging account of his force: "It consists of about twenty-seven hundred continental troops; of **July 27.** militia from the state of Connecticut, one major, one captain, two lieutenants, two ensigns, one adjutant, one quartermaster, six sergeants, one drummer, six sick and three rank and file fit for duty; the rest, after remaining three or four days, deserted us: of those from the county of Berkshire (in the Massachusetts), who consisted of upward of twelve hundred, half of which were to have remained, somewhat more than two hundred are left, the remainder having also deserted: of Colonel Moseley's regiment from the county of Hampshire (Massachusetts), about ten or twelve are left, the rest having deserted: of Colonel Porter's regiment of the county of Hampshire, about two hundred left: of the militia of the county of Albany, ten hundred and fifty are left, being forty-six more than half of what were upon the ground, when it was resolved to let half return to their habitations."

"That torpor," adds Schuyler, as a commentary upon the facts he had just stated, "criminal indifference, and want of spirit, which so generally prevails, is more dangerous than all the efforts of the enemy. Nor is that jealousy and spirit of detraction, which so unhappily prevails, of small detriment to our cause."

Major-General Arnold, flattered by the complimentary preference of Washington, and eager for action, did not hesitate to proceed to the North when ordered by Congress, in accordance with the advice of the commander-in-chief. Although he would thus be obliged to serve under St. Clair, who was one of the five major-generals whose promotion above him had so grievously wounded Arnold's spirit, he yet for the present generously waived all personal feeling, and took the subordinate position. On joining General Schuyler, at Fort Edward, Arnold moved with the army to Moses' creek, and received the command of the left division, encamped on one side of the Hudson river; while Major-General St. Clair commanded the right, on the opposite side.

General Burgoyne, after lingering three weeks at Skenesborough, at length began his march toward the south. Instead of returning to Ticonderoga, and thence proceeding by Lake George to Fort George (whence there was a good road to Fort Edward, which was his object), he determined to strike across the country by a more direct route. Fearful, however, that turning back would appear like a retreat, and thus destroy the *prestige* of his late

triumph, or influenced by the opinion of the tory Major Skene, of Skenesborough (who is suspected of having advised the land-route, that the value of his property, of which he was an extensive holder in that neighborhood, might be enhanced by a military road), Burgoyne marched forward. His route was naturally a difficult and laborious one, through a country of forest and swamp, where he had to cut down trees, plunge into morasses, and throw bridges across the numerous creeks, ravines, and gulleys. The weather, too, was sultry, and the musketoes abounded, greatly tormenting his men, whose European freshness seemed to provoke these annoying insects to more than ordinary bloodthirstiness. Schuyler's precautions in destroying the bridges, and obstructing the roads and passes with felled trees, also added greatly to the difficulties and delays of Burgoyne's march. He, however, continued his route toward Fort Edward; while General Phillips, with the artillery, provisions, and baggage, guarded by a strong detachment of troops, proceeded by the way of Lake George, with the purpose of forming on the Hudson a junction with the main body, which had preceded him by land.

In the course of his progress, while the country was impressed by his recent triumphs and his overwhelming force, Burgoyne strove to induce the inhabitants to abandon the American cause. He issued a swelling proclamation, abounding in the usual promises of reward for compliance and threats of punishment for disobedience. General Schuyler put forth a no less rhetorical counter-edict, in which the people, being reminded how the British in New Jersey had "cruelly butchered, without distinction of age or sex; ravished children from ten to women of eighty years of age;" burned, pillaged, and destroyed, not even sparing " in their sacrilegious fury those edifices dedicated to the worship of Almighty God," were told that the same fate awaited them.

While everything thus appeared so disastrous for the American cause in the North, an event occurred in Rhode Island which, however trifling in itself, greatly stimulated the spirit of the country. General Prescott was in command of the British troops at Rhode island, and held his headquarters at a farmhouse near the water, about five miles from Newport. Lieutenant-Colonel Barton, in command of a regiment of Rhode-Island militia, determined to surprise him and carry him off. He accordingly selected thirty-eight men, in whom he had confidence, and set out on the expedition one dark night. From Warwick neck they rowed over in two boats, with muffled oars, to the opposite side of the bay, a distance of ten miles. Having passed the British men-of-war and guard-boats without exciting alarm, they landed, and silently proceeded on. Upon reaching the house, they secured the sentinel, and entered. Arriving at the door of the room where the British general slept, they found it locked; whereupon a negro of the name of Prince, who was at Barton's side, and is spoken of as his " confidential friend," with a leap " plunged his head against the door, and knocked out the panel, through which the colonel entered."[*] Prescott was found in bed, and immediately secured. His aid-de-camp attempted to escape from the house by leaping through a window, but was caught and carried over to the mainland together with the general. Barton and his party returned with their prize across the bay, silently and cautiously as they came. Prescott, who seemed greatly surprised at the success of Barton's enterprise, remarked to him as they landed, " Sir, I did not think it possible you could escape the vigilance of the water-guards."

The boldness, skill, and success, with which the enterprise had been conducted, were highly lauded. Congress voted Barton a sword, and promoted him to the rank of a colonel of the continental army. The country exulted more particularly over the capture of Prescott, because in an officer of his rank they held an equivalent for Major-General Lee, still a prisoner, for whom Washington immediately proposed to exchange the British commander. In the meanwhile, Prescott was ordered to be " genteelly accommodated, but strongly guarded," and removed into some place " where the people are generally well affected." He was refused his liberty on parole, and it was determined to treat him in every respect as Lee was treated by the British.

* Holmes's Annals of America.

CHAPTER LI.

Puzzling Conduct of General Howe.—He is supposed to seek a Junction with General Burgoyne.—Lord Stirling sent to Peekskill.—The Departure of the British Fleet from New York.—A Pithy Letter from General Putnam.—A Trick of the British exposed.—The Enemy off the Capes of Delaware.—They sail away again.—Washington perplexed.—He moves his Army to Germantown.—Washington in Philadelphia.—Meeting with the Marquis de Lafayette.—His Life and Character.—His Devotion to the American Cause.—His Interviews with Franklin and Deane.—His Escape from France.—Arrival in America.—His First Impressions.—His Joyous Progress.—His First Rebuff.—Final Success.—Appointed Major-General.—Becomes a Member of Washington's Family.—Washington's Opinion of Him —Count Pulaski.—His Life and Character.—He is appointed Major-General and Commander of the Cavalry.

1777. GENERAL HOWE'S " conduct is puzzling and embarrassing beyond measure; so are the informations which I get," writes Washington. " At **July 22.** one time the ships are standing up toward the North river; in a little they are going up the sound; and in an hour after they are going out of the Hook." Washington, however, was for awhile so far persuaded that Howe's object was to form a junction with General Burgoyne, by the Hudson, that he sent Lord Stirling with his division to Peekskill, and moved with the rest of his army to Ramapo. But, while here, he learned that **July 24.** Sir William Howe had left New York, with a fleet of two hundred and sixty-seven sail, and a land-force of about sixteen thousand men, made up of thirty-six British and Hessian battalions, a powerful artillery, a New-York corps called the Queen's Rangers, and a regiment of light-horse. Sir Henry Clinton was left at New York with seventeen battalions, a regiment of light-horse, and a corps of American loyalists. Clinton had been to Europe, and his return was first made known to General Putnam by receiving from him a flag of truce, with a demand to give up Lieutenant Palmer. This provoked the following memorable reply :—

" HEADQUARTERS. 7 *Aug.*, 1777.

" Edmund Palmer, an officer in the enemy's service, was taken as a spy, lurking within our lines; he has been tried as a spy, condemned as a spy, and shall be executed as a spy, and the flag is ordered to depart immediately.

" ISRAEL PUTNAM.

" P. S.—He has been accordingly executed."

Washington also received such information as induced him to believe that the Delaware was General Howe's destination. It became necessary, therefore, to move the army back again in that direction, and to recall the divisions of Lord Stirling and General Sullivan from the Hudson river.

As Washington was preparing for his march toward the Delaware, he received through General Putnam the following letter, addressed to General Burgoyne, which a young man had brought into the American camp at Peekskill :—

"NEW YORK, *July* 20, 1777.

"DEAR SIR: I have received your letter of the 14th of May, from Quebec, and shall fully observe the contents. The expedition to B——n [Boston] will take place of that up the North river. If, according to my expectations, we may succeed rapidly in the possession of B——, the enemy having no force of consequence there, I shall, without loss of time, proceed to co-operate with you in the defeat of the rebel army opposed to you. Clinton is sufficiently strong to amuse Washington and Putnam. I am now making demonstration to the southward, which I think will have the full effect in carrying our plan into execution. Success attend you!   "W. HOWE."

The story of the young man who had presented himself, and given up the letter, was this: He had, he said, been a prisoner in New York, and was offered a handsome sum for carrying the letter to General Burgoyne, which at first he refused to do, but subsequently consented, with the intention of taking it to the American camp. Washington no sooner read the letter, than he saw that it was a trick. "It was evidently intended," says he, "to fall into our hands. The complexion of it, the circumstances attending it, evince this beyond a doubt in my mind." He accordingly urged Putnam to lose no time in sending on General Sullivan and Lord Stirling with their divisions, while Washington himself moved the main body to Coryell's ferry on the Delaware, in order to be ready to cross that river as soon as the enemy made a movement toward Philadelphia. To General Gates, who was then in that city, Washington wrote, urging him to be on the alert for information, and to transmit it as soon as he had ascertained it to his satisfaction; for he declares that he himself will pay no regard to any flying reports of the appearance of the fleet.

From Philadelphia soon came the intelligence that the enemy had arrived off the capes of Delaware. Next day, however, an express came hurrying into the camp with the news that the fleet had borne away again, taking an easterly course. "Now, surely the North river must be their object." thought Washington; and he orders General Sullivan back again to Peekskill, for the "importance of preventing Mr. Howe's getting possession of the Highlands, by a *coup de main*, is infinite to America." Washington, thus perplexed by the strange movements of the enemy, finally moves his army across the Delaware, and encamps at Germantown, about six miles from Philadelphia. His letter to his brother Augustine at this time is the best exposition of his movements and perplexities:—

Aug. 5.

"Since General Howe removed from the Jerseys," writes Washington, "the troops under my command have been more harassed by marching and countermarching than by any other thing that has happened to them in the course of the campaign. After he had embarked his troops, the presumption that he would co-operate upon the North river, to form a junction with General Burgoyne, was so strong, that I removed from Middlebrook to Morristown, and from Morristown to the Clove, a narrow passage lead-ing through the Highlands, about eigh-teen miles from the river. Indeed, upon some pretty strong presumptive evidence, I threw two divisions over the North riv-er. In this situation we lay till about the 24th ultimo [July], when, receiving cer-tain information that the fleet had actu-ally sailed from Sandy Hook, and upon the concurring sentiment of every one, though I acknowledge my doubts of it were strong, that Philadelphia was their object, we countermarched, and got to Coryell's ferry on the Delaware, about thirty-three miles above the city, on the 27th [July], where I lay until I received information from Congress that the ene-my were actually at the capes of Dela-ware. This brought us in great haste to this place [Germantown], for the defence of the city [Philadelphia]. But, in less than twenty-four hours after our arrival, we got accounts of the disappearance of the fleet on the 31st [July]; since which, nothing having been heard of them, we have remained here in a very irksome state of suspense; some imagining that they are gone to the southward, whilst a majority, in whose opinion upon this oc-casion I concur, are satisfied that they are gone eastward. The fatigue, however, and injury, which men must sustain by long marches in such extreme heat as we have felt for the last five days, must keep us quiet till we hear something of the destination of the enemy."

While the army was encamped at Ger-mantown, Washington was frequently in Philadelphia. On one of these occasions he for the first time met the marquis de Lafayette, at dinner. When the party was breaking up, Washington took him aside, and, having complimented him up-on the noble disinterestedness which he had shown in behalf of the American cause, invited him to headquarters, telling him that he might always consider it as his home, and himself as one of the fam-ily. The American commander, however, remarked in a tone of pleasantry that he could not promise him the luxuries of a court, or even the conveniences which his former habits might have rendered essential to his comfort; but added that, since the young nobleman had become an American soldier, he would doubtless try to accommodate himself to the char-acter which he had assumed, and submit to the manners, customs, and privations, of a republican army.

. The marquis GILBERT MOTTIER DE LA-FAYETTE was born on the 6th of Septem-ber, 1757, at Chavagnac, in the province of Auvergne, France, and was married be-fore he was eighteen years of age to the grand-daughter of the duc de Noailles. Like most French youth of rank and for-tune at that time, he entered the army; and, while on duty at Metz, he tells us that his enthusiasm in behalf of the Amer-ican cause was first awakened. The duke of Gloucester, a brother of King George III., happened to be on a visit to Metz, where he was complimented with a din-ner by the commandant of the place. The young marquis de Lafayette was one of the guests on the occasion. The Ameri-can war *(apropos to some despatches late-ly received in England)* became a topic of conversation at dinner; and, although the royal English duke was not likely to have given a very favorable coloring to the cause of the "rebels," Lafayette's interest was at once so much awakened by his grace's talk, that, even before he arose from the table, the thought suggested itself to him of offering his services in behalf of a people struggling for independence.

With his young heart filled with enthusiasm for liberty, the marquis hurries to Paris, and there seeks out his two bosom friends, Count Ségur and Viscount de Noailles, to whom he announces his intention to go to America, and entreats them to join him in the enterprise. They readily consent; but, on consulting their parents, upon whom they are dependent for support, they are forced to abandon the scheme. They, however, kept their friend's secret. Lafayette, being in the enjoyment of an income of nearly forty thousand dollars a year, was in a position of greater independence than his youthful companions, and therefore resolutely clung to his original plan. He soon obtained an interview with the count de Broglie, then prime minister under Louis XVI, who, with the cautious prudence of age, strove to deter the young enthusiast from what appeared to him a rash and dangerous enterprise. "I have," said the veteran, "seen your uncle die in the wars of Italy; I witnessed your father's death at the battle of Minden; and I will not be accessory to the ruin of the only remaining branch of the family."

De Broglie continued urgently to counsel the youthful marquis against the undertaking; but, finding his efforts useless,

he introduced him to Baron de Kalb, a Prussian officer, who had been in America, in order that the inexperienced Lafayette might obtain from him the introductions and information he desired. De Kalb presented him to Silas Deane, the American commissioner in Paris. "When I presented my boyish face to Mr. Deane," says Lafayette, "I spoke more of my ardor in the cause than of my experience; but I dwelt much upon the effect my departure would excite in France, and he signed our agreement." The purport of this agreement was, that the young marquis should, on joining the American service, receive from Congress the appointment of major-general, and be conveyed to America in a vessel about to sail, with munitions of war for the patriot armies. In the meantime, news having arrived of the success of the British at Fort Washington, and of the subsequent retreat of the American army through New Jersey, the activity of French sympathy was so far checked, that the despatching of the French vessel with supplies was necessarily abandoned.

The enthusiasm of the ardent Lafayette was, however, proof against the most disastrous news. When urged to give up his scheme, he answered: "My zeal and love of liberty have, perhaps, been hitherto the prevailing motives; but now I see a chance for usefulness, which I had not anticipated. I have money: I will purchase a ship, which shall convey to America myself, my companions, and the freight for Congress." Accordingly, he did purchase a ship; and, while it was fitting at Bordeaux, for sea, Lafayette took the occasion of visiting England. His wife's uncle, the marquis de Noailles, was the French embassador in London; and under such auspices he was, of course, readily admitted to the court and the society which gathered about it. His first visit, however, was to an American, Mr. Bancroft. He was subsequently presented to the king; he danced at the homes of Lord George Germain, then minister of American affairs, and of Lord Rawdon, who had just returned from New York; and joined General Sir Henry Clinton in his box at the opera, whom he was destined afterward to meet as an enemy on the field of battle. Lafayette says, in regard to these intimacies with the society of London: "Whilst I concealed my intentions of going to make war in America, I openly avowed my sentiments; I often defended the Americans; I rejoiced at their success at Trenton; and my opposition spirit obtained for me an invitation to breakfast with Lord Shelburne. I refused the offers made me to visit the seaports, the vessels fitting out against the *rebels*, and everything that might be construed into an abuse of confidence."

On Lafayette's return to France, he concealed himself for some days at Passy, where he saw but a few of his personal friends and some Americans, among whom was Doctor Franklin, who, with Arthur Lee, of Virginia, had become joint commissioners with Deane. Franklin admired the spirit and generous disinterestedness of the marquis, and furthered his objects. On Lafayette's leaving for Bordeaux, to embark, the French government, through the complaint of the British embassador

in Paris, was on the alert, and strove to prevent his departure. His family also, with the exception of his young wife, who shared in her husband's enthusiasm for the American cause, were anxious that he should abandon his scheme. He succeeded in reaching Bordeaux, and immediately set sail for Passage, a small seaport in Spain, where he proposed to wait for the ship's papers. Here, however, followed him a *lettre de cachet* from the king, forbidding his departure, and letters from the government ministers and from his family, insisting up the abandonment of his enterprise. But finally, after some hair-breadth escapes from pursuit, and meeting with one or two romantic adventures, he got safely to sea, leaving his young wife and child behind him. Baron de Kalb and several other military personages, looking for service in America, accompanied him. The ship arrived at Charleston, and the young marquis's impressions seem to have been of the most agreeable kind. The democratic features of American life were the first to catch the eye of the high-born nobleman fresh from the ceremonious court of Versailles, but the effect was apparently no less delightful than new.

"I will now tell you," writes Lafayette to his wife, "about the country and its inhabitants. They are as agreeable as my enthusiasm had painted them. Simplicity of manners, kindness, love of country and of liberty, and a delightful equality, everywhere prevail. The wealthiest man and the poorest are on a level; and, although there are some large fortunes, I challenge any one to discover the slightest difference between the manners of these two classes respectively toward each other. I first saw the country-life at the house of Major Huger. I am now in the city [Charleston], where everything is very much after the English fashion, except that there is more simplicity, equality, cordiality, and courtesy, here than in England.

"The city of Charleston is one of the handsomest and best built, and the inhabitants among the most agreeable, that I have ever seen. The American women are very pretty, simple in their manners, and exhibit a neatness which is everywhere cultivated, even more studiously than in England. What most charms me is, that all the citizens are brethren. In America, there are no poor, nor even what we call peasantry. Each individual has his own honest property, and the same rights as the most wealthy landed proprietor. The inns are very different from those of Europe: the host and hostess sit at table with you, and do the honors of a comfortable meal; and, on going away, you pay your bill without higgling. When one does not wish to go to an inn, there are country-houses where the title of a good American is a sufficient passport to all those civilities paid in Europe to one's friend."

Receiving everywhere a flattering welcome, the young Lafayette goes on joyously from South to North Carolina, and thence through Virginia to Maryland and Pennsylvania. On reaching Philadelphia, where Congress was assembled, he submits his letters to Mr. Lovell, the chairman of the committee of foreign affairs,

The next day, Lafayette presents himself at the hall of Congress, where Mr. Lovell comes out to meet him, with the discouraging intelligence that, as Congress had been embarrassed with the applications of so many foreigners, there was but little chance of his success. The young marquis, however, was not to be driven away by such a rebuff: so he immediately wrote to the president of Congress, asking permission to serve in the American army, on these two conditions: that he should receive no pay, and that he should act as a volunteer. These terms were so different from those asked by the crowd of foreign military adventurers, that they were at once accepted; and the youthful Lafayette, not yet twenty years of age, was appointed major-general in the American army.

His encouraging reception by Washington, added to the success of his final application to Congress, greatly inspirited Lafayette, and he became eager for service. His horses and equipage were immediately sent to the camp at Germantown; and he availed himself of the commander-in-chief's invitation, and became, as it were, a member of his family. On the very next day after making his acquaintance at the dinner-party, Washington invited him to ride out with him, to inspect the fortifications on the Delaware. These courtesies flattered the marquis, but did not satisfy his desires. He did not seem to understand the honorary nature of his major-generalship, and expected the rank to be accompanied by a command. "It is true he has said," writes Washington, "that he is young and inexperienced, but at the same time has always accompanied it with a hint that, so soon as I shall think him fit for the command of a division, he shall be ready to enter upon the duties of it, and in the meantime has offered his services for a smaller command; to which I may add, that he has actually applied to me, by direction, he says, from Mr. Hancock, for commissions for his two aids-de-camp." Washington was perplexed by the pertinacity of the young and ardent Frenchman, and asked for instructions from Congress. That body replied that Lafayette's appointment was only honorary, and that Washington was at liberty to use his own judgment in regard to the bestowal of a command. The young marquis was accordingly left for the present in the enjoyment only of the rank of a major-general, while he served in the army as a volunteer.

Lafayette is described as being at this early period nearly six feet high, large but not corpulent, and not very elegant in person, his shoulders being broad and high. His features were irregular, his forehead remarkably high, his nose large and long; his eyebrows projected prominently over his eyes, which were full of fire, and of a hazel color. He spoke but few words of broken English.*

Baron DE KALB, who came over from France with Lafayette, was also (though subsequently to the appointment of the marquis) made a major-general. The services of most of the other French officers, however, who accompanied them, were not accepted, and they returned home.

* Thacher.

Another distinguished foreigner soon presented himself at the headquarters of the commander-in-chief. "Count Pulaski, of Poland, an officer famous throughout Europe for his bravery and conduct in defence of the liberties of his country against the three great invading powers of Russia, Austria, and Prussia, will have the honor of delivering this into your excellency's hands," were the words of Doctor Franklin, in the letter written by him at Paris to Washington, introducing the illustrious Pole.

Count CASIMIR PULASKI, in the rebellion against King Stanislaus Augustus, of Poland (who, as a creature of the empress Catharine II., was upheld on the throne against the wishes of the nation), had already given proof of his devotion to liberty. His father had sacrificed his life in the same cause, and the son succeeded him as the leader of the insurgents; but, failing to gather a sufficient force to resist the efforts of Russia, in conjunction with the Polish king, to subdue his country, young Pulaski determined to possess himself of the person of Stanislaus, and compel him to head the people in their struggle for independence. Accordingly, Pulaski, with thirty-nine bold associates, entered Warsaw, seized the king, and were carrying him off, when the guard came up and rescued the royal prisoner. Pulaski's meager force of patriots was soon after beaten by the combined armies of Russia and Prussia, and he himself forced to fly from the country. He subsequently joined the Turks, in whose service he fought against his old enemies the Russians. When the war was over, Pulaski went to Paris, where he met Franklin, by whom, on his resolving to go to America, he was commended, as we have seen, to Washington.

The commander-in-chief proposed that Pulaski should have the command of the cavalry, in which hitherto there had been no officer of higher rank than colonel. General Joseph Reed had been offered the appointment, but had declined. Washington recommended Pulaski for the command, saying to the president of Congress: "This gentleman, we are told, has been, like us, engaged in defending the liberty and independence of his country, and has sacrificed his fortune to his zeal for those objects. He derives from hence a title to our respect, that ought to operate in his favor, as far as the good of the service will permit."

Count Pulaski was raised to the rank of brigadier-general by Congress, and, after the battle of the Brandywine, given the command of the cavalry, in accordance with the suggestion made by the commander-in-chief.

CHAPTER LII.

Burgoyne's Progress.—General Schuyler moves his Camp to Fort Miller.—Alarm of the Country.—Schuyler rebukes the Cowards.—His Efforts for Defence.—Burgoyne rallies the Savages.—Unchecked Ferocity.—Story of Jane M'Crea.—Burgoyne horrified.—Impotent Attempt to punish the Murderers.—The Effect of the Tragedy upon the Country.—Burgoyne pushes on to Fort Edward.—The Americans retire to Stillwater.—The British besiege Fort Stanwix.—A Summons unheeded.—Peter Gansevoort in Command.—Old Herkimer to the Rescue.—A Struggle.—A Fratricidal Fight.—The Patriots in Possession of the Field.—Death of Herkimer.—Schuyler sends Relief to the Patriots on the Mohawk.

1777. GENERAL BURGOYNE continued his toilsome march toward the Hudson, and so slow was his progress, that he did not reach Fort Anne till the end of July. On his approach, General Schuyler abandoned his position at Moses' creek, and moved down the Hudson to Fort Miller. The inhabitants of the country were still in great alarm, and fled from their houses and their farms, abandoning to the enemy their flocks and ripening harvests as the British advanced. The people even in Albany were panic-stricken, and called upon Schuyler for protection. Vexed at their unmanly fears, Schuyler strove to inspire them with greater fortitude. "Is it," he writes, "becoming rational beings, when a misfortune has happened to them, to despond and not to counteract the evil? Surely not; and, if the militia would do their duty, we should soon make the enemy repent their ever having come into the country, and retreat with infinitely more loss than we have experienced; but if the militia will sit still, folding their arms, and not make use of those exertions which God has put in their power to make use of for their own defence, they certainly will become the victims of an enemy whose very mercies are cruelty."

General Schuyler in the meantime was unwearied in his efforts to bring all the resources of the country to bear in its defence. He wrote the most pressing letters to the governors of New England, to the committees of safety, and to Washington, asking for reinforcements. From the commander-in-chief he soon received the encouraging response that he would despatch General Lincoln, of Massachusetts, to use his great influence in calling out the militia of New England; and Colonel Morgan, with his riflemen, to protect the country against the barbarous Indian allies of the British.

General Burgoyne had gathered together a large force of Indian warriors. To those which he had brought with him from Canada were now added the Ottawas and allied tribes. It was supposed by the British government that these savages would terrify the country, and such had been its object in employing them. Burgoyne, naturally a humane person, had hoped to keep the cruel instincts of the Indians in check by the exercise of military discipline, and the influence of the French-Canadians who led them on. These wild denizens of the forest fully served the purpose designed of inspiring terror, but it was soon found impracticable to keep them within the constraints of civilized warfare. A tragic incident now occured, which proved how useless had been Burgoyne's attempt to tame the ferocity of his Indian allies. The British army had reached Fort Anne, and was preparing to move on to Fort Edward. The Americans had retired with their main body, leaving a rear-guard at the fort, ready to evacuate it on the approach of the enemy in force.

Near Fort Edward lived a Mrs. M'Neil, who, being a royalist in sentiment and a kinswoman of General Fraser, remained, awaiting without alarm the approach of the British troops, while most of the inhabitants were flying. With Mrs. M'Neil there lingered one, however, who, though belonging to an American family, did not share in the anxious alarms of her countrymen. This was Jane M'Crea, the daughter of a Scotch Presbyterian clergyman, of New Jersey. Her father was dead, and she had gone to live with a brother residing near Fort Edward, but who, as he was a patriot, had abandoned his home on the approach of the enemy, and fled to Albany. He strove to persuade his sister to accompany him, but without success. He wrote to her again and again, to entreat her to join him, but she still lingered behind. She was now a guest of Mrs. M'Neil, and, like that lady, fearlessly awaited the approach of the British, for she knew that she had one among them who would protect her to the utmost of his power. This was her lover.

In the neighborhood of her brother's home at Fort Edward there lived a youth of the name of David Jones. He and Jane M'Crea became lovers, and were betrothed. His family, however, were loyalists, while hers were whigs; and, when war broke out, a separation took place. Young Jones volunteered to serve in the royal army, and, leaving his betrothed at the home of her patriot brother, went to Canada, where he received the king's commission as a lieutenant. Having joined

Burgoyne, he was now marching, with the division under General Fraser, toward his former home, and with eager expectation of meeting his beloved.

As rumors reached Miss M'Crea's brother, at Albany, of the advance of the enemy, and of the terror with which their savage allies were filling the whole country, he sent a peremptory command to his sister to go down to him. She finally though reluctantly consented, and prepared to leave, in company with several families, in a large batteau, which was about to sail. On the morning of the day proposed for departure, the whole region was suddenly alarmed by the intelligence that some of Burgoyne's Indians were prowling in the neighborhood.

The home of Mrs. M'Neil was one of the most exposed, and the household was soon thrown into great consternation by a negro-boy, who came running in, crying that the Indians were close by, and then scampered away to the fort. Before the people in the house could hide themselves, the savages had entered. Seizing Mrs. M'Neil and Miss M'Crea, the Indians —dividing into two parties, each with a prize—bore them off toward Burgoyne's camp. Those who had charge of Miss M'Crea had not gone far, when they halted at a spring. Here the Indians quarrelled among themselves for the possession of their captive. All their savage ferocity was aroused; and one, in his wild rage, settled the dispute by killing the poor girl. They then tomahawked her, and bore her scalp as a trophy to the British camp.[*]

* Wilkinson.

This is the commonly-received account of the tragic event. There are, however, other versions of the sad story. Every annalist has his own. One tells us that the fatal shot came from the Americans at Fort Edward, who, observing the Indians escaping with their prize, fired at them, and unfortunately killed the fair captive, whereupon the savages immediately scalped her. Another reports that the Indians had been hired by Lieutenant Jones to bring his betrothed to the British camp, and that in their quarrel for the reward (a keg of rum) they tomahawked her. This is the more popular version; but, as it was solemnly denied by Jones himself, who asserted his entire ignorance of the affair until he beheld the reeking scalp of the victim, it should no longer be accepted.

Burgoyne was no less horrified than every other civilized being at this act of savage ferocity. He determined, moreover, to punish the murderer. A council of his Indians was called, and a demand made upon them for the surrender of the criminal. This, however, greatly angered the savages, for he who had done the cruel deed was a chief. Burgoyne would, notwithstanding, have still persisted, had not those who were supposed to be more familiar with the Indian character, together with some of his officers (fearful lest the savages might become so indignant as to abandon the British alliance), persuaded him no longer to urge his demand.

The story of the murder, however, was everywhere told with an exaggerated account of the complicity of the British, and served to inflame the feelings of the whole country against them. "The story," says Lossing, "went abroad with all its horrid embellishments; and the blood of Jane M'Crea pleaded eloquently for revenge. Burke, in the exercise of his glowing eloquence, used the story with powerful effect in the British house of commons, and made the dreadful tale familiar to the ear throughout Europe." Burgoyne's civilized notions of justice, moreover, so far disagreed with the sentiments of his savage allies, that they became discontented, and deserted him so rapidly, that he was soon left with but few Indians in camp.

General Burgoyne now reached Fort Edward, while the Americans continued to retire farther down the Hudson, moving first to Saratoga, and thence to Stillwater. The British commander in the meantime **Aug. 3.** halted, to await the arrival of General Phillips, with the artillery and baggage, and to receive intelligence from the detachment of the army sent under Colonel St. Leger to make a diversion by the way of Oswego, and with whom it was intended to form a junction at Albany.

Word soon came that St. Leger was investing Fort Stanwix (or Schuyler, as it had been lately called) situated at the head of navigation on the Mohawk river. Colonel Peter Gansevoort, of Albany, who had served under Montgomery at Quebec, commanded the post, with a garrison of seven hundred and fifty regular troops from Massachusetts and New York. The fort had been built during the French War, and was of considerable strength, but had been allowed to decay. The Americans, however, had lately repaired it, though not in such a manner as to make its defences complete.

Colonel St. Leger now threatened the post with a large and very miscellaneous force, composed of nearly seventeen hundred men in all, among whom there were a few British, Hessians, Canadians, and American loyalists, while the majority were Indian warriors, under Brant, the Mohawk chief, and Sir John Johnson.

On the 3d of August, St. Leger sent in a flag, with a summons to surrender, and a copy of a pompous proclamation which he had spread over the country. The garrison took no notice of either, but resolved upon defending their post. On the next day, the English com- **Aug. 4.** mander commenced the siege by throwing a few bombs, and sending out parties of Indians to approach close to the fort, and, under cover of the trees, to pick off those at work on the parapets; while at night the savages were ordered to keep up a wild howl, with the view of frightening the garrison.

Although the country had been panic-stricken by the advance of the enemy, the aged Herkimer, general of the militia of Tryon county, had succeeded by great efforts in gathering eight hundred men, with whom he had marched to Oriskany, within eight miles of the fort. He now sent to inform Colonel Gansevoort of his approach, and to request him to signify the arrival of his messenger by firing three guns. On hearing these signals, General Herkimer proposed to force his way through St. Leger's troops, to the besieged garrison. As the enemy were on the alert, and had surrounded the fort, with the view of cutting off its communication with the neighboring country, the messenger had great difficulty in reaching Gansevoort. He finally succeeded by wading through a swamp supposed by the enemy to be impassable, but only after a long delay; for, although he had started in the night, with the hope of delivering his message before morning, he did not arrive until ten o'clock the next day.

Old Herkimer, in the meanwhile, remained at Oriskany with his militia, anxiously awaiting the discharge of the three guns, which were to be the signal for his advance. His men chafed at the delay, and their officers, sharing in their impatience, urged Herkimer to press on. The veteran, with true Dutch phlegm, smoked his pipe, and did not heed their importunities. At last, two of his officers (Colonels Cox and Paris), irritated by the obstinate prudence of their cautious commander, lost all self-control, and in their anger charged Herkimer with cowardice and treason. The fact that he had a brother and other relatives in the ranks of the enemy appeared to give some show of probability to the accusation. The old man, however, was true as steel, and, conscious of his integrity, calmly replied, "I am placed over you as a father and a guardian, and shall not lead you into difficulties from which I may not be able to extricate you." His officers, notwithstanding, persisted in their ungenerous taunts, when Herkimer yielded, and gave the order to advance; but he took care to tell those who were so anxious to press forward, and were so boastful of their courage, that they would probably be the first to run at the sight of the enemy.

Colonel St. Leger had received intelligence of General Herkimer's approach, and sent out Major Watts, with a party of Johnson's Greens, Colonel Butler with his Rangers, and a considerable body of Indians under Brant, to oppose it. Colonel Gansevoort had observed from the first this movement of the enemy, but was unconscious of its object, until Herkimer's messenger arrived, when it became obvious that St. Leger's object was to cut off the old veteran's party. Gansevoort immediately fired the three signal-guns, and ordered out a detachment of two hundred men drawn from his own and Wesson's regiments, with a single iron three-pounder, to make an attack upon the position occupied by Sir John Johnson's division, which had been weakened by the detachment sent off against Herkimer.

Lieutenant-Colonel Willett, a veteran Long-islander, who had served in the French Wars, and like Gansevoort fought under Montgomery at Quebec, had charge of this enterprise. Willett drew up his men and prepared to make a sortie from the fort, when the rain fell in torrents, and prevented his departure. It proved, however, but a summer shower, and after a short delay he was able to sally out. Willett's charge upon Sir John Johnson's "Royal Greens" and Indian allies was so impetuous, that the advanced guard was pushed in upon the encampment, and the whole force driven in confusion from its ground. Sir John was so taken by surprise, that he had no time to put on his regimental coat, and, thus unaccoutred, strove to rally his troops. His efforts, however, were unavailing, and he and his Royal Greens were forced to cross the river and seek refuge in St. Leger's camp on the opposite bank, while the Indians fled in all directions through the surrounding forests. A large quantity of stores, five British flags, and the papers and baggage of Sir John Johnson, fell into the hands of Willett, who had not lost a single man in the enterprise. On his return to the fort, the English flags were hoisted beneath the American standard; and his men, mounting the ramparts, gave three loud hurrahs.

Herkimer moved on, in no complacent humor; and his undisciplined militia, sharing in the contentions of their officers, followed him with little order or caution. The enemy, in the meanwhile, had prepared an ambuscade. Across the road by which Herkimer was advancing there was a ravine, through which he would be obliged to march. The enemy, on reaching this, posted their few regulars in the front, toward the fort, and concealed the Indians in the thick wood on each side of the road. The latter were ordered to let the Americans pass through the ravine, and only attack them when they had pushed on in the struggle with the small party of British in front. In this manner it was intended to surround Herkimer's force, and completely hem it in — front, flank, and rear.

The Americans came on carelessly and without suspicion. Their main body had got fairly into the ravine, followed by the baggage-wagons, while the rear-guard was still some distance behind on the road, when suddenly the Indians, too impatient to wait for orders, shouted their terrible war-whoop, and rushed impetuously from their cover down upon Herkimer and his men. The rear-guard immediately turned and fled, leaving those in advance to bear the whole brunt of the attack. General Herkimer was brought down at the first fire, by a musket-ball which killed his horse, and shattered his own leg near the knee. The brave old man, however, refused to be carried from the field, and ordered his men to bear him to the foot of a beech-tree near by, where, sitting on his saddle, and calmly lighting his pipe, he remained, giving orders.

The fight continued for more than an hour with great spirit, when the enemy strove to settle the engagement with a charge of the bayonet. The Americans, however, formed in circles, by which they were enabled to present a front to their assailants from all sides, and keep them off by their effective musketry. The day had been cloudy and unsettled, and now came a heavy rain, with thunder — the same shower which, as we have seen, delayed Willett's sortie from the fort. The storm for awhile put an end to the struggle, and both parties sought a cover in the woods.

During this temporary lull, the Americans shifted their ground, and determined to change their manœuvres. The savages had been observed to await the discharge of the muskets, and then rush upon each man of the scattered troops while he was separated from his fellows, and tomahawk him. To guard against this, it was resolved by the Americans to post themselves, two together, behind the trees, so that when one had fired his musket and prepared to reload, the other might come forward ready to take his place and cover his comrade. With this improvement in their tactics, the Americans found the Indians much less formidable, and soon got so far the advantage of them, that they began to lose spirit and disperse.

Major Watts now brought up a detachment of the "Johnson Greens," which had hitherto been kept in reserve. These were men belonging to the Mohawk valley; and, being thus brought into conflict with the American patriots, among whom there were not only those who were neighbors, but some even who were their kinsmen, the horrors of a fierce family feud were added to the usual terrors of warfare. The old quarrels and animosities which had before occurred between those taking separate sides in the early controversies and troubles of the colonies, growing out of the dispute with the mother-country, were now aroused to increased fury. There was no check to passion, and no scruple to forbid the shedding of blood. Actual war authorized all, and neighbor joined in deadly struggle with neighbor without a qualm of conscience. The engagement was fierce, and the result terribly fatal.

The battle was so pertinaciously contested on both sides, that neither seemed disposed to give way. The Indian allies of the British, however, were the first to lose heart; and, shouting their retreating cry, "*Oonah! oonah!*" these ruthless warriors at length fled precipitately to the adjoining forests. The white men heard these ominous shouts of their savage confederates, and saw their hasty retreat to the woods, but nevertheless continued to fight, and did not cease their deadly struggle, until the distant firing from the attack of Colonel Willett (in his sortie from the fort) began to be heard; whereupon, the British commander, anxious for the safety of St. Leger's camp, withdrew his troops from the field, leaving the patriots in possession, and marched back to reinforce the arch-leader of the "tories," Sir John Johnson.

The victory, in the engagement thus abruptly brought to a close, remained undecided. The loss in killed and wounded on both sides was about equally great, amounting to over three hundred each. Of the American officers, Colonel Cox and Captain Van Sluyk were killed at the first fire. The brave old commander, Herkimer, and the rest of the wounded, were borne off the field on litters made from the branches of trees. The general died ten days after the battle, at his own residence, on the Mohawk river. His shattered leg was amputated, but (from the complex nature of the wound) so unsuccessfully, that he never recovered from the effects of the operation. He bore his sufferings cheerfully, and calmy awaited his death, smoking his pipe and reading his Bible, to quote the graphic words of an annalist, "like a Christian hero." His patriotic example was greatly venerated by his countrymen, and his illustrious name was subsequently conferred by the legislature of New York upon one of the newly-formed counties of the state.

The enemy had retired from the field of action in such haste, that one of their officers (Major Watts, who was severely wounded) was left for dead. He there remained for two days, when he was discovered by an Indian scout, near a spring of water, where he had crawled to quench his burning thirst, and was borne into St. Leger's camp.

When General Schuyler received intelligence, at Stillwater, of this tragic contest, he despatched a force of eight hundred continental troops, under the command of Brigadier-General Learned, to reinforce the patriots.

A few days subsequently, General Arnold volunteered his services, which were accepted by Schuyler, who ordered him to proceed immedi- **Aug. 13.** ately to the "German Flats," where he was to assume the chief command, and, calling out the militia of the neighboring country, relieve Fort Schuyler, if practicable; otherwise, to adopt such precautionary measures as would most effectually cover the settlements of the Mohawk valley from the ravages of General Burgoyne's advancing British and Germans, and their more terrible Indian allies, who filled the country with consternation.

END OF VOL. I.